A HISTORY OF THE UNIVERSITY OF CAMBRIDGE

This volume brings to completion the four-volume *A History of the University of Cambridge*, and is a vital contribution to the history not only of one major university, but of the academic societies of early modern Europe in general.

Its main author, Victor Morgan, has made a special study of the relations between Cambridge and its wider world: the court and church hierarchy which sought to control it in the aftermath of the Reformation, and which at the same time gave it patronage and exploited it mercilessly; the 'country', that is the provincial gentry who provided much of the patronage and many of the recruits to Cambridge, especially in the sixteenth and seventeenth centuries; and the wider academic world. Morgan also seeks to revive his readers' interests in institutional history, and finds the seeds of contemporary problems of university governance in the struggles which led to and followed the new Elizabethan statutes of 1570.

Christopher Brooke, General Editor and part-author, has contributed chapters on architectural history – showing how imaginative study of the buildings of Cambridge provides a chronological framework for the whole period; and among other themes, a study of the intellectual giants of the late seventeenth and early eighteenth centuries, Robert Brady, physician and historian, Richard Bentley and Isaac Newton.

A HISTORY OF
THE UNIVERSITY
OF CAMBRIDGE

VOLUME II
1546–1750

VICTOR MORGAN

With a contribution by Christopher Brooke

CAMBRIDGE UNIVERSITY PRESS

Cambridge, New York, Melbourne, Madrid, Cape Town, Singapore, São Paulo, Delhi

Cambridge University Press
The Edinburgh Building, Cambridge CB2 8RU, UK

Published in the United States of America by Cambridge University Press, New York

www.cambridge.org
Information on this title: www.cambridge.org/9780521350594

First published 2004
Reprinted 2009

Printed in the United Kingdom at the University Press, Cambridge

A catalogue record for this publication is available from the British Library

ISBN 978-0-521-35059-4 paperback

CONTENTS

Contents

Contents

Contents

PLATES AND FIGURE

List of plates and figure

List of plates and figure

FIGURE

Cambridge University Press and the authors gratefully acknowledge the
permission of all those noted above for the Plates. The photographs
by Wim Swaan were originally taken for C.N.L. Brooke, J.R.L. Highfield and W. Swaan, *Oxford and Cambridge* (1988), and are reproduced
with the generous approval of the Director of the Research Library, the
Getty Research Institute, Los Angeles (reference 96. P. 21, Wim Swaan
Photographic Collection).

TABLES

GENERAL EDITOR'S PREFACE

The core of this book comprises the deep research of Victor Morgan, with a strong emphasis on the links between Cambridge and the wider world of Court, parliament and 'the country', and with its main orientation in the period 1546 to 1640. It was originally planned to be a thematic study, in which each of these elements would be carried through to 1750. But time has passed and the earlier chapters have grown: completion on this scale of a book in which every period and every theme was given equal weight would take many more years and a much larger book. So we have harvested what has been achieved and I have attempted to sketch some major themes not covered by Victor Morgan's chapters, and above all what happened after 1640. This is not a perfectly balanced book, but I think it is in some ways more interesting than if we had tried drastically to reshape it. For those who seek some outline of the whole period, I have provided in chapter 2 a history of the university and colleges as it is reflected in the most vivid of all the materials for its study, in its buildings. For those who wish to know what academic legacy Cambridge acquired, chapter 14 attempts to penetrate the supreme intellectual adventures of the last two generations of our period. The rest will speak for itself.

In my Preface to the first volume in this series – Damian Leader on *The University to 1546* – I paid tribute to *The History of the University of Oxford* and humbly observed that 'perhaps beside the great battleship launched by the Oxford Press there is room for a modest, serviceable frigate, sent from Cambridge'. Both are now complete, and the Oxford series will remain an incomparable monument of scholarly achievement, unequal in execution, but in the mass an immensely impressive statement of scholarly endeavour.

Our own aim and achievement have been much more modest; but oddly, one of the chief faults of my own volume IV, *1870–1990*, was that it was too long, so that the reviewers did not read it all. The late Lord Annan – failing to use the index – was astounded to find no mention of Lord Adrian. Another reviewer found a lack of 'edge' in the book. If he meant a lack of fashionable polemic, I plead guilty: I have tended in the past too much to avoid polemic, which I have thought fed its author's vanity more than the cause of historical science. If he meant lack of subtlety and nuances, he had read a different book from the one I wrote. If he meant that I presented too bland and optimistic a view, that may be: such a book cannot be the vehicle for debates on university politics; but the book contains some of the most searching criticisms – for example of the treatment of women in Cambridge and the fissures between university and colleges – which I have seen in print.

There is however a serious point here. One of my main concerns was to expound some of the ways in which Cambridge had won high international esteem; and this can only be achieved by dwelling on the heights. John Prest, in a genial review in the *Journal of Ecclesiastical History* (46 (1995), 344–6) took me to task for concentrating on the leaders and ignoring the rank and file. He commended my courage but doubted my wisdom in attempting as a single author to do what twenty-four contributors provided in the twentieth-century volume of the Oxford *History*. It is notoriously unwise to answer reviewers, but Prest raised serious issues in what he both said and did not say. One central problem in the history of Oxford in the twentieth century is how a very traditional university was able not only to hold its own as a great centre of humanist studies but to win international fame in the natural sciences too. Future readers of volume VIII will look in vain for answers to this question: even the excellent chapter on the medical sciences fails to bring to life such central characters as Sir Charles Sherrington; and research in the humanities between the two World Wars is represented by a list of books, in no particular order. Prest says nothing of the colleges – wisely, for the Oxford *History* was conceived in conscious reaction against the pious college histories of a former generation, and never fully came to terms with the problem of doing justice to the individuality of the colleges in a unitary history. Doubtless the same is true of our venture; but we have tried. Prest encourages his readers to compare Greenstein's chapter on junior members with mine. Greenstein has indeed provided an ample stock of charts and tables, the outward and visible sign of a marvellous database provided for him by the staff of the *History* – the envy of those of us who have had to work with much inferior tools in Cambridge; but his analysis of them, though full of interesting detail, is sometimes superficial. Social categories too often are reduced to 'middle class' and the like without consideration of the meaning of 'class', and there is no serious discussion of the changing nature of schools or the bewildering patterns of their relation to the social and economic standing of parents; nor are the categories of parents and occupations subjected to adequate critical analysis. In other words, Prest was in a measure criticising me for not falling victim to the inadequate analysis lying behind most current university statistics. I cited as many figures as I thought were reliable: I believe profoundly in the value of statistics, and for that reason am sceptical of the value of much which social historians parade before us. Even the much more sophisticated chapters in the nineteenth-century volumes of the Oxford *History* rely heavily on the university's matric-ulation records, which have provided often ambiguous material for the statistical analysis of parents' status in the world for which Cambridge has nothing to compare – though the authors have been at infinite pains to check their evidence to the limited extent to which this is possible (see Curthoys and Howarth 1999, pp. 576–9). Some of Greenstein's tables are valid and interesting – but their value cannot be assessed except by the kind of close analysis I attempted. Several reviewers noted that I was more given to narrative and exposition than to analysis; but the truth is that my closely woven analyses of student backgrounds and of what I called the 'anthropology' of the late twentieth century – its relation to the world-wide movements and prejudices of the age – were less readable than my vignettes of the men and women who have made Cambridge internationally famous. But a closer look even at my studies of major figures might have revealed the element of reflection which I thought and think the chief mark of my volume.

Yet, though I admire the Oxford *History* – as Ben Jonson said he loved and honoured Shakespeare – 'this side idolatry', I freely admit that the authors of the Cambridge *History*, and all students of academic history, are deeply in its debt. For the present book I have myself found particular guidance and inspiration in the contributions of Mordechai Feingold to the seventeenth-century volume; but our debts are many, and widely scattered among volumes iii–v of the Oxford *History*. In my own studies of university and college history, the contrast between Oxford, which had the courage in the 1960s to form a department out of university resources to write the *History*, and the failure of the Cambridge History Faculty to make even the most modest provision for research in the field has been painful. In my last years as Dixie Professor, indeed, I was allowed to teach a segment of Cambridge history – roughly that of the present volume – with the aid of a generous and enthusiastic group of colleagues; and Barrie Dobson and I took regular courses on the physical evidence for medieval and early modern Cambridge, which helped to enlarge my knowledge of the theme of chapter 2.

General Editor's preface

History in my eyes is first and foremost the scientific study of evidence about the past; and in all the volumes of this series one of the first aims has been to deploy our current knowledge of what the historical evidence reveals. One imperceptive reviewer claimed that there was little original research in Peter Searby's volume: as it is virtually all written from sources, most of them little tapped by earlier historians, it is hard to know what he meant. For historical research is the investigation of historical evidence, no more and no less. As a portrayal of the spectrum of university activities and institutions – and of the variety of the colleges – this volume, like its predecessors, is selective. That it must be, for three reasons. We have attempted to portray in depth the themes we pursue, and space would not permit an encylopaedic coverage. Nor would the time we have to spare: the book has been long in the making, and the tyrannical demands of the RAE – to which Victor Morgan is still subject – no longer permit most members of faculty to engage in large research projects.

The third reason is that our aim is to combine an intelligible survey of the current state of knowledge of our theme with revelation in depth of the sources we have been able to plunder. Thus chapters 13 and 15 are greatly indebted to Twigg (1990) and Gascoigne (1989); and we have made very full use of the recent college histories of Trinity Hall, Caius, Queens', Magdalene, Sidney and Emmanuel. For many years Victor Morgan has been accumulating material from the very rich gold-mines in the PRO and local collections, and in the printed literature of the sixteenth and seventeenth centuries, throwing new light into many dark corners. There are many more corners to be explored; but the generous reader will appreciate that any attempt to compass a stretch of history in 500 pages which took the authors of the Oxford *History* close on 2,000 must be highly selective, or else superficial; and that we have avoided. I generously gave the reviewers of volume IV some amusement by frequent references to my own memories and experiences, though with less generosity none gave me credit for my purpose – which was precisely to underpin a broad survey of an enormous subject with as much authentic evidence as possible. The present volume ends well past the memory of man or usable oral tradition; but in our collaboration we have tried to combine Victor Morgan's exceptional knowledge of the byways of sixteenth- and seventeenth-century written sources with my own knowledge of the buildings, colleges and books of early modern Cambridge.

C.N.L.B.

PREFACE

While the analogy is not perfect, a parallel can be drawn between the biography of an individual and the history of an institution. In the representations of the 'ages of man' and the 'steps of life' that were so popular in the sixteenth and seventeenth centuries, characters representing the different ages are shown, variously, as withdrawn and inward to themselves or as being defined by their engagement with the wider world. Here, in examining the life of Cambridge University, for the most part the story is of one such period of active engagement.

Another institution, in another place, has been able to devote two volumes and dozens of authors to telling its story over the same period. Necessarily, this more modest offering has had to be more selective and more thematic. The dominant theme is the relationship between the University and the wider society of which it was part. It has selected itself and it has done so for two reasons. The first is to do with where we are now in terms of our understanding of the wider historical context. The second is to do with the nature of the period.

Any history is itself the history of the moment of its doing, and the present moment is one in which we enjoy the fruits of that efflorescence of historical curiosity that had its roots in the mid-1960s. This volume attempts to place the history of the university within the context of at least some of the understandings that we now have as a result of that revivification of historical inquiry. While attempting to attend to the quiddities and quirks of the places and people gathered on the banks of the Cam it also broaches upon such things as the royal Court, provincial society, the social order, parliament, urban history, intellectual endeavour and religious thought and practice. In attempting this broad purview it cannot but be that much more imperfect than a more constricted and inward-looking project might have been, in and of itself. But it is what the moment demands. In time others will replace it with the insights brought to the history of the university by the concerns of their moment.

Incidentally, it will be gratifying if what is said here goes some way to reassert the status of institutional history as a genre. Much of the impulse for the growth of the 'new' history to which allusion has just been made arose as a reaction to the aridities to which political and institutional history can too easily degenerate. Perhaps, after all this time, we need to consider the possibility of a new type of institutional history: one that infuses the history of the institution with an understanding of the broader context but also one that attempts to gauge the impact of the institution on the shaping of that context.

The second reason for the approach adopted here is simply that this is a period when the two English universities were drawn ever more closely into relationships with the central institutions of the state while also and in a variety of ways being tied more intimately to a diversifying kaleidoscope of provincial societies. At the same time the Reformation and Renaissance impulses projected them into a continent-wide traffic of ideas. Related to these considerations is the issue of the balance of the relationship between the institution and its context. To what extent does the institution place its imprint on the wider society and how far does the wider society intrude its values and 'style' into the institution, possibly subverting some of its core purposes in the process?

These questions also have implications for how we do institutional history. The danger is that if we chronicle only the internal doings of the institution we will not be able properly to judge the significance of those activities. Thus, in essence, the argument adopted here is that between – roughly – the 1560s and the 1680s the English universities were remarkably influential in setting the tone for the learned, pedantic, latinate culture that then prevailed. Thereafter, and contrary to much received opinion, Cambridge continued to generate much lively intellectual endeavour. However, an appreciation of that endeavour has to be tempered by a realisation that by then much of the action was elsewhere. That 'elsewhere' was an emergent metropolitan-based, cosmopolitan-orientated culture that favoured wit above sagaciousness. For, as a primary source of the pedantic, 'Jacobethan' culture, Cambridge was swept up in the consequences of a reaction to what was a broad dismissal of 'pedantry' – a word that when used abusively implied more than simply a style of academic practice. In this it was one of the victims of that broader reordering of thinking and doing that we might term the 'English Resolution' of the late seventeenth century.

In writing this book I have engaged many obligations. As best as I can recall these are recorded in the acknowledgements. However, here I wish to record my profound gratitude to the General Editor of the series in which this volume appears. Christopher Brooke has done far more than a General Editor should have to do in order to ensure that it has got to press without – as he clearly feared – another fifteen years of gestation. In bringing an outsider's eye and an outsider's interests to the history of the institution to which he and others like him are devoted I hope that in my judgements I have not been too unkind to the object of their affections. For, in the final judgement, in the moving and stirring times recounted here, the university was a doer and a mover, as even again it is in these latter days.

Victor Morgan

ACKNOWLEDGEMENTS

This book has been aided over many years by kindly advice in editorial meetings from William Davies and Peter Searby; by deeply valued support and help from William Davies and many of his colleagues in the Cambridge University Press, especially Frances Brown in copy-editing, in production Alison Powell, and Barbara Hird who has made the index; and by the resources and the generous help of the staff of the Cambridge University Library and University Archives, the Library of the University of East Anglia, the British Library, the Bodleian Library, Oxford, the Public Record Office, the Institute of Historical Research, the Folger Shakespeare Library, the Lambeth Palace Library, and the Libraries and Archives of several Cambridge colleges, especially Corpus Christi, Emmanuel, Gonville and Caius, Jesus, St John's, Trinity and Trinity Hall. We owe a particular debt in the University Archives to the late Heather Peak and Dorothy Owen, and to Elisabeth Leedham-Green, Patrick Zutshi and Jacky Cox; and in the Manuscript Room also to Godfrey Waller; in Emmanuel to Janet Morris, Sarah Bendall and Frank Stubbings; in Gonville and Caius College to Philip Grierson, Jeremy Prynne and their colleagues; in St John's College to Malcolm Underwood; in Trinity College to David McKitterick and Jonathan Smith; in Trinity Hall to Sandra Raban; in the UEA Library to David Palmer and his staff of the Inter-Library Loan service. Chapter 2 owes much to the generous help of Hugh Richmond.

Victor Morgan wishes especially to thank Hassell Smith and Robert Ashton for the inspiration and support from which his researches have sprung. He thanks the Princeton University Press for permission to reproduce the article on which chapter 6 is based; and the authors of the theses listed in the bibliography for allowing their works to be cited. He is grateful to the marquess of Salisbury, the earl of Iveagh and the Marquis Townshend for the use of unprinted material in their possession.

Acknowledgements

We are both deeply indebted to help in word-processing by Edna Pilmer and Rosemary Brooke. We have constantly depended on the support, advice, help and tolerance of our wives, Rosalind Brooke and Jane Key – above all, on their patience, and occasional impatience. Of what we owe to each other, something is said elsewhere.

C.N.L.B.   V.M.

ABBREVIATIONS

BL	The British Library
Bodl.	The Bodleian Library, Oxford
CJ	*House of Commons Journals*
CSPD	*Calendar of State Papers, Domestic Series*
CUA	CUL, Cambridge University Archives
CUL	Cambridge University Library
DNB	*Dictionary of National Biography*
EHR	*English Historical Review*
HLRO	House of Lords Record Office
HMC	*Historical Manuscripts Commission*
JEH	*Journal of Ecclesiastical History*
LJ	*House of Lords Journal*
LP	*Letters and Papers, Foreign and Domestic*
NDR	Norwich Diocesan Registry (in NRO)
NRO	Norfolk Record Office
NRS	Norfolk Record Society
ODCC	*The Oxford Dictionary of the Christian Church*
OED	*Oxford English Dictionary*
P.C.	Privy Council Papers
PRO	Public Record Office, Kew
SCH	*Studies in Church History*
S.O.	PRO, Signet Office papers
SP	PRO, State Papers
VCH	*Victoria County History*

Chapter 1

PROLOGUE: CAMBRIDGE SAVED

A fundamental theme in the history of the University of Cambridge in this period is the intimacy between the university and the state. From the 1530s onwards the university, its individual colleges and many of its members enjoyed the benefits arising from this new-found relationship. In due course we will see the advantages that this gave the university in its conflicts with the city of Cambridge.[1] But intimacy also brought its perils and corruptions, and at no time were they greater than during the unsettled 1530s and 1540s. At times during these decades the very survival of the university – or at least, of the colleges – was in question. That they did survive was in no small measure because university men already constituted influential voices in the corridors of power. But then and in the future theirs were not to be the only voices. Covetous eyes were not for the last time cast in the direction of Cambridge and her sister university.

When we speak of the state in this period we need to avoid any too grandiose a level of abstraction. In particular, we need to avoid imputing an undue degree of homogeneity. Indeed, the struggle over the fate of the universities in the 1530s and 1540s was in itself a significant indicator of what at the time was a relatively new configuration within the central institutions of the early modern English state. The outcome of the struggles in the 1530s is also an indicator of the relative balance of power between the major components within that new configuration. In working with this new type of central political institution the Cambridge men who saved the university in the 1540s were dealing with an entity that had taken on a new form in the previous twenty years. This was the royal Renaissance Court that had been created by Henry VIII at the beginning of his reign. Its splendour caught the contemporary eye and perhaps has beguiled modern historians. But apart from these flashy splendours there were 'the men in dark suits' who provided new levels

[1] Below, chapter 7.

of administrative expertise to the burgeoning aspirations of the Tudor state.[2] They also provided what passed for intellectual justifications for what Henry wanted. Essentially, then, within this new type of Court we need to distinguish between the members of the recently elaborated royal household and the new administrative cadre. This cadre served mainly the great departments of state, and within the relatively new and flexible secretariat. From the viewpoint of Cambridge, the significance of the 1530s and 1540s was survival itself. In the larger scene the fortunes of the university illustrate the relative balance of influence at that time between these different types of men who met together within the bearpit that was the royal Court. Not for the last time the universities became an arena in which were to be played out conflicts that were inherent in the emerging political structures of Tudor England. In the 1530s and 1540s the universities were especially vulnerable; the paradox is that they were also especially useful to the Tudor state. The politically driven necessities of the 1530s took on an ideological component: as always, university men were well equipped to provide justifying ideologies. There were two aspects to the growing intimacy between state and university. The first involved the increasing familiarity with the universities among men at the heart of government; the second reflected the uses to which these men, and others anxious to advise government, put the universities and individual academics in the service of the state in the years down to the 1560s.

The crucible for these developments was the tumultuous decade of the 1530s, witnessing the king's divorce, the Reformation Parliament, the breach with Rome and the dissolution of the monasteries. The monasteries were dissolved in the 1530s and the colleges saved in the 1540s by a similar process with dramatically different outcomes. Under Thomas Cromwell's direction, a group of commissioners visited the monasteries in 1535, very well aware that the appetites of the king and courtiers had been whetted by the *Valor Ecclesiasticus*, the great survey of ecclesiastical revenues conducted earlier in the same year. In his classic account of the Dissolution, David Knowles described the visitors as 'adulatory, pliant, time-serving . . . ready to accuse or ruin any man, friend or foe, stranger or relative, in order to retain the favour of Henry or Cromwell, but they were often sagacious, moderate and good-natured in their personal dealings when neither career nor cash was at stake'; and among the four leading visitors he drew some distinction between the career ecclesiastics

[2] Cf. Starkey 1987 and the classic presentation of the administration of Henry VIII and Thomas Cromwell in Elton 1953.

and the laymen. The two clerics, Richard Layton and Thomas Legh, were pluralists who rose in Cromwell's wake in the royal service, were employed on many missions, and died before they could be promoted to bishoprics – or be burnt as heretics. The two laymen were markedly different in character, but equally unprincipled. John ap Rice or Price became a respected country gentleman on his Welsh estates – once those of Carmarthen and Brecon priories – and a noted bibliophile; under Mary it seems to have been forgotten that he had been actively engaged in persecuting the Carthusian monks and Fisher and More. John Tregonwell 'added a tomb to what is now one of the most exquisite monuments of the monastic past' – to quote Knowles again – at Milton Abbas, and like Price enjoyed the fruits of monastic spoil in a comfortable old age in which he was actually knighted by Mary.[3] They were all professional lawyers and royal servants; it goes without saying that none of them had been a monk or a friar. In contrast the Commissioners who reported on the Oxford and Cambridge colleges in the 1540s were all themselves heads of colleges, and all well known in the circles of the Court. The contrast immediately reveals the very different preparations for the two commissions – and that in a measure the outcome of the commission on the colleges was already a foregone conclusion. But it had not been so at first.

The utility of the universities for ideological purposes first became evident in Henry VIII's pursuit of a divorce from Catherine of Aragon. Henry was thwarted by the papal legate, Cardinal Campeggio's suspension of proceedings in London in June–July 1529 on the grounds that the prevailing temperature in Rome precluded further meetings. To make matters worse Clement VII then removed the case to Rome. In pursuit of some sort of authoritative learned legitimation of Henry VIII's urgent need for a divorce, Thomas Cranmer had suggested an appeal to the opinion of the universities. With some difficulty suitable opinions or 'determinations' were extracted from Oxford and Cambridge. Emissaries were also sent on continental tours to solicit favourable opinions from other universities, from religious houses and from individuals.[4] It was the provost of King's, Edward Fox, who did much of the footwork. During 1529–30, Fox was also a member of a hastily convened think tank charged with finding justifications for the king's wishes. It was these men that

---

[3] Knowles 1959, pp. 270–4.

[4] Mullinger 1873, pp. 612–22; Heywood 1840, p. 195; Scarisbrick 1968, pp. 164–5, 255–8. Initially this was in pursuit of opinions that marriage to a dead brother's wife was unlawful; then there was a second circuit of France and Italy in pursuit of determinations by the universities that the king's cause should be heard in England (Scarisbrick 1968, pp. 267, 289).

produced the 'king's book', which probably was finished in October 1529 although not published until April 1531.[5] Levitical law was invoked as divine authority and Pope Julius' grant of dispensation to Henry VII for his son to marry Prince Arthur's widow was, it now appeared, *ultra vires*. To marry a deceased brother's wife was also found to be forbidden by the law of nature.[6] It was these findings, the deliberations of Convocation and the determinations of the universities that, in May 1533, provided Cranmer, by then archbishop, with the grounds for declaring void Henry's marriage to Catherine.[7]

In addition to the use which Henry and his advisers made of the universities, there were also those men of learning who at this time spontaneously proffered their services to the state. For theirs was the 'new learning' that sought to marry intellect with action.[8] We need to recognise the type as a phenomenon of the greater part of the period with which we are concerned: we will encounter more of them in later pages. No doubt for some it was a convenient creed, and, as in the 1520s, personal opportunism often combined with high principle so that neither the historian, contemporaries, nor least the individuals themselves could easily segregate motives. The higher principle was grounded in the desire to infiltrate the new ideas into society, and the church and into the highest counsels of government. The new articulate citizen, who was usually a graduate and often the attendant in the antechambers of the powerful, was often still a member of the university.[9] In an hierarchical world articulated by patronage and clientage those who sought social reform and religious change did so by soliciting the men with power and influence about the Court. They were successful, at least as reflected in the background of the graduate laity who became prominent in central government during the 1530s and 1540s. Increasingly, university alumni could be found in government, or quasi-government offices, or as informal advisers to government. What began in the 1530s was to be a characteristic feature of the English state until the late seventeenth century.

The larger changes afoot during the 1530s and 1540s underlined the need of the university for the ear of influential men in government. At Cambridge this realisation had already dawned. Since the mid-fifteenth century the university had commonly sought protection through the

---

[5] Surtz and Murphy 1988. For the issues in the divorce proceedings, see Brooke 1989c, pp. 162–9 and refs.

[6] Guy 1997, pp. 213–33.   [7] Scarisbrick 1968, p. 312.   [8] McConica 1965; Elton 1972a.

[9] McConica 1965; Ferguson 1965; Jones (W.R.D.) 1970; Elton, 1973; Jordan 1966, p. xv; but see Elton 1979a.

election as chancellors of great dignitaries of state.[10] In 1504–5, they had elected John Fisher as chancellor, an office he was to hold, with only a brief intermission, till his death. On his demise he was replaced by Thomas Cromwell. Recalling Cromwell, the seventeenth-century historian of the university, Thomas Fuller, wrote of 'How easy it was for covetousness in those ticklish times, to quarrel the college lands into superstition? Sacrilege stood ready to knock at their gates: and alas it was past their porter's power to forbid it entrance, had not the Lord Cromwell vigorously assisted the university on all occasions.'[11] Cromwell's role may have been more equivocal than Fuller suggests, yet it is true that the defence of the interests of the universities against the threat posed by the dissolution of religious houses was the first major occasion on which were manifest the benefits of university alumni and patrons in government.

As a result of the dissolution of the monastic houses, both universities had lost their friaries and most of their monastic halls of residence. But Buckingham College had survived, transformed into Magdalene College; and the university had actually benefited from the premature demise of St Radegund's nunnery and St John's hospital, which had been converted into Jesus College in the 1490s and St John's College in the 1510s.[12] Nor may the disappearance of the house of Augustinian or Austin canons at Barnwell greatly have affected the university. But the four major friaries were in effect very grand colleges; and their disappearance was both a disaster to the university and a hint to the greedy of what else might be done. Yet curiously enough they did not wholly disappear: the sites of the Dominican and Franciscan friaries were to be converted into Emmanuel and Sidney Sussex colleges much later in the century, and part of the Austin friars' buildings became the Perse Grammar School in the 1610s. More immediately, that subtle courtier William Mey, president of Queens', looked over his college's boundary wall and observed that the Carmelite friary was a ripe plum ready to pick – and with the expert aid of his vice-president, the eminent civilian Thomas Smith, he arranged with Thomas Cromwell (for a price) its amalgamation with Queens'.[13]

In 1545 the Chantries Act empowered the king to dissolve any corporation within the universities and to seize its possessions.[14] Contemporary

---

[10] Brooke 1989b, pp. 50–2, 233–4.   [11] Fuller 1655/1840, p. 214.   [12] See below, p. 17.
[13] Stein 1988, p. 191; Searle 1867–71, pp. 222–32; Mullinger 1884, pp. 23 ff. Cf. Twigg 1987, p. 31.
[14] 37 Henry VIII c. 4; Scarisbrick 1968, p. 519.

comment suggests that the threat was not so much from the king but from 'certain officers in the Court and others . . . in authority under the king' who were 'importunately suing to him to have the lands and possessions of both universities surveyed, they meaning afterwards to enjoy the best of their lands and possessions by exchange of impropriated benefices and such other improved lands'. In February 1546 the university wrote formally to the king, professing itself still willing to put its possessions at his service.[15] Less formally, a campaign was mounted against the threatened depredations by courtiers.

This campaign was forwarded through resort to others about the Court who were familiar with the universities and who could be relied upon to defend their interests. On the same day as Cambridge made its formal submission to the king, it also wrote to the secretary of state, William Paget. Paget was reminded of the importance of the universities to the state, and asked to protect the cause of learning.[16] Paget was an appropriate man to importune: the very model of the new, academic, government official and courtier. Educated at Trinity Hall, he had afterwards studied at Paris. Employed on numerous missions foreign and domestic, he had served as a clerk to the privy council for four years, and had become a privy councillor, clerk of parliament, chancellor of the duchy of Lancaster and secretary of state.[17] The university was further aided by another of its native sons, Sir Thomas Smith. Smith was a former fellow of Queens' and public orator. In 1544 he had been vice-chancellor, and at the time was Professor of Civil Law. In 1548 he was to succeed Paget as secretary of state.[18] Smith interceded on behalf of the university with the queen, Catherine Parr, to whose council he was clerk.[19] In her turn Catherine spoke on behalf of the university to the king. For her part the queen favoured not only the reformed religion, but also the reformers, and, therefore, by extension, university men. She had already, or was subsequently, to call upon Cambridge dons to educate the children of the royal household that she had inherited from her predecessors.[20] First William Grindal, the pupil of Roger Ascham, and after Grindal's death in 1548 Roger Ascham himself, became tutors to Princess Elizabeth.[21] John Cheke was summoned to Court as tutor to Prince Edward. Informally, the university had jointly appealed not only to Smith, but also to

---

[15] Lamb 1838, p. 59; *LP* XXI, i, p. 99, no. 203.   [16] *LP* XXI, i, p. 99, no. 204.

[17] Venn, III, p. 296b; Gammon 1973.   [18] *DNB*; Dewar 1964; Stein 1988, ch. 13.

[19] Dewar 1964, pp. 24–5; *DNB*.   [20] Hudson 1980, pp. 68–75.

[21] William Grindal was a Greek scholar and fellow of St John's in 1542–3 (Venn, II, p. 270a; Ryan 1963). He was apparently related to the future archbishop Edmund Grindal, although the precise relationship is not clear (Collinson 1979, pp. 26, 222).

his close friend, Cheke.[22] It was Cheke who had been appointed as the first Regius Professor of Greek, in 1540, and it was Cheke who was the inspiring tutor to many men who subsequently went on to influential positions in public life.[23]

In the immediate circumstances of 1545–6 the invocation of the influence of the university men about the Court was remarkably successful. The university had asked Paget that the proposed enquiry into the revenues and expenditure of the colleges should not be consigned to 'such as know better *quid pecunia solet facere quam quo in loco doctrina debet esse* [what money is accustomed to do than where learning should reign] but to such as can rightly esteem both'.[24] The outcome of this and similar requests was the appointment of a commission consisting of Matthew Parker, John Redman and William Mey.[25]

At the same time Richard Cox was appointed sole commissioner for the University of Oxford.[26] They were all men high in royal favour; like Cromwell's commissioners, they were the king's men. But they were also, and much more, leaders of the Oxford and Cambridge establishment; and Cox was head of Henry VIII's own college, soon to become Christ Church. They were also beneficiaries of the new cathedral establishment. Between 1538 and 1542 all the ex-monastic cathedral chapters were refounded as secular chapters, and among other refoundations, most notably, Westminster Abbey acquired a dean and chapter who enjoyed all the privileges of a royal peculiar long since usurped by the abbot and monks.[27] Among the canons of Ely might be found Richard Cox, archdeacon and canon from 1540 to 1553 (and later bishop), and Matthew Parker and William Mey, canons from 1541 to 1554.[28] Among the first canons of Westminster was John Redman (1540–51), who as warden of the King's Hall had a privileged role in the Chapel Royal.[29] William Mey was to be dean of St Paul's from 1545 to 1554 – and briefly again in 1559–60.[30]

At the time Parker was the newly elected master of Corpus, and had just been elected vice-chancellor as successor, and under the sponsorship, of Thomas Smith.[31] Neither was Parker innocent of the workings of the Court. In 1535 he had been appointed chaplain to Anne Boleyn, and through her patronage had become dean of the collegiate church of

[22] Mullinger 1884, p. 78; Dewar 1964, p. 19.
[23] Hudson 1980, pp. 53–7.   [24] *LP* XXI, i, p. 99, no. 204.
[25] Lamb 1838, p. 58.   [26] Brooke, Highfield and Swaan 1988, p. 132.
[27] See, most recently and authoritatively, Rex and Armstrong 2002, with a table of the new foundations on p. 402.
[28] Horn 1992, pp. 13, 15, 17, 19.   [29] *Ibid.*, p. 72.
[30] Horn 1969, p. 5.   [31] Hudson 1980, p. 58.

Stoke-by-Clare in Suffolk. His revival of the school at Clare appears to have provided one of the grounds for the recommendation – supposedly from the king – that Corpus elect him as its master.[32]

William Mey was a pluralist, a civil servant and an expert lawyer, notionally (as academic lawyers had to be) a civil or Roman lawyer, but in practice also an expert on canon law: he was appointed to the commission to reform ecclesiastical laws in the same year, 1546, that he was appointed to the Cambridge commission. His civilian training helped to prepare him also for diplomatic service; and again during 1546 he was dispatched with Sir William Petre on a diplomatic mission to France. Petre described his colleague as 'a man of the most honest sort, wise, discrete, and well lernyd, and one that shall be very mete to sarve his Majestie many wayes'.[33] The most senior commissioner was John Redman, warden of the King's Hall, itself a part of the Chapel Royal, though located in Cambridge. He had been public orator in 1537, was twice Lady Margaret's Professor of Divinity, and a royal chaplain. He was a noted Greek scholar, who as Lady Margaret's Professor had espoused the cause of the new pronunciation of Greek, in alliance with Cheke: Cheke and Smith were his disciples. He was a relatively conservative figure among the reformers, although he repented on his deathbed in 1551, under Edward VI, of having striven against justification by faith alone, and revised his views on the Eucharist. But among the commissioners he was the supreme beneficiary and the most revolutionary. He was, as Patrick Collinson has said, 'in reality the true founder of Trinity'. Under his influence his own King's Hall (already the largest college in Cambridge and long dedicated to the Trinity) was converted by Henry VIII into a yet larger college, mopping up Michaelhouse and Physwick Hostel (hitherto a wholly owned subsidiary of Gonville Hall) in the process – along with an ample store of monastic and other ecclesiastical loot.[34] His most notable acquisition was the lion's share in the prebend of Masham in York Minster, reckoned the most valuable prebend in England (Redman had evidently studied the *Valor*), and previously dedicated to the support of cardinals.[35] Redman has a right to be considered the most underrated master of intrigue of Tudor England.

Certainly the benefits of having university men in government were evident in the report of the commission. The poverty of the colleges

---

[32] *DNB*; Brook 1962, p. 23; below, pp. 455–7.

[33] Quoted in *DNB*, art. May, Mey or Meye, William.

[34] *VCH Cambs.*, III, pp. 462–3; Collinson 1991, p. 3. Mullinger 1884, pp. 80–6, is a Victorian period piece, but full of useful information.

[35] Cross 1977, pp. 196–7.

was recorded, as was the inadequacy of their revenues to meet their expenditure. Parker and the other commissioners presented the report to the king at Hampton Court, in the presence of a number of courtiers. Henry expressed surprise at their findings and avowed that he 'thought he had not in his realme so many persons so honestly maynteyned in lyvyng bi so little lond and rent'. Therefore, he thought it unreasonable that their lands should be exchanged for worse.[36] Parker wrote that at this remark some courtiers 'were grieved, for that they disappointed *lupos quosdam hiantes* [wolves with their mouths wide open]'.[37] However, the king had not fully removed the threat, by saying merely that he would not press the colleges to exchange their lands.[38]

The successful campaign mounted in opposition to the threat posed by the Chantries Act of 1545 has a fourfold importance. First, it helped to preserve the colleges – in every sense the most vital parts of the new type of university that was emerging during the course of the sixteenth century. If the colleges had been plundered and emasculated the university might still have expanded during the second half of the century but it would have been a very different institution from the one that did emerge. Second, it demonstrates the extent to which university men, and particularly those of a reformist disposition, had infiltrated the Court in pursuit of their aims. It also demonstrates that they could wield effective influence on behalf of the universities even against the interests of a more traditional type of courtier. Third, it indicates the increasing dependence of the government on university-trained men. Perhaps inevitably this was combined among those about the Court with an increased familiarity with the affairs of the universities. As events on this occasion demonstrated, but not for the last time, familiarity might bring benefits and influence, but it also had its dangers. Finally, from the viewpoint of Cambridge it confirmed within the university an understanding of the benefits that might accrue from access to suitable patrons at Court. This was a lesson that was not lost, either on the institution, or on many of the individuals within it. In this the university was partaking in the wider elaboration of the patron–client system at this time: a system of patrimonial patronage that was the concomitant of an emergent system of curial politics.[39]

A further set of events during 1545–7 emphasised the potential threat to the university during a period of political and religious upheaval, and the virtues of influential connections at Court.

---

[36] Lamb 1838, p. 60; Parker 1853, pp. 35–6. The Commission's Report is in *Cambridge Documents 1852*, I, pp. 105–294.
[37] Parker 1853, p. 36.   [38] *Ibid.*   [39] Morgan 1986, 1988.

There was perennial conflict between the authorities of the university and the town of Cambridge and these were to continue well into the seventeenth century.[40] In the 1540s 'the townsmen of Cambridge began now to hope their time come, to cast off the yoke (as they counted it) of the University, as if on the alteration of religion the ancient privileges of scholars should be abolished, under the notion of superstition'.[41] A minor dispute over the appropriation of 'an ambling nag' belonging to the master of Peterhouse was blown up into an issue of principle. Further disputes arose over the conduct of Stourbridge Fair, and the university's prisoners, malefactors taken at the fair, were liberated by the mayor's son. These petty disputes prompted Roger Ascham, the Orator, to appeal to the patrons of the university at the heart of government. Ascham 'belettered all the Lords of the privy council', and amongst the rest Sir Thomas Wriothesley the lord chancellor of England,[42] whom 'the University partly commandeth as once a member, partly requesteth as now a patron thereof'. The 'belettering' also encompassed some gentlemen of the king's bedchamber. In itself this is an indication of how far university men such as Ascham were up-to-date with the configuration of politics at the centre. For we now know the extent to which the privy chamber (in referring to the 'bedchamber' Fuller was using a later term) had become a centre of power in the Henrician Court.[43] To round off the drubbing given to their municipal neighbours the university procured the confirmation of its privileges in the following parliament.[44]

The significance of the outcome of these events needs to be judged within the broader context. It was not only in Cambridge that municipal authorities saw the upheavals precipitated by religious changes in the 1530s and 1540s as an opportunity to outwit their neighbours. In many English towns independent religious or quasi-religious corporations occupied substantial parts of the townscape and often affronted the civic dignity with their immunities, privileges and ceremonial. These 'corporations within corporations' not only took the obvious form of cathedral closes within towns that were episcopal seats. In many cities there were also extensive areas occupied by friaries, hospitals and secular colleges. In some towns substantial numbers of properties were owned by religious bodies and rented out as a source of income.[45] The equivalent in Cambridge were the colleges and the readily associated institutions of the

---

[40] See below, chapter 7.   [41] Fuller 1655/1840, pp. 240–1; Lamb 1838, pp. 73–9.
[42] Venn, IV, p. 479b. Wriothesley was educated at Trinity Hall.
[43] Starkey 1977, 1987; Loades 1992.   [44] Fuller 1655/1840, pp. 241–2.   [45] Tittler 1991.

regulars, the monks, nuns, canons and friars.[46] Because they represented liberties within the framework of municipal corporations disputes often arose over the issue of boundaries and jurisdiction. The dispute over miscreants at Stourbridge can be seen as one instance of this type of dispute. In short, religious institutions within towns were often a running sore for their host municipalities. In this broader context it is illuminating to contrast what happened at Cambridge with what happened some 60 miles away at Norwich.[47] There, in 1517, Cardinal Wolsey had enforced a settlement between the monks at the cathedral and the city. However, in the 1540s, with the monastic cathedral dissolved the city was able substantially to reverse this decision. Moreover, with the dissolution of the friaries this decade saw the opening up of vast tracts of the townscape. At the same time the city effectively municipalised those former religious institutions such as the Great Hospital and the school the services of which they appreciated. They also acquired the former Blackfriars as a new municipal hall. What formerly had probably been part of an episcopal crozier was refashioned as a municipal mace. In most of this it is possible to detect the doings of Alderman Augustine Steward, the 'Mr Fixit' of Henrician Norwich and a man with all the right connections. The municipal leaders of Cambridge simply were not in the same league. But the difference between what happened in a place like Norwich and what happened in Cambridge was not simply a question of differing municipal status or the presence or otherwise of personal acumen on the part of municipal leaders. It is also both a measure of how far the universities had already acquired a special status within the Tudor state and an indicator of much that was to come. By the 1540s, municipal Cambridge faced formidable opponents in the persons of academics in high places and with connections in high places. And however much contemporaries may have seen the colleges as simply another type of religious institution ripe for the picking, by the time that the Cambridge burghers reached for the promised fruit, they had it whisked from their hands. Not least this was because the university and university men had begun to play a role that they were to fulfil for decades to come as apparatchiks of the Tudor state. In the crisis surrounding Henry's divorce the early modern equivalent of ideology was suddenly important. As we have seen, it was the new humanist scholars from the universities, who were sent scuttling around Europe whipping up support. It was the same

[46] As we have seen above. For details, see Brooke 1985a and below, pp. 17–20.
[47] For what follows, see Morgan 1996; Pound 1988.

men who concocted the footnoted justifications that Henry required. When he sat there at Hampton Court listening to the apologia from the universities, no doubt Henry would have liked to gratify his importunate courtiers; but by then he had learned the lesson that these pendants could be useful: better leave them their paltry manors and the lead on the roofs of their college halls.

Chapter 2

THE BUILDINGS OF CAMBRIDGE

GREAT ST MARY'S AND KING'S CHAPEL

Supreme among the documents for the history of the University of Cambridge are its buildings and their setting, for Cambridge wears its heart on its sleeve. It has a tiny ancient centre with Great St Mary's church, the Senate House and the Old Schools at its heart; and round this centre the colleges cluster.[1] Great St Mary's was there long before the university; and the first students flocked to it as they had been accustomed to gather in and around St Mary the Virgin in Oxford. Probably from the thirteenth century its nave had come to be used as the chief meeting place of the university, in which its ceremonies took place – and so it remained until the eighteenth century, when the Senate House was built. In the late fourteenth and fifteenth centuries permanent buildings replaced the temporary lecture rooms and other quarters in which the university had squatted in its early years; and these naturally were as close to Great St Mary's as the close-knit housing of the region permitted. Hence the site of the Old Schools, the centre of the faculties and libraries throughout our period. Hence too the site of most of the early colleges – Clare, Gonville Hall, Trinity Hall, the King's Hall and Michaelhouse – the last two translated into Trinity College from 1546. In the 1440s Henry VI and his young queen (who was seventeen when she founded Queens')[2] had swept clear a whole quarter of the town between the High Street (King's Parade and Trumpington Street) and the river to make way for their colleges of King's and Queens'. The old court of Queens' is a perfectly preserved fifteenth-century college, protected by a massive castle gate – the first of the great castle gates which are a special feature of the Cambridge colleges of the fifteenth and sixteenth centuries – with

---

[1] See Plate 1. For what follows, see esp. Willis and Clark 1886/1988; Brooke, Highfield and Swaan 1988, esp. ch. 6. On Great St Mary's, Brooke 1999a.
[2] Brooke and Ortenberg 1988.

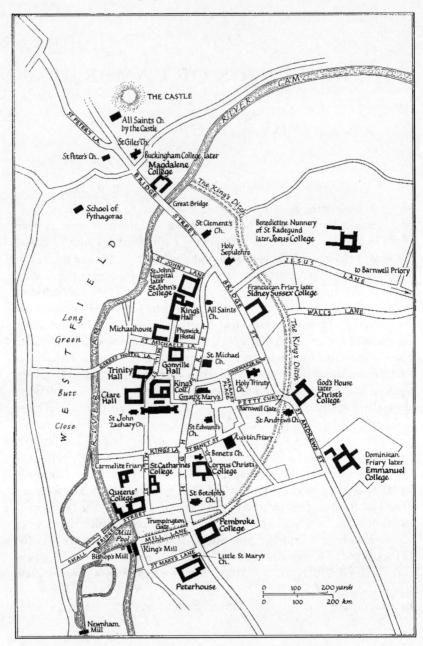

THE CASTLE

All Saints Ch.
by the Castle

ST PETER'S LA.

St Giles' Ch.

St Peter's Ch.

Buckingham College, later
Magdalene College

RIVER CAM

The King's Ditch

Great Bridge

BRIDGE STREET

School of Pythagoras

St Clement's Ch.

Benedictine Nunnery of St Radegund later Jesus College

to Barnwell Priory

Holy Sepulchre

JESUS LANE

St John's Lane

St John's Hospital later

St John's College

Franciscan Friary later
Sidney Sussex College

WALLS LANE

BRIDGE ST

King's Hall

All Saints Ch.

Long Green

W E S T   F I E L D

Michaelhouse

Physwick Hostel

ST MICHAEL'S LA.

St Michael Ch.

GARRET HOSTEL LA.

SHOEMAKER ROW

The King's Ditch

Trinity Hall

Gonville Hall

MARKET PLACE

Holy Trinity Ch.

God's House later Christ's College

Clare Hall

King's Coll.

Great St Mary's Ch.

Butt

Close

St John Zachary Ch.

PETTY CURY

Barnwell Gate

St Andrews Ch.

ST ANDREW'S ST

R I V E R   C A M

St Edward's Ch.

Austin Friary

KING'S LA.

ST BENET ST

St Benet's Ch.

Dominican Friary later
Emmanuel College

Carmelite Friary

St Catharine's College

HIGH ST

Corpus Christi College

Queens' College

St Botolph's Ch.

Trumpington Gate

Pembroke College

BRIDGE STREET

Mill Pool

MILL LANE

King's Mill

Little St Mary's Ch.

SMALL BRIDGES ST

Bishop's Mill

ST MARY'S LANE

Peterhouse

| 0 | 100 | 200 yards |
| 0 | 100 | 200 km |

Newnham Mill

Plate 1 Cambridge in the early sixteenth century

GREAT ST MARY'S,
The University Church.

Plate 2 Great St Mary's in 1813

chapel, library, hall and chambers.[3] King's was designed to be a larger
New College by the Cam; but Henry VI's resources were never adequate
to his dreams, and when he was deposed, only a modest foundation in
what is now the university Registry, a fair-sized first chapel (long since
demolished) on the grass beside it, and the shell of the great chapel which
is now his monument were left as the shadows of a great design.[4]

---

[3] Twigg 1987, Parts I and II, esp. ch. 1; Brooke, Highfield and Swaan 1988, pp. 108–14 and
pls. 68–73.
[4] Recent discussion of the extent of Henry VI's personal involvement does not concern us. Strong
arguments can be mounted for substantial input by leading figures in his entourage; but the well-
documented case in Lovatt 1981 for seeing the chapel and the priorities established in the statutes
as reflecting a very strong personal interest by the king is very convincing. On the architectural
history of the building see Woodman 1986.

The nave of Great St Mary's was rebuilt in and about the 1490s in a campaign partly or largely orchestrated by the vice-chancellor and proctors. The tendentious evidences gathered by Matthew Parker and his friend John Caius give the impression that it was wholly the work of the university – and the greatest benefactor was undoubtedly Thomas Barewe, whose gift was made on the amazing condition that Richard III be enrolled among the university's benefactors, at the height of Henry VII's reign.[5] Doubtless in fact it was a cooperative venture between town and gown – a reminder that cooperation was a normal part of life, but more rarely recorded than the conflicts. Yet it remains a monument to the practical needs and purposes of the leaders of the university of the 1490s (including the young John Fisher) and their devotion to the Blessed Virgin Mary. But if we stand near the north entrance to King's chapel we can see at a glance the contrast between the chapel thought fitting for the devotions of one single college and the church which reflects the aspiration of the whole university. King's chapel was first conceived in the megalomaniac fancies of Henry VI and his advisers, and it is a vast church which encompasses a royal chapel, a chantry for the souls of Henry and his family, and a chapel for the devotions of an academic community. It was completed by the munificence of Henry VII and Henry VIII, and its great fan vault and the plethora of Tudor and Beaufort emblems which fill the walls and ceiling of the ante-chapel were the work of John Wastell, the eminent architect who also designed the nave of Great St Mary's. But perhaps the most astonishing thing about King's chapel is its glass. It is surprising enough that it survived all the vicissitudes of the iconoclasm of the Reformation and the puritan revolution. Even more surprising is the story of its making. In 1515 Bishop Richard Fox of Winchester devised for Henry VIII the highly sophisticated iconographic scheme, full of types and ante-types. Basically, the glass portrays the life of the Blessed Virgin Mary, from her immaculate birth to her assumption into heaven – and within the scheme the life of her son forms the central group of incidents, culminating in the great crucifixion in the east window. The ensemble is one of the most elaborate and dramatic expressions of devotion to Mary, and of late medieval religious sentiment, in Europe. Henry VIII continued to fund and support it to the end of his life – the whole scheme was finished in 1548.[6] Yet long before this the king had given his blessing to the Henrician Reformation and to the first wave of iconoclasm. King's chapel is a strangely ambivalent historical document, a reminder of the

---

[5] Brooke 1999a, pp. 18–20, 23–4.
[6] The fundamental study of the King's glass is Wayment 1972.

paradoxes of which Reformation history is compounded, especially in Cambridge.[7]

The lawns of King's form one of many open spaces reflecting the predicament of late medieval and early modern Cambridge. Henry VI swept this whole quarter of Cambridge clear; but the space between King's chapel and the river simply remained a building site – a neglected open space, like some of the precincts of religious houses, till a later generation tidied it up. It is surprising how many of the medieval religious houses of Cambridge were converted into colleges, before as well as after the dissolution of the monasteries in the 1530s. In the 1490s John Alcock, bishop of Ely, had suppressed the house of nuns of St Radegund and converted it, very grandly, into Jesus College. In 1511 John Fisher was able to save a substantial sum from the treasury of the Lady Margaret Beaufort, take over the old Hospital of St John and convert it into St John's College. In 1539 the beautiful monastic Buckingham College was dissolved, since it was a house of monks; or was it? Peter Cunich has shown that, surprisingly enough, the last students of Buckingham College failed to depart – until in 1542 they were able to catch the ear of Lord Audley, a leading royal official and a major beneficiary of the dissolution of the monasteries, who in turn helped them to win the king's consent to the conversion of Buckingham College into a secular college – that is to say, to recognise the status quo.[8] It seems clear that, unlike most college founders, Audley was interested neither in masses for his soul nor in students; what incentive he had to consent to found a college is not clear. But he and his widow, Lady Elizabeth Audley, who usurped from the king the title of foundress, have won a strange immortality. To whom Buckingham College was dedicated is entirely unknown. The dedication of the college to St Mary Magdalene seems to be the result of a pun – M-Audley-N, Magdalene as it was pronounced then and now.[9]

This strange story reveals that there were active and powerful figures in Cambridge determined not to let the legacy of the religious houses be entirely lost; and this is reinforced by the survival of the precincts of the four major orders of friars, all of which avoided becoming absorbed (as

[7] See below, chapter 12; Porter 1958/1972; Brooke, Highfield and Swaan 1988, ch. 7.
[8] Peter Cunich in Cunich, Hoyle, Duffy and Hyam 1994, pp. 33–6.
[9] *Ibid.*, pp. 40, 281 n. 24.

in so many towns of the age) into building development. The precinct of the Carmelite friars was adjacent to Queens' College, and the canny president of Queens', William Mey (who was to die archbishop-elect of York at the opening of Elizabeth I's reign), attached it to Queens' just before the dissolution – though he had to pay a large price for it thereafter.[10] Much of the Austin friary survived long enough to offer a home to the free grammar school established under the will of Stephen Perse of Caius in 1615–18.[11] The precincts of the Dominican and Franciscan friars (though not the buildings) survived intact to be refounded in 1584 and 1596 as Emmanuel and Sidney Sussex colleges. Emmanuel and Sidney are symbols of continuity. They remind us that the dissolution of the monasteries must (at first) have appeared an unmitigated disaster in Cambridge – and many, even of those who welcomed some of the changes, will have regretted the passing of what amounted to a notable group of colleges. For all the conflicts of regulars and seculars in the university, it had to be recognised that the friars had been a major creative force: for in the Franciscan convent Duns Scotus had probably taught; and in the Dominican, almost certainly, Robert Holcot, one of the most eminent biblical scholars of the later Middle Ages, had spent a part of his career.[12] Nor was the outcome of the Reformation clear or clear-cut: who could say, in the 1540s and 1550s, that a return to the papal allegiance might not be followed by some revival of religious houses? This must have been an especially teasing question to those leading academics like John Redman, first master of Trinity – and almost as much its founder as Henry VIII – who on his deathbed still hovered on the edge of old and new doctrines, or Andrew Perne, master of Peterhouse, who seemed equally at home with the regimes of Mary and Elizabeth.[13] The spacious gardens and lawns of Emmanuel, with the Dominican fishpond in their centre and surrounded by a medieval wall, remind us that the Dominican precinct survived intact from 1539 to 1584, its future uncertain. The Franciscan church in particular had been a favourite meeting place for the university, a rival to Great St Mary's as the place for ceremonies and sermons; and soon after the dissolution an attempt was made to move the king to make a grant of it to the university.[14] Henry VIII, meanwhile, was debating whether to suppress

---

[10] Twigg 1987, p. 31; Searle 1867–71, I, pp. 222–32, and addenda, pp. vi–vii.
[11] Now the Whipple Museum of the History of Science. See Pevsner 1970, p. 206. Cf. Brooke 1985/1996, p. 101.
[12] For the evidence that Duns taught in Cambridge, see Emden 1963, p. 198; cf. Moorman 1952, p. 173. On Holcot, see Bendall, Brooke and Collinson 1999, p. 11 and refs.
[13] See above, p. 8. On Perne see esp. Collinson 1991.
[14] Willis and Clark 1886/1988, III, pp. 465, 470, etc.

Plate 3 Emmanuel College, from the air

the colleges or enhance them. Eventually he was cajoled by an obscure court intrigue into putting the matter into the hands of leading local divines; and he became convinced by the remarkable, and admirably tendentious, visitation of the colleges undertaken by John Redman, Matthew Parker and William Mey (and in Oxford by Richard Cox), that they should be preserved and enlarged; and so he converted the King's Hall into Trinity College, mopping up Michaelhouse and Physwick Hostel in the process.[15] He also endowed the college with the site and buildings of the Franciscan house; and the college immediately set to work to quarry stone and other materials from it for their own building works – to such good purpose that little remained of the Franciscan buildings when arrangements were made to sell the site to the executors of the Countess of Sussex to found her college in the 1590s. The founding of Sidney Sussex College seems to have been delayed by objections from the master and fellows of Trinity, who may have played for time to complete the process of quarrying stone from the friars' buildings – for the great works of

[15] Brooke, Highfield and Swaan 1988, pp. 152–4; Mullinger 1884, pp. 79–86; Dawson 1984.

Plate 4 Emmanuel College, the Founder's Cup: silver-gilt *tazza*, made in
Antwerp, 1541. The finial is enamelled with the arms of the Founder,
Sir Walter Mildmay, on one side and his monogram on the other.

Thomas Nevile in Trinity were just beginning in the mid-1590s – or to
command a higher price; perhaps for both. In the end they gave way with
a good grace, and Sidney could enter into the Franciscan inheritance.[16]

---

[16] On Sidney, see Willis and Clark 1886/1988, III, pp. 724–36, 752; on its Franciscan inheritance
and early buildings, see Salway 1996; Wyatt 1996. Nevile's works at Trinity included Great Court,

Needless to say, continuity is in some ways less apparent in the new foundations which then sprang up: both Emmanuel and Sidney were (in some sense of the term) puritan foundations. It is true that the statutes of Emmanuel provided by Sir Walter Mildmay – Elizabeth's chancellor of the exchequer and a notable moderate puritan – were in large measure based on those given by John Fisher to Christ's (where Mildmay had spent his university career); and that there was a striking affinity between a community training professional Catholic preachers and one training professional puritan preachers. But Mildmay himself was at some pains to emphasise the differences the Reformation had brought. He took over quite substantial parts of the medieval buildings, but adapted the chapel to a dining hall, and the southern range of the cloister to student rooms on the conventional college pattern. The chapel was at the heart of his idea of a college; but it was a new chapel – a preaching box, deliberately oriented not east and west, but north and south. When the heyday of puritan Emmanuel was passing, in the euphoria of the Restoration after 1660, William Sancroft – who somehow contrived to be both a high churchman and a dyed-in-the-wool Emmanuel man – called in Christopher Wren to provide the college with a chapel properly oriented, portraying the beauty of holiness.[17]

THE ACADEMIC QUARTER

Thus the dissolved religious houses were not wholly lost in the Cambridge of Renaissance and Reformation. Meanwhile, the most powerful symbol of continuity is the academic quarter with its centre in Great St Mary's and the Old Schools, and the line of colleges along the river. These were the notable creations of the late Middle Ages, and the line of colleges is above all a monument to the fifteenth and sixteenth centuries. At the southern end of this line lies Queens'; and on the river's edge lies the relic of a beautiful red-brick lodging of the mid-fifteenth century. It is a part of the original design of the college by Andrew Docket, its academic founder, who was aided by Margaret of Anjou, the first of the queens he cajoled into paying for his dreams.[18] It is a relic because it once extended further to the south; but enough remains to provide one of the notable puzzles among college buildings. It is the only part of Docket's

---

the hall (see pp. 38–9) and the beginnings of Nevile's Court: Willis and Clark 1886/1988, III, pp. 474–95.

[17] On Mildmay's buildings, see Bendall *et al.* 1999, pp. 43–4 and refs. in n. 3.

[18] On it, see Brooke in Bradshaw and Duffy 1989, pp. 57–8; Brooke, Highfield and Swaan 1988, p. 112 and pl. 70; Twigg 1987, pp. 130–1.

Plate 5 Emmanuel College, the Founder's Cup: *repoussé* decoration inside the bowl, showing the poet Arion being rescued by a dolphin, surrounded by a frieze of fantastic sea-creatures

design which was not already a conventional element in a college court: chapel, hall, library, president's chamber, fellows' parlour, students' rooms formed the basic pattern of late medieval colleges. The lodge by the river was not. The only plausible explanation which has been proposed is that Docket provided comfortable lodgings for his royal patrons; and it seems highly probable that it was used to house Henry VII when he visited Queens' in 1507.[19] It was ideally situated for a royal barge to moor beside it, and carry the king or queen or other grand visitors along the Cam, past the panorama of the academic quarter. Andrew Docket was a fund-raiser of genius. We are inclined to think the profession a modern invention; and indeed it has returned to Cambridge and its colleges – as to all universities – in the late twentieth and early twenty-first centuries as a new specialism. But medieval Cambridge had the friars in its midst, orders who lived mainly – the Franciscan entirely – by begging; mendicancy was a highly developed profession. Nor was it confined to the friars: some of the most accomplished beggars of the late Middle Ages were seculars, including Edmund Gonville, founder of Gonville Hall and two other religious houses besides in the early and mid-fourteenth century, and Andrew Docket himself.[20] The profession declined as a result of the dissolution of the monasteries, and this may be part of the reason why so few new colleges were founded in later centuries – before the twentieth. But it had one of its most notable recruits in the early sixteenth century in John Fisher.

Fisher was a devout Yorkshireman who became a leading Cambridge academic in the 1480s and 1490s; and in 1494–5 he lunched with the Lady Margaret and soon after became her favourite chaplain, with a special dispensation to be absent from Cambridge in her service. From this notable collaboration came a string of benefactions to Cambridge – especially the Lady Margaret's Professorship of Divinity and the colleges of Christ's and (after her death) St John's. Meanwhile, in 1504 he became both chancellor of the university and bishop of Rochester, rarely visiting Cambridge thereafter – save in his dreams; for his own benefactions to Cambridge, in collaboration with his patroness, went on unabated. For a time Fisher was president of Queens'; and it is hardly a coincidence that the red brick of Queens' at the south end of the academic quarter, so characteristic of later Cambridge building, so different from anything in Henry VI's King's, came to be imitated in Fisher's St John's at the north end in the early sixteeenth century. Queens', and Cambridge red brick, are monuments to the inspiration of Andrew Docket and (perhaps) of Queen Margaret. By the same token it could be said that the completion of the academic quarter is a monument to Fisher and the Lady Margaret. Yet Christ's is on the other side of the town by the Barnwell Gate. In a similar way, one might say that Fisher's central concern with the education

---

[19] Cf. Brooke in Bradshaw and Duffy 1989, pp. 58, 65 n. 63; Underwood, in *ibid.*, p. 43 n. 22.
[20] See Brooke 1999c, ch. 16.

of north country boys was matched by the yales who support the coat of arms of the Lady Margaret in Christ's and St John's, symbols of her lordship of Kendal. But the yale is a mythical beast and it is not clear – not likely indeed – that she ever visited Kendal; and it is in Westmorland (currently Cumbria) not Yorkshire.[21] None the less, however much we qualify them, there are real links here.

What the academic quarter undoubtedly symbolises is the manner in which the colleges were taking over the university in the fifteenth and sixteenth centuries. In 1440 there were eight colleges, mostly very small – only the King's Hall was a major institution; the vast majority of the students were either in hostels or in friaries. By the mid-sixteenth century the friaries were gone and the hostels rapidly disappearing: between 1570 and the mid-nineteenth century a student had to belong to a college.[22] The reasons for the change are not easy to discern. It is evident that the new foundations of the fifteenth century added considerably to the spaces available in colleges and even more to their prestige; and the more authoritarian attitude of the government and the university officials, including the heads of colleges, made it seem first desirable, then essential, to round up unruly students within the walls of those academic fortresses, the colleges – whose fortress-like quality is symbolised in the massive gates stemming from that at Queens' of the mid-fifteenth century. Furthermore, the prestige and courtly links of the new foundations of the mid-fifteenth and mid-sixteenth centuries gave an authority to the colleges which is a vital part of the story; and of this their buildings are the outward show – and symbols. Most conspicuous are the perfect court of Queens', enhanced by the lodging by the river – in Elizabethan times enhanced still further by the greatly enlarged president's lodge (see pp. 308–9); King's chapel; the amalgamation of the King's Hall, Michaelhouse and Physwick Hostel into Trinity College in 1546 – and their remodelling as a single architectural unit, Great Court, by Dean Nevile at the end of the century; and beyond Trinity the growing splendour of St John's, monument to Henry VIII's grandmother. They all reflect (in varying degrees) the grandeur of their royal and courtly patrons, and prepare us for the age when church and state were dominated by Cambridge

---

[21] For all that concerns the Lady Margaret, see Jones and Underwood 1992.
[22] On the history of the hostels, see Leader 1988, pp. 45–8, 258–9.

The absence of non-collegiate students is implicit in the statutes of 1570, c. 50: see *Cambridge Documents 1852*, I, pp. 490–4 – and already *c.* 1544 it was assumed that all students were in colleges, halls or hostels (*Statuta 1785*, pp. 122–3): the disappearance of halls and hostels gave the colleges a monopoly. I am indebted to Dr Elisabeth Leedham-Green for help with this: the documents cited are entered at the opening of the first University Matriculation Register.

men – Burghley, Parker, Whitgift and the others – and the university had to accept in return a much reduced intellectual freedom.

JOHN CAIUS AND THE LAY ELEMENT IN CAMBRIDGE

The university had always been a clerical community, and remained so in great measure until the nineteenth century. To this there were two notable exceptions. In the sixteenth and seventeenth centuries there were laymen who came to Cambridge to study and enjoy themselves, for a time – often leaving without a degree and going on to serious education in the Inns of Court. This element increased substantially in the late sixteenth and early seventeenth centuries; but we have no idea when it began. It is often said that it started about 1560, but that is only because the first document which reveals the presence of laymen in large numbers is the Caius Matriculation Register, which starts in 1559.[23] William Cecil, later Lord Burghley, Sir Walter Mildmay and Sir Thomas Gresham – to name only the most famous – were there before 1559. The early history of the lay presence is wholly obscure, but it is beyond doubt that they formed a very significant element in the university from 1560 on (see pp. 131–46).

There was also a small number of laymen holding office in the university and the colleges. A man who wished to practise law in the church courts had (in effect) to be a layman at this time, and this largely accounts for the lay presence in Trinity Hall.[24] Many physicians were laymen, and the medical faculty also had lay members. But few college statutes allowed for lay fellows – Trinity Hall and Caius were the most notable exceptions; and the most eminent lay heads in this period were John Caius, physician, founder and master of Caius (1559–73), and Thomas Legge, his chosen successor, civil and canon lawyer, tutor of Jesus, and master of Caius (1573–1607).

The building works of John Caius largely survive, and tell a strange story. After refounding the college in 1557–8, he built three gates to mark the entries and the exit, and he built a court to house about sixty fellows and students and an extension to the master's lodge. The court is beautifully finished with fine thirteenth-century ashlar bought by Caius

[23] Venn 1887; summaries in Venn 1897–1901, I–II; cf. Brooke 1985/1996, pp. 80–4.

[24] Serious practice in church courts involved entry to Doctors' Commons in the city of London, which was prohibited to the clergy (Squibb 1977, esp. ch. 1; Brooke 1985/1996, p. 85). The reasons for this are not entirely clear; but late medieval popes had prohibited the study of civil (Roman) law to the clergy, and civil law was the essential background to the study and practice of canon law in sixteenth-century England, especially after the closure of the canon law faculty by Thomas Cromwell (for the survival of Roman canon law through the Reformation, see Helmholz 1990). On Trinity Hall, see Crawley 1976, ch. 4.

from Oliver Cromwell's impecunious grandfather, and quarried from the ruins of Ramsey abbey. But in most other respects it is a highly conventional copy of a medieval court. A fourteenth-century founder like William of Wykeham would have felt quite at home in it. There was no essential novelty in the living and working conditions Caius envisaged. Each of four staircases linked ground and first floor;[25] and on either side of the stairway was a unit, with a loftier, tutor's room, above, to house a fellow-tutor and up to three students, and a more modest students' room below for three or four more. This was the tutor's group; the social and educational unit. It is clear that the tutorial group in Caius did not necessarily – perhaps rarely did – exactly number six or seven students; but the framework was the traditional unit which Wykeham had provided in New College in the late fourteenth century. So far, there was nothing new.[26]

Caius provided in his statutes that only pensioners or commoners should occupy his court down to 1580.[27] The precise purpose of this is not clear; but it is a reminder that even a college in the hands of a rich benefactor looked to commoners' rents as an essential part of its economy. William of Wykeham had provided only for scholars in New College. But that was unusual: it is clear that the Old Court at Corpus, also of the second half of the fourteenth century, was designed to hold many commoners from the start.[28] In the event, all these plans had to be modified. The college was not highly popular while Caius himself lived; but Thomas Legge was the most genial and tolerant of men: he brought many or most of his old pupils from Jesus with him, and attracted many more, so that in his time the college rapidly filled up. But the tutorial groups rarely numbered a tidy six or seven.[29]

[25] Also a half-staircase (now M) next to the chapel. For the master's lodge, see Watkin, Brooke and Richmond 1999.

[26] It is often asserted that the tutorial system was a novelty in Tudor, or more specifically Elizabethan, Cambridge. But the architectural evidence, which shows a clear line of continuity from Wykeham's New College in the fourteenth century to Caius Court in the late sixteenth – and can probably be traced back before New College, perhaps even to the late thirteenth century – makes it clear that in some senses there was continuity in the relation of tutors and pupils. For the architectural evidence at New College, very similar to Caius Court but without the third storey, see Jackson-Stops 1979, pp. 183–4 and esp. fig. c on p. 186; and see the discussion of its significance in Brooke 1989b, esp. pp. 164–5; Brooke 1987.

Willis and Clark 1886/1988, III, pp. 302–3, suggest that Caius' statutes put two students in a chamber; but the passage has to do with rents, not with room allocation (Venn 1897–1901, III, p. 364).

[27] 'pensionariis tantum elocentur' (Venn 1897–1901, III, p. 364).

[28] On Corpus Old Court see Brooke 1989b, pp. 163–4; for the architectural evidence, see esp. Rackham 1987–8.

[29] Brooke 1987.

Caius allowed himself two remarkable innovations. In some courts of this period a third storey came to be added to fit more students into the space of one court. Caius attempted nothing so revolutionary; but he provided attics or cocklofts approached by stairs within the tutors' rooms. By day the students worked in cubicles within the upper or the lower chamber, under the tutor's eye; by night the tutor could dismiss the men who shared his room to the cockloft above, and enjoy a modicum of privacy. The cocklofts are lit by windows on the outer side of the court – from without the buildings seem to have three storeys. But from within the court the traditional arrangement is preserved, to emphasise the highly conservative nature of Caius' conception.

The other innovation is that the court has only three sides: two, to east and west, of rooms for tutors and students; one, on the north, comprising the chapel, which at that date still wore its Gothic costume of the late fourteenth century. But the south side was left open: 'We have decreed that no building be constructed which closes the whole of the south side of our foundation, to prevent the free circulation of air and make it shut in and corrupt, which might damage the health of those dwelling in Caius and (especially) Gonville Courts and speed the coming of illnesses and death.'[30] The south side is still open to the sun and fresh air – and Caius court started a new fashion for three-sided courts.[31] But in the early eighteenth century the Senate House was to come perilously close, and the master of Caius had to sue out a writ in Chancery to prevent it closing the southern vista in defiance of the wishes of Dr Caius.[32]

Caius himself meanwhile planned to set a small gate in the middle of the south wall of the court: he did not live to see it finished, but the concept is highly characteristic of him. The Gate of Honour is a Renaissance fantasy: it was set facing down a small street no longer extant, which led to the Old Schools – and Senate House Passage, the route to Great St Mary's. Through the Gate of Honour his students were to proceed to their degrees: it is a triumphal arch commemorating their successes in the schools. On its faces lay a series of sundials, and in the court was a pillar with many more.[33] In almost every respect these fantasies were in striking contrast to the conservative nature of the court behind it. When

---

[30] Venn 1897–1901, III, p. 364: 'valetudinem nostrorum et maxime Collegii Gonevilli offendat'. In Caius' statutes and the Matriculation Register, 'collegium' is used where we would say 'court'.
[31] Examples in Cambridge of three-sided courts were Nevile's Court at Trinity and Sidney Sussex as originally planned, both facing west (Willis and Clark 1886/1988, II, pp. 517–19, 736–7 and fig. 4), and St Catharine's, facing east, although St Catharine's was originally designed to have an east wing (see below, p. 34).
[32] See pp. 60–1.   [33] Brooke 1985/1996, pp. 65–7.

North Front of the Porta Honoris
One of the Entrances to Caius College Cambridge.

Plate 6 The Gate of Honour, Gonville and Caius College, from within: pen drawing by William Wilkins, *c.* 1800, Society of Antiquaries

the works of John Caius were complete, one entered the college from the east by the Gate of Humility, passed through into Caius Court by the Gate of Virtue, and went out by the Gate of Honour to take one's degree. The Gate of Humility was modest in scale and originally had charming miniature pillars with Corinthian capitals. Over the inner face of the

28

Gate of Virtue, facing Caius Court, is written an inscription – identical to that formerly visible on the foundation stone of the court – to Wisdom: 'John Caius set this stone [in dedicating the court] to Wisdom.'[34] The Gate of Virtue has Renaissance symbols of wisdom and plenty on it; even more striking is the peaceful, Italianate face it presents to the world. Superficially, one enters Caius Court by a noble gate, as in other colleges; but a glance at it shows that it is no castle gate, like that at Queens' – that the college is not a fortress, as most of the other gates proclaim, but a peacful home of learning. Like General Moncrieff in *The Importance of Being Earnest*, John Caius was essentially a man of peace, except in his domestic life among the fellows. Contemplating the Gate of Virtue, one might be in Padua, even in Florence; in the court itself one might be in Oxford.[35] Dr Caius was equally intoxicated by what we call Gothic and Renaissance tastes: in the Gate of Honour a four-centred arch, typical of the Gothic of its period – adjacent to a plain Tudor Gothic court – is surmounted by a riot of Renaissance ornament. The dedication of the court to Wisdom can be equally interpreted as a Greek idea characteristic of a very notable humanist, or as an invocation of one of the most powerful ideas in the Old Testament. There is a puzzle here, which can illuminate not only the eccentric personality of Dr Caius, but the intellectual and aesthetic world of Cambridge at large.

Dr Caius had been a young fellow of Gonville Hall in the early 1530s, when it was a notorious seedbed of Protestants – moderate Protestants, one has to say, some of whom prospered for a time in the service of Queen Anne Boleyn, alongside her most notable chaplain, Matthew Parker, master of Corpus, whom Anne's daughter Elizabeth was to make archbishop of Canterbury. Parker and Caius both came from Norwich; in later years, at least, they were intimate friends; and it seems likely that their friendship went back to their early days in Cambridge. It was probably not quite true, as the conservative bishop of Norwich, Richard Nykke, asserted in 1530, that 'I hear of no clerk that hath commen out lately' of Gonville Hall 'but savoureth of the frying pan';[36] but the young Caius moved among Protestants, and is likely to have been sympathetic towards them. In later life he was conservative – he was evidently happy with traditional rituals, he kept the college's mass vestments and books, and was tolerant in religious matters: the evidence strongly suggests that he had no serious

---

[34] *Ibid.*; Willis and Clark 1886/1988, I, pp. 171–85, esp. p. 172 (foundation stone), 177 (inscription on the Gate of Virtue).

[35] Brooke 1985/1996, pp. 65–7, 306.

[36] Quoted Brooke 1985/1996, pp. 51–2, and n. 41 for the MS. On John Caius and his career, see *ibid.*, ch. 4 and p. 306, citing Nutton 1987 on Caius as humanist.

Plate 7 The Gate of Virtue, Gonville and Caius College, from the east

theological interests, at least not of a confessional nature. William Butts, alumnus of Gonville Hall and royal physician who recruited chaplains for Queen Anne, turned John Caius towards Padua, where he could indulge the two academic passions of his life, Greek and medicine. In Padua he supported himself by lecturing on Aristotle as 'Professor of Greek Dialectic', and studied medicine. The two coalesced then and in later years in his studies of manuscripts of Galen, which have established him as one of the most notable textual scholars of the century.[37] But they also inspired him with fundamentalist reverence for Galen; and in his later career as a physician in London and Cambridge he combined very strangely a notable talent for practical medicine which brought him a handsome fortune, a deep interest in practical research including dissection after the best Paduan models, and undeviating devotion to the words of Galen.

He refounded Gonville Hall as Gonville and Caius College in 1557–8, and after the last master of Gonville Hall had died in 1559, he was prevailed on to take up the office – at the urging not only of the fellows but of the vice-chancellor and heads of the colleges, one of the earliest references to joint action in the body which was later to dominate the university.[38] As head of an unruly group of young fellows, he was out of his depth: he was autocratic and cantankerous, attempting to expel the more difficult, and put the lesser offenders (so it was alleged) in the stocks. But he was tolerant in matters religious: the great experiences of his early life, outside Cambridge, had been in Catholic Padua and Protestant Zurich, home of the naturalist Conrad Gessner, a close friend and academic ally; his court and his gates remind us that though conservative in some of his tastes, Renaissance ideas and values were deeply meaningful to him. He was a Christian, probably a devout Christian; but not a man of sects. He suffered for this in later years, because the young Protestants among the fellows raised the cry of popery against him. Matthew Parker knew better, and protected him from afar. Meanwhile, Caius continued to pour the money earned in his prosperous medical practice in the City of London into the endowment of the college and its buildings. There is a heroic dimension to his generosity, as his buildings still bear witness, for as they went up he was increasingly under siege from his colleagues. His successor, Thomas Legge, was an ecclesiastical lawyer, commissary of the university and of the diocese of Ely, offices which prove him a loyal Anglican and help to explain why he too was accused of popery.[39] But the burden of the accusation against Legge was that he harboured papists in the college, and this was undoubtedly true; he also harboured and tolerated the fiery Protestants who accused him. There is no doubt that he was a man who cared deeply for toleration, which was possible for a layman, more difficult for a cleric – and it was the lay chancellor of the university, Lord Burghley, who protected him in the end.[40]

---

[37] Nutton 1987.   [38] See pp. 37–8. For what follows, see Brooke 1985/1996, pp. 70–8.

[39] On Legge, see Brooke 1985/1996, ch. 5 and in *Oxford DNB*, forthcoming; Stein 1985. For the reputation of the civil lawyers, and the view of canon law as 'a dangerous popish relic', see Helmholz 1990, pp. 52–3.

[40] Brooke 1985/1996, pp. 88–92.

CHAMBERS

Just as John Caius represented both tradition and innovation, continuity and change, so the buildings of seventeenth- and early eighteenth-century Cambridge reflect the slow pace of change and the remarkable innovations which none the less occurred. The chamber remained the fundamental unit, in which tutors and students lived together, until the mid-seventeenth century – and was then only slowly modified as the tutor came to seek, and find, greater privacy; and as the number of tutors and their intimacy with their charges declined. By the 1610s the community had expanded beyond the buildings provided by Dr Caius. The building which enabled Robert Willis to reconstruct the basic pattern of the medieval and early modern chamber was one of those built at Caius out of the legacies of Thomas Legge and his close colleague for well over thirty years, the philanthropist Stephen Perse.[41] These two buildings, set to the north of the Gate of Humility where the corner of Tree Court (of 1868–70) now stands, reflect the peak of student recruitment in the college in the period 1610–30.[42] In the upper floors of the Perse building the young Willis found a chamber with partitions forming cubicles or studies, as had evidently been the norm from the fourteenth to the seventeenth centuries. While the Perse and Legge buildings were in the making, a well-to-do young student in Trinity was observing the sizars performing domestic duties about him – and not long after, as a fellow, George Herbert wrote the lines, addressing his divine tutor:

> Who sweeps a chamber for thy Laws,
> Makes that and th'action fine.

On reflection, aiming for a wider audience, he changed 'a chamber' to 'a room as' – the words familiar in the hymn we still sing today, though unmindful of the sizars who inspired it.[43]

The chamber was the unit of accommodation still; but in the course of the seventeenth century its context and its design and furnishing were gradually modified. Caius Court had provided two and a half storeys of chambers; the Perse and Legge buildings at Caius of the late 1610s had three storeys and a garret floor, also divided into chambers. This design allowed almost twice the number of students to be accommodated on

---

[41] On Stephen Perse, see *ibid.*, pp. 98–103.

[42] For statistics of student numbers, see Venn 1897–1901, III, p. 392 and chart following; Brooke 1985/1996, pp. 833–4; Twigg 1990, p. 289.

[43] For George Herbert, see Charles 1971, fo. 75. For Willis, see Willis and Clark 1886/1988, II, ch. 3, esp. pp. 305–27, the classic statement of the evidence. For sizars, see below, pp. 330, 493.

a staircase; and it also reflects the beginning of a change in the relation of tutor and pupil. The tutorial groups were becoming larger, the small intimate unit favoured still by Dr Caius was giving way to units designed above all to maximise the numbers which the limited size of a Cambridge court could hold.

The effect of increasing numbers is reflected most dramatically in Clare College. In the late 1630s a plan was devised to open the college to the west and provide it with an approach from the meadows which now form the Backs, and to rebuild it completely. The first aim involved a fierce battle with King's to win the plot of land to the west of the old college – to give Clare a lung towards the Backs. With the help of the king and a team of episcopal arbitrators Clare was successful: it could open the path which led across the river, and build the bridge which still stands, sagging a little in memory of all the cartloads of stone it bore in the mid-seventeenth century.[44] Clare as we know it comprises a complete college of that period, with a slightly later chapel, otherwise unaltered until the new Clare was built beyond the Backs in the twentieth century. It is a monument first of all to the expansion of student numbers of the late sixteenth and early seventeenth centuries. It consists mainly of traditional student rooms, but the staircases comprise four storeys each, and there is thus much more accommodation than in Caius Court, let alone the medieval courts of Oxford and Cambridge. It is also, in a curious way, a monument to the Civil War; for the building was interrupted in 1642, when the parliament-men began a series of depradations of its materials for the better fortification of Cambridge Castle.[45] A visitor today who walks through the court from east to west contemplates fine Jacobean façades; but if he goes to the bridge and turns round, he sees only a Baroque face – and another Baroque façade within the court lines hall and combination room. Desultory work went on in the interval; but the major step forward, which led to the completion of the court with Baroque façades, came in and after 1669, when Wren's master mason, Robert Grumbold, was called in to marry the new world to the old.

Ironically, the pressure of numbers was already beginning to ease in most colleges by 1669. The exception was St Catharine's, which enjoyed a golden age under the mastership of John Lightfoot, a very notable Hebrew scholar, an enlightened divine and a popular master. He stood for learning, not for 'enthusiasm'; and he prepared the way for the new

---

44 Willis and Clark 1886/1996, I, pp. 89–92; for what follows, see *ibid.*, pp. 93–112.
45 *Ibid.*, p. 100.

Plate 8 Clare College, 1769: engraving by Lamborn, showing the Baroque west front of the college, with King's chapel and the end of the Gibbs building of King's beyond

world in St Catharine's and Cambridge by changing the dedication of one of his books from Cromwell to Charles II. Even more to the point, he gave every encouragement to the career of his younger colleague John Eachard, a lively, witty, genial man who gathered students around him as Thomas Legge had done in Caius a hundred years earlier – and collected money here, there and everywhere (including from his own pocket) to build a new college to house them. The three sides of the court which were built by Eachard were primarily designed to house increased numbers of students, in chambers somewhat larger than their medieval predecessors, but essentially the same in purpose. Eachard also provided hall and combination room; but the other public buildings, especially the library, planned for the east wing, were never built; so St Catharine's to this day has a three-sided court, by accident not design. When Eachard died, there were large debts still to pay, in spite of his heroic efforts; and although St Catharine's continued to flourish in the early eighteenth century, its heyday was passing. Eachard died in 1697; the chapel was added by 1704; and in the 1750s James Essex completed the south wing and gave the college its symmetrical appearance – at the

34

same time clearing the houses which cluttered its face to the east, and creating the open view from Trumpington Street which completes the work which Eachard had begun.[46]

Meanwhile, from 1660 on, a steep decline in student numbers had brought the undergraduate population of the university as a whole to little more than half the size it had been early in the century, and it was not to rise again till after 1800, nor achieve the level of the 1620s till about 1850 (see p. 464). As at Oxford, this period was none the less one of great achievement in college building; and one of the fundamental puzzles of the period is the contrast between declining prosperity and a never-declining will to build.

The much smaller intake of students meant that there was more space for those who came. In Caius, a hopeful college order had rather prematurely assigned a whole chamber to every student as early as 1652.[47] By 1696 the decline was being matched by rising living standards, and to the late 1690s and the early years of the eighteenth century belong the elegant panelling of the upper chambers in Caius Court and the more modest wainscotting of the rooms below.[48] When the north wing of Gonville Court was entirely rebuilt in the mid-eighteenth century to the designs of the tutor, later master, James Burrough, larger and more elegant chambers than their medieval predecessors were created.

The changing pattern of student rooms is apparent in many buildings of the late seventeenth and eighteenth centuries. Among the most sumptuous are those of the Garden Quad in New College, Oxford, of the 1680s.[49] New College, like King's at Cambridge, escaped the decline in numbers because it had a fixed number, seventy, of fellows and scholars; in consequence the modest chambers provided by William of Wykeham, with four scholars to a room, now seemed cramped. The college was also following the fashion in trying to attract noblemen and fellow commoners – rich pensioners who paid handsomely, but expected extensive accommodation in return. This had in the past been provided for the rich by adding chamber to chamber; but the answer in New College was to build Garden Court, with ample rooms – some for two students to a room; but in the long run for one. In similar fashion, King's at Cambridge (after toying with schemes devised by Hawksmoor and approved by Wren) called in the great architect James Gibbs to provide

---

[46] Brooke, Highfield and Swaan 1988, pp. 215–16; Luckett 1973, pp. 14–22; Willis and Clark 1886/1998, II, pp. 98–106.

[47] Venn 1897–1901, III, p. 103.

[48] Brooke 1985/1996, p. 156 and pl. 15; for what follows, *ibid.*, pp. 172–3.

[49] For what follows, see Brooke, Highfield and Swaan 1988, pp. 203–6 and pl. 129.

Plate 9 A chamber in Caius Court, Gonville and Caius College:
built 1565–9, probably wainscotted in 1697

ample rooms for most of its fellows in one of the large spaces left over by
the failure of Henry VI's building schemes. Gibbs was asked to design a
complete court, with the chapel preserved as its northern wing, and with
chambers to the west and east and public rooms on the south. But in the
event only the range of chambers on the west was built, between 1724 and
1731. It is a monumental building, though relatively unadorned – much
less so than Hawksmoor would have provided – and it is as strong a statement of what was thought right for privileged fellows and students in the
early eighteenth century as Caius Court is for the 1560s.[50] Twenty-four
apartments were provided, each of three rooms, each apparently designed
for two students – to give them space, company and also privacy.

The Gibbs building at King's was to house a high proportion of the
resident population – for by this date some, in the end many, of the fellows
had ceased to reside. Other colleges were providing for quite a different
student body. For many students the old accommodation could prove
adequate: they could spread out more spaciously in it as their numbers

[50] Willis and Clark 1886/1988, I, pp. 560–3.

declined; the chambers could be readily adapted, as in Caius, to house a single student in a single chamber, with perhaps one of the earlier studies converted into a bedroom. But this would not suffice for resident fellows, still less for noblemen and gentlemen commoners. An interesting model for their accommodation was provided in the Westmorland Building at Emmanuel.[51] An appeal was launched in 1718 for the rebuilding of the main residential wing of the front court, provided by the founder in the 1580s. As was not uncommon in such appeals, it was claimed that the buildings were ruinous and needed rebuilding – the modern jargon is to say that 'they have reached the end of their useful life'. They were not at all ruinous when drawn by David Loggan in or about 1690; and a close study of what actually happened makes it clear that it was not the state of the fabric but the shape of the rooms which inspired the rebuilding. The south wall was moved 11 feet to the south, and the whole building made to comprise sets of one large chamber with two smaller rooms behind: this is a less ample version of the Gibbs building, but luxurious compared to what the fellows and students of Emmanuel had had to live in in the more crowded days of the early and mid-seventeenth century. It is clear that the Westmorland Building was designed for fellows and fellow commoners: Emmanuel was one of the colleges which succeeded in the course of the eighteenth century in attracting relatively large numbers of fellow commoners. In the years 1715–19 only three had entered the college; in 1723–4, as the new building was completed, five came at once. But the chief beneficiaries were undoubtedly the fellows, who were thereafter amply housed. The current head of the founder's family, the twelfth earl of Westmorland, made a modest contribution of £500 – and of his architect, John Lumley. In return, his coat of arms presides over a noble stone façade, and his name has been attached to it ever since. Later in the century James Essex was to provide a classical western wing to the court, and so complete what Ralph Symons in the 1580s, Sir Christopher Wren in the 1660s[52] and Lumley in the 1710s and 1720s, had begun. We need not doubt that the Westmorland Building was inspired by the desire both for better housing and for a more monumental, fashionable south wing to the court.

HALLS

The common meal in the college hall had been almost as much a central feature of the life of a medieval colleges as common worship in the chapel.

---

[51] Bendall *et al.* 1999, pp. 322–7.   [52] See below, p. 46.

Thus in Wykeham's New College and Docket's Queens', chapel and hall form together one wing of the quad or court. The hall was part of the fundamental provision of the new colleges of the sixteenth century. But then as now, eating was not the only activity within its walls. One of the most remarkable achievements of that fanatical builder, Thomas Nevile, at Trinity, was the hall, completed in 1608. In shape and dimensions it is closely modelled on the hall of the Middle Temple in London; but whereas the Caius hall of the 1850s reproduced the style and idiom of the Middle Temple hall, the hall at Trinity is in a very different style, with many strange Jacobean devices.[53] It was clearly intended from the start to be a theatre. Cambridge enjoyed at the turn of the sixteenth and seventeenth centuries its own version of the dramatic fashions of the age. They attracted the interest of seniors and juniors alike: one of the most notable dramas performed in Tudor Cambridge was a play about Richard III, *Richardus Tertius*, by Thomas Legge, master of Caius, performed in the hall of St John's in 1579, which has an honourable place in the dramatic prehistory of Shakespeare's *Richard III* of the early 1590s.[54] Comedies were the most favoured; Terence was the model; and the language was Latin. The extreme popularity of lengthy pieces in Latin has puzzled modern commentators; but there is no doubt of the facts. As Patrick Collinson writes,

> College plays . . . were the most popular and well-attended public events of early modern Cambridge, on the success or failure of which individual and corporate reputations depended heavily. A large part of the rationale for the building of the great hall at Trinity seems to have been theatrical, to steal the thunder of St John's, which had the strongest dramatic culture in Cambridge in the sixteenth century, and to put Trinity in the forefront of attention on the occasion of royal visits. Completed under Thomas Nevile's mastership in 1608, this is England's oldest surviving theatre. The comedies were an important point of contact between the colleges and the Court, and a star performance could be the first step to a glittering career. Sometimes colleges called back from London their 'auncient good actors' . . . Plays were defended as an important academic adjunct, 'for the emboldening of their Iunior schollers, to arme them with audacity'.

---

[53] Its adornment is described as a 'barbaric profusion of strap-panels, caryatids, etc.' in Pevsner 1970, p. 170; cf. Brooke, Highfield and Swaan 1988, pls. 88–9. On it see Willis and Clark 1886/1988, II, pp. 489–94; cf. Brooke 1985/1996, p. 215.

[54] Legge's plays have been admirably edited in Sutton 1992; cf. Nelson 1989, II, p. 713; 1994, p. 61.

Plate 10 The hall, Trinity College, looking north; designed to be used additionally as a theatre

And he goes on to describe the conflicts brought on by shortage of tickets, which led the disappointed students to throw stones at hall windows and to a major riot at Trinity's Great Gate in 1611, when the Trinity bouncers attempted to exclude 'divers northern tuffe laddes' from St John's.[55]

---

[55] Collinson in Bendall *et al.* 1999, pp. 77–9, citing Nelson 1994, pp. 425–86 and Clark 1906.

In 1614 James I came across from Newmarket in wintry weather to see four plays on four nights, including George Ruggle's *Ignoramus*, a farcical attack on the common lawyers. Although John Chamberlain thought the play 'more than half marred with extreme length', the king loved it, 'laughed exceedingly and offentymes with his handes and by wordes applauded it'.[56]

COLLEGE CHAPELS

The colleges were religious communities, dedicated to worship and learning. The nature of the worship was profoundly affected by the Reformation, but the way of life and the purposes of the communities changed much less. John Fisher's statutes for Christ's of the early sixteenth century were the chief source of Sir Walter Mildmay's statutes for Emmanuel of the 1580s.[57] The Dominican precincts, designed for the training and life of Friars Preachers, became a training ground for godly preachers once more. The chapel remained one of the central, focal buildings of the collegiate community; it lost none of its importance. But there were notable changes.

Of these, with one proviso, the surviving buildings are our chief and most accurate witnesses. The proviso is that over the generations, over the centuries, their furnishings have undergone many changes. The best witnesses of this among the Oxbridge colleges are the accounts of Merton College chapel, which reveal quite dramatically the local consequences of the Reformation – especially in the accounts of the Oxford carpenters who made a handsome living changing the furnishings at each vicissitude of the English Reformation.[58] But there are some dramatic evidences of change in the buildings themselves, both in the mid-sixteenth and in the mid-seventeenth centuries. In the late 1630s, for example, the fellows of Caius, following the example of Peterhouse – surprisingly, since the master of Caius was a moderate puritan – filled the ceiling of their chapel with innumerable cherubs, and gave it other indications of a Laudian tendency, notably fine altar rails. In 1643 the puritan iconoclast William Dowsing removed the cherubs from both Peterhouse and Caius, and the chapels settled down to a more puritan regime. But not for long: after the Restoration the altars returned to the east ends and in Caius (though not in Peterhouse) the cherubs returned to the ceiling.[59]

[56] Collinson in Bendall *et al.* 1999, p. 79.
[57] See above, p. 21; Collinson in Bendall *et al.* 1999, pp. 23–30; Stubbings 1983.
[58] Fletcher and Upton 1983.   [59] Brooke 1985/1996, p. 127; Dowsing 2001, pp. 156, 163.

Plate 11 The chapel, Gonville and Caius College, with the ceiling of the late 1630s, showing the cherubs set in coffered panels, removed in 1643 and later restored; from Ackermann's *Cambridge*, 1815.

The outer shells and fabrics of the chapels are, in the nature of things, more lasting, and several colleges – even apart from King's – still have medieval chapels or chapels with a medieval nucleus. The most impressive of these is the chapel of Jesus College, or in other words the convent church of the nuns of St Radegund. For the convent was suppressed in 1496 by John Alcock, bishop of Ely, and in the liberal process of conversion the church was cut down in size, but remained far more

41

ample than most college chapels. It is indeed a chapel within a church, for an enclosed choir of elaborately carved woodwork, now replaced by the exquisite version of a late Gothic choir devised by Pugin in the 1840s, was formed within the eastern limb of the church.

In spite of the medieval legacy, it was rare for a generation to pass between 1550 and 1750 without a new college chapel being built here or there. The new Trinity of the mid-sixteenth century needed a larger chapel than the King's Hall had provided, especially in Mary's reign; Corpus (1579) and Peterhouse (1628) abandoned the parish churches which had formed their chapels till then; the new colleges of Emmanuel and Sidney had new chapels built for them at the turn of the sixteenth and seventeenth centuries. After the Restoration came the noble Wren chapels at Pembroke and Emmanuel; and the rebuilding of St Catharine's culminated in the chapel at the end of the century (1699). Then there was a pause: the next new chapel was Clare's, in 1763.[60] But the eighteenth century none the less laid its hand on many chapels: several acquired eighteenth-century dress, starting with Caius chapel in the 1710s. It is often said that the Reformation brought a caesura in church building; it was certainly not so in the chapels of Cambridge colleges. It used also to be alleged that Gothic gave way to Classical styles of various kinds in the sixteenth and seventeenth centuries; but Peterhouse chapel and the library of St John's show that new and inventive modes of Gothic could be devised in Cambridge in the 1620s.

One of the significant changes was the abandonment of parish churches. The founder of Merton provided for a college chapel which was to be the old parish church of St John the Baptist with a grand new chancel for the college.[61] The founder of Peterhouse, Hugh of Balsham, bishop of Ely, as in so much else, imitated Merton on a more modest scale, and he selected the old parish church of St Peter without Trumpington Gate – now Little St Mary's – as the nucleus of his college chapel. In the mid-fourteenth century the fellows of Peterhouse contrived to rebuild its chancel on the model of Merton's.[62] This used to be thought a marriage of convenience, and there is surprisingly little evidence in college statutes of any parochial function in the colleges which shared their chapels with a parish. But the evidence of the buildings leaves no doubt that in the fourteenth century a combination of academic and pastoral function was thought proper for a college. The church of St Michael in Cambridge was entirely rebuilt by Hervey de Stanton in the 1320s as part of the basic

[60] Willis and Clark 1886/1988, III, p. 516.   [61] Martin and Highfield 1997, esp. pp. 39–40.
[62] Brooke 1985a, pp. 64–6.

provision for his new college of priests, Michaelhouse: two-thirds of it (by a most unusual division) forms the chancel for the college, one third the nave for the parishioners. Similarly, it is clearly significant that the oldest complete medieval court in Cambridge, Corpus Old Court of the mid-fourteenth century, has provision for everything a college needs except a chapel: it was founded adjacent to the ancient church of St Benet by a group of Cambridge citizens to be a link between town and gown. And such it was in a very genuine sense – though its absorption of the town's revenues also aroused such passionate jealousy that it was sacked in the so-called Peasants' Revolt of 1381: so-called, because in Cambridge it was an urban revolt. Of such paradoxes, of such ambivalence, is the history of Cambridge made.[63] Corpus was indeed commonly known as Benet Hall or Benet College in the sixteenth century; but Matthew Parker, master of Corpus and archbishop of Canterbury, was as tenacious of the traditions of Corpus and Cambridge as he was – for all his Protestant convictions – of the traditions of the English church. The college retained its name of 'Corpus Christi' (as did its Oxford namesake) in spite of the popish connotations of the cult; but Corpus did not venture to build a chapel separate from St Benet's until Parker was securely dead. Then the 'master and fellowes . . . most humblie and earnestlie made suyte' to the Lord Keeper, Sir Nicholas Bacon, who had been a contemporary of Parker in Corpus and had a considerable hand in his promotion to Canterbury, to provide, or rather open the appeal, for a chapel within the walls of the college; and this was built in 1579–84, with the help of many other contributors. It was a handsome Tudor Gothic box, with fine Jacobean woodwork, but was totally destroyed by William Wilkins in the 1820s, when he built the New Court and the new chapel.[64]

To the high churchmen of seventeenth-century Cambridge a college was an inward-looking religious community. However much its students might go on to pastoral work in the parishes of the kingdom, their devotions in college chapel should be unspotted by the world, wholly apart. This image of a college chapel is most perfectly preserved in the new Peterhouse chapel, of the 1620s and 1630s. It is a tiny box in which a community of scholars could feel the intimacy of common worship to the full. It was built on the initiative of Matthew Wren, master of Peterhouse and later bishop of Ely, with the help of John Cosin, who was to succeed him as master, and much later, when he was bishop of Durham, was to provide funds for clothing the whole building in stone. It is a charming evocation of early seventeenth-century Gothic, with occasional Classical

[63] *Ibid.*, pp. 65–8.   [64] Willis and Clark 1886/1988, I, pp. 289–95; Sandeen 1962.

motifs; and the stalls still evoke the personal taste of these two powerful exponents of the beauty of holiness in the heyday of William Laud.[65] An eminent puritan complained in the 1640s

> that in Peter House Chappel there was a glorious new Altar set up, and mounted on steps, to which the Master, Fellowes, Schollers bowed, and were enjoyned to bow by Doctor Cosens the Master, who set it up; that there were Basons, Candelstickes, Tapers standing on it, and a great Crucifix hanging over it . . . that there was likewise a carved Crosse at the end of every seat, and on the Altar a pot, which they usually called the incense pot . . . and none of them might turne their backs towards the Altar going in nor out of the Chappell . . . and the common report both among the Schollers of that House and others, was, that none might approach to the Altar in Peter-house but in Sandalls, and that there was a speciall consecrated Knife there kept upon the Altar, to cut the sacramental bread that was to be consecrated.

J.W. Clark commented that 'the account is probably much exaggerated', but it rings true to all that we know of Cosin's tastes and the best Laudian practice of the 1630s, including altars, candles, stately ritual and, on occasion, incense.

In the era of puritan revolution, Matthew Wren was to spend many years in the Tower of London; but he emerged in time to summon his nephew Christopher to plan the work nearest to his heart, a new chapel for Pembroke College where he had been a student and fellow.[66] The younger Wren was Savilian Professor of Astronomy at Oxford and a notable scientist. Pembroke chapel was his first major building, and it doubtless played a part in forming his careeer as an architect. It was built in 1663–5, and by 1664 he was at work on the Sheldonian Theatre in Oxford; from then on his buildings grew apace. Of Matthew's contribution, the family chronicle, the *Parentalia*, observed:

> The first money he receiv'd after his Restitution, he bestow'd on Pembroke-Hall, and to the honour of Almighty God, to whose service he had wholly devoted himself; for the Ornament of the University, which he always affected with a fervent and passionate Love; and in a grateful Remembrance of his first Education, which was in that Place receiv'd, and thankfully acknowledg'd, he built that most elegant Chapel there.[67]

[65] Whatever doctrinal differences may be discerned between Cosin and Laud, they were both upholders of the majesty of the tradition of the English church and of the beauty of holiness. For what follows, see Willis and Clark 1886/1988, I, pp. 45–6, quoting William Prynne.

[66] Willis and Clark 1886/1988, I, pp. 146–7; on Wren's work in Cambridge, see also RCHM, *Cambridge*, I, pp. 62–6; II, pp. 148, 153–4, 213–14, 236–41; McKitterick 1995, chs. 1 (by David McKitterick), 2 (by Sir Howard Colvin).

[67] Wren 1750, p. 33, quoted in Willis and Clark 1886/1988, I, pp. 146–7.

Plate 12 Pembroke College chapel, by Christopher Wren, interior; the east
end added in 1880 by George Gilbert Scott

It is a singularly evocative building: not richly adorned, but relatively
simple, of supremely elegant proportions with fine plasterwork and carved
panelling, an enclosed space in which the regular hours celebrated in a
hall-shaped choir could join at times in the beauty of holiness behind the
Laudian altar rails at the east end. Peterhouse chapel has been darkened
by later stained glass, but was always in appearance an enclosed, inward

looking Gothic choir, not far removed in conception from the choir of Jesus chapel. The Wrens brought light and space into Pembroke chapel: it is still an enclosed sanctuary, set apart from the world, and inward-looking; but it is a spacious, well-lit sanctuary, with nothing Gothic about it.

William Sancroft, the master of Emmanuel – hereditary Emmanuel man turned high churchman (see pp. 475–7) – was meditating meanwhile a similar new chapel for his college. The Dominicans had provided a very spacious church, but Mildmay had converted it into a dining hall, building in its place the classic puritan preaching box, oriented north and south, which later became the library, and since the early twentieth century the 'Old Library'. Sancroft meanwhile was rapidly climbing the ladder of promotion which was to culminate in Lambeth in 1677–8. He was dean of York in 1664 and of St Paul's later in the same year; and St Paul's led him to friendship with Christopher Wren. Together they were planning a new classical face to St Paul's when, in 1666, the Fire of London made them partners in a much more radical scheme for a wholly new cathedral. In March 1665 Sancroft had resigned as master of Emmanuel, but he remained in close touch with his successor, John Breton, another 'staunch high churchman'[68] produced by puritan Emmanuel. The chapel was begun in 1668 and consecrated by the bishop of Ely, Peter Gunning, on 29 September 1677. Sancroft himself retained a generous interest throughout, leading the appeal with a substantial grant at the outset, and rounding it off by paying for the woodwork and other fittings – including the elaborate classical altarpiece, only completed in 1687, not long before the Revolution of 1688 and Sancroft's fall.[69] Pembroke chapel sits almost by itself, linked to the neighbouring buildings by a modest cloister. At Emmanuel, Sancroft and his successor doubtless briefed Wren to provide with the west end of the chapel an extension to the master's lodge. Hence the design completes the fourth side of the front court, setting a long gallery for the master and his guests above a cloister walk for the less privileged. The long gallery is now the meeting room for the master and fellows, and the lodge has gone elsewhere. But the long gallery offers, with those at Queens' and St John's (now the fellows' combination room), a striking reminder of the social standing of the head of house in the sixteenth and seventeenth centuries (see pp. 305–12).

The chapels of Pembroke and Emmanuel provide a powerful image of the worshipping community as conceived by high churchmen of the

---

[68] Collinson in Bendall *et al.* 1999, p. 272; for what follows see *ibid.*, pp. 272–5; Willis and Clark 1886/1999, II, pp. 703–9.

[69] On Sancroft, see the immortal portrait by Patrick Collinson in Bendall *et al.* 1999, esp. pp. 248–56, 272–82.

mid- and late seventeenth century. Eminent nineteenth-century architects looked at them with disdain and offered to rebuild them. Merci-
fully the fellows of Pembroke and Emmanuel had the sense to restrain
them. At Pembroke, after the dismissal of Alfred Waterhouse, G.G. Scott
was allowed to extend the east end in a discreet and sympathetic manner: the proportions, the sense of enclosed space, are diminished, but
not seriously. At Emmanuel Sir Arthur Blomfield was allowed to make
modest changes to the east end, and the celebrated theologian Fenton
Hort master-minded inscriptions on the walls and a splendid show of
Emmanuel worthies in the glass (including some honorary members,
such as Origen and St Augustine): the inscriptions have been covered
over, and the glass has its own beauty. In the main both chapels still
clearly reflect the aims of the eminent seventeenth-century divines who
inspired them, and the genius of their architect.[70]

The puritan image is not so well served by surviving chapels, for none
can now convey the bare simplicity of preaching halls, with the Lord's
table set in their midst. Only the old library at Emmanuel – currently
furnished as a meeting room and adorned with many portraits – now
represents a special creation by a puritan founder to set beside the statelier
creations of the high churchmen. There one can still in imagination
see the godly meeting of Laurence Chaderton and the first fellows of
Emmanuel – and the first students – in what remained, during most of
the old library's time as a chapel, the most thriving religious community
in Cambridge.

LIBRARIES

William Sancroft was also much concerned with Emmanuel's library. He
had tried, and failed, to secure for the college the great collection of
books left by an earlier master, Richard Holdsworth, at whose feet he
had sat. In its place Emmanuel was able to garner the greater part of
Sancroft's own even more considerable library: the 5,000 volumes in the
Emmanuel library today represent one of the largest private collections
of the seventeenth century to survive.[71] But it took many years effectively to house them, for the special building Sancroft had dreamed of
was never built. The seventeenth and early eighteenth centuries were
a great age of library building in Cambridge – both in the sense of
the provision of large libraries in search of books, and of the gathering
of large collections of books seeking adequate housing. These libraries

[70] See Brooke *ibid.*, pp. 510–12.   [71] On Sancroft's library, see Collinson in *ibid.*, pp. 281–2.

Plate 13 The Elizabethan pulpit from the original chapel (now the old library) of Emmanuel College, now in the church of St Mary and St Michael, Trumpington

are unique legacies of the successes and failures of seventeenth-century Cambridge.

One reason for the rise of the colleges in the fifteenth century had been their relatively lavish provision of books. Granted the cost of medieval academic manuscripts, access to libraries was a first necessity for poor, and not so poor, students. Cambridge, moreover, was slow to provide adequately for a university library. One wing of the Old Schools sufficed in the early and mid-fifteenth century, to be enhanced by another wing when the chancellor, Archbishop Rotherham, provided for his own large collection of books in the 1470s. As time passed – and especially when printed books became common and profuse – the books crept further and further into the nooks and crannies of the Old Schools, gradually driving the scholars (when not engaged in reading) to seek other homes. But Cambridge had no Sir Thomas Bodley in the sixteenth or seventeenth century to transform its university library. For this, it had to await the Royal Library in the 1710s – and the urgent and critical demand for space which this implied (see pp. 58–9).

Few historical myths are so persistent as that the advent of printed books made a sudden and fundamental difference to the supply – not to mention the cost – of academic books.[72] In Cambridge, symbols of continuity are more in evidence than of change; and the greatest of sixteenth-century libraries is to be found in Matthew Parker's books in Corpus, among which the manuscripts are justly more famous than the printed. The fourteenth- and fifteenth-century statutes of Oxford and Cambridge colleges – starting with Bateman's for Trinity Hall and Gonville Hall – presuppose an ample library, with much of the collection being freely lent to poor fellows and scholars (that is, no doubt, to those not rich enough to buy their own books), and the rest kept chained in the library.[73] The characteristic college library of the fifteenth century was a room with five windows on either side with white walls – as light as possible since it was lit wholly by natural light – with six bays containing lecterns for the chained books, and space for the books to lie beneath. Such an arrangement still survives in the old library of Queens', though the lecterns are mostly hidden in later bookcases, built up as the books grew more numerous.[74] It can be reconstructed at Caius, where the shell of the Gonville Hall library survives, and its furnishings can be deduced from early documents; and a borrowing register of the early fifteenth century shows the lending process in action – as chain marks on surviving manuscripts also preserve a memory of the chained

---

[72] For the arguments that mass production of books started in the thirteenth rather than the fifteenth century, see d'Avray 2001, pp. 15–30.

[73] For this and what follows, see Willis and Clark 1886/1988, III, pp. 389–418.

[74] Willis and Clark 1886/1988, II, pp. 50–1; Brooke, Highfield and Swaan 1988, p. 109 and pl. 69; cf. Twigg 1987, p. 104. The extensions of the cases took place piecemeal: some can be dated 1529–30, and especially 1612–13 (Willis and Clark 1886/1988, II, p. 50 n. 2).

library.[75] The most important of these documents is the catalogue of 1569, which shows that the lecterns and the chained books were still there; and that printed books had not wholly ousted manuscripts. The library, in outward show, was little altered, it seems clear, from the way it was built and furnished in the 1430s – though some provision must already have been made for growing numbers of unchained books. Yet there is no record before 1675 of any major change: in that year new windows were provided to improve the light, and improvement was much needed since the much larger, delightful though restrained in taste, Baroque bookcases which still survive replaced the lecterns; and the chamber overhead was converted into a library for old books and manuscripts.[76]

The most remarkable evidence of continuity lies in the old library of Trinity Hall: it is in form a perfectly preserved fifteenth-century library, with square-headed Gothic windows and lecterns for reading the chained books. But it is in fact a purpose-built, detached library of the late sixteenth century.[77] It is indeed remarkable that the fellows of Trinity Hall never felt compelled to make any fundamental changes till the nineteenth century. The college was dedicated to the study of civil and canon law, and this had two consequences for the library. First, the basic textbooks the fellows needed did not change in the sixteenth century: print might (or might not) replace manuscripts; but Justinian and his late medieval commentators still ruled in civil or Roman law; and the medieval *Corpus Iuris Canonici* – though its teaching was officially proscribed by Henry VIII and Thomas Cromwell – still reigned in canon law until the seventeenth century. In any case many of the fellows of Trinity Hall were professional canon lawyers practising in Doctors' Commons in the city of London, and satisfied their needs for new books there.[78] A medieval library sufficed.

In marked contrast is the history of the library of St John's. The original provision of the 1510s had been just such a room with five windows on either side as was provided for Gonville Hall in the 1430s. But in St John's the books were taking over by the early seventeenth century: it was one of the most active colleges academically, and had more need than Trinity

[75] Brooke 1985/1996, pp. 25–7, 33–7. For the early fifteenth-century borrowing register see Clarke and Lovatt 2002, pp. 256–73. For the catalogue of 1569 see Brooke 1985/1996, pp. 36–7, and Leedham-Green 1981.

[76] Willis and Clark 1886/1988, I, p. 200. The bookcases have twice been moved, in the 1850s and the 1990s: they are now in the new college library, the Cockerell building of the 1830s (see p. 53).

[77] Brooke, Highfield and Swaan 1988, pp. 94–5, pls. 54–5. Willis and Clark 1886/1988, I, pp. 222–3, III, pp. 412, 415, date the library to the mastership of Henry Harvey (1557/8–1585) or to about 1600. See Crawley 1976, p. 35.

[78] Crawley 1976, esp. p. 57; Brooke 1993b, pp. 61–3. For the history of canon law, see Helmholz 1990.

Plate 14 Trinity Hall library: the lecterns, late sixteenth century

Hall of space for purchases of new books, and gifts of books from ex-fellows and others. Temporary quarters were found elsewhere in 1616, and plans laid for a new building – on the first floor as was usual to avoid the danger of damp in a room with no artificial heating; but better still, with an open cloister below to ensure a steady flow of air.[79]

[79] Willis and Clark 1886/1988, II, pp. 263–5.

It was not until 1623 that finance was secured for this ambitious project. From April to October of that year negotiation was carried on with the bishop of Exeter, Valentine Carey – who had been a fellow of St John's and master of Christ's, and a hammer of the puritans. He made it clear that he was agent for a shrewd and cautious benefactor, who wanted to be the sole donor of the library, and yet to be sure the estimate of costs was not overrun. In October, 'Lord Keeper Bishop Williams (hitherto very artfully concealed) owned and declared himself to be the founder.'[80] John Williams, ex-fellow of St John's, bishop of Lincoln – later archbishop of York – and a leading minister of James I's last years, is perhaps mainly remembered as William Laud's chief rival and enemy on the bench of bishops. In modern parlance, Laud was a great high churchman, Williams middle of the road – neither was a puritan, though that did not help them to be friends. Their rivalry indeed extended to extravagant patronage, Williams to St John's Cambridge, Laud (a few years later) to St John's Oxford. Williams funded a magnificent, monumental library, Laud a whole quadrangle.[81] Laud's building works actually included two libraries, though neither was on the monumental scale of Williams'. But Laud did more, for he was a scholar and a princely book collector, whose agents operated beyond the limits of Europe in pursuit of Greek and oriental manuscripts and other treasures, so that Laud is remembered as a major benefactor to the Bodleian Library as well as to his college. Williams was not a scholar, but his generosity was abundant. In 1623 he offered £1,200; by 1626, when the work was finished, he had given over £2,000 – and the rest, nearly £1,000 more, had been found by the college and Sir Ralph Hare. The earl of Southampton meanwhile had bequeathed a collection of books which was largely responsible for the urgent need for space. The result was a beautiful working library; but it was on a much larger scale than any of its predecessors: it is a monument as well as a library; a statement of the values of a college and of the grandeur of a minister-bishop. When it was finished, its founder was no longer artfully concealed: the western gable, overlooking the river, was completed in 1624, and bears the inscription 'ILCS', 'Iohannes Lincolniensis Custos Sigilli, John bishop of Lincoln, Keeper of the Great Seal'. It is a magnificent room, light and lofty, in structure a splendid example of early seventeenth-century Gothic, but with timberwork full of Renaissance and Jacobean detail. The alternation of reading desks and bookcases showed the adaptation of the medieval model to the proliferation of books in the seventeenth

---

[80] Baker and Mayor 1869, I, p. 209, quoted Willis and Clark 1886/1988, II, p. 265.
[81] Colvin 1988.

Plate 15 St John's College: the old library, 1623–8, the gift of John Williams, bishop of Lincoln, later archbishop of York

century; as did the scale of the room, 110 feet in length and 30 feet wide.[82]

The old library of St John's is the first of four monumental libraries in Cambridge: it has been followed by the Wren Library at Trinity (1676–95), the Cockerell Building of the old University Library, now the library

---

[82] Willis and Clark, 1886/1988, II, pp. 266–71. For the exterior, see Brooke, Highfield and Swaan 1988, pl. 17; for the interior, *ibid.*, pl. 95.

of Caius (1837–42), and the new University Library completed in 1934.[83] The tower and façade of the last are monuments to the generosity of John D. Rockefeller, Jnr. The Wren and the Cockerell were paid for by subscription; but both were monumental statements, in imitation of their predecessors. The Wren, as well as being one of its architect's noblest buildings, is a memorial to Wren's friend, Isaac Barrow, the master of Trinity who conceived the enterprise and set it in motion.[84] Barrow was a devout man and a noted preacher as well as first Lucasian Professor of Mathematics and Newton's patron; we cannot suppose that he intended by his library to make the worship of books vie with the worship of God as represented by King's chapel. But he and those who completed his work made a statement which we do well to bear in mind when contemplating the supposed decline of the university in the late seventeenth and early eighteenth centuries (see pp. 485–6, 510).

The story was told that Barrow planned a theatre for the university in imitation of Wren's Sheldonian Theatre in Oxford, to replace the nave of Great St Mary's as a more permanent and dignified setting for university ceremonies; and when the plan failed, he vowed in dudgeon to lay out at once the foundations of a new library to complete Nevile's Court.[85] It is true that Barrow was vice-chancellor in 1675–6, and may well have canvassed a great scheme, for many attempts had been made earlier in the century to launch a new 'Commencement House', and he was clearly a man of large vision. But it seems certain that he had laid plans for the Trinity library before that, since the work on it began in February 1676. Very sadly, Barrow died of a fever in May 1677, at the age of 46: he was only two years older than Wren, who lived to 1723; and the history of Cambridge and Trinity might have been very different if he had lived as long as Wren.[86]

Wren's designs comprised both one for a circular library surmounted by a dome and the rectangle that was eventually built. It seems that at an early stage it was explained to him that Barrow and his colleagues contemplated extending Nevile's Court and its cloister, so that the library would form the western wing, with the cloister running beneath it.

---

[83] See the summary account of the University Library, old and new, in Brooke 1998.

[84] On the Wren, see above all McKitterick 1995; also Willis and Clark 1886/1988, II, pp. 531–47; on Barrow, Feingold 1990.

[85] From the life of his successor, John North, quoted in McKitterick 1995, p. 5; Willis and Clark 1886/1988, II, p. 532.

[86] For the age of Newton and Bentley, see below, chapter 14. For earlier attempts to found a new 'Commencement House', see Willis and Clark 1886/1988, III, pp. 35–43. For what follows, see esp. Colvin in McKitterick 1995, pp. 32–7 and *ibid.*, pp. 142–5.

Plate 16 The arms of Isaac Barrow surmounted by a squirrel, by Grinling Gibbons, 1690–3, Wren Library, Trinity College

Wren's specifications for the building show that he had been carefully briefed by Barrow, and had thought deeply about the buildings and its context.

On the ground floor was 'the substruction Cloister . . . I haue chosen middle pillars and a double porticoe and lightes outward rather than a middle wall, as being the same expence, more gracefull, and according to the manner of the aunciens who made double walkes (with three rowes of pillars or two rowes and a wall) about the forum.'[87] In the main library on the first floor he designed bays along the walls: 'the best way for the Students will be to haue a little square table in each Celle with 2 chaires' and four lesser cells at the corners, 'to be shut up with some neat Lattice dores for archives'. The main library is very large – 150 feet by 38 feet – and very lofty, to allow space for big windows above the bays,

---

[87] This and the following quotations are from McKitterick 1995, pp. 142–5; also in Willis and Clark 1886/1988, II, pp. 534–6. For photographs, see Brooke, Highfield and Swaan 1988, pls. 18, 139–42; McKitterick 1995, *passim*.

Plate 17 The Wren Library, Trinity College: interior, from Ackermann's
Cambridge, 1815

to maximise light as well as space for books and readers, though in contrast
to other Cambridge libraries the central space not occupied by shelves is
very large indeed. He describes the main front on Nevile's Court, with
its many classical features, thus. I 'haue filled the Arches with relieues
of stone, of which I have seen the effect abroad in good building . . . I
have given noe other Frontispeice to the middle then statues according
to auncient example.' He goes on to explain that the outside face next
to the river will be 'after a plainer manner to be performed most with
Ashler'. The beauty of the ashlar, some of the finest work of Wren's
mason, Robert Grumbold, and the splendour of the proportions of the
building make an inspiring vista from the Backs; but most thought and
care was lavished on the eastern face, within the court, with its classical
motifs and surmounted by statues representing Divinity, Law, Physic and
Mathematics, set up in 1681 by the sculptor Gabriel Cibber. Within the
library, it was arranged that a subscriber who paid for furnishing one of
the bays could have his coat of arms carved over it by Grinling Gibbons,
and a row of generous benefactors are thus recorded – most delightfully, a
grasshopper and a shield of oak leaves and acorns commemorate a donor

56

Plate 18 The Wren Library, Trinity College: the east front from Nevile's
Court

(probably Dr William Lynnett) who spurned the aid of heralds; a squirrel
adorns the arms of Isaac Barrow.[88]

Wren, evidently inspired by Barrow, had spoken of the needs of students; and there seems no doubt that a prime consideration in its design
had been not only to house a great and growing collection of books,

[88] Brooke, Highfield and Swaan 1988, pl. 141; McKitterick 1995, figs. 8–9.

but to provide for readers. This is remarkable, since the reaction of many librarians to the spread of books was to let them fill all the available space and not concern themselves unduly with the readers. From the early eighteenth century the Wren Library has been open as of right (so far as we know, uniquely among colleges libraries at this early date) to all the students of the college.[89] A cynic might observe that in Trinity, notoriously well provided with aristocratic layabouts, a place set apart for peace and quiet was essential to the reading men. To this it might be answered that Trinity in the age of Newton and Bentley – though not a peaceful place – enjoyed a dedication to learning hardly paralleled elsewhere (see chapter 14).

THE UNIVERSITY LIBRARY AND THE SENATE HOUSE

In the grandiose schemes, and uncertain performances, of early eighteenth-century Cambridge, there is an element of comedy. It began in 1715, when Lord Townshend persuaded George I to celebrate the university's loyalty in the face of the Old Pretender's rebellion by buying and giving to Cambridge the magnificent library of the late bishop of Ely, John Moore. Over the years Moore's books drove the human flock out of the Old Schools, and the Senate House had to be built to provide for some of their activities.[90] The advent of Moore's library was the fulfilment of a dream; but the sudden incursion of 30,000 volumes into the University Library caused a crisis.

> The King, observing with judicious eyes
> The state of both his universities,
> To Oxford sent a troop of horse, and why?
> That learned body wanted loyalty;
> To Cambridge books, as very well discerning
> How much that loyal body wanted learning.[91]

Thus Joseph Trapp (1679–1747), the Professor of Poetry at Oxford, in commemoration of the event which converted the University Library from a mediocre to a great collection of books. Richard Holdsworth's books, when they eventually reached the University Library in the 1660s, numbered over 10,000.[92] This was a major event; Bishop Moore's library – the Royal Library – was an avalanche.

---

[89] Gaskell and Robson 1971, pp. 33, 36; McKitterick 1995, pp. 65–7.
[90] Ringrose 1998; McKitterick 1986. For what follows, Willis and Clark 1886/1988, II, pp. 29–34.
[91] Nicholls 1812–16, III, p. 330: 'by an Oxonian'.
[92] Oates 1986, pp. 314–26 (on the University Library). Cf. pp. 478–9 and McKitterick 1991, esp. pp. 35, 56 (on Perne's library); Brooke 1985/1996, pp. 104–6 (on Branthwaite's); Collinson in

Plate 19 The Senate House, engraving by Lamborn, 1768, from the south, mainly of the 1720s, designed by James Gibbs with the help of James Burrough

First of all, a new room with a dome was built at the south-west corner on land formerly belonging to King's: here the manuscripts were housed. Then bookcases spread along the west wing and round the corner, threatening the last bastion of the medieval university, the Regent House.[93] All this took time, and many of the books lay for years unsorted and unshelved. In 1721 the young James Burrough, fellow of Caius – later tutor and master – at the beginning of his career as a distinguished amateur architect, proposed a major enlargement of the Old Schools facing Great St Mary's, with one wing for the Senate House, another for the university offices. In March 1722 James Gibbs was summoned from London, and entrusted with 'Mr Burrough's plan of the intended publick buildings' to improve as he thought fit, and he was to be 'retained to supervise and conduct' the building work. To Burrough and Gibbs jointly must, most

Bendall *et al.* 1999, pp. 270–1, 281–2 (on Sancroft's). For an edition of some sixteenth/seventeenth-century private library inventories, see Leedham-Green 1986.
[93] Now the University Combination Room, in which the regents had met and disputations had been held – an essential supplement to Great St Mary's.

probably, be ascribed the credit for the design of the Senate House.[94] But not for its shape.

When the land on which it stands was being acquired in the late 1710s, the vice-chancellor was the recently elected master of Caius, Thomas Gooch; and he and Burrough were evidently allies in the project. But as the Senate House was being built, and gradually spreading to the west, it occurred to the fellows of Caius that it was going totally to obscure their view to the south – the precious southern aspect which Dr Caius himself had declared must never be closed. Caius had intended that the Gate of Honour, in the middle of the southern side of Caius Court, should stand as a triumphal entry for Caius students proceeding down the little street straight ahead (see p. 28); and if the Senate House as planned had been completed, the street would have been closed. The fellows of Caius (it seems) detected James Burrough in the act of surveying for the foundations of the building as it would proceed across their view; and they insisted that the master intervene.[95] The master was in residence as a canon of Chichester on 31 May 1727, and from that safe distance he issued an eloquent plea to the vice-chancellor against closing the street. This would 'so effectually shut out all view of that noble fabric King's Chapel, that I wonder how the University or that College can bear it; and [it is] a scheme so injurious to Caius College, that I am fully resolved not to bear it. What ground you have already to build on I myself contracted for: but I am sure I never contracted for the street in front of the Schools, nor could anybody convey it to me.' On 6 July a college order was passed empowering the master to procure an order from the Court of Chancery to protect the king's highway. Thus Burrough's scheme was frustrated, though he himself remained a loyal fellow, later tutor, of Caius – an amiable man who helped to keep the peace between Gooch and his colleagues, and was to succeed him as master.[96] Meanwhile, building ceased; the Senate House achieved approximately its present form – with the west end left unfinished in the expectation that Burrough's scheme would be revived. This never happened, and it fell to his successor as master, John Smith – when he was vice-chancellor – to lay the coping

[94] Willis and Clark 1886/1988, III, p. 44, quoted in Brooke 1985/1996, p. 171. See *ibid.*, n. 53, for doubts about Burrough's share, which was, however, confirmed later in the eighteenth century by William Cole (quoted in Willis and Clark 1886/1988, III, p. 64); see also Friedman 1984, pp. 225–6.

[95] Brooke 1985/1996, pp. 171–2; Willis and Clark 1886/1988, III, pp. 43–54. There must have been a long argument before the master's letter (see below) was written, since the digging seems to have taken place in 1726 (Willis and Clark 1886/1988, III, p. 49).

[96] Brooke 1985/1996, pp. 170–4, esp. 171–2; Willis and Clark 1886/1988, III, pp. 49–55.

stone on the present west end. The Senate House was jointly designed by James Gibbs, James Burrough and the Court of Chancery.

The Court of Chancery also provides a postcript to the story of the relations of the colleges and the university. At the outset of this chapter, we witnessed the colleges growing to maturity, ceasing to be decorative appendages to the medieval university and becoming in a sense the university itself. But in the process they retained a remarkable degree of independence, in law and endowment, and in their own inner social, religious and academic lives. This was to protect them for many generations to come from being overwhelmed by the university or becoming mere satellites to it. But it also meant that as power shifted from the regents and the proctors to the heads of house and a vice-chancellor who was himself one of the heads (as the next chapter will show) the university became a slow-moving federation. The shape of the Senate House today is a reminder of what the veto of a single college could do to frustrate the university's most treasured plans.

Beside the austerely classical Senate House one contemplates the flowery Baroque of the east front of the Old Schools; and this reflects another fundamental aspect of eighteenth-century Cambridge: the incursion of national politics, of Whig and Tory, into academic affairs. The university had always contained a large number of clergy hoping for patronage, and in earlier days this had encouraged them to seek links in the royal Court. In return, the Court and government were deeply concerned to ensure the loyalty of the young clergy coming out of Oxford and Cambridge. In the early eighteenth century the Court still counted for much.[97] The chancellor of the university, the duke of Somerset, was a relic of a former age: he had won the office for his support to William and Mary in the revolution of 1688, but by 1748 he had been living in retirement for over thirty years. The duke of Newcastle greatly coveted his office; and when Somerset was thought to be dying, Newcastle gathered supporters in Cambridge, including 'our old friend' Dr Gooch, master of Caius and bishop of Norwich. Early in 1748 Gooch was translated to Ely; in December the duke of Somerset died at last – and Newcastle was elected. He was immediately active in the affairs of the university, promoting building works to give the Old Schools a new east front, covering a further limb of the University Library. For this Burrough, the author of the Senate House, naturally had a design. The duke, however, had his own candidate, Stephen Wright; and the members of the Senate – many of them loyal Whigs, some mindful of the fount of patronage, some

---

[97] See below, pp. 533–41.

(we may suppose) genuine admirers of Wright's design – voted with the duke. Later, however, Newcastle and Burrough were to be on good terms. The most important events in the university year, in Newcastle's view, were the loyal addresses to the king. In 1759 when he was master of Caius and Tory vice-chancellor, Burrough helped Newcastle past an awkward corner and Newcastle in gratitude arranged for Burrough to be knighted.[98] But Senate House Yard still carries a memorial of the political parties of the eighteenth century. As has been said, 'a Whig Old Schools to this day frowns at a Tory Senate House'.[99]

For the story told in this chapter the historian has a fundamental tool in *The Architectural History of the University of Cambridge*, the masterpiece of the great engineer and architectural historian Robert Willis, completed with loving care by his nephew J.W. Clark and published in 1886 – a book universally admired and readily available since it was reprinted in 1988 – and for the most part neglected by historians. The buildings of Cambridge, university and colleges alike, are a palimpsest: if the palimpsest is read with care and penetration, and imaginatively, they are among the most authentic documents of this history.

---

[98] Brooke 1985/1996, pp. 173–4; Winstanley 1922, pp. 37–54, esp. p. 44 on Gooch. For what Whig and Tory meant in eighteenth-century Cambridge, see Brooke 1985/1996, pp. 162–3 and refs.
[99] Brooke 1985/1996, p. 174.

Chapter 3

THE CONSTITUTIONAL
REVOLUTION OF THE 1570s

. . . your statutes being antiquated, semi-barbarous, and obscure, and for
the most part unintelligible on account of their age, you may henceforth
obey royal laws framed under our auspices.
(Preamble to the University Statutes of Edward VI,
Heywood 1855, pp. 4–5)

THE MAKING OF THE ELIZABETHAN STATUTES

Constitutional history is not fashionable at present among historians. In
the last two generations little attention or importance has been paid to
the study of formal constitutional forms and of practice, either on the
national scale or in the more modest circumstances of the universities.
More recently some early modern historians have suggested that ideas
and ideals may have some place in our explanations. Even so, this new
eclecticism has not extended to a positive resuscitation of constitutional
history. This broad disdain for constitutional history was repeated on a
more local scale as the new social history of the 1960s extended its bounds
to encompass the history of the universities. The purpose of this chapter
is to argue the case for the importance of considering, first, that changes
in constitutional forms may tell us something about changing ideas of
power, in itself no trivial matter in an institution which for at least half
the period with which we are concerned in this volume had an important
formative influence on the opinion-makers of the day. Secondly, it may
be that our neglect of matters constitutional reflects our own present
disdain for the legal niceties: we simply no longer have a constitutional
frame of mind. This may have cut us off from an understanding of periods
when such things were important to contemporaries.

On Elizabeth's accession in 1558 the university was being governed
under the statutes promulgated under her predecessor, Mary, by Cardinal
Pole.[1] That even under the pressure of business arising from the setting up

---

[1] For which see Mullinger 1884, pp. 156–7; Lamb 1838, pp. 237–74; Peacock 1841, pp. 39–40.

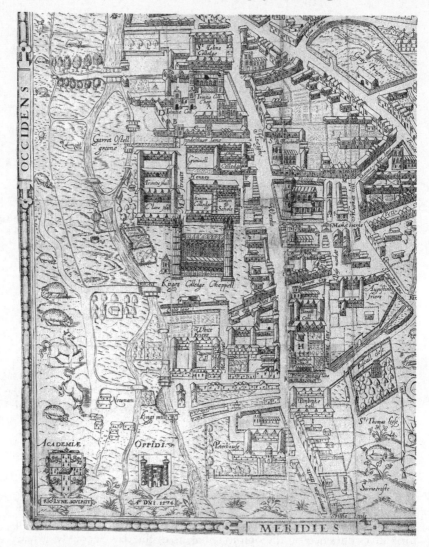

Plate 20 Cambridge in 1574: a part of Richard Lynes' map

of the new Elizabethan regime affairs at Cambridge were immediately taken in hand is indicative of the significance that the universities had already acquired within the Tudor polity by this date. It was as part-and-parcel of this larger process of acquiring control of the various levers of power in the state that Elizabeth's new secretary of state, William Cecil, later Lord Burghley, had been nominated and installed as chancellor of

Cambridge University in February 1559.[2] Under pressure from Matthew Parker, Cecil instigated a visitation of the university, under royal authority, in May of the same year. This was carried through during the following summer.[3] It has been judged to have been 'thorough', though 'undramatic' in its effects.[4] Two Marian masters were deprived of office, although death or prudence had removed six more. Eleven Elizabethan masters were appointed, but only three had been Marian exiles, whereas six had held ecclesiastical or university positions under Mary, and two, Baker and Caius, were later to be accused of popery.[5] These changes were hardly sufficient to satisfy the younger fellows with more radical religious convictions. The cautious conservatism of the Elizabethan visitation had created a situation inherently liable to generate disharmony between those placed in positions of authority as masters, and those subject to this authority. The situation was exacerbated by the combination of two further circumstances.

The first was the rapid increase in the number of new, young, fellows in the colleges.[6] The second was the power these young fellows derived from the relatively democratic constitution of the university. By the orders resulting from the royal visitation of 1559 the Marian statutes had been replaced by those of Edward VI.[7] Whereas the Marian statutes had begun to accumulate power in the hands of the masters of colleges, the Edwardian statutes gave relatively greater authority to the regents.[8] However, Burghley seems to have expected the heads to act with the authority that had been granted to their Marian predecessors. When trouble was brewing in November 1569 over the election of proctors, he had written 'wishing yow the heades to conserve such quietnes in the inferior members as is mete to be amongst men of that profession and study'.[9] Earlier, in June 1562, exasperated by the contention in the colleges, Burghley had written to the vice-chancellor, threatening to resign. He complained that

---

[2] PRO, SP 12/2/21; Porter 1958, p. 102. This is not to suggest that the university was averse to associating itself with the patronage and influence which attached to a powerful alumnus such as Cecil. The acquisition of influential chancellors was an already well-established practice by this time (see below, p. 93; Brooke 1989a).

[3] PRO, SP 12/4/33; Porter 1958, p. 104; Lamb 1838, pp. 276–7, 576.

[4] Porter 1958, p. 104. Cf. the conclusions to be drawn from the making of the first Elizabethan government at the centre (MacCaffrey 1968, pp. 22–92).

[5] Porter 1958, p. 106; above, p. 31.   [6] Below, pp. 221–2.

[7] CUA, Lett. 10.B.35; Mullinger 1884, p. 178.

[8] Regents were MAs of not more than three years' standing. Later, the Elizabethan statutes of 1570 extended this period to five years (below, p. 86n). 'Regency' had originated in the medieval university as a means of providing itself with a continuous supply of teachers (Leader 1988, p. 22).

[9] CUA, Lett. 10.3.a.

I cannot find such care in the Heads of Houses there, to supply my lack [that is, absence], as I had hoped for, to the ruling of inordinate youth, to the observation of good order, and increase of learning and knowledge of God. For I see the wiser sort that have authority will not join earnestly together to overrule the licentious parts of youth in breaking of orders, and the stubborness of others, that malign and deprave the ecclesiasticall orders established by law in this realm.[10]

For their part, the heads were aware of the problem, but felt ill equipped to deal with it. In 1564 they complained of the uninhibited power of the regents, and proposed that it should be curbed.[11] Later, in 1569, during the turmoil over Cartwright's lectures, William Chaderton, president of Queens', expressed his doubts as to whether the then vice-chancellor, Dr John Mey, would be able to contain the young regents. For 'although he be minded to call them to accompt, yet, I think he will not or cannot minister sufficient punyshment to suppresse their errors: Satan will have the upper hande and we shall be all in a hurlye burlie and shameful broyle'.[12] In fact, the expectations of the government as to the degree of control to be exercised on its behalf by the heads were incommensurate with the powers the heads derived from the existing statutes and the magnitude of the problems with which they were confronted. Thus, the first Elizabethan visitation of the university was too conservative to satisfy the religious radicals and the participatory pretensions of the increasing number of young regents. At the same time it was too liberal in restoring the Edwardian statutes. It was a recipe designed to enhance the conflicts that were soon astir.

In many respects the university became a cockpit in which were played out with a concentrated intensity the clashes between the old and the new religious ways. In assessing the character and consequences of those clashes we need to divest ourselves of the certainties imposed by hindsight. It was far from apparent to contemporaries in the 1560s that the religious settlement at the commencement of Elizabeth's reign would be more lasting than the settlements imposed in the preceding three reigns. The Protestantising was certainly not complete, and observation of events on the Continent, especially as in France, demonstrated that the high tide of Protestantism could be reversed.[13] Moreover, the lessons to be drawn

---

[10] Cooper, *Annals*, II, p. 173. See also Burghley to the heads, 12 Nov. 1566 and 13 Aug. 1569 (CUA, Lett. 9.3.1–2).

[11] BL Lansdowne MS 7, fo. 160 (item 790), 18 Jan. 1564; Strype 1822, I, pp. 15–16. A number of these proposals were later incorporated into the rewriting of the statutes in 1570.

[12] PRO, SP 12/71/11. On Cartwright, see below, pp. 68–70.

[13] Prestwich 1985; Cameron 1991.

from the experience of both the conflict itself and of the ultimate victory and defeat on religious matters within the university were carried forth into the broader reaches of English society and informed attitudes and behaviour for generations to come. The defeatist decision on the part of many Catholics to retreat into upper-class enclaves owed something to the coterie retreatism practised at Cambridge in the 1560s, passively sitting it out in expectation of the next turn of the tide.[14] Equally, the unrealistic expectations embodied in some Protestant triumphalism in part emerged from the experience garnered in the formative conflicts in Cambridge in the 1560s and early 1570s. The uncertainty of outcome, with all to be played for, and the broader influence of the university, widely recognised at the time, both served to intensify the clashes within Cambridge.

The constitutional arrangements prevailing at Cambridge in the first decade or more of Elizabeth's reign were ill suited to the containment of the religious factions which appeared determined to thrash out their differences within its confines, and with a view to the influence of their battles far beyond its walls. This alone would have been enough to focus attention on the constitution of the university and it is also possible to detect at work in the revision of the university's statutes a set of changing assumptions about the nature and sources of power in the Tudor polity.

With regard to both its religious precipitants and the formative pre-conditions of political theory, the constitutional revolution at Cambridge in the 1570s affords one of the most evident demonstrations of an underlying argument of this volume. The very centrality of the universities to many aspects of English life for the greater part of this period means that what we see happening at Cambridge had ramifications for our understanding of wider issues in early modern society and polity. In this chapter we will look at the immediate religious circumstances which precipitated constitutional change at the level of the university, examining the formal provisions and the practical consequences of the new constitution which was the outcome of this crisis, and of the implications of these developments for our understanding of the changing contemporary perceptions of the sources of power in Elizabethan society.[15]

From the middle of the 1560s there was a series of disputes over questions of religious observance that served to reveal the inadequacies of the existing constitutional arrangements from the viewpoint of a government intent upon maintaining strict control in such matters. The

---

[14] On the more general phenomenon of Catholic retreatism in the wider society, see Bossy 1975.
[15] For constitutional change in the colleges, see below, pp. 78–9.

luckless Robert Beaumont, as master of Trinity and vice-chancellor, was to be publicly humiliated when his processional horse was shaved and he was accused of treachery by his former friends for attempting to enforce Archbishop Parker's demand for uniformity in doctrine, rites and apparel.[16] The most notorious clash was between a kaleidoscope of shifting alliances at St John's: in Burghley's words, 'this wild fury broken loose in the college of St John's'.[17] Initially the master of St John's, Richard Longworth, had aligned himself with William Fulke in throwing away surplices, demolishing the steps at the east end of the chapel, and sanctioning the wearing of hats rather than the square academic caps. Against Longworth and his supporters had been set Richard Curteys, the president of the college, who appears to have acted as Burghley's agent in the disputes.[18] Concurrently, similar disputes over vestments had stirred at Trinity College, with Thomas Cartwright taking the lead, before discreetly retiring to Ireland, for the moment.[19] At Peterhouse, even the young John Whitgift could be found in opposition to the surplice – until, in the words of Edward Dering, he being a man, God suffered him to fall into great infirmities, and he succumbed to the temptations of advancement proffered by Burghley.[20] It was these disputes in the 1560s – mainly over the retention of 'popish' vestments – which convinced those in the university charged with their suppression of the inadequacies of their constitutional arrangements. However, the immediate precipitant of constitutional changes in the university was a series of lectures on the Acts of the Apostles delivered by Thomas Cartwright in the spring of 1570.[21]

In 1569 Cartwright had returned to Cambridge from serving as a domestic chaplain to Archbishop Loftus of Armagh, to be elected under the prevailing democratic franchise Lady Margaret's Professor in succession to William Chaderton. In the arguments that followed on the delivery of his lectures he was accused of resurrecting aspects of the vestments controversy that had animated the years 1565–7. This point is debatable, but what is certain is that he gave new emphasis and urgency to an existing element in radical Protestant thought: the incompatibility of the offices of archbishops, bishops, deans and archdeacons with the model of the

---

[16] For Beaumont's tribulations, see Porter 1958, pp. 114–18, and below, p. 258.

[17] PRO, SP 12/38/13, fos. 71–4, quoted in Porter 1958, p. 129.

[18] For the disputes at St John's, see Porter 1958, pp. 119–35; Cooper, *Annals*, II, pp. 217–25; CUA, Lett. 8, pp. 14, 15. The definitive treatment is in Bauckham 1973 and 1975.

[19] Pearson 1925; Collinson 1967, p. 112.   [20] Collinson 1964, pp. 120–200.

[21] For a discussion of their content and their place in the development of the puritan movement, see Collinson 1967, pp. 112–13.

primitive church to be derived from the Acts of the Apostles.[22] There is, moreover, a Cambridge dimension to Cartwright's propositions which seems not to have been recognised hitherto: there are parallels between the rule of a presbytery, which in effect was what Cartwright was advocating, with the prevailing rule of the regent masters at Cambridge. It is at least worth contemplating the possibility that the enthusiasm for presbyterianism owed something to the experience of formative years at Cambridge no less than to the experiences of continental exile or the model to be found in the Acts of the Apostles. Conversely, the increasing abhorrence with which the relative democracy of university government was viewed by those in positions of responsibility may have owed as much to the parallels which could be drawn between the house of regent masters and a presbytery as to the coincidence of the individuals who exploited the former in promoting the latter.

In June of 1570, Cartwright's predecessor in the Lady Margaret's Professorship, Dr William Chaderton, president of Queens', wrote to Burghley emphasising the general undermining of authority implicit in what had lately been adumbrated:

> True it is suche seditions, contention, and disquietude, suche errors and schismes openlie taught and preached, boldlie and without warant, are latelie growne amongst us, that the good estate, quietnes, and governance of Cambridge, and not of Cambridge alone but of the whole church and realme, are for great hasarde unles severlie by authoritie they be punished . . . For his daylie lectors teache suche doctrine as is pernitious and not tollerable for a christian commonwealth.

With Cartwright, Chaderton associated Robert Some of Queens' and Edmund Chapman of Trinity College, both of whom had preached along similar lines, as aiming 'to overturne and overthrow all ecclesiasticall and civill governance that now is, and to ordeyn and institute a newe founde policie'.[23]

Under further pressure from Edmund Grindal there was correspondence between Burghley and the vice-chancellor and heads. The outcome of this was that at the Congregation on 29 June a letter from Burghley was read to the assembly, and plans were laid by Cartwright's opponents to block his *supplicat* for the doctorate of divinity. The resurrected Edwardian statutes required the caput to present the grace for

---

[22] Pearson 1925, p. 33; Collinson 1967, pp. 112–13; CUA, Lett. 9.c.4, Burghley to the heads, 3 Aug. 1570.
[23] SP 12/71/11.

the degree to the Congregation for approval.[24] However, at this time the caput was appointed afresh at each Congregation, and although the nominations were in the hands of the vice-chancellor, or in his absence, the proctors, the regent masters then had the right to approve or reject the nominations. On this occasion the regents non-placeted all the nominations until they achieved a body that they thought would approve of Cartwright's degree. However, the vice-chancellor, Dr John Mey, refused to admit him. In the furore that followed, Cartwright's salary was sequestered, he was suspended from lecturing and later, towards the end of 1570, ejected from his chair. Thereupon he retired to Geneva.[25]

Although the more immediate crisis was over, with a victory for those in authority, another loomed in November, with the annual election of the vice-chancellor. Again, as with the caput, the Edwardian statutes (see p. 65) gave considerable power to the regents who elected the vice-chancellor by simple majority. It was unlikely that they would elect anyone who had thwarted their aims in June, and it was even possible that they might attempt an act of defiance and – horror of horrors – elect Cartwright to the office. It was the threat posed by these immediate circumstances that precipitated a thorough-going revision of the statutes. The constitutional drafting that occupied the summer of 1570 was to have a fundamental effect in shaping the alignments of the academic community at Cambridge until their replacement in 1856.

The proposal to revise the statutes appears to have emanated from Whitgift, possibly in close consultation with his old acquaintance and an equally authoritarian personality, Andrew Perne. Following discussions with Burghley he consulted with other heads of houses remaining in Cambridge, including Mey, Perne, Hawford, Harvey and Ithell. Working over the summer, they had the new statutes ready by mid-August, and Whitgift wrote to Cecil suggesting that if he did not have time to scrutinise them, he should pass them on to Parker, or someone else qualified to vet them. In fact they received the royal assent and passed the Great Seal a little over a month later, on 25 September. One of the first results of their implementation was that under the new and restricted franchise they created, Whitgift was elected vice-chancellor in November.[26]

---

[24] Grindal was at this time bishop of London and an absentee master of Pembroke Hall (SP 12/71/23; Strype 1824, I, ii, p. 376; CUA, Lett. 9.C.3). For the caput, see below, p. 84.

[25] Mullinger 1884, pp. 217–18; Collinson 1967, p. 113.

[26] Strype 1822, III, pp. 16–17. Collinson 1991, pp. 11–12, leans in favour of the role of Perne in their drafting, but the evidence is only circumstantial. It was subsequently claimed that two of the heads, Dr Pory and Dr Baker, Perne's closest associates, 'were gone from Cambridge' while at least some of the new statutes were being formulated (Heywood and Wright 1854, I, p. 89), and

The new statutes effected a major shift in the basis of power within the university, from the regent masters to the heads of houses, and they were not submitted to without a struggle. That struggle again illustrates both the immediate alignment of opposing forces within the university and the contrary views on governance which informed their positions. Things were fairly quiet during the year of Whitgift's vice-chancellorship, but in the following years there arose 'diverse controversies betwene the masters [of colleges] and heades of the Universitie . . . on the one part, and the masters [of arts] and regents playntife on the other part'.[27] Under the old constitution the proctors, as representatives of the regent masters, had wielded considerable power which in constitutional terms had flowed up to them from below. It is hardly surprising that in the campaign of opposition to the new statutes, the proctors elected in the Michaelmas term of 1571, Arthur Purefroy of Peterhouse and John Becon of St John's, were the leading opponents of the revision.[28] One of their accomplices, a fellow of Pembroke, had initiated the assault by inveighing against the new statutes 'and that bitterly' in the presence of the vice-chancellor, most of the heads, 'and divers straungers . . . to the great offence of all hearers'. This had occurred in the relative privacy of the master's chamber at Corpus. However, the issue was really joined in an oration made by Becon in the Regent House at the election of the vice-chancellor, 'to the diffaming of the queens majesties statutes, and to the great discrediting of the heades of colleges, using such insolance against them as the like have not been harde'. Such an obvious affront, by one in authority, on such an occasion, released a torrent of criticism by lesser men; the heads later complained of Becon that through his 'audasitie the inferior sorte have been sithence the more encouraged and embouldened boeth to speak and to sett themselves against their seniors and heades'.[29]

By the beginning of May 1572 the dissidents had raised a petition of 164 names which they submitted to their chancellor, Lord Burghley. They also remitted to their leaders the furtherance of their cause through approaches to the earls of Sussex, Huntingdon and Bedford, Sir Ralph

---

this lends some additional weight to the argument for the influence of Perne in their drafting: Strype 1822, III, p. 17 (19 Aug. 1570); *Cambridge Documents 1852*, I, p. 454; Heywood and Wright 1854, II, p. 610.

[27] Heywood and Wright 1854, I, p. 63, the heads to Burghley, n.d. The heads claimed that the officers elected at Michaelmas 1571 'did find the Universitie very quyet and obedient to the queens majesties statutes at theneterynge of their offices' (Heywood and Wright 1854, I, p. 65).

[28] For the transformation in the powers of the proctors, see below, pp. 81–4; Heywood and Wright 1854, I, p. 61. See Porter 1958/1972, pp. 167–8, and the documents brought together by Heywood and Wright 1854, I, pp. 58–122, from State Papers, Lansdowne MSS, and Corpus Christi College, Cambridge, MS 118, parts of which are also in Lamb 1838.

[29] Heywood and Wright 1854, I, pp. 109–10.

Sadler, and Edmund Grindal and Edwin Sandys, leading Cambridge dons now on the bench of bishops.[30] Although the opposition to the new statutes drew on a wider constituency for support than would have been prepared to assist Cartwright in the controversies that had initiated the constitutional changes, it is clear from the mere enumeration of the names of those who it was thought might further their cause at Court that the opposition was inspired by the religious radicals whom the new statutes were intended to curb. Burghley referred the hearing of the matter to Grindal and Sandys, but under Whitgift's leadership the heads requested that Matthew Parker, archbishop of Canterbury, Richard Cox, bishop of Ely, Robert Horne, bishop of Winchester, and Thomas Bentham, bishop of Lincoln, should be added to the hearers. Ostensibly this was because of their knowledge of Cambridge, most of them having been educated there, and 'allso have good experience sithence that tyme of the estate of the Universitie of Oxforde'. However, it may be that they feared that, despite his earlier criticisms of Cartwright, Grindal would be too kindly disposed to the puritans amongst the opponents of the new statutes. Equally, the heads may have hoped sincerely that by adding to the hearers men who were known to the university and respected by many, 'their judgmentes and consent maye make more for the better likinge of the said statutes hereafter'. As it was, the cause was finally heard before Parker, Grindal and Sandys at Westminster towards the end of May.[31]

Whatever the hopes and fears of the various parties to the dispute, there was no equivocation in the conclusions of the adjudicators in their report to Burghley: 'We think that the statutes as they be drawen maie yet stande, and no greate cause whie to make anie alteration. We think also that theis younger men have been farre overseen to seek their pretended reformation by disordered meanes.'[32] Although this judgement may have ordained that the new statutes would be upheld, it did not quell the immediate controversy. A few days later, on 10 June, in the Regent House, under the terms of the new statutes the heads were to choose four lecturers. John Becon was no doubt smarting from the criticisms contained in the recent determination of the dispute over the statutes. He contrived to create confusion by claiming that Burghley had informed him that the lecturers and other officers were to be chosen in a way that deviated from the rules formally laid down. But he had overstepped the mark with the man from whose equable hand those of his faction had most to hope. Five days later Burghley wrote to the vice-chancellor, judicious as ever, but warning that 'I may be moved . . . to lett

[30] *Ibid.*, I, p. 61.   [31] *Ibid.*, I, pp. 64, 108–9.   [32] *Ibid.*, I, pp. 108–9.

Mr. Proctor taste of the frute of his rashnesse and untrue reporte of me.'
If Becon continued in his opposition, he was to be sent up 'To answere
thereto . . . for I maye not suffre thiss manner of rashnesse to encrease
without temperynge it with some colder humor, to reduce the same to
modestie.'[33]

Busied as Burghley was with other affairs during the summer, it is
not clear what was the outcome of these ructions. However, writing
at the end of September, he ruled on the issue of the procedure to
be followed in electing lecturers. Not for the first time he concluded
with the hope that he might employ his authority amongst them 'for
the benefit and preferment of the University, [rather] than to bestow
the little leasure I have from greater affairs in the compounding of your
quarrells. Wherefore I trust, through your discreet government, I shall not
much hear hereafter.'[34] A forlorn hope, a misplaced trust: the changing
social composition, the very order of government that had only recently
been imposed with such contention and strivings, and the increasing
numbers within the university, were to ensure that both Burghley and
his successors as chancellor would ever have the matters of Cambridge
clamorously about their ears.

During the 1560s, 1570s and 1580s a series of measures at the level both
of the university and of individual colleges transformed the constitutional
framework within which Cambridge operated. Cumulatively the most
important change was the augmentation of the powers of the heads of
houses within the university, and of those same heads as masters of their
individual colleges. It is the constitutional changes of these decades that
provide the formal framework for later events, and the framework for our
understanding of those events. At the same time, the means by which
these changes were brought about, the specific powers they gave the
heads of houses, and the subsequent manner in which that group often
exercised those powers go a long way towards explaining the marked
antagonism that was felt towards the men who were heads and masters,
an antagonism which is a *leitmotif* of life at Cambridge in succeeding
years. In chapter 8 we will have occasion to examine the sociological
transformation in the role of masters, which also served to bolster the
new, formal, powers and to reinforce the antagonism.

THE STATUTES OF 1570

What then was the constitution imposed on Cambridge in these decades,
against such clamorous opposition? The constitution provided for the

---

[33] *Ibid.*, I, pp. 113–15.   [34] *Ibid.*, I, pp. 121–2.

university by the Elizabethan statutes was the outcome of a few months' work in the summer of 1570 in response to the immediate crisis created by Cartwright's lectures. But its drafting embodied responses to longer-term structural changes to which the institution was subject. These included a changing social composition and the increasing concern of the government with its activities. This interpretation is borne out by the other constitutional changes to the university that occurred in the latter part of the sixteenth century. Moreover Oxford University shared many of the same problems and elicited similar responses from government. A summary of the changes experienced by Cambridge's sister university also tends to support the suggestion that modifications to the administration and constitution of the universities were, at least in part, a result of a fundamental change in attitude and interest on the part of the government.

The letters patent of 1561, the new statutes of 1570 and the Act of Parliament of 1571 together provided the constitutional framework for Cambridge University over the ensuing years.[35] The letters patent recognised the corporate status of the university, and mainly served to establish its rights and privileges *vis-à-vis* the outside world. In particular they defined the relations of the university with the Corporation of Cambridge, and established the university as a liberty, partly insulated from normal jurisdictions. The university was granted or confirmed in its rights as clerk of the market at Barnwell and Stourbridge, and in its jurisdiction over regraters and ingrossers, the sale of victuals, and policing in the town. The mayor and bailiffs were instructed to assist in these activities. The university was further relieved from the payment of subsidies or provision for military service, and the boundaries within which these rights and privileges pertained were clarified. It was further endowed with an explicit jurisdiction in cases involving its members. This jurisdiction was to be exercised in a court – the Consistory – that henceforth was to be a court of record. The special problems of supplying the necessities and regulating the behaviour of the increasingly large numbers that constituted the university are reflected in these provisions of the letters patent. They are of further significance in granting immunities, privileges and special jurisdiction.[36] This they did at a time when Tudor policy had long been intent on eradicating those liberties in which the royal writ did not have immediate passage, where there was immunity from certain types of

---

[35] There were no major changes in the bases for the government and administration of the university, and of many of the colleges, until the major reforms of the 1850s and 1860s – a profound witness to the forces of institutional inertia.

[36] Clark 1892, pp. 1–33.

taxation, and where local jurisdictions excluded or curbed the authority of the increasingly pervasive quarter-sessional and assize system of local government.

The grant of seats in the House of Commons in 1604 was a further acknowledgement of this exceptional status. The anomaly thus created by this grant involved a significant recognition by the government of the special circumstances of the university as an unusually constituted institution of a scale not normally encountered in early modern society. Equally, the new statutes of 1570 were a recognition of the increasingly important role of the university in national life and therefore of the need to maintain a stricter and a more reliable grasp on its internal activities. The culmination of these developments was the parliamentary statute of 1571 (13 Eliz. c. 29). This incorporated both universities and confirmed their right to hold endowments and their existing rights and privileges, including those granted by letters patent to Cambridge ten years earlier.[37]

This combined flurry of regulative activity was mainly concerned with Cambridge (although the Act applied to both universities) and it is normally assumed that the constitution of Oxford was not revised along lines similar to those that had long been operating at Cambridge until the reception of the revised statutes of 1636. However, in the 1560s there were proposals for the revision of the Oxford statutes.[38] In practice, although there was no full-scale revision of local statutes as there was at Cambridge, piecemeal organisational changes and codification of existing statutes seem to have had much the same effect. These alterations were largely carried through as a result of the influence wielded by Oxford's chancellor, the earl of Leicester, who was elected to the office in December 1564. Following his election, in 1565, the earl placed as vice-chancellor his protégé Thomas Cooper, fellow of Magdalen, and compiler of the great *Thesaurus Linguae Romanae et Britannicae*.[39] Subsequently, Leicester appears to have nominated Cooper's successors. These included the puritan Lawrence Humphrey, whom he kept in office for five years between 1570 and 1575. It was mainly under the earl's auspices that the university's statutes were revised and codified in the mid-1560s.[40] It was Leicester who instigated the creation of a committee consisting of

---

[37] Shadwell 1912, I, pp. 183–8. Blackstone makes the point in this context, citing Sir Mathew Hale, that the letters patent were not considered adequate of themselves (Blackstone 1829, III, pp. 84–5).
[38] Lawrence Stone, 'The Ninnyversity?', *The New York Review of Books*, 16 (28 Jan. 1971), 21; *HMC* [70] *Pepys*, p. 9; Williams 1986, pp. 397–440.
[39] Williams 1986, pp. 423–31; Rosenberg 1955, pp. 124, 126n, 130.
[40] Mallet 1924–7, II, pp. 116–19.

the vice-chancellor, the doctors, the heads of houses and the proctors to arrange the business of Convocation prior to its meeting. In practice, as at Cambridge, these moves had the effect of depriving the guild of regent masters of their powers of government.[41]

Precedent is all, even in the matter of establishing autocracy, and it could be argued that the alterations instituted by Leicester at Oxford in the 1560s were one of the sources of inspiration for Whitgift's (or Perne's) more systematic changes to the statutes at Cambridge in 1570. One might even speculate that at the back of Whitgift's mind was the idea of using the same type of organisational changes as those initiated by the earl of Leicester at Oxford, but with quite different ends in view. To some extent Leicester's interventions at Oxford had served to promote the puritan cause in that university. The purpose of Whitgift's actions was to curb the worst excesses of puritanism at Cambridge. None the less, even with these divergent aims, both men sought similar means to their realisation, through a concentration of power and responsibility in the hands of a small group of identifiable men who could be held answerable to an external political authority.

Oxford was experiencing the same type of increase in the number of its students and the same type of change in its social composition as were taking place at Cambridge. The changes in the effective constitution of the university instituted at Oxford in the 1560s suggest that the reaction of those in power at the centre was similar to similar problems. As we have seen, the constitutional changes at Cambridge had been precipitated by the specific circumstances of the crisis brought on by Cartwright's lectures in 1570. But these changes should also be seen as part of a response to longer-term changes in the size and composition of both the universities. To these we must add the effects of a general desire for detailed regulation and control of, and information about, numerous aspects of economy, society and polity which surpassed the pretensions of any previous regime. Indeed, so long as we recognise that aspiration is not the same as achievement it would not be inappropriate to describe the actions arising from these aspirations as the rise of the Tudor interventionist state.[42] Parallel to and intimately interlinked with this new intrusiveness seems to have been a sea change in the understanding of the sources of authority in the polity. The following exposition of the import of the constitutional revisions at Cambridge may, indeed, throw some light on

---

[41] Rosenberg 1955, p. 133; Mallet 1924–7, II, p. 119; McConica in Stone 1975, p. 151.
[42] See below, chapter 4.

this. What is certain is that the treatment meted out to the universities needs to be seen in this broader perspective. Nor is it possible to interpret changes at Cambridge in purely domestic terms.

Writing to the University of Cambridge in 1569, the earl of Leicester had addressed himself to 'Mr Vitz channcelor as to the rest of the Regentes and rulers in the universitye'.[43] Similarly, the letters patent of 1561 had confirmed grants and privileges to the 'Chancellor Masters and Scholars of the University of Cambridge'; it was the whole number of these that constituted the body politic of the university.[44] However, the statutes of 1570 helped to tip the balance of power within this body politic away from the relatively democratic grouping of regent and non-regent masters to a small clique composed of heads of colleges. How this occurred is obscure, for the heads of houses as a standing committee have no place in the statutes of 1570. They had no place in the caput, no special role in the Senate. They nominated two candidates for the office of vice-chancellor – of whom the Senate chose one – already under Edward VI's statutes. By later convention the vice-chancellor was (with very few exceptions) one of them, and he regularly consulted them; but it was a convention, no more. The statutes of 1570 gave the heads a major say in all university appointments. But the real source of their power lay in meetings of heads with the vice-chancellor, which had no statutory force but increasing authority. As early as 1559 Dr Caius had been prevailed on to become master of his college by the united voices of the senior fellows and the vice-chancellor and heads. Meetings of heads are rarely recorded before the 1620s; but they clearly occurred.[45] It was the vice-chancellor, who after 1587 was invariably master of a house, and who as the chancellor's deputy was an ex-officio member of the caput, who presided in the reconstituted Consistory Court. In the years which followed it was this body which was to become the forum for some of the most celebrated disputes which rent the calm of Cambridge. Assisted by a doctor of law, the vice-chancellor came to sit weekly in term time with five or six

---

[43] CUA, Lett. 9.C.2a. The phrase is used in the body of the letter. It is addressed to 'the vicechancellour and other the regentes and rulers'. See also a letter of 1562, addressed to the vice-chancellor, or in the event of the vice-chancellorship being void, to the proctors (CUA, Lett. 9.B.3).

[44] 'Concedimus prefatis Cancellario, Magistris, et Scolaribus . . .' (Clark 1892, p. 8). Cf. Shadwell 1912, I, p. 184; Cooper, *Annals*, II, p. 602; *HMCS*, XII, p. 224.

[45] See p. 31; Venn 1904, pp. 77–8; Brooke 1985/1996, p. 64; Brooke, Highfield and Swaan 1988, p. 163. Gonville and Caius College was ruled from the 1590s to the 1850s by a committee of senior fellows: it had no place in the statutes of the college, but was set up by an act of usurpation in the 1590s, similar to that which gave authority to the heads in the university itself (Brooke 1985/1996, pp. 96–8).

heads of colleges to hear causes.[46] Indisputably, the overlap of roles and the concentration of power were very considerable. There was also a further accretion of power by the heads of houses that occurred in the ensuing years as a result of a semantic confusion and the combination of a number of functions in the same few persons. The impression to be gained from numerous documents for the period after 1570 is that in the minds of those outside the university there was sometimes confusion between two notionally separate bodies, the *caput senatus* (see pp. 84–8) and the heads of houses. And well there might be, for the *caput senatus* had become a permanent committee nominated by, partly elected by, and partly composed of individuals drawn from the less formally constituted group composed of the heads of houses. The cliquish nature of power at the apex of the university is also manifest in the complaint by the objectors to the new statutes that five or six heads had met to decide the nomination of candidates for the vice-chancellorship under the new electoral procedure for that office.[47] Moreover, subsequent revisions of the statutes of individual colleges greatly augmented the powers of their individual heads at the expense of the rest of their members, and of the Visitors of the colleges to whom dissatisfied members might appeal;[48] and their authority was further enhanced by the rule (implicit, though not explicit, in the statutes of 1570) that every student must be the member of a college; and by the heads' role as interpreters of the statutes to their flock.

The concentration of responsibility for the government of the university in the hands of the heads of houses is characteristic of Elizabethan attempts to ensure the greater answerability of subordinate units of government through a more precise allocation of authority. As Elizabeth pointedly indicated in the letter accompanying the new statutes, the heads and others in authority were to 'exact from all others a diligent observance of them'. However, if 'it shall happen that these statutes are contemned, neglected, or not observed, we shall hold you, to whom execution thereof is intrusted, and who have undertaken the government of others, responsible for the transgression'.[49] The ambiguous intermediary

---

[46] 'At a Monday Cort' (BL Harl. MS 7033, fo. 200). For some examples of the vice-chancellor and heads meeting to conduct business in the Consistory, see BL Harl. MS 7033, fos. 201, 205, and CUL MS Mm. vi. 54, fo. 16 (vice-chancellor and ten other heads, 1632); CUL, Baumgartner (Patrick) MS 22, fos. 12v, 13v (over a disputed election of a master, 1626); *ibid.* MS 23, fo. 36 (re archiepiscopal visitation, 1636); CUL MS Mm. i. 38, p. 42 (1597, over a disputed election of a master); Porter 1958, p. 156.

[47] Heywood and Wright 1854, I, p. 67.

[48] In general, see Winstanley 1935, ch. 2; Brooke, Highfield and Swaan 1988, pp. 40–1 and ch. 6.

[49] *Statutes 1570* in Heywood 1838, p. 2. Similarly, it was to the heads that Cecil (Burghley's son and successor as chancellor) addressed admonitory letters in 1602, reminding them of the duties

position in which this injunction placed the heads is readily apparent in the years that followed, and is not dissimilar to the position in which many local justices found themselves during the same years: the role of intermediary between Court and community was not an easy one to occupy in the political culture of the period. Thus the statutes and their interpretation assisted the process whereby, increasingly, the heads were set apart from the rest of the members of the university. For example, with the exception of those exercises required for the purpose of taking a higher degree, the heads of colleges were exempted from all scholastic exercises, both in the university and in their individual colleges (c. 50, 12).[50] These privileges were resented, and in 1580 the doctors expressed their discontent at being excluded from the government of the university by – among others things – attempting to force the heads to preach on Sundays and holidays.[51]

The new statutes recognised the increased importance of the colleges in the life of the university as compared with the individual faculties or the whole body of regent masters. A cycle of colleges was established to supply the opponents and disputants in public exercises (c. 27), and in the regular sermons (c. 45). This acknowledgement of the importance of the colleges also had the indirect effect of increasing the overall authority of the heads through the new powers they gained within their individual colleges.[52] Attendance at lectures was to be monitored and enforced on a college basis (c. 5). Anyone wishing to be admitted MA had first to seek the approval of the head and the majority of fellows, or senior fellows of the college to which he belonged (c. 19). In general the grace for any degree required the prior approval of the head and a majority of the fellows (c. 21). This power within colleges was further increased by supplying the heads with a veto in all college elections and all grants of leases (c. 50, 29) and in effect they were given a further veto over the punishment of any of their own number (c. 42).

Finally, the statutes of 1570 laid certain responsibilities on the heads as a group. Where no specific punishment was expressly designated by the statutes, the chancellor in conjunction with the heads was to determine an

---

attached to their offices, and upbraiding them for having failed to act on his earlier instructions (CUA, Lett. 9.B.24.i). Whitgift had drafted the accompanying articles (*ibid.*). Peacock 1841, p. 61, no. 1, was in error to suggest that the archbishop took no steps to reform the abuses complained of at this time.

[50] The Elizabethan statutes are printed in Heywood 1838 and *Cambridge Documents 1852*, I. They are referred by chapter and clause in the text.

[51] SP 12/139/20.

[52] The augmentation of the powers of the heads of houses *within* their colleges is examined more fully in chapter 8.

appropriate punishment (c. 50, 39), and, similarly, all ambiguities arising from the statutes were to be settled by the chancellor in conjunction with the majority of the heads of houses (c. 50, 43).[53] However, the most immediately obvious accretion of power was in the control the heads were now given over the election of officers of the university. This was done by giving the nomination of candidates to the heads, although leaving the final election from this restricted list of candidates with the regents. Previously, the regents had enjoyed much freer elections.[54] In the case of the taxors, who were to be nominated by the cycle of colleges (c. 37), individual heads exercised indirect control through their veto within the colleges.[55] A procedure like that for the election of taxors was also to be followed in the election of proctors. The regents were now required to select the proctors from amongst the nominees presented to them by the cycle of colleges in their turn.[56] If they disliked the nominees the regents could appeal against them, but only to the vice-chancellor and a majority of the heads of colleges: the very men from amongst whom, in their role as masters of individual colleges, the nominations had received initial approval (c. 35). The potential for chicanery by masters in the nominations from within colleges is evident in the story of how in 1593, John Jegon, master of Corpus, jobbed his brother, a young fellow of the college, into a proctorship.[57] It is again implicit in the case of the dispute between the heads and the doctors in 1580. On this occasion a doctor suggested that, at the instigation of the heads, one of the proctors had withheld a key necessary to the conclusion of the procedures that the opponents of the heads were pursuing.[58]

---

[53] In effect this often meant the vice-chancellor, acting on behalf of the chancellor, of whom he was considered an entire deputy (see *Statutes 1570*, c. 42; Peacock 1841, p. 46 n. 3).

[54] *Statutes 1570*, c. 35; Venn 1910, p. xx.

[55] Moreover, changes in the organisation of the university, most notably the rise of the colleges, had reduced the importance of the office. Originally, they had been responsible for pricing the lodgings available in the town. But as Fuller put it with his usual pithiness, although the name remained, the 'office is altered at this day. For after the bounty of founders had raised Halls and Colleges for Scholars' free abode, their liberality gave the Taxors a writ of ease, no more to meddle with the needless prizing of townsmen's houses' (Fuller 1655/1840, p. 25).

[56] At Oxford, the failure to establish a set cycle of colleges for the election of proctors resulted in an 'endless contention' between colleges (SP 16/119/34). At Cambridge, however, earlier proctorial cycles had been initiated in 1514 and 1557 (Tanner 1917, p. 34; Heywood 1838, p. 22). As those who objected to the new statutes complained, 'the authority of liking or mislikinge of proctors and taxors, [is] wrested now from the bodie to the masters [of] howses' (Heywood and Wright 1854, I, p. 73).

[57] BL Lansdowne MS 75, fos. 15v, 113, 124 (nos. 7, 51, 57). For a dispute in 1582 over the choice of a proctor from Gonville and Caius College see BL Lansdowne MS 36, fos. 84–108 (nos. 33, 34, 35, 37, 42, 44–5) and SP 12/155/47. For an animated election of proctors in 1569, see CUA, Lett. 9.c.2a–b.

[58] BL Lansdowne MS 30, fo. 166v (no. 59), John Hatcher to Burghley, 26 July 1580.

The constitutional revolution of the 1570s

The alteration in the status and powers of the proctors that was brought about by the Elizabethan statutes had a significance over and above the practical control that the heads could now exercise in their election. Previously, as we have seen, they were elected from the body of the regents. As a result, during the disputes of the 1560s and early 1570, they had tended to act as the representatives of their constituency in opposition to authority. Even under the new statutes the control of the masters over the election of the proctors was not absolute. Thus, as might be expected, the proctors had taken a leading part in the opposition to the new statutes during 1571–2.[59] But this role as spokesmen for the body of the university is manifest even later; it was a tradition that survived. Possibly this was a result of the curtailment of the freedoms in most other respects previously enjoyed by the majority of the university and the need for *some* focus of opposition. For example, it is evident in 1612 in the boastful claims of the never modest John Williams – later bishop of Lincoln (1621–41) and archbishop of York (1641–50) – to Sir John Wynn as to his achievements while serving as a proctor. Williams was no doubt right to claim that 'The opposition twixte the maisters of Colleges and the bodie of the Universitye, wch is the companye of our Regent and Non-regent Maister of Artes, hath beene soe longe a foote as any Cantabrigian can enforme you thereof.'[60] For Williams this opposition was epitomised by the clash between the vice-chancellor and the proctors, as representatives of the two interest groups; 'but it is most of all perceived in that twixt the vice-chauncellour and the proctoures, who are in a maner Tribuni Plebis, and represent the bodye as the vice-chauncelour doth the heads of Colleges'.[61]

Despite these intermittent assertions of opposition to the heads through the proctors, the Elizabethan statutes had marked a further decline in the proctors' powers. In the fifteenth century they had exercised an authority equal to that of the vice-chancellor, but it had since faded.[62] The new Elizabethan statutes attempted to restrain further their authority to the supervision of academic proceedings (c. 42). Even this the heads curbed by

[59] Heywood and Wright 1854, I, p. 61.

[60] Yorke 1887, p. 153. The Edwardian statutes had decreed that MAs were to become non-regents after three years. During their preceding three-year period of regency the injunctions of 1549 required them to keep their disputations (Heywood 1840, p. 13; also p. 234, Pole's Ordinances). Under Elizabeth, regents were declared to be MAs of less than five years' standing, doctors of less than two years' standing, and some university officers. Non-regents were MAs of more than five years' standing, and doctors of more than two years' standing, These two groups constituted separate houses in the Senate (Heywood 1840, pp. xii n, xiii; Cooper, *Annals*, II, p. 602); they are referred to below as the 'body' of the university.

[61] Yorke 1887, p. 153.

[62] For their powers under the old statutes, see *Statuta antiqua*, cc. 53–64, 84, esp. c. 54.

a decree of March 1571.[63] Thus the revised statutes embodied the aggrandisement of the heads and of the vice-chancellor on the one hand, and the derogation from the powers of the proctors on the other. Underlying this change were more than simply practical considerations. As Williams' remarks seem to imply, the authority of the proctors derived from the body of the university, whereas the authority of the vice-chancellor derived from the external authority represented in the royal statutes that defined his office, and the lay chancellor whose deputy he was. Therefore, at a philosophical level, the new statutes marked a shift from an ascending to a descending theory of authority in the government of the university.[64] In at least this particular aspect of the revision of the university statutes, the principle adopted by the Crown and its agents is, perhaps, indicative of fundamental attitudes. The detailed evidence provided by these constitutional changes at Cambridge suggests that it might be worth resurrecting an old debate on the aspirations of Tudor government – was there a Tudor despotism?[65]

The opportunity to control still further the already severely circumscribed freedom of elections was facilitated by a shift from a secret to an open ballot. It was reported that 'Men dare not give their voices according to their conscience, for feare of displeasure.' A fear, it was claimed, that was 'not without cause; for D[r] Whitgift in a scrutinie [that is, a vote] some gyvyng theire names, was exceedinglie moved, and called for pen and ynke to write theire voices simplie and freely, thinking that with so terrefying of them, they wold for feare give as he would have them'.[66] In their role as fellows of colleges the members of the Regent House were highly dependent upon the goodwill of the masters of their colleges. Their further degrees, profitable offices and future livings all depended on their approbation. Therefore, it was no little power that had been granted to the supervising oversight of the heads when the secret ballot was removed; 'this opening of voices enforces men, agaynste their

---

[63] Heywood and Wright 1854, I, pp. 57–8, 177.

[64] For the background to these ideas, see Skinner 1978, pp. 48–65; Ullmann 1961, pp. 20–6; 1979, pp. 30–2; Pocock 1975, pp. 334–5, 353–60. Under the old statutes the proctors received their powers through election from among their fellows: 'duo magistri artium actualiter regentes rectores seu procuratores per majorem partem magistrorum in artibus regentium, eorum judicio, in virtute juramenti praestiti, ad hoc magis idonei in diversis scrutiniis eligantur, omnibus et singulis magistris in eadem congregatione praesentibus specialiter juratis de magis idoneo in electione praeponendo' (*Statuta antiqua*, c. 53).

[65] Hurstfield 1967; Elton 1972.

[66] Heywood and Wright 1854, I, p. 77. Neither were free elections fostered by masters acting as scrutators, or tellers of votes (*ibid.*, I, p. 79).

othe and mynde, to give their voices according to their masters' request or commandment, for feare of his heavie indignation'.[67]

Later, following the acquisition by the university of seats in parliament in 1604, the heads attempted to construe their statutes in order to remove the parliamentary election from the body of the university to themselves; they claimed that the procedure to be used should be that followed in the election of the vice-chancellor where – as we have seen – although the election was with the body of the university, the nomination of candidates remained in the hands of the heads of colleges. On the occasion of a dispute in 1614 the chancellor, the earl of Northampton, denied this restriction, and thereafter the broader of the two franchises employed within the university was retained for parliamentary elections.[68] The election of the chancellor of the university was also by means of this broader franchise and it seems that the *cause célèbre* of the election of the duke of Buckingham as chancellor in 1626 was, in effect, carried through by the masters of colleges in the teeth of a substantial part, perhaps even a majority, of the body of the university. Undoubtedly on that occasion the cumulative corporate experience of the preceding sixty years, and the accustomed influence of the heads of houses in determining the outcome of elections through the powers given them by the statutes of 1570, contributed not a little to their success.[69] Buckingham had been elected by the narrowest of margins. Yet, some four years later, following the assassination of the duke, the then vice-chancellor was still willing to make a guarded promise on behalf of himself and his fellow heads to the king for the successful engineering of the election of another royal nominee. 'I am but one of many and therefor, (having to doe wth a multitude) cannot absolutely assure the effectinge your Maities pleasure yet I dare undertake for my self, with rest of ye heades, & many others, truly & faithfully to labour in your Maties desires – and now presume to send faire and stronge hopes to give them full satisfaction.'[70]

The new statutes of 1570 gave the heads very considerable powers to influence the outcome of elections through the nomination of candidates and the abolition of the secret ballot. This influence was further augmented by subsequent changes in procedure. A grace, passed during the 1570s, modified the free election of the scrutators to the course followed in the election of proctors. This gave the heads the nomination

[67] *Ibid.*, I, p. 78.   [68] Mullinger 1884, pp. 463–5; Rex 1954, p. 59; Morgan 1983, ch. 9.   [69] Morgan forthcoming.   [70] SP 16/114/60.

of the key officers responsible for the conduct of votes in the Senate.[71] The preceding analysis of election procedures suggests that there was considerable justification in the complaint by the opponents of the new statutes that 'all elections be now taken from the body, and derived to masters of houses'.[72]

THE CAPUT AND THE HEADS

The curtailment of the powers of the houses of regents and non-regents and of their representatives, the proctors, on the one hand, and the augmentation of the powers of the heads on the other, was carried further by the clarification of the status of the caput – the small committee which vetted graces (or motions) laid before the Senate.[73] The caput had first been mentioned in the Grace Books in 1520.[74] Under the Edwardian statutes it had been nominated afresh at every congregation. Mary had revoked the Edwardian statutes, and the Ordinances of Cardinal Pole that replaced them had established annual elections to the caput, and given a veto in its deliberations to each of its members. The readoption of the Edwardian statutes at the beginning of Elizabeth's reign had resulted in a reversion to the former, loosely regulated, method of appointment to the caput, and as we have seen, this had played a part in the fracas surrounding Cartwright in 1570.[75] At Oxford, in the 1560s, the earl of Leicester, as chancellor, had encouraged the formation of a similar small body of men at the apex of university administration. The potential for control inherent in the concentration of responsibility represented by such a body also appealed to the drafters of the new statutes at Cambridge, and had its parallels in other areas of government: as always, events at Cambridge need to be judged in this broader context. For example, in its relations with the counties the Privy Council sought to facilitate communication and to enforce responsibility by specifying a smaller group of justices within each commission of the peace.[76] In its relations with

[71] BL Lansdowne MS 30, fo. 134 (no. 52), citing c. 36 of the Elizabethan statutes which had allowed free election. Burghley was said to be privy to the change.

[72] Heywood and Wright 1854, I, p. 82.

[73] Peacock long since noted that 'There is no point in the ancient constitution of the university more obscure and uncertain than the composition and powers of the caput' (Peacock 1841, p. 21, no. 1).

[74] Venn 1910, p. vii. This is about twenty years earlier than the date implied in Roach 1962, p. 120.

[75] Heywood 1855, pp. 3–26, 216–18; Peacock 1841, pp. 38, 41. There had been some confusion over which colleges had had their statutes revised in 1559 (BL Harl. MS 7033, fo. 18v, Matthew Parker to William Cecil).

[76] Initially this consisted of members of the quorum. Over time, demand expanded the numbers in the quorum until it was practically coextensive with the commission as a whole. There is evidence

Cambridge the government sought a similar convenience and control. The Elizabethan statutes of 1570 (c. 41) reverted to the practice, initiated by Cardinal Pole, of requiring the election of the caput for a whole year. This ensured greater stability and answerability amongst its members. The procedure for nominating candidates for election also appears to have been altered. Those who defended the new statutes claimed that prior to their introduction the joint nomination had been in the disposal of the vice-chancellor and proctors who named such persons 'as might best serve for their purpose and private commoditie'.[77]

The caput comprised the vice-chancellor and five others.[78] Under the new arrangements the vice-chancellor, the senior proctor and the junior proctor *each* nominated five candidates. In each group of five there was one doctor of divinity, one doctor of law, one doctor of medicine, one non-regent and one regent. In other words, there was a maximum of three candidates for each position on the caput, and the election took place between these three nominees. Now, although the new procedure resulted in the presentation of three distinct lists of nominees, and might therefore be considered an improvement on previous practice, what the defenders of the new statutes failed to mention in their justification was that the electorate had been severely curtailed. Under the former practice the caput had been elected by the whole body of every congregation.[79] In the case of the rejection of Drs Perne, Baker and Porie it is clear that this procedure did indeed permit some discrimination to the body of the university.[80] Under the new statutes this broad franchise had been abolished. It was replaced by an electoral college composed of three groups: the heads of colleges, the doctors and the scrutators.[81] In practice the procedures for nomination and election to the caput seem to have been even more circumscribed than they might appear to have been

---

that the Privy Council tended to communicate with a limited number of justices. These men were responsible for the forwarding of central government missives. This is based on a reading of numerous commissions of the peace and justices' notebooks and correspondence for Norfolk and Suffolk.

[77] Heywood and Wright 1854, I, p. 88.

[78] The vice-chancellor and a doctor from each of the faculties of theology, medicine and law, a non-regent and a regent master. The chancellor and, in his absence, the vice-chancellor, was an *ex-officio* member (Peacock 1841, p. 47). Under the medieval statutes the senior doctor who was a monk or friar had represented the interest of the religious houses in Cambridge. By a grace of 1547 he had been replaced by the public orator but there is no evidence of his subsequent attendance (Venn 1910, p. xxvii; *Statuta antiqua*, Grace of 17 Nov. 1547; *Cambridge Documents 1852*, I, p. 451; Peacock 1841, p. 21n.1). When acting with the two proctors it was called the 'septemviri' (*Cambridge Documents 1852*, I, p. 486).

[79] Heywood and Wright 1854, I, p. 89.   [80] Lamb 1838, p. 366.

[81] The election procedure in 1636 is recorded in CUL, Baumgartner (Patrick) MS 22, fos. 91–2; MS 23, fo. 48v. See also Peacock 1841, p. 47.

from the letter of the new statutes. Those who objected to the new procedures argued that the freedom of nomination was more apparent than real, and that those whom the vice-chancellor named, 'they are sure to be chosen'.[82] Initially, the doctors, having been divested of all power in other areas, and able to do nothing in this, absented themselves from proceedings.[83] The scrutators were accused of being the puppets of the masters of colleges. Certainly, as we have seen, the change in the procedure for *their* nomination had brought them under the influence of the heads. As a result of these changes it was said to be possible to arrange matters so that 'most of the heads [that is, members of the caput] be masters of colleadges: wherebie it falleth out that nothinge can passe all the whole yeare whereof they dislike, or anie one of them'.[84] That, indeed, was the gravamen of objections to the changes wrought in the caput by the new statutes: the heads of houses had gained an effective dominance in this crucial body.

The importance of the caput lay in its powers to control the business that came before the houses of regents and non-regents. This was all the more important because the powers of these two houses were not substantially changed by the new statutes. But the caput provided an effective filter on their deliberations. Each member of the caput had a veto, and no grace for whatever purpose could be submitted to the body of the university without the prior approval of the caput (c. 41).[85] In addition, the new statutes provided that in appeals from the judgement

---

[82] Heywood and Wright 1854, I, p. 70. Peacock 1841, p. 47 n. 2, notes that the vice-chancellor's list was almost invariably chosen. Moreover, if the election was not settled within the first three votes, the choice devolved on the vice-chancellor and two senior doctors, as happened in 1636 (CUL, Baumgartner (Patrick) MS 22, fo. 91).

[83] Heywood and Wright 1854, I, p. 70. However, they were back and voting in the 1630s (CUL, Baumgartner (Patrick) MS 22, fo. 48v). Under the old statutes the doctors had enjoyed joint power with the vice-chancellor to correct abuses (*Statuta antiqua*, c. 19, *Cambridge Documents 1852*, I, p. 317).

[84] Heywood and Wright 1854, I, p. 70. Most of the heads of house were qualified as doctors in one or other of the three higher faculties, while another head might be qualified to stand as a member of the non-regent house (cf. the complaints of those who objected to the new statutes, Heywood and Wright 1854, I, p. 78). One might add to those a point which may not have been apparent at the time. The new statutes extended the period of regency from three to five years, and included in the membership of the house of regents doctors of not more than two years' standing. This would have made it possible to select a regent representative with some considerable years of experience.

[85] In a dispute in 1580 one of the enemies of the heads claimed that when the Senate was asked to assent to the sealing of certain letters, 'the heads [of colleges] began to fume and play their parte; and would have had the lettres brought into a hedde [i.e. the caput], that any one of them might have denied the seale' (Heywood and Wright 1854, I, p. 274). In 1627 Matthew Wren used his position as representative of the Faculty of Theology in the caput to veto the incorporation of Isaac Dorislaus as a doctor of the university (SP 16/86/87). See also the role of the caput in the election of the duke of Buckingham as chancellor in 1626 (BL Sloane MS 1775, fo. 27).

of the vice-chancellor, the nomination of delegates to hear the appeal lay with the caput, joined with the two proctors (c. 48).[86]

The concentration of power in the hands of the caput and, because of its mode of appointment, effectively in the hands of the heads of houses, must have been much to the liking of central government. As Burghley remarked in reply to those who objected to the restrictions on the nomination to university offices imposed by the new statutes: 'I thynk ye st[atute] very good as it is, to reduce the nomination . . . to be doone by a nombre nether too few for lack of consideration, nor committed unto too many for feare of confusion: and none better can I thynk, than the heades of Colledges.'[87] Here Burghley was clearly applying to Cambridge a principle of broader application: it was precisely this limitation of numbers and concentration on the quality and experience of membership that Burghley and others repeatedly expressed as a preference with regard to the commissions of the peace.[88]

After 1570 the once-ephemeral caput became a permanent and a key part of the constitution of the university. Certainly, by 1600 the development of the caput had reached the stage where it was being described as one of the three distinct entities that constituted the Senate, the others being the upper house, or Regent House, and the lower house.[89] Thus it would appear that the answer to Dr Roach's question, as to when the term 'Senate' became general, may lie in the late sixteenth century.[90] Then, it became necessary to find a word that encompassed the older entities, the house of regents and non-regents, and the *caput senatus*, in its permanent and enhanced post-1570 incarnation. For the early modern historian this formulation carries obvious echoes of the increasingly clear contemporary view of the three entities which constituted a parliament.[91] With their taste for analogical reasoning this parallel is hardly likely to have been lost on pedantic academics. Here lie some intriguing possibilities.

The transformation of the caput into a permanent body and an instrument of the heads of houses was certainly a reversal of its original role as an ephemeral committee representing the interests of the regent and non-regent houses at individual congregations. Moreover, the powers of veto possessed by each individual member of the caput had probably

[86] CUL, Baumgartner (Patrick) MS 22, fo. 4.
[87] BL Lansdowne MS 102, fo. 183r–v (no. 99). This general preference on Burghley's part can be found expressed in a particular instance even before the revision of the statutes. In 1567 he wrote that, in a matter to be adjudged, he would prefer it settled by the vice-chancellor and the heads (CUA, Lett. 9.c.1.d, Burghley to the university, 20 July 1567).
[88] Smith 1974, pp. 77–8. [89] Cooper, *Annals*, II, p. 602. [90] Roach 1962, p. 120.
[91] See Loach 1991; Graves 1985.

originated in a desire to protect the interests of the separate faculties or religious houses of the medieval university.[92] With the changes introduced by the statutes of 1570, that power had, in effect, been transferred to the heads of houses. While it is true that the heads remained members of their faculties it is also true that their primary loyalty was to the group constituted by their fellow masters. This is true even of individuals such as John Cowell, Regius Professor of Civil Law and master of Trinity Hall in the early 1600s, who was intent upon reinvigorating that faculty.[93] It is this transformation in the powers and allegiances of the caput which may well help to explain why the faculties are such shadowy and ill-documented entities in early modern Cambridge as compared with what appears to have been the case at Oxford.[94] But there may also be a wider importance embodied in the changes in the powers of the caput at this time.

The caput was an institution that had originally derived its power from below, from the regent and non-regent masters as a body, and from those same individuals as represented via their particular faculties. The changes of 1570 converted this institution into a body deriving its authority from the power of its main nominators, electors and members, the heads of houses. They in their turn derived much of their power and drew many of their directives from above, from the royal statutes of the university and the statutes of their individual colleges, in turn derived from royal charters. The faculties can be envisaged as vertically integrated interest groups, composed of various levels of academic achievement. The exercise of the veto on behalf of one of these groups was therefore the exercise of a power originating from below. By contrast, the exercise of the veto within the caput after 1570 articulated the interests of a horizontally integrated interest group, composed of the masters of colleges. In their hands the veto was essentially an exercise of power derived from above, and intended to regulate and censor those matters that were to be committed to the deliberation of the body of the university. From this viewpoint the assumptions underlying the reform of the caput are the same as those governing the shifts in the relative power of proctors and vice-chancellor.

THE ROLE OF THE VICE-CHANCELLOR

The final but major change in the government of the university affected the office of vice-chancellor. There was no major and immediately

[92] See above, n. 78. [93] Simon 1968, pp. 260–72; below, pp. 438, 440.
[94] McConica 1986, pp. 151–334.

obvious addition to his powers *qua* vice-chancellor to affront the university. At the time of the changes in the statutes the main objection was to the alteration in the mode of his election. Previously, it had lain with the regents, and it was contended that this led to 'contentions and labours . . . by factiouse regents for un meete and unfitt men'. This canvassing was said to go on for half a year before the election, 'with greate spight, bitternesse making of factiouse changes and losse of time'.[95] Under the new statutes the heads of houses convened annually on 4 November to select two candidates for the office. The following day the regents and non-regents were allowed to vote for either of the two nominees (c. 34). However, it was claimed that even this very restricted choice was removed in practice, with the heads pressing hard for one candidate. Conversely, the previous form of election was said to have encouraged heads to be responsive to popular needs in order to gain election – 'that they might be thought worthy, by the judgement of the body, to be preferred to that credite'.[96] In addition, those who objected to the new statutes foresaw that the new electoral procedure would ensure that only heads of houses would be nominated for the vice-chancellorship, and the exclusiveness of the governing oligarchy would be maintained. They were answered that anyone from MA upwards could be nominated.[97]

For their part the protagonists of the new statutes argued that there was a natural relationship between the vice-chancellor and the masters of colleges that was both close and reciprocal. The heads of colleges, 'havinge the chief charge and care in government, doe best knowe who are most mete for that office', while 'they are greatly assisted for their better and quyet regimen of their severall colledges' by the authority of the vice-chancellor.[98] The relationship between the vice-chancellorship and a mastership came to seem so natural that it is necessary to remind ourselves that it was not always so. Before 1570 there was no necessary relationship or overlap of office between the heads and the vice-chancellor, but after that date the fears expressed by the opponents of the new statutes proved well founded, and the vice-chancellorship ceased to be an office open to any of the more senior doctors of the university, and came to circulate within the narrow circle composed of heads of houses. For example, of the five senior doctors who received the royal injunctions from the king at Newmarket in 1616, all were masters of colleges. Only

[95] Heywood and Wright 1854, I, pp. 66–8; *Statuta antiqua*, c. 8, *Cambridge Documents 1852*, I, p. 311; CUA, O.A. no. 8; Heywood and Wright 1854, I, p. 86.
[96] Heywood and Wright 1854, I, pp. 66–7.   [97] *Ibid.*, I, p. 67, and c. 5, p. 85.
[98] *Ibid.*, I, p. 84.

one, John Davenant, never served as vice-chancellor, mainly because of his duties as Lady Margaret's Professor of Divinity. The other four were either the present, or past and future vice-chancellors.[99] Indeed, the relationship between the two types of office was if anything even more marked than might at first appear.

In the period between 1570 and 1640 the vice-chancellorship tended to be occupied by those masters who enjoyed long periods of office as masters. With a number of explicable exceptions, all vice-chancellors served as masters for more than ten years.[100] The evidence of individual careers suggests that the vice-chancellorship was closely associated with those who had served, at the time of their election, or in subsequent years were to serve long periods, as masters. Looked at from another viewpoint, only five men occupied the headship of a house over twenty years and failed to serve as vice-chancellor.[101] Amongst those who served for less than twenty years as masters, a number of special circumstances explain their failure to become vice-chancellor.[102] Some occupied chairs.[103] Others were ecclesiastical pluralists who seem to have treated their mastership as only one in a clutch of offices. In addition, many of these had influential and time-consuming offices that kept them away from Cambridge. However, these are perhaps not sufficient reasons for their failing to become vice-chancellor: other men with similar

---

[99] CUA, folder in plan press.

[100] The exceptions are twelve in number. They include a group who served early in the period: John Young, 1553–4, Edmund Cosin, 1558, Matthew Hutton, 1560–2, John Stokes, 1565–6, Richard Longworth, 1567–8, John Still, 1575–6, John Copcot, vice-chancellor 1586–7; a group of three who served towards the end of the period: John Mansell, 1624–5, president of Queens' for nine years, 1622–31; John Cosin, 1639–40, with nine years in all as master of Peterhouse, 1635–43. In addition, Fogg Newton became vice-chancellor in the year he was elected provost of King's, in 1610. Robert Scott, master of Clare 1612–20, served only eight years as master, and was vice-chancellor in 1619–20. The exceptions can be accounted for by the unusual political and religious circumstances, especially at the beginning and end of the period, or by premature death or promotion.

[101] See below, n. 104.

[102] Edmund Hownde, master of St Catharine's 1577–98, Edmund Barwell, master of Christ's 1582–1609, Laurence Chaderton, master of Emmanuel 1584–1622, Samuel Collins, provost of King's 1615–45, Thomas Batchcroft, master of Caius 1626–49. Barwell and Chaderton may have been excluded because of their radical religious opinions. Alternatively, they may have wished to avoid the office because its authoritarian image clashed with their view of a pastoral and proselytising mastership. Chaderton was busy with his lectureship at St Clement's church, Cambridge, for nearly fifty years (on him see now Collinson in Bendall *et al.* 1999, chs. 2, 6). Hownde was a chaplain to the queen and the earl of Leicester. The reason for Batchcroft's exclusion is not clear. Collins was Regius Professor of Divinity during most of his provostship, and the occupancy of a chair explains why a number of these men never served as vice-chancellor.

[103] In addition to Samuel Collins (n. 102), the following masters also occupied chairs and failed to become vice-chancellors: William Whitaker, Regius Professor of Divinity, 1580–96; John Overall, Regius Professor of Divinity, 1596–1607; John Davenant, Lady Margaret's Professor of Divinity, 1609–21.

preoccupations did manage to serve in the office.[104] Overall, and as might be expected, there was a fairly close correlation between the locally active and experienced masters and the vice-chancellorship. The emergence of this oligarchy is reflected archivally in the preservation of joint orders by vice-chancellor and heads, from 1574 onwards.[105]

After 1570 only two men served as vice-chancellor without already being master of a college, and in both these cases the circumstances were somewhat anomalous. The first of these was John Hatcher, elected in 1579. In the disputes between the heads and the doctors that ensued during Hatcher's year of office it became clear that even this election was the result of a ruse employed by the heads. Their attempt to manipulate the nomination to the office had been turned back on themselves by their opponents. In arbitrating these disputes, Edmund Grindal recommended to Burghley that he should admonish the heads that 'for the [election of the] vice-chauncellour alwaies to pricke two fitt men; and never hereafter to practize, that of the two nomynated, one shulde be an unfitt man, and as it were a staale, to bring the office to the other (which they did nowe in nomynatinge Doctor Hatcher, and taste of the frutes thereof) which ministreth a juste offense to the reste of the universitie'.[106] The last non-head to be elected vice-chancellor before the end of the twentieth century was John Copcot, in 1586. At the time, he was a fellow of Trinity, and he even became master of Corpus during his tenure of the vice-chancellorship. This anomaly, and his subsequent election at Corpus, can probably be explained by his connections with Burghley and his chaplaincy to Archbishop Whitgift.

Copcot's connections with Burghley and his somewhat anomalous election as vice-chancellor while still only a fellow of a college suggest that the heads themselves were subject, on occasion, to external pressure over election to the office. At least at Cambridge the situation was not

---

[104] The following were not vice-chancellors: John Caius, a practising physician normally resident in London, President of the College of Physicians, lecturer in anatomy at the Barber Surgeons Hall; Lancelot Andrewes, chaplain to the queen and dean of Westminster; his brother, Roger Andrewes, whose pluralities included the chancellorship of Chichester; Samuel Brooke, chaplain to James and Charles, and Professor of Divinity at Gresham College in London; Thomas Eden, LLD, professor at Gresham College; Edward Leeds, LLD, a master in Chancery and vicar general of Ely diocese; Edward Martin, pluralist and chaplain to Laud; James Montague, DD by special grace as first master of Sidney Sussex, pluralist and dean of the Chapel Royal to James I; John Preston, chaplain to Prince Charles and preacher at Lincoln's Inn; Richard Sterne, chaplain to Laud. Samuel Harsnett was vice-chancellor while bishop of Chichester, but employed a deputy in Cambridge (CUA, Lett. 11.B.A.6).

[105] CUA, CUR 44.i, nos. 137–222.

[106] BL Lansdowne MS 30, fo. 135 (no. 152), archbishop of Canterbury to Lord Burghley, 30 June 1580; BL Lansdowne MS 102, fo. 178r–v (no. 97). For vice-chancellors who were not heads, see Cooper, *Annals*, II, p. 429 n. 1.

like that at Oxford, where, from 1568, the vice-chancellor was appointed directly by the chancellor.[107] In 1602, partly out of annoyance with the perennial disputes between the town and the university, Sir Robert Cecil, who had succeeded his father as chancellor, ordered a general tightening up of regulations. This reveals something of the thinking about the nature of the office of vice-chancellor. The admonition included a vague instruction to the effect that the statutes governing the choice of the vice-chancellor and of officers were to be properly observed: 'Those Elections being done and by the heads of Colledges accordingly with speciall Regard of such men whose wisdome and learning may most avayle to the good and peacable government and the creditt of the universitye.'[108] This admonition appears to have had some effect. In particular, John Jegon seems to have been a particularly successful vice-chancellor: five years later Cecil was acknowledging that he would 'give credit to the report made to me of the good endeavours of some late Vice-Chancellors in the service of that place' – while he protested that the choice 'is wholly in yourselves', that he would 'not so much cross the liberty of your own choice as to recommend any particular to your nomination', he nevertheless remarked that if earlier vice-chancellors had begun the reform of abuses 'you would so dispose of your succedent elections that the Vice-Chancellorship may be cast on such men as you shall truly judge most like to prosecute all those good offices which any precedent Vice-Chancellor has begun'.[109] Like the heads of houses, the vice-chancellors also enjoyed a considerable accretion of power as a result of the various alterations to the government of the university during the 1560s and 1570s. Not all of this was the result of specific statutory changes; in part it was the result of a change of attitude of which the changes in the statutes were only one manifestation. In the early 1560s, Burghley was expressing what appears to have been a genuine doubt as to whether he could intervene in the troubled situation at St John's. He had been informed by those with experience of the university that the chancellor or vice-chancellor 'hathe not used heretofore to medle in matters pertyninge to private statutes of Colleges' except where expressly permitted to do so; a few years later Parker was reporting on the troubles at Gonville and Caius in very similar

---

[107] Mallet 1924–7, II, p. 116. At Cambridge the vice-chancellor normally wrote to the chancellor, informing his superior of his own election (e.g. *HMCS*, XII, p. 465; CUA, Lett. 9.B.14, 9.B.22a; BL Harl. MS 31, fo. 98; CUA, Misc. Collect. 8, fo. IV; SP 16/175/36; CUL, Baumgartner (Patrick) MS 23, fo. 41v).

[108] CUA, Lett. 9.B.24.ii.

[109] CUA, Misc. Collect. 8, *passim* (Jegon's notebook while vice-chancellor); *HMCS*, XIX, p. 459. By the eighteenth century the choice of vice-chancellor normally followed a rota of heads (Winstanley 1935, p. 10; but see below, p. 536).

terms and expressing doubts as to 'howe yor vicechancellor can deal in order with ther college matters'.[110] But attitudes were soon to change. After the ructions and the statutory changes of the early 1570s, Burghley can be found peremptorily instructing the fellows of Caius to move to the election of a new master, and ordering the vice-chancellor to see that the statutes of the college are fulfilled in this respect.[111] They were: but they permitted Dr Caius himself to choose his successor, which he did, to very happy effect.[112]

From the mid-fifteenth century on, the chancellor had ceased to be resident – commonly to provide a friend at, or near, the Court for the university.[113] As a result the importance of the vice-chancellor began to increase.[114] From 1535 this was overtaken by the desire on the part of the central government to have a member of the inner circle with direct oversight of the university. Thus John Fisher was succeeded by Thomas Cromwell in 1535.[115] The university had reaped benefits from having a direct relationship with a man of prominence: it was Fisher who acted on behalf of Lady Margaret in the foundation of Christ's in 1505, and St John's in 1511.[116] Henceforward, the office of chancellor was always held by a great officer of state or an eminent nobleman. Consequently, in the now habitual absence of the chancellor the position of the vice-chancellor increased in importance within the university.

Nor was this all: the vice-chancellor now became the local deputy of a great man of the realm, whose prestige, and the authority derived from the other offices he held, confused the precise limits of his jurisdiction within the university. This confusion also devolved ill-defined additional authority to his deputy. Moreover, the vice-chancellor was known to have the ear of the influential, and the mixed blessing of serving as the main intermediary between the chancellor and the university. This development was recognised in the statutes of 1570, where powers granted to the chancellor were from the first exercised on his behalf by the vice-chancellor. The statutes specifically stated that 'whatever is appointed to be done by the Chancellor of the University in our Statutes, let it be done in his absence by the Vice-Chancellor' (c. 42).

[110] CUA, Lett. 9.B.3; SP 12/38/26.
[111] SP 12/95/10. See below, p. 204; Brooke 1985/1996, pp. 77, 87 and n. 28. Burghley was misinformed by those who wished to set aside Dr Caius' exceptional but legal nomination of his successor.
[112] Brooke 1985/1996, pp. 77, 87.   [113] Brooke 1989a.
[114] For the earlier chancellors, see Tanner 1917, p. 18, corrected in Brooke 1989a, esp. pp. 50–2, 233–4.
[115] For Cromwell's impact at Cambridge, see Elton 1973, pp. 32–4.
[116] Tanner 1917, p. 18; Underwood 1989; Jones and Underwood 1992, ch. 7.

THE VICE-CHANCELLOR AND THE COURTS

The privileges granted to the university by the letters patent of 1561 in part depended upon the exercise of authority by the vice-chancellor as an ex-officio member of the commission of the peace. As such, he enjoyed all the additional powers and responsibilities accruing to this office at that time.[117] The subsequent evidence also suggests that the vice-chancellors extended their use of their powers as justices beyond the matters to do with markets and fairs with which the letters patent of 1561 were mainly concerned.[118] Eleven years after the reception of the statutes, the defenders of the new regime were arguing that 'It is very requisite and necessarie that the vice-chauncellor, and others of the Universitie, should have thaucthoritie of a justice of peace, to committ seditiouse and rebelliouse persons and breakers of the peace unto warde', without the possibility of escape through appeal to the university's system of justice.[119] From the viewpoint of those who advocated them, these police powers increasingly were necessary in a sensitive institution where it was important to restrain the seditious and potentially rebellious. However, circumstances suggest that there was some justification in complaints that when confronted with intractable opponents on whatever issue vice-chancellors exploited the confusion of jurisdictions that they exercised, 'And commonlie, for maintenance of there extremyties, they will say they do yt, not as vice-chancellors, but justices of peace, and therebie refuse appelations to the bodie [of the university]: so that we know not under which jurisdiction we live, and libertie of appelations is wreasted out of our handes by there oppression.' It was even claimed that 'the moderators of publike disputations exercise the like authoritie, by vertue of their justice-shippes, in publike disputations in the scholes', and that erring disputants had been ordered to the Tollbooth, the town's lockup.[120]

---

[117] Smith 1974, pp. 87–111. For the grant of a request for JPs drawn from the university see a Privy Council letter of 1552 (BL Lansdowne MS 3, fo. 31 (no. 16), and copy in Lansdowne MS 115, fo. 169 (no. 65)); and a further request for representatives of the university in the Commission for the County of Cambridge, 'Reasons to have Justices of Peace of ye University' (BL Lansdowne MS 51, fo. 146v (no. 62)). These requests all originated in disputes with municipal and, later, county authorities.

[118] Clark 1892. For the argument that the chancellor or the vice-chancellor had authority to hear causes concerning the peace, see below.

[119] Heywood and Wright 1854, I, p. 92.

[120] *Ibid.*, I, pp. 74, 77, 106. For some examples of a vice-chancellor exercising powers that were indubitably those of a JP in matters of sheep-stealing and bastardy, see CUL, Baumgartner (Patrick) MS 22, fo. 76. Sometimes those powers clashed with those of a fellow JP, the mayor of Cambridge. In 1575 Andrew Perne forbade the roasting of an ox at Barnwell, for fear of the crowds it would attract and the danger of plague. With an eye to the commercial advantage of

They also had jurisdiction in the Consistory Court. This essentially ecclesiastical jurisdiction dated back to the time of Edward I. It was confirmed by the Elizabethan grant of 1561, which in its turn received parliamentary sanction in the Act of 1571. In the same year a room on the east side of the Schools quadrangle was fitted out as a court. Its meetings, however, cannot be distinguished from the regular meetings of the heads, discussed above. It was to become the scene of many heated encounters, and the focal point of much business. Here, on Mondays, the vice-chancellor kept his court, with the assistance of his fellow heads.[121]

Under Elizabeth the Consistory became the main means of enforcing religious conformity in sermons, commonplaces, public lectures or other public expositions.[122] The new statutes of 1570 required that offenders should recant and publicly confess their error. If they were unrepentant, or failed to accede to the required form of submission, they were to be expelled from their colleges and banished from the university (c. 40). Recantation and submission often took place before the heads in the Consistory.[123] For it was the vice-chancellor and heads who sat as judges and enforced conformity, using civil law procedures.[124] Indeed, there are indications that by the 1590s some radical precisian masters felt that they had a right to define doctrine through the Consistory.[125] The reinvigoration of the Consistory Court in the early 1570s probably represented a

---

the town, the mayor had licensed the roasting (Hatfield MS 136.6). For confirmation of the right to maintain a gaol, see PRO, S.O. 3, 2/June 1603.

[121] For a note of 'the charge of making the Consistory', see CUA, V.C. Ct. III, i, p. 2. This was in 'the Little Schole, now the place of Judgment for the Vicechan:' (CUL MS Mm. ii. 25, fo. 35). Matters dealt with included points of theology, both in the Consistory and, according to a letter from Jerome Beale to Samuel Ward, at the Consistory door (Bodl. Tanner MS 71, fos. 10v–13, 28 May 1629). For its growth in the 1590s, see below, pp. 149–50. For examples of the range of business dealt with 'At a Monday Court', see BL Harl. MS 7033, fo. 200; for examples of the vice-chancellor and heads meeting to conduct business in the Consistory, see BL Harl. MS 7033, fos. 201, 205; CUL MS Mm. i. 38, p. 42 (1597, over a disputed election of a master); CUL, Baumgartner (Patrick) MS 22, fos. 12v, 13v (over a disputed election of a master, 1626); CUL MS Mm. vi. 54, fo. 16 (the vice-chancellor and ten other heads, 1632); CUL, Baumgartner (Patrick) MS 23, fo. 36 (1636, on archiepiscopal visitation). For meetings in the 1620s and 1630s, see esp. Hoyle 1986.

[122] For a notorious example of the exercise of the authority of the vice-chancellor and heads through the Consistory, see the case of the religious radicals Francis Johnson and Cuthbert Bainbridge, fellows of Christ's, in 1589. Johnson claimed that 'I was there (for anything I heard) by the sole authority of the vice-chancellor charged the next day to depart the university' (Porter 1958/1972, pp. 157–63).

[123] E.g. Ralph Brownrigg's submission to the Consistory in 1617, before the vice-chancellor and the heads, after disputing points of doctrine (BL Harl. MS 7033, fos. 202v, 204r–v).

[124] CUA, V.C. Ct. III, i, *passim*.

[125] Cf. Collinson in Bendall *et al.* 1999, p. 40. 'Precisian' was an alternative for 'puritan' much favoured in the sixteenth and seventeenth centuries.

further reduction in the number of those exercising authority in the university. There were complaints that, 'Whereas before by auncient statutes the proctors and doctors did assist the vice-chancellor in corrections and judgements, now they have no place nor anie thing to do.'[126]

A second court, that of the Commissary to the Chancellor, was more concerned with the regulation of matters of trade, especially at Midsummer and Stourbridge fairs.[127] None the less, certain matters were reserved to the Consistory Court, and as appeal from the Commissary's Court was to the Consistory, all contentious matters were likely to end up under the scrutiny of its limited number of judges.[128]

ARISTARCHIE TO MONARCHIE

Little wonder, then, that in 1611 one of the proctors was of the opinion that a particularly assertive vice-chancellor – Barnaby Gooch – was 'endeavouring by all meanes possible to reduce our Aristarchie to a Monarchie (as they terme it) but, as we understand, an absolute Tyrannie'.[129] Furthermore, disputes between the master and fellows of individual colleges, or between a master and groups outside the university, were frequently referred to the determination of the discomforted master's fellow heads. This procedure could arise because the vice-chancellor was the statutory Visitor, or joint Visitor, of a number of colleges, and it was to the Visitor that appeal was made in such cases.[130] In internecine quarrels between master and fellows, appeals to the Visitor by disgruntled fellows were likely to find little favour. In part this was because of a decline in

---

[126] Heywood and Wright 1854, I, p. 74.

[127] Cooper, *Annals*, II, p. 610; for examples of business in the Commissary's Court, before Thomas Legge (himself master of Caius) as Commissary, on such matters as servants, tenants, carriage of dung, etc., see CUA, Comm. Ct. 1.1.

[128] Moreover appeal from the Consistory was circumscribed, and effectively in the hands of the heads (CUA, 0.11.216, 217, Vice-Chancellor's Box 1, discussion of right of appeal). The delegates appointed to hear the appeal were appointed by the caput (CUL, Baumgartner (Patrick) MS 22, fo. 4).

[129] Yorke 1887, p. 153.

[130] At Corpus, the vice-chancellor and two senior doctors were said to be Visitors, or, at the least, to occupy the influential position of interpreters of the statutes (*Cambridge Documents*, II, pp. 460–1, 468n.). For instances of the exercise of this power, see Masters 1753, Appendix, p. 62; HMCS, XX, p. 94; CUA, Lett. 9.B.16. The same arrangements applied at Gonville and Caius and Christ's. For Caius, see BL Harl. MS 7031, fo. 123 (1581); CUL MS Mm. i. 35, p. 384. Jegon, Cowell and Ward, all masters, acted as Visitors in 1607. For Christ's, BL Harl. MS 7031, fo. 35 (1570s); CUL MS Mm. v. 48, fo. 67v. Hill, Comber and Collins determined the dispute. Laud was to argue that the chancellor, or in his absence the vice-chancellor, had the right to visit colleges with no special Visitor (Laud 1847–60, v, ii, p. 570). There was general resentment at the interference of the vice-chancellor within colleges (see the complaints of Christ's in 1586–7, BL Harl. MS 7033, fo. 41v; and Queens' in 1575, Hatfield MS 136.5).

the statutory powers of Visitors, relative to the master, as a result of the revision of the statutes of many colleges.[131] In part this was because there was a natural inclination on the part of visitors to tend to favour the side of the master – as in the 1580s the fellows of Gonville and Caius feared would be the case.[132] As active statesmen, clergymen and senior officials, the Visitors of colleges were likely to prefer the side of authority in the guise of the master. Perhaps of greater importance was the fact that some colleges had Visitors who in other capacities were currently masters. Yet other Visitors were bishops. The visitatorial bishopric might well be occupied by an individual who had gained the see through the acumen he had displayed at an earlier stage in his career as governor of a college. The Visitor of St John's, Peterhouse and Jesus was the bishop of Ely. In this period three occupants of this see had been masters of Cambridge colleges. In addition, the remaining bishops shared similar academic or administrative backgrounds, at Oxford or elsewhere.[133] It is particularly significant that the Visitors appointed to revise the statutes of St John's were all masters of other colleges.[134]

Disagreements between parts of the university and outside bodies were also, on occasion, subject to the decisive influence of the heads of houses. This is illustrated during the early 1620s in a dispute which arose between the master of Corpus, Samuel Walsall, and the Corporation of Norwich over the allocation of Norwich scholarships at that college. Initially, the Privy Council had referred the matter to arbitration. The local interests represented by the city authorities were dissatisfied with its outcome, and further petitioned the Privy Council that indifferent arbitrators should be appointed. This is not surprising, considering that initially the matter had been referred to the bishop of Norwich and one Clement Corbett. On further appeal the matter had been referred to the visitors of the college. The bishop at the time was Samuel Harsnett, a former master of Pembroke Hall. Clement Corbett, although a Norfolk man, was at that time master of Trinity Hall. The visitors of the college were the vice-chancellor and the two senior doctors of divinity. Leonard Mawe, the vice-chancellor, was also master of Peterhouse. The two senior doctors were

---

[131] E.g. Strype 1824, II, ii, pp. 647–8.   [132] BL Harl. MS 7031, fo. 123.

[133] Lancelot Andrewes, Nicholas Felton and Matthew Wren had been Cambridge heads. Richard Cox (bishop 1559–81) had been canon of Cardinal College, headmaster of Eton, dean of Christ Church, Oxford, chancellor of Oxford and dean of Windsor. Martin Heton (bishop 1599–1609) had been vice-chancellor of Oxford in 1588, and dean of Winchester. John Buckeridge (bishop 1628–31) was a former president of St John's College, Oxford. Francis White (bishop 1631–8) was a former fellow of Gonville and Caius and from 1625 had been dean of Sion College, London. (*DNB*.)

[134] Scott 1898, p. 286.

John Richardson and John Hills. The former was master of Trinity College, and the latter was master of St Catharine's. There is, it would seem, at least *prima facie* justification for the city's plea for more disinterested arbitrators![135]

It is evident, then, that the new statutes of 1570 marked a distinct accretion of power to the heads of houses, both in the university and within their individual colleges. The accession of power within colleges was in many instances further augmented by the subsequent revision of college statutes.[136] In addition, over a longer period, and in more indirect ways, the vice-chancellor gained a new eminence and authority. From the end of the 1580s, occupants of the office were drawn exclusively from the narrow circle of the heads. Furthermore, the university courts and the arbitration of disputes came almost exclusively under the sway of the vice-chancellor and the heads. This all occurred at the expense of the relatively democratic gatherings of the regent and non-regent masters, and their tribunes, the proctors. All in all, one cannot but admire the sophistication of the arrangements hastily drafted into the new statutes during the summer of 1570, and the relative efficiency with which democracy was transformed into oligarchy. However, it will become evident that under the pressures to which they became subjected, the new constitutional arrangements were to have consequences for which their originators could not have provided.

[135] Norwich City Muniments, Case 25, shelf d (1361), Petition; SP 14/133/66; Venn, II, p. 319b; I, p. 396a; III, p. 165a; III, p. 452a; II, p. 371a.
[136] See above, pp. 78–9.

Chapter 4

CAMBRIDGE UNIVERSITY AND THE STATE

During the sixteenth and early seventeenth centuries the universities became more intimately connected with provincial society in general, and specific local and regional communities in particular. The endowment and growth of the colleges, statutory limitations and a changing and more varied social mix which provided the opportunities for developing links of patronage and clientage – all these developments took place within the context of a rapid increase in numbers that drew the country into the universities and the universities into the country.[1] But these were not the only manifestations of the ever-closer links between university and society in this period, nor were the provincial communities the only parts of that society which began to display an interest in the universities: to an unprecedented degree the central government and a more diffuse and variously motivated set of Court interests also became increasingly involved in their affairs. The roots of this interest of the centre in the universities can be traced back to the 1530s and beyond.[2] Not unnaturally, these diverse interests were not always compatible, and on occasion were positively antagonistic. Consequently, the universities became an arena in which were to be played out conflicts that were inherent within the political structure of late Tudor England. Neither was theirs a purely passive role: there were numerous reasons why the universities and the colleges as corporations, and individuals within them, should seek the attention and favour of the Court, thereby multiplying the likelihood of clashes of interests.

Moreover, by encapsulating those conflicts, the universities also positively contributed to the sharpness of the encounter and thereby to the creation of the particular character of the political culture of the period. They did this, first, simply by providing two more arenas in which the conflict could be seen to be taking place. Secondly, because they were centres of intellectual activity this tended to contribute to the ideological

[1] Below, chapter 6.   [2] Above, chapter 1.

component of the encounter. Thirdly, because during the late sixteenth and early seventeenth centuries the universities housed large numbers of the articulate elite – both lay and clerical – during a formative period in their lives, and, we may surmise, contributed to a heightened awareness amongst these individuals of the political realities of the wider society they were about to enter.

On the nature of the early modern state, the blood of distinguished scholars of past generations has fertilised the historiographical battlefield and the nurturing hand of aged learning has carried the scars of ungrateful youth;[3] and there are some essential features of the early modern state that we need to understand before we proceed.

Although the sixteenth century inherited a long-established and so-phisticated system of central administration in England, it would be anachronistic to think of this as a bureaucractic state as in our mod-ern understanding of the term. Even that supposed pioneer of Tudor bureaucracy, Thomas Cromwell, advanced his purposes more by way of breaking the bureaucractic rules than by applying them.[4] Rather, the structures of government performed two functions, one manifest and the other latent. The manifest functions were those which ensured, for exam-ple, that – eventually – taxes were brought in and the more reprehensible forms of anti-social behaviour were punished. But stretching across and enveloping this bony skeleton was a whole tissue of relationships and obligations. These constituted the latent functions of government and – usually – they ensured loyalty and adherence to the regime through the continuing filaments of personal obligation and reciprocal needs. This was a patrimonial state constituted by the ties, rewards and too frequent frustrations of patronage and clientage.[5] Furthermore, as the universities expanded and became central to the interests of the state, and as those within the universities sought to advance their personal or corporate in-terests, so the universities became ever more intimately enmeshed within these networks of obligation. This, then, was one facet of the type of state within which the universities operated in this period.

The second feature of the early modern state of which we need to take note and that contemporaries would have grasped with an intuitive understanding was the centrality of the royal Court to both the manifest

---

[3] The more recent disputes have centred on the relative importance of the Departments of State, the Council and the Secretaries and, on the other hand, the Household, the Privy Chamber and the Favourite: see Starkey 1987, pp. 1–24; 1989; Elton 1988. One of the most seminal and illuminating contributions is Starkey 1977.

[4] Much of this can be discerned in the Elton–Starkey debate alluded to above.

[5] Morgan 1988, 2000, 2001; McCaffrey 1961; Adams 1991, 1995.

and the latent functions of government. This was, moreover, a new type of royal Court in the sixteenth century, both in England and elsewhere in Europe. It provided the stage and focus for a new type of Renaissance monarch. For the greater part of the period with which we are concerned it was the dominant permanent central institution of both politics and society. Indeed, the period between the accession of Henry VIII in 1509 and the Revolution Settlement of the 1680s and 1690s can be characterised as a period of curial politics, and by extension and to some degree, the era of the curial state. In the late seventeenth century a conjunction of circumstances saw the achievement of the long-sought practice of annual parliaments. Although the royal Court continued as a component in the political and social system it was no longer the only or dominant element at the centre. From the viewpoint of the universities, this transition from an era of curial politics to an early form of parliamentary politics was one among a number of extraneous circumstances that helped to demarcate the change in the character of the university in this period and that made of Cambridge a very different institution in the 1730s from what it had been in the 1660s.[6]

We also need to consider the issue of purposefulness with regard to the early modern state. Here a distinction can be drawn between state-building and state-formation. There are those who see the undoubted developments in the state in this period as arising from purposeful intent among at least some of those involved in the processes of government. A variant of this view is the determinist notion that seems to impute to the state a motivation of its own. Once again, anachronism may be at play. This notion of *state-building* owes more than a little to the political agenda of the post-colonial era.[7] When looked at in detail it is indeed evident that there is a process in train in this period that we might care to call *state-formation* but it has about it less of purposeful construction and more of ramshackle accretion. These accretions occurred in response to immediate imperatives. None the less, *in toto*, the involvement of government in areas such as poor relief, the regulation of the markets and the encouragement of industries[8] might justify the claim that the sixteenth century sees the rise of the Tudor interventionist state. To a large extent the history of the universities runs parallel to what was also happening elsewhere in the broader reaches of Tudor society. This is not to say that there are not differences between, say, provisions for poor relief and the management of the universities. However, those differences are in part a measure of the distinctiveness of the perception of the universities in

[6] Below, chapters 13 and 14.   [7] Slack 2000.   [8] See above, p. 74.

this period. Nor need we adhere to too simplistic a model of what was involved in Tudor interventionism. Events at Cambridge demonstrate that we are not contemplating a monolithic intrusiveness of the centre in the peripheries.[9] It is also the case that those on the peripheries were induced to resort to the centre, and often to involve it in parochial concerns against its own wishes and judgement. In the late seventeenth century there was a measure of withdrawal:[10] in the sixteenth and early seventeenth centuries there was an increased intimacy of state and university, forged in the stirring times of the 1530s and 1540s. Facing for a time the possibility of meltdown, Cambridge emerged, but in many respects cast in a new mould.[11] In these decades we saw the increasing familiarity with the university amongst men at the heart of government, and the uses to which these men, and others anxious to advise government, put the universities and individual academics in order to meet the immediate need created by Henry's divorce. That having been met, Cambridge might have retreated again to the peripheral vision of government. But this did not happen, and it did not happen because a combination of other circumstances kept it fully within the field of view. Managing the universities became part of the portfolio of those in power, while riding post-haste to Court became second nature to academics in pursuit of their own interests in two otherwise sleepy English provincial towns. By the end of the sixteenth century there can have been hardly a week in which university matters were not hammering at the doors of secretary of state or royal favourite.

We have examined in some detail the ways in which, during the 1570s, the statutes of the university and of individual colleges were substantially revised.[12] In the short term these alterations can be seen as the government's response to the turmoil created in the university by those who believed that the Elizabethan settlement was a compromise, a half-way house; that the true Reformation was still to come.[13] Looked at in a larger perspective the constitutional changes introduced under Elizabeth can be viewed as a recognition of the importance to the state of the universities and as the culmination of the process set in train under her father. This was true in both the religious and the secular spheres — in so far as these may be distinguished in this period.

The combination of secular and religious motives is evident in the use made by the Crown of the universities in the 1530s.[14] But it was not only that confronted with the crisis of the divorce the Crown found a

[9] Morgan 1984.   [10] Below, pp. 533–4.   [11] Above, chapter 1.   [12] Above, chapter 3.
[13] Cf. Peel 1915, I, p. 142.   [14] Above, chapter 1.

new use for academics and intellectuals. In addition to the use which Henry and his advisers made of the universities, there were also those men of learning – more especially the new lay proponents of the new learning – who at this time spontaneously proffered their services to the state. Personal opportunism often combined with the desire to infiltrate the new ideas on society and the church into the highest counsels of government. The new 'articulate citizen', who was usually a graduate and often the attendant in the antechambers of the powerful, was often still a member of the university;[15] outstanding examples were William Mey, Matthew Parker and Sir Thomas Smith. Thereafter and for generations to come, those who sought social reform and religious change did so by addressing the men with power and influence about the Court. They were successful, at least as reflected in the background of the graduate laity who became prominent in central government from the 1530s and 1540s onward. This was a phenomenon both observed and applauded by contemporaries. Roger Ascham was thinking of his own time at St John's and honouring his former college when he looked back admiringly at the achievements of Nicholas Metcalf, appointed in 1518 as the third master of the reconstituted St John's. But what Ascham said of Metcalf could be as well applied to the whole university in terms of its increasing influence in the wider world. In Ascham's view, when Metcalf ceased to be master of St John's, 'he left such a company of fellows and scholars in . . . [the college], as can scarce be found now in some whole university: which, either for divinity on the one side or other, or for civil service to their prince and country, have been, and are yet to this day, notable ornaments to this whole realm'.[16]

The role of university men in general, and of Cambridge men in particular, in helping to shape the formulation of major policies of national significance is evident on Elizabeth's accession. Then, some fifteen years on from the events of 1545–6, many of the same cast of university graduates had come to play yet larger roles on the national stage. What has been called 'the Cambridge Connection' has been held responsible for promoting the more radical version of religious settlement during 1558–60.[17] This connection consisted of both clergy, and laymen with strong university backgrounds, such as William Cecil.[18] However, as we

---

[15] McConica 1965; Ferguson 1965; Jones 1970; Elton 1973, 1979a; Dowling 1986; Fox and Guy 1986.
[16] Wright 1904, pp. 278 ff. [17] Hudson 1980.
[18] *Ibid.*, 1980, pp. 5, 63. William Cecil was an able Greek scholar. He was tutored by Cheke, his first wife was Cheke's sister and his second wife was a Greek scholar in her own right. When contemplating a new translation of the Bible, Matthew Parker expressed the hope that Cecil would translate the Epistles.

will see, it would be wrong to assume that the scholarly standards and the disinterested idealism represented by this group at this time continued to be evident in ensuing years in the relationship between the university and the government and Court.

Increasingly, university alumni could be found in government offices, or as informal advisers to government. This was to be a characteristic feature of the English state until the late seventeenth century. It is worth remarking upon because it is so like the situation with which we are now familiar that there is a danger that we may take it for granted. Moreover, the laicisation of government in the late fifteenth and the first half of the sixteenth century was made possible by the new type of men that the universities were training. It is also to be distinguished from the earlier role in government of many who had been to university but the majority of whom were clerics.[19] It is to be distinguished again from the lay governmental elites of the greater part of the eighteenth and nineteenth centuries, most of whom were not graduates.

The pattern of relationships established in the stirring and dangerous times of the 1530s and 1540s was maintained, and university men sought and found places in government and about the Court. As Ascham observed, this was true both of prominent clergy and of laymen. As the number of lay university men in government multiplied, increasingly it was possible for the universities and their constituent colleges to appeal directly to their own alumni. Thus in its dispute with Westminster School in the early 1600s, Trinity College appealed to Robert Cecil to act as its intermediary to the king.[20] In 1617 Fulke Greville, later Lord Brooke, wrote to the master of Jesus, his former college. Brooke alluded to his employments about the Court (while the king was away in Scotland) and regretted that he would not be able to visit Cambridge: 'Yet my love is such to my old nurse, that I would not have her good neglected by my absence.' He therefore asked for detailed costings for the erection of new chambers that he intended to sponsor.[21] In 1629 Brian Duppa, dean of Christchurch, Oxford, wrote to an alumnus of the college, Dudley Carleton, Viscount Dorchester, by then secretary of state. Duppa expressed the happiness of the university at 'having so active a Sonne to sollicite

---

[19] For examples of the clerical element in government and the shift to lay 'civil servants' in the late Middle Ages, see Brooke 1957, pp. 52–6, 97–9, 363–5.

[20] Trinity College Muniments; folder, Westminster School; 'Petitions and Various Extracts (c. 1608)' including, 'The Humble Petition of the Master and Fellowes and Scholars of Trinity College in Cambridge' (a contemporary copy).

[21] Jesus College Archives, Ant. 2, p. 29. Brooke had been a fellow-commoner at the college in 1568. He was secretary for the Principality of Wales from 1598, and had been treasurer of the wars, and of the navy. From 1614 to 1621 he was chancellor of the exchequer. (*DNB* and Rees 1971.)

for her'.[22] In 1622, in the person of Lord Keeper Williams, the clerical and the lay roles were combined. He asked his former college, St John's, to which he gave its new library, to grant a favour to his chaplain, and went on to reflect that 'what favour you shall shew him herein I shall acknowledge as reflecting upon my intercession'.[23]

At the same time, as the instance of Lord Keeper Williams illustrates, those in positions of power in the state had direct and personal experience of the universities and could invoke their institutional associations or personal connections. Thus in 1607 the then master of Trinity, Thomas Nevile, pointed out that the college had fathered eleven deans, seven bishops and two archbishops.[24] Not all Cambridge colleges enjoyed the same achievements – or the same boastfulness – as Trinity. None the less, during the period 1558–1640, fourteen masters of Cambridge colleges were elevated directly to bishoprics, and a further three eventually achieved this dignity.[25] Consequently the bishops were familiar with the workings and the personnel of the university, and this was reflected in their subsequent attitudes and behaviour when as senior clerics they were inevitably drawn into the orbit of the government for the purposes of both ecclesiastical and civil administration. Matthew Parker, as archbishop of Canterbury, and Edmund Grindal, as bishop of London, jointly expressed 'the good zeale and love that we beare to the universitie sumtyme our loving nurse'.[26] Individuals such as John Jegon, master of Corpus, addressed himself to Archbishop Whitgift, 'in regard of your singular good favor shewed to my selfe in Courte and otherwise'.[27]

When matters at issue involved individual colleges there was a natural inclination to turn to those men in government who were familiar with

---

[22] SP 16/149/19. Duppa went on to reveal the other side of this intimacy: 'As for our Society (of wch we glory that your Lordship hath beene Once a Part) I dare promise for them a ready obedience to his Maiesties commands.'

[23] CUA, Lett. 11.A, Appendix D, fo. 5E. The letter was on behalf of Henry Downhart who was required to attend on Sir Edmund Herbert's embassy to the king of France (Venn, II, p. 54b, 'Donhalt').

[24] Ball 1918, p. 168.

[25] Those *directly* elevated were: Lancelot Andrewes (Chichester, 1605); Valentine Carey (Exeter, 1621); John Davenant (Salisbury, 1621); Nicholas Felton (Bristol, 1617); Edmund Grindal (London, 1559); Samuel Harsnett (Chichester, 1609); Richard Howland (Peterborough, 1585); John Jegon (Norwich, 1603); Leonard Mawe (Bath and Wells, 1628); John Mey (Carlisle, 1577); James Pilkington (Durham, 1561); John Whitgift (Worcester, 1577); Matthew Wren (Hereford, 1634); John Young (Rochester, 1578). This list omits three masters whose tenure of a mastership and elevation to episcopal office falls outside the dates selected for this sample: Ralph Brownrigg (Exeter, 1642); John Cosin (Durham, 1660); Benjamin Lany (Peterborough, 1660). Those masters who eventually became bishops were: Matthew Hutton (Durham, 1589); James Montague (Winchester, 1616); John Overall (Lichfield, 1616). Richard Sterne, who became bishop of Carlisle in 1660, falls outside the sample dates selected here. See also Fincham 1990.

[26] CUA, Lett. 10.II.1a.   [27] CUA, Misc. Collect. 8, fo. 1.

the ways of these institutions. Sometimes, as in a row that arose over the felling of timber at Queens' in 1579/80, a former president, who had become bishop of Chester, could advise on the finances of the college and the necessity or otherwise of felling.[28] However, anyone acquainted with this world of clientage and connection might not have avoided the suspicion that favour and advantage would be sought through these old connections. There must have been some doubts in the minds of provincial burghers when, in the 1620s, it was suggested that a matter in dispute between the Corporation of Norwich and Corpus should be referred to the bishop of Norwich, Samuel Harsnett, and a diocesan official, Clement Corbett, because both had been masters of Cambridge colleges.[29] But it was not only on particular local issues that bishops and other influential clergy could exercise their knowledge of the universities and advise government. Nor was such influence always to the liking of the universities.

In 1636 it was claimed for Laud, a former president of St John's College, Oxford, that 'his nearness to his majesty in a place of that eminency' had been 'a chief operation in advancing this great work' of the new statutes then being forced upon Oxford.[30] Sometimes the presence of alumni in government might afford some protection and favour. In 1572 members of the Court of High Commission wrote to Cambridge threatening the exercise of their powers unless the university sent up the erring Thomas Aldrich for examination. They recalled that they had recently purged Oxford, but as they were for the most part Cambridge men, 'and zealous to the same', they were writing first informally to the vice-chancellor.[31]

Certain key offices within the ecclesiastical establishment gave their incumbents immediate access to the monarch and allowed them to deploy their personal influence. Consequently word of university matters could be whispered directly in the royal ear. Thus during the early years of James' reign James Montague, master of Sidney Sussex, had exercised considerable influence over the king in his capacity as dean of the Chapel Royal.[32] An office of equal significance within the royal Court was that of clerk of the closet. This was occupied in the early 1600s by Richard Neile, a former member of St John's and a former Cecilian agent in the university. From the vantage of his later office, Neile was able to use

---

[28] CUA, Lett. 9.B.15.a, b. The bishop of Chester was William Chaderton, who had been president of Queens', 1568–79.

[29] SP 14/122/128. Harsnett had been master of Pembroke, and Corbett had been master of Trinity Hall.

[30] Laud 1847–1860, v, ii, p. 128.   [31] CUA, Lett. 9.C.6.a.

[32] Fuller 1655/1840, p. 297; *VCH Cambs.*, III, p. 485.

his knowledge of the university to forward the Arminian interest in the church by procuring the appointment of clergy of that persuasion.[33]

On a longer view, a fundamental change was effected in the relationship between the state and the university as a result of the religious changes during the 1530s and 1540s, including the renunciation of papal authority.[34] Previously, the universities had won their privileges and considerable independence by playing off the Crown against the papacy.[35] After the Reformation the universities were wholly dependent on a royal will that now combined authority in the state with power over the church. Deprived of any alternative authority to which they could resort, the Protestant universities in general, and the English universities in particular, could hardly avoid slipping more fully under the control of the governments of the various secular states in which they found themselves. From the viewpoint of these universities the removal of papal authority increased yet further the importance to them of the Court. As we will see, the protagonists in disputes within Cambridge University over matters of ecclesiastical discipline, and of doctrine, inevitably sought support at Court for their antagonistic positions. Inevitably, recourse was now to the king where it had been to the pope.[36]

During the course of the sixteenth century the universities underwent a substantial change in their social composition, they acquired a new ideological significance, and became the source of the sort of trained personnel that was required by a new type of government. For its part, the Crown responded to these changes by attempting an unprecedentedly detailed oversight of the universities. But the motivation for this new interest cannot wholly be ascribed to changes in the nature of the universities. It is also the case that the aspirations of government itself had changed, and it now aspired to oversee, to inquire into and to regulate vast tracts of society that had once been beyond the ambit of central government. That desire for control and regulation of the universities arose not only because they were in and of themseves nodal points in early modern society. It also derived from an awareness of the wider influence of the universities as increasing numbers of university men spread throughout the realm, and beyond.

---

[33] *HMCS*, xv, p. 199. For Neile's appointment, July 1603, see *HMCS*, xix, p. 204; Foster 1978, pp. 210, 298.

[34] Heywood 1855, I, pp. 193–5; Fuller 1655/1840, pp. 211–13, for the instrument rejecting papal claims. An Act of 1536 required that every person proceeding to a degree in the university should take an oath before the Commissary of the university, 'that he from hensforth shall utterly renounce refuse relinquish or forsake the Bishopp of Rome and his auctorite power and jurisdiccion' (28 Henry VIII c. 10, §§6 and 7).

[35] Reeves 1969a, pp. 61–84.   [36] Above, chapter 3, and below, chapter 12.

The recognition of the influence of the universities throughout the realm in the spheres of both church and state is encapsulated in the images that were applied to them as 'fountains', 'seminaries' or 'nurseries'. Cambridge is 'that fountain from whence the public state derives those streams tht must hereafter minister knowledge, religion and government to the whole realm'.[37] It is further characterised as 'that famous Nourserye of Lerninge from whence (as from a cleare fountayne) should dayly spring the sweete streames of peace and godlines'.[38] All the more reason, then, to ensure that the unsullied purity of those streams was maintained. Thus, at a time when it was harbouring crypto-Catholics, Gonville and Caius College was commended to Burghley's care, 'least it prove a nursery of corruption to the greate daunger of the realme'.[39] Some members of the college confessed themselves ashamed of those fellows who 'for many yeares have made the colledge as a seminarye, to poyson the common wealth with corrupted gentlemen'.[40] Moreover, dissension in religion could all too easily lead to disaffection in the state. As Andrew Perne put it in a cautionary letter to Burghley in 1585, if 'fantasticall humors . . . should take root in the universitie as they doe in other places, bothe the Church, and consequentlye the comon weale shall soone come to ruyne thereby'.[41]

This telling and influential image of the universities persisted through from the mid-sixteenth to the late seventeenth centuries. It both reflected a contemporary perception and provided the grounds for concern and justification for intervention. In both symbol and reality it marked out the period. It could not have been applied in mid-fifteenth-century England nor would it have made sense in the mid-eighteenth century: it did encapsulate both the realities and the perceptions of the greater part of the sixteenth and seventeenth centuries. Thus the preamble to the Edwardian statutes for Cambridge has the king turning his eyes to 'our academies as to fountains and seminaries of learning from whence the knowledge of truth coming forth may flow into and be propagated amongst all our possessions'.[42] His sister and successor, Queen Mary, wished that all might travail in their vocations and God be feared, served, and obeyed. She therefore thought good

> for a beginning, to wish that the examples hereof may first begin in our Universities, where young men and all sorts of students, joining godly conversations with their studies in learning, may, after, as well by their

---

[37] *HMCS*, xix, p. 459.   [38] CUA, Lett. 11.A.C.6.b (another version in *HMCS*, xvi, p. 390).
[39] SP 12/169/39.   [40] BL Lansdowne MS 34, fo. 33.   [41] BL Lansdowne MS 45, fo. 125v.
[42] Heywood 1855, pp. 3–4.

doings as by their preachings, instruct and confirm the rest of our subjects both in the knowledge and fear of Almighty God; in the due obedience towards us, and all other their superiors; and in their charitable demeanours towards all men.[43]

Doctrine might change yet again, but the perception of the persuasive role of the universities did not. In this at least, Elizabeth concurred with her sister. For her, Cambridge was 'placed as it were before the eyes and in the mind of all', through which example she wished that it might 'lead and bring the rest of our people to a like observance of our laws, and to peace and concord, and to true obedience'.[44] In his turn King James animadverted on the need to maintain religious uniformity and truth 'deriving of both out of the nurseries & fountaines of our Church & common wealth (our universities)'.[45] He described Cambridge as 'one of ye principall seminaries of this state, for Church & Comonwealth'.[46] For Charles the universities were 'renowned Nurseries of relligion and learning', and at the beginning of his reign he expressed the hope that they 'should not in least measure decline from their former integrities and reputacon'.[47] From the mid-sixteenth century, then, increasingly, the universities were perceived by the government as important in both the religious and the secular life of the state. Neither was this view of the importance of the universities limited to government circles. The prevailing 'utilitarian' attitude towards education[48] served to enhance the value placed on the universities throughout society.

Men claimed to study at the university 'to the benefite . . . [of] both gods church, as also the common wealth',[49] in preparation for the time 'that they shall bee called forth into the Church or Commonwealth'.[50] Those thus engaged were wished 'the grace of God to direct yor studies to his glorye and to the profit of the Common wealth',[51] and 'learned men' were described as endeavouring 'by their studies to deserve well in the Church or Commonwealth'.[52] Schemes for provincial universities proposed that men should study 'untill that by learning and degree they shall be fit for some good place in the Church or Commonwealth'.[53] The process of endowment during the sixteenth and seventeenth centuries both of the colleges and of lectureships in the provinces in part at least reflected the desire of the laity to create a proselytising ministry throughought the land, while at the heart of this project itself was the assumption that the universities would become powerhouses designed

---

[43] Lamb 1838, p. 165. [44] Heywood 1838, p. 2. [45] CUA, Lett. 11.A.A.6.
[46] CUA, Lett. 11.A.A.7. [47] SP 16/19/59. [48] See below, pp. 131 ff. [49] SP 12/155/69.
[50] SP 16/281/54. [51] CUA, Lett. 10.1.b. [52] CUA, Lett. 12.C.5.
[53] Quoted in Bussby 1953, p. 158.

to pump out ministers to labour in the benighted provinces.[54] On the secular front Edward Coke referred to Cambridge as 'one of the famous eyes of the Comonwealth'.[55]

In short, a plethora of pious platitudes can leave us in no doubt as to what had become the perceived role for the universities within the wider community. Here was a conception of the university in which it was deeply embedded within its environing society while at the same time its tentacles of influence expressly were intended to reach out into both Court and country. Here, then, was a type of institution made anew and now explicitly intended by both government and members of the wider society to have a far-reaching effect on its environing culture. But this new conception of the universities was born into a society that was at the same time intensely anxious about the maintenance of 'order' in the face of 'discontent'. Much of this anxiety was rooted in the historical experience of the 1540s and 1550s and by the end of the century was probably misplaced.[56] By then it was the palace coup – as with Essex's abortive efforts in 1601 – that was the most serious threat rather than the old-fashioned popular revolt or magnatial rebellion. None the less, annual memorial sermons and popular myths sustained the conventional fears.[57] And in turn it was these fears that inspired policy and action. For their part these newly influential institutions, the two universities, were swept up into the consequences of this wider perception and the policies that flowed from it. Oversight, regulation and control were the order of the day.

THE URGE TO IDEOLOGICAL CONTROL

Queen Elizabeth – or her draftsman – justified the new statutes for Cambridge in 1570 'On account of the again increasing audacity, and too great licence of men', and in doing so articulated the common platitudes.[58] The problem was that the early modern state lacked in practice the resources for sustained enforcement of the aspirations to good order that it voiced in principle. The consequence of this was that there were periodic bouts of enthusiasm for enforcement, usually occasioned by a particular abuse that had come to the notice of those in authority. For example, this pattern is evident in the instructions issued to the judges of assize prior to their riding on their biannual circuits. It is also evident at Cambridge. Thus, the orders sent to the university by their chancellor in

---

[54] The classic statement on this project is Hill 1963. See also Seaver 1970.
[55] CUA, Lett. II.A.E.3.c.   [56] For the roots of this see Elton 1972.
[57] Morgan 1999b.   [58] *Cambridge Documents 1852*, I, pp. 454–5; Heywood 1838, p. 1.

1602 were initiated by a desire to restrain the propagation of free-will doctrine. However, they also took in a wider sweep of abuses and provided
a veritable vade-mecum of contemporary requirements for good order.
They condemned 'common frequenting of the Towne by day or nighte
sittinge and drinkinge in Tavernes and other houses', ordered the restraint
of the 'Idle common wandring abroade of the younger sort of Schollers
into the feildes and townes adioyninge, with their dogges goones etc.',
and commanded the academics to look to their gates, which were 'to
be shutt in dew and accustomed tyme and not to stand open most parte
of the night giving lybertie to night gaddinge in the Towne, and divers
other Inconveniences'.[59] But in a period when religious differences were,
to a considerable extent, contained within rather than excluded from the
universities, it was especially important to supervise these institutions,
and to circumscribe the worst excesses of doctrinal error.[60] King James
well saw, 'considering . . . to how little effect our care & endeavour
of preserving as well uniformtie in order, as unitie of truth in this our
Church will tend if we should not carefully provide for the deriving of
both' out of the universities.[61] On the occasion of the election of the
Lady Margaret Reader in Divinity, in 1608, Cecil wrote to the university with his recommendation for the place, 'consideringe how neerely
it concernes me in matters of such consequence to be carefull for you'.[62]
On another occasion Cecil opined that it was 'especially in matters ap-
pertayninge to Religion' that 'a dewe observation, ether [i.e. both] of
the statutes of universitye, or [i.e. and] of the publicke constitutions of
the Church for Conformytye' were required. This care was especially
necessary in the university because of its far-ranging influence through
its students. Thomas Ball noted that 'a preacher in the university doth
generare patres, beget begetters, and transmit unto posterity, what God is
pleased to reveal to him'.[63]

---

[59] CUA, Lett. 9.B.24.ii. See also the royal injunctions of 1616 (CUA, folder in plan press). The
orders from the chancellor in 1602 are similar in these respects to those promulgated by the
vice-chancellor, John Jegon, in 1600 (see CUA, Misc. Collect. Admin. 8, fo. 2). Wren's orders as
vice-chancellor in 1628 are mainly concerned with the conduct of disputations, but also include
topics dealt with by Jegon (Northants Record Office, Finch-Hatton MS 590).

[60] See below, chapter 12.

[61] CUA, Lett. 11.A.A.6. James I to Valentine Carey, as vice-chancellor, 30 June 1615.

[62] SP 14/35/34. Cecil's influence was effective and John Davenant was elected (Tanner 1917,
p. 73). Major disruptions had resulted from Thomas Cartwright's tenure of the office, in 1569 (see
above, p. 68). The 'readership' or 'professorship' had been founded in 1502 by Margaret Beaufort,
mother of Henry VII. The office was held for two years (see Clark 1904, pp. 57–65).

[63] Thomas Ball, 'Life of Preston' in Clarke 1651, p. 494. For concern over the maintenance of
religious conformity and the suppression of popery at Cambridge see, for example, CUA, Lett.
9.C.16; Lett. 9.C.7; Lett. 9.C.8.a, b; Lett. 9.C.9; Lett. 9.C.10.

Dissension in religion was not only disliked in itself: it could all too easily lead to disaffection in the state. In 1565, Burghley wrote to the bishop of Ely over the disturbances at St John's that he was 'inwardly afrayd, that if feare shall not staye this ryotous insoleneye, these rash young heades, that are so soone rype to clyme into pulpittes will contente themselves with no limittes ether in the Church or in the pollicy'.[64] The responsible authorities in the university agreed with their chancellor.[65]

From the government's viewpoint there was a need for vigorous ideological control of the concentration in the universities of men devoted to the pursuit of ideas. This is illustrated by the events outlined by Ralph Brownrigg of Pembroke Hall, in a public recantation made by him in 1618. He described how various men 'comming togither to my chamber' occasioned a 'suddaine disputation' in which he had taken exception to 'a booke sett forth by public authority' and which had led to 'a rash mentioning of two scandalous questions'. That is – following Calvin and Beza – Brownrigg appears to have maintained 'the seditious and treacherous questions' that a king breaking fundamental laws might be opposed.[66]

Freedom of thought and liberty of teaching indubitably were not attributes of the early modern university that were favoured by the state. Cecil did not doubt 'How necessarye it is, that a good conformtye be had and observed, in all the members of the universitye, with the avoydinge both of distraction in opinion, and diversitye in practice . . . there is no man of any upright judgment but will acknowledge', nor that 'there can be noe greater Enemye, to all good order, then Libertye in the education of all yonge gentlemen and scholers'.[67]

In addition to the dangers of oral debate exemplified by the case of Ralph Brownrigg, the availability of the printing press had introduced a further means of disseminating disruptive ideas. The problem had two sides to it. First, there was the possession of books antipathetic to established authority. During the doctrinal disputes of the 1590s, Whitgift ordered an investigation, and 'many Divines studies' were searched. To the horror of puritan heads, the presence of numerous popish books was revealed.[68] Second, on the part of those in authority there was felt to be a need to regulate the press and to censor new publications. Thus, in

---

[64] Scott 1907, p. 159.   [65] See above, p. 108 and n. 41.

[66] CUA, Lett. 11.A.9.a. The book in question was David Owen, *Herod and Pilate Reconciled: or the concord of papist and puritan* (Cambridge, 1610), licensed by the university (Heywood and Wright 1854, I, p. 292).

[67] CUA, Lett. 11.A.C.6.b, and with minor differences of wording in *HMCS*, XVI, p. 389, Cecil to the university, December 1604.

[68] BL Harl. MS 7029, fo. 8.

1584 a volume by Walter Travers was issued in which he expressed presbyterian opinions. Whitgift wrote to Burghley that 'Ever sens I hard that
they had a printer in Cambridge I dyd greatlie feare that this and such
like inconveniences wold follow.' The archbishop then addressed himself
not only to the immediate issue – suggesting that Travers' work should
be burned – but also to the general problem. He urged 'that (yf printing
do styll there continew) sufficient bondes with sureties shold be taken
by the printer not to print anie bokes unlesse they be first allowed by
lawfull authoritie; for yf restrante be made here [in London] and libertie
graunted there, what good can be done?'[69]

The problem was a general one, although perhaps more acute with
regard to the ideas likely to be disseminated from the universities. The
Star Chamber Decree of 23 June 1586 finally established the procedure
for regulating the press as a whole, effectively concentrating it in London,
under immediate and watchful eyes. The only concession to the nascent
provincial press was permission for one press only to be maintained in
each university.[70] The following August, Whitgift wrote to Cambridge,
forbidding the printing of any books in the university that had not been
authorised by the bishop of London or himself, and referring to the
recent decree.[71]

OXFORD AND CAMBRIDGE'S MONOPOLY

The policy of exercising control through a concentration of activities and
responsibility that was manifest in the regulation of printing was also evident in the continued restriction of higher education to the two centres
of Oxford and Cambridge. During the period 1560–1660 there were a
variety of proposals to establish separate universities, or university colleges, in the regions, especially in those areas that contemporaries came
to describe as 'the dark corners of the land', in the north and the west.
In large part proposals of this type were simply a natural extension of the
practice of attempting to bring enlightenment to what were perceived
to be the benighted parts of the kingdom by establishing schools there as
beacons of Protestant illumination.[72] The 1650s saw a flurry of proposals
for 'decentralisation' of the universities, and the establishment of colleges

---

[69] Heywood and Wright 1854, I, p. 381.
[70] Siebert 1965, p. 61; Elton 1965, pp. 179–84; McKitterick 1984.   [71] CUA, Lett. 9.C.12.
[72] E.g. John Bridges, *A Defence of the Government Established in the Church of Englande for Ecclesiasticall
    Matters . . .* (London, 1587), p. 523, rebutted a radical puritan proposal for 'reforming universities,
    by erecting of Doctors and teachers in as many places as may be'; Bussby 1953.

in the regions.[73] One critic pointed to the practical difficulties that arose as a result of having to send young men from distant parts to the two universities and asked consideration 'whether they that Founded our two great Universities, seem not more to have consulted the Honour than the conveniency of the Nation, since if that had been respected, the Colleges should rather have been dispersed at convenient distances throughout the severall Counties'.[74] However, by the mid-seventeenth century a further consideration may have motivated such proposals. By then it would have become evident that the social engineering implicit in the creation of schools and of bursaries from schools to the universities in the dark corners had had an unforeseen consequence. There is some evidence to suggest that it created an internal brain drain, with bright lads being recruited from the north and the west.[75]

It is worth noting the peculiarities of the English in organising their higher education. There has been, perhaps, a tendency to see the expansion of the universities throughout Europe in this period as a common phenomenon. The trend for increased numbers of students over the course of the sixteenth and the greater part of the seventeenth century may indeed be a shared phenomenon, but equally revealing is the fact that this increase was realised in different ways in different places. As Scottish historians never tire in telling us, the northern kingdom in the British Isles had more universities than its wealthier southern neighbour. On the Continent, in those areas where the Counter-Reformation prevailed, a rather different system of higher education was created. In 1555–6 Cardinal Pole had been decisive in creating the diocesan seminaries later advocated by the seventh session of the Council of Trent, in 1563.[76] Ironically, in England the 'prophessyings' of the puritan 'church within a church', that reached their height under James I, and which were held in local market towns, shared the characteristics of decentralisation and dispersion to some extent evident in the creation of diocesan seminaries on the Continent.[77] The emergent custom for aspirant preachers to reside for a time with established puritan gurus in their provincial livings was in some degree an extension of forms of sociability found within

---

[73] See below, pp. 471–2. A more modest proposal of the 1650s involved the appointment of local Visitors to replace the bishops and archbishops nominated as Visitors by most college statutes (BL Add. MS 22579, fo. 21r–v).

[74] William Sprigge, *A Modest Plea For an Equal Commonwealth Against Monarchy* . . . (London, 1659) p. 49.

[75] Morgan 1987; below, p. 190.

[76] This established diocesan seminaries, of which there were thirty-six by 1626. See O'Donohoe 1965.

[77] Collinson 1967, pp. 168–76; Hill 1966, p. 47.

the universities, but also afforded a contending model for pedagogic practice.[78]

The proposals for provincial universities, the pattern developing on the Continent, the practice of prophesying and attendance upon the pulpits and dining tables of puritan panjandrums, all presented the prospect of alternative means of educating a significant number of those intent upon a clerical career who otherwise would have to enter the universities. All these possibilities considered, it is worth noting what did not happen, or what did not happen in substantial degree in England and why it is unlikely to have happened.

While men such as Burghley and Walsingham seem to have lent their names to proposals for the establishment of a religious seminary at Ripon,[79] the repetition of similar proposals from various localities, and the failure to bring them to fruition before the heady days of the 1640s and 1650s, suggests that, apart from general inertia and numerous practical difficulties, the government had set itself against the proliferation of such sensitive institutions throughout the land. To have permitted such a development would merely have exacerbated the difficulties of supervision and control. At the beginning of Elizabeth's reign the north and the west were unruly areas and potential seedbeds of subversion that might threaten the stability of the whole regime, as in 1569. The royal writ ran uncertainly and was felt to require the reinforcement provided by locally based provincial councils. To permit the establishment of provincial colleges would have removed too many men originating in these sensitive areas from the close and often direct personal supervision it was possible for the government officials to exercise over Cambridge, and – perhaps to a lesser extent – Oxford. Moreover, the special royal links with Trinity College, and the close family connections of the Cecils with St John's, ensured an even closer control of the two largest colleges at Cambridge, both of which drew many of their students from the north. The corollary of this was the magnification of the importance of Oxford and Cambridge as the nodal institutions through which it was possible to attempt to control the education of both the lay and the clerical elite of the entire realm. Similarly, but on a smaller scale, the control of the Court of Wards by the Cecils combined with high levels of paternal mortality to give the government control over the education of young men of hereditary standing and potential influence. Significantly, although some wards were brought up in Burghley's own household, yet others were sent to Cambridge, the university over which

---

[78] Webster 1997; Collinson 1983, ch. 20, esp. pp. 543–4.   [79] Bussby 1953.

the Cecils exercised most influence, and especially to their own college, St John's.[80]

Thus far we have considered some of the contemporary perceptions of the universities as institutions with an influence beyond their own walls, and some of the positive and negative means by which the government attempted to regulate that influence. We now need to examine some of what might be described as the internal characteristics of Cambridge, to review some of the problems to which these characteristics gave rise, and some of the regulatory responses that they elicited.

KEEPING ORDER AND STUDENT NUMBERS

Throughout the early modern period, governments were easily unnerved by large gatherings of individuals. Such gatherings posed a potential threat to good order, and even to the stability of the regime. This was as true of the universities as of elsewhere. For example, in 1580, the vice-chancellor joined forces with the influential local JP, Roger, Lord North, to suppress an attempt to organise games on the Gog Magog hills. North wrote that he did 'utterly mislyke any of assemblye of people without the [purpose of] service of god or hir majestie'.[81] One of the first sets of orders that James sent to the university was a prohibition of 'all manner of unprofitable or idle games plays or exercises' within 5 miles of Cambridge, 'whereby throngs concourse or multitudes are drawn together'.[82]

In contemporary perception and sometimes in reality, violence was just below the surface. In 1603 the bishop of Lincoln reported to Cecil on his effort to exercise his responsibilities as Visitor of King's College, 'but the younger factious sort . . . grew into such an outrageous uproar and tumult . . . that I, fearing riot or violence to myself, was constrained like an Ephesian town clerk to prorogue my visitation . . . and to dissolve the assembly and depart my ways'. The bishop went on to request correction of 'the authors of the aforesaid garboile and tumult. Otherwise I do not see how there can be any good order or government in that College or University.'[83] Affronted dignity no doubt exaggerated the threat, but the provost also saw fit to report the weakness of those in authority 'by reason of the multitude of delinquents'.[84]

The difficulties of social control created by the growth in the size of the universities from the mid-sixteenth century onwards posed a new and intractable problem for Elizabethan government. It was this problem as

---

[80] Hurstfield 1958, pp. 118–19.   [81] CUA, Lett. 9.E.7.c.   [82] Cooper, *Annals*, III, pp. 6–7.
[83] *HMCS*, xv, p. 76.   [84] *HMCS*, xv, p. 80.

much as any other that induced the Crown and its ministers to interfere to an unprecedented degree in the running of the universities, and in ways comparable to their attempt to control in detail the broader reaches of provincial society. Furthermore, in many respects Cambridge University posed problems with a persistence and on a scale only intermittently encountered elsewhere.

The problem posed for the government by the university was compounded of four main elements. First, Cambridge, and Oxford similarly, were uniquely *large* institutions, and institutions that were growing ever larger before the disconcerted eyes of onlookers. The irony here is that, on the one hand, the government wanted better-educated clergy, and cultivated laymen who could service the emergent needs of the Renaissance state. On the other hand they often found themselves living uncomfortably with the practical outcome. Second, there was the threat that was posed by the function of the university as a place for the generation and mediation of ideas.[85] Third, there were the difficulties that arose from the social composition of the universities. To this part of the problem alone there was a variety of aspects.

They included the effects of taking young men from relatively humble backgrounds, and training them to become part of the clerical intelligentsia, thus cutting them off from identification with the social group of their origin, and inducing an ardent commitment to the clerical group and the associated ideas into which they had been inducted. This sociological characteristic may well in part explain the fervency and assertiveness of puritan clerics and academics in the 1590s no less than that of their Arminian successors in the 1620s, as they sought social identity and justification. Equally, one reason for the decline of clerical 'enthusiasm' after the Restoration may be to do with the sociology of what by then was an assured and substantially self-replicating profession.[86]

If in the high Elizabethan period the problem with this group in the university arose from an overassertive purposefulness, that with their aristocratic[87] fellow-students originated in precisely opposite circumstances. On the one hand, students from aristocratic backgrounds entered the university with an assurance of their own social standing and an inclination to display this assurance through the rituals of college life and the minutiae of social relationhips. On the other hand, there was considerable confusion in the minds of students, parents and tutors as to precisely

---

[85] See above, pp. 67–70.　　[86] Cf. e.g. Stone 1975, pp. 50–1.

[87] Here, as elsewhere (see esp. p. 221 n. 112), I use 'aristocratic' as a convenient portmanteau term in order to encompass the scions of both the nobility and the gentry.

what an aristocratic student should be *doing* during his sojourn at Cambridge. This bewilderment over the purpose of aristocratic education in terms of means, if not ends, helps to account for the wide variety of expectations and behaviour that is so evident in this period. These difficulties were on occasion exacerbated by the propinquity of these two major social groups within the narrow confines of the same college walls. Finally, there was the paradox that the university was to a marked extent an age-segregated institution permitting – at least until 1570 – a high degree of youthful autonomy and self-government. This was all the more remarkable in a society characterised by the integration of all age groups within the predominant institution, the household, and a society in which, if anything, the patriarchal principle was being reinforced at this time.[88] Something of the overall nature of early modern Cambridge emerges from an examination of these factors in somewhat more detail.

There continues to be much uncertainty about the precise details and chronology of the increase in the numbers attending the universities during the sixteenth century. This is partly because the laxer requirements for matriculation and the more informal and therefore undocumented rules governing residence may mean that a proportion of students in the first half of the sixteenth century have gone unrecorded. More seriously, the college registers only begin with Caius in 1559 and are few and far between for some generations after that. None the less, it is clear that by 1600 Cambridge had undergone an expansion that shifted it from one order of magnitude in terms of size to another.[89]

The significance for the government of this expansion is all the more marked when the English situation is compared with that on the Continent. There, in large part the appetite for higher education was catered for by the proliferation of new universities and the establishment of the diocesan seminaries, as much as by the expansion of existing institutions.[90] By contrast, and as the Privy Council noted, 'the Universities of this realme, whereof in the whole there are but two',[91] absorbed the whole of the increase in the number of English students. In fact, this was the other side of the coin of the positive disinclination of the government

---

[88] Schochet 1975, pp. 37–98; Stone 1977, pp. 151–9, 216–20; Thomas 1976a, pp. 205–48, esp. p. 214.

[89] See esp. Stone 1975, pp. 3–110; Brooke 1985/1996, pp. 82–4; Cressy 1972. Professor Cressy's thesis contains much of importance on the numerical and social composition of the Cambridge student body.

[90] Thus by the early seventeenth century, Spain had thirty-three universities, while in parts of northern Europe confessional differences had also led to their proliferation (Richard Kagan in Stone 1975, II, p. 357; and compare the map in Rashdall 1936, III, at end, with that in Eulenburg 1904).

[91] Heywood and Wright 1854, I, p. 185.

to permit the proliferation of universities, or similar institutions, in England and Wales.[92] But while this preference for concentration rather than dispersal may have assisted the maintenance of control in some respects, in others it accentuated the problems of control arising from the size and scale of Oxford and Cambridge.

When effectively recorded matriculation was introduced in 1547, at a liberal estimate and *in toto* there were perhaps somewhere of the order of 500–600 undergraduates on a four-year course. By the 1580s estimated total admissions alone were running at over 460, and in the 1620s these had risen to over 500.[93] At the time of the queen's visit in 1564 there were said to be 1,267 residents in the university.[94] In 1569, Archbishop Parker was informed that the figure was 1,630,[95] while, in the 1570s, William Harrison estimated that altogether there were 3,000 students at both Oxford and Cambridge.[96] By the 1590s numbers at Cambridge were touching 2,000,[97] and in 1621, John Scott calculated that the whole number in every college who were registered and then residing was of the order of 3,000 persons.[98] There were, and remain, considerable complications in arriving at these figures. As, for example, Scott himself noted, there were 'many poare Scholars . . . not accounted' in his overall calculation.[99] Moreover, as one historian of Pembroke has noted,[100] the prevalence of pre-elections to fellowships obviously complicates the calculation of the number of fellowships in so far as that number must include what we might term 'fellows in waiting'. None the less, all these qualifications admitted, the broad trend of increase in numbers over the course of the second half of the sixteenth and first two or three decades of the seventeenth centuries is evident to us and was disconcertingly apparent to contemporaries.

The response to the trend in numbers is reflected in the flurry of orders made for the regulation of matters that had previously been left in quiet informality. For example, in 1568, tutors at Trinity Hall were made

---

[92] Numerically, very few students appear to have sought education abroad. Some Catholic parents, but by no means all, sent their sons abroad to acquire a doctrinally acceptable education. At the other end of the religious spectrum small numbers sought the purity of doctrine provided, initially, by beacons of Protestantism such as Leiden. The Scots seem to have been more interested in coming to England than were Englishmen in going to Scotland. The Inns of Court on the whole appear to have provided an addition, rather than an alternative, to the universities in the educational careers of most students.

[93] Cressy 1972, p. 222, tables 24–5.   [94] Mullinger 1884, p. 214.

[95] Cooper, *Annals*, II, p. 269.   [96] Harrison 1968, p. 70.

[97] Cooper, *Annals*, II, p. 568. The document is ambiguous: the number may have been around 1,700. Moreover, the 1590s were a period of relative slump in admissions, before picking up again in the early 1600s; cf. the table in Twigg 1990, p. 289.

[98] Pembroke College Library, MS I.C.II.76.   [99] *Ibid.*

[100] Pembroke College Treasury, MS B.5, pp. 84–5 (Ainslie's excerpts).

formally responsible for the payment of their pupils' commons every six weeks.[101] It is also evident in what became a positive frenzy of the building activity at late sixteenth- and early seventeenth-century Cambridge.[102] Masters such as William Fulke at Pembroke, in the late 1570s, sponsored the rebuilding of property in the ownership of the college in order to accommodate more students.[103] There is, indeed, considerable evidence for the architectural response to the increase in numbers. Within the constraints imposed by the narrow confines of the city of Cambridge, a number of options were adopted. 'Pensionaries' were built. These were ranges of chambers standing by themselves beyond the main court of a college. Some were newly and cheaply built to rather low standards. Others utilised former storehouses and stable-blocks.[104] Within the main buildings of a college it was often possible to insert a ceiling in the roof of upper-floor rooms, and form attic rooms in the roofspace.[105] There are analogies here with the type of modifications being made in domestic buildings in this period in order to provide for more differentiated social space. One wonders to what extent what the gentry saw in the universities was then copied in their own houses. The external architectural evidence for the insertion of attic rooms are the dormer windows so characteristic of Loggan's views of the colleges.

The result of all this packing and crowding was evident in the increase in the size of the colleges, and it was the college that provided the formative institutional context for the life of each student. In the 1570s Harrison suggested that each of the larger colleges was housing between 140 and 200 scholars.[106] By the 1620s, five out of the sixteen Cambridge colleges had over 200 members.[107] To us, the scale of the colleges and of the university as a whole may not seem large, familiar as we are with large corporate institutions, and their physical embodiments in architecturally distinct buildings such as factories, office blocks, prisons, shopping malls, media centres, and even the modern university in its various incarnations. But to the sixteenth-century eye the colleges must have presented a remarkable and unusual picture of permanent corporate existence on a scale that was almost unrivalled. By way of contrast there were no large bureaucratised government departments; until the late seventeenth century,

---

[101] Trinity Hall Archives, Liber Actorum, fo. 47 (26 Sept. 1568).   [102] See above, pp. 32–3.

[103] Bauckham 1973, p. 108.   [104] Ball 1960, p. 108; Baker and Mayor 1869, I, pp. 183–4.

[105] Ball 1960, p. 105.   [106] Harrison 1968, p. 70.

[107] Masson 1859, I, pp. 89–91; Twigg 1990, p. 289 (Trinity College, 440; St John's, 370; Christ's, 265; Emmanuel, 260; Queens', 230; Gonville and Caius, 180; Clare, 144; Peterhouse, 140; Pembroke, 140; King's, 140; Jesus, 120; Magdalene, 90; St Catharine's, 56; Trinity Hall, 56). These statistics were compiled by John Scott, notary public, in 1621. The original is BL Add. MS 11720. The figures have clearly been rounded out.

most administrative activity continued to be conducted on a small scale in the often private and semi-domestic accommodation clustered around Chancery Lane and the Inns of Court.[108] Clerks to government officials were part of their domestic establishment.[109] By the early seventeenth century the only institutions that were really comparable with the universities were the Inns of Court. These probably accommodated around 1,000 transient residents during the brief periods of the law terms.[110] But the Inns were themselves set within the unique urban environment of London, and were dominated by it. After the dissolution of the monastic houses in the 1530s the royal Court appears to be the only example of an institution of a scale comparable with the universities.[111]

More or less permanent agglomerations of large numbers of individuals at the universities, at the Inns, or about the royal Court; the concentration of large numbers in urban centres; and the more ephemeral gatherings encouraged by occasions such as the assize weeks of county towns, the summer musters and large fairs such as that at Stourbridge in Cambridgeshire, or Harleston in Norfolk: all these aroused considerable and not unjustified fears amongst those charged with the maintenance of public order. In the context of the university this concern is, for example, reflected in a letter from the vice-chancellor, John Jegon, to Chief Justice Popham. Jegon alluded to disputes between the university and the town, and wrote of his fears for the maintenance of good order, 'the multitudes of both bodies being to much intemperate'.[112]

THE SECULARISATION OF PATRONAGE

We have also noted that the university posed particular problems arising from its role as a generator and mediator of ideas. The Reformation had actually removed some of the institutional constraints that had helped to contain too free a pursuit of these activities by overly enquiring minds. Before the Reformation most of the regular clergy, and some of their secular confrères, were answerable to an individual religious house, and ultimately to the chapter of their order, or to the diocesan authority which was promoting their education.[113] Although the practice was less evident

---

[108] Aylmer 1961, pp. 150–2. Incidental information on the location of government offices in London can be gleaned from the miscellanea of the Chancery and the Exchequer (PRO, C.181, E.163) and from family correspondence.

[109] Smith 1968, pp. 481–504. The clerk of the pipe lived at Ealing and appears to have accommodated his clerks in his own household (PRO, E.163/24/35).

[110] Prest 1972, p. 16.   [111] See above, n. 3.   [112] CUA, Misc. Collect. 8.

[113] Knowles 1955, pp. 14–28, 354. See Brooke 1985a for the religious houses in the context of all the churches of medieval Cambridge.

at Cambridge than at Oxford, the regular clergy sometimes had lived on staircases, the building of which had been financed by their individual houses, in an establishment under the general oversight of their chapter. Architecturally, this arrangement was evident in one of the courts at Magdalene.[114] From the 1540s these sources of external authority were removed. At the same time would-be clerics began to look not to a religious house or the diocesan authority for future preferment, but to the laity. The dispersal of former monastic property took with it appropriated (or 'impropriated') livings and meant that in most instances the local gentry were the ultimate beneficiaries of former monastic patronage that had extended to about two-fifths of the parochial benefices in England.[115]

In the diocese surrounding the university, Ely, before the Reformation the bishop had direct presentation to only nineteen benefices. At the same period the colleges had twenty Ely livings in their gift, and this was to increase to thirty after the Reformation. However, the main accretion of patronage was to the laity. In the decade 1526–36 the laity had promoted candidates to nineteen livings, while other patrons promoted to fifty livings. In the period 1566–76 the comparable figures were forty-six and sixty.[116] Of the 399 benefices in the county of Essex the post-Reformation church retained the presentation to only fifty-two, the Crown held thirty-eight, but the majority passed into the hands of the gentry.[117] A survey of the archdeaconry of Norwich in 1603 – effectively half of the county of Norfolk – suggests that 207.5 of the livings, some 70 per cent, were controlled by the laity.[118]

Individual families such as the Riches in Essex and the Townshends in Norfolk wielded considerable influence through the concentration of patronage in their hands. Moreover, that influence was greater than any merely statistical measure might indicate, for they were often both willing and able to place individuals whose opinions were not necessarily in

---

[114] Magdalene College was founded on the site and in the buildings of the former Benedictine establishment in Cambridge, Buckingham College (see p. 17). 'The existing south range of the First Court of Magdalene is not a homogeneous structure but a series of separate staircases built by different monasteries.' John Caius was to write that in the fifteenth century the houses of Ely, Walden and Ramsey each built chambers (McDowall 1950, pp. 3, 5, 10). At Gonville Hall the canons of Butley, Suffolk, had had specific rooms assigned to them (W.W. Buckland 1895, pp. 14–17; Heywood 1855, p. 54).

[115] Hill 1958/1962, p. 54. Hill states that at the dissolution the advowsons of perhaps one-third of the livings in the country passed from ecclesiastics to laymen.

[116] Heal 1975–6, pp. 143, 150–1. The colleges usually gave their patronage to their own fellows. There is a mid-seventeenth-century list of livings in the gift of the colleges at the universities in Dugdale MS 8199 (at Blyth Hall, Coleshill, Warwickshire; I am indebted to Sir William Stratford Dugdale, 2nd Bart., for a copy of this MS). It is incomplete for Oxford but appears to be complete for Cambridge.

[117] Quintrell 1965, pp. 273–5.   [118] Morgan 1983, p. 748.

accord with those of the hierarchy. For example, strenuous efforts were made by Dorothy Bacon to find a suitably learned and virtuous man to fill the livings at Raynham, and to act as chaplain in the household of Norfolk's godly magistrate, Sir Roger Townshend. Lady Dorothy described how, if the man in question, Thomas Day, satisfied the criteria of 'scolarshep and suffecyency', then 'ashewredly yf so, then lyeth his prefarment near him for Sir Rodgar hath Ranham now at his disposeng, [and] yf not that many more [livings] to present unto as anye mane In Norfocke yf he find worthe in the mene'.[119]

As a result of these shifts in the control of ecclesiastical patronage and the not infrequent discrimination with which it was exercised, the parochial clergy, and those who aspired to that status, became increasingly dependent on their lay patrons.[120] As one academic put it, 'if the patron be precise so must his chaplain be; if he be papistical his clerk must be so, or else be turned out. These are those clerks which serve their turn, whom they commonly entertain and present to church livings.'[121] Somewhat less sardonically, Lady Dorothy Bacon expressed a view that none the less led to a similar conclusion: 'it is a matar that all good mene and wemeng Ought to be carefull of in the choise of a menestar in To Our housses and paresche'.[122]

Over and above the control that accrued to the laity through the right of presentation to established parochial preferments, from the late sixteenth century onwards there developed a parallel system of support for the clergy in the ever expanding number of lectureships. As Bancroft was quick to point out, these lectureships were even more under the control of lay patrons than were livings within the church.[123] At Norwich, as at Ipswich and Colchester, the town preacher was on an indefinite contract with the corporation.[124] At Bury St Edmund's appointments were affected by the puritan proclivities of the local gentry active in the district, Sir John Higham and Sir Robert Jermyn.[125]

The danger of clerical populism fostered by this type of patronage was present even within the universities. James I required that 'no new erected lectures or sermons be permitted in any parish church of ye towne' for fear that they might attract scholars from the more readily controlled services in their colleges, or distract them from their academic

---

[119] Key 1993, pp. 95–6.   [120] Quintrell 1965, p. 285; Cliffe 1960, pp. 374 ff.
[121] Burton 1621/1932, p. 322.   [122] BL Add. MS 41654, fo. 50.   [123] Cross 1976, p. 157.
[124] Seaver 1970, pp. 88–117.
[125] *Ibid.*, p. 86. Jermyn was also given control of an endowment intended to establish an exhibition from Bury St Edmund's school to a college in Cambridge. Significantly, he selected St John's as the college to which it should be attached as one which – in the 1560s and 1570s – had earned an unimpeachably radical reputation.

exercises.[126] Subsequently, the two town preachers at Cambridge, Bentley and Sibbes, were required to subscribe to the three articles of Canon 36. According to the vice-chancellor, Sibbes hesitated to do so, not because he had any resolved opinion against the articles, but 'for feare to displease his crasie Auditors'.[127]

The measure of the flow of university men into these lectureships is to be seen in the fact that between 1560 and 1602, of about 700 lecturers active in London, at least 82 per cent are known to have attended a university.[128] As the number of graduates increased, so did the likelihood of university men being forced to take up lectureships. When the 'dignity of the cloth' was being reasserted in the late 1620s, the heads of colleges reported – with evident distaste for the circumstances – that certain statutes of Emmanuel College forced even BDs and DDs 'either to stand idle, or to betake themselves to Lecture and to seek meanes of Lively hood from the benevolence and favour of the people'.[129]

The prospects for future preferment depended increasingly on lay patronage. The fact that this patronage inevitably embraced a wide spectrum of theological viewpoints cannot but have encouraged the pursuit by the individual student within the university of his own religious proclivities, especially if he happened to enjoy a pre-existent connection with a local impropriator of known religious views. In this way the diversity of opinion inherent in the increase in lay patronage penetrated the universities and there, no less than in the localities, it subverted attempts to maintain a doctrinal hegemony, and generally undermined the effectiveness of the control exercised by the representatives of established authority within the university.

STATE CONTROL OF SERMONS AND LECTURES

Two further and related aspects of the university education of aspiring clerics created additional problems, and elicited a number of responses from those responsible for the maintenance of good order and established opinions at Cambridge. Problems arose because of the taste for sermons and the characteristic method of teaching through disputations. The authorities in the university encountered these in a particularly acute form when, during the sixteenth century, the incantation of carefully prescribed Latin formulae was superseded by a demand for a preaching clergy

---

[126] CUA, Lett. 11.A.A.7.
[127] CUA, Lett. 11.A.A.8.d. Part of the phrase is struck through in the original.
[128] Seaver 1970, pp. 181, 309.   [129] CUA, Lett. 12.A.9.

and for what one bishop disdainfully described as 'preaching in season and out of season'.[130] The very act of preaching was redolent with all the anarchic dangers of individual explication and expounding. By the mid-seventeenth century a former fellow of Corpus was of the opinion that preaching had 'driven many into a fugitive Faith, that can endure no Profession long, but like the wild Ass used to the Wilderness, travers the wayes of every Religion [Jer. 2:24], and are never to be found until they have lost themselves: Thus Preaching hath almost *preacht* it self out of doors, and the effusion of the Sermon is the confusion of it self and the hearers too.'[131] Careful oversight of those who preached in the university, and were later to preach in the countryside at large, was but the first note in what became a general policy of tuning the pulpits.

In 1589 Burghley was expressing his grief to the vice-chancellor, having recently heard of 'contentious persones, and that in open preach, taking upon them verie rashlelie to condemne the doctrine, ministerie, and other Orders of the Realme established for Ecclesiasticall discipline'.[132] Earlier, in mitigating the offences of William Charke, Burghley noted that the offending sermon had been 'delivered in the Latin tongue, and not popularly taught'.[133] None the less, Burghley was alive to the dangers inherent in the unfettered expression of opinions through the medium of sermons and lectures. In a circumspect yet weightily worded warning addressed to the university in the summer of 1570, and clearly alluding to Cartwright's lectures, the university's chancellor articulated the government's concern with this Pandora's box. He wrote that he had heard

> that some parsons in that university having occasion by their vocation in reading or preaching or both, do enter into certen new assertions unprofitable to edify either in doctrine or good manners . . . And yet to descend more particularly, I heare they leave their office of interpreting of scriptures which is proper for readers of divinity, and of teaching and declaring the way of salvation or pardition, which belongeth to preachers of the Gospell, and divert their braynes and tongues to dispute of garmentes, of civill offices allowed in the Ecclesiasticall government etc.

[130] Lambeth Palace MS 943, fo. 125. The phrase is ascribed to the bishop of Norwich during a Visitation sermon at King's Lynn in 1627. The catalogue ascription to Bishop Corbett is incorrect, as is the MS correction in the Lambeth copy of the catalogue. From internal evidence the sermon can be dated to May 1627, and therefore must have been delivered by Samuel Harsnett, who was not translated to York until January 1629.
[131] Edward Boys, *Sixteen Sermons Preached Upon Several Occasions* (London, 1672) sig. a². Boys had been a fellow of Corpus in the 1630s (Venn, I, p. 195a).
[132] CUA, Lett. 9.C.13. See also CUA, Lett. 11.A. Appendix D, fo. 4, Privy Council to the university, 31 May 1622, regarding a subversive lecture at Oxford in the Lent term.
[133] CUA, Lett. 9.C.5.a. Charke was expelled from Peterhouse for his puritan opinions (Venn, I, p. 324a; *DNB*).

These 'unquiett rash braynes' were to be suppressed and secluded 'both from reading and preaching untill they shall reforme their errors'.[134]

There were, indeed, repeated attempts to regulate preaching and lecturing at Cambridge. The royal Injunctions, delivered to the university in 1616, banned preaching in the town by any who were not conformable, required all students to attend the sermons at St Mary's, and restrained attendance at other churches at the time of the St Mary's sermons. On the more strictly academic front no one, 'either in pulpitt or in Schooles', was to be permitted to 'maintayne dogmatically any point of doctrine that is not allowed by the church of England'. Annual reports on conformity to these regulations were supposed to be made personally by the vice-chancellor and heads to the king.[135] The Injunctions of 1616 in part reiterated the orders issued by Cecil following the Hampton Court conference, in 1604. Then, the university was instructed to observe its existing statutes, to be vigilant against private conventicles, and to ensure that no 'sermons be suffered to be preached by unconformable men or at unseasonable times, contrary to the ancient orders of the university, either on Sundays or Holy Days in the time of ordinary prayers in the colleges; or in the weekdays in the time of lectures or other exercises'.[136]

While such orders might curb the too public expression of opinions by the more judicious individuals within the university, there was always a minority of individuals whose sense of commitment or whose quirks of personality drove them beyond acceptable limits. Moreover, when this happened on the occasion of lectures or sermons the damage was done, and could not easily be redressed. For example, in the early 1630s a London preacher, Nathaniel Barnard, had taken the opportunity of a sermon preached at St Mary's in Cambridge to inveigh against the new ceremonialism – an attack that Laud took personally, and that still rankled ten years later.[137] Within a few weeks of this incident Richard Spinks used the occasion of a college commonplace to condemn non-residency, to advocate a stipendiary clergy, and presumably indirectly to attack Laud in the demand that 'the Ministers of God should not leave theire charges to serve at tables, noe not [even] the councell table'.[138]

[134] CUA, Lett. 9.C.3.
[135] CUA, folder in plan press, CUA, Lett. 11.A.A.7. The doctrinal disputes behind these Injunctions are discussed in Morgan 1983, pp. 530–636.
[136] *HMCS*, XVI, p. 390 (Dec. 1604).
[137] SP 16/216/70. For another outburst by Barnard and the consequences of his sermon, see Seaver 1970, pp. 144, 248–9.
[138] SP 16/216/67, 70.

Certainly the most notorious, and probably the ultimate realisation within the university of the inherently anarchic propensities in preaching, was the *cause célèbre* created by the sermon preached in St Andrews church by Thomas Edwards at midsummer 1627. Milton's 'shallow Edwards', subsequently the author of *Gangraena*, was later to progress through pres-byterianism to independency. Even at this time among his friends he had the reputation of being a 'young Luther'.[139] The more judicious Dr Fuller recalled him as a college contemporary 'who often was trans-ported beyond due bounds with the keenness and eagerness of his spirit, and therefore I have just cause to suspect him'[140] – as did the authorities following a sermon in which he had severely rattled the great chain of being, allegedly preaching that

> When there arise any doubts about the way, and thou knowest not well which way to take, if thou beest a servant, thou must not go to thy carnal master to enquire of him; if thou beest a wife, thou must not go to thy carnal husband to aske; if thou beest a son, thou must not go to thy carnal father; if thou beest a pupil, thou must not go to thy carnal tutor to ask him: but thou must finde out a man in whome the spirit of God dwells, one that is renewed by grace, and he shall direct thee.[141]

The serious implications of these remarks were such that they were eventually reported to the king, who clearly saw them as a threat to his own position, for in response he wrote to the vice-chancellor and Senate, referring to 'some errours of opinion lately published in a lecture amongst you savoring of faction and popularity, and too much trenching upon the soveraigne Right of Kings: which wee have ever maintained a[nd] Will'.[142] Judgement was given against Edwards at the end of March and within a few days he was back in St Andrews, voicing a formal recantation of his error in preaching 'against obedience to superiors'.[143] Significantly, he was made to cite biblical texts (1 Tim. 1:6 and 1 Peter 2:18 and 3:1) to the effect that superiors should be obeyed, whatever their faults – significant, because in the offending sermon he was reported as having declaimed 'If all this be not true, then this book (clapping his hand upon the holy Bible) is full of falsehoods, and God himself is a lyar, and Christ himself a deceiver.'[144] On this occasion Edwards certainly realised, if ever anyone did, the subversive potential of individual explication of the greatest book of ambiguities.

---

[139] Mullinger 1911, p. 77.   [140] Quoted in *ibid.*, p. 77.
[141] Heywood and Wright 1854, II, p. 362.   [142] CUA, Lett. 12.A.3.
[143] Heywood and Wright 1854, II, pp. 362–3.   [144] *Ibid.*, II, p. 362.

CONTROL OF DISPUTATIONS

In addition to sermons and lectures the procedure by disputation provided a further opportunity for the assertion of opinions opprobrious to authority. For, in this procedure, proponent or opponent would adopt a position, 'for the sake of the question' that was considered wrong, in order that it should be defeated. This form of proceeding continued as part of academic life well into the eighteenth century. Steele was to remind his readers that 'Those who have been present at publick Disputes in the University, know that it is usual to maintain Heresies for Argument's sake. I have heard a Man a most impudent socinian for half an hour, who has been an Orthodox Divine all his Life after.'[145] As Steele suggests, this procedure seems positively to have encouraged the maintenance of perverse opinions for the sake of displaying forensic skills. During periods of intense religious differences, disputations provided an opportunity to voice dissentient opinion. Thus at St John's in the 1570s it was claimed that 'factyious & seditious Questions are sometyme propounded & contradictions maynteyned in bravery which move altercation & strife'. Moreover, the procedure known as 'questions' was also a potential source of contention: protagonists might skirt serious 'controversyes or poynts of Learning', preferring, rather, hubristic displays of 'witty & affected conceits'.[146] But even if a question was defeated, its maintenance in the disputation provided a forum for expounding views contrary to those established by authority. The authorities were not unaware of this possibility and Cardinal Pole's Ordinances (c. 13) had required that in disputations, if either opponent or respondent proposed anything contrary to orthodox faith, at the beginning or end of the disputation he was to announce that the truth was in the contrary proposition, and that he only propounded the views for the sake of disputation. Presumably it was an oversight that this requirement was not repeated in the Elizabethan statutes of 1570 (cf. c. 45).

The situation was exacerbated at certain times by the general disputatiousness of college life and preoccupation with matters of theology when theology was a matter of intense concern. All this hardly discouraged the airing of unacceptable opinions, whatever those opinions may have been at any time. For example, during Elizabeth's reign the allegedly crypto-Catholic fellows at Gonville and Caius were said to have defended dissimulation during a disputation before the scholars of the house at the common table – pointedly choosing to do so just prior to a

[145] *The Spectator*, no. 485, Tues. 16 Sept. 1712, reprinted in Bond 1965, IV, p. 220.
[146] CUL MS Mm. i. 38, p. 79.

communion enforced by the vice-chancellor.[147] They were also reputed to be so bold as to 'dyspute openlye as well in the colledge Court as in their chambers'.[148] Later, in 1607, when another fellow of Gonville and Caius was accused of maintaining popish opinions in the college, he did not deny that 'he had some reasoning about points of religion', but claimed that it was 'in way of disputation'. Stung by the accusation, the accused party further rejoined that others amongst the fellows 'had so talked and reasoned about points of religion as well as he', they answering 'little thereunto but that it was for argument sake'.[149] Nor were these disputatious encounters limited to matters of religion: matters of political theory might also be voiced.[150]

Such circumstances were difficult to avoid when both universities were deeply imbued with the attitudes and skills that went along with the essentially medieval procedure of disputation. A measure of the extent to which a preoccupation with these procedures suffused academic thinking and thinking beyond academe is the uses to which, on occasion, they were put in circumstances which to us might seem extraordinary. Thus, in 1554, Convocation had agreed upon certain test propositions to be put to the bishops – Cranmer, Ridley and Latimer – accused of heresy and imprisoned at Oxford. They were to be allowed to dispute against the propositions if they wished, and a deputation of Cambridge dons was dispatched to assist their Oxford brethren. Proceedings were conducted in the Divinity Schools with regular syllogisms, with major, minor and conclusion![151]

The draftsmen of the Elizabethan statutes at Cambridge were so obsessed with this mode of proceeding that they missed the opportunity for radical change by permitting the continuance of this potentially subversive form of academic exercise. Indeed, the requirements for disputations were regulated with some minuteness,[152] and a cycle of disputations between different colleges was confirmed that contributed to the often violent inter-college encounters characteristic of the period.[153]

In the late sixteenth and early seventeenth centuries, disputations were hardly genteel encounters. Indeed, for their enthusiastic observers they seem to have constituted a form of academic bloodsport or the equivalent of the vitriolic review of a later time. The Cambridge orders of 1600 admonished those who attended the exercises in public schools to

---

[147] BL Lansdowne MS 33, fo. 92.   [148] *Ibid.*, 33, fo. 106.   [149] *HMCS*, XIX, p. 382.
[150] See above, p. 112 and n. 66.
[151] Neale 1909, p. 8; Venn 1910, p. 100; MacCulloch 1996, pp. 562–8.
[152] Elizabethan statutes, cc. 6, 7, 22–32, 45 (*Cambridge Documents 1852*, I, pp. 459, 464–70, 481–2).
[153] c. 27. In addition, c. 25 positively encouraged diversity of assertions amongst disputing MAs.

abjure 'standinge upon stalles, knockinge, hissinge and other imoderate behaviour'.[154] At Oxford, Anthony Ashley Cooper recalled the violence on these occasions in the 1630s, and at the same period an Oxford don referred to 'the great riots, tumults, abuses and disorders at ye time of disputations in schooles', made worse by the repeated encounter of the same colleges in the cycle of colleges required to provide disputants.[155]

The sermon, the lecture, the commonplace and the disputation were characteristic features of university life during the late sixteenth and early seventeenth centuries. They were often conducted before large and enthusiastic audiences in a period when feelings ran high on the issues under exposition or in debate. Moreover, by the late sixteenth century the admixture to the university of young lads from gentry backgrounds means that they were – if they chose – exposed to the content and familiarised with the process of academic discussion. The result was four or five generations of laymen who, later in their lives, as JPs and and as MPs, took an unprecedentedly engaged and active interest in the issues of religious debate that had been batted around their heads in their formative years. Moreover, they imbibed as much the process as the substance of debate; and their correspondence often catches the style of pedantic disputatiousness that had enlivened their youthful years.

Repeated injunctions to conformity suggest only partial success on the part of those responsible for regulating the conduct of academic exercises. Moreover, the favoured mode of redressing errors when they were detected was through public recantation. Often this seems only to have focussed further attention on the erring individual and his errant thoughts.[156] We have noted that the exuberant Thomas Edwards was forced to recant his opinions in the place and in front of the audience before which he had expressed them.[157] When news of Ralph Brownrigg's recantation was brought to James, the king expressed the hope that 'it will be a good example for others not to be to[o] busy'.[158] Others, with perhaps more insight and less *amour propre* than James, seem to have realised that suppression was more effective than refutation. Burghley advocated this policy in the early stages of the Cartwright controversy, in his order to suppress the memory of the controversial sermon preached by Charke,

---

[154] CUA, Misc. Collect. 8, fo. 85.   [155] Boas 1935, pp. 10, 42–3.
[156] A printed example of the manner in which erring opinions were set out *in extenso*, prior to refutation, is John Bridges, *A Defence of the Government Established in the Church of Englande for Ecclesiasticall Matters* . . . (London, 1587). John Cowell also got into trouble for a heavy-handed piece that managed to provide further circulation for the opinions of his opponent (Morgan 1983, p. 589).
[157] Above, p. 127.   [158] CUA, Lett. 11.A.A.9.b.

and the heretical and seditious sermons preached by John Browning.[159] Whitgift attempted to follow a similar line in suppressing the doctrinal disputes that threatened the peace of the university in the 1590s.[160]

In these situations it was often the local academics who wished to extract recantations from their doctrinal opponents or inferiors within the institution. In part this desire arose from an extension to these larger issues of the practice of exemplary punishment that was inflicted for more trivial breaches of discipline within the university. In its turn, and at this lowlier level, government policy had actually encouraged the adoption within the university of a psychological means of control that it also favoured in other contexts. In part, a natural academic predisposition to argumentativeness also tended to favour public refutation rather than silent suppression. In part, the adoption of the procedure of recantation within the context of the university represented the adoption of practices employed by ecclesiastical courts on cognate issues. Last, and not least, quite evident personal dislike combined with detestation of opposing viewpoints and encouraged academics with the upper hand to seek the public humiliation of their opponents. As those with a more Olympian perspective on academic squabbles such as Burghley and Whitgift re-alised, this was not a sensible policy. The retraction of academic points on scholarly subjects before a small circle of peers and experts was one thing. It was, however, an altogether inappropriate means for regulating the circulation of ideas when played out – as it so often was in early modern Cambridge – before a large, youthful and overexcited audience, agape for spectacle, with which they were often rewarded.

THE SOCIAL COMPOSITION OF THE UNIVERSITY: THE 'ARISTOCRATIC' CURRICULUM

As with precise details of the increase in the number of students, so also with the changing social composition of the universities: much remains unclear in detail, open to debate and subject to further investigation.[161]

---

[159] CUA, Lett. 9.C.4 (Burghley to the vice-chancellor and heads, 3 Aug. 1570); CUA, Lett. 9.C.5.a.; CUA, Lett. 9.C.5.b, c, p. 552.

[160] For example, in his warning to the heads (Trinity College Library, MS B.XIV.9, fo. 15 and Morgan 1983, p. 552).

[161] This issue was once at the fore of concerns as a leading element in the 'new' history of the universities that emerged during the mid-1960s and 1970s. Major contributions that also summarise much other work can be traced in the following: Cressy 1970; McConica 1973, pp. 543–54; 1977, pp. 115–34; 1986, pp. 666–93; McConica in Stone 1975, pp. 151–82; Stone 1975; Russell 1977; Morgan 1978, pp. 147–8; O'Day 1982, pp. 77–131. There is an excellent discussion of the social makeup of seventeenth-century Oxford by Stephen Porter in Tyacke 1997, ch. 1.

None the less, the overall picture of an addition in the form of an influx of students from 'aristocratic' backgrounds is hardly likely to be modified in its essentials. This created a new set of problems in terms of managing the lives of individuals within the university. The attempts to regulate the formative years of this elite came not only from individual parents, but also from the government – concerned as it was with the maintenance of due order and hierarchy.

A number of developments in the university during the sixteenth century facilitated, and were no doubt encouraged by, the desire on the part of aristocratic parents for personalised supervision and education of their offspring. Important amongst these developments was residence in colleges, rather than in the less formalised halls that the colleges were superseding, or promiscuously, about the town.[162] Perhaps the most important development in this regard was the emergence of the tutor as the key figure in the education of young men in the university, the theme of chapter 9 below.

Governmental concern with the supervision of the aristocratic element in the university is evident in a reading of the statutes and ordinances of the period. These show that the more minute and careful regulation of such matters as residence that has been noted by previous historians was mainly directed at controlling the offspring of the elite. Pole's Ordinances in the 1550s had required that no member was to pass the night outside the college (Ordinance 26), and this was also provided for in the statutes of 1570 (c. 50, para. 34). However, while both Pole and the draftsmen of 1570 attempted to inhibit at any time the wandering of pupils in the town without the permission of someone in authority (Pole's Ordinance 25, 1570, c. 47), by implication these provisions appear to have been directed to the protection of the more prestigious students. Exception is made for poor students and sizars who needed to go out unattended to follow their own business, or that of their masters.

Solicitude on the part of individual parents and of the central authority for the well-being of aristocratic students encouraged intervention in the affairs of the university. At the same time the very presence of these students had a number of other disruptive effects on university life. Among other things, their presence encouraged a diversification of the subjects studied and the methods of teaching employed. They also created new problems of social control, importing into the academic context the youthful version of aristocratic values and attitudes.

---

[162] Curtis 1959, p. 39; above, p. 24.

Although there have been much debate and some advances in our understanding of what was taught at the early modern English universities, there remain uncertainty and continuing opportunities for further investigation.[163] Here, our concern is with the way in which changes in the social makeup of the university affected what was taught. Essentially, the influx of aristocratic students led to a broadening of the curriculum that was taught, if not of that which was required. In effect there was created a diverse 'informal curriculum' for those aristocratic students who did not need to study in order to take a degree and to pursue a career.

However, the various types of teaching that went on at Cambridge did not exist in separate compartments. Both 'career track' and aristocratic students seem to have been taught by the same tutors. The tutors were themselves on the career track yet in order to succeed as tutors they needed to be able to teach aristocratic students. Therefore, even before they became tutors, but with that prospect in view, they are likely to have been inclined to acquire the expertise that would be required. It was also the case that some aristocratic students were simply grabbed by what was going on around them and became immersed in the theological and linguistic culture of the universities far beyond what was required of them, and beyond what their often startled parents had expected. Evidently – at least until the late seventeenth century – for many students the universities were exciting places in which to be.

At the same time there were aspects of both the formal and the informal curricula that were perceived to be of use to the social group for which they were not primarily intended. So, for example, elements of the religious training intended for career-track students were considered worthwhile for aristocratic students. Equally, the predominantly linguistic training that had been fostered by humanistic impulse had placed a premium on rhetorical skills. The aim was to acquire a persuasive eloquence. Consequently, and as we have just noted, many of the student exercises involved observation of or participation in verbal encounters. But, of course, eloquence and a more specific mastery of languages was of use not only in the pulpit. It also equipped a layman to operate in many other theatres of the public sphere that emerged or that were transformed during the sixteenth century. These included the royal Court, parliament or diplomatic missions. But at a more workaday level, and for what was substantially the largest number of individuals, it was the law courts, and the local arenas provided by the judicio-administrative-political meetings of quarter sessions and assizes that were to become the primary scene

---

[163] See below, chapters 12 and 15.

for rhetorical display. Occasionally, as with the tabletalk of the Lestranges of Hunstanton, one catches a glimpse of a further transformation: rhetoric in the domestic sphere.[164] Moreover, in these contexts we need to see that the eloquence inculcated by the more formal aspects of the teaching provided by the universities was not entirely distinct from many of the other activities that formed part of the emergent informal curriculum for aristocratic students. For eloquence was a display skill. As such it sat alongside other display skills that were acquired in the arena provided by the universities. These included aspects of dress, swordplay and deportment. But also encompassed were yet other skills required in an honour-based patron–client society, such as leadership, deference and condescension. The presence of aristocratic students may have added French fencing masters to the services provided in Cambridge, but in the larger equation the intrusion of such things into academic life was as nothing compared to the unprecedented impact made by the concerns and the procedures of the academy on the wider culture between the 1570s and the 1680s. For a number of generations the latinate, linguistically sophisticated, pedantically theological culture of the early modern universities, together with the premium that they placed on eloquence, largely set the style of that wider culture. So we should not be misled by the intermittent bleatings of academics and governors in this period about the intolerable behaviour of students – especially aristocratic students. The odd bit of illegal swimming, intermittent swordplay and perennially ostentatious dress did not, in the long run, distract the universities from their larger concerns which were also the larger concerns of the wider society. Worse was to come and in a more fundametal way. For from the late seventeenth century there were fundametal shifts in the focus and the style of both state and society. True, as is argued below,[165] there was more vibrancy to academic life in the period after *c.* 1670 than cruder interpretations have allowed. But the real problem was that there were fundamental changes in the structure of state and of the interests and concerns of the wider culture. In the first place, there was a reaction against much that the universities practised, and the way that they practised it. In the second place, the flow of influence largely was reversed. In the earlier period it is the case that there had been piecemeal intrusion of aspects of the environing aristocratic culture. This was carried in the persons of large numbers of aristocratic students. But after the 1670s, increasingly, a metropolitan-based, cosmopolitan-orientated culture came to penetrate the universities through the lifestyles and interests of new generations

---

[164] See Lipincott 1974.   [165] Chapters 14, 15 and 16.

of academics. The world of the coffee house and the newspaper now reached into the university in the way that the academic exercise had once reached into the provincial pulpit. Pedantic eloquence was held at a discount against scintillating wit. Moreover, in affairs of the mind there was a shift from institutionalised intellect to uninstitutionalised intellect, or intellect in institutions in addition to but apart from the universities: it had become a more pluralistic world. Therefore, as with any modern history of an institution, it cannot be understood simply in, of and for itself.

As universities were originally and primarily institutions for the education of the clergy, most aristocratic parents expected that their children should receive at the least a sound religious education while at university even though they were not intended for a clerical career. Sometimes what was required was not overly strenuous and demands were pitched at capacities. Lady Katherine Paston expected her son to 'ruminat over all thy Psalms and Chapters and textes of scripture', which long since he had learnt by heart and not to forget his 'Conduit of Comfort . . . for they will be to the[e] in time to com, both Comforters and Cownselers'. The college also provided 'such excelent means' to prepare him to receive his first communion.[166] William Denton expressed to Ralph Verney his hope 'that divinity and especially the pracktique (for knowledge alone doth not save) be ever att both ends of your other studys, for without that there can be noe true content in any study'.[167] Francis Gardiner wrote to his son's tutor that 'Above all, my desire is, that Sundays, fast days, and the like, may have their particular employment in divine studies, beside his constant reading the scriptures each morning and evening.'[168] When Robert Wilton sent his son Thomas up to Cambridge from Norfolk in April 1621, he confided to his notebook the hope that God would bless him 'with a gracious progresse in grace and learning in the dewe feare of his heavenly name to my comfort heere & to bothe our endles joyes & comfort everrlastingly'.[169] From Oxford, Anthony Bagot informed his mother that he and his companions studied rhetoric, logic and history during the week, and on Saturdays and Sundays read parts of Nowell's *Catechisme*, 'wherein I trust we shall so profite as shall be to your desyer & our owne furthereunce'.[170] William Whiston recalled that, in his time as a

[166] Hughey 1941, pp. 83, 90–1, 102.
[167] Microfilm of uncatalogued Verney MSS, Claydon House, Bucks., William Denton to Ralph Verney, *c.* 1630.
[168] Cary 1842, p. 152.
[169] CUL Buxton MSS, Box 96, Notebook of Robert Wilton, p. 155.
[170] Folger Shakespeare Library, MS L.a.36.

tutor, in the evenings he sometimes read over to his pupils Dr Hammond's *Practical Catechism*,[171] while the biographer of John Conant, rector of Exeter College, Oxford, remarked with approbation that 'his first and chief Care was to plant the fear of God in the youth there to see that they had well laid the foundation of sincere Piety & true Religion', to which end 'he was very careful to recommend the youth to pious as well as learned Tutors'.[172]

However, in addition to building on their earlier religious educa-tion, most aristocratic parents would have concurred in Lady Katherine Paston's hope that 'that is the plase I trust shall doe the[e] good more ways then on[e]', and that her son should come 'from that plase adorned bothe with devine and humayne Learinge', imbued with 'vertuous and Civill behaviour' and 'furnished with grasses as a bee comms laden to her hive'. Her hope that he should 'be furnished with those liberall sciences, which that Nurcery affordethe to the studious and best mindes'[173] would have met with the concurrence of Brian Twyne's father, to whom the son was forced to justify himself: 'I studie not divinity too much. I say unto you father I doe not so . . . I have spent my time in such sort as one of my standinge doth reqyre it, good Liberall artes', although he was brought to admit that 'I have by stelth obtained to some meane knowledge in the Hebrewe toonge'.[174] As in Twyne's case, some aristocratic students evidently got the scholarly bit between their teeth, and pursued elements of the reading and exercises intended for aspiring clerics. This was true of Sir Symonds D'Ewes at St John's. Although he performed only a few formal public exercises he applied himself to the improvement of his written style and later was to expostulate on the benefits of observation and conversation:

> Nor was my increase in knowledge small, which I attained by the ear as well as the eye, by being present at public comencements, at Mr. Downes his public Greek lectures, and Mr. Harbert's [Herbert's] public rhetoric lectures in the University; at problems, sophisms, declamations, and other scholastical exercises in our private college; and my often conversation with learned men of other colleges, and the prime young students of our own.[175]

It is worth noting that while referring to the enhancement of his writing skills D'Ewes also mentions the essentially verbal exercises of the univer-sity. Sir Thomas Isham was more direct and explicitly recommended the

---

[171] Whiston 1749, p. 10.   [172] BL Add. MS 22579, fo. 10v.
[173] Hughey 1941, pp. 65, 72, 74, 83.   [174] Twyne 1927, p. 214.   [175] Halliwell 1845, I, p. 121.

acquisition of the oratorical skills that would serve a gentleman well in later life:

> if hereafter yow be not taught to make a verse instead of Lucan yow may learne Plutark, yet poetree I commend boeth for matter and meothhard and thinke not him to be a sufficient scholler, that is not somewhat practised therein. the best orrators in tymes past as Cicero amongst the Romans, and Demostines amongst the Grecians were Poetes, and learned of stage players to pronounce playnelie to speake ellequentlie, to act there speeches properlie and to conclude there sentences with compendious brevitie. lett not then that be contemptable unto yow which wise menn hereto fore highlie have esteemed

an example in itself of practising that which was recommended.[176]

Much of what was required in aristocratic education by way of religious, linguistic and oratorical skills could be adopted and adapted from the curriculum intended for the professional scholar. However, more was often required and this enforced an enlargement of teaching. Although the earl of Salisbury complimented his son's tutor on 'the respect you have had to instruct him towards God', he also complained that 'if you had given yourself a little more to put him into the ways that men provide for such as he is, without tying him and yourself to the old and dry exercises' he would not have 'made so little use of a University life'.[177] When William Clark became tutor to the son of Sir John Hobart he expressed the intent that the education of his new pupil should be not 'disagreable to his calling, and answerable to your content'.[178]

As in the case of Harvey Bagot, the reading of histories was one of the studies considered suitable for gentlemanly study. It was probably at the universities that the 'ordinarily qualited Gentlemen of England' acquired 'a superficiall Master of the warres of Alexander . . . Of the christians against the Moores . . . The Spanyards against the Infidels in the Indies. Or Henry fifte and other English Kinges in France'.[179] Music certainly seems to have been part of the aristocratic curriculum, although not always meeting with the approval of the more puritanically inclined.[180]

---

[176] Northants Record Office, Isham Correspondence, 14.

[177] *HMCS*, XIX, pp. 465–6. For further expressions of the notion of an education appropriate to an aristocratic status, see *HMC 24: Rutland*, I, p. 296.

[178] Bodl. Tanner MS 285, fo. 28. Clark was a fellow of Trinity Hall, 1609–34 and at the time of this letter had just received his LLB (Venn, I, p. 348a).

[179] William Bradshaw, *A Brief Censure Upon the Pamphlet* ([np], 1603), p. 78. See also Ball 1918, p. 249 and SP 12/288/27, books borrowed by Mr Bedingfield of Mr Owen (in the hand of Martin Man, secretary to Sir Nathaniel Bacon, who was guardian of Owen).

[180] Venn 1913, pp. 88–9; Knappen 1933, p. 111; Bodl. Tanner MS 286, fo. 38. It could well be that the practice of music in small groups around an enthusiastic university tutor helped to foster the efflorescence of domestic music in England in this period.

Despite regulations to the contrary, provision was made for the teaching of social graces such as dancing. Students 'entreated to have Learned to daunce' and, at least at Oxford, tutors justified it as 'an exercise well beseminge a gentleman and noe hindrance to his study'.[181] Somewhat more tentatively, a Cambridge tutor wrote to Sir John Hobart that he had sent his son to the singing school, partly by his own desire and partly because the tutor had some skill therein, and they could practise together, 'being a qualitie in it selfe not to be discomended'.[182] There was, then, some force in Seth Ward's complaint in the 1630s that the nobility and gentry 'send their sons hither . . . that their reason, fancy and carriage [may] be improved by lighter institutions and exercises, that they may become rational and graceful speakers, and be of an acceptable behaviour in their counties'.[183]

There were, however, those extreme cases, like the future duke of Newcastle. His 'education was according to his birth; for as he was born a gentleman, so was he bred like a gentleman' and 'To school learning he never showed a great inclination.' His tutors at Cambridge failed to 'persuade him to read or study much, he taking more delights in sports than in learning'.[184] Unlike those students who were dependent on obtaining a degree for their future advancement, many of the offspring of the aristocracy viewed their time at the university as a purgatorial withholding from the excitements afoot elsewhere. Robert Morrell, tutor to William Cecil, the son of Lord Salisbury, had constant difficulties with his pupil for this reason. Morrell rebutted Salisbury's complaints of lack of progress by his son by referring to the long periods of interruption in his studies, suggesting that 'The delights of the Court (if I may say so without offence) have greatly estranged, if not quite alienated his mind from his books.' The Pandora's box of princely pleasures having once been opened to the student so, 'As Themistocles could not sleep in the night for dreaming of Miltiades triumphs, so neither can he go to his study all the day for revolving in his mind the sports and pastimes abroad in the world.'[185]

The lack of interest in academic study or their distraction by other excitements of aristocratic students such as the future duke of Newcastle

---

[181] Elizabethan statutes, c. 47 (*Cambridge Documents 1852*, pp. 483–5); SP 46/24/98; Folger Shakespeare Library, MS L.a.13; Throckmorton Account Book, fo. 15, mentions a dancing master (1654).

[182] Bodl. Tanner MS 285, fo. 59.   [183] Ward 1654, pp. 49–50.   [184] Firth 1886, p. 104.

[185] *HMCS* XVI, p. 82 (4 March 1605). Sir Christopher Heydon also disrupted the education of his ward in order that he should return into Norfolk at the behest of some of his friends who wished to see him (Bodl. Tanner MS 75, fo. 247), as did Sir Edward Montagu with his protégé (*HMC 45: Buccleuch and Queensberry*, III, p. 22).

or the future earl of Salisbury created new and not easily resolved problems of control, not only for the individual tutor, but also for the university at large, and for those at the centre of government concerned with the good order of the universities. For example, it seems clear that it was primarily to curb the sporting activities of students such as Newcastle that it was necessary to order that 'no student of anie condicon or degree' was to keep any weapon or firearms, 'or at anie time [to] shoote in the same, eyther with in the Coll[ege] or in the precinctes of thuniversitie, or abroad in the country'.[186] The keeping of greyhounds was also banned.[187] The sporting preoccupations of many aristocratic students are epitomised by the exasperated if rather crack-brained remarks made by Alexander Akehurst to the fellow commoners of Trinity College in 1654. One Sunday, at supper in the college hall, he was reported to have told them that 'In Heaven they should have a Tennis-Court, and Bowling-greenes & cry spiritually Rub, rub, rub.'[188]

Despite repeated attempts to regulate ostentation of dress the propin-quity of numerous children of rank fuelled the fires of sartorial emulation and created new business for the tradesmen of both university towns.[189] At Oxford, Brian Twyne noted the ever-rising standards of dress.[190] At Cambridge in 1578, Burghley complained of the excesses in dress and laid the fault at the door of those in authority who had permitted 'sondry yong men, being the children of gentilmen and men of welth . . . to use very costly and disguised manner of Apparrell, and other attyres, unsemly for students in any kynd of human lerning, and therby not only to be more chargeable to thier frends then is convenient, but by their example to induce others of les habilitie to change and cast awey ther modesty and honest frugallitie, to overcharging of ther frends'.[191] Despite this and similar attempts to impose restraint, the correspondence of parents and students is full of pleas for a new suit for Christmas, 'for my best shute is quite out of fashion',[192] or of anxious mothers invoking divine guid-ance and sartorial restraint: 'I . . . pray to god, so to guide the[e]: that thou mayest not adicte thy selfe to that vayn garbe: which is most in

---

[186] CUA, Misc. Collect. 8, fo. 85v.   [187] CUA, CUR, 44.i, no. 144 (23 Feb. 1617).
[188] CUL, MS Dd. iii. 88, fos. 2v, 3v; Cooper, *Annals*, III, pp. 457–8.
[189] Cooper, *Annals*, II, pp. 455–6, Burghley to the vice-chancellor, permitting the nobility distinctive clothing, and requiring a more precise adherence to the social gradations of dress. See also Andrew Perne to Burghley, 27 April 1588 (BL Harl. MS 7031, fos. 97v–98); CUA, Misc. Collect. 8, fo. 2v, item 2 (Nov. 1600).
[190] Twyne 1927, p. 216.
[191] Cooper, *Annals*, II, p. 360. The order recognised that the sons of the nobility, and of knights and other men of standing, could wear more expensive clothing. See Hargreaves-Mawdsley 1963; Harte 1976.
[192] Folger Shakespeare Library, MS L.a.176, William Bagot to Walter Bagot, Oxford, Nov. 1619.

fation amongst youthe in these times. which to my thinkinge is such for the most part: as promisethe no hope of grase in them for the present much lese a blessinge for the worlde to come'.[193] Tailors' bills became a regular part of undergraduate expenditure for the better-off student, and arrears on such bills became a matter of supplication to parents.[194] Students recommended their favourite Cambridge tailors[195] while others claimed that 'in London they cannot make a gowne soe well as they can heere in Oxon'.[196]

As Burghley's complaints make clear, there were a variety of motives for wishing to curb the sartorial excess evident in the universities.[197] Some of the materials used were unnecessary imports. There was much wasteful expenditure by those who could ill afford it. There was also, too often, an emulation in dress that was felt to transgress the boundaries between the different levels of the social and academic hierarchy. In these circumstances it became all the more necessary for the gentry to assert their status. When a tutor informed an uncle that he had provided his nephew with 'a suit of apparell' he also assured him that 'nothing of decencie shall be wanting unto him'.[198] Sartorial affectation was extended from students to academics: it became necessary to punish masters of arts who turned up in college 'so disguised in apparell (unmeet for a Scholler)'. The 'disguise' included, under an academic gown, 'a cut taffety dublet of the fashion, with the sleves out, & a great payer of Gally gastion Hose'.[199]

It can hardly be doubted that the arrival of the scions of the aristocracy in Cambridge, and Oxford too, helped to fill the coffers of their tailors and to brighten up the streets of these English provincial towns. But their ostentatious display also created problems for a government intent upon enforcing a due decorum in dress as a means of maintaining the distinctions of social hierarchy. Moreover, the gathering together of so many young men in one place encouraged competition in matters of dress for want of other means to assert the status, and to express the distinctions between one gradation of aristocracy and another. The situation in the university towns was no doubt similar to that in London, and more

---

[193] Hughey 1941, p. 95.

[194] E.g. Folger Shakespeare Library, MS L.a.179; BL Add. MS 27396, fo. 140; SP 46/24/98; Leeds Reference Library, T4338, tutor's accounts for Henry Ingram in 1709. The latter include payments to the mercer, the tailor, the hatter and the shoemaker totalling £10-13-6 compared with an expenditure on books in the same period of £2-0-0. Henry entered Oriel in 1708; he was the son of Arthur, Viscount Irwin (Foster 1891–2, II, p. 787b); Staffordshire Record Office, Paget Accounts, D/w 1734/3/4/124.

[195] BL Add. MS 27396, fo. 140, Robert Gawdy to Framlingham Gawdy, 17 April 1639.

[196] Folger Shakespeare Library, MS L.a.56, Harvey Bagot to Walter Bagot, Oxford, 17 June 1610.

[197] Cf. Cooper, *Annals*, II, p. 360; above n. 191.   [198] Bodl. Tanner MS 286, fo. 17.

[199] BL Harl. MS 7031, fo. 9.

particularly, in the Court. Except for a few great noble houses whose standing was recognised throughout the realm, the majority of aristocratic families enjoyed a status that normally was articulated within the context of a particular provincial community. Especially for those families – the majority – whose head did not sport a formal title, that status was 'achieved' rather than 'ascribed'. Once removed from the local community in which the social position of their family had been carefully located by a multitude of circumstances over a period of years, what did the offspring of such families do? They resorted to a variety of means to assert their standing, of which ostentatious dress was one aspect, and sartorial innovation was another. Thus the attraction of aristocratic families to the Court and of their sons to the universities helped to create the notion of fashion at this time.[200]

A further means of manifesting status in the arena provided by the university was through the maintenance of servants. Charles Gawdy looked 'to keepe a man in Cambridge',[201] and John Isham had a servant while at the university.[202] The accounts of Robert Towshend at Jesus in 1594 include payments to 'his boy',[203] and those of William Cornwallis, a student at Trinity College in 1560, mention payments to his man.[204] At Sidney Sussex, in the 1630s, Laurence Minshull had the services of a sizar.[205] Nor were these isolated instances. In 1602 it had been necessary for the vice-chancellor to promulgate a regulation to the effect that no student was to 'reteine or have belonging to them . . . anie boyes or persons whatsoever' who had not been formally admitted as students to the appropriate college, 'under pretense to waight upon them at their Chambers or else where'. Even then it had been necessary to make exception for those who were considered to be of suffcient standing to enjoy this privilege.[206]

The maintenance of servants phased over into the intermittent support of clients and dependants within the university. Just as aristocratic values and lifestyle had been imported into other spheres of activity in the university, so were they in this regard. At the universities, members of the aristocracy learned the social skills of creating obligation, and practised the arts of brokerage and patronage that they would require in their subsequent careers. Moreover, for students from humble backgrounds the

[200] See Harte 1976, pp. 132–65.   [201] BL Egerton MS 2716, fo. 4.
[202] Northants. Record Office, Isham Correspondence, 13, 14.
[203] Rainham Hall MSS, Box 50. His ascription to Jesus College is tentative: see Venn, IV, p. 260a.
[204] Venn, I, p. 399b; Elveden Hall, Suffolk: Cornwallis MSS, Box 3, no. 2, account book.
[205] *HMC 45: Buccleuch and Queensberry*, III, p. 369; Venn, III, p. 185b. On sizars, see below, pp. 330, 493.
[206] CUA, Misc. Collect. 8, fo. 85v.

presence of the aristocratic element opened up opportunities for cultivating connections that were likely to be of utility in their future careers.
At its simplest, prospective clergymen were now rubbing shoulders with
laymen who, during the course of the sixteenth century, had become
the main type of patrons of parochial ecclesiastical livings.[207] Moreover,
these developments took place against a background in which the patron–
client system was becoming both more elaborated and more complex.[208]
Indeed, the development of relationships in the universities as a result
of their emergence as new arenas for the creation of patron–client relationships itself positively contributed to these processes' elaboration and
increased complexity.

Within the university at large, but more especially within individual
colleges, activities and relationships intended to cultivate patron–client
connections between students shifted the balance of power and influence
as between them and the fellows and master. From one viewpoint it is evident that by exercising their skills of condescension and patronage within
a college, aristocratic students helped to bind together its usually diverse
social elements. In its mildest forms these activities were unexception-
able, and in some instances positively beneficial. Lady Katherine Paston
encouraged her son, William, to aid the needy in his college: 'good child
let not a poor hungry siser want a reward from the, but lett the poorest and
least be frinded, reape a kindness from the[e]. Let such not want bread or
beer, in a moderat maner, but be a healp to the healples in ther most need.
and the lord will blese the[e] if thow beest kinde to the poor and nedy
on[e]s.' In Lady Katherine's admonition we hear articulated the wholly
admirable Christian roots of condescension.[209] This small-scale largesse
is likely to have been widespread; but because it was by its very nature
essentially piecemeal and informal it is not readily documented, although
occasional fragments of evidence do occur. Thus, when William Cornwallis was at Trinity College in the 1560s the family accounts include a
gift of money to 'master Watkinson skoller of Cambryge', in addition to
8 pence given on another occasion to 'ii pore skollers of Oxfford'.[210] But
other circumstances were less innocuous.

On occasion the leadership provided by aristocratic students supplied
an alternative focus of loyalties, and a challenge to those in authority
both in the university and in individual colleges. Thus, after the drunken
riot that followed the choosing of a lord of misrule at Pembroke Hall

[207] See above, p. 122.   [208] Morgan 1988.   [209] Hughey 1941, p. 72.
[210] Elveden Hall, Suffolk: Cornwallis MSS, Box 3, no. 2, account book.

at Hallowmas 1628, it was two fellow commoners who were punished as 'the Ringleaders'.[211] At Trinity College in 1610–11, it was Francis Neville, the eldest son of a Yorkshire gentleman, who seems to have been the ringleader of a group of youths who caused disturbances in the college. On one occasion he violently attacked the butler in the buttery, 'to the dangerous and pernicious example of this society'.[212]

Attention has been drawn to the new model of top-down authority that was imposed upon the university in the 1570s.[213] But that is only part of the story. Although we have not yet fully penetrated it, beneath the formal structure of authority in the university there was a counter-culture of those subject to this authority. Indeed, it may well be that the counter-culture became both more necessary and more emphatic as the powers of those in authority were increased. Certainly, the presence of the aristocratic element gave it new impetus and more independence. Moreover, we now know that the existence of various realisations of this counter-culture was a characteristic feature of many parts of pre-modern society.[214] In this as in so many other ways, the circumstances of the university need to be understood within the context of the wider environing society. There, as Sir Keith Thomas has pointed out, 'When a normally repressive regime was punctuated by interludes of conviviality and misrule the result could be explosive.'[215] As we have seen, such an explosion seems to have taken place at Pembroke Hall in 1628, over the election of a lord of misrule. The reasons for these explosions were well understood by contemporaries. At St John's in the 1570s one group of fellows requested 'That noe Lord of Misrule, Lottery, or Salting be used in the Colledge'. They explained that these were occasions for the release of pent up frustrations: 'there is nothing sought herein, but disgrace, defaminge, & abuse of some persons, & such things be taken up usually for revenge, being but a more cunninge kind of libelling reteyned of many, specially for such a purpose'.[216]

Academic theatricals were sanctioned by the classical models that were held in high regard and the texts of which figured within the curriculum.[217] The putting on of plays provided an ideal opportunity for display on the part of aristocratic students. Indeed, on the occasion of the

---

[211] SP 16/160/55 III.
[212] Venn, III, p. 243b; Trinity College Muniments, Admissions and Admonitions, 1560–1759, p. 400.
[213] Above, chapter 3.
[214] For the seminal early papers on this theme see Thompson 1972; Davis 1975.
[215] Thomas 1976b, p. 25.   [216] CUL MS Mm. i. 8, p. 79.
[217] Nelson 1989, 1994; Legge 1992.

intermittent visits by royalty to the university they afforded the occasion for posturing even before the greatest in the land – albeit the plays seem to have elicited boredom among courtiers with short attention spans. At Trinity College in January 1594, Thomas Nevile alluded to a forthcoming production as intended 'for the exercise of yonge Gentlemen & Scholers', and we may surmise that it was the former who would play the parts of 'sondry personages of greatest estate to be represented in auntient princelie attire'.[218] But theatricals were also liminal occasions with a potential for disorder – as proved to be the case when plays were mounted in a number of the colleges. At Trinity, as at other colleges, there were considerable revelries at Christmas.[219] On these occasions it seems that it was the undergraduates themselves who punished those of their number who refused to participate by 'stanging' them.[220]

The counter-culture of the college also manifested itself in the ritual of 'salting and tucking'. This was an initiation rite, common in its essentials to both Oxford and Cambridge. The statutes enforcing decorous behaviour were tacitly suspended and, unlike on other nights, students absented themselves from their chambers and the oversight of their tutors.[221] The freshmen were summoned to the hall to meet their student seniors, the senior and junior sophisters. There, they were obliged to pronounce a witticism that would make their audience laugh. If they succeeded they were rewarded with sack or beer. If they failed, they were made to down a salt-based concoction, and were tucked. This involved making an incision with the finger-nail in the lip, or an abrasion from the chin to the lip, sufficient to cause a flow of blood. The rite might also include the administration of an oath by the senior cook, to be sworn upon an old shoe which each initiate was required reverently to kiss.[222] The prevalence of these practices can be indexed in student accounts,

[218] BL Harl. MS 7031, fo. 27v.
[219] These did not meet with the approval of all members of all colleges. At St John's in the 1570s, one group asked for the abolition of games at Christmas (CUL MS Mm. i. 38, p. 79). Similarly, in 1586, John Smith of Christ's used the occasion of an Ash Wednesday sermon to attack the custom of allowing plays to be performed in the colleges on Saturday and Sunday evenings as a breach of the sabbath (Gray 1926, p. 113). For subversive drama at Cambridge, Folger Shakespeare Library, MS v.b.303, pp. 301–3.
[220] Ball 1918, p. 215. The stang was a wooden pole on which the victim was tied, and carried ignominiously through the courts of his college. 'In some colleges in the University of Cambridge; to stang scholars in Christmas, being to cause them to ride on a colt-staff or pole for missing chappel' (John Ray, *A Collection of English Words not Generally Used*, London, 1674). There are references in the account books of Trinity, St John's, Queens' and Christ's to the place where the pole was kept.
[221] Trinity College Muniments, Masters' Old Conclusion Book, 1607–73, p. 188.
[222] Mullinger 1884, pp. 400–1; Marsden 1851, p. 15; Bowers 1941–2.

for the freshmen were required to pay for the beer consumed on the occasion.[223]

These saltings were evidently riotous occasions that threatened the authority of the college authorities. At Trinity College, in 1646, complaint was made of 'the Sophisters pronesse, to unsufferable Abuses, which arise by the permission of salting nights'. Future meetings were banned and the sophisters were admonished to carry themselves in all 'Civilitie and without noyse or upon those nights . . . formerly soe called'.[224]

Many of these practices, such as the election of a lord of misrule, had their roots in a period before any significant influx of aristocrats into the universities. Yet their presence cannot but have reinvigorated the counter-culture of these institutions. Unlike those students intent upon obtaining a degree, aristocratic students were a positive source of income to their college, and they knew it. Unlike those students who were held by necessity to the rigours of the curriculum, aristocratic students had to a much greater extent the resources and the opportunities to plot mischief. They also had the inclination to do so as a means of asserting their role as leaders. Numerous details support this interpretation, but nowhere is it better exemplified in a coherent manner than in the recollections of Anthony Ashley Cooper, the future earl of Shaftesbury. Although he was a student at Oxford rather than Cambridge, the evidence suggests that in these respects the two universities were quite similar.[225] As well as being a moderately benevolent gang-leader in town and country, he attempted to reform the college.[226] He sometimes manifested those skills of leadership and management that he so notably displayed in his maturity. The senior

---

[223] Maitland 1847, p. 520, 2 shillings paid for the salting of Henry Gates in 1570; Elveden Hall, Suffolk, Cornwallis MSS, Box 3, no. 2 (no foliation), 'The chordges of Mr William at skoll in Cambrigg . . .', 1561–2.

[224] Trinity College Muniments, Masters' Old Conclusion Book, 1607–73, p. 188.

[225] See below, pp. 249–51; Christie 1871, I, pp. 15–18.

[226] Christie 1871, II, Appendix I, pp. xi–xiii. However, not all parents or guardians were willing to indulge their offspring and wards in this way. Sir Christopher Heydon criticised the manner in which his son 'sequestreth him self from the commons in the hall and associateth him self wth others in his privat chambre. it was not wont to be the manner of studentes when I was in Cambridge, neyther can I lyke it in him; For besides the disordre, though I have not fayled to furnishe him with all that is neces-sary, yet I meane not to maynteyne others under his charge' (Gonville and Caius College Library, MS 73/40, fo. 369. Sir Christopher Heydon to Giles Fletcher, fellow of the College, August 1602). In the 1660s, Sir Edward Bagot expressed his fears of the consequences of the similar popularity of his son, 'hee haveing the good fortune to be liked by most, they doe some of them too much to his face Commend him; which I feare may Create in him too heigh an oppinion of him selfe . . . too high thoughts off his owne merits; may make him incapable of good Counsell' (Folger Shakespeare Library, MS L.a.47). Ashley Cooper's subsequent career persuades one that Sir Edward's fears for his son may have been well placed.

fellows at Exeter attempted to reduce the strength of the college beer; 'I hindered their design.' News of their intention

> put all the younger sort into a mutiny; they resorting to me, I advised all those were intended by their friends to get their livelihood by their studies to rest quiet and not appear, and that myself and all the others that were elder brothers or unconcerned in their angers should go in a body and strike our names out of the buttery book, which was accordingly done, and had the effect that the senior fellows, seeing their pupils going that yielded them most profit, presently struck sail and articled with us never to alter the size of our beer, which remains so to this day.[227]

The universities, along with schools,[228] could be repressive regimes, concerned with the inculcation of youth with an established body of knowledge through rigorous and well-tried techniques of teaching. The psychological and intellectual pressures thus generated had called into being brief periods during which the normal rules were suspended and steam let off. Therefore, a counter-culture had existed in the universities even before the major influx of aristocratic students during the late sixteenth century. What then happened was that the leadership of this counter-culture was taken over and exploited for its own purposes by the aristocrats. Because of their relative independence and assertive demeanour, under their leadership the counter-culture became less of a safety valve and more of a real threat to the formally constituted authorities in the universities and in individual colleges. Thus threatened, senior academics either attempted to regulate the occasions of misrule, as in the case of college plays, or else attempted to abolish them, as in the case of saltings at St John's and Trinity. In adopting either tactic in response to the threat from below, masters and senior fellows ultimately could only turn to the greater authority represented by the central government in order to bolster their standing in general, or on particular occasions. Thus, in effect, the changing sociology of the university prompted its managers to invoke the powers of central government in support of their own authority.

[227] Christie 1871, II, Appendix I, pp. xi–xii.   [228] Thomas 1976b, p. 14.

Chapter 5

CAMBRIDGE AND PARLIAMENT

PARLIAMENT AND CAMBRIDGE

The history of the relationship between the state and the universities has always involved a paradox. As the preceding chapters have amply demonstrated, when the universities have been of serious concern to the wider society they have not been able to avoid the attentions of the government of the day. For the universities, an untroubled somnolence has only been bought at the cost of irrelevance to the vital concerns of the moment. If this is indeed a recurrent paradox in the history of the universities there are, none the less, distinctions to be drawn. For example, it is in the sixteenth and seventeenth centuries that the universities first become objects of sustained concern to the legislature and not just on the part of the executive. Far more often than is the case today, parliament articulated the diverse and often competing concerns of a wider society with what they saw in wholly new ways as 'their' universities.[1] The story of the universities in parliament in this way demonstrates yet again the increasing centrality in the sixteenth and seventeenth centuries of the universities in general and of Cambridge in particular to the concerns of the state and of the wider society. This was followed by the relative marginalisation of the universities from the 1670s onwards. The same trajectory is repeated in the case of the universities in parliament.

The issues related to the universities that are embedded in parliamentary debate and legislation are but one facet of more broadly seated concerns with those institutions and that manifest themselves in other contexts in both Court and country. This consideration of the place of Cambridge University in parliament may serve as a corrective to an all too discernible practice of treating issues in parliament in this period in isolation from the broader context in which they occur. This approach

---

[1] I have attempted elsewhere to provide an initial demonstration of the 'seamless' perspective of contemporaries as a corrective to the too often 'compartmentalised' viewpoint of the modern historian: see Morgan 1984.

may help to shift our perspective on parliamentary history; it may help us to perceive it as others at the time saw it.

There are, then, two main themes that run through the handling of the universities in parliament in these years. The first manifests the proprietorial attitude adopted by the majority of the aristocracy towards these institutions. This attitude derived from the direct investment by many families in providing endowments for the colleges: they were, in effect, protecting their investments, or those of their ancestors. The second theme was manifested as part of a larger concern with the maintenance of religion, or, more often, the attempts to use parliament to complete a reformation that many considered had stalled and to remodel a church 'but halfly reformed'.[2] In the context of religion the universities were important on three grounds: first, as institutions where an increasing proportion of the scions of aristocratic families were receiving their education; second, as seminaries in which were educated the clergy who were to spread the gospel in the countryside; third, as unique centres of theologically directed scholarship, for the universities brought together the men and the books that were required to provide the armoury for international doctrinal disputation.[3] It was these roles that underlay contemporary allusions to the universities as at one and the same time 'nurseries', 'seminaries' and 'fountains'.

While on the one hand the aristocracy claimed a proprietorial interest because of their investments, and manifested a broadly based concern with the religious functions of the universities, on the other hand the Crown could not but resist the encroachments on its prerogatives implicit in these concerns, as they were articulated in parliament. For while the conflict of interests was for the most part latent rather than realised, it remains true, none the less, that the Crown considered the universities as very much part of its own bailiwick. The universities as such, and individual colleges within each university, depended for their corporate existence on an exercise of the royal prerogative under the Great Seal. More broadly, under Elizabeth and the first two Stuarts, the Crown and its ministers continued to oppose what it considered to be meddling in religious matters by members of the Commons: matters that the Crown considered were none of their business. Therefore, whenever the subject of the universities arose in parliament there arose also a potential clash of interests as a consequence of the new and intense concern with the universities on the part of both the aristocracy and the Crown. If the attention given to the universities in parliament was not always welcome

[2] Collinson 1967, p. 29.   [3] Below, chapter 12.

to those institutions, nor to individuals or factions within them, it is also true that the changing nature of the universities, and of individual colleges, made them seek parliamentary protection for their interests. The ebb and flow of parliamentary interest in the universities is in itself a useful indicator of shifts of interest in other contexts.

In 1604 James I granted the universities the right to send their representatives to sit in the Commons. This was the outcome of an agitation for representation that stretched back at least as far as 1566.[4] During the intervening period there had been a number of requests for the right of representation, and in the arguments supporting these requests can be found two types of evidence: the first is for the changing status and interests of the universities; the second the changing social and legislative environment with which the universities had to deal. The grant of parliamentary representation was, in a general sense, a recognition of the unique status that the universities had acquired during the sixteenth century. At this time the universities experienced a change in their social composition, an increase in their scale, and the acquisition of a much augmented role as seminaries and a newly important role as arsenals for doctrinal disputation. The grants of a charter in 1561, and of new statutes in 1570, were recognitions of these developments that, at the same time, enhanced the identity of Cambridge University as a corporation.[5] The creation of this jurisdictional and administrative enclave is all the more remarkable when it is recalled that the overall trend of Tudor policy was towards the reduction of the number and privileges of traditional liberties and immunities.[6] Further evidence of this enhanced corporate identity is the apparently greater activity of the university's Consistory Court, and that of the Commissary, together with the enhanced role of

---

[4] *De Burgensibus*, Letters Patent, 12 March 1604; CUA, Charter of James I (Luard 195); CUA, c.3.c, Attorney General Coke to the university. The standard study of university representation in parliament is Rex 1954. For the agitation for representation, see Rex 1954, pp. 24–5; Humberstone 1951, p. 16.

[5] Above, chapter 3.

[6] For the general Tudor policy on the reduction of liberties see a thoughtful and neglected review article, James 1967; Morgan 2001, pp. 298–9. There is evidence for the treatment of the universities as in some senses 'liberties', even before the process of Elizabethan corporatisation. In part this may have derived from the ecclesiastical privileges they enjoyed *vis-à-vis* the dioceses in which they were located, and the immunities they had acquired from municipal regulation (for the latter see ch. 7). However, in the sixteenth century their standing was carried beyond these local exemptions. In the parliamentary context the claim to the status of liberties is evident, for example, in a debate on a Marian bill for the regulation of purveyors. The purveyors were prohibited from taking within 5 miles of the universities (*CJ*, I, pp. 45b, 46a). See also similar proposals for exemption in *CJ*, I, pp. 91a,b, 92a,b, and for the addition of a proviso in a bill for towns, preserving liberties of the universities, *CJ*, I, p. 40b. Subsequently, the universities were treated as if they were on a par with the Cinque Ports and the stannaries (Notestein, Relf and Simpson 1935, III, pp. 37, 39, 85; also IV, pp. 242–3).

vice-chancellor as JP. Characteristically, in 1587, a request to Burghley for parliamentary representation was combined with a petition for separate JPs.[7]

From later comment it is clear that contemporaries considered that it was primarily the corporate institution rather than the individuals within it which was to be represented in parliament. In a petition for representation of the clergy that probably dates from the last years of Elizabeth's reign the two notions of representation are combined:

> Though the clergy and the universities be not the worst members of this common-wealth, yet in that respect they are of all the other in worst condition; for in that assembly every shire hath their knights, and every incorporate town their burgesses, only the clergy and the universites are excluded.
>
> The wisdom and justice of this realm doth intend, that no subject should be bound to that law, whereunto he himself (after a sort) hath not yielded his consent; but the clergy and the universities may now be concluded by law, without their consent, without their just defence, without their privity.[8]

However, in the minds of many contemporaries there was an equation of scholars and fellows within a college with the status of servants within a domestic household.[9] As such the theory and practice of the time held them not to be eligible for direct representation of their interests: as servants they were not enfranchised members of the political nation. This attitude was evident in the disputes that arose over the franchise that was to be employed within the university for the election of its MPs. Not unnaturally, the majority of its members favoured a broad franchise to ensure the representation of their interest and as a means of ensuring a platform in parliament for voicing discontent with the oligarchic authority of the

---

[7] Above, pp. 94–6; BL Lansdowne MS 51, fo. 146v (no. 62), 'Reasons to have Justices of Peace of ye University', '. . . To have ii burgesses in parliament, expedient for the necessary defence of the lib[er]ties of ye universities lest any thing through untrue nisriance[?] or ignorance of some thinges might be enacted, or pretermitted to the hinderance of the universitie.' In their conflicts with the town, the university had previously obtained the appointment of JPs in 1552 (Cooper, *Annals*, II, p. 63 (request for JPs); BL Lansdowne MS 3, fo. 31 (no. 16); copy in Lansdowne MS 115, fo. 169 (no. 65), Privy Council letter 27 Nov. 1552 implying appointment of JPs to oversee persons privileged by the university).

[8] 'Reasons to induce her majesty, that deans, archdeacons, and some other of her grave and wise clergy, may be admitted into the lower house of parliament', clauses 6 and 7. The original of this MS cannot be traced. It is printed in Burnet 1865, V, p. 175. These two notions of representation are also combined in Glanville's remark that the purpose of university representation was 'to serve for those students who, though useful members of the community, were neither concerned in the landed or the trading interests, and to protect in the Legislature the rights of the Republic of Letters' (Glanville 1768, p. 11).

[9] This concept is discussed more fully on p. 268 below.

heads of colleges: the enfranchised 'masters' of great 'households'. In part at least this seems to be one of the motivations behind the disputed election of 1614.[10] In a debate in 1623 the conception underlying the more restricted franchise was unequivocally stated. Members of the university had attempted to vote at the county election, but, it was argued, 'He, that hath a Chamber, cometh not in by Livery and Seisin, nor by Deed enrolled: No assise lieth. The Freehold of it is in the Corporation [of the college]: His Fellowship, [is] like Wages and Dyet, given a Servant.'[11]

It was, then, the institution, rather than the persons within it, that was represented. Furthermore, it was a true measure of the peculiar structure and status of the university as it had developed during the sixteenth century that this doctrine should have prevailed in a period in which the liberties, immunities and privileges of most other corporations were being reduced.[12]

The desire on the part of the universities to enhance their separate corporate identities by means such as the acquisition of their own JPs and MPs arose in part from their long-standing conflicts with their environing boroughs. Perennial though this conflict had been, changing circumstances exacerbated it during the sixteenth century. From the viewpoint of the university the dissolution of the religious houses may have removed one source of intervention in its affairs – from religious houses to which a few were attached – but it had also abolished influential corporations, and cut it off from a clerical elite of priors and abbots who could have exercised themselves on behalf of the university against the town through their influence both outside and inside parliament. The dissolution left the university that much more exposed not only to the Crown, but also to its immediate neighbour.[13]

The changes in the social composition and the scale of the university created problems for the city authorities no less than for the university itself. The presence of the university in the town enhanced the problems of policing, social control and poor relief experienced by most urban places

---

[10] Rex 1954, pp. 58–60, 63–5; Moir 1958, pp. 39–41; Jesus College Cambridge Archives, Dr Duport MSS.

[11] *CJ*, I, p. 714b, 28 May 1623. For the electoral franchises operated at Cambridge, Rex 1954, pp. 58–60. For discussion of contemporary notions of what was represented in parliament, see Dean 1990; Dean and Jones 1998, pp. 2–5.

[12] Interestingly, by 1621, it was being argued in parliament, in a debate on the commission of the peace, that 'Universityes have their priviledges, Mechanicall Trades divers encouradgments' (Notestein *et al.* 1935, IV, p. 284). In the same parliament, in the debate on a petition by Magdalene College, Coke argued that Dr Gooch spoke not for himself but for the corporation of the college (*ibid.*, III, p. 159). See the remarks attributed to Wentworth (*ibid.*, IV, p. 700).

[13] See below, p. 275; Fuller 1665/1840, pp. 240–1.

in this period.[14] Physical expansion alone encroached upon the jurisdiction of the corporation. The invigoration of the university's Commissary Court intruded upon the regulation of commercial affairs normally dealt with by the civic authorities in comparable boroughs. The supervision of Stourbridge Fair must have constituted a similar challenge.[15] The exemption of privileged individuals from the jurisdiction of the borough was a slight both to its status and to its income.[16] In these circumstances of continuous and intensifying local warfare it was necessary for the university to cultivate its contacts at Court in order to protect its interests.[17] The acquisition of MPs was simply an extension into the parliamentary arena of this general policy of seeking representation and protection. As such it affords a contemporary and a more seamless perspective on attitudes towards parliament than appears when that institution is studied in isolation. It helps to explain the practice of the university of electing courtiers as their parliamentary representatives. This not only gave the universities influential representatives in parliament: it also helped to create an obligation to the university on the part of the courtier that would last beyond the termination of a brief parliament. It was likely to be of lasting value in that permanent central institution of politics at this time – the Court.[18]

Following the acquisition of representation, the burgesses for the universities were provided with an *aide-mémoire* to justify their presence in the Commons. This included the argument that 'commonly, the Townes are aginst the Universities, and ever ready to oppugne their lib[er]ties: and there fore it is necessary for them [the universities] to have some to enforme' the House of Commons, '. . . lest Prejudicial action be taken against the Universities'.[19] The sixteenth century had seen the augmentation of the position of the colleges within the university. Unlike most of the ephemeral halls which they superseded, the colleges were

---

[14] In general see Clark and Slack 1976, and for Cambridge, Goose 1980.

[15] Cooper, *Annals*, II, pp. 468–9; Siraut 1978.

[16] Rex 1954, pp. 25, 34, for discussion on this motive for acquiring MPs. Rex does not place her discussion in the appropriate context: the social and economic expansion of the university.

[17] This was one of the main roles of the newly created office of Orator, and is evident in both his rhetorical and his epistolary efforts. For further example see a letter from the university to Sir Robert Clarke, one of the barons of the exchequer. Sir Robert is asked to dismiss the case against certain Cambridge brewers, who had been granted a privilege by the university. The university goes on to complain of its poverty as a result of 'the continuall mayetenaunce of these pr[i]vileges' (CUA, Lett. 11.A.C.3.A).

[18] For the tendency to elect courtiers, see Rex 1954, p. 35 and *passim*; and for their ongoing commitments, Willson 1940, pp. 75–6.

[19] BL Cotton MS Faustina c.VII, fos. 183–6 (no. 28); and see the claim in 1587, quoted above, p. 150 n. 7. See also, e.g., SP 14/124/31, 'Advertisementes for the universitie of Oxford', which includes matters to be watched over in parliament in 1621.

institutions in perpetuity, capable of holding and acquiring property. Indeed, the university can be envisaged as a federal structure. Within that structure there were numerous differences of financial resources and statutory requirements between one college and another. The augmentation of endowments during the sixteenth and seventeenth centuries served to elaborate these complexities yet further.[20] It was the interests of the corporations of the individual colleges, as much as that of the university as a whole, that required representation in parliament. Attorney General Coke recognised this in the letter which accompanied the patent granting the right of representation. Coke recalled matters relating to the universities that had arisen during his time as Speaker and noted that the colleges had 'Locall Statutes and ordynances prescribed to them by their founders, as well for the disposing and preserving of their possessions as for the good government and vertuous educacon of studentes and Schollers', and it was not 'possible for any one generall Lawe to fitt every particuler Colledge especially when their pryvate Statutes and ordynances be not knowne'. Consequently, Coke claimed to have initiated the suit for two burgesses 'that may informe (as occasion shall be offered) that high Court of the true State of the University and of every particuler Colledge'.[21]

It could have been argued that the predominantly clerical element in the universities was adequately represented in Convocation, and at one time this might have been true.[22] But as the colleges became substantial landowners, and as both the volume and the range of concerns of parliamentary statutory provision increased, there were many aspects of the temporal role of the colleges that were best represented and safeguarded in the Commons rather than in the Convocation House. It is notable that the petition of *c.* 1603 in favour of representation equates the universities with the clergy, claiming that compared with all other groups they are 'in worst condition'.[23] In addition there was an associated complex of reasons for the pursuit of clerical and university representation in the Commons.

In the first place, if the lower clergy had been restored to the Commons they would have gained a platform from which to conduct their disputes with the spiritual peers in the Lords, and one in which the

[20] Below, pp. 186 ff.
[21] CUA, Lett. 11.A. C.3.c. Coke was Speaker in 1593. The need of which Coke writes is evident in the number of bills promoted by individual colleges, and most notably in the election of Barnaby Gooch, the master of Magdalene, as MP for the university in the 1620s. Gooch used his position to pursue in parliament the dispute of his college with the earl of Oxford over the ownership of a lucrative estate in London. For a summary of the circumstances of this dispute see below, pp. 175–6.
[22] Graves in Dean and Jones 1990.
[23] Burnet 1865, V, p. 175, quoted above, p. 150.

ecclesiastical authorities would not have been able to exercise the degree of control with which they manipulated Convocation.[24] In the second place, we may speculate as to the influence of the developing notion of the university as seminary. This encompassed a view of the universities as arsenals for the manufacture of the weaponry for international theological disputation.[25] As such there may have developed a belief that these vital institutions should articulate their findings in the forum of parliament and inform the debates on religion that animated that institution. It is probably no coincidence that the unsuccessful petition of 1584 by the universities for representation was followed by a petition to parliament on ecclesiastical matters. This had as one of its aims the enhancement of the opportunities for study for the purpose of furthering disputatious scholarship.[26] The second of these proposals, and no doubt the first too, met with a dismissive rebuttal on the part of the bishops.[27]

Finally, we may conclude that the pursuit of parliamentary representation on the part of the universities was a reflection of the increasing importance of parliament in and of itself as one of a number of means for the resolution of a wide range of difficulties. It is now increasingly clear that much of the legislation of the late sixteenth and early seventeenth centuries arose from local experience and private initiatives.[28] Along with other institutions and individuals, the universities and individual colleges within the universities resorted to parliament to achieve their ends. For example, the executors of the countess of Sussex wished to purchase the site of the dissolved house of the Greyfriars at Cambridge as the site for Sidney Sussex College. However, the current owners, Trinity College, were prohibited by both their own statutes and the statutes of the realm from making any such permanent alienation. Clearly, the executors wished to secure a firm title for the new foundation, and they therefore obtained a private Act to permit Trinity to make the sale.[29]

Again, parliament could be used to ratify and make more secure agreements reached in lower courts. For example, disagreements had arisen between King's College as landlord and its tenants of the manor of

---

[24] A similar point is made by Mullinger 1884, pp. 305–6. Rex is rather dismissive of it, but it tends to be supported by more recent work on both parliament and puritanism.

[25] Below, pp. 441–54.   [26] Strype 1824, III, pp. 320–9 and III, 2, pp. 278–317.

[27] Neale 1957, pp. 58–71.

[28] See, for example, Bindoff 1961, pp. 59–94; Pound 1962, p. 149; Smith 1979, pp. 93–110; Elton 1979b; Morgan 1984, pp. 39–64; Elton 1986, pp. 43–61, 303–18; Dean and Jones 1990; Dean 1996; Cust 1992; Smith 1999.

[29] House of Lords Record Office, Main Papers, H.L., 24 March 1593, draft of 'An Act that the site of the later dissolved house of the Gray Friars . . .', and 35 Eliz. c. 2 (Private Acts); *LJ*, II, p. 181a; see above, pp. 19–20.

Ruislip over fines and rentals. These contentions had been ended by an agreement by consent, and a decree in Chancery was obtained to establish the indenture of agreement. Subsequently, the tenants sought further assurance of their composition, purportedly with the agreement of the college. They petitioned parliament for an Act so that 'the said Composicon and agreement maye soe be established ratyfied and confirmed, as that the same maye never hereafter be ympugned dissolved or ympeached'.[30]

Parliament could also be used to reverse the decisions of lower courts. This is what Magdalen College, Oxford, attempted to do in connection with a decision in Chancery which had gone against them over some of their lands in Northamptonshire.[31] Doubts about the corporate status of a college such as Wadham could be finally resolved by an Act of Parliament, as could uncertainties over a grant of property to Cambridge by letters patent, for no 'other conveyaunce or assurance might be had or devised so effectuall and sufficient in the lawe as by authority of Parliam[en]t they might be made'.[32] On occasion individuals petitioned parliament for the redress of grievances that had arisen in the context of the university. In 1641, Dr Metcalfe petitioned the Commons that as Hebrew Professor at Cambridge he was eligible for a senior fellowship, whereas he was only preferred to a junior fellowship.[33] As in Metcalfe's case, the House was loath to intervene in these instances of individual local grievance. We may surmise that those in charge of business in the House were unwilling to clutter up its proceedings with the time-consuming specifics of cases of this type. Also, the very localised and specific nature of many such

[30] HLRO, Main Papers, H.C., 1 June 1614, draft of 'An Act for the Confirmation of an indenture . . .'. For some further evidence of colleges in pursuit of parliamentary action see *HMCS*, XVIII, p. 43; Willson 1931, p. 73 (Corpus Christi College, Oxford); *ibid.*, p. 252 (All Souls College, Oxford); Brentnall 1980, p. 295 (Oriel College, Oxford). But it was not only Oxford that had business in James I's first parliament: the vice-chancellor of Cambridge also seems to have been in attendance in London 'this Parliament time' (*HMCS*, XVIII, p. 47), probably about an Act for the confirmation of a grant to the university (HLRO, Main Papers (Supplementary), H.L., 26 February 1606). There were also to be attempts to resolve a long-standing dispute over Emmanuel College by means of parliamentary legislation (D'Ewes 1942, p. 326). See also Private Acts, 27 Eliz. 'An Act for Confirmation of her Majesty's Letters, Patent to the Queen's College in Oxford'; 27 Eliz. c. 2; 35 Eliz. c. 2; 43 Eliz. c. 8. These references are illustrative rather than exhaustive.

[31] HLRO, Main Papers (Supplementary), H.L. [? 1623], draft of 'An Acte for the Reversinge of a decree unduely obteyned in Chauncery . . .'. Similarly, in 1621, Pym noted that Dr Gooch preferred a petition on behalf of Magdalene College 'for Remedie against a Decree of Chancery . . .' (Notestein *et al.* 1935, IV, p. 299).

[32] HLRO, Main Papers (Supplementary), H.C., 1 March 1621, a version of 21 James I c. 1 (Private Acts); HLRO, Main Papers (Supplementary), 26 February 1606. In order to resolve his dispute with Magdalene College, the earl of Oxford petitioned an Act of Parliament 'for the better confirmacon and corroboracon of . . . severall decrees in Chauncery', in the Court of Wards, and by letters of Privy Seal (HLRO, Parchment Collection (Box 178), H.L., 4 March 1624).

[33] Notestein 1923, p 415 n. 2.

grievances meant that they were unable to elicit a broad interest within the House. As with similar matters brought before the Privy Council or the assize judges there was a general inclination to refer these matters for resolution elsewhere by those who could be better informed and who had more leisure to evaluate the merits of the case.

In 1628 the supposed preoccupation of the bishop of Lincoln with the business of the House of Lords was used as a pretext to resolve a dispute over an election from Eton to King's. Kenelm Jennour petitioned the House to settle the matter themselves, or refer it to the bishop as Visitor of the college. The House took the latter course.[34] Similarly, when a dispute arose over an election at Caius in 1624, a disgruntled fellow was advised that if he did bring it before parliament it would only be referred back to the Visitors of the college.[35]

These instances illustrate three points. First, the extent to which institutions and individuals looked to parliament for the redress of particular grievances has perhaps not been fully appreciated by historians preoccupied with the set pieces of constitutional conflict. Second, they suggest that in some cases a complaint to parliament was just another gambit in waging law. It could serve as a means of prompting a more expeditious settlement of issues elsewhere, and the petitioners had no especial desire for a specifically legislative resolution of their difficulties. Third, they indicate that at this prosaic level parliament was familiar enough with a custom in which university issues were brought before it. So, when a large set-piece political matter such as the election of the duke of Buckingham as chancellor of the university arose in 1626, both Lords and Commons were habituated to dealing with the affairs of the universities. The difference was that the matter of the duke raised issues that had not arisen on most of the relatively trivial occasions when they had been acquiring their habits. This *cause célèbre* brought elements in the two houses into a conflict with the Crown's prerogative.[36] But even this conflict had been implicit over a longer period during which colleges and individuals sought by parliamentary means to confirm or reverse grants by the Crown.

To the evidence for the occurrence of university business in parliament must be added the familiarity of parliament-men with the universities as a result of their own earlier educational experiences. The evidence is substantial for the increase in attendance of future MPs at Oxford and

---

[34] HLRO, Main Papers, H.L., 20 May 1628, petition and endorsement. Jennour seems to have failed to achieve the ultimate purpose of his supplication, although a son, Henry, entered Trinity College in the autumn of 1628 (Venn, II, p. 471b).

[35] Cosin 1869–72, I, p. 16.   [36] Morgan forthcoming.

Plate 21 Two of the three Esquire Bedells' maces given by the duke of
Buckingham when he was chancellor, 1626–8

Cambridge.[37] Nowhere was the awareness of this familiarity more manifest than in the regular debates on the Subsidy Bill – and what was a
parliament without a subsidy? In almost every parliament this became
the occasion for the display of eloquence and loyalty on the part of

[37] Cf. below, p. 232.

157

alumni who attempted to argue the precedence in naming of Cambridge or Oxford.[38] Just as the Court and the Crown became more intimately involved with the universities during the course of the sixteenth and early seventeenth centuries, so too did parliament and parliament-men take an increasing interest in their affairs. In 1621, John Chamberlain noted that both the universities and the towns of Cambridge and Oxford 'have had but yll proofe this parlement' because for various reasons their MPs had not been sitting.[39] Chamberlain's passing comment encapsulated the significance that parliament had acquired in the life of the universities, and the importance of the universities, and of university alumni, in the deliberations of both Lords and Commons. All in all, there was an increased familiarity with the affairs of the universities on the part of parliament-men. Consequently, parliament became an arena within which there was articulated both intervention in the affairs of the universities, and an opposition to that intervention, as it manifested itself both inside parliament and outside its confines.

When the universities, their constituent colleges or individual members resorted to parliament they were doing no more and no less than many other groups and individuals were doing at this time: they were using one of the many instruments provided by the state for the resolution of their problems. The difference was that – increasingly – parliament appeared to offer the most certain, the most secure and the most conclusive resolution of these problems. Therefore, as part of a spectrum of means, and as the most certain of those means, the parliamentary option must often have been there in prospect, as a thought in mind. If this was the case then this brief examination of university concerns in parliament has implications for the current debate on whether parliament was an event or an institution.[40] For one of the criteria for the existence of an institution must be its continuity. One of the arguments in favour of parliament being an event and not an institution was its undoubtedly brief and intermittent existence, a circumstance that – discounting the anomaly of the 1640s – prevailed until the very late seventeenth century. But continuity surely resides in something more than simply regularity and permanence of session: in some degree it must also reside in the minds of those for whom it was something in prospect, a thought in mind. Paradoxically, the very prosaic nature of some of the concerns taken to parliament helped to anchor it within the thoughts of a wide range of individuals. Its

[38] See, for example, *CJ*, I, p. 275a and Willson 1931, pp. 55–6; Notestein *et al.* 1935, IV, I, pp. 144–5, cf. *ibid.*, IV, pp. 34–5; VI, p. 381; Notestein 1923, p. 212. See also *CJ*, I, p. 449b; Notestein *et al.* 1935, VII, p. 618.

[39] Chamberlain 1939, pp. 369–70.   [40] Russell 1976, pp. 1–27; 1979; 1983.

perceived role as one means among many, albeit at the furthest end of a whole spectrum of means, to achieve the ends of individuals and groups, gave it a life and meaning beyond the irregular and intermittent nature of its summons or the brevity of its sessions.

A recurrent theme of this volume has been the intricate interconnectedness in this period of the history of the university with the wider society. In the relationship between university and parliament we have another instance of the way the university became firmly embedded in its environing society over the course of the latter half of the sixteenth century. Furthermore, the perspective afforded by the history of one institution, the university, helps to clarify something of another, parliament.

CORRUPT ELECTIONS

The corruption of elections in colleges was one of the areas in which there was criticism in parliament over practices within the universities. As such, the initiative for these criticisms arose from outside the universities and can be viewed as an intervention in their affairs. However, over the years the role of external mediators – patronage brokers – in facilitating these corruptions became more pronounced. In this respect criticism of corruption in college elections was criticism of their increasing involvement with outside intervention, and an intervention that, as we have seen, was often solicited at Court.[41]

There are indications that the criticism of corruption in elections at the universities had been voiced prior to the major changes they underwent during Elizabeth's reign. As early as 1513 there were complaints of open bribery in the election of university officers 'so as to arouse the indignation of the good, the derision of laymen, and the talk of the vulgar', while in 1554 a bill was introduced into the Commons that from its title appears to have been directed towards the same problem. However, as we have seen, the first clear indication of parliamentary criticism of such practices came in the session of 1575–6.[42] Having passed both Houses the bill proposed for the reform of these abuses was vetoed by the queen.[43] The issue came up again some eight years later, in the parliament of 1584. There, it occurred in a petition for a preaching and learned

---

[41] Above, pp. 104–6.

[42] Heywood 1855, I, p. 135; *CJ*, I, pp. 34b, 35a. The Bill for Elections of Scholars in the Universities: see below, p. 356.

[43] The first reading in the Commons followed the second reading of a bill for the maintenance of the colleges in the universities. Their interrelated progress can be traced in *CJ*, I, pp. 108b, 110a, 111b, 112a, 113b; D'Ewes 1682; *LJ*, I, pp. 743b, 745a, 746a; Strype 1822, I, pp. 148–9. I presume that it is this bill that is referred to allusively by Elton 1986, p. 125.

ministry. The petition complained of electors who admitted scholars and fellows in return for bribes, and of others who resigned their places for money. Electors were enjoined to consider only the aptness and poverty of the candidates, and in doing so to respect the wishes of the founders of the colleges. In context, it is clear that this attempted intervention in the affairs of the universities arose from the efforts of puritan clergy to achieve further reformation through the activities of their lay supporters in the Commons.[44] As such, the remarks on corruptions in the universities made in their petition implied two propositions. First, that, as in the church-at-large, those in positions of responsibility – such as the heads of colleges – were prepared to tolerate the corruptions that were being criticised. Second, that increasingly the universities were looked to as the unique fountains from which were to issue forth both a godly learned ministry and a stream of exegetical and disputative scholarship.[45]

It is hardly surprising that, emerging from this context, these proposals for the universities were not proceeded with. However, some five years later, similar complaints did result in an Act intended to deal with the corruptions complained of in 1584. The Act of 1589 (31 Eliz. c. 6) outlawed the taking of bribes by electors on pain of the election becoming void and the right of presentation then devolving to the queen. To deal with those who resigned their places for payment, a fine was set for the recipient of double the amount paid. Those for whose entry payment was made were declared ineligible for election on that occasion. To assist in the maintenance of due procedures in elections it was required that the relevant local statutes should be publicly read at the time of the election. Those who defaulted on this responsibility were subject to a fine of £40.[46]

---

[44] Strype 1824, III, 2, p. 299; Neale 1953, pp. 60 ff. Elton has noted that in the parliaments between 1559 and 1581, Elizabeth was most active in blocking bills touching on religion and in vetoing bills that seemed not to serve the general interest (Elton 1986, pp. 123, 125). More recent work enforced a revision of Neale's original conception of a 'puritan opposition'. None the less, even Elton acknowledges that parliament became 'one of the arenas where those dissatisfied with the condition of the Church tried to promote reform' (Elton 1986, pp. 198–9, 350–5. See also Graves and Silcock 1984, ch. 6).

[45] Below, chapter 12.

[46] HLRO, Main Papers (Supplementary), H.L., 6 March 1589 [1 and 2], two drafts substantially the same as that printed in *Statutes of the Realm*. Version 1 is entitled 'An Acte for the avoiding of abuses in chosing of Fellowes schollers & other p[er]sons into Rowmes & places in colleges, Churches collegiat Churches Cathedrall halles hospitalls scholes & other like societies'; version 2 is entitled 'An Acte for the Avoydinge of Abuses in choseinge of Fellowes & . . . Scollers into Colledges Churches collegyeat and other Lyke societies'. The general tenor of version 2 is more narrowly restricted to the circumstances of fellows of colleges, compared with the more sophisticated wording and wider terms of reference in version 1, which more nearly approximates to the version in *Statutes of the Realm*.

The petition of 1589 had also complained of the 'ill usage of the masters of colleges', and it may be that the passage of the Act of 1589 served to shift parliamentary attention from elections in general to the role of the masters within colleges. Certainly, during the 1590s and early 1600s, this is the more dominant theme. This preoccupation may also owe something to a wider awareness of the crucial changes in masterships that were taking place in those years.[47] None the less, the cases that are examined below indicate that irregularities continued, and there is evidence of continuing concern in parliament with the problem of corrupt elections in the universities. It next emerges as a theme in the parliaments of the 1620s.

A bill was introduced into the 1621 parliament 'to prevent Simony, and Abuse of Elections in Colleges and Halls', but was not proceeded upon.[48] A bill with the same title was introduced into the Commons in the following parliament, in March 1624. Again, it proceeded only a little further than its predecessor, being lost in committee.[49] In the 1624 parliament a bill with a similar purport but a somewhat different title received a first reading in the Lords. As in a number of other instances in the parliamentary context, as for example in the petition of 1584, the title suggests that the universities were being treated as part of a larger clerical apparatus.[50] The Oxford Parliament of 1625 was, perhaps, too busy with other matters even to entertain a general bill on this theme, but a version again appears in the equally fraught parliament of 1626, proceeding as far as the committee stage. The title recalled that of its equally abortive predecessor, introduced into the Lords in 1624.[51] It seems likely that these two bills, originating in different Houses in different parliaments, are generally related. If this is the case then it provides further evidence of the co-operative relationship between elements in the Lords and in the Commons that have been detected at work on matters relating to Cambridge and to other matters during the parliaments of the 1620s.[52] The issue of elections at the universities does not arise again in general terms in the later parliaments of that decade, although in the parliament of 1628 the Lords did receive a private petition complaining

---

[47] See below, chapter 8.   [48] *CJ*, I, p. 626a, first reading.
[49] *CJ*, I, p. 684b, first reading; p. 735b, another similar bill, preferred by Sir Walter Earle; p. 762b, second reading and commitment.
[50] 'An Act for avoiding of corrupt and simonical Contracts for Churches and Benefices and for preventing of undue Elections in Colleges and Halls' (*LJ*, III, p. 393b).
[51] *CJ*, I, pp. 818b, 819a, 'An Act to Prevent Corruption in Presentations and Collations to Benefices, and in Elections to Headships, Fellowships, and Scholars places, in Colleges and Halls'.
[52] Morgan forthcoming; Russell 1979.

of the corrupt practice of Samuel Collins in manipulating an election to Kings.[53]

The abortive nature of the various bills introduced during the 1620s may have encouraged some members to turn to other means of correcting the abuses in the universities. Amongst the papers of Sir Henry Spelman, the leading member of the contemporaneous commissions on fees, is a tantalising memorandum. 'To enquier of exacted fees in the Univ[e]rsities And buying & selling degrees schollerships Felowships etc. . . . for o[u]r Commission being only to enquier of Courtes perhaps reacheth not these.' Evidently on further consideration Spelman and his fellow commissioners concurred with his hesitation – no doubt to the relief of many contemporary academics and to the frustration of later historians. The archives of Cambridge University, and the records of the commissioners contain no evidence of such an enquiry.[54] Nevertheless, the miscellaneous evidence from other sources, adduced elsewhere in these pages, suggests that there would have been cases aplenty to justify the fears of those who from the 1570s through to the 1600s introduced bills to regulate the conduct of elections within the universities.

In the 1630s parliament never met, and this frustrated the attempts of those who had sought to curb corrupt elections by legislative means. Criticism, however, flowed into other channels. In 1636 two masters of Cambridge colleges reported to Laud on the disorders of the university. Their distaste for the low church practices at Trinity College no doubt encouraged them to retail the 'common report there goes (and not without probabilitie) that here both Fellowes & Schollers & Officers places are sold'.[55] But Laud would be no more successful than his predecessors who had operated via parliament in curbing what had become a perennial feature of university life. When parliament met again in 1640, a number of complaints were rapidly forwarded to the Commons, and a Committee for the Universities was established to deal with issues, some at least of which had attracted parliamentary attention over the preceding sixty years.[56]

There is a threefold significance in these repeated attempts to eradicate corrupt elections in the universities. First, it demonstrates the continuity of interest that could be sustained in an issue from one parliament to another. Indeed, there are indications that the same or similar bills relating to the universities may have been carried along from one parliament to

---

[53] HLRO, Main Papers, H.L., 20 May 1628.
[54] BL Add. MS 34601, fo. 70; PRO, E.215 *passim*; Aylmer 1958. As a former member of the university and as a distinguished scholar, Spelman is likely to have known what was going on.
[55] Cooper, *Annals*, III, p. 282.   [56] Notestein 1923, p. 399 and n. 2; Twigg 1990, p. 47.

another. Contrary to what appears to have been orthodoxy in the 1990s, parliaments were more than a series of discrete events. Not least this was because continuity was encouraged by the unresolved character of the problems that men brought to them for legislative resolution. Second, on a number of occasions, as with the bill of 1576 and the petition of 1584, it is evident that the initiative for introducing the issue of elections at the universities originated amongst the non-governmental members of the Commons. The repeated loss of bills on the same theme creates a strong presumption for similar origins on other occasions. This conclusion is re-inforced when we recall the proprietorial attitude adopted by the Crown towards the universities. Both the universities and their constituent col-leges derived their corporate existence from acts of the royal prerogative under the Great Seal. Viewed from this perspective, the criticisms voiced in parliament, and the proposed remedial legislation, were unwelcome encroachments upon the Crown's prerogatives. This was likely to result in governmental or royal obstruction of bills that impinged upon the prerogative, whatever intrinsic merits these bills may have had. More-over, the generally held perception of the universities as seminaries as, effectively, part of the structure of church and ministry, also contributed to the distaste with which proposed legislation touching on the uni-versities was viewed. This was because religious matters were treated as matters for royal rather than parliamentary settlement. Therefore, what larger conclusion is to be drawn from looking at these issues over the longer term but in the light of this fairly narrow review specifically of proposed legislation affecting the universities? Any matters relating to the universities introduced into parliament were seen as challenging the royal prerogative.[57] The interests in the universities of both the Crown and the wider community increased – as we have seen it doing in this period – as it became a cynosure of their concerns; ultimately they were likely to come into conflict in that ultimate forum, parliament. Finally, the larger framework of ecclesiastical reform within which some of these proposals were couched indicates the intense clerical and theological interests of the laity. The universities had come to play a crucial role in the thinking of these laymen in their pursuit of further reformation, and they inevitably took every opportunity to intervene in the affairs of the universities to achieve their ends. Looked at overall their efforts in parliament were per-haps the least successful of their means of intervention compared with

---

[57] Alluding to this and a wider range of proposed legislation in the early years of Elizabeth's reign, Sir Geoffrey Elton mistakenly wrote that 'Whatever may have been the rights and wrongs of these cases, plainly the veto here served the general interest and not the Queen's' (Elton 1986, p. 125). This is clearly wrong.

the influence they had come to wield through the process of endowment and the provision of patronage.

We have seen that in the late sixteenth century there was an accretion of power in the hands of the heads of colleges.[58] It was, perhaps, inevitable that this should lead to jealousies and accusations of the misuse of these powers, and that in at least some instances there were good grounds for these accusations. Given the proprietorial attitude of the gentry towards the universities it was almost equally certain that criticisms would be voiced and remedies propounded in parliament.

Three components can be identified in these parliamentary criticisms. The first derived from the simple misapplication of the considerable initiatives available to masters. The second focussed on the special pressures to which some heads were thought to be subject as married men with family responsibilities, and the potentially corrupting influences with which resident wives were thought to pervade the college. The third involved something of a paradox. It derived from the more puritanically inclined critics and their notion of the university as an arsenal for exegetical criticism, and international theological disputation. Under the statutes of 1570, fellows might not marry; but masters claimed not to be fellows and, by custom, ignored this prohibition. One can detect a sense that in this quarter wives were felt to be a distraction not only for the youthful troopers of further reformation currently under instruction, but also for the great leaders of precisian scholarship under whose tutelage the troops were marshalled. At Cambridge in the 1590s there emerged a new precisian Calvinism, distinguished by a dogmatic reference to the works of Calvin and Beza, and by neo-scholastic schematisation of Calvinism that endowed this brand of Protestantism with many of the structural characteristics of post-tridentine Catholicism.[59] At the same time, and in the social sphere, there evolved a new image of the dedicated puritan scholar, working all the hours that God sent, and with little time or motivation for the distractions of a conjugal relationship. There was much that was monkish and ascetic about this image, albeit not all the puritan masters at Cambridge adhered to the high expectations of their lay supporters. Therefore the parliamentary criticisms of masters of colleges not only derived from specific knowledge or suspected corruptions but also

---

[58] Above, chapter 3; cf. also below, chapter 8.   [59] Below, pp. 445–6.

arose from a more diffused sense of the changing ideal of the demeanour appropriate to a man in the position of a master.

Amongst the accusations levelled at Roger Goad, provost of King's, in 1576, was that he overawed the senior fellows and coerced them into a spoil, that they made 'a dividend of the Colledge money . . . Public dilap-idations of the College money . . . Neglegint in hudling up accompts to de-fraud the Coll[ege] . . . Deteyning the Coll[ege]: money and diverting it another way'.[60] There appear to have been few real grounds for these particular accusations, but the concentration of power in the hands of the masters of colleges, the uncertain arrangements for the administration of some college accounts, and the opprobrium they encountered as a re-sult of attempting to fulfil their disciplinary responsibilities, made them peculiarly liable to such accusations.

At St John's in the early 1570s the fellows were renowned for their ability to make life intolerable for their master. In one of the disputes that arose at this time they accused the then incumbent, Nicholas Shephard, of engrossing the profits of various college leases. They described how there had been 'a rumour that all unreasonable leases made by Colledges should be made frustrate at the parliamente'. Spurred on by the threat of this imminent curtailment of his discretionary powers, Shephard was said by the fellows to have fraudulently procured a lease for himself. However, the terms of the legislation of 1571 frustrated his designs and 'at his return from the Parliament, he did rente the foresaid lease in a rage'.[61] The legislation of the early 1570s, intended to regulate the granting of college leases, although ostensibly of a general purport, may have been aimed particularly at abuses that were most readily available to masters.

The puritan element in the criticism of masters is evident in the peti-tion to parliament of 1584. Here, there is a glancing reference to masters as participating with the fellows in accepting bribes at college elections.[62] Again, amongst the church grievances presented to parliament by a pu-ritan petitioner in 1589, was the 'ill usage of Masters of Colledges' who were said to be converting college profits to the preferment of themselves and their wives and children.[63] Furthermore, during this parliament an attack on pluralities was clearly seen to involve a criticism of a practice common amongst the masters of colleges. The bishops replied that the

---

[60] Mullinger 1884, p. 385 n. 3.
[61] 13 Eliz. c. 11 (1571), 'Fraudulent deeds made by Spiritual Persons', especially clauses III, IV; Scott 1909, p. 300.
[62] Strype 1824, III, 2, p. 297.
[63] Mullinger 1883, p. 330; Cooper, *Annals*, II, p. 597, attributes this to 1597, following Strype 1822, II, p. 375; BL Lansdowne MS 119, fos. 94–101v (no. 6).

deans of cathedral churches and the masters of colleges could not continue their residence and duties without the income from a benefice.[64]

The parliament of 1597 saw a frontal attack on the masters of colleges. During the first session John Davies, the poet, initiated proceedings by 'shewing Many Corruptions in the Masters of Colledges in their abusing of the Possessions of the . . . Colledges contrary to the intent of the Founders, converting the benefit of the same to their own private Commodities'. Davies asked the House to reform these abuses, and had to hand 'a Bill drawn to that purpose'. A committee of lawyers was appointed for the better digesting of the said bill.[65] Davies' own religious inclinations at this time are uncertain, although later he was a scourge of recusants in Ireland.[66] However, the quarters of the House in which the bill was likely to win approval are indicated by the comments of another member. Sir Edward Hoby expressed himself 'liking very well of the said Motion', and moved 'that like consideration may be had of Deans and Chapters as of the said Masters of Colledges'. Hoby was a not inconsiderable scholar and also something of a puritan. Like Davies, he was a member of the Middle Temple.[67] It was to those MPs that were members of the Middle Temple that the draft bill had been referred by Mr Speaker, together with two other members named to the committee: Sir Francis Moore, also, later, of the Middle Temple, but as counsel and under-steward to Oxford University a likely opponent, and Mr Bois, also of the Middle Temple.[68] Something in the way of an orchestrated attack seems to be indicated, and one in which religious inclinations played their part amongst both those for and those likely to oppose the bill.

The directness and the public nature of these criticisms stung into action the heads of both Oxford and Cambridge. Within a week they jointly petitioned their respective chancellors, Buckhurst and Burghley. They complained that Davies' speech tended 'to the utter discredit of the Governers and Heads of Colledges', and asked that he might be made to provide proofs of his assertions. They protested that they did not wish to conceal any fault with which those of their office might be

[64] Neale 1957, pp. 224–7.
[65] D'Ewes 1682, p. 559b, not elaborated on in Townshend 1680, p. 106.
[66] *DNB*; in the 1601 parliament he may have owed his seat to another critic of colleges and patron of puritan academics, Sir Edward Coke (Hasler 1981, II, p. 22b). For Coke's predilection for the puritan academic Edward Playfere, below, pp. 376–7.
[67] D'Ewes 1682, p. 559b; *DNB*, although it has been suggested that he did not share the puritanism of his younger brother, Thomas Posthumous Hoby (Hasler 1981, III, p. 681b).
[68] Moore: *DNB*; Hasler 1981, III, p. 72a; John Bois was almost certainly a potential opponent of the bill, as member for Canterbury and steward of his liberties to the archbishop of Canterbury (Neale 1957, p. 416; Hasler 1981, I, p. 477a).

charged, but they strongly objected to 'this libertie of speache, uttered to
the discreditt of so many persons of our place if there be noe just cause
thereof, nor that for the faults of a few (if any such be) a general Sclander
and Infamy may be brought upon all the rest'.[69] As always when they
were subjected to criticism, the masters played upon the fear felt by their
political masters that any impugning of those placed in authority carried
with it the threat of general social disruption: they asserted that as a result
of these accusations 'we may . . . be less regarded of those who are to
lyve under our government'. They also spoke out quite clearly against
the passage of the intended Act, expressing their 'feare, that, by colour of
these scandalous Informations, published against us in that place, some
new Statute may passe, to the generall prejudice of both the Universities,
whereof ourselves being Members would not willingly be thought to give
the occasion of makinge any such Statute'.[70] Their protest appears to have
been successful, for nothing more was heard of Davies' bill that session.
However, there are indications that other business in the parliament of
1597 may have touched on the universities in general and the masters
of colleges in particular. In the following month a bill for establishing
good order in grammar schools received its second reading but was refused
commitment.[71] This can almost certainly be identified with an undated
draft Act to be found amongst the State Paper miscellanea.[72] In a related
but less exalted academic context to that of Davies' bill, the draft for
schools attempted to deal with a similar problem but in a different way.
The schools bill noted that the revenues 'have byn of late tyme converted
to the private lucre and profit of such confidentiaryes, who perverting
the trust and good intent of the Founders' place unfit men as teachers,
men willing to accept whatever stipend the feoffees might offer. Out of
increased revenues feoffees were said to provide little supplementation to
the masters and scholars, 'but wholly divert it to their own commodity'. It
was proposed that henceforth surpluses should be allocated to the masters
and 'the poor scholars for their maintenance & support there, or at the
universities'.[73]

Thus far one might suspect that this bill came from the same stable
as that for the masters of colleges. After all, it attempted to deal with a
similar problem: the misapplication of funds in trust given for educational
purposes, in this case by trustees who, like the masters, exercised considerable control over the funds in question, and an undoubted influence over

---

[69] Cooper, *Annals*, II, p. 587.   [70] *Ibid.*   [71] Townshend 1680, p. 113 (9 Dec. 1597).
[72] SP 46/16/57. It is headed, 'An acte for the establishing of good order for free scholes, and for the
due imployment of the recvenues thereof'.
[73] SP 46/16/57.

their inferiors, whether fellows or schoolmasters. However much those in favour of Davies' bill may have endorsed these principles, the means proposed to remedy the failings detailed in the schools bill must have guaranteed its rejection. The schools bill claimed that the appointment of schoolmasters and the oversight of revenues properly belonged to the bishops of diocese, 'who in all reason are the most meet and competent iudges in all matters of learning'. The bishop was to have power to examine trustees, to appoint and dismiss schoolmasters, to oversee accounts and to direct their use.[74] Whereas Davies' bill represented an attempted encroachment by the laity in parliament on the regulation of the universities, the schools bill aimed to curtail the increasing grip of the laity on educational patronage in schools. Moreover, in so far as the funds from free-school endowments were employed as university bursaries, the bill would have extended episcopal patronage within the universities. This was a type of intervention that men of Davies' persuasion could well do without.

All this suggests that the two major Statutes of Charitable Uses of 1597 and 1601 need to be seen in this broader context of a contested concern for the regulation of funds for educational purposes. There are apparent inconsistencies within the Acts, and as with similar inconsistencies in other legislation of this period this is likely to indicate amendment during their passage. The inference to be drawn is that, as with Davies' bill, the heads of the universities fought a successful campaign. The Statutes of Charitable Uses of 1597 and 1601 arose out of a concern with the misappropriation of funds donated for charitable purposes.[75] The preamble of the 1597 Act refers to gifts for 'Scholes of Learninge', and 'for the Maintenance of Fre[e] Schooles and pore Schollers', and that of 1601 enumerates 'Schooles of Learninge, Free Schooles and Schollers in Universities' and 'Education' as objects of both benefaction and legislation. None the less, both Acts contain provisos that they shall not encompass the colleges, halls and houses of learning in the two universities and at Westminster, Eton and Winchester – presumably on the grounds explicitly stated elsewhere in the Act of 1601 that it should not extend to 'any Colledge Hospitall or Free Schoole whiche have speciall Visitors or Governours or Overseers appointed them by their founders'.[76]

---

[74] It is possible that the bill was Whitgift's work.

[75] 39 Eliz. c. 6 and 43 Eliz. c. 4; Townshend 1680, pp. 120, 124. The legislation and its working are discussed in Jones 1969, pp. 16–56.

[76] In practice, subsequent strict construction might implicate the colleges of the universities in investigations (Jones 1969, pp. 29 n. 5, 38, 39). For what follows, see above, n. 28.

The allusive references to educational purposes in the preambles, the addition of a specific reference to 'Schollers in Universities' in the preamble to the second Act, and a repetitious redundancy in the exempting provisions hint at modifications and cobbling together of a number of drafts in committee such as we know to have taken place with other bills. The additional specific reference to scholars in the universities permitted investigation of benefactions granted not directly to colleges, but to other trustees. All this suggests the possibility – the evidence is too circumstantial to bear a greater weight of argument – that some MPs saw these Acts as additional instruments with which to investigate those very corruptions in the universities of which we have heard them complain in that self-same parliament which passed the first Statute of Charitable Uses in 1597. The supposition is that in the parliaments of 1597 and 1601 contemporaries would have seen a relationship between these pieces of legislation or proposed legislation. That relationship has not hitherto been noted by historians. All three instances – Davies' bill for masters, the anonymous bill for schools, and the two Statutes of Charitable Uses – manifest an interest in the regulation of the funds that the laity had provided for educational purposes. However, the details of their wording or their parliamentary passage indicate that intervention in this sphere could originate in quite different quarters: amongst the laity in the case of Davies' bill, and probably with the episcopate in the case of that for schools. The Statutes for Charitable Uses may indeed have been a compromise between these two otherwise opposed interests.

This supposition would lend substance to Coke's remarks in 1604 that he had 'found by experience in former Parliamentes (and especially when I was speaker) how necessary it were for o[u]r university to have Burgesses'.[77] Indeed, the immediate cause for the agitation on the part of the universities for MPs of their own may have been the issues raised in the parliaments of 1597 and 1601. In so far as those issues had impugned the integrity and threatened the authority of the masters, it may have been they who most desired parliamentary representatives. Certainly, with their Court connections, they were the men in the universities who were best placed to obtain it. If this is so, they were soon to be in need of parliamentary defence of their interests. Notestein suggested that two lists of legislation proposed for James' first parliament may have originated amongst the backbench MPs who had been active during the later Elizabethan parliaments.[78] This may well have been the

---

[77] CUA, Lett. 11.A.C.3.c. Coke was Speaker in 1593. He did not sit in 1597 and 1601.
[78] Notestein 1971, pp. 47–74.

case, for in the lists is a proposal for visiting the universities and reforming certain points in their administration.[79] In this parliament the issue of the masters of colleges emerges towards the end of the first session, in June 1604. On this occasion the proposed legislation enjoyed greater success than in 1597, and progressed through the Commons to the Lords, where it was lost in committee.[80] Luckily, the text of the engrossed bill has survived.[81] It appears to differ somewhat from what we may infer was contained in Davies' bill of 1597, in so far as his remarks on introducing the bill can be assumed to have summarised its contents.[82] These had dwelt upon the corruptions of masters, and their abuse of college possessions. The bill of 1604 restricted itself to attempting to prohibit what many saw as the root of these corruptions – married masters. No married man was to be eligible as a master. Any incumbent master who married voided his office, 'as if such maried persons had bene naturally dead'. No woman was to be permitted to lodge in a college. A master who procured such a lodgement was to be penalised by the loss of his office.[83] Draconian though these measures were, their diplomatic avoidance of aspersions on the integrity of incumbent masters may help to explain why this bill progressed so much further than its predecessor of 1597. But ultimately having failed again, on this occasion an almost identical bill was introduced into the Commons during the following session.[84] It was 'much disputed', but upon the bill being put to the question the House was reported to have divided for the first time that session, producing a healthy eighty votes in the bill's favour.[85] Behind this bill we may once again detect the sponsorship of the proponents of the bill of 1597, and it may be more than coincidence that when the bill was committed, it was entrusted to members appointed to meet in Temple Hall – as had been the bill of 1597.

---

[79] *Ibid.*, pp. 52–3.   [80] *CJ*, I, pp. 237a, 238b, 243a, 244a, 245; *LJ*, II, pp. 327a, 330b, 332a.

[81] 'An act prohibiting the resiance of maried men with their wives and families in Colledges, Cathedrall Churches, Colledgiat houses, and halles of the universities of Oxford and Cambridge.' It is printed *verbatim* in Bond 1962, pp. 87–8.

[82] D'Ewes 1682, p. 559b.

[83] Bond 1962, pp. 87–8. See p. 298 in the meantime Laurence Chaderton, a married man, had become first master of Emmanuel.

[84] HLRO, Parchment Collection (Box 1E), H.L., 6 March 1606. See also a version in BL Lansdowne MS 487, fos. 28–9 (no. 7).

[85] Birch 1849, I, p. 63. For the progress of the bill see *CJ*, I, p. 259a (24 Jan. 1606); *CJ*, I, p. 260a (second reading and commitment, 25 Jan. 1606); Willson 1931, p. 9 (28 Jan.); *CJ*, I, p. 272 (22 Feb. 1606) amendments from committee reported, and engrossment; *CJ*, I, p. 275 and Willson 1931, pp. 55–6 (26 Feb.); *CJ*, I, p. 276b, third reading and vote: for 169, against 104. Compare Birch 1849, I, p. 63; Willson 1931, pp. 58–9 (3 March); *CJ*, I, p. 278b, sent to Lords (6 March); *LJ*, II, p. 388a, brought from House of Commons and first reading (6 March); *LJ*, II, p. 396a, second reading and on the vote refused commitment (17 March).

The debate on third reading gives some idea of the issues that members perceived as lying behind the bill. Speaking for the bill, William Hakewill alluded to the corrupting influence of marital responsibilities on the actions of heads, and the perverse influence of wives: he asked rhetorically, 'who knoweth not how covetous hedds of howses are to maintaine preferre and provide for their wyves and children: Who knoweth not how much women prevaile with their husbands to the overthrowe of learninge discipline yea and of the colleges?' This perverting female influence was also perceived as a direct threat to students: again Hakewill appealed to the lascivious imagination of his parliamentary audience. He asked them to contemplate how the 'manners of younge men are corrupted and drawen from their studyes by the ordinary sight and conversacion with women'. The diarist Robert Bowyer was prepared to dismiss these arguments with a show of academic parody, but it seems clear that for Hakewill, and for a proportion of the well-filled House to which he was appealing, they carried weight. The preceding speaker in favour of the bill, John Hoskyns, had asserted 'Virginity a virtue: Marriage not of necessity'. He also referred to the need to keep to the wishes of the original benefactors: 'the founders would that the heads of their houses should be single and unmarried'. This was clearly a spurious argument, alluding to pre-Reformation circumstances, and in his reply Bowyer had some fun at Hoskyns' expense – 'if you will enferre there fore he must be unmarried I must conclude *ergo* preist may not marrie and yet this ientleman saieth he is not popish' – presumably a glancing blow at Hoskyns' known puritan sympathies.[86] But both Dr Caius and the immaculately Protestant Sir Walter Mildmay had prescribed celibacy on all members of their colleges, including masters. What we have in the speeches by Hakewill and Hoskyns is an articulation of the high expectations that an increasing number of the laity held of university divines: they expected ascetics, devoted to study, not the 'men of business' preferred by the government. When those expectations were disappointed the laity were driven to intervene in the affairs of the universities – not least, as here, through action in parliament.

As with others that had preceded it, the bill on whose behalf both Hakewill and Hoskyns had waxed eloquent was also lost in the Lords.[87] Not that the issue was dropped. This parliament saw a continuing campaign for a learned and preaching ministry. Indeed, the bills against married masters need to be seen as part of that campaign. This is evident

---

[86] Willson 1931, pp. 8, 9, 58, 59. For what follows, see p. 298.
[87] HLRO, Parchment Collection, H.L., 6 March 1605/6, recto, endorsement.

in another bill promoted during the 1605–6 session. It attempted to ensure a resident preaching ministry by attacking those who held livings in
plurality. Among other things it laid rigorous obligations on the heads of
colleges. They were to be present at their benefices and to preach every
other Sunday. To make this practically possible, from henceforth no head
was to hold a benefice with cure of souls more than 20 miles from the
university. Anyone elected as a master who held a benefice beyond this
limit lost it within three months of his election. Moreover, within the
wording of the bill we can detect the high expectations and special role
assigned to the heads of colleges by the puritan laity: 'forasmuch as the
non-residence of heades and cheife Governors of Colledges and Halls in
the Universities which are the seminaries of the Ministrie, is by example
very hurtfull and likely to infect the younger Scholers trained up under
them for the Ministrie with a light and carelesse respect of their duties
when they [themselves] shall [be] beneficed'.[88] These words would have
sounded of ill omen in the ears of Dr Nevile, master of Trinity and dean
of Canterbury. On the part of at least some activist laymen there existed
a model of the university as a seminary and of the masters of colleges
as exemplars of godly virtues. It was in pursuit of the realisation of this
model that those lay activists who were MPs attempted to intervene in
the affairs of the universities through action in parliament.

We hear relatively little of the heads as such in succeeding parliaments.
In part this was no doubt because the attack on the heads was part of a
larger drive for the further reformation of the ministry. But by the parliaments of the 1620s those who promoted this cause were being thrown on
to the defensive against the onslaught of fundamental doctrinal innovations: a generation on they were no longer the innovators.[89] Nevertheless,
the sustained parliamentary campaign of the 1580s to early 1600s makes
it clear that parliament was familiar with the power and the potential
for corruption of the heads of colleges and the envy they inspired. Individual parliamentarians and the corporate parliamentary memory no
doubt carried that knowledge through to inform the understanding of
the *cause célèbre* of 1626, the election of the duke of Buckingham as
chancellor of Cambridge – an event in which the heads incurred no little opprobrium.[90] Not that the agitation in James' first parliament had
absolutely no impact. In 1597, acting as vice-chancellor and master of
Corpus, John Jegon had signed the letter complaining of the speech by

---

[88] Bond 1962, pp. 104–5. As with the other bills discussed above, this one was lost in the Lords. Its
provisions recall those of 1589 (Neale 1957, pp. 226–7). For Nevile (below), see pp. 262–3, 296.
[89] Below, pp. 445–6.   [90] Morgan forthcoming.

John Davies in which Davies had accused the heads of colleges of corruption. In 1607–8 his brother and successor as master, Thomas, became involved in a dispute with one of the fellows, Edmund Gurney.[91] The matter had reached Cecil, and Cecil wrote back to Cambridge with a rebuke that makes it clear that Jegon's marital status was one of the things that Gurney held against him. Cecil asked the Visitor of the college, Dr Goad,

> to have an eye upon it, as you shall see cause, out of which imputations I wish all the Heads of Colleges would take a friendly admonition from me, and that is the inconvenience which Colleges sustain by the having of wives and families within the College. I did think that that which was lately attempted in Parliament for the reformation thereof would have made them more careful of this University's blemish, but it does not appear to be so. I pray you at the next assembling of the Heads to you to advertise them hereof from me.[92]

Even the chancellor could not approve of the practice, although clearly neither could he condone the incursion into his bailiwick represented by the attempts at parliamentary reform of what was perceived by some as a pernicious vice: the marriages of masters.

The king himself seems to have taken to heart the parliamentary agitation over the heads of houses during the early years of his reign. In settling the dispute over the election to Christ's in 1609 he plumped for one of the candidates because 'he is a single man without charge of wife or children, a condition which me think prefers him who has it in the choice of a headship of a house before other concurrents, *ceteris paribus*, for it gives him less cause of diverting the revenues of the house to private uses, and has besides less occasion of offence and scandal amongst youth than marriage has'.[93] The puritan promoters of the bills against heads would have approved of the king's criteria. Ironically, they could hardly have approved of his choice: Valentine Carey, a man who was a scourge of puritanism at Christ's.[94]

LANDS AND LEASES

We have noted that one of the reasons why the universities sought representation in parliament was to protect the expanding corporate interests

---

[91] Cooper, *Annals*, III, p. 597.
[92] *HMCS*, XX, p. 65, 11 Feb. 1608. Goad subsequently reported that Jegon's wife lived in a very private and convenient lodging on the backside of that College, without any trouble to the Company, burden to the College or offence to any (*HMCS*, XX, p. 84).
[93] *HMCS*, XXI, p. 160 (20 Nov. 1609).   [94] See above, p. 372.

of themselves and their colleges as landowners.[95] We will also see that as individuals some masters and some fellows were tempted to manage the property of which they were trustees in a manner that was to their immediate advantage but to the long-term detriment of the foundation.[96] But there were those laymen associated with the universities who took an appropriately proprietorial and often critical interest in matters such as these. As the original donors, or as the representatives of the families, that had originally provided the colleges with their endowments, it was not unnatural that they should try to ensure the appropriate employment of their benefactions. Exertions on their part were all the more likely when we recall the institutional means and informal local connections by which benefactors retained links with the colleges through their benefactions.[97] The proprietorial interest was not terminated once endowment had taken place; rather, it was encouraged by the procedures established to manage many of these endowments.

Just as on other issues men who were in a position to provide endowments turned to parliament to provide them with the righting of particular wrongs, or the solution of general problems, so also did they in their relationships with the universities. In many respects the criticism of corrupt elections, of the depredations inflicted by predatory masters, and the attempts to ensure the purity of those fountain-heads of the ministry were all aspects of a proprietorial presumption on the part of the aristocracy towards the universities. But in no area was this proprietorial attitude more likely to manifest itself than over endowments. Moreover, while it is true that individuals might benefit from laxity or irregularities in the administration of college properties, even men such as these had a personal vested interest in the general principle of maintaining the letter of testamentary or other bequests. They would themselves need the assurance that their own wishes would be respected in the transmission and administration of their own property within their families. This is surely the root of the repeated emphasis in argument, both in parliament and without, on the need to maintain the wishes of founders.[98] Furthermore, the parallel to be drawn between the

[95] Of course, a presence in the intermittent and irregular meetings of parliament was only one of the devices they employed to protect their interests as landowners. In addition to seeking representation at the royal Court for this purpose, they also used the Crown's courts. Space does not permit of an examination of the measures of the colleges in protecting their interests as landowners in the courts; but see, for example, PRO, c 78/20/1 (Gonville and Caius College v. Sir Thomas Ragland, 1561); c 78/60/7 (Trinity College v. William Ascough Esq., 1580); c 78/80/23 (Magdalen College, Oxford v. Christopher Layer, 1587). See below, n. 99.

[96] Below, pp. 273–82.   [97] Below, pp. 206–10.

[98] For example, in the debate in March 1607 (Willson 1931, p. 59).

colleges as landowners and individuals in the same capacity provided a potential for leverage in debate that was not lost on parliamentary tacticians. This is evident, for example, in the debate in 1621 arising from the long-drawn-out attempts by Magdalene College to regain the Covent Garden property earlier sold to the earl of Oxford. On this occasion Sir Edward Coke argued that the lord chancellor had no right to issue decrees contrary to the general tenor of parliamentary legislation, and he warned, 'This particuler involves a generall; it toucheth everye man in his inheritance.'[99]

The legislation to which Coke alluded was the statutes of 1570 and 1576.[100] These had constituted an attempt to prevent one of the most obvious abuses arising from the development of the colleges as landowners. The ever-present temptation for the current fellows of a college was that they would attempt to reap the maximum benefits from the college properties during their incumbency, to the long-term detriment of the interests of the college. This could be done by taking large entry fines and small rentals on long leases.[101] The first of these two Acts limited leases to a term of twenty-one years or three lives. Both the need for and the effectiveness of the procedures embodied in this Act are evident in the immediate steps that were taken to circumvent its provisions. These included the calling in and remaking of leases long before the period of the existing lease had run its course. Some five years later a further Act was required in explanation of the first. This prohibited the surrender or ending of a lease within three years of making a new lease.[102]

One of the aims of the Elizabethan legislation had been to encourage intervention by the Crown in the granting of leases.[103] In the case of the disputed Aldgate property of Magdalene College, a lease had been granted to the Crown on condition that it was re-leased by the Crown to the intended ultimate beneficiary, the importunate earl. This was subsequently described as 'Most dishonourable to the said Queene who was onlie used as an instrument to defeat her owne good Lawes made for the maintenance of Lerninge and Religion.'[104] But in the event private interests were encouraged by the restrictions now imposed by the

---

[99] Notestein *et al.* 1935, III, pp. 158–9. For the history of the Covent Garden property, see Hoyle in Cunich *et al.* 1994, pp. 77–83.

[100] 13 Eliz. c. 10 and 18 Eliz. c. 11. On the effects of these Acts, see Sarah Bendall in Bendall *et al.* 1999, p. 130. They were also an attack on one of Elizabeth's favourite ways of raising money (Hoyle in Cunich *et al.* 1994, pp. 77–83).

[101] The issues were in fact even more complicated than this: see pp. 273–82.

[102] 18 Eliz. c. 11.   [103] HLRO, Main Papers (Supplementary), 8 March 1621, *breviat*.

[104] *Ibid.* See also the concerns expressed in 'An Acte for the assurance & establishment of grants heretofore made to the late Queene Elizabeth by Collegiate & Ecclesiasticall Corporations & Persons' (HLRO, Main Papers, H.L., 13 March 1621).

Acts to attempt to circumvent their provisions by inciting the use of the Crown's special exemptions from the legislation. As we have seen, one consequence of this was further to enhance the importance of the Court as the forum in which exemptions from the legislation might be won as a result of invoking the mechanisms of patronage and clientage that articulated power at the centre.[105] From the perspective of the universities it certainly demonstrates the complexity of relationships between the central institutions of the state. Ultimately, in the case of legislation such as this, the unforeseen effect of increased attempts at regulatory legislation by parliament was to enhance the importance of the royal Court.

In addition to being of considerable significance in constituting a major source of wealth lost to the college in question, the issue of Magdalene College lands was also something of a test case for all colleges during the fifty years in which it wended its way through Common Pleas, the Court of Wards, the five occasions on which points of law were argued in King's Bench, thence through Chancery and into Exchequer Chamber, until the college finally sought an unravelling of these labyrinthine legal complexities in parliamentary legislation.[106] Specifically, there were many parliamentarians whose families had a vested interest in maintaining the inviolacy of the collegiate endowments that they had provided. Generally, there were many more who as landowners were sensitive to argument from the unhealthy precedent provided by the exploitation of college property such as was epitomised by the treatment of Magdalene College and its lands. Nor was Magdalene alone in trying to exploit the sensitivities of landowners in parliament as a means of winning support for its case when all else had failed.[107] The resort to a parliamentary resolution of these long-drawn-out disputes served to alert benefactors and potential benefactors to the threats to their benevolence, and to make it clear that from, at the latest, the time of the legislation of the 1570s the active intervention of those about the Court, and the connivance of the Crown, had been necessary in procuring the circumvention of the legislation that had been designed to protect their investments in

---

[105] Below, pp. 278 ff and Morgan 1988.

[106] HLRO, Main Papers (Supplementary), 8 March 1621, *breviat*. See also HLRO, Main Papers, H.C., 13 May 1614; Main Papers, H.L., 13 March 1621; Parchment Collection (Box 178), H.L., 4 March 1624; Main Papers, H.L., 20 March 1624; Main Papers, H.L., 22 March 1624. See Hoyle in Cunich *et al.* 1994, pp. 77–83.

[107] Merton College also attempted to regain possession of property 'unduly procured' from it (*CJ*, I, p. 818a, 11 Feb. 1626), as did Magdalen College, Oxford (HLRO, Main Papers (Supplementary) [?1623], 'An Acte for the Reversinge of a decree unduely obtained in Chauncery . . .', not mentioned in the *Journals*). See also SP 14/124/31.

learning. By pursuing their own interests and bringing these cases into the parliamentary arena it was unavoidable that the colleges helped to focus attention in a very public way on the none too savoury machinations that went on at Court. In doing so, the voicing of university issues in parliament positively contributed to the colouring of attitudes towards the Court among the political nation. Through debates on issues such as college leases and endowments the universities in this period made a not insignificant contribution to the shaping of the contemporary political culture.

A REFORMED MINISTRY

A further topic on which at least a section of parliamentarians displayed an active interest was the reformation of the ministry. Inevitably this led to a concern with the universities as the training grounds for proselytising ministers and as the citadel of exegetical and disputatious scholarship.[108] Linked to attempts to improve the quality of the ministry were further attempts to curtail pluralities and to ensure that all cures enjoyed a resident minister. Once again, this focussed attention on the universities, not least because some of their leading members were notable pluralists or non-residents.

In the contemporary mind there was seen to be a connection between the provision of a godly ministry, pluralities and the universities. What was sought was a constant flow out of the universities of learned ministers. Pluralities were seen to inhibit this – as they had for four centuries at least. On the same day in 1604 that a bill for provision of a godly and learned ministry was introduced, so also was a bill against pluralities of benefices. It was argued that pluralities 'hath hindred the increase of many learned Preachers, which the Universities would have sent forth'.[109] The same arguments were employed in debate on a similar bill in 1621, when Sir Benjamin Rudyard described how 'Many a poore, honest sufficient Minister sitts shutt up in his study, stifling his good parts, smotheringe the use of his Callinge.'[110]

---

[108] This encouraged the transformation of the clergy into a graduate profession and effectively created an obligation for the universities to ensure that their graduates were also preachers (Bond 1962, pp. 80–1). A similar bill was introduced in 1606 (*ibid.*, pp. 98–100). See below, pp. 469 ff; and O'Day 1979.

[109] Bond 1962, pp. 81–2. A bill of 1606 contains many similarities to this of 1604, including the argument for the inhibitory effect on the sending forth of ministers (HLRO, Uncatalogued MSS, MS 25).

[110] Notestein *et al.* 1935, IV, p. 343. The same argument is employed in the preamble of a bill for impropriations (HLRO, Main Papers, H.C., 18 April 1621). See also Dr Williams' Library, Morrice MS E, p. 136, for related remarks by Rudyard.

Against this was to be set the case for pluralities as a reward and support for scholarship: as Whitgift remarked, 'the cheefest reward for learned Divines in this Kingdome are Bishopricks and Cathedrall and Collegiat Churches, which speciallie consist of Impropriacions'.[111] In the debate in 1621 it was argued that to limit everyone, whatever their qualifications, to one benefice would lead to the decay of the universities because parents would be discouraged from entering their sons upon a clerical career with the prospect of only the most meagre of rewards.[112] In 1610, the bishop of London countered yet another bill against pluralities and non-residence with the argument that 'If this bill proceed, it will overthrow the universities and bring in barbarism and I know not what, as we see an example in Scotland; for the parity and meanness of the provision of livings for ministers hath rooted out almost all learning in that Kingdom. *Honos alit artes.*' Reversing the logic of what was to be Rudyard's argument, the bishop suggested that, 'If men's preferments be worse when they come abroad than they be in the university, they will be like drones and never come abroad.'[113] We may also discern here an implicit but never fully articulated conflict between two of the roles assigned to the universities: that of the proselytising seminary and that of the intellectual arsenal.

Wherever we may consider the truth of this contemporary debate to lie, it is clear that the desire to provide a preaching, resident, ministry led to a concern in parliament with impropriations, pluralities and non-residence. This inevitably drew attention to the universities whenever the issue arose, for both sides of the argument accepted the role of the universities as centres for training and scholarship. Moreover, it is evident that during the first thirty years of the seventeenth century there was an intensity of concern with the issue despite the repeated loss of bills on the subject. As on other issues that we have examined relating to the universities, there was a continuity of concern that belies recent attempts to present individual parliaments as discrete and unconnected events.

The issue of a reformed ministry arose in 1604, while in the session of 1605 there were at least three relevant bills.[114] That 'for the providing of a learned and godly Ministery' would have required testimonials on

---

[111] I.e. the endowments (of some colleges) include substantial appropriations of tithes from parishes. Quoted in Scott 1908, p. 134. For the attack on the universities and impropriations in the Millennary Petition of 1604, see Mullinger 1884, pp. 447–51.

[112] Notestein *et al.* 1935, IV, p. 343. For an articulation of the assumption that a small stipend was 'not worthie of a scholler' and required supplementation by members of the parish see Eliot 1832, I, p. 4.

[113] Foster 1966, I, p. 73.   [114] Bond 1962, pp. 80–2.

behalf of a would-be incumbent from his university or college. Another bill attempted 'to repeale and alter certaine clauses in divers Statutes towching Residence of beneficed Men'. Amongst its other provisions was the requirement that the masters of colleges were to be present at their benefices, and there to preach on alternate Sundays, unless their obligations to their university required them to preach there. This particular bill displayed an acute awareness of the role of the universities in creating a resident, preaching ministry, and of the influence of the masters within their colleges. Its drafters were well informed about life at the universities.[115] The issue of residence was easily confused with that of the 'impropriation' or 'appropriation' of tithes to an institutional rector – a very common practice in the late middle ages designed to redistribute some of the church's revenues – but easily read as an abuse, especially in an age like that of the Tudors, when many impropriations fell into lay hands. Little wonder that, with the sentiments abroad that were expressed in this bill, earlier in the session Cambridge University had sought parliamentary confirmation of the letters patent that had annexed the income from the rectories of Somersham (Huntingdonshire) and Terrington (Norfolk), to the divinity readers in the university, with provision for the maintenance of a vicar to minister to the needs of the parishes.[116] In the session of 1606–7 a further bill was introduced 'against non residence and pluralities of benefices' that bore many similarities to the equally abortive bill of 1604.[117] The matter arose again in 1610,[118] and once more in 1621.[119] In 1642–3 the inhabitants of Somersham petitioned parliament and expressed their pent-up resentment at the convenience made of them by the annexing of the living to the Regius Professorship.[120] At the same time the fellows of Trinity College petitioned parliament in an attempt to preserve the right of some of their fellows to retain a benefice with their fellowship.[121]

As with the issue of lands and leases, so with the debate on the best means of providing a learned, resident and preaching clergy, matters close to the pockets and souls of many parliamentarians led them to take an interest in the universities, and to attempt, however unsuccessfully, to intervene in their affairs. Moreover, the recurrence of these topics from

---

[115] *Ibid.*, pp. 98–100.
[116] HLRO, Main Papers (Supplementary), H.L., 26 Feb. 1606. The bill was lost with close of the session in May.
[117] HLRO, Uncatalogued MSS, MS 25, possibly arising from a suggestion by Wentworth in January 1607 (Willson 1931, pp. 3, 9, 16n.).
[118] Foster 1966, I, pp. 71–3, 219–27.
[119] Notestein *et al.* 1935, IV, pp. 342–3, and HLRO, Main Papers, H.C., 28 April 1621.
[120] Bond 1962, pp. 348–9.   [121] BL Egerton MS 2651, fo. 81.

parliament to parliament ensured some familiarity with the universities in the context of parliamentary deliberations, and a presumption of the right to deal in these matters. This occurred at a time when, for its part, the Crown-out-of-Parliament was multiplying the occasions on which it was employing the prerogative to intervene in the affairs of the universities, and evolving a theory to justify that intervention. These intrusions coincided with developments within the university, most notably the increase in the landholding endowments of the colleges. This drove these corporate landowners to seek the protection of their interests at Court, in the courts of law, and, ultimately, in parliament. At the same time the accentuation of the difficulties encountered with the host towns of Oxford and Cambridge also drove the universities into the parliamentary arena. Finally, the multiplying of the topics with which parliament was concerning itself inevitably affected the interests of these large and increasingly complex institutions. Thus circumstances combined both to draw and to drive the universities into the parliamentary fray.

Chapter 6

CAMBRIDGE AND 'THE COUNTRY'

The overall pattern of the educational revolution in sixteenth- and seventeenth-century England is now well established. In the first burst of enthusiasm for a new educational history in the mid-1960s it was registered in terms of numbers.[1] But, even more, it has come to be recorded in the very evident transformation in the cultural and intellectual life of English society. For the gentry, it is to be read in both the articulate nature of parliamentary debates and the unlaboured facility of expression which emerges over the years within large collections of family correspondence. To draw examples from one area of the country: in East Anglia evidence of this transformation is to be found in the articulate religious and political interests of Sir Nathaniel Bacon, the musical compositions or patronage of the Fermours, Knyvetts, Kytsons and Pastons, the antiquarian and linguistic interests of the Spelmans, the genealogical curiosity of the Lestranges, Townshends, and numerous other county families, the Spenserian compilations of 'the rhyming Woodhouses', the Senecan translations of Sir William Cornwallis, the occult indulgences of the Heydons, the artistic predilections of the Gawdys, the book collecting and libraries of the Knyvetts and the Townshends, and the range of virtuoso interests magnificently portrayed in the painting 'The Oxnead Treasure', which now hangs in Norwich Castle Museum.[2] This cultural transformation is pre-eminently visible still in the primary surviving art-forms of the provincial gentry: their houses and their gardens, which owe not a little in form and decoration to college architecture and college gardens. Nor was this transformation confined to the provincial gentry. During the second half of the sixteenth century the cultural life sponsored by the urban elite of a major regional capital such as Norwich and implemented by its schoolmasters and painter-stainers was also transformed.

[1] This is a revised and updated version of Morgan 1975. For fuller documentation see Morgan 1983. For a brief technical discussion of some statistical problems, see Appendixes I and II, below, pp. 238–40.
[2] See Morgan 1992 and 1999b, and below.

They created a new world of civic ritual incorporating classically inspired ceremonial, a civic portrait collection and a new civic library, founded in 1608, designed to gratify an apparently insatiable appetite for well-turned sermons.

Beyond Norwich lay London. 'The gentlemen of all shires do flie and flock to this citty', wrote John Stow of Elizabethan London; 'The swarming metropolis dominated English life', says Professor Rabb.[3] Exposed to novel educational experiences and immersed in the delights of a scintillating capital, who can doubt that the gentry shed their provincialism and acquired a new urbanity unknown to their rustic forebears; that they became articulate participants in a more homogeneous nation, and that the universities were the main instrument in effecting this transformation?

But the creation of a more informed, refined and integrated cultural and intellectual milieu was only one contribution of the universities to the complex changes within English society during this period. That some of these other developments have been largely ignored is in part a reflection of the degree to which the 'new' history of education was espoused by those historians who defined their special interest as 'social history'. This approach has largely consisted of a conscious reaction against the aridities to which constitutional and institutional histories too easily degenerate. But change in constitutional forms and procedures and changes in institutional organisation do assist in shaping and reshaping the social realities; they do contribute to the political consequences of these reshapings. The social historian cannot ignore them.[4]

Studies of changing patterns in English education have often been concerned with establishing the secular trends, the proportions of classes, and the total of individuals who received higher education. In addition to reflecting our current concerns, this preoccupation with the social composition of higher education has concentrated attention on particular classes of documents, especially the college and university registers which remain in muniment rooms and archives at Oxford and Cambridge: witness the considerable energies expended on the interpretation of the Register of Gonville and Caius College.[5] However, equally important elements of university history are revealed by other documents in the great national repositories in London and in innumerable smaller collections throughout the country. While aggregate statistics are a

[3] Stow 1908, II, p. 212; Rabb 1967, p. 22, see also pp. 26, 96 ff, 101, 138. For what follows, see esp. Curtis 1959, ch. 10.
[4] Talbott 1971, p. 144. This theme is pursued further in chapters 3, 10 and 11.
[5] The debate can be traced in Cressy 1970; cf. Brooke 1985/1996, pp. 80–4.

necessary prerequisite to further research they do not reveal the whole story: the upswing in the line of a graph looks the same whether it is depicting enrolments at university in seventeenth-century England or our present aspiration for a 50 per cent participation rate in the United Kingdom. But what it means depends on an understanding of the society based on a study of non-quantitative materials.

One result of the statistical approach was the unproved assertion that the increase in university education under the Tudors and early Stuarts dissolved local loyalties and created a more homogeneous nation. In truth this is a Whiggish conception stalking in a once modish statistical garb, and a conception that was not altogether unaffected by late twentieth-century interests. In fact the institutional and social arrangements of Tudor and Stuart Cambridge do not support the assumption that the universities erased that sense of local attachment for which there is so much evidence in this period, and which led men to talk of Norfolk or Suffolk or Kent or Somerset or Yorkshire as their 'country', and which impelled some men ultimately to oppose a king in defence of what they considered to be 'the just liberties thereof'.[6]

The extent of the symbiosis between universities and their environing society fluctuates from one age to another. In the eighteenth century it was a highly attenuated relationship.[7] In the late sixteenth and early seventeenth centuries the universities and society achieved a high degree of intimacy not to be equalled until the present age. It behoves us to try to discern with which sections of the wider society the universities were connected, and in what ways, and with what consequences for both of them.

THE RISE OF THE COLLEGE

The 'rise of the college' is generally accepted as one of the most important developments in the history of the English universities during the

---

[6] At one time the notion of 'the countrey' and the 'community of the county' received much attention, largely as the result of the seminal work of Professor Alan Everitt (Everitt 1966, 1969a, 1969b; Hexter 1968; Roots 1968). Arising from a broader European framework, the idea of a court–country dichotomy was a central theme in Hugh Trevor-Roper's interpretation of the period (see esp. Trevor-Roper 1953, 1957). The retreat to the Court implicit in the revisionism of the 1970s distracted attention from provincial labours (a revisionism reviewed and criticised in Cust and Hughes 1989). In 1980 Clive Holmes published a paper purporting to undermine much of what Everitt and his followers appeared to argue, and which has been cited since as grounds for a too summary dismissal of the notion of 'the countrey'. Detailed criticism of Holmes 1980 cannot be undertaken here; in any case it does not detract from the broad evidence of contemporary awareness of 'countrey', further evidence of which is deployed in this chapter.

[7] As we shall see, below, pp. 533 ff.

sixteenth century. It is a rise compounded of both the decline of alternative institutions and the burgeoning of old-established colleges combined with the creation of virile new ones.[8] Both of these developments affected the relationship of the universities with the communities from which their students came, and the lives of those students both at the university and in their subsequent careers. The disappearance of monastic sponsorship for students at the universities broke a chain of dependence which – even in the nationalistic world of late fifteenth-century English monasticism – linked the student to the ultimately supranational institution of the Catholic Church.

In his *History of the University of Cambridge*, Thomas Fuller concludes a list of the old hostels and houses for friars with an enumeration of the variously eminent religious who 'lived in the aforesaid houses in Cambridge belonging to their orders', and having graduated in divinity 'were afterwards dispersed into their respective convents all over England'. Significantly, he also goes on to suggest that many of these buildings eventually passed into the hands of laymen intent upon the founding of colleges.[9] By 1550 only eight halls survived at Cambridge, although they lingered on in a somewhat modified form for slightly longer at Oxford. They were more than adequately replaced by the twelve new colleges founded or refounded at Oxford and Cambridge during the sixteenth century, nine of which were endowed before the reign of Elizabeth.[10]

This transformation in the institutions available to students wrought a radical change in their social life, for which the college now became the main focus. In 1575 William Soone reported to a friend in Cologne that 'none of them live out of the colleges in townsmen's houses'. Harrison noted with enthusiasm that the daily life of students was conducted within college walls rather than in the promiscuous circumstances and miscellaneous habitations of the continental counterparts of the English university towns. Alone of the colleges founded in universities throughout Europe in the sixteenth century, those of the English universities grew into flourishing institutions dominating the university and providing Oxford and Cambridge with their idiosyncratic federal structure.[11]

---

[8] For the architectural evidence at Cambridge, see above, chapter 2, and below, pp. 303–12; cf. Newman 1986 for Oxford.

[9] Thomas Fuller, quoted in Heywood 1855, I, pp. 47 ff, see Stokys, p. xvi n. 1, in Peacock 1841, and *VCH Suffolk*, II, p. 302.

[10] See above, pp. 17–25; Kearney 1970, p. 20; Stone 1975, ch. 1.

[11] Kearney 1970, p. 20; Curtis 1959, pp. 5, 34–7, 282; Cooper, *Annals*, II, pp. 329, 350. The custom of college residence became so universal that in the 1630s, when the pressure of numbers forced some students to reside outside their college 'where no governor or tutor can look after their pupils as they ought', it was a cause of automatic reprehension. *Ibid.*, III, p. 283.

It was the college which evoked the emotions of affectionate gratitude for the benefits which membership entailed – benefits spiritual no less than material. 'I pray God make me thankfull for that he should bring me first unto this college of any stranger', Samuel Ward confided to his diary after his admission to Emmanuel College. 'God's benefits' included that 'He hath set thee in a College where thou sufferest not contempt for the true service of God', and such gratitude was a spur to industrious action, 'How that I ought often to remember how I am placed in a most excellent place for knowledge and grace, and therefore to be carefull to spend my time well.'[12] It was to his former college that the daughter of Dr Foulkes applied for a contribution towards the cost of printing her father's *Works*. It was the college which was constrained to assist the indigent son of one of its recent benefactors. It was college politics which continued to fascinate a former fellow of Caius in his distant Devonshire parsonage. It was college gossip and affairs which played a large part in persuading a Leicestershire preacher to revisit his old university: 'You see I cannot get off from college', he wrote to a friend.[13]

The rival college became the institution which helped to define one's own identity. By the late sixteenth century the typical expression of student violence – that most useful indicator of loyalties and hatreds – is for the students of Trinity to attack those of St John's, while a more mild-mannered and introverted youth found it necessary privately to re-prove himself for 'my pride is walking in the middest of the orchard when St John's men were there'.[14] These expressions of corporate consciousness often took place on those occasions when one college met another either in sporting activities or in public disputation. The repeated attempts to prohibit confrontation on the playing fields testify to their occur-rence: 'That the hurtfull & unscholarlike exercise of Football & meetings tending to that end, do from henceforth utterly cease (except within places several to the colleges & that for them only that be of the same colleges).'[15]

Conflicts between different colleges were also occasioned by the public disputations that were part of the academic curriculum at both Oxford and Cambridge. The most ornate of these events occurred at the

---

[12] Knappen 1933, pp. 107, 118, 129.
[13] Boas 1935, p. 25; Masters 1831, pp. 116, 337; Cosin 1869–72, I, pp. 18 ff; SP 16/540/pt. IV/446/31.
[14] Cooper, *Annals*, II, p. 601; Knappen 1933, p. 113.
[15] Cooper, *Annals*, II, p. 538 (dated 1595); cf. p. 382 for a similarly worded prohibition in 1580. The new dons of the nineteenth century turned to corporate games – mainly rowing – as a means of stimulating the pride of students in their colleges, and to give them a sense of identity. See Rothblatt 1981, ch. 7; Brooke 1993b, pp. 37–9, 290–3.

graduation ceremonies, the Act and the Commencement. Contemporaries present a picture of 'the great crowding in the Commencement-House' and of the general air of excitement engendered by these events.[16] But also at other times in the year there were opportunities for conflict that were exacerbated by the custom of selecting the disputants from different colleges. The possibility of these conflicts occurring became more likely as the antagonisms increased between the Calvinist and the Arminian parties within the universities. Thus, in 1630 the provost of Queen's College, Oxford, having been informed 'of the great riots, tumults, abuses and disorders at the time of disputations in schools', found it necessary severely to admonish his scholars 'not at all to meddle with Wadham College in disputation or otherwise'. In 1627–8 there had been 'Great disorder at Schools' between Exeter and Magdalen Colleges.[17]

The evidence suggests that during the sixteenth century the college became one of the main foci of loyalty and of activity in the life of the university man. For Professor Kearney these burgeoning foundations are 'the educational equivalent of the centralising institutions which formed the basis of Tudor monarchy'.[18] But were they? Do the institutional arrangements – do the specific expressions of gratitude and loyalty towards, and identity with, the college which we have just seen expressed in a general sense – do the daily experiences of college life provide some grounds for demurring from this judgement?

ENDOWMENT

As corporate bodies the colleges were both able and eager to accept endowments. As part of the general transformation in the nature of charitable gifts during the sixteenth century, those received by the colleges took on a more rational and permanent character. Before the Reformation, in return for prayers for the souls of himself and his family, John Lestrange had given to Gonville Hall 'seven hundred ewes and three hundred lambs' which were 'to be delivered to the . . . Master and fellows at midsummer'. By the 1560s another Norfolk man, Archbishop Parker, sought to express his affection for his country and his love of learning: he gave lands to Corpus Christi College by a complex legal instrument designed to ensure the perpetuity of the scholarships and fellowships he was

---

[16] See Mede 1677, p. XLIII; Peacock 1841, p. 28 n. 3; and see below, n. 119.
[17] Boas 1935, pp. 10, 43; for disorders at Cambridge in the 1630s see Mullinger 1911, pp. 131 ff; Cooper, *Annals*, III, pp. 280–3.
[18] Kearney 1970, p. 22.

creating.[19] Writing at the end of the sixteenth century, Andrew Willet asserted that 'of all other times . . . this space of forty years profession of the Gospel, under the heading and direction of our happy Deborah, hath excelled: I cannot rehearse the hundredth part of such fruits as the Gospel hath brought forth in his land'. But he does attempt to catalogue 'the charitable benevolence, bountifull liberality, large expenses bestowed' on his beloved Cambridge.[20]

Professor Jordan has provided statistical confirmation of Willet's assertions: 98 per cent of the sum known to have been given for educational purposes in the early modern era was in the form of endowments. Jordan has gone on to argue that gifts to the universities may be regarded 'as gifts for the benefit of the whole nation' and to suggest that 'the charitable giving of our period was in consequence a most important solvent of the parochialism which marked the English society at the outset of our long period'.[21] But was it? For if in the sixteenth and seventeenth centuries endowment commonly equalled land, land implies a place. Transformed into landowners, the colleges were drawn into the local communities of the landowning classes. As one of those classes they developed vested interests in the localities where they held their lands – and those localities developed a vested interest in the colleges.

Statutory restrictions frequently reinforced natural inclinations: 'One chief part of our college endowment issues out of the counties of West-morland and Yorkshire', explained the fellows of Trinity College, 'And therefore it is provided by our local Statutes that in our elections, both of scholars & fellows, principal regard should be had of those counties.'[22] The endowments of other colleges also tended to be concentrated in one or more areas of the country. Such endowments had the effect of taking at least some of the fellows of a college on an annual circuit through

---

[19] Venn 1897–1901, III, pp. 24–5; cf. *VCH Norfolk*, II, p. 265; Strype 1821, I, p. 495. A similar concern is evident in the legal instruments creating and regulating Sir Nicholas Bacon's endowment of six scholarships at Corpus: see indenture quadripartite with elaborate provisions to prevent default by his heirs (NRO, NRS MS 13915).

[20] Willet 1601, p. 960. (A more comprehensive survey of educational endowments at the two universities is contained in the 1634 edition, pp. 1,233–43).

[21] Jordan 1959, pp. 292, 361, 363. However, the figure of 97.89 per cent is to an unknown extent an exaggeration: endowments are normally matters of record; very often other forms of benefaction are not.

[22] SP 14/52/14. In this document and in many others the phrase 'our local statutes' refers to the statutes of the particular college. In the few ambiguous instances where it is unclear whether the phrase refers to the statutes of the college *per se*, or to the local limitations ordained by those statutes, I have always preferred the former interpretation. It should be added that certain readerships and professorships were also 'bodies corporate', and therefore, the university reasoned, capable of accepting the security of income to be derived from permanent endowment, see SP 16/169/8.

these regions: there developed the office of 'Riding Burser' who went on 'Progress . . . to visit their tenants, reform abuses, punish misdemeanours'.[23]

Local gentry and many of that fast-growing, ubiquitous but ill-defined semi-professional class of 'estate administrators' became involved in running the agricultural and financial side of the college endowments. John Winthrop the elder was for more than sixteen years auditor of both St John's and Trinity Colleges, making regular trips to Cambridge from his home at Groton Hall in Suffolk to discharge his duties. During the 1570s the annual expenses of Corpus included payments of 26s 8d to the auditor and surveyor, £3 10s to the general steward, 40s 'To the steward of our courts', and 40s each to the bailiffs of their six various estates.[24]

The closeness of contact with the local gentry could lead to arrangements of mutual benefit. In a period of intensive building activity the colleges were in great need of ready funds for capital expenditure. In these circumstances they appealed to the alumni. As the fellows of Trinity College realised, such an appeal placed them under a special obligation to their prospective benefactor: 'We think ourselves not a little beholding, that you will be pleased so lovingly to regard us in time of our college['s] present want occasioned by the very chargeable building, which we have in hand.' When the need became urgent, 'Your favour herein showed shall be so much more acceptable, by how much you do the more kindly regard us in this our urgent need; and we for our part will be right ready (besides security) to return unto you that meet thankfullness which we hope will give you both now and hereafter very good contentment.'[25]

The loan of £100 by Sir Francis Barrington, a leading Essex gentleman, was not to be requited with mere effusive thanks. For at the time of these negotiations he was also attempting to persuade the college to renew his lease of the parsonage of Hatfield Broadoak, which still had twelve years to run. Sentimental attachment conveniently coincided with business interests:

> It should be more fit for me to renew my lease so in regard of love I bear to that house, wherein I was bred & to which both my Father and my self have ever been much beholding, I shall be ready . . . to lend one hundred pounds and to be taken as part of the Agreement when I shall renew my lease. And this I do not offer only in regard that the parsonage is near me,

---

[23] Macray 1894–1915, II, pp. 17, 176; Boas 1935, pp. xxi, 1, 10, 15, 64; SP 16/388/15. Cf. S. Bendall in Bendall *et al.* 1999, pp. 135–8.

[24] Mullinger 1911, p. 172; *Winthrop Papers*, I, 46, 48–9, 58–9, 65, 73n, 78, 82, 87, 91, 103–5, 112, 117, 126, 135, 137; NRO, NRS MS 23372 (299), 'The Annual Expenses of the College'. This document is undated, but internal evidence places it in the late 1570s.

[25] BL Egerton MS 2644, fos. 159, 161. Cf. Bendall in Bendall *et al.* 1999, ch. 4.

but also to show my true affection to that place which I must ever love &
honour and my desire that no adversaries should prevent me of continuing
a tenant to so worthy a society.[26]

Sir Francis was not to be disappointed. The college promised that 'as you
shall afford us a very great pleasure, so be assured, that when time doth
come, that we can qualify you in the particular mentioned . . . we will
respect you with all loving friendship, and do you therein all the pleasure
we are able'.[27] Nearly thirty years later the Barringtons were still the
tenants of the parsonage of Hatfield Broadoak.[28]

Not all such relationships were to the benefit of the colleges involved.
In the disputes which raged at Gonville and Caius in the 1570s the opponents of the master and president accused them of allowing the father of
one of their students to cut down the timber on a college estate, and of
attempting to pass a fraudulent lease to the brother-in-law of one of their
party in the college.[29] As impecunious institutions in need of financing
for large building projects, and as individuals frequently dependent for future preferments on those who sought their leases, the colleges and their
fellows easily slipped into close and not always advantageous relationships
with the gentry of those areas where lay the college estates. However, the
disadvantages of these connections with the local gentry were as nothing compared with the depredations inflicted by the importunities of
predatory courtiers. But that is another story.[30]

During the sixteenth century the foundation of grammar schools to
which were attached closed exhibitions to colleges became a very popular
form of endowment.[31] Once again, this created institutional and customary ties which linked particular localities with one or more of the colleges
in the universities. Thus, Alexander Nowell, dean of St Paul's, endowed
Queen Elizabeth's Free School at Middleton, Lancashire, for the benefit of Middleton and the inhabitants of the surrounding townships. The
school was to send thirteen (eventually six) poor scholars to Brasenose
College, Oxford. This endowment is characteristic of the expressions
of enduring affection for a man's native country. Although Nowell had
achieved distinction in an ecclesiastical career and an important position
in the capital, his endowment was intended to benefit 'that end country of Lancashire' where he had been born, and where he had been a

---

[26] BL Egerton MS 2644, fo. 157. For the connections of the Barringtons with Trinity College see
Venn, I, p. 97. For their status in county society: Quintrell 1965, pp. 14, 18.
[27] BL Egerton MS 2644, fo. 159.   [28] BL Egerton MS 2646, fo. 56.
[29] BL Lansdowne MS 33, fos. 91, 93, 107, 115v.
[30] See above, pp. 175–6; below, pp. 277–8, 284.
[31] See Jordan 1960, pp. 206 ff, 252; Charlton 1965, p. 131; Simon 1968; Cressy 1980.

proselytising preacher in the 1560s.[32] Archbishop Grindal founded a free school in his native parish of St Bees in Cumberland, and provided for fellowships and scholarships at his old colleges of Pembroke and Magdalene at Cambridge, and at Queen's College, Oxford, 'all these eight places to be furnished out of the said school of St Bees'.[33] Robert Johnson, founder of Uppingham and Oakham schools, left an endowment which gave scholars from these schools access to Clare, St John's, Emmanuel and Sidney Sussex.[34] Earlier, in 1601, Thomas Cave had made a bequest which linked Clare with Wakefield Grammar School.[35] The preponderance of students at St John's from certain localities is partly attributable to the connections of the college with particular schools, in the north with the schools of Sedbergh, Giggleswick, Bradford, Pocklington and others; in Lancashire with Lancaster and Manchester; in Wales with Bangor and Ruthin; in Shropshire with Shrewsbury Grammar School.[36]

As with Dean Nowell's foundation at Middleton, the establishment of schools in the 'dark corners of the land' – the north and the north-west – was part of a concerted effort to bring Protestant enlightenment to these otherwise preponderantly Catholic areas. Grindal himself described his native district of Cumberland as 'the ignorantest part in religion, and most opressed of covetous landlords of any one part of this realm'. Both Sidney Sussex, and St John's in the earlier part of Elizabeth's reign, were essentially puritan seminaries and both had strong connections with the north fostered by the acquisition of scholarships tied to schools in the northern counties. By the early seventeenth century nearly two-thirds of the pupils of Hull Grammar School went in roughly equal numbers to one of these two colleges. Sidney Sussex in particular had benefited from the spate of early seventeenth-century grammar school foundations, the majority of which were concentrated in the dark corners of the land.[37] Puritan missionary zeal exploited and reinforced local connections.

---

[32] BL Lansdowne MS 15, fo. 136; *CPR Eliz.*, V, no. 2448; and see Curtis 1959, p. 282 and refs.; BL Lansdowne MS 15, fo. 136; *DNB.* The connections between the Nowell brothers and Archbishops Parker and Grindal would bear further investigation. They had common interests in education, preaching and antiquities. See Flower 1935.

[33] Collinson 1979, pp. 27, 280 and 347 n. 58; Willet 1634, pp. 1,222–3; Purnell 1904, p. 10; *Cambridge Documents 1852*, II, p. 206; *VCH Cambs.*, III, p. 351; Cunich *et al.* 1994, pp. 26–7.

[34] Harrison 1953, p. 77.   [35] *Ibid.*, p. 66.

[36] Mayor 1893, p. x; see also Simon 1954–5, p. 50 n. 1; Spufford 1970, p. 118 and n. 2. One motive for endowment was to bring enlightenment to the 'dark corners of the land'. However, there is some evidence that its effect was to create something like an internal brain-drain. Bright young men were siphoned out of northern places by university endowments and thereafter redirected to softer southern climes (Morgan 1986).

[37] Collinson 1979; *DNB* s.v. Grindal; *VCH Cambs.*, III, p. 482; Lawson 1963, pp. 126–7; Jordan 1959, p. 288; 1960, p. 227; see the important article Hill 1963b. The relation of the colleges to the production of a preaching ministry is delightfully illustrated in the statutes of Corpus Christi

There are some indications to suggest that one of the effects of this spate of foundations was to make these schools the main channels through which students from the northern counties gained access to, and support while at, the universities.[38] In East Anglia, a much richer region during the early seventeenth century, there seems to have been less reliance on these major feeder schools, and a greater overall availability of education. There a learned clergy spread out into small and intimate parishes, and religious proclivities combined with the greater wealth of a numerous local gentry to provide more diversified sources of individual patronage for promising local boys intent upon a university education. Again, in East Anglia geographical proximity brought both gentry and would-be students into more intimate and more frequent acquaintance with Cambridge.

The conditions attached to many endowments, and the provisions enjoined by numerous statutory regulations ensured that college and local community were constantly participating in each other's lives. In their relationship with the endowed schools, the colleges were not merely passive receptacles for students. They were also involved in the appointment of schoolmasters and participated in the selection of scholars. Candidates for the headmastership of Pocklington, and for the head- and under-masterships of Shrewsbury, were required to become members of St John's. On most occasions the college used the opportunity of a vacancy to advance one of its own graduates, and in doing so often preferred to the school one of the latter's former pupils.[39] In the case of Alexander Nowell's foundation, the principal and fellows of Brasenose College were to be the governors of Middleton School. Sir Robert Hitcham's bequests eventually made Pembroke the trustee of property in Suffolk, mostly for schools and almshouses in the county.[40] The exhibitioners of Thomas Cave at Clare were elected conjointly by the college, the vicar of Wakefield, and the governors and masters of Wakefield School.[41] In Suffolk, Sir Nicholas Bacon endowed his school at Botesdale with six scholarships tied to Corpus Christi, the college in which he had spent his 'younger time'. Selection of the students for these scholarships was by consultation between the schoolmaster, Sir Nicholas' heirs, and a fellow of the college sent over from Cambridge for the purpose.[42]

College, 1570; see Auerbach 1954, plate 38. Note the text on preaching and the detail of a sermon in progress.

[38] Jordan 1959, p. 291; 1960, p. 428.
[39] Mayor 1893, pp. x, 97, 130, 139; *HMC 47, Shrewsbury Corporation*, p. 45.
[40] *CPR Eliz.*, v, no. 2448; *VCH Cambs.*, III, p. 349.   [41] Forbes 1928, II, p. 638.
[42] NRO, NRS MS 10129, a leather-bound book embossed 'Botesdale', no foliation; NRO, NRS MS 13915, Indenture quadripartite; NRO, NRS MS 23372, miscellaneous pieces, sixteenth to

Such arrangements are typical of the active and continued participation of the godly magistrates of Elizabethan England in encouraging further reformation through the patronage of educational institutions. Thus, it was only natural that Sir Robert Jermyn, a puritan gentleman with considerable influence in the town, should be nominated to oversee the establishment of a scholarship from the school at Bury St Edmunds to St John's College, Cambridge.[43] Across the border, in Norfolk, another puritan magistrate, Sir Christopher Heydon, underwent the expense of a suit in Chancery in order to gain some say in the nomination of the schoolmaster and usher at the school recently founded by Sir John Gresham at Holt. In endowing a scholarship at Caius for a pupil from this school Heydon again displayed his desire for a supervisory control of the educational institutions which served his locality: he and his descendants retained a right to nominate to the scholarship and this involved communication between the Heydons and the college whenever the scholarship became vacant.[44]

Other families exercised similar rights. At Christ's the Berkeleys had the right of nomination of one scholar from the county of Gloucester; at Clare the family of Edmund, Lord Gorges, as descendants of the executors who created the Freeman scholarships, continued to exercise the right of nomination until the mid-seventeenth century. At Magdalene, Sir Christopher Wray gave the parsonage of Gainsthorpe, Lincs., for the maintenance of two fellows and six scholars. He retained the right to nominate both fellows and scholars during his lifetime. After his death the right passed to the dean and chapter of Lincoln, who, with the concurrence of his heirs, were to nominate the scholars from among the pupils of the Free School of Kirton-in-Lindsay, or in the absence of suitable candidates, from Lincoln School. Similar conditions attached to some of the separately endowed fellowships.[45]

In addition to particular individuals and families, corporations also enjoyed the right of nomination and exercised a supervisory authority over the endowments of certain colleges. The mundane but annually repeated administrative procedures, no less than the exercise of the powers

---

eighteenth centuries. For evidence of a college fulfilling its supervisory duties see Boas 1935, pp. 29–30, 34, 37. For a critique of the nineteenth-century failings of this system of appropriated scholarships or exhibitions to meet the needs of a transformed socioeconomic structure see Rothblatt 1981, p. 43.

43 BL Add. Charter 27701. For Sir Robert's puritanism and connections with Bury, see Collinson 1967, pp. 188, 204–5. See also NDR, Box 1109, Bury School Agreement, 1583.

44 Linnell 1955, pp. 28–9; SP 16/246/98.

45 *Report of the Commissioners*, 1852–3, . . . *Evidence*, p. 328; Forbes 1928, II, p. 640; Purnell 1904, p. 81; Venn 1897–1901, III, pp. 214–15.

of patronage which these duties involved, were a constant reminder of the connections of college and community. At Norwich the corporation appears to have maintained a tight control over the nomination of students for scholarships.[46] The complicated indenture tripartite establishing Archbishop Parker's endowment for Norwich scholars at Corpus permanently tied the college to the city, and in addition obliged the corporation to augment this endowment with scholarships out of its own revenues.[47] Under the ancient statutes of Bishop Bateman, Gonville Hall was obliged every September to make a yearly report to the bishop and to the dean and chapter of Norwich of the names and number of their fellows. Trinity Hall was under a similar obligation.[48]

The administrative form of other scholarship endowments also ensured a continuous, if not always harmonious, connection between the college and members of the local community. At Clare the Marshall scholarship took the form of one-third of a rent-charge on lands in Lincolnshire. In 1636, John Borage of North Barsham, Norfolk, gave to the same college a rent-charge of £15 per annum to support a bye fellowship for natives of Norfolk. The foundation of exhibitions to St John's, Cambridge, and Magdalen College, Oxford, by Sir Ambrose Cave involved their half-yearly payment by his heirs out of the rents of lands designated for this purpose. According to Peacock, even after the decays of the eighteenth century, the incomes of many scholarships and fellowships continued to be rent-charges on 'foreign' estates, beyond the direct control of the colleges to which they were appropriated.[49]

During the sixteenth century there was a transformation in the magnitude, the sources, the forms and the ultimate consequences of endowments for the colleges of the English universities. College architecture no less than the statistics of charitable endowments cannot fail to convince us of the change in the magnitude of giving. During the fifteenth and earlier centuries endowments — such as there were — had tended to come from

---

[46] Saunders 1932, p. 174. I am indebted to Mr Ian Dunn, formerly of the NRO, for assistance in searching city records for mention of these nominations.

[47] Norwich City Muniments, City Chamberlain's Accounts, VI, no foliation, *passim*, record these annual payments and 'Rewards' to the messengers 'for carrying the stipend to Bennet college'. The Bacon family papers, formerly at Redgrave Hall, and now in Chicago University Library, contain a long and fairly continuous series of acquittances for payments to Corpus of the quarterly stipends of the six scholars established by Sir Nicholas Bacon; Typescript Calendar of Redgrave MSS, 334.

[48] BL Lansdowne MS 33, fo. 115. Writing in the 1920s Venn surmised that these documents had been destroyed (Venn I, pp. i, x). They do indeed appear to be missing for earlier centuries, but from the reign of Elizabeth there is a fairly continuous series of returns preserved among the MSS of the dean and chapter of Norwich. I am indebted to Mrs Elizabeth Rutledge for facilitating my consultation of these documents.

[49] Forbes 1928, II, p. 642; I, p. 77; BL Add. MS 36906, fos. 237 ff; Peacock 1841, p. 117 n. 1.

the great princes of the church. Members of an international institution, their aspirations appear to have transcended their original local loyalties. If they did attach local restrictions to their benefactions, they thought in terms of their often very extensive dioceses. Thus, William Smith, a fifteenth-century bishop of Lincoln, founded a fellowship for his diocese. Bishop Bateman had endowed Gonville Hall and Trinity Hall primarily to serve the needs of his diocese of Norwich.[50]

By the second half of the sixteenth century, on the other hand, even eminent clerics appear to have been thinking in terms of achieving their larger ends through favouring those local societies from whence they came. Grindal's endowments were intended to bring enlightenment to his native parish of St Bees in Cumberland; Archbishop Parker's foundation was intended for the benefit of his beloved native city of Norwich. But it was no longer the episcopate which was the great benefactor of the university for by then this distinction was shared by local gentry and merchants, men who thought primarily in terms of their native community.

The form of the gifts provided by these new benefactors also changed. They were directed towards the colleges, and provided support for a specific scholarship or fellowship in preference to a simple addition to the general funds of the college.[51] In the guise of land or rent-charges for exhibitions from particular schools they created permanent connections which increasingly tied individual colleges to specific localities.

Therefore, one of the consequences of the great sixteenth-century endowments of the universities was to take the colleges into the country, and bring the country into the colleges. As in many spheres, so also in education: to some extent the creation, and to a very large extent the control, of the institutions of local society were passing into the hands of the county gentry and the oligarchs of the larger towns.

STATUTORY LIMITATIONS

The growth in the number of locally tied endowments merely served to accentuate and further complicate the requirements created by the pre-existent statutory limitations. The origins of these limitations lay in the distinction between northerners and southerners in the medieval English universities. In the fifteenth century the major conflict between different groups of students at Cambridge was that between the northerners and

---

[50] McMahon 1947, p. 56; *VCH Cambs.*, III, p. 356; Brooke 1985/1996, p. 15; see below, p. 199.
[51] Forbes 1928, II, p. 637; *Report of the Commissioners . . .* , 1852–3, pp. 164–5.

the southerners on the occasion of the Minor Commencement. Significantly, as we have seen, by the late sixteenth century these events had become the catalysts of conflicts between the students of different colleges.[52] The broad division between northerners and southerners was of many centuries' standing. This peculiarly English version of the often violent conflicts between the *nationes* of the medieval European universities continued into the first half of the sixteenth century: northerners and southerners were still breaking one another's heads at Henrician Oxford.[53] Whereas at Paris and other continental universities the organisation of the student – and sometimes the teaching – body was into broad groups of nations, such as German, French and Italian, there were so few foreigners at medieval Oxford that the distinction which developed there was between Englishmen coming from north or south of the Nene. Whereas on the Continent individual 'nations' such as the Picards or Burgundians were adopted as sub-units within the larger grouping of the *nationes*, in England as early as 1297 there are references to representatives being drawn from the counties *within* the northern and southern divisions.[54] This feeling of difference between northerners and southerners continued to affect English society throughout the sixteenth and seventeenth centuries, but by then it was subsidiary to the sense of county identity which had developed from within it.[55]

The early statutes of most of the first batch of Cambridge colleges founded between the late-thirteenth and the mid-fourteenth centuries do not appear to have enjoined any local limitations. However, the second series of foundations extending from the mid-fifteenth century into the early 1600s did introduce these regional restrictions, while at the same time similar limitations were incorporated into the statutes of the colleges of earlier foundation. Lady Elizabeth de Clare's Foundation Statute of 1359 enjoins that no inquiry shall be made, nor shall any objection be raised against candidates for a place in the college on the grounds of the place of their birth. This clause was changed in the statutes of 1551

---

[52] See above, pp. 185–6.

[53] Mullinger 1867, p. 10; cf. Peacock 1841, p. 111 n. 1; Emden 1964, p. 9. The conflicts of northerners and southerners were, however, much more marked at Oxford than at Cambridge (Leader 1988, p. 28). At Oxford the last recorded clash between northerners and southerners occurred as late as 1578.

[54] Kibre 1947, pp. 160–7; Rashdall 1936, III, pp. 55–60; see Emden 1964, p. 7, for correction of the traditional view that the dividing line was the Trent. At Oxford, in addition to the north–south division, there was also a practical, but apparently not formally organisational, distinction between the English and the Welsh (Cooper, *Annals*, II, p. 329); see also Cole 1969–70, pp. 185–91; Macray 1894–1915, II, p. iv; *VCH Cambs.*, III, p. 454.

[55] For an eloquent expression of the sense of difference a man from one part of the country felt when he ventured into a foreign region see Kinge 1597, Sig. *14 (*STC* 14976).

which laid down strict regulations as to the place of birth of candidates for membership in the college.[56] The early restrictions as to locality divide elections between men from the north and men from the south of the Trent. They seem to have originated in an attempt to curb the monopolisation of all the places in a college by a group of kin or a local faction whose members sought fellowships as safe havens from the uncertain life of the halls whose existence ebbed and flowed around the more permanent and endowed collegiate institutions. This appears to be the logic behind the late fifteenth-century statutes of Peterhouse, reconfirmed by Richard Redman, bishop of Ely and Visitor of the college in 1516.

> Since reason persuades us that there is no one but who deservedly owes much to the country from whence he took his birth . . . it constantly happens, that upon election of fellows being announced, domestic discords and detestable quarrels easily arise, to the no small detriment of learning, the fellows being all desirous of putting forward their countrymen and those they affection most, some one, and others another.

To avoid these domestic discords it was enacted that half the fellows should come from the northern dioceses and counties, and half from the southern; if one part came to preponderate over the other the larger part was not to be increased until the smaller part was rendered equal in number.[57]

The effect of such regulations was twofold. In the first place they facilitated the conduct of rivalries within the universities. Indeed, it is worth contemplating the possibility that the north–south division in the medieval university was actually exacerbated by such well-intentioned regulations. In the second place they narrowed down the possible geographical range of rivalries *within* the northern and the southern divisions; if you could not gain an advantage over your opponents from the north or the south, perhaps you could engross all the benefits of the northern or southern division for your faction within the college? At the time of Bishop Redman's reconfirmation of the Peterhouse Statutes the college also found it necessary to agree, 'for the furtherance of goodwill, peace and quiet in our elections, and for other considerations specially moving us thereto . . . that it shall not be lawful to have more than two fellows or scholars together out of any county of England, whatever diocese it may be'. Peterhouse was not alone in having these regulations; they also pertained at St Catharine's and were introduced at St John's in 1545 and

---

[56] Peacock 1841, pp. 28, 111; Forbes 1928, II, p. 33; Heywood 1855, II (ii), p. 126.
[57] Heywood 1855, I (ii), pp. 63–4; *VCH Cambs.*, III, p. 336.

Clare in 1555. At the same period similar regulations were introduced at Pembroke, where it was laid down that the number of fellows from any one county was not to exceed a fourth part of the total number of fellows.[58] In the decade that Bishop Redman confirmed the Peterhouse Statutes, Nicholas West provided Jesus College with statutes which fixed the number of fellowships at six, to be drawn alternately from two groups of northern and southern counties, with never more than one fellow from the same county, except for those counties where the college owned sufficient property to support two. At Queens' a statute of 1475 enacted that not more than one fellow was to be elected from any one county, and not more than two from any one diocese. When Emmanuel was founded in the 1580s it was laid down that the college was not to have two or more fellows from the same county at any one time.[59]

The need to enact these statutes testifies to the prevalence of regional sentiment, the strength of which appears to have been on the increase from some time in the late fifteenth century. They created one group of colleges which had a reasonably wide geographical intake. King's College occupied a unique position which was reflected in its lack of private endowments and its statutory limitations: 'increase of Scholarships and Fellowships they have none by reason their foundation is certain, consisting of 70 Schollars and fellows: some other helps they have had, but not many: men otherwise well disposed, not presuming . . . to add to such a princely foundation'. One also suspects that the sixteenth-century gentleman and merchant was not inclined to endow an institution peculiarly subject to royal interference and in the administration of which they could exercise only a minimal influence. King's scholars were recruited from its sister college of Eton. First preference was to be given to candidates from parishes in which the two colleges owned property, and second preference to candidates born in Cambridgeshire and Buckinghamshire.[60]

The renewal of statutes during the sixteenth century modified the character of their regional limitations for some of the colleges. As we have seen, at Clare the general preference for candidates from the parishes of the churches belonging to the college was transformed into a strict limitation of never more than two fellows from the same county. The Henrician statutes at St John's brought the college into line with the

---

[58] Heywood 1855, I (ii), pp. 65–6; *VCH Cambs.*, III, pp. 422, 439 n. 39; Winstanley 1935, p. 195; Heywood 1855, II (ii), p. 187; see Peacock 1841, pp. 110–11. Oxford colleges had comparable statutes: see Bloxam 1853–5, I, pp. i, vii, and Stone 1975.
[59] *VCH Cambs.*, III, pp. 411–12, 474; Bendall *et al.* 1999, p. 63, 422.
[60] Willet 1634, p. 1,234; *VCH Cambs.*, III, pp. 382–3.

pattern which was beginning to prevail at other colleges. The original foundation statutes had ordained that *at least* half of the twenty-eight 'foundress's fellows' should come from the nine northern counties. This regional bias had been augmented by subsequent endowments, most notably the endowment by Bishop Fisher of four fellowships and two scholarships. The scholars and three of the fellows were to be Yorkshiremen while the other fellow was to come either from the diocese of Rochester or from Richmondshire. Under the new dispensation northern fellows were to constitute *at most* half of the total body of fellows. These changes appear to have been inspired by the desire of the king – or of his advisers – to reduce the influence in the college of northern fellows with unaccommodating Catholic sympathies. A measure of their success was its reputation as a seminary of puritanism during the early years of Elizabeth. The college again received new statutes in 1580. Under their terms, and the terms of most private endowments, the great majority of fellowships were limited to candidates born in the counties to which each fellowship was specifically attached.[61]

In common with the provisions of the Edwardian revisions of statutes at other colleges, those at Trinity ordained that not more than three natives from any one county could hold fellowships simultaneously. A further revision of the statutes in 1560 abolished the county limitation on fellowships, but required that, all other things being equal, candidates from places where the college owned property were to be preferred. Thus, Trinity was transformed from a college having a theoretically equal distribution of fellows to one with a considerable regional bias in favour of the northern counties.[62]

Another group of colleges was more or less tightly tied to specific localities. Often regional in inception, if anything the strength and multiplicity of these local connections were augmented during the sixteenth century. The original Beaufort Statutes for God's House – later to become Christ's College – established a preference in elections to fellowships in favour of the natives of the nine northern counties, of which only one was to come from each county. Students were to be selected according to the same local preferences, with an upper limit of three students from any one county. Magdalene was essentially a college for Lincolnshire men, although it did acquire one or two benefactions to augment its plundered resources which provided it with links in the West Riding and Norfolk, and to Wisbech and Shrewsbury. The Foundation Statutes of Sidney

[61] Forbes 1928, II, p. 33; *VCH Cambs.*, III, pp. 438, 443.
[62] *VCH Cambs.*, III, p. 464; SP 14/52/14.

Sussex established a preference in the election of fellows from Kent and Rutland; those from the latter county being drawn in particular from Oakham and Uppingham Schools. The leaning towards Kent was no doubt due to the Sidney family connection with that county, while the favour shown to Rutland originated in the fact that one of the executors of Lady Sidney's will – Lord Harrington – was seated in that county at Exton.[63] In this respect Sidney Sussex is better compared with Wadham at Oxford than with Emmanuel, the Cambridge college with which it is otherwise most closely associated.

The remaining three colleges had strong regional connections with East Anglia. Trinity Hall, like Magdalene, was a small and very poor college. It had originally been established by Bishop Bateman of Norwich to provide civil and canon lawyers for his diocese. Naturally, it had suffered from the abolition of canon law studies at the Reformation, and the uncertainties created by the subsequent encroachments of the common lawyers into the domain of civil law. But Trinity Hall's statutes ensured that its legal bias should continue, and in 1604–5 only three of its members were ministers. It also retained its connections with East Anglia through its few estates, most of which lay in Norfolk, through those of its statutes which established a preference for students from Gonville and Caius College (with a population dominated by East Anglians), and through a general preference for fellows and students from the diocese of Norwich.[64] The statutes of Gonville Hall given by Bishop Bateman in 1353–5 were augmented in the late fifteenth century with a clause which had initiated the territorial preferences and limitations which intimately connected the college with the eastern counties. The effect of the statutes promulgated between 1559 and 1573 by Dr Caius after his refoundation of the college was to accentuate these territorial limitations. Their effects are evident in an analysis of the county origins of students when this information becomes available after the beginning of the college register in 1560 (Fig. 1).[65] Corpus Christi College already had a strong bias in favour of the diocese of Norwich before Archbishop Parker founded four new fellowships and several new scholarships in 1569. These tied the college even closer to Norfolk, and more particularly to Norwich.

[63] *VCH Cambs.*, III, p. 431; Purnell 1904, pp. vi, 207; Hoyle in Cunich *et al.* 1994, p. 90; Scott-Giles 1975, p. 26.

[64] *VCH Cambs.*, III, pp. 362–70; Scott 1884, p. 164; cf. Peacock 1841, p. 32, App. A, p. xlix, n; SP 14/10A/72; HMC 23 *Cowper*, II, p. 100: documents among the muniments of the dean and chapter of Norwich, where they are in some instances wrongly attributed to Trinity College. On Trinity Hall, see Crawley 1976, chs. 1, 3, 4.

[65] See p. 200 and Fig. 1. *VCH Cambs.*, III, pp. 356, 358. The relevant statute, attributed to Bishop Bateman, was in fact a fifteenth-century forgery (Brooke 1985/1996, p. 16 and n. 35).

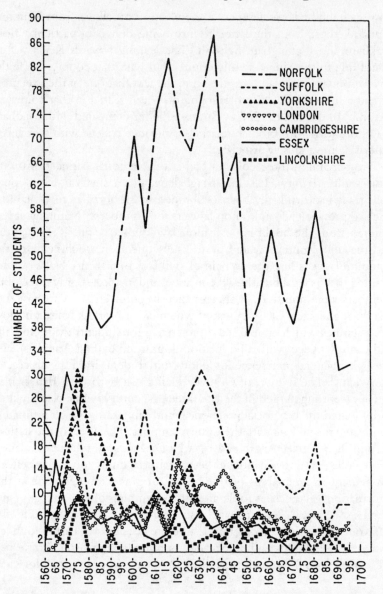

Fig. 1 Gonville and Caius College: quinquennial totals of membership by predominant counties, 1560–1700

Ten years later there were thirty-seven men and youths on the foundation. Of these, twenty-one came from Norfolk, of which number seven came from Norwich.[66]

Once a bias had been established it became cumulative, with students and fellows from the favoured county engrossing even the open fellowships on the foundation. In a dispute between the city of Norwich and Corpus in the 1620s, the arbitrators noted that the college 'have ever had more of the Norwich Scholars in their society then they are bound by Covenant to have'. And earlier in the dispute in a very spirited letter the college had asked indignantly, 'If to make them more allowance, to admit more of them in better Fellowships than they can challenge, be not, in your valuation, thankworthy.'[67] In the 1630s one of the fellows of Gonville and Caius accused the master of preferring men from counties other than Norfolk and Suffolk. The arbitrators of the dispute found that, on the contrary, 'the present Master of the said College hath so carefully pursued that Statute as at this time (of the 12 Senior Fellows of that house) 11 are of Norfolk'.[68] These examples suggest the way in which patterns of regional association, created by endowment at Corpus and statutory limitation at Caius, were reinforced by customary patterns of patronage and connection accumulated about these formal links between the colleges and the local communities which they served.

One would expect these patterns to be most obvious among those students who entered a college with the intention of taking a degree and in the hope of enjoying the benefits of the college endowments. Presumably, they would be less obvious among those students who entered a college as pensioners or fellow-commoners. As such they could expect no direct financial assistance from the college. Yet even among these students there is some evidence to suggest that the choice of college was influenced by regional ties. A sample of Norfolk gentry from the early years of the reign of Elizabeth provides some very crude indications of the pattern of college attendance among the social elite of the county (see Table 1). If choice was unaffected by regional considerations, distribution between colleges should be scaled according to the relative size of the colleges. To some extent this is so; Christ's, St John's and Trinity were very large colleges and this is reflected in the proportion of the Norfolk elite which was attracted to them. In particular the prestigious reputation of Trinity College is reflected in the large number of students

---

[66] NRO, NRS MS 23372, 'The Revenues of Corpus Christi College in Cambridge'.
[67] Norwich City Muniments, Case 25, shelf d (1361); 31 Oct. 1622 and 14 Dec. 1619.
[68] SP 16/315/11.

Table 1. *Distribution by college and college status of a sample of Norfolk gentry alumni c. 1563, 1578 and 1585*

College	Fellow-commoner	Pensioner	Scholar	Sizar	Status unknown	Total	Total %
Peterhouse				1		1	0.85
Clare	1	4				5	4.2
Pembroke		2.5				2.5	2.1
Gonville & Caius	1	13.5	1	1		16.5	14.1
Trinity Hall		8		2	1	11	9.4
Corpus	5.5	7		3	4	19.5	16.2
King's			2			2	1.7
Queens'	4	3				7	5.98
Catharine Hall						–	0
Jesus	1	2.5				3.5	2.99
Christ's	2	11	2			15	12.8
St John's	2	10.5		2		14.5	12.3
Magdalene						–	0
Trinity	7	8		0.5	1	16.5	14.1
Hostels		3				3	2.5
Total	23.5	73	5	9.5	6	117	
Total %	20	62	4	8	5	100	

Gonville & Caius Trinity Hall Corpus	47	(40%)
	All other college and hostels	24 (21%)
Christ's St John's Trinity	46	(39%)

Sources: The composite list from which these figures derive was compiled from Dashwood, Bulwer *et al.* 1878–95; Hatfield House MS 161, fos. 41–6, and Bodl. MS Barlow 13, fos. 507–9.

entering as fellow-commoners. However, Gonville and Caius and Corpus were medium-sized colleges during the period in which most of the individuals in this sample were entering university. Trinity Hall was in the process of declining to the status of the numerically smallest college in Cambridge. Even so, they attracted just as many Norfolk students as the three largest colleges and nearly twice as many as all the other colleges and hostels put together. A less randomly selected sample of Norfolk residents *c.* 1630–3 shows the continued favour accorded to Gonville and Caius (see Table 2).[69] However, what these figures conceal rather than reveal is the extent to which the choice of college was determined for members of the elite by acquaintance with the prospective tutor. A detailed analysis of the connections between tutors and students at Gonville and

[69] See Kearney 1970, pp. 56–7 for a convenient reproduction of Venn's graph depicting numbers at the different Cambridge colleges. For the sources of this sample, see notes to Tables 1 and 2.

Table 2. *Distribution by college and college status of a sample of men resident in Norfolk c. 1630–3*

College	Fellow-commoner	Pensioner	Scholar	Status unknown	Total	Total %
Peterhouse	3	6			9	14.8
Clare					–	0
Pembroke	1				1	1.6
Gonville & Caius	7	6	2	1	16	26.2
Trinity Hall			1		1	1.6
Corpus	2	3			5	8.2
King's	2		1		3	4.9
Queens'	3	1			4	6.6
Catharine Hall					–	0
Jesus		1			1	1.6
Christ's	3	5			8	13.1
St John's	2	2			4	6.6
Magdalene					–	0
Trinity College	1				1	1.6
Emmanuel	3	4			7	11.5
Sidney Sussex		1			1	1.6
Total	27	29	4	1	61	
Total %	44	48	6	1.6	100	

Sources: This sample is based on a composite list of Norfolk residents c. 1630–3, who were required to compound for knighthood; PRO E.407/35 (incomplete), E.178/5520 (severely damaged). See J.P. Cooper, 'The social distribution of land and men in England, 1436–1700', *The Economic Hist. Rev.*, 2 ser., 20.3 (1967), 429–30. A more comprehensive list of names is to be derived from a copy-book now in the library of Ickworth House, Suffolk, case 1, shelf 3 (I am indebted to the late R.W. Ketton Cremer for making this document available to me). Where students migrated, or transferred from one status to another they have been attributed as halves to each category.

Unfortunately the listings used in Tables 1 and 2 were compiled originally for different purposes and the two samples will not sustain detailed comparison.

Caius suggests that this acquaintance was frequently based on common local origins. Statutory regulations ensured that most of the fellows at Gonville and Caius were Norfolk or Suffolk men; in their capacity as tutors they tended to attract other East Anglians of both high and low social status.[70] It would require a similar analysis of other colleges to determine how many Norfolk 'statistical strays' – as in these figures – can

---

[70] I hope to publish the results of this analysis at a later date.

be accounted for by the presence of a fellow from Norfolk tutoring local boys. Connections determined by custom and statute variously affected the development of both the colleges and their regions. Influence on the preservation or propagation of particular religious beliefs is one aspect of the interplay between college and local community.

Contemporaries certainly believed that the religious tenor of a college could affect the character of the areas it served. At a time when Gonville Hall appears to have been suffused with advanced religious views, Bishop Nykke of Norwich, in commenting on the conformability of his diocese, complained in 1530 that 'I hear of no clerk that hath commen out lately of that College, but savoureth of the frying pan, though he speak never so holily.'[71] Later in the century, under the aegis of the conservative and tolerant Dr Caius, the college became a refuge for men of a like persuasion. The effects of the toleration of Catholics maintained in the college led Dr Sandys, archbishop of York, to request that Dr Legge, Caius' nominee as his successor, should be allowed to accept no more pupils 'to breed and train up in popery', for all 'the popish gentlemen in this country [Yorkshire] send their sons to him [and] he setteth sundry of them over to one Swayl [Swale], also of the same house, by whom the youth of this country is corrupted: that at their return to their parents, they are able to dispute in the defence of popery: and few of them will repair to the church'.[72] Legge came from a Norfolk family, and had acquired his northern connections during the tenure of his former fellowships at Trinity and Jesus. His popularity as a tutor is suggested by the group of pupils who migrated with him to Caius, including six boys from Yorkshire. Two years later he was followed from Jesus by Richard Swale, who was himself a Yorkshireman by birth and whom his enemies described as a close friend of the new master.[73] In this instance religious attitudes served to reinforce a natural dependence on local connections. After all, a man prepared to maintain his religious convictions in the face of increasing political pressure was likely to be fastidious in the choice of a tutor for his children. What better guarantee of doctrinal acceptability was there than the reputation or the recommendations of a man with established local connections, or a man of local birth in distant Cambridge?

The college affected the character of the local community, but the character of the local community also affected the nature of the colleges.

[71] Brooke 1985/1996, pp. 51–2 and refs.; Strype 1812, II, pp. 695–6.
[72] Strype 1824, II, pp. 2, 341–2; III, pp. 1, 73.
[73] Venn 1897–1901, I, pp. 73–4, 85; III, pp. 64 ff; Venn, IV, p. 189a; BL Lansdowne MS 33, fo. 91.

It is a reasonable hypothesis that, as the number of endowments with all their various restrictions increased over the years, access to higher education became relatively more available for some groups in society. As the form and number of endowments varied very considerably from one area of the country to another, this may well have contributed to the differentiation between regions. Conversely, differences between regions could affect the size and social composition of the colleges. At Norwich there is evidence to suggest that a powerful and independent corporation attempted to fulfil the wishes of the founder for locally tied exhibitions by preferring genuinely poor scholars and by enforcing the restriction to boys born within the city. Shrewsbury, a less powerful corporation, allowed its school and therefore its exhibitions to be infiltrated by the local gentry.[74]

The selection of students for university did not occur in a sociological vacuum; rather, they emerge at Cambridge from the swirling mists of patronage and influence which cover so much of the Elizabethan and early Stuart landscape. Within this dusky world the cross-currents and breezes varied considerably from one region to another. As the country settled down after the uncertainties of the middle of the century and the early years of the Elizabethan regime, local families became more assured of their position in the community, and more ready to provide educational patronage for their clients. Once again, the inclination and resources available to provide individual sponsorship must have varied from area to area.

The effect of the colleges on the social structure of their localities did not cease after the process of recruitment. Did colleges such as Gonville and Caius at Cambridge, with its strong connections with East Anglia, and Exeter at Oxford, with its equally strong connections with the West Country, add to the resources of these regions by returning to them the men they had educated? Did other colleges such as Jesus at Oxford, in relation to Wales, and Christ's, St John's and Trinity at Cambridge, in relation to the North Country, 'where great need is that nurture, learning and religion should be planted', syphon off local talent and redirect it elsewhere? John Penry thought they did. If he was right, social mobility may have been beneficial for the individual but detrimental for the region. In these circumstances the numerous educational endowments in the dark corners of the land may have retarded development in Wales and the north by providing for its more able youth an escape to the universities, where

---

[74] Saunders 1932, p. 174; *HMC* 47, *Shrewsbury Corporation* . . . (1899), pp. 44–5.

they acquired an eligibility for employment in more hospitable southern counties.[75] To what extent did the nomination to itinerant preacherships in the gift of individual colleges offset this drain on northern manpower resources?[76]

There appear to be considerable variations in the availability and the quality of education accessible from region to region. East Anglia, with the massive advantage of its tied endowments at Corpus and its statutory preference at Caius, together with lesser preferences at other colleges, appears to have been far better served than Lincolnshire with its relatively meagre provision at Magdalene. Did the university have the same effect on regions served by only two or three fellowships and scholarships at each of a number of colleges, with an intake dispersed over a broad area, as on regions like East Anglia which received special preference at one or two colleges? Answers to these questions can be provided only by local historians who are aware of the larger national context as they work in detail on their own chosen localities. But it does seem that it would be advantageous for the social historians of education to adopt a different viewpoint: to cease treating the universities like encapsulated components within an anonymous twenty-first-century society; to treat higher education as an integral part of a larger analysis of the social structure within the communities with which the university was so intimately connected. One suspects that the college would then emerge in the realm of social history as it appears within the realm of political history and the history of ideas: not as the educational equivalent of the centralising institutions of the Tudor state, but as one of the mechanisms which contributed to the regional differentiation which is the characteristic feature of English socioeconomic structure at this time.[77]

THE COLLEGE AND ITS BENEFACTORS

The origins of the regional limitations lay in an attempt – albeit it unsuccessful – to curb the worst effects of regional patriotism and to subdue the quarrels between different areas of the country. With the major series of endowments during the sixteenth century there was an inversion of purpose. Now the aim was actually to favour the community of birth or some other area of the country for which the donor felt a special sense of

---

[75] SP 14/52/14; Hill 1963b; Penry 1960, pp. 38–9; Seaver 1970, pp. 180–1; Stone 1964, pp. 47 and n. 14; Morgan 1987.

[76] SP 38/8/14, Nov. 1607; *CSPD*, VIII, p. 382.

[77] See Spufford 1970; Simon 1954–5, 1968. The best summary of earlier work and a major contribution in its own right to our understanding of regional differences is Thirsk 1967.

affection or in which he detected an urgent need for improvement. It was the merchants and gentry who provided the majority of endowments, and they thought and acted at the level of the communities which were their natural habitats. In this respect the college did not simply foster the development, but also provided an outlet for the expression of local sentiment.

W.K. Jordan went to some lengths to emphasise the massive impact of charitable bequests emanating from London. Fired by a radical religious ideology, the merchant class of the metropolis is presented as the catalyst of change throughout society. 'Very evidently, then, these [London] donors saw the needs of their age from the point of view of the realm as a whole, and they were moved by an evangelical fervour as they sought to secure the translation of their cultural and historical aspirations into institutional form.' London merchants are presented to us as 'the men who were the architects of modern England . . . of the western world'.[78] Even after due allowance is made for the limitations in his statistics pounced upon by critics, much remains of the original argument. It is fairly clear that dwellers in London and other large towns were influenced by the radical forms of Protestantism, and were enthusiastically willing to propagate good works and the gospel. Perhaps conscious of their own early difficulties and subsequent successes, they appear to have been intent upon spreading those skills and attitudes which sociologists – and even some historians – consider the prerequisites for modernisation. But the motives of these benefactors were probably less innovative than Jordan allows. The effect of their benefactions in breaking down the sense of regional identity is certainly more debatable than his unequivocal superlatives would seem to suggest.

Members of the urban merchant societies were temporal transients. The successful passed through the city in one or two generations and moved back to the countryside at a higher social level than that at which their fathers had left it. The urban economy was subservient to the vagaries of agrarian production. With the exception of London, even the greatest towns in the land – Norwich or Bristol – were visually circumscribed entities set within the rural landscape. The dominant social and political ethos was that of the aristocrat and his landed estates. As much as anyone, the hopes and expectations of the merchant were conditioned by this environment. As much as gentleman or nobleman, he lived in a world dominated by the rural ideal of the continuity of the family, an

---

[78] Jordan 1960, pp. 309, 318.

ideal which elided into the desire for personal immortality based on some great act worthy of memorialisation.

For reasons of finance and health it was land and the physical reality of the country estate which offered the best guarantee of that continuity. But in adverse demographic conditions an endowed charity ensured the continuity of a name which could not otherwise be provided for through a lack of lineal descendants.

> Here dead in part whose best part never dieth,
> A benefactor William Cutting lyeth,
> Not dead, if good deeds coulde keepe men alive,
> Nor all dead, since good deeds doe men revive.
> Gunvile and Kaies his good deeds may record,
> And will, no doubt, him praise therefore afford.

And no doubt they did, for in addition to his gifts to the parish of East Dereham, Norfolk, this London merchant instructed his trustees (many of them East Anglians, or London merchants and scions of Norfolk families) to endow four scholarships at Gonville and Caius: 'And that the said scholarships shall be called Cutting, his poor Scholarships.'[79] The deed of foundation for two additional fellowships and two scholarships at Sidney Sussex ensured that 'they be called the Fellows and Scholars of Mr Peter Blundell'. Blundell was a London merchant who had made very considerable benefactions to his native town of Tiverton in Devon. These included the establishment of a grammar school from which the scholars and fellows were to be chosen.[80] It was required of his fellows that at all their public sermons and commemorations they were to mention Mr Blundell as their founder and as a special benefactor to the college.

In bequeathing money for scholars and fellows to Gonville and Caius in 1587, Joyce Frankland had established a similar requirement. One fellow was to be known as her chaplain and 'to take oath to make 12 sermons or exhortations yearly in the college chapel, making mention and commending the charitable devotion of me, Joyce Frankland'. Her only son had been killed in a riding accident, and Dr Nowell, dean of St Paul's, took the opportunity when consoling her to suggest that she should found endowments at the universities. Nowell later described the episode to Archbishop Whitgift:

---

[79] Venn 1897–1901, III, p. 231; BL Royal MS 7. F. XIV (4), fos. 33–42; Jordan 1961, p. 106; 1959, pp. 215–28.

[80] Edwards 1899, pp. 50–1; Jordan 1960, pp. 371, 234, 106.

And I found her crying, or rather howling continually, Oh my son! my son! And when I could by no comfortable words stay her from that cry and tearing of her hair; God, I think, put me in mind at the last to say: 'Comfort yourself good Mrs Frankland, and I shall tell you how you shall have twenty good sons to comfort you in these your sorrows which you take for one son.' To the which words only she gave ear, and looking up asked, 'How can that be?' and I said unto her. 'You are a widow, rich and now childless, and there be in both universities so many poor toward youths that lack exhibition, for whom if you would found certain fellowships and scholarships, to be bestowed on studious young men, who should be called Mrs. Frankland's scholars, they would be in love towards you as dear children, and will most heartily pray to God for you during your life; and they and their successors after them, being still Mrs. Frankland's scholars, will honour your memory for ever and ever.'[81]

This revealing passage suggests one of the ways in which personal grief, the desire for family continuity, and a personal memorial could be turned to the advantage of the universities. These desires are always there, but in some ages and places they appear to be stronger than in others; both sixteenth/seventeenth-century English and nineteenth/twentieth-century American colleges have especially benefited. Thomas Fuller exposes the same idea at work in a typically revealing aside. He is cataloguing the beneficence of Sir Francis Clerke in establishing fellowships and scholarships at Sidney Sussex College for men from Clerke's native county of Bedfordshire. Fuller considers this donor to have been especially bountiful, for 'he had a daughter; and generally it is observed that parents are most barren and the childless most fruitful in great expressions of charity'.

Apart from the need to dispose of their accumulated wealth in some way at their death, the specific conditions of many endowments suggest that the college provided a means of continuing the family name for those who did not have heirs, and a source of personal immortalisation for those so inclined to be commemorated. By limiting his charity to a particular locality or school, a benefactor did not simply aim at creating the most efficient form of endowment. He was also ensuring that he should be remembered by the community where he had been born. The attachment of the merchant to his native rural community was not forgotten in life or unacknowledged at death. One London merchant endowing scholarships at both universities requested that the benefiting

[81] Venn 1897–1901, III, pp. 218, 229–30; Brooke 1985/1996, p. 96; for what follows Edwards 1899, pp. 50–1.

colleges 'would be pleased to prefer at every election my countrymen of Cheshire if they deserve not the contrary'. W.K. Jordan has noted that many London merchants showed a preference for establishing charitable institutions in the county of their or their family's origins.[82] The changes wrought by urban life were married to the residuum of ancient rural ideals among the mercantile benefactors of the universities. The offspring of this marriage were institutional arrangements which served to accentuate the consciousness of locality among its beneficiaries.

THE EXPERIENCE OF COLLEGE LIFE

'How much . . . are we all bound that are scholars, to those munificent Ptolemies, bountiful Maecenases, heroical patrons, divine spirits, who gave us all this comfort, for never can I deem him less than God, that have provided for us so many well-furnished libraries, as well in our public academies in most cities as in our private colleges!' We should not expect a less effusive eulogy from the doyen of seventeenth-century bookworms, Robert Burton. But neither should we read too much of our own cynicism into these profuse expressions of gratitude. The evidence adduced at the beginning of this chapter suggests that there was a genuine appreciation of the benefits bestowed by the college. The arrangements enjoined by benefactors and the daily life of the college ensured that that sense of gratitude was given a local habitation and a name.[83]

When Edward Lucas undertook to finance the wainscotting of the hall in Magdalene College, the college recognised his generosity by erecting his arms.[84] As the colleges were rebuilt and enlarged, it became customary to place the arms of the various benefactors in the glass of the college chapels. For the boys at daily prayer in the chapel in the sixteenth and seventeenth centuries, this glass spoke of the benefactors who had made possible their presence there. Because of continuing local connections many boys would have recognised in the arms of their benefactors the quarterings of families of importance in the localities from whence they came.

Distaste for 'Gothic' in the eighteenth century no less than the ravages of time has seriously reduced the number of surviving sixteenth- and seventeenth-century portraits. But as the colleges bloomed, the faces of benefactors and fellows spread across the walls of hall and parlour. An

---

[82] SP 14/78/88, I; Jordan 1960, pp. 311–18.
[83] Burton 1932 edn, II, p. 92; cf. C.P. Snow. *The Masters* (Penguin edn), pp. 108–11.
[84] Purnell 1904, p. 20.

attentive student may have detected in their lineaments the likeness of those families which habitually attended the college and some of whom may have been his contemporaries. He would certainly have recognised the iconographic function of all such portraiture, and have been reminded once again of his peculiar dependence on local generosity.[85]

As we have seen, Joyce Frankland ensured the remembrance of her generosity by requiring her fellow-chaplain to preach twelve sermons a year commending it in the college chapel. Other benefactors did like-wise. Sometimes, in addition to the sermons in the university, the college was also required to provide a preacher to deliver a sermon in the bene-factor's native parish. On these occasions the connections of college and community once again were augmented. In 1573, Sir Thomas Smith en-dowed 'a moderate feast' to be celebrated annually in Queens' College in his memory.[86] All these miscellaneous occasions for commemoration were in addition to the major festivals of remembrance enjoined by both college and university statutes. The foundation statutes of Magdalene enjoined that at the beginning and end of each term, after service, Ec-clesiasticus 44 was to be read, and the whole proceedings concluded with prayers for the soul of the founder and for the welfare of his successors and other benefactors. At Pembroke, 'The commendations also of the foundress and of those who have deserved well of the college shall be read after the statutes.'

In this respect the changes wrought by the Reformation brought only slight alterations, and it was in keeping with Elizabeth's conservative tem-perament that her statutes should reiterate a requirement first enunciated in their Edwardian precursors. In every college on the next day after the end of each term the whole college was to assemble in the chapel, and after the traditional verses from Ecclesiasticus there was to be a com-memoration of the founder and benefactors, followed by prayers to be preceded by the words, 'The memory of the righteous shall remain for evermore.'[87] It was to the advantage of the college that it should. Apart from the sincere symbolism of the ceremony – which we should not discount – it also acted as an inducement to potential benefactors and a guarantee of the form that their own immortalisation might take. It was a matter to be taken seriously. The acquisition of benefactors was of major importance and they could best be encouraged by seeing that the

---

[85] Scott-Giles 1975, p. 112; for the background to these remarks see Strong 1969, and the relevant sections of the college histories in *VCH Cambs.*, III.

[86] For the commemoration sermons, see below, pp. 228–9; *VCH Cambs.*, III, p. 411.

[87] Purnell 1904, p. 42; Heywood 1855, II, pp. 2, 197; I, pp. 34–5, and App., pp. 42–3, Elizabethan statutes, c. 50.

conditions enjoined by their predecessors were observed. In the 1630s the fellow of one college had warned that the overriding of local limitations damaged its interests, discouraging 'well disposed people both there and elsewhere from all such pious and charitable beneficence'.[88] Most colleges took steps to see that their benefactors were not forgotten. In 1615, Gonville and Caius paid £5 to John Scott, the notary of Cambridge, 'for writing two tables of the founders and benefactors of the college with their several coats portrayed in them'. Three years later he compiled a history of the university which was, in effect, a catalogue of the founders, benefactors, officers and members of the several colleges. A copy, with armorial embellishments, was presented to every college.[89]

On these numerous occasions of remembrance each fellow and scholar would know to whom he was individually beholden, for each scholarship and fellowship was a separate and frequently a named endowment, and in the minds of the men who heard those names intoned in the college chapel, with the name would be associated a place, usually the place to which their particular endowment was limited, often the name of a county or locality which was native to both benefactor and beneficiary. Because the perpetuity of their name was a large part of the purpose behind endowment, and because in the sixteenth century 'name' was so intimately connected with 'place', and because benefactors chose to express their charity in institutional forms which tied individual communities to specific colleges, those who benefited from that charity could not fail to be reminded of their benefactor's name, and of their own dependence on the accident of their local origins for the enjoyment of his beneficence.

In addition to these formal spurs to the recollection of regional origins and dependence on local connections, the college environment also provided numerous other informal but persistent reminders. In the sixteenth and seventeenth centuries, men displayed their regional origins in the intonations of the language they spoke. Most of the East Anglian gentry received their early schooling within the region, usually by local men, and often in the company of neighbouring children of lower social origins. Their earliest years would commonly have been spent in the care of wet-nurses who normally would be local women speaking the regional dialect. Even after the initial one or two years, children continued to keep the company of women. Sir Thomas Elyot recommended taking them away from the women of the house when they were seven years old. In Yorkshire Henry Slingsby was sent to school with the local parson at the

[88] SP 16/303/31.   [89] Venn 1897–1901, III, p. 278n.

age of six. With a few notable exceptions, women did not have access to Latin, nor was their English standardised, if one is to believe the evidence of the very idiosyncratic spelling in the letters of this period. It was in this environment that the inflections of speech were originally established in early childhood and it is unlikely that they were seriously affected by the subsequent experience of the university. The old antagonism between northerners and southerners suggests one of the ways in which it may have found expression there. In the sixteenth and seventeenth centuries it may have helped to identify colleges dominated by particular areas.[90]

There is some evidence to suggest that men were conscious of these variations. Venn conjectures that these regional differences may have been the source of some scribal peculiarities in university documents. Samuel Ward suffered from a speech impediment which caused some trouble prior to his election to a fellowship at Emmanuel. His problems could have been made worse by his north country accent, for he prayed God to 'bless all good means . . . I shall use to procure the amendment of my speech and pronunciation'. It was their accent and vocabulary which allowed early nineteenth-century Norfolk men to identify foreigners whom they contemptuously referred to as 'sheer men' because they came from other counties of England, while in the seventeenth century it was remarked of Sir Walter Raleigh that, 'notwithstanding his so great mastership in style, and his conversation with the learnedest and politest persons, yet he spake broad Devonshire to his dyeing day'.[91]

After 1500 the preoccupation of the humanists with the classics ensured that the main developments in the English language were in the fields of word choice and syntax. There had been very considerable and self-conscious debate about the correct pronunciation of Greek and Latin. If there was any standardisation, it is here that it is likely to have occurred. It was standardised Latin and Greek pronunciation which the graduate teachers would have taken back to their schoolchildren in the counties. It was a familiarity with Latin and a mastery of complex syntax rather than a pronunciation distinct from that of the popularly shared varieties of English regional dialects which distinguished a gentleman from the people in early seventeenth-century England.

There was also an expectation that men from different parts of the country would display differences of mind and character which

[90] T. Elyot, *The Book called The Governor*, ed. S.E. Lehmberg, London, 1970, p. 19: Parsons 1876, p. 3.
[91] Venn, I, pp. i, xxii; Knappen 1933, p. 128; Wilbraham 1821, p. 16; Raleigh 1829, VIII, p. 743.

predisposed them to different occupations. Norfolk men were believed to be argumentative and therefore to favour the law. Fuller believed that 'each county is innated with a particular genius, inclining the natives thereof to be dexterous, some in one profession, some in another; one carrying away the credit for soldiers, another for seamen, another for lawyers, another for divines etc., as I could easily instance'.[92]

The symbolism of these local communities was carried into the college. Fellow-commoners were required to provide themselves with plate which they were expected to present to the college on their departure. The appearance of the tankard during the last quarter of the sixteenth century may owe something to this social development. Frequently the plate combined the arms of the donor's family with those of the college. Thus the quality of the plate was not simply a measure of the student's standing in the college. It was also implicit with the significations of family connection and the relative social gradations of the county community represented in the innumerable quartering of arms characteristic of the heraldic frenzy of the Tudor age. For the fellow-commoner who used it, and the sizar who cleaned it, the donative plate was resonant with the niceties of provincial hierarchy.[93]

For some fellows and scholars the conditions governing the arrangements for their daily life enjoined by their benefactors ensured that they were constantly reminded of their local connections. Archbishop Parker's endowment at Corpus required that the Norwich scholars should be taught by the Norwich fellows. At Sidney Sussex, Mr Blundell's fellows were to tutor his scholars *gratis*. At Corpus the Norwich scholars were assigned to a specific set of chambers, and the Norwich fellows had the monopoly of the studies (the sixteenth-century equivalent of a modern library carrel) within their chambers, which they assigned to their Norwich students. Similar conditions governed Sir Nicholas Bacon's endowment at Corpus. When Sir Christopher Wray built twelve chambers with studies at Magdalene, the two holders of the fellowships which he had endowed were assigned rooms at the south-east corner of the court – with the reservation that Sir Christopher's descendants should have the right to occupy these rooms if they should enter the college.[94] Back at Corpus, Parker had left various pieces of furnishing and bedding to be handed on from one generation of Norwich scholars to the

[92] See Partridge 1969; Ong 1959; Mason 1884, pp. 4–5; Fuller 1655/1840, I, p. 73.

[93] See Purnell 1904, pp. 78, 208; Lyons 1910, p. 219; Venn 1913, pp. 208–9; 1897–1901, III, p. 302; BL Harl. MS 374, fo. 38.

[94] Norwich City Muniments, Case 25, shelf d (1361); Edwards 1899, p. 52; NRO, NRS MS 10129; Purnell 1904, p. 16. For studies in chambers, see above, pp. 32–3.

next.[95] In the very process of daily study the Norwich scholars were reminded of their benefactor and through him of their common local origins. For Parker had enjoined that the books which he gave to Corpus should 'remain within the under chamber of the xth chamber on the East side for the common use of all 6 Norwich scholars'.[96]

It requires an effort of the historical imagination to grasp the reality of this much simpler university society, so different from the world of transience and abstraction with which we are most familiar. It was a society based on land, and therefore always anchored in a physical place. It is surely this dependence which is embodied in the statute of Jesus College to the effect that a fellow was to be supported out of the income from the lands held by the college in the county from whence he came. It is embodied in an Elizabethan emendation to the statutes of Pembroke that 'the management of these lands and the receipt of their rents shall be placed in the hands of one of the persons deriving advantage from them'. It is there in the idea implied by the statutes of Christ's, King's, Trinity and other colleges, that they should take their students and fellows from the college estates or the areas of the country where the college held its lands and from which it derived its revenues.[97]

Of what loyalties was a boy conscious as a student at early seventeenth-century Cambridge? Surely one loyalty was that to his home 'country', as he pored over books reserved for boys from that country, perhaps used and marked in his days as a student by the schoolmaster who had started him on his academic career; working in a study built out of the benefactions of a man from his own country, sharing a chamber with a boy from the same town or region, overseen by a tutor who was a member of the college by right of the same regional dispensation, whose acquaintance or companionship he could expect to enjoy in his subsequent careers; surrounded by other boys from other parts of the kingdom, attending the college under analogous regulations; his sojourn there financed by the fruits of those fields he had known as a child, would know again as a man, perhaps tilled by his father and brothers or leased by his patron. Herein lay the roots of that strong bond of sentiment attaching him to his country: sentiments originating in the realities of a physical place and reinforced in the college by the ever present mnemonics of his dependence. But the factious world of Tudor Cambridge was unlikely to leave this spirit of

---

[95] BL Royal MS, App. 66, fo. 75. There is an ambiguous reference which suggests that perhaps a numerous family like the Gawdys also found it convenient to store similar domestic items at Cambridge and pass them on from uncle to nephew: Venn 1913, p. 211.

[96] BL Royal MS, App. 66, fo. 75.

[97] Heywood 1855, II, pp. 2, 137, 199; *VCH Cambs.*, III, pp. 378, 429, 431; above, p. 197.

generous gratitude unsullied by a more sordid appreciation of dependence on county origins.

Gratitude was one source of regional consciousness; frustration and conflict were others. One possible, although not necessary, source of frustration was the need to migrate from college to college in search of endowments designed for men of one's own county. Gabriel Harvey, born at Saffron Walden in Essex, was tempted to migrate from Trinity Hall, for 'there is at this present a fellowship void at Christ's College for Essex, and some of the fellows have desired me to stand for it'. In the 1680s John Tillotson recommended the son of a friend, a minister in Yorkshire, to Dr Blythe of Clare College: 'His father hath thought fit to remove him from Brazen-nose College in Oxford for no other reason but because he is not there by reason of the Statutes capable of preferment: there being I think but one Yorkshire fellowship, which is full.' At Clare the statutes of 1551 restricting to a maximum of two the number of fellows from the same county was a constant cause of migration. Religious proclivities could combine with the requirements imposed by regional limitations; Samuel Ward, who as a student was a member of Christ's, was inhibited from entering on a fellowship in the college by a statute prohibiting two men from the same county holding fellowships at the same time, for the college already had a fellow from Ward's native county of Durham. Luckily, he was able to migrate to a fellowship at the newly founded Emmanuel College.[98]

At Emmanuel the complications which similar limitations could cause, and the ramification of local connections, are illustrated by the experience of Joseph Hall, later bishop of Exeter and Norwich. As a student at the college, Hall was tutored by Nathaniel Gilby, son of the famous puritan divine, Anthony Gilby. The father had supervised the school at Ashby-de-la-Zouche which the 7th earl of Huntingdon had established in 1567, and where Hall had received his earlier education. The complications arose over Hall's election to a fellowship in 1595. The college was allowed only one fellow from Leicestershire, and that place was occupied by Nathaniel Gilby. To make room for Hall, the earl of Huntingdon offered Gilby a chaplaincy in his household, and Gilby resigned his fellowship. Unfortunately, the earl then died, and for a time Gilby was left without a position, as Chaderton, the master, insisted on moving to fill the vacancy even though Hall offered to withdraw his candidature.[99]

---

[98] Scott 1884, p. 178; Wardale 1903; Forbes 1928, II, p. 33; Knappen 1933, p. 39; Collinson in Bendall *et al.* 1999, pp. 82–3.

[99] Davenport 1949, pp. xiv–xvi. On Hall, see also Collinson in Bendall *et al.* 1999, pp. 88–90.

Undergraduates as well as would-be fellows were made aware of their local dependence as they sought an adequate scholarship. John Catlin was admitted as a sizar at Christ's in January, but in August 1639 he migrated to Caius to take up a scholarship in the nomination of the local family of the Heydons. Whenever a man stood for election he would have to prove that he was eligible 'by his country'. At Oxford, Brian Twyne had obtained the patronage of Lord Treasurer Buckhurst in an attempt to gain a fellowship at Merton. He reported to his father that the warden of Merton had 'enquired much of my country, because he said he knew that you dwelt in Sussex, but I told him that I was born in Southwark in London, and by that I held my place at Corpus Christi as a Surrey man'. At Cambridge it had been necessary to include in the Elizabethan statutes (1570) a definition of county origins 'as that county to which it shall appear that their father belonged'.[100]

Obviously, the availability of locally restricted places was not always equal to the supply of talent capable of filling them. Most endowments made some attempt to reconcile the criterion of ability with the expression of local sentiment. Sometimes the overriding of local statutes was carried smoothly – 'He was not eligible by his country, but being the best learned of all that stood we consented to choose him, and he had every voice' – but usually it was not. Even if the college agreed, the local patron might object. The city of Norwich argued that the Norwich fellows at Corpus should be chosen from among the Norwich scholars. The college rejoined that these scholars were not always of sufficient merit to justify election to a fellowship, 'of which want there hath been too much experience, and is still just fear in so small a number as five'.[101] The clauses enjoining consideration of a student's ability were always open to conflicting interpretations and were a seedbed of divergent judgements in colleges constantly torn by factional strife. The commendable desire to place learning before local piety too easily degenerated into concessions to the insistent pressure of special interest groups. Increasingly, the Court used the claim of superior ability as an excuse to interfere with elections without having taken proper cognizance of the true capacities of its candidates.[102]

Sixteenth- and seventeenth-century Oxford and Cambridge resounded to complaints that local restrictions were being circumvented. So they were. And a candidate disappointed by this means had little

---

[100] Venn, I, i, p. 308a and SP 16/437/50; Twyne 1927, p. 218; Heywood 1855, I, App. p. 40, Elizabethan statutes, c. 50.24.
[101] SP 16/441/117; Norwich City Muniments, Case 25, shelf d (1361).
[102] On the nature, extent and effects of Court interference, see below, chapters 10–11.

consolation save the thought that in his suffering his country had been wronged. But if an opportunist fellow was willing to wink at an election transgressing the restriction of a fellowship to some 'foreign' locality, he was unlikely to favour a similar move when it threatened to reduce the influence of his own region in the college. There was complaint but never a solution because, although all were sinned against, all were sinners. Whenever a disagreement arose, whatever the specific matter at issue, it was always possible to include the accusation that local restrictions had been abused. It was one of the charges levelled at Lawrence Humphrey of Magdalen College, Oxford, in the 1580s. It was among the complaints made against Dr Batchcroft, master of Gonville and Caius, during an imbroglio in the 1630s. Thomas Cooke, the complainant, had a personal grudge against Batchcroft, and as far as one can tell there was only a minimal truth in his accusations – but they are very revealing of contemporary attitudes. Cooke pointed out that 'the said College is endowed with rich and great revenues, by the Founders and Benefactors (being Norfolk and Suffolk men) for the maintenance of one Master and certain fellows ever to be chosen out of the said Countries'. He went on to complain that although most elections had been made accordingly, 'and the present Master enjoys his preferment in right of both the Countries and the Statutes', yet contrary to his office and oath he

> hath broken many statutes, and caused of his own accord many elections to be made of strangers of other countries; to the great wrong of the will of the founders, the great prejudice of his Country, the ill example of future elections, the great damage of the college, and the discouragement both of the students of that Country, and all well disposed people both there and elsewhere from all such pious and charitable beneficence.

Cooke goes on to say that he had urged Batchcroft to act according to his oath and the statutes, and as 'love to his Country required'.[103]

Disagreements were also engendered by other ambiguities among the restrictive statutes. In a further attempt to marry merit to local piety, many statutes took the form of graduated preferences or alternatives. If a suitable candidate was not available from a favoured school, then two or three other schools in the locality were to be canvassed. If there was no suitable candidate from one county, then the electors were instructed to consider aspirants from one or more alternative counties. As the arbitrators reported in the dispute between Cooke and Batchcroft, they found that the Statute of Elections 'doth not absolutely require that Norfolk and

---

[103] Macray 1894–1915, II, p. iv; SP 16/715/111, 115; SP 16/303/31.

Suffolk men and such as are of the Diocese of Norwich be preferred'.[104]
Fellows intent upon building up their faction in the college often based
it on the supply of young students recruited through their local connections.[105] Quite clearly, the preferential statutes would exacerbate the
rivalries between fellows in their capacity as electors. Apart from this, all
the numerous disputes within a college were brought to a head on the
occasion of elections. Statutes of this nature would tend to focus these
disputes into confrontations over differences of locality.

In the early seventeenth century not even the regional colleges were
totally isolated enclaves within the university, monopolised by any one
area; the arbitrators in the dispute at Caius had also reported that 'we find
that in all times there have been some of other countries admitted'.[106]
There was always sufficient contrast within a college to stimulate a consciousness of dependence on regional origins for the size of the bounty
received. It could arouse envy of better-paid fellowships attached to other
regions and a jealous pursuit of the most lucrative fellowship for which a
man was eligible by right of birth in a particular place.[107] This situation
had arisen from the desire of donors to perpetuate their memory through
the means of the college – which had in its turn led to the establishment
of many inequalities between the various scholarships and fellowships.
For, to ensure the continued remembrance of their name, benefactors
attached it to a financially distinct endowment. Discussing the establishment of Sir Simon Bennett's bequest to University College, Oxford, the
fellows of the college reported that they had consulted with his kindred,
'And they being earnest for a number, as if therein consisted the only or
the chief honor of a benefactor, whether the maintenance allotted were
sufficient or not.'[108]

This led to the creation of bye-fellowships and sub-scholarships. It was
a process favoured by the established fellows of a college. Ideally, no doubt
they would have preferred new benefactions to be merged with the general funds of the college to augment their own stipends. But if a donor
was insistent on separately named endowments, it was to the advantage of
the established fellows to see that the new additions to the college were
supported from financially distinct resources which excluded them from
sharing in the dividend derived from the college's general endowment.
The majority of scholarships appear to have consisted of sub-foundations
supported by separate estates and providing differing emoluments. One

---

[104] SP 16/315/111; see above, n. 68. For mention of preferential statutes see *VCH Cambs.*, III,
pp. 363, 378, 431, 438, 464; Harrison 1953, pp. 15–16; above, p. 199.
[105] SP 16/159/16; SP 16/160/58 III, 2d complaint; Masters 1831, p. 165; above, pp. 199 ff.
[106] SP 16/315/111; Stone 1975, ch. 1.   [107] SP 16/203/70.   [108] SP 16/281/54.

reason why the Norwich fellows did not like being shuffled around from one fellowship to another at Corpus was the difference in income between the various fellowships. Naturally, most men pursued the most remunerative endowments.[109] Equally naturally this encouraged disputes within the college; the foundation fellows warned that the scheme for Sir Simon Bennett's endowment would create a body separate from that of the ancient foundation. 'So there shall bee two several bodies with the same walls, under one head. And how apt this device is to occasion murmurings and heart-burnings, if not factious division, may easily be conjectured by any men of experience.'[110]

But the cause of disputes was not simply that the bye-fellowships had sometimes been poorly endowed at their inception. They also had the disadvantage of providing a fixed income during a period of unprecedented inflation. The deeds of endowment normally stated a specific sum that the fellow was to receive from the endowment. Obviously, the real value of these fellowships decreased as inflation progressed. We have seen that there was every incentive to exclude the bye-fellows from a share in the dividend enjoyed by the foundation fellows. The advantage of the dividend was that its size was not fixed by statute. Derived from the corporate income of the college, it was protected against inflation by the Elizabethan Act requiring one-third of all college rents to be paid in kind. Increasingly, the major source of a fellow's income was not his fellowship stipend, but his share in the college dividend.[111] There was an ever-widening gap between the income of foundation fellows and of bye-fellows, and all the more reason to intrigue for a place on the foundation. One need only add that bye-fellows had little or no say in the government of the college and the administration of its estates, in order to see in this distinction one of the reasons why the bickering and disputes at sixteenth- and seventeenth-century Cambridge were maintained at an intensity far above that which is normally endemic within academic circles. Rivalry for the most generous of any one of a number of similarly restricted local endowments encouraged conflict between men from the same county community. These conditions were almost certain to ensure that the participants in these conflicts were made keenly aware of their common local origins.

[109] Peacock 1841, p. 117; Willet 1634, p. 1,238; Norwich City Muniments, Case 25, shelf d; BL Egerton MS 2715, fo. 235.

[110] SP 16/281/54. The fellows of Caius, threatened by the invasion of six new Frankland fellows in 1591, invented the distinction between 'senior' and 'junior' fellows in imitation of King's, Trinity and St John's (Brooke 1985/1996, pp. 96–8).

[111] Venn 1897–1901, III, pp. 217 ff; *Report of the Commissioners*, 1852–3, *Report*, pp. 107–8; 18 Eliz. c. 6 (1576).

During the sixteenth and seventeenth centuries the unprecedented acquisition of endowments and their attendant statutory limitations created an environment in the college within which the grateful scholar or fellow was constantly reminded of his native community. Concurrently, attempts to override these local restrictions through external interference with the college statutes may have severed him from their advantages. Such attempts certainly made him more conscious of the importance of his place of birth as the justification for his continued enjoyment of them. A further effect of the increase in the number of endowments was to multiply the variations of stipend and terms of tenure among the fellowships and scholarships which they created. This induced rivalries between men from the same locality seeking the same place, or vying for the most remunerative of a number of locally restricted endowments. Whether as grateful beneficiary or as disappointed aspirant, a university man during the reigns of Elizabeth and the early Stuarts could hardly fail to be aware of his 'country'.

THE UNIVERSITY AND THE COUNTRY

The increasing intimacy between specific colleges and localities occurred within a general context of greater intercourse between the university and the larger society of which it was part. The effects engendered by the series of unprecedented endowments during the sixteenth century were reinforced by two other developments characteristic of the university at this period. The first was the revolutionary increase in the number of students. The second was the expanded proportion of the aristocracy represented within that number.[112]

The universities had suffered from the pessimism and uncertainties of the mid-century, but under Elizabeth they had more than recovered in numbers so that by 1601 contemporaries were enthusiastically referring to Cambridge as 'that place from whence so many famous learned men are dayly produced into the world'.[113] It seems likely that about 9,800 students entered Cambridge in the period 1620–39. At the beginning

---

[112] For a discussion of the social composition of higher education see Stone 1975, ch. 1. The word 'aristocracy' is employed here and elsewhere in this book as a portmanteau expression to include both the nobility and the gentry (see MacCaffrey 1965, p. 52; Stone 1965, pp. 7 ff). MacCaffrey's criterion for gentility, 'all those who enjoyed the coveted distinction of bearing heraldic arms', is unrealistic, as is his assumption that this group was coextensive with the political nation: rather, this should be taken to include numerous non-armigerous gentry, an increasingly large electorate reaching well down into the yeomanry, and a number of very influential and articulate preachers.
[113] Cooper, *Annals*, II, pp. 16, 26, 52; SP 12/281/15; Stone 1975, ch. 1.

of these years the overall population of the university at any one time was reported to be in the region of 3,000. This would suggest a body composed of around 1,960 (65 per cent) undergraduates and 1,040 (35 per cent) fellows and officers of the university.[114]

When these clergymen and gentlemen departed from the university they did not forget it, nor were they forgotten by it. In its effects the increase in the size and the change in the social composition of the student body drew the university into the country and ensured that countrymen would recollect Cambridge.

As the heirs of important county families flooded into Cambridge it became necessary to exercise greater care over the well-being of these prestigious students. At the beginning and end of term many of them were collected from or delivered to their parents either by their tutor, a young fellow of the college, or their former schoolmaster.[115] This was only one of numerous occasions on which tutors could meet the parents of their students.[116] Part of the endowments of most colleges included a manor house in the countryside to which the fellows could retire when the university was closed because of plague. This was an especially necessary provision at Cambridge, with its poor drainage and 'fenny air'. The provision of these retreats can be traced back to the arrangements provided by a partly monastic university. But by the late sixteenth century it was equally likely that a fellow who was also a tutor would retire for a few weeks with some of his students to the home of one of their parents in a nearby county. As the numbers and the crowding increased at Cambridge, so did the risk of infection. The development of this habit may have received an impetus during the periods of heavy infection in the 1590s, 1620s and 1630s.[117]

As the number of those who could claim some connection with the university increased, and as they spread out into the countryside, the universities were caught up in the rhythm of a provincial year which was itself acquiring a more clearly defined pattern at this time. It was not only the resident members of the university who were attracted to the considerable festivities associated with the first Tuesday in July, the day fixed by the Elizabethan statutes (c. 20) for the beginning of the Great

---

[114] Earlier estimates produce similar figures; cf. Stone 1964, table II. See brief discussion of technical problems, in Appendix I, II, below.

[115] Smith 1953, p, 10; *Winthrop Papers*, I, p. 84, probably a reference to Thomas Newton, fellow of Trinity, 1597, see Venn, I, iii, p. 253b; Macray 1894–1915, II, p. 36.

[116] See below, chapter 9.

[117] Creighton 1965, I, pp. 282–3, see also pp. 261–2, 527; Shrewsbury 1970, pp. 167, 172, 181, 219, 232, 246, 282, 298–9, 307, 356–9, 395–7; Hughey 1941, p. 83.

Commencement.[118] The university musicians seem to have provided a welcome 'with their loud Music', but the star attraction was the performance of the praevaricator. Akin to the court fool or the boy bishop of the medieval drama, the praevaricator lacerated his audience and the university authorities with a punning jocularity which must have appealed to their verbally sophisticated sensibilities, if not to their sense of propriety. The authorities are not likely to have looked kindly upon the suggestion of one praevaricator that they should provide roast beef for all the country clergy there present. St Mary's was fitted up with a stage where – according to Laud – the praevaricator 'acts and sets forth his profane and scurrilous jests besides other abuses and disorders'. Occasionally, sections of the speeches were in English: a concession for the delectation of the ladies present. It is the commencement at an American college, with its bands, beer and alumni, rather than the more stately congregations at the English universities which today more nearly approximates to the festivities at seventeenth-century Cambridge.[119] It also had its serious side. Professor Collinson has shown how these festivities were used as a 'cover' for a general meeting of the puritan graduates who since leaving the university had spread out into the country parishes.[120]

At the other end of the summer, in September, Stourbridge Fair provided another opportunity for clergy and university to meet informally once more before the onset of winter.[121] In the intervening weeks the development of the Long Vacation provided an opportunity for the members of the university to go visiting in the country. Conveniently, this break coincided with the proliferation in the countryside of activities sufficient to constitute a 'summer season'. Characterised by the growth of sporting events, it culminated in the harvest home and the reckoning-up at Michaelmas. The two great social as well as administrative–judicial occasions were the midsummer quarter sessions and the festivities surrounding the summer assizes. Joseph Mede's biographer noted that 'in the Vacations he was wont to be invited into the country by a kinsman and a Knight'. With luck, a university man aspiring to a secure country living might be given the opportunity to display his theological leanings and sermonising skills before those gentry who he hoped would provide

---

[118] Peacock 1841, pp. 11, 49; 'Buck', in Peacock 1841 (separate pagination), p. lxv; Marsden 1851, pp. 83, 99, 104 ff; Morison 1935, pp. 72–4; the Batchelors' Commencement occurred during Lent and was not such a great occasion.

[119] 'Buck', in Peacock 1841, p. lxxxii; for the crowd-pulling capabilities of the praevaricator see above, nn. 16–17; 'Stokys', in Peacock 1841 (separate pagination), pp. xxix–xxxv, n; CUL MS Dd. vi. 30, fos. 19v, 21v and *passim*; Morris and Withington 1967, pp. 56–7, 147–9.

[120] Collinson 1967, pp. 219, 305, 320.

[121] *Ibid.*, pp. 320, 492 n. 10; Collinson 1961, p. 149; see also Venn 1913, p. 267 n. 2.

him with preferment. More immediately, the payment for these services provided a useful addition to a fellow's stipend. If these were not sufficient inducements, business required their presence, for it was towards Michaelmastide that the riding bursars were active in visiting the college estates.[122]

Theoretically the universities were supposed to be in session throughout the year but circumstances had combined to favour the development of the Long Vacation during the summer quarter. At Oxford during the fifteenth and early sixteenth centuries there had been occasional removals on account of the plague and the insanitary condition of the town. Magdalen men had retired to their manor of Brackley, and other places, and at the same college, in August 1555, leave of absence was granted to the majority of the fellows because of the scarcity of corn in the town. By 1570 the relaxation of the requirements for residence during the summer had become so habitual that Bishop Horne could speak of 'the great vacancy after the Act to Michaelmas' and in 1584 one of the complaints brought against Humphrey as president of Magdalen was that the lectures during the vacation were not properly maintained.[123] In 1568 the vice-chancellor and the heads of houses at Cambridge wrote to Sir William Cecil suggesting that 'there should be intermission and a time of breathing: that mens wits, being by such recreation refreshed, might the more earnestly and greedily desire the former studies: [and] so it hath been observed with us, as a necessary help to learning from time to time'. Unfortunately, the King's Readers were required by statute to 'keep their ordinary days of reading in the vacant quarter betwixt Midsomer and Michaelmas'. The vice-chancellor and his associates asked that the readers might be absolved from this responsibility, 'considering as well the auditors' absence that quarter as also the contagiousness of the same time, and the dangerousness both for the readers and also for the hearers: so that there cannot be meeting for the most part, without great peril of sickness, and other inconveniences'. Where a dispensation was not obtained, the performance of the required exercises became merely perfunctory: the 'wall lectures'. By the 1620s, Symonds D'Ewes, that most rigorous and punctilious of young men, was complaining of the sloth of the fellows in missing the college exercises, or common places during

---

[122] Mede 1677, p. XLII; BL Add. MS 27396, fo. 162; BL Harl. MS 389, fos. 12v, 31, 45, 59, 99, 110; BL Harl. MS 374, fo. 42; BL Sloane MS 7380, fos. 13v–14v (this reference is to the year 1670); Boas 1935, p. 64.

[123] Macray 1894–1915, II, pp. iii–v, 30–1, 41, 43, 45. The Act was the Oxford equivalent of the Cambridge Commencement. Creighton 1965, I, p. 283.

the vacation.[124] While a lonely fellow was maintaining the letter of the statutes by mumbling at a blank wall at Cambridge, the likelihood was that the majority of his colleagues were preaching to large audiences in the country and enjoying the hospitality of their pupils' parents.

It was not only by the visits of country clergy and gentry to the university, and of university men to the country, that an intimate acquaintance was maintained between the two. Cambridge acted as an exchange for the social, political, theological and cultural information explosion of the late sixteenth and early seventeenth centuries. This information explosion occurred within the context of an improved system of communications. The inflation of numbers and the influx of the social elite ensured that the university became an important locus within the communications net created by the development of the carrier trade. London was the main focus of this network, but the importance of the university for provincial society ensured that there were cross-country connections – for instance, between Cambridge and Norwich. It was the presence at the university of a wealthy elite with numerous personal possessions periodically requiring transportation which made these connections economically viable. Similarly, Milton's Hobson (of 'Hobson's Choice') made a comfortable living by hiring out hackneys to the young gentlemen flooding into Cambridge and back again to their country. It is impossible to quantify, but the impression made by repeated references to the carrier in collections of family correspondence is that the communications net based on the system of carriers would never have achieved the density it did without the size and social composition of the university being what they were, for as Lady Katherine Paston's son knew, the carrier 'is the young students joy and expection'.[125]

The universities played their part in developing the means of disseminating news throughout the society by means of the proliferation of letters and primitive news-sheets. In a general way the experience of the university developed the habit of correspondence and the skills required in a letter-writing society. It is surely not altogether fortuitous that the great collections of family correspondence began to expand in number and substance in rough coincidence with the expansion of the universities. In a more specific way the universities contributed to these developments

---

[124] Strype 1822, III, p. 10; Marsden 1851, p. 65.

[125] Blomefield 1805–10, III, p. 374; BL Egerton MS 2983, fo. 11; Hughey 1941, p. 69; Osborne n.d., p. 37. There is no entirely adequate description of English land communications at this time, but see Jackman 1962; Crofts 1967; Housden 1903, pp. 713–18; Thompson 1918, pp. 234–43; Chartres 1977. The standard contemporary guide is Taylor 1637, *STC* 23740.

by providing an institutional framework for the exchange of news. Correspondence took different forms. There were the letters of solicitous parents to their children, and of impecunious students to their parents. This was often supplemented by the correspondence between parents and tutors. Usually, these are concerned with academic progress, or the lack of it; with the need of the student for pillows, towels and similar items; with periodic requests for a sword or a new suit; and occasionally with recommending a *douceur* to the master of the college as the best means of obtaining a vacant scholarship. On other occasions the letters contain items of social and political news relating to the student's own county society. The fellows of the colleges continued to correspond with their native communities: Ward received advice from Durham throughout his distinguished university career; at Oxford, Crosfield usually maintained his correspondence with the north via other north-countrymen. The example of Lady Katherine Paston's correspondence with her son William suggests that it was frequent and, in the case of socially prestigious students, also involved his tutor and sometimes the master of the college. This form of communication became so common that typical examples of letters to and from the university came to be included in books of advice on epistolary form.[126] It implies a world very different from that inhabited by the modern undergraduate or member of faculty. Today, the dependence on family and the ties of locality are less strong and the student has greater opportunity within the university to identify with an independent youth culture antagonistic to both parents and teachers.

The university environment created friendships and connections which in some instances were continued after the departure of one of the participants from Cambridge. As a university-educated clergy spread out into the parishes the sources of information in provincial society were multiplied and the means of disseminating that information were increased. Men carried with them into the country a continuing interest in college politics and a persistent interest in university theology at a time when that theology was of more than parochial concern. From his country living at Tawstock in Devon, Oliver Naylor continued to advise his former colleagues at Gonville and Caius on the intricacies of college elections. But he expected a recompense; he wrote to one of his

---

[126] Hughey 1941; Venn 1913, ch. 11; Gawdy family letters, BL Egerton MSS 2715, 2716; BL Add. MSS 27395, 27396; SP 46/24/72; SP 46/21/82, 85; Knappen 1933, pp. 112, 128; *A President for Young Pen-Men, or the Letter Writer* (London 1625), *STC* 20584a, provide the specific evidence for the remarks made in this paragraph. However, it is based on impressions gathered from a more extensive reading in MS and printed sources.

contemporaries at college: 'I have heard from Cambridge of Mr Simpson's last sermon. If that or any thing about that cause be worth your writing I pray you let me hear. I am in a place of very good contentment, but so far is a banishment.' A Leicestershire lecturer wrote to a compatriot in Newcastle that 'I was at Cambridge Xmas holidays. Mr Docket greatly desires to be remembered to you', and goes on to promise notes of 'an admirable sermon upon John 3.19 [preached] last Xmas day'. In university politics, the corruptions of the duke of Buckingham in interfering with the election of fellows and masters of colleges, and the news of the coercive means employed to obtain his own election to the chancellorship, found a ready ear among the country gentry who corresponded with the college fellows.[127]

The university also fed the scholarly interests which it had originally stimulated among the gentry during their residence. Symonds D'Ewes maintained a long correspondence with Tuckney, successively master of Emmanuel and St John's. Through Tuckney's mediation he borrowed various manuscripts from the University Library for use in writing his general history of Great Britain. D'Ewes never completed the proposed volume, but he did make use of the manuscripts in attempting to prove the antiquity of Cambridge to the House of Commons. The dispute as to the precedence of Oxford and Cambridge in parliamentary bills had become a traditional part of House of Commons banter by the time D'Ewes came to cite his manuscript sources in 1640–1. He preferred to decide the matter by documented precedent rather than by a vote, suggesting that it would not 'be any glory to *Oxford* to gain it by voices here, where we all know the multitude of Borough towns in the western part of England do send so many worthy Members hither, that if we measure things by number, and not by weight, Cambridge is sure to lose it'.[128] In 1625 Dr Collins wrote from King's College to Sir Henry Spelman in praise of the scholarly qualities of his *Glossarium*. Later, in the 1640s, the Spelmans were in correspondence with Abraham Whelock, the Anglo-Saxon scholar whom Sir Henry had nominated to the chair in that subject which he had established in the university.[129] Earlier, Sir Christopher Heydon had been engaged

---

[127] Cosin 1869–72, I, p. 1; SP 16/540/pt.IV/446/31; BL Harl. MS 390, fo. 151; BL Sloane MS 1775, fos. 23–30; Harvard University, Houghton Library, MS Eng. 1266 (v. 2), fos. 257–73; Marsden 1851, pp. 25–6.

[128] Marsden 1851, p. 26; BL Harl. MS 374, fos. 283–5; Notestein 1923, p. 212; Parker 1721, p. iii. D'Ewes' remark suggests that contemporaries were conscious of the regional pattern of attendance as between the two universities.

[129] BL Add. MS 34599, fo. 89; Add. MS 5845, pp. 332–3; Add. MS 34601, fos. 55, 56. See below, pp. 458–60. The Spelmans were associated with the Hares, another Norfolk family with a strong interest in Cambridge, BL Add. MS 34599, fos. 50, 86v–87, 90; NRO, Hare MSS.

in correspondence with Giles Fletcher, tutor to his son at Caius College and an authority on the occult and astrological subjects which excited Sir Christopher's curiosity.[130]

A Star Chamber Decree of 1586 had prohibited all printing outside the city of London except at Oxford and Cambridge. By inhibiting the development of provincial printing, this regulation stimulated the intercourse between London and the intellectually curious members of the various provincial societies. It also magnified the importance of the university towns as sources of supply. The presence there of men concerned with matters of the intellect, and who possessed long-standing connections with others of similar inclination in the localities, ensured that these towns became sources of supply not simply of books from the university presses, but also of books originating in London and from abroad. Students and fellows were the obvious agents in these transactions. William Paston supplied his mother with books, candles and writing paper from Cambridge. Robert Gawdy also sent books into Norfolk, for the use of his brother. Joseph Mede provided a similar service for Sir Martin Stuteville in Suffolk. At Oxford, Crosfield bought books on behalf of his former school at Kendal in Westmorland.[131] On occasion the books no less than the newsletters for which Cambridge acted as an exchange could be considered politically and theologically subversive by the authorities. In the 1570s crypto-Catholics in Caius College sent popish books into the country while the Bacon brothers exchanged volumes in the Admonition controversy.[132] These activities spilled over into the provision of a whole variety of services for local gentry and townsmen with connections in the university. Joseph Mede saw to the binding of Sir Martin Stuteville's court rolls; Crosfield compiled a genealogy for Mr Lee, the mayor of Abingdon.[133]

The offer to compile Mr Lee's genealogy had occurred when Crosfield visited Abingdon to preach a sermon which appears to be associated with the election to his college of pupils from Abingdon School. Mr Lee must have found Crosfield's style to his taste, for he concluded their meeting by asking him to preach his funeral sermon, in addition to compiling his

[130] Venn 1897–1901, I, p. 95 (Gonville and Caius Coll. MS 73/40, fos. 348–89).
[131] Siebert 1965, p. 69; Hughey 1941, pp. 65, 73, 98, 100; BL Add. MS 27396, fo. 178; BL Harl. MS 389, fos. 118v, 142, 166, 175, 176; BL Harl. MS 390, fos. 9, 13, 148; Boas 1935, pp. xiii, 41; see also Cosin 1869–72, I, pp. 1–2.
[132] BL Lansdowne MS 33, fo. 100v; Bacon MSS *penes* T.S. Blakeney Esq., formerly on deposit at the Institute of Historical Research. Anthony Bacon to Nathaniel Bacon, n.d. Anthony Bacon was in residence between April 1573 and Christmas 1575, during the period of the Admonition controversy.
[133] BL Harl. MS 389, fos. 133v, 137; Boas 1935, pp. 56, 59, 128.

genealogy.[134] It is a commonplace that this age had an insatiable appetite for sermons. Both Emmanuel and Sidney Sussex had been founded with the purpose of educating a preaching ministry. But even before leaving the college, fellows had the opportunity and the obligation to preach. As we have seen, it was an opportunity because it enabled them to augment a meagre income and to display their talents before potential patrons. It was an obligation because frequently it was enjoined in the conditions regulating the endowments which the colleges were receiving during these years. By including the financing of a sermon among his bequests a benefactor could ensure the perpetuity of people's remembrance of him in his own locality.[135] Thus, Mr Slade of Ellington provided £13-6-8 to support two scholars 'and for a sermon in his parish'. Sir Henry Williams (alias Cromwell) endowed a sermon against witchcraft to be preached by a fellow of Queens' on 25 March each year in a church at Huntingdon.[136] Quite naturally, the provision of sermons by fellows tended to reinforce the connections of individual men or colleges with specific localities. John Smith, fellow of Queens' College, was praised for the flexibility of his sermon style when preaching 'in lesser country auditories (particularly at a church near Oundle in Northamptonshire, the place of his Nativity)'. The provost of Queen's College, Oxford, and nephew of the newly appointed bishop of Carlisle, preached his uncle's consecration sermon and then 'sent several copies . . . to gentlemen in the country, especially to such as had sons of our house [i.e., college]'.[137]

Through the occasions of reunions and of visits, through the means of correspondence and newsletters, in the process of providing a whole range of miscellaneous services for the local gentry, the university as a whole was drawn into the orbit of provincial society. It would be wrong to exaggerate the extent of the exclusiveness of regional connections but it is impossible not to notice the way in which many of these doings tended to entwine some individuals and colleges in the social world of some localities more than of others.

UNIVERSITY ALUMNI IN COUNTRY SOCIETY

The influx of nobility and gentry did not reduce the number of poor scholars, most of whom were intent upon a clerical career. On the

---

[134] *Ibid.*, pp. 56, 59.   [135] See above, p. 208.
[136] Willet 1634, p. 1,233; *VCH Cambs.*, III, p. 411; Smith 1673, p. xxv.
[137] Smith 1673, p. xxv; Boas 1935, p. 34. The fathers mentioned by Crosfield were mainly north-countrymen.

contrary, the increase in the number of scholarships provided by endowment, the need for personal services on the part of the aristocracy, the demand for a preaching ministry, and a general ethos which placed a premium on educational certification ensured an increase in their numbers. The indications are that the major changes in the social composition of the student body at the English universities occurred *before* the accession of Elizabeth and *after* Charles II's departure from Breda.[138] Here, we are concerned to suggest the extent of familiarity with the university environment among members of provincial society. How many men had observed the workings or experienced the effects of the county limitations and local preferences which riddled the English universities? J.H. Hexter supported his contention that the nobility and gentry were flooding into the universities by showing the extent of university education among deputy lieutenants and justices of the peace by the end of the century: 'Bookish learning had gone with them out into the shires and was widely scattered among the men who ruled the countryside.' It is a contention amply borne out by subsequent research.[139]

Lawrence Stone has suggested that in the peak decade of the 1630s no fewer than 1,240 young men were entering higher education every year. Of these perhaps 430 (35 per cent) went into the church and another 190 (15 per cent) into law and medicine. This means that the country was producing some 600 (48 per cent) educated laymen who were not entering the professions.[140] Not all of these were gentry likely to return to landed estates in their native communities. Some became the professional writers who supplied London's first Grub Street, located in St Paul's Churchyard. The emergence of the professional author roughly coincides with the overproduction of graduates postulated by M.H. Curtis. P. Seaver has shown that a London lectureship was often the first step in an ecclesiastical career; graduates destined for a less uplifting future were also attracted to the metropolis. There is some statistical and very considerable literary evidence to suggest that a proportion of the superfluity of graduates from Oxford and Cambridge subsequently became the penurious writers of Elizabethan London. Essentially of humble origins, these are the men who helped to create Elizabethan literature in the formative period between 1530 and 1580. In the years after 1580 they provided much of the ephemeral scribbling which is the feverish but fertile background to the greatest products of Elizabethan and Jacobean

---

[138] Stone 1964, pp. 57–80, and 1975, ch. 1; Cressy 1970.
[139] Hexter 1961, pp. 55–6 and *passim*; Heal and Holmes 1994, pp. 263–4.
[140] Stone 1964, pp. 56–7. See Appendix 1.

Table 3. *University experience among a sample of about 470 gentry resident in Norfolk c. 1563, 1578 and 1585*

Degree of certainty in identification	Number	% of total identifications	% of total sample
Certain[a]	50	42.01	10.63
Probable[a]	28	23.53	5.95
Uncertain	14	11.76	2.97
Informed guess	27	22.68	5.74
Totals	119	100.00	25.30

Notes: Total in sample = 470.

Even given a reasonable familiarity with the history of Norfolk families in the Elizabethan and early Stuart period it is not always possible to identify individuals in one list with those in another. In these circumstances I have tried to provide some measure of the certainty of my statistical statements.

[a] 'Certain' + 'Probable' = 78 (16.59%).

Sources: Same as for Table 1.

literature.[141] It is worth noting that the idea of 'the country' receives some attention in their work. It is also present in the writings of men who were not necessarily members of this new social group; perhaps it is related to the fact that of 200 poets alive between 1525 and 1625 at least 76 per cent had attended university.[142]

Alan Everitt and Peter Laslett have painted a picture of the educated pursuits of the Kentish gentry.[143] A similar canvas is required for Norfolk (Tables 1–3). As early as the 1570s, between 17 per cent and 26 per cent of a sample of 470 resident Norfolk gentry had attended university.[144] In Yorkshire in 1642, of the 679 heads of families investigated by Dr Cliffe, 169 (25 per cent) had attended an English university. There are important technical problems with regard to the comparability of sources and methods, but this does suggest some interesting contrasts with Norfolk, although Yorkshire was anything but an intellectual backwater.[145] Dr Lloyd tells us that between 1540 and 1640 at least 343 men from

[141] Curtis 1967; Seaver 1970, p. 179; Williams 1965, pp. 256–7; Harbage 1952, pp. 96–7; Miller 1959. See also Saunders 1964, ch. 4.

[142] Calculated from App. II to Sheavyn 1967, pp. 210–38. This figure is undoubtedly an underestimate of the extent of university experience. It does not allow for defects in registration during the earlier years or for the increase in the habit of attendance during the period.

[143] Everitt 1957, pp. 22–5; 1966, pp. 45 ff; Laslett 1948.

[144] See note to Table 3.

[145] Cliffe 1969, p. 74; see Dickens 1952, 1963.

south-west Wales matriculated at Oxford. Of these, 132 (38 per cent) were entered as the sons of gentry, of whom at least fifty (38 per cent) obtained degrees. The pattern of attendance from this region follows that estimated by Lawrence Stone from the vantage of aggregate statistics compiled for the nation as a whole.[146] A study of knighthood in England suggests that members of this group initially emulated the peerage by educating their eldest sons privately, but after about 1580 they also succumbed to the attractions of public higher education[147] – at the point when the nobility was temporarily withdrawing its patronage from the universities and transferring it to the Inns of Court and then the Grand Tour.[148] The improvement in the educational attainment of MPs is in large part a measure of the attainments of the leading local gentry.[149] This is especially true of the parliaments of the 1620s and 1640s when the electorate preferred that their community should be represented by local men of standing and was most unwilling to accept carpetbaggers and Court nominees.

From the viewpoint of this essay, the most significant increase in the extent of university experience was among the justices of the peace. As the Court nobility and the episcopacy lost effective control of the localities, as the miscellaneous medieval institutions of local government decayed and were supplanted by the quarter sessional system, and as the county bench of magistrates acquired extensive new administrative responsibilities and assumed quasi-legislative functions, it was the justices of the peace and the elite formed by the deputy lieutenants who became the effective governors of the shires.[150] Christine Black's study of Derbyshire and Nottinghamshire in the period from 1529 to 1558 suggests some legal training among local JPs, but shows that there is positive evidence for only one JP from Nottinghamshire and two from Derbyshire having attended a university.[151] In Lancashire it is only after Elizabeth's accession that the gentry begin to display a really active interest in education.[152] In contrast to this, Joyce Mousley found that in 1580, of those who were heads of her eighty-seven selected families or family branches in Sussex,

---

[146] Lloyd 1968, pp. 194–5. Thirty men from this region went to Cambridge; Stone 1964, p. 53.
[147] Leonard 1970, pp. 34–41.   [148] Stone 1965, pp. 648, 688 (fig. 21).
[149] Stone 1964, p. 63, summarises and qualifies the evidence.
[150] There is no adequate published description of the interrelationship of these developments. However, for a summary of some of the relevant considerations see Smith (A.G.R.) 1967, ch. 7; Elton 1965, ch. 10. The best description of how the Commission of the Peace worked in practice – as distinct from theory – is Smith (A.H.) 1959a. For a description of the quarter sessional system in operation, see Smith (A.H.) 1967, pp. 93–110.
[151] Black 1966, pp. 48–51.   [152] Watson 1959, pp. 33–5.

Table 4. *New members of the Wiltshire Commission of the Peace with experience of higher education*

Decade	Total of new members	Higher education		None	
		No.	%	No.	%
1581–90	31	16	51	15	48
1591–1600	27	20	74	7	26
1601–10	23	14	61	9	39
1611–20	28	23	82	5	18

Source: Allison D. Wall, 'The Wiltshire Commission of the Peace 1590–1620. A study of its social structure' (MA thesis, University of Melbourne, 1966), p. 46. Unfortunately, Mrs Wall does not distinguish between university and other forms of higher education.

22 per cent had attended university, whereas 29 per cent of their sons did so. Of those among this number who were office-holders, over half had some higher education.[153] A study of the Wiltshire Commission of the Peace displays the growth in the number of educated justices.[154] Professors Hexter, Barnes and Owens have revealed the extent of university education among the governors of Jacobean Northamptonshire and Caroline Somerset and Norfolk.[155] Finally, J.H. Gleason's exploration of the background of justices between 1562 and 1636 provides further evidence of the developments noted in these other local studies (Table 5). By the 1620s at least half, and often more, of the Commission of the Peace had personal experience of the university world. As they sat on the justices' bench – these proud governors of the county community – their understanding of that community and its place among the other shires, which together composed the comity of England, owed something to the self-consciousness of local origins engendered by that experience at the university.

Many of these men looked upon themselves as a godly magistracy with a mission to raise a city as upon a hill – a godly community – within their county societies. In this they were joined by many from among the other segment of the articulate provincial elite: the members of an often godly and increasingly well-educated ministry. As an educated gentry began to

[153] Mousley 1956, pp. 131, 331–4, 340, and Leonard 1970, p. 34. As Dr Mousley noted, a limitation to her statistics – which also applies to these which I have provided for Norfolk in Table 1 – is that they aggregate men from different generations.
[154] See Table 4. These figures are derived from Wall 1966.
[155] Hexter 1961, p. 55; Barnes 1961, p. 31; Owens 1970, pp. 560–72.

Table 5. *Percentage of 'working members' of the Commission of the Peace with experience of the universities*

Date	Kent	Norfolk	Northants	Somerset	Worcs.	N.R. Yorks	Total	Diff. incr.
1562	2.27	5.88	5.88	3.44	5.26	11.76	4.89	
1584	16.38	41.66	16.66	15.38	15.38	38.63	23.17	18.28
1608	40.20	59.61	18.91	35.55	20.58	56.25	40.51	17.34
1626	62.71	52.94	53.70	50.00	51.72	58.82	55.47	14.96
1636	68.25	67.30	71.79	54.90	50.00	48.71	61.65	6.18

Note: The numbers in each individual commission are often too small for too much significance to be read into them. However, the percentage for the total in each year is more reliable, while the trend over the years within every county is obvious and very considerable.

Source: Gleason 1969, pp. 86–8.

fill the quarter sessional bench, an educated clergy were occupying the parish pulpits. In the pursuit of their degree they could not have avoided being reminded of their local dependencies. Within the local community their more radical members looked to the justices who wielded power in county government to protect them from the diocesan institutions utilised by the episcopate. Estimates suggest that at Elizabeth's accession 10 to 15 per cent of the nation's parish churches were without incumbents. This is probably optimistic, and a truer picture is that something nearer 22 per cent of all benefices were void in 1558.[156] Many of these deficiencies were quickly remedied by the flow of graduates supplied by the universities. This overall improvement is evident in a comparison of the situation in the diocese of Norwich in 1563 with that which prevailed in 1612. In 1563, 434 benefices (over 36 per cent) were void or served by curates (Table 6). At that time the archdeaconry of Sudbury had been the best provided for in the diocese, with only forty-two (19 per cent) livings void or served by curates. It occupied a similar relative position in 1612, with only two vacancies – and those from recent deaths – and with three livings served by curates. In 1563 the archdeaconry of Norwich had had eighty (27 per cent) livings void or served with curates, but by 1612 they were reduced to three (Table 7). The archdeaconries of Norfolk and Suffolk had been the worst provided for, with deficiencies of over 45 per cent

---

[156] Curtis 1967, pp. 314–15; Tyler 1967, p. 84. See also, for further details on the parochial clergy, Christopher Hill's inimitable study, *Economic Problems of the Church from Archbishop Whitgift to the Long Parliament* (1956).

Table 6. *The diocese of Norwich in 1563*

Archdeaconry	Parish churches		Rectories or parsonages full		Vicarages full		Void, but some served with curates	
	No.	%	No.	%	No.	%	No.	%
Norwich	289	24	168	58	41	14	80	27.7
Norfolk	402	33.5	184	45.8	36	9	182	45.3
Suffolk	286	23.8	114	39.9	42	14.7	130	45.5
Sudbury	224	18.7	151	67.4	31	13.8	42	18.8
Totals	1,201		617	51.4	150	12.5	434	36.1

Source: NDR, sun/3 (Box 806), Miscellaneous Register, fos. 96ff.

Table 7. *The diocese of Norwich in 1612*

Archdeaconry	Number of parish churches	Vacancies	Vacancies %
Norwich	289	3	1.03
Norfolk	402	20	4.97
Suffolk	286	–	–
Sudbury	224	2	0.89
Total	1,201	25 + ?	2.08 + ?

Note: The returns are missing for Suffolk archdeaconry in 1612.
Source: Barton 1964, II, pp. 304–5, 305–9, 320–1.

(182 and 130 respectively). By 1612, in the Norfolk archdeaconry four of the vacancies had been caused by recent avoidances, and in the remaining thirty-nine (10 per cent) cases sixteen were vacant and twenty-three were served by curates.[157]

A further survey of the diocese conducted in 1605 provides some indication of the extent of university experience among this segment of the articulate elite (Table 8). By this date there was a licensed preacher in almost every other parish. Of the 579 beneficed preachers within the diocese only seventy were licensed non-graduates, although there were

[157] NDR, sun/3 (Box 806), Miscellaneous Register, fos. 96ff. See Tables 6–7; Barton 1964, II, pp. 304–5, 305–9, 320–1. The returns are missing for Suffolk archdeaconry in 1612. For a summary of evidence from other dioceses see Curtis 1967, pp. 320–1; Spufford 1970, pp. 115–16; cf. Lloyd 1963a, pp. 180–1. Christopher Hill is not convinced of the sufficiency of these improvements: Hill 1956, p. 207, and 1963, p. 87.

Table 8. Institutions in the diocese of Norwich of clergy surviving in 1605

Date	Totals			DD & BD			MA			BA			NG		
	I	II %	III	IV	V %	VI	IV	V %	VI	IV	V %	VI	IV	V %	VI
1556–60	2	0.2	1	—	—	—	1	0.3	0.0	—	—	—	1	0.4	0.0
1561–65	12	1.3	4	1	1.1	−3	—	—	—	4	2.9	0.0	7	2.5	+3
1566–70	36	4.1	12	—	—	—	4	1.1	−8	2	1.5	−10	30	10.5	+18
1571–75	62	7.1	15.5	2	2.2	−13.5	13	3.6	−2.5	10	7.3	−5.5	37	13.0	+21.5
1576–80	91	10.4	22.75	14	15.7	−8.75	29	8.0	+6.25	12	8.8	−10.5	36	12.6	+13.25
1581–85	129	14.8	32.25	8	9.0	−24.25	50	13.8	+17.75	20	14.6	−12.25	51	17.9	+18.75
1586–90	133	15.2	33.25	15	16.9	−18.25	48	13.3	+14.75	21	15.3	−12.25	49	17.2	+15.75
1591–95	116	13.2	29.0	15	16.9	−14	48	13.3	+19	27	19.7	−2	26	9.1	−3
1596–1600	150	17.1	37.5	20	22.5	−17.5	83	22.9	+45.5	20	14.6	−17.5	27	9.5	−10.5
1601–5	142	16.3	35.5	14	15.7	−21.5	86	23.8	+50.5	21	15.3	−14.5	21	7.4	−14.5
Totals	873			89			362			137			285		

Key:

Col. I: Total number of institutions per quinquennium.

Col. II: Percentage of the total number for the whole period, 1556–1605.

Col. III: Mean of the total per quinquennium. (Col. I divided by the number of types of degree plus 'non-graduates' represented in the total.)

Col. IV: Number of institutions of clerics with the specified degree per quinquennium.

Col. V: Percentage of the total number with specified degree instituted during quinquennium.

$$\frac{\text{Col. IV } (quinquennium)}{\text{Col. IV total}} \times 100$$

Col. VI: Deviation from the mean for the quinquennia = Col. III (quinq. mean) − Col. IV (quinq. total)

It must be emphasised that these figures are subject to severe limitations. As at present calculated they imply similar demographic characteristics among the different classes of clergymen. They also assume a similar rate of mobility among holders of different types of degrees. Neither of these possibilities is likely to hold true. The figures refer to institutions, not to individual clergymen.

Source: Barton 1964, I, pp. 191–212.

a further 215 non-graduate clergy. An examination of the dates of institution to livings provides a very rough indication of the improvement of educational standards and the extent of university experience among the clergy. There is a noticeable decline in the proportion of non-graduates instituted to livings. In counterpoint to this is the increase in the proportion of MAs. The below-average figures for BAs are probably compounded of the effects of an inadequate supply of BAs compared with non-graduates in the early years and an increasing availability of MAs in the later decades.[158]

The two groups which had known each other at college were drawn together again in the counties. Nicholas Bownde had matriculated as a sizar from Peterhouse in 1568, took his BA in 1571–2, became a fellow and proceeded to his MA in 1575, then received his DD in 1594. John More had been a fellow of Christ's between 1568 and 1572. At the termination of his fellowship he became minister of St Andrew's, where he earned the title of the 'Apostle of Norwich'. Bownde married More's widow, eventually succeeded him at St Andrew's and also posthumously edited his sermons. In doing so he dedicated them to the justices of Norfolk for, as he explained in the dedication, they had been preached first before the justices at quarter sessions, 'and afterwards (the Lord so effectually blessing him and moving some of you with his Holy Spirit) being written out at the earnest request (as it seemeth) of your Worships, himself in his lifetime dedicated them in a sort unto you'.[159] In the 1620s, Thomas Scott delivered the sermon before the judges and the justices of the peace at Norfolk assizes. The intensity of political antagonisms in the 1620s fires the invocation of the idea of 'the country' which he employs in an annex to the sermon. He tells his audience that in the forthcoming parliamentary elections they should choose one 'that is religious, will stand for his Country's good', and he urges them on to action: 'Let none amongst you be seen idly to sit at home whilst these things are doing in the full County, as if it did not concern you; but ride, run and deal seriously herein, as for your lives and liberties which depend hereupon.'[160] For many of those among his audience the implications of this admonition must have owed something to their sojourn in Cambridge. There they had learned to identify 'the country' with the social world of their own regional societies. While the experience of college life aroused in them

---

[158] Barton 1964, I, pp. 191–212. See Table 8.
[159] Venn, I, p. 186b; III, p. 205b; Nicholas Bownde, 'Epistle Dedicatory', in John More, *Three Godly and Fruitful Sermons* (1594), no pagination.
[160] Scot[t] 1623, pp. 87–8.

a sense of local identity, the institutional arrangements of the English universities provided an increasing temptation for men to identify 'the country' with the administrative and political entity: the community of the county.

Thus the concept of 'localism' in this period has been too narrowly conceived, and I have suggested the beginnings of an alternative framework of analysis. In this period social historians have unduly neglected the shaping influence of institutions on the society they study; and some too easily made assumptions about the effects of education in that society – assumptions originating in our present preoccupation with the social consequences of education – need to be questioned. It is equally important to know where men go to as to know where they come from: the experience of college life no less than the contents of his books and the precepts of his tutor influenced a man's views and allegiances.

APPENDIX I (SEE P. 221)

Later estimates tend to confirm the accuracy of Professor Stone's earlier calculations (Stone 1964; 1975, pp. 91–2). Stone suggests that in the 1630s there was a combined average annual entry to Oxford and Cambridge of 996. The discrepancy with his previous estimate of 1,055 is only fifty-nine (5 per cent). The earlier set of figures suggested that 59 per cent of university entrants did not immediately enter upon a profession on leaving university. The revised estimates suggest a figure of 57 per cent. These figures do not appear to take into account graduations in music and medicine. The omission is not serious. However, it is not clear if graduates in civil law are included among aspirants to ecclesiastical offices. This would constitute a slightly more significant omission. In addition it should be noted that Professor Curtis' original suggestion (Curtis 1967, pp. 319–20) was that there were 327 vacancies in the church each year. This implies an annual residue of 100 men who may have hoped to find a place in the church, but were more likely to be disappointed. Combined figures for laymen and prospective clergymen suggest that 67 per cent of university men did not enter immediately upon a recognised professional career. Of the 566 (57 per cent) laymen, many were likely to find their way back to county society and positions of authority.

A number went on to the Inns of Court. Professor Prest calculates a total of 2,644 admissions to the Inns of Court for 1630–9 (Prest 1965, p. 385), giving an annual average of 264. Professor Stone calculates that about 50 per cent of entrants to the Inns of Court had previously attended university. This suggests that, on average, each year 132 men went on from university to an Inn of Court. An as yet unknown proportion of this number eventually entered the various levels of the legal profession. In this decade a total of 536 men were called to the bar (Prest 1965, table xiv), giving an annual average figure of fifty-four. We may then make the hazardous assumption that the extent of university education among men called to the bar is the same as that among entrants to the Inns. This suggests that each year twenty-seven men entering the higher levels of the legal profession had had experience of university life.

APPENDIX II (SEE P. 222)

The estimate of a total university population of between 2,998 and 3,050 is derived from Cooper, *Annals*, III, p. 148. In the following calculations the difference is halved to produce a compromise figure of 3,024. The estimate of the undergraduate population is derived from Stone (1975, p. 92). Accepting a yearly entry of 490 (*c.* 1610–19) combined with a four-year course of study suggests a student population of 1,960, constituting 65 per cent of the university community. Accepting a yearly entry of 513 (*c.* 1620–9) suggests a student population of 2,052, or 68 per cent. However, not all students stayed the course. At present we have no means of estimating the drop-out rate. Apart from the difficulties likely to be encountered by poor students, other considerations also contributed to reducing the number of *resident* as distinct from *entering* students. Those of noble parentage were allowed to proceed to their degree in three years rather than four. In addition they, and most of the sons of the gentry who entered as fellow-commoners or pensioners, did not intend to take a degree and therefore had no incentive to stay the whole length of the course. These calculations are further complicated by the fact that during Michaelmas and part of Lent term there were four years in residence, but in Easter term there were only three. Moreover, by the early eighteenth century it seems to have been assumed that freshmen might not arrive until after Christmas (Waterland 1730, p. 17). Assuming a student body of 65 per cent suggests a faculty-and-administration/student ratio of 1:1.84. This does not seem realistic. Very rough calculations for the four years 1632–5 suggest a faculty/student ratio of 1:2.97 at Gonville and Caius. However, not all fellows acted as tutors. The tutor/student ratio was nearer 1:4.76. However, this obscures the fact that by the 1630s the 'professional' tutor had emerged.

In fact, twenty-two tutors accepted under ten students each, producing a ratio of 1:2.40, whereas three tutors accepted over ten students, producing a ratio of 1:22. Further work is required on this subject but the present very uncertain figures suggest a faculty/student ratio that would offend the desire for cost-effective throughput of today's academic administrators.

Chapter 7

A LOCAL HABITATION:
GOWNSMEN AND TOWNSMEN

There is, perhaps, a temptation to conceive the relationship between a university and its urban context simply as bipartite. This is particularly evident, for example, in more popular studies of town–gown relationships.[1] But I suspect that the relationship is rarely as simple as this. To borrow a phrase of the anthropologists, universities and their urban environs are almost always 'part societies', and the relationship between these two particular constituent elements can only be fully understood within the larger context.

Be that as it may, the form of the relationship between Cambridge university and town cannot be fully understood simply within this restricted local framework. In part this is because of two salient characteristics peculiar to universities. First, in most instances they draw their clientele from a wider circuit than that of the town. Consequently a wider and possibly more socially and politically influential group of individuals will have an interest in the locality than would be the case if the university was absent. Second, to a greater or lesser degree and while never an essential characteristic, universities are inclined to be concerned with the ideas of the day. This interest is likely to be seen as of use to the central authority – but at the same time to be potentially dangerous. Both conditions induce intervention in the locality by outside forces. This was quite markedly true of Cambridge in the sixteenth and seventeenth centuries.

The history of Cambridge has usually been written by university men as the history of the university or by those bemusedly and admiringly looking in from the outside.[2] We need to look afresh at the history of Cambridge *tout court*, in the light of what we have come to know since the 1970s of the history of towns as such in early modern England.[3] Only

---

[1] For a good example of its type see Parker 1983.
[2] The notable exception to this is Cooper's *Annals*, but that is more of a compilation than a history.
[3] For convenient reviews of much of this literature see Clark 2000; Clark and Slack 1972, 1976; Corfield 1972.

then will the generic and the singular in the town's experience become fully evident. Furthermore we need to contemplate the possibility that ultimately it may be developments beyond the strict limits of the history of the universities or of urban history which create the terms of engagement from which emerge at any one period the specific forms of the relationship between university and town.

In every age the relations of town and gown have been deeply ambivalent, but antagonism is always better recorded than friendship. Yet there is little doubt that there was exceptionally intense antagonism between university and town in the greater part of the sixteenth and the first half of the seventeenth centuries. One reason for this may have been that in this period the two entities were becoming increasingly and recognisably distinct on the ground. There was what might be described as at first a physical disentanglement of the university and the town and then a process of recolonisation by the gownsmen of the townsmen's space. These processes were a result of what might be seen as both negative and positive developments.

The negative element came with the dissolution and the disappearance of religious foundations which could be compared with the buildings and institutions of the university. In some of these, such as Corpus Christi College, founded by the citizens, and God's House, the college of grammarians which had been converted into Christ's College at the beginning of the sixteenth century, and above all the hospital of St John converted into St John's College, the town had had an interest.[4] The sixteenth century witnessed intense building activity on the part of the colleges, so that by 1600, and with the exception of the parish churches, all the major physical structures within Cambridge carried about them, as it were, the signature of the university rather than that of the town.[5] This is to be contrasted with the experience of other urban places in this period. For example, in Norwich there was a substantial acquisition of former monastic property by the corporation. This was used both for practical purposes such as the creation of a municipal granary and for the elaboration of civic ceremonial space.[6] Furthermore, it is, I think, easy for us, accustomed as we are to moving among large physical structures, and buildings distinguished in function by their appearance, to underestimate the impact made on contemporaries in this relatively small market town of the line of aberrant structures that appeared during the Tudor period, stretching from Queens' and King's, through Caius'

---

[4] Above, p. 17; Rubin 1987.
[5] Above, chapter 2; Lobel and Johns 1975; Willis and Clark 1886/1988.   [6] Coby 1992.

rejuvenated Gonville Hall to the truly monstrous presences of Trinity and St John's.[7]

If we are to believe contemporary complaints, these imposing new structures were to be juxtaposed with the jerry-built speculative building intended to house the contemporaneous influx of poor into the town. These were the 'unwholesome and base cottages' which in 1616 the university complained were built 'and pester every lane and corner'.[8] Some sense of the likely appearance of these single-cell cottages is to be gained from the twelve surviving examples of such buildings which have been discovered in nearby Norwich and from the complaints in 1619 of the fire risk arising from thatching in reed and straw. We may therefore conclude that the distinctions between town and university were accentuated as the predominant character and quality of the housing stock of the two bodies moved in opposite directions.

It is worth noting that what we are seeing in these buildings is not mainly the embodiment in stones and mortar of the aspirations of relatively penurious and uninfluential scholars. One must recall that, then as now, poor scholars could be very accomplished beggars; and the new buildings of Caius and Trinity remind us that not all scholars were poor. Yet much of the building activity in this period represents an intrusion into the town of the aspirations of the predominantly secular elite. In effect the colleges became the convenient focus of activity in a particular locality of the aspirations not only of kings and ministers but also of an increasing number of gentry and merchants. The motivations were varied which led to this focus of investment in Cambridge. It included the desire to provide a preaching clergy and the less elevated wish to purchase advantage in seeking the prospective education of one's offspring. But it also included a peculiar transmutation of the late medieval concern for a form of continuity which had manifested itself in the endowment of chantries for the salvation of souls.[9] Indeed, it can be argued that if anything the Reformation served to enhance rather than to diminish the importance of the universities and their colleges as institutions through which the personal aspirations of the laity could be realised. True, what was sought was no longer a solidly established institution which could offer some guarantee of being able to provide the service of praying

---

[7] See above, pp. 21–30.
[8] Cooper, *Annals*, III, p.110. Such complaints were fairly conventional, like those which adduced the ruinous condition of buildings as the excuse for rebuilding them. For the Norwich structures (below), I am indebted to my late colleague, the former Director of the Norwich Survey, Alan Carter; CUL, CUR Town 37.7, 1a.
[9] See the succinct statement in Brooke 1985/1996, p. 8.

souls out of purgatory.[10] But it would be anachronistic to conclude from this that the laity lost all interest in the facilities which could be offered by corporations in perpetuity such as were represented by the colleges. Moreover, the dissolution had, of course, massively reduced the number of institutions of this type. For this reason if for no other, the collegiate bodies in a couple of English market towns acquired a new attraction. However, what was now sought was a form of memorialisation and continuity of the family name and celebration of the dear departed at a time when an increasing number of families were displaying pretensions and sensibilities of this type. Between the 1520s and the 1680s they generated new business for the heralds and genealogists; they took over their local churches and effectively converted them into family mausolea, stuffing them full of their mannerist monuments, and not least an increasing number of families ensured their memorialisation by an astute investment in a named benefaction at a Cambridge college.[11]

For example, when Joyce Frankland lost her son she was offered consolation by Alexander Nowell – a notable ecclesiastical mendicant – with the thought that she could have many more sons if she would invest in the provision for students at Gonville and Caius, Emmanuel, Brasenose and Lincoln colleges. Sir Christopher Wray effectively purchased a family interest in a set of chambers at Magdalene; and at Sidney Sussex Mr Blundell's fellows and students were locked into a mutual interdependence which relied upon a continued recollection of their benefactor.[12] Thus the increasingly lengthy roll-call in the prayers in commemoration of benefactors within colleges was in effect also a register of the extent to which – at one remove – an increasingly wealthy gentry were quite unwittingly intruding their interests into a particular provincial market town.[13]

But to return to the issue of the topographical consequences of these investments: the growth of the university at this period was manifested through the growth of the colleges; permanent and physically distinct, unlike the more ephemeral hostels that previously had been interspersed about the town.[14] The sixteenth century saw a developing concentration

---

[10] Cf. Duffy 1992, pp. 381, 393; clause 22 of the *Thirty-Nine Articles* (Hardwick 1876, pp. 319–21).

[11] For recent studies of the first two of these phenomena and surveys of the relevant literature see Bujak 1992; Finch 1989. The apotheosis of hubris expressed in monumental form by a local family is, perhaps, the Tollemache memorial at Helmingham in Suffolk, where a dormer window has been inserted in the nave in order to accommodate the soaring pretensions of the family.

[12] Above, pp. 208, 214.

[13] The cumulation of this evidence leads me to conclude that Lawrence Stone exaggerated the extent of the decline of a concern with lineage in the late sixteenth and the seventeenth centuries (Stone 1977, pp. 85–91, 123–9).

[14] See above, pp. 21–5.

of the collegiate property to the west of a line described by what are now Trumpington Street, King's Parade and Trinity Street.[15] For townsmen who were still heavily dependent on rural resources for their day-to-day needs, this blocked convenient access to the very useful watermeadows to the west and there were numerous disputes over the exploitation of this area.[16]

This restriction to the west combined with the limitation imposed by the line of the King's Ditch in the east to constrict the physical development of the town. Finally, through a process of endowment and purchase and over a long period of time, the colleges had been acquiring the dominant interest in the town's common fields, both the West Fields and the East or Barnwell Fields.[17] There was only a slight element of exaggeration in the claim by the vice-chancellor in 1587 that 'the colleges are in effect owners of all the land in the fields of Cambridge'.[18] This effectively placed the town within a circuit controlled by gownsmen. Again, this is to be contrasted with the situation in towns such as Norwich and requires us to take a broad view of the urban space. There, it is true that urban expansion all took place within the ample confines of the city walls. However, it is also true of Norwich that individual townsmen and the corporation as a whole had substantial and in this period growing interests in the adjacent countryside, especially to the west of the city.[19] This is to be contrasted with the situation at Cambridge, where the overall increase in the town's population in this period took place within a very restricted area and in circumstances in which there was only constricted access to the resources available in the immediate environs of the town. There can be little doubt but that this exacerbated the problems arising from the combination of tenements, multiple occupation and sustained inward subsistence migration which was a characteristic feature of the majority of urban places in this period.[20]

This *de facto* topographical bifurcation of the town must have been worrying enough for the burghers but it did not stop there. Within what we may care to think of as the townward or eastern side of the urban area

---

[15] See above, pp. 21 ff.

[16] There is, perhaps, a tendency to forget the close and immediately dependent nature of urban life on the surrounding countryside in the early modern period. Given the very high cost of transport, it was an important source of constructional materials such as reed for thatching. It was an essential source of perishable supplies such as milk, fish and vegetables, and to some extent of herbal curatives. It was increasingly important as a space for 'parking' and 'refuelling' the main means of locomotion and power: the horse; in Norwich the developing commercial centres represented by inns owned pasturage just outside the town: Garrard 1986; Branford 1988.

[17] Hall and Ravensdale 1976.   [18] Parker 1983, p. 103.

[19] For Norwich in this period see Corfield 1972, 1976; Pound 1971, 1988; Griffiths and Smith 1987.

[20] Clark and Slack 1972.

there was a second threat posed in the late sixteenth century by a second phase of collegiate expansion. This was represented by the foundation of Emmanuel and Sidney Sussex in the 1580s and 1590s.[21]

Although it is less easy to document, there was also the intrusion represented by the investment in property in the town by the wealthier and more entrepreneurial academics. In effect these individuals came to constitute something like an alternative economic elite. There are parallels and contrasts elsewhere, in this instance with the patterns of behaviour of the rural gentry in their relationships with their local towns. The city of Norwich once again provides a benchmark in the form of a major provincial capital. For the greater part of the sixteenth and seventeenth centuries the provincial gentry seem to have 'withdrawn' from active involvement in their local urban centres, including active interference in the politics of major places such as Norwich, or investment in urban property.[22] Perhaps because Cambridgeshire was a relatively small county with few substantial resident gentry they seem to have played little part in the life of the county's main town. Against this negative factor is to be set the circumstances of the university's more plutocratic academics. Perhaps because some of them were resident for most of the year these men became actively involved in urban affairs.[23] There is, for example, the case of Andrew Perne, the long-serving master of Peterhouse. He appears to have exploited the pressure for accommodation arising from increased student numbers by running up a hostel adjacent to the college. He also owned a number of tenements in the town which he exploited as a source of rental income. Finally, he had what he refers to as his 'new mansion house': this may have provided even more luxurious accommodation than that afforded by the master's lodgings at Peterhouse.[24]

---

[21] Bendall *et al.* 1999, chs. 2, 4, 5.

[22] However, there are two qualifications to make to this general picture. There is considerable evidence of the way in which the periodic meetings of the increasingly elaborate quarter sessions and the assizes for a week or more at a time converted the city into a forum for the playing out of conflicts among the gentry and into a stage for their strutting pretensions. Administrative necessity and social practice also encouraged the acquisition of town houses by the leading local gentry. See Smith 1974, p. 15.

[23] Here, in so far as the distinction can be made, I am concerned only with their involvement as 'private' individuals, rather than in their capacity as representatives of the university. Aspects of the latter role are discussed below, pp. 248–9.

[24] Leedham-Green 1991. Perne owned a house in Trumpington Street, occupied by Wallis the brewer of Trinity, which backed 'on to Swinescroft [and was] apparently the northernmost of a set of some four tenements acquired by Perne at various times, that immediately to the south of the one occupied by Wallis being the site of his "new mansion house"' (*ibid.*, pp. 81, 86, 88). He alludes to 'the hostil bilded by me the which cost me one hunderith pownde' [adjacent to college] (*ibid.*, p. 88).

Table 9. *Cambridge population excluding colleges*

Date	Source	Approx. number
1524–5	Exchequer lay subsidy	2,600
1563	Ecclesiastical census	2,400
1587	Vice-chancellor's estimate	5,000
1620s	Inmate census	7,750
1674	Hearth tax	8,000

Source: Goose 1980, p. 353.

The more marked physical presence and increasingly frustrating constriction imposed by the university was reinforced by what must have been a very evident and fairly rapid shift in the overall makeup of the population in the mid-Elizabethan period. On the one hand there was a marked increase in the number of 'townsmen'. The town's population was relatively stable or even declined in the first half of the sixteenth century, but an increase seems to have taken off by the 1570s, which may have roughly trebled the population by the 1620s, if we can rely on the figures available (see Table 9).

But this increase in the town's population arose largely as a result of an influx of those trying to escape endemic poverty in the countryside. In this the experience of Cambridge was of a piece with many other urban centres at the time, such as Norwich.[25] By the mid-1630s adverse comment was being made on the 'multitude of poor people [who] have been received out of the Countrie Towns adjoining and divers other parts of this kingdom'.[26] In 1584 the Privy Council had remarked disapprovingly upon the 'public hurt and incommodity' which had arisen as a result of the promiscuous building infill of sites in and around the town and the division of houses 'into many small tenements (for the rudeness and straitness of them not fit to harbour any other than of the poorest sort)'.[27]

From the viewpoint of the town's governors, such individuals were *in* but not *of* the town, except as a new and intractable problem with which they had to deal. As the Privy Council went on to acknowledge, as a consequence of the accommodation of this influx both university and town were likely to be 'overburthened in yearly allowance towards the maintenance of the poor' and to be put at further risk from plague and infection 'by reason that so many poor people are so narrowly and

---

[25] Pound 1971; and in general Beier 1985.   [26] Cooper, *Annals*, iii, p. 272.
[27] Goose 1980, pp. 349–50.

unwholesomely thrust and thronged together in diverse places'.[28] In the admittedly extreme circumstances of the plague year of 1630, the vice-chancellor suggested that there were 'five thousand poor and not above one hundred who can assist in relieving them'.[29]

On the other hand there was also a massive increase in the number of gownsmen. By the early 1620s the university probably numbered in the region of 3,000, with something like 1,960 undergraduate students constituting 65 per cent of the university's total number. At this time members of the university therefore constituted some 28 per cent of a total population of the urban area of upwards of 11,000, of which nearly one-fifth were made up of undergraduates.[30] Here was a specific local twist to the problems created by a general increase in urban populations in this period.[31]

The situation was one, then, in which Cambridge shared in the general problems of most urban centres arising from a rapid increase and continuing turnover of a semi-destitute population.[32] In various ways the resultant difficulties were exacerbated by the further addition to the town's population by the increase in the number of gownsmen. Finally, a further twist was given to this last element in the situation for, from as early as the 1560s, there was a transformation in the character of these university recruits.

First, the increase in numbers may have shifted the age balance among members of the university, but there had always been an element of young and riotous students in it from its earliest days. As the university authorities themselves complained, one of the problems which they confronted in the 1560s and early 1570s was an increase in what they characterised as 'licentious youth'. Within this they included not only students but also young regent masters. In part the new university statutes of 1570 were an attempt to contain this problem.[33] However, from the viewpoint of the town there was nothing comparable that they could do to contain the youthful excesses of gownsmen when indulged too often at the expense of the town and its officials. This situation appears to be all the more anomalous, and therefore we must presume frustrating, when looked at from the perspective of the usual assumptions and practices of the period.[34] The increased Tudor fear of social unrest – justified or

[28] *Ibid.*   [29] Cooper, *Annals*, III, p. 227.   [30] Goose 1980, p. 353.
[31] For the argument for a general increase in the size of urban populations, and for a summary of the evidence, see P. Griffiths *et al.* in Clark 2000, pp. 195–209.
[32] Goose 1980.   [33] See above, chapter 3.
[34] A comparable problem naturally occurred in Oxford, and in London with the younger members of the Inns of Court.

not – was matched by the desire to contain this threat by the imposition of a strict system of control. As older forms of control through community and clientage declined, the household acquired a new significance for this purpose. It is this development which lies behind the regime's reinforcement of the principles of patriarchy. The problem at Cambridge was that students and young regent masters when about their business in the town had much of the character of masterless men.[35] Now it is true, and I have argued elsewhere, that there was an attempt to solve this problem *within* the university by equating students with children and fellows with servants under the authority of the paterfamilias of the master of a college. The college itself was equated both architecturally and conceptually with a great country house.[36] There was some merit in this equation within the university, but this did not redound to the benefit of the town in its dealings with 'licentious youth'. First, because the analogy was inexact: if the colleges were great country houses – as seems to have been the thinking – they were highly unusual in being set in the urban context of an English market town. The concentration of numbers and the propinquity of habitation had no real parallel. Moreover, in the wider world the effectiveness of the favoured model of patriarchal social control depended upon the local community being able to exercise some oversight; and the community could censure those heads of households who failed to exercise satisfactory control over those in their charge. Here again, the parallel at Cambridge was inexact. The burghers of the town had no effective means of censuring the master of a college when its members ran amok in the town.[37]

There were also the problems which arose from the changing social composition of the university. Earlier formulations in terms of lay successors to medieval clerks have long since proved to be too simple a view of the complex transformations in the social composition of Tudor Cambridge; and the full ramifications of this issue cannot be pursued here. However, what is germane in this context is that one of the elements in this transformation included an influx of students from gentry and wealthy urban backgrounds. These young men brought with them a wholly new set of expectations and patterns of behaviour which arose in large part from their anticipation of their future role in what was still predominantly a patron–client society.[38] Indeed, in some instances it is possible to demonstrate in detail the way that they practised with their fellow students the skills involved in the articulation of eminence and deference natural to their inherent social position. The most articulate

---

[35] Beier 1985.   [36] See below, pp. 303–12.   [37] See below, pp. 250–3.   [38] Morgan 1988.

statement of these attitudes and practices is to be found in the memoirs of Anthony Ashley Cooper, from the viewpoint of this book unfortunately an Oxford man! However, the use of this Oxford evidence in the Cambridge context can be justified in so far as piecemeal and less coherent evidence can be found which indicates that much the same practices could be found at Cambridge.[39]

With no undue modesty the future champion of English liberties could not resist recounting the stories of his leadership of the young men at Exeter College in the 1630s. He recalled that he 'kept both horses and servants in Oxford', and how, because he 'was allowed what expense or recreation I desired', this permitted him to cultivate his equals and patronise his inferiors; 'it gave me the opportunity of obliging by entertainments the better sort and supporting divers of the activest of the lower rank with giving them leave to eat, when in distress, upon my expense, it being no small honour among those sort of men, that my name in the buttery-book willingly bore twice the expense of any in the university'. This and his other qualities, he claimed, purchased for him the leadership of his contemporaries: 'This expense, my quality, proficiency in learning, and natural affability easily not only obtained the good-will of the wiser and elder sort, but made me the leader even of all the rough young men of that college.' He explained how he 'always relieved them [the sturdy youths who supported him] when in prison and procured their release, and very often was forced to pay the neighbouring farmers, when they of our party that wanted money were taken in the fact, for more geese, turkeys, and poultry than either they had stole or he had lost'. Cooper goes on to recall that the stirling virtues that, clearly, he was not backward in recognising in himself won him the leadership of the college in its disputes with Christ Church and elevated him to the leadership of those who opposed the established power structures – both formal and informal – within the college.[40]

The occasion for his 'seizure of power' at Exeter was his successful opposition to college saltings. He had initiated opposition by boxing the ears of the son of the earl of Pembroke, another aristocratic member of the college. In the scrimmage that ensued, the 'bachelors and young masters' came to the aid of the older students, but were also set upon by Ashley Cooper's faction 'and had been beaten very severely, but that my authority with them stopped them, some of them being considerable enough to make terms for us . . . Dr Prideaux the Master being called

[39] Some of this more fragmentary material is drawn together in Morgan 1983.
[40] Christie 1871, I, pp. 15–18 – also for what follows.

out to suppress the mutiny'. Other instances could be cited of the ways in which Ashley Cooper's inherited social position allowed him a freedom of manoeuvre unavailable to those other students who were 'intended by their friends to get their livelihood by their studies'.

Traditionally the universities, along with schools, were repressive regimes, concerned with the inculcation of youth with an established body of knowledge through rigorous and well-tried techniques of teaching. Inevitably, the psychological and intellectual pressures thus generated had called into being brief periods during which the normal rules were suspended.[41] Therefore, a counter-culture existed in the universities even before the major influx of aristocratic students during the late sixteenth century. What then happened was that the leadership of this counter-culture was taken over and exploited for its own purposes by the aristocrats. Because of their relative independence and customarily assertive demeanour, under their leadership the counter-culture became less of a safety-valve and more of a real threat to the formally constituted authorities in the universities, in individual colleges and in the university towns and their environs. Thus challenged, at least senior academics had the option either to attempt to regulate the occasions of misrule, as in the case of college plays, or else to attempt to abolish them, as in the case of saltings at St John's and Trinity. Unfortunately the indulgence in periods of misrule was not restricted to the confines of the colleges. However, the town authorities and the local parish constables were not in so advantageous a position in that they were ill equipped psychologically to attempt to exercise control over youth groups, the leaders of which were their social superiors; and the exceptional privileges of the university meant that they simply did not have jurisdiction over its members.[42]

The tensions created by this changing structure of circumstances also had ramifications for the relationship between the local authorities, both university and town, and the central institutions of the state. On occasion the vice-chancellor and the heads of houses were not averse to seeking the reinforcement of the authority of their chancellor or of the Privy Council against wayward and recalcitrant youth.[43] However, whenever the town had a similar recourse the effect was to bring them into conflict with their near neighbours. Given the second-rank status of their patrons at Court, not surprisingly, they usually came off second best.

Here again we need to view town–gown relationships within the broader context of their relationships with the wider 'country' and with

---

[41] See Thomas 1976.
[42] See above, pp. 94–6. For the special corporate privileges of the university, see below, pp. 253–4.
[43] See above, pp. 247–8.

the Court. The managerial problems thus posed prompted these local bodies to take the initiative in seeking the intervention of the Court as a means of bolstering their own authority. Much of the intervention by the central institutions of the state in the affairs of the university arose, not as a consequence of initiatives at the centre, but as a result of the recourse to the centre from the localities. This situation at Cambridge has close parallels with what we know of the relationship of county and urban societies elsewhere in England at this time in their relationship with the Court.[44] But let us return once again to the licentious youth of Cambridge.

There is considerable evidence of concern on the part of the university authorities with the problems posed by an increase in the proportion of its more youthful members.[45] It was usually members of the youthful tendency who were to the fore in the frequent conflicts with their contemporaries in the town. There has been an inclination to treat these encounters as a perennial feature of Cambridge life. What has not perhaps been fully appreciated is that this change in the age structure of the university was paralleled by a similar change in the age structure of the town. At least inferentially, we can see from the demographic evidence that a significant reason for the increase in the town's population was caused by a disproportionately large influx of young persons. Moreover, many of these youthful incomers were inmates or lodgers, and only loosely under the supervision of a responsible elder. Again, the low mean household size for Cambridge perhaps suggests that the household as a mechanism of social control was relatively weak within the town.[46] There may also have been some effect arising from the occupational structure of the town. Thus, compared with Norwich, it had a relatively high incidence of service and transport trades compared with crafts and manufactures. Employers in the former sectors tended to favour servants as against the preference of the latter for apprentices.[47] The degree of control of masters over servants and the period of continuity of service was less than that over apprentices.[48] Indirectly this may also have contributed to the presence of a loosely regulated body of youth within the town. Overall,

---

[44] For further comment on this phenomenon and another example of its manifestation at Cambridge see Morgan 1984.

[45] See above, p. 248.   [46] Goose 1980, pp. 354, 362–3, 365.

[47] Goose 1980, p. 375. Again, this was a natural consequence of the distorting effect of the types of demand created by the university and colleges.

[48] 'Servants' are, of course, an unsatisfactorily broad catch-all category. Kussmaul has tended to read back the eighteenth- and nineteenth-century evidence into the sixteenth and seventeenth and to suggest that servants were recruited on an annual basis (Kussmaul 1981). However, more detailed evidence from the period itself indicates that in the earlier centuries servants were likely to come and go at all times of the year (Campbell 1985; Smith (A. H.) 1989). There are likely

what we may be seeing here is a series of indirect and on the whole unwelcome outcomes from the viewpoint of both the university and the town of the university's dominance over the commercial and economic life of the town.

Although in theory all students should have been resident in colleges, the evidence from the censuses of the town in the 1630s suggests that the pressure of numbers and desire for more luxurious living may have driven some into lodgings;[49] and the less well off may have competed with youthful poor rural incomers. The conjunction of a young university with the migration of indigent youth to towns produced in Cambridge a particularly volatile concoction.

Finally, the presence of the university divided the loyalties of many of the more prosperous of the town's inhabitants. A growing and prosperous university required and sustained a level of skills and services in the town which it would not have enjoyed if the university had not been there. Thus there were many who lived in the town, but depended upon the colleges for their prosperity. This was obviously true in the case of specialist artisans such as the stationers, printers, bookbinders and booksellers.[50] It was also true of the laundresses, brewers and victuallers.[51] Less evidently, but no less significantly, it was true of other groups of artisans such as bricklayers, plumbers, carpenters, stonemasons and carvers, who no doubt undertook commissions for patrons outside the university, but whose numbers and diversified skills were sustained by the almost continuous campaigns of college building during the latter half of the sixteenth and first half of the seventeenth centuries.[52] This particular division of loyalties within Cambridge accentuated a more general and widespread difficulty. An increasingly urgent problem facing urban governors throughout England in the late sixteenth century was how to persuade their colleagues to

---

to have been crucial and perceived distinctions between servants and apprenticeship. On the one hand, servants were more likely to be providing fairly unspecialised domestic services or assistance to semi-commercial households, and employing elements of skills they already had, albeit those skills might be refined during the course of time in service. On the other hand, apprenticeship usually required a capital investment in the form of a premium paid to the master. This had two consequences. First, apprentices were likely to come from somewhat better-off families and to have higher social and economic aspirations than did servants. Second, the investment was a powerful inducement to stay the course: those who attempted to withdraw from it risked parental wrath. A further inducement to stay was inherent in the necessarily cumulative skills-based character of craft apprenticeship. It is worth speculating that in the contemporary mind this division among the plebeian elements of the town's youth could also be read into the situation of young men at the university: their social background and their experience at Cambridge was akin to that of apprentices rather than that of servants. Distinctions and antipathies among the town's youth may have helped to colour attitudes to students.

[49] Goose 1980, p. 362.   [50] Leedham-Green 1986, I, pp. xvi–xix.
[51] See e.g. Parker 1983, pp. 127ff; Twigg 1987, pp. 123–5.   [52] See above, chapter 2.

sacrifice their private time and personal income in order to provide the increased executive oversight required to meet the needs created by the pressing social problems posed by the changing character of urban life. Furthermore, it was necessary to accustom a yet broader spectrum of the moderately prosperous to the need to contribute to the provision of communal services in those areas where individual initiative was no longer adequate. This included such prosaic matters as the supply of clean water, control of the disposing and collection of refuse, and the provision of paving and lighting. Most notably it also involved acceptance of the need to provide for those subject to endemic poverty. In itself this required a change in perception in circumstances in which, increasingly, poverty was a consequence of an intensifying dependence on the labour market – which was itself subject to the cyclical fluctuations imposed by the trade cycle and further complicated by the vagaries arising from intermittent disruption of international markets. In addition, the urban communities, along with all others, had to meet what in *in toto* were the increasing fiscal demands of the central government in a period when it was fumbling towards the transition from a domain state to a tax state. In many towns and cities facing these demands a perennial problem was that those who made or had made their wealth in town avoided the increasing burdens and costs of urban life by decamping beyond its confines. In Cambridge this phenomenon took a particular turn as a result of the presence of the university. In effect an increasing number of the town's more prosperous inhabitants won exemption from the increasing responsibilities of urban life by claiming the privilege of being a servant of the university. For example, in 1635 the town was required to raise £100 as ship-money. The corporation complained to the Privy Council against the claim of exemption by 'privileged persons'. These were individuals who, they claimed, had purchased the status of being scholars' servants. According to the town they constituted something like a third of the inhabitants of Cambridge.[53]

Furthermore, the impact of the university on the life of the town may have contorted urban politics: there are some indications that it had the effect of exacerbating factional divisions among the leading burghers. For example, there was the furore that blew up between town and university in 1587, ostensibly over Hammond's pigs. The porcine details need not detain us; the point is Hammond's status. He was a brewer and also a bailiff of Jesus College. As such he was a privileged person and when the mayor

[53] Parker 1983, p. 128.

literally impounded the pigs Hammond resorted to the vice-chancellor for protection against his fellow burghers.[54]

Towns need to be assessed in the context of the wider urban hierarchy and of the regions which they served.[55] Again, Cambridge was at the centre of a region with relatively few competing market centres compared – say – with the situation in counties such as Hertfordshire and Devon.[56] Its apparent failure to realise its natural potential in this regard may owe something to the academic incubus in its midst. Furthermore, the growth of many other urban centres in this period arose from the enlargement of existing or the acquisition of new manufacturing activities. Late medieval Cambridge appears never to have had any significant manufacturing sector; and in many practical ways the presence of the university inhibited the development of such a sector during the course of the sixteenth century. In some degree it was in the interests of the university to stifle this independent development in order to ensure that it received the services of its urban host.

These effects were, one might say, diffuse although fundamental. But there was also a more direct consequence for the town of the existence of the university and the presence within it of both the precious scions of gentry families and the country's present and future intelligentsia. Quite apart from the intrusion into the town's affairs which arose intermittently as a result of appeals against it by the university to the Crown, the central government was itself especially concerned with what it often referred to as this 'well' or 'fountain' of the nation. For example, although the Privy Council manifested concern with urban conditions in many towns it only required that censuses be made of Oxford and Cambridge.[57]

---

[54] *Ibid.*, pp. 103–4.   [55] Patten 1978.
[56] Goose 1980, p. 351; Everitt 1967.   [57] See p. 247.

Chapter 8

HEADS, LEASES AND MASTERS' LODGES

... and although the name of the pope be here banished it is indeed still here, and in steade of one, not only Englande, butt Oxford also hath mani, eche companie his pope, a fayre swarme.

> Nicholas Gybharde to Lawrence Tonson on the heads of colleges at Oxford, 5 July 1575 (SP 12/105/4)

... those little living idols, or monuments of monarchy.

> W. Sprigge, *A Modest Plea for an Equal Commonwealth*
> (London, 1659, p. 45)

The basis for the antipathy to the heads of houses expressed in these quotations at both Oxford and Cambridge can be located in the constitutional and organisational changes that were effected at both universities in the early years of Elizabeth's reign. As we have seen, informally at Oxford and formally at Cambridge, their constitutions were revised, and the heads, masters or presidents of colleges came to form a governing oligarchy in their universities at large. Within the individual colleges, piecemeal reform of the statutes endowed their heads with far-reaching powers and privileges.[1] Both corporately and individually, the heads became charged by the central government with the responsibility for maintaining political order and doctrinal conformity amongst the volatile mix of youthful intelligentsia and aristocracy that gathered in unprecedented numbers in the rapidly expanding colleges of Oxford and Cambridge in the late sixteenth and early seventeenth centuries.[2]

But over and above these self-evident grounds for antagonism between the majority of the heads and the other members of their universities, there seemed to be an edge, a sharpness, a rankling discontent that derived from something more and something less than the institutional changes that we have surveyed in an earlier chapter. It was more because it was more frequent and continuous than the famous – and some would have said infamous – occasions on which the heads most ostentatiously

[1] Above, p. 78.   [2] Above, ch. 4.

256

exercised their new authority. It was less because it was compounded of many small incidents, patterns of behaviour and pointed confrontations. Trivial though these were in themselves, none the less cumulatively, between roughly 1560 and 1640, they served to set apart the heads from the other members of the university. This occurred despite the variety of talents and dispositions to be found amongst the hundred or so men who served as masters of Cambridge colleges in this period.

There were significant similarities in the circumstances of both Oxford and Cambridge, even though those circumstances might take slightly different local forms, as for example in the precise type of provision for the master's lodging. We will miss something of the full significance of the changes taking place in Cambridge if we fail to place those changes in the larger context. In this instance in no small part the style of life adopted by most masters at both universities arose from the same external causes. For example, many of the heads at both universities had aspirations to promotion into the same ecclesiastical hierarchy. At the same time, the pressures to which they were subjected came from the same source, the Court, although in so far as the survival of documents permits of systematic comparison, the evidence suggests that the extent of inroads into each institution did vary. Finally, as we will see, the equation of the masters with the heads of large households encouraged them to adopt the forms of domestic arrangements that were emerging in such households at this time.

This chapter therefore examines some of the multifarious and repetitive minutiae of university life; some of the nagging saws and perennial irritants that over time can take on a quite irrationally exaggerated importance. The purpose is to draw a composite picture of the lifestyle and modes of conduct of masters. This may help to explain the antagonism so evidently felt towards the heads on celebrated occasions such as the disputed election of the duke of Buckingham as chancellor in 1626, an antagonism that cannot wholly be ascribed to political or doctrinal differences.[3]

THE HEADS' LIFESTYLE

Over and above the differences between masters and fellows that arose as a result of their different responsibilities and divergent career patterns, in the period from the 1560s to the 1640s the whole style of life of the two groups was moving apart. Writing of the heads of the Oxford colleges in

---

[3] Morgan forthcoming.

1613 the French classicist Isaac Casaubon considered that they lived 'like noblemen'.[4] This had not always been the case, and the transformation as much as the difference was what was resented. This is evident in an incident that occurred during Robert Beaumont's vice-chancellorship at Cambridge, in 1565.[5]

Beaumont had been one of the Protestant exiles at Geneva in Mary's reign. The irony is that in his subsequent position of authority in the university he found himself in the invidious position of being required to impose Parker's 'Advertisements', an attempt to extort some conformity from his hotter Protestant brethren. Thomas Wood, the well-known Leicestershire puritan, reported to Anthony Gilby, at Ashby-de-la-Zouche, on the opposition that Beaumont encountered at Cambridge. Although the main motive behind this opposition is to be found in a distaste for what the more radical puritans saw as a turning back 'to the toyes of popery and pudles of superstition', it is also clear that there was a considerable admixture of resentment at the social pretensions with which this became associated. Wood claimed that 'Upon a certen daye, Mr Beaumont rode with his footeclothe to the churche (a maner not used in our tyme as you knowe).'[6] Beaumont quickly attempted to justify himself to the influential Gilby: 'I mervayle one of Mr Wodds yeares wolde so lightly eyther credite or write of so unlyke a matter. I ryde styll as homely as you do, or at least as homely as ye have sene me ryde in Leicestershire in all points.' Possibly – but the resentment at Beaumont's style and equipage found symbolic expression through the unfortunate medium of his horse. For while he was preaching, 'certen of the boyes clipt of[f] all the heere of his horse tayle and toppe, and made him a crown like a popishe prest'. Not content with this, the following Sunday, 'The said boyes to make . . . amends cutt all tho heere of his horse taken before in short peces and strewde it in the waye as he went (instead of a carpet) from his chambre to the churche.'

As in the heady days of the 1960s when the vice-cancellarial limousine was a frequent target for artistic daubing, so also in this period the availability of superior means of transport for heads was an object of continuing resentment: the maintenance by masters of good riding horses

---

[4] Quoted in Mullinger 1884, p. 381.

[5] The following paragraph is based on both the editorial matter and the document printed in Collinson 1960, pp. 24–5. This corrects Porter 1958, pp. 115–18. Beaumont was master of Trinity College, 1561–7.

[6] A large, richly ornamented cloth laid over the back of a horse and reaching to the ground on either side: a mark of state. Wood had probably been at Cambridge in the 1530s, and Gilby had been there 1531–(?)1553 (Venn, I, p. 215b). Wood is not recorded by Venn, but see Collinson 1960, p. iv n. 2.

both asserted their equivalence with the heads of gentry households and served to distinguish them from other academics. In a dispute at King's in 1603, two of the fellows entered the college stable 'where the Provost's geldings are kept' and, ignoring the protests of the horse-keepers, took away two of them, 'notwithstanding the Provost's charge to the contrary for that himself that very same day was to use them in his journey on College business – so upon the sudden putting him to provide common hackneys'.[7] Clearly, the need to resort to the use of common hackneys was an insult to the dignity of the provost of King's.

The possession of horses by the heads of colleges clearly had a symbolic significance over and beyond any additional convenience their availability might provide. In 1546–7 a major row over principle between the university and the city of Cambridge had been precipitated by the appropriation by the king's purveyor of fish of the ambling nag used by the ageing master of Peterhouse. But no doubt of equal importance was the resentment engendered among fellows of colleges at the recurrent expense of this privilege of office. At Christ's the cost of maintaining his horses figures largely in the master's expenses, as did the master's stable and geldings at Queens'. At Trinity College in 1616 there was a dispute between the master and fellows over their respective rights to pasturage for horses on the back green.[8]

If the maintenance of a stable was one symbol of the difference between masters and fellows another distinction of equal importance was the privilege of masters to retain servants. In 1589 the heads and other senior officers of the university had had this right confirmed as part of the wider confirmation of the university's privileges in Stourbridge Fair.[9] The symbolic and psychological significance of this right was that it again equated the masters of colleges with the heads of domestic households. From a practical viewpoint the main effect was to place considerable powers of patronage over Cambridge tradesmen in the hands of individual heads. But masters such as Thomas Bainbridge at Christ's also retained personal servants, both male and female. At Queens' College in 1588 the president had his own gardener. In 1634 an increase in the income of Sidney Sussex College permitted additional payments to the master for

---

[7] *HMCS*, xv, p. 80.
[8] Fuller 1655/1840, p. 241; CUL, MS Mm. v. 46, p. 197 (1569); Queens' College Archives, Bk 5, Journale 1587–1621, *passim*; Trinity College Muniments, A: The Masters' Old Conclusion Book, 1607–73, p. 59. In 1660 the fellows of Corpus declared that the new college stable had not been built for the sole use of the master, but that they might have a share in it, the master having sole use of the old stables (BL Harl. MS 7033, fo. 42).
[9] PRO, S.O. 3/1, August 1589.

wages to a man, and liveries for two of his servants.[10] There was, then, a marked difference of lifestyle permitted to masters compared with fellows as a result of the right of masters to keep servants. In addition, this helped to confirm the status of the masters of colleges as the equivalents of the heads of households.

RESIDENCE AND NON-RESIDENCE

The multifarious business of the college which the provost of King's had been forced to pursue on the undignified discomfort of 'common hackneys' was one of the original reasons for permitting masters longer periods of non-residence than were the fellows, as for example at Jesus and Corpus.[11] In great part this business arose from the process of endowment. In so far as this involved regular supervision of college estates, the work was frequently delegated to the subsidiary official, the riding bursar. However, corruption is the daughter of habit, and an energetic master such as Whitgift still found the necessity and the time to go on his own visitation and check on the work of the subsidiary college officers. The provost of King's, Roger Goad, also went on a progress about the college estates when he entered office, and on later occasions.[12]

At the prior stage of obtaining endowments it was usually the master who played a crucial part in negotiations which might take him away from the college for considerable lengths of time. When a lucrative endowment was in immediate prospect this might be acceptable. But when the long-drawn-out cultivation of potential benefactors was being pursued, this could arouse resentment: to fellows already suspicious of a socially distant head the cultivation of benefactors could appear to be no more than their master's social junketings with his betters at the college's expense. And no doubt sometimes it was: the boundaries in such matters are never precise. Characteristically, the fellows of Corpus complained that their master, Thomas Aldrich, made himself 'too much acquainted with the gentlemen of the country' around Cambridge, while the fellows of King's accused Roger Goad of 'Deludeing and glossing with noble and Honourable persons'.[13] But it was primarily the master who had to cultivate useful connections. Apart from his college status it was he who was likely to

---

[10] CUL, MS Mm. v. 47, fo. 104; Queens' College Archives, Bk 5, Journale, 1587–1621 (June 1588); *Cambridge Documents 1852*, III, p. 592.

[11] *VCH Cambs.*, III, pp. 422, 372. The master of Corpus was required to reside for only three months during the year, whereas no fellow was to be absent more than sixty-five days.

[12] Maitland 1847, pp. 365–6; BL Harl. MS 7031, fo. 8. For further evidence of the heads of colleges going on their own progresses, see Howard 1935, p. 15; Eland 1935; Martin 1976, pp. 159–78.

[13] Lamb 1838, p. 127; BL Harl. MS 7031, fo. 7.

have the necessary contacts. As Court interference in the appointment of the heads of houses increased, the very achievement of a mastership was itself an index of connections in influential circles. John Lightfoot (master of St Catharine's, 1650–75) was commended for his contribution towards the cost of the rebuilding which he initiated, 'and moreover was instrumental by his interest with his Friends to procure good benefactions for the same use from others'. The work was completed by his energetic successor John Eachard 'and those very many generous persons in *London*, and elsewhere, whose love of Learning, and favour to him, have excited them freely to contribute thereunto'. The austere Laurence Chaderton was able to enhance the fortunes of Emmanuel through his friendship with godly laymen. Lancelot Andrewes raised money for his college, Pembroke. When Fulke Greville, Lord Brooke, contemplated erecting a building at his old college, Jesus, it was with the master, John Duport, that he communicated about schemes for building. At Oxford the sugared eloquence of William Lewis, provost of Oriel, is said to have done much to assist in raising the funds necessary for the building activities of that college.[14]

Despite intermittent absences many of the masters spent long years in Cambridge. Such, for example, was Owen Gwynn, master of St John's from 1612 to 1634. This meant that, over those years, as most of the seniors moved on, it was the master who remained the person of first resort and the link at their alma mater for those older alumni who might be reaching the stage of contemplating making provision for an academic endowment. Again, long-serving masters had good connections with aristocratic families through their predilection for accumulating the scions of such families as pupils under their own charge.[15]

The failure of masters to reside in their colleges for all or part of the year is reflected in their ownership or occupation of separate houses. John Cowell left his house in Cambridge to Trinity Hall, and maintained a house in London, as did Roger Goad, the provost of King's.[16]

---

[14] For the increase in the connections between the Court and the university see chapter 4. For St Catharine's, see above, pp. 33–5, and Bright 1684, I, p. xxviii; for Chaderton, see Bendall in Bendall *et al.* 1999, pp. 108–13. For Andrewes, Welsby 1958, p. 47; for his earlier display of financial acumen as successively junior and senior treasurer at Pembroke in 1580–2 see Bauckham 1973, pp. 107, 109n; Jesus College Archives, Ant. 2.29; Venn, II, p. 265a; Emden 1948, pp. 44, 190–2.

[15] William Jessop to Owen Gwynn, 30 June 1617, 'And hearinge that all mye ould Acquaintaince are worn out there, longe agoe And that youe onelie Sr, are the nowe resident survyver there of my Tyme', asks for a favour to the son of a friend (Scott 1897, pp. 144–5. See also Emden 1948, pp. 44, 89); John Preston, master of Emmanuel, was described as 'the greatest pupil-monger in England' (Collinson in Bendall *et al.* 1999, p. 217, citing Thomas Fuller 1662, p. 291).

[16] Crawley 1976, p. 94; BL Egerton MS 2644, fo. 165, see also fo. 164v; Lake 1988, p. 196.

One reason for the occupation by masters of houses in and around Cambridge arose from the criticism of the wives and families that some masters attempted to maintain in their lodges.[17] Some form of accommodation in London was necessary for those masters who were energetic men of business. His friends expected that Nevile would be at his house in London at the time of the meeting of parliament. In addition, work arising from his various deaneries and a chaplaincy to the queen would also have drawn this busy master to the capital. As the case of Thomas Nevile suggests, a further cause of non-residence was pluralism amongst the heads of colleges. With one or two notable exceptions, such as Laurence Chaderton, most heads held a variety of ecclesiastical preferments. It was said of Lightfoot that it was not want of affection for his college that made him rarely reside there, but a sense of his prior responsibility to his flock. John Jegon apologised to Attorney General Coke for not having sent him a present since his last term as vice-chancellor and explained that in the first half of the year he had been sick, and the second half he had spent at his parsonage in Lincolnshire.[18]

Masters such as Samuel Ward took the opportunity of the easier travel afforded by the summer months to visit their ecclesiastical livings.[19] It was also during this period that masters could most conveniently visit potential benefactors. Moreover, towards the end of the summer they were likely to be absent on a progress around the college estates. During both the long vacation and at Christmas they took the opportunity to socialise with their friends in the country. Indeed, these powerful distractions for masters from the ever-present problems of governing Cambridge helped the further differentiation of academic term and vacation that is evident in this period, and contributed its part to the development of the summer season in the English countryside.[20]

A number of careerist heads combined their masterships with other appointments as archdeacons, deans and even bishops. When this practice was at its height, during the early 1600s, Nevile of Trinity was dean of

[17] See pp. 297–303.
[18] BL Egerton MS 2644, fo. 165; Venn, III, p. 244b; Bright 1684, I, p. xxviii; CUA, Misc. Collect. 8, fo. 3. Jegon is referring to the rectory of Beckingham, Lincs., which he had acquired in 1595 (Venn, II, p. 466b). The letter of apology was written from Corpus in November 1600.
[19] Bodl. Tanner MS 71, fo. 172, visit to Wells; Tanner MS 72, fo. 146, expectation of visit to western parts; Tanner MS 73, pt i, to Ward as archdeacon of Taunton, from Cambridge.
[20] For evidence of the absence of masters from Cambridge during the summer months see, e.g., BL Harl. MS 7029, fo. 8 (June 1595); BL Harl. MS 7029, fo. 12 (16 July 1595); Ussher 1847–64, X, p. 53 (6 July 1608); BL Harl. 7033, fo. 204 (1632); Laud 1847–60, V, ii, p. 560 (August 1635); *ibid.*, pp. 573, 575 (May 1636). For absence in the Christmas vacation: BL Harl. MS 7031, fo. 120 (23 Dec. 1595); BL Harl. MS 7031, fo. 110v (Jan. 1596); BL Harl. MS 7029, fos. 46, 46v (Jan. 1596); Laud 1847–60, V, ii, p. 572 (Dec. 1635).

Canterbury; Tyndall of Queens' was chancellor of Lichfield, archdeacon of Stafford and dean of Ely; Clayton of St John's was dean of Peterborough; John Jegon of Corpus was dean of Norwich; John Hills of St Catharine's was successively archdeacon of Stow and archdeacon of Lincoln. James I's favourite preacher, Lancelot Andrewes of Pembroke, was dean of Westminster. James Montagu of Sidney Sussex was successively dean of Lichfield and of Worcester, and dean of the Chapel Royal.[21] The latter was a position that gave him direct access to the king, but withheld him from university business.[22]

There were considerable economic inducements to hold academic and ecclesiastical offices in plurality. Jegon at Corpus became involved in a dispute over his retention of the mastership of Corpus after the delivery of the *congé d'élire* effectively appointing him to the bishopric of Norwich. He claimed that the bishopric was compatible with the mastership and justified the claim by reference to similar instances of plurality.[23] In practice, the overlap between the appointment to bishoprics and the resignation of masterships may have been a result of the difficulties the new bishops experienced in gaining access to the temporalities of their see. As Jegon somewhat plaintively complained, if he had resigned, he would have had nowhere to go.[24] John Davenant, president of Queens', explained his own situation with some forthrightness following his election to the bishopric of Salisbury. 'I hope in regard of ye excessive chardges of first fruits Subsidies & Tenths, wch amount as I am tould to above £600 yearly I shall obtain leav to hould my Mastership some time.'[25]

The problems arising in the relationships between master and fellows as a result of the absences of the former were such that the unusual unanimity between the absentee president of Queens' in the 1640s, Herbert Palmer, and his fellows was seen as a matter for surprised comment. Better recorded were the conflicts that arose from these absences. The most notorious and unhappy example of the combination of episcopal office with

---

[21] CUA, Lett. 11.A.C.2.a.; *HMCS*, XIV, p. 382; Venn, I, p. 466b; II, p. 371a; I, p. 30b.

[22] Venn, III, p. 201b. See his letter to Cecil: *HMCS*, XIV, p. 375. Montagu was involved in James' literary efforts and later was to edit the king's works. (Both *DNB* and Venn fail to list Montagu's important office as dean of the Chapel Royal.)

[23] SP 12/287/19. For similar situations at Winchester College and at New College, Oxford, see *HMCS*, VI, p. 221; and see below for the cases he had in mind.

[24] SP 12/287/19. Jegon's *congé* was dated 10 January 1603; he received the temporalities on 14 May (Horn 1992, p. 38). However, Jegon was being somewhat disingenuous: in his case the delay was also part of a plot to ease his brother Thomas into the mastership. This done, John then proceeded to use his new position as bishop to appoint his brother as archdeacon and arrange his appointment as a prebendary of Norwich (Venn, II, p. 466b; Horn 1992, pp. 45, 53).

[25] Bodl. Tanner MS 73, i, fo. 26, see also fos. 31, 66. Davenant was elected bishop of Salisbury 11 June, and consecrated 18 Nov. 1621 (Horn 1986, p. 2). His successor at Queens' was elected 29 April 1622 (*VCH Cambs.*, III, p. 415a).

a mastership was that of Samuel Harsnett as bishop of Chichester (1609–19) and master of Pembroke Hall (1605–16). The fellows complained that he had been absent seventeen out of twenty-seven terms within the preceding nine years. Not that his physical absence had relieved them of his demands: 'For seven whole years and more we have suffered in silence almost every extremity from our overbearing warden.' Neither were the fellows of Pembroke happy with one of Harsnett's successors as master, Jerome Beale, whom they also accused of the exquisitely combined vices of extortion and absence from college. And that was part of the problem: repression and extortion were possible through only an intermittent presence or an amenable deputy; good government required continuous attendance.[26]

A resident and active master could be irksome to the fellows of a college but from the 1560s onwards it is evident that an absent master was resented even more by many fellows. In the 1630s, Roger Andrews, master of Jesus, was forced to resign after absenting himself from the college for two years, and thereby arousing the resentment of other members. At St John's in the 1580s the fellows had complained at the absence of their master, William Whitaker. The criticisms levelled at Roger Goad, provost of King's, suggest that the fellows checked the redit book for the number of days he was absent. Even such a puritan ascetic as the young Samuel Ward mellowed in later life. While master of Sidney Sussex he also became a prebendary of Wells (1615) and canon residentiary (1617), archdeacon of Taunton (1615), rector of Great Munden, Hertfordshire (1616), and a canon of York (1618). Another puritan master of an earlier generation was William Fulke. He seems to have spent as much time in his parish of Dennington, Suffolk, after as he had done before he became master of Pembroke in 1578. During most of the time that Humphrey Tyndall was dean of Ely he resided at Ely rather than in the president's lodge at Queens'. Even in the 1650s, Charles Hotham was driven to complain that the then master of Peterhouse, Lazarus Seaman, had not spent one year in eight in residence at Cambridge, absenting himself from the college 'to attend upon a richer Benefice in London'.[27]

---

[26] Clarke 1651, p. 436. (Palmer was a member of the Westminster Assembly of Divines and it was no doubt this that kept him away from Cambridge: Venn, III, p. 300a); Heywood 1855, II, ii, pp. 203, 207; SP 16/160/58/111. The fellows of Pembroke had complained about the activities of his deputy in their case against Harsnett (Heywood 1855, II, p. 207; BL Harl. MS 7029, fos. 174v–5).

[27] BL Harl. MS 7033, fo. 64v; CUL, MS Mm. i. 38, p. 90; BL Harl. MS 7031, fo. 8; Horn and Smith 1975, p. 21; Horn and Bailey 1979, pp. 17, 102, 110; Venn, IV, p. 334b; Bauckham 1973, p. 100 n. 5; Clarke 1677, p. 476. Tyndall was dean of Ely 1591–1614 and president of Queens' 1579–1614 (Horn 1992, p. 11; Venn IV, p. 284ab). *A True state the Case of a Negative Voice*, printed, to be found

Non-residence was, however, a point of conscience with the more radical divines, and in his day Ward had the case of William Fulke held up to him as an example by one of his own former pupils. Ward was admonished, 'If you fasten at Cambridg you have no need of ye country or if you fasten in the country you have no need of yet other', and, it was argued, 'this course of non-residency as it is commonly used is . . . one of ye worst sores & grievances of our church'.[28] The charge was indeed a familiar one, and had been levelled against members of the university in general and the heads in particular on occasions throughout these years.[29]

The problem with pluralism on the part of academics arose because of the obvious parallels and the direct connections with the practice of pluralism in the church. On the one hand many of those in the higher reaches of academe might expect to become members of what for want of a better term we might describe as the 'cathedral clergy'; as prebendaries, deans and even bishops. Here, pluralism and absenteeism were rife. On the other hand, as the expectation of the standard of pastoral care rose during the sixteenth century, the model of the parochial clergyman was revived, available and ever attentive to the spiritual needs of his flock.[30]

The masters of colleges were placed in an awkward position in attempting to respond to the competing demands made on them. Increasingly, the general demand for a new level of pastoral care could be interpreted as requiring a new level of commitment on the part of masters both to their private students and to the general spiritual oversight of their college. At the same time a plurality of ecclesiastical offices was necessary in order to provide them with additional sources of income and to help to maintain them in the style that came to be appropriate to the inflated dignity of the office that they occupied.[31] This made it difficult for them satisfactorily to meet their pastoral obligations to parish, close or college. Therefore,

in BL Harl. MS 7032, fo. 234. See [British Library] *Catalogue of Printed Books*, 107, cols. 463–4, and *DNB*.

[28] Bodl. Tanner MS 72, fo. 170v. His correspondent was Thomas Whitfield of Marholm, Northants. He argued that there was no need for the additional income for Ward. Whitfield had taken his MA from Emmanuel in 1609 (Venn, IV, p. 393b).

[29] Strype 1824, III, I, p. 721 (1587). In a sermon Charles Chadwick, of Emmanuel College, reflected upon the non-residence of some of the university, 'particularly such as were governors of the colleges'.

[30] These remarks are based in part on a study of the career patterns of parochial clergy in the diocese of Norwich and on a study of Norwich cathedral clergy. One of the characteristics of the cathedral clergy was that they held numerous parochial livings. But that did not necessarily make them pastoral parochial clergy: indeed it made it more difficult for them to provide a satisfactory level of pastoral care. And no one in this period was promoted to the episcopal bench from a primarily pastoral-parochial background. Bishops were part of the same career pattern, though they rarely held ecclesiastical pluralities.

[31] Bodl. Tanner MS 72, fo. 170v, Samuel Ward.

the lay criticism of pluralism and non-residence that found expression in parliament and elsewhere was also a criticism of the universities in general and the masters of colleges in particular.[32]

Pastoral responsibilities at a plurality of livings was only one of a number of causes that drew masters away from Cambridge. The needs of souls were more than equalled by the newly emergent needs of the state for the talents that Cambridge harboured.[33] From the viewpoint of the majority of members of the university throughout this period, it was not somewhere to stay for life but somewhere to pass through on the way to other places. For the high-flying and successful academic, absence from the university was often the means to further preferment. For the ambitious master in particular, intermittent absences were part of the transition to operating on a larger stage. The original statutes of Trinity College had envisaged that the master might be called from the college not only on its affairs, but also on service to the state, or by royal command. The sending of masters such as Davenant and Ward as emissaries to the Council of Dort was a very obvious and no doubt justifiable use of their talents.[34] However, less immediately justifiable and far more irritating to the fellows was the way in which the chaplaincies to leading noblemen or the Crown that many masters held took them off to preach or to consult in high places. For the master these activities were an important means of catching the rays from the suns that radiated the warming preferments of the courtly world. But with their eyes ever upon the dawn in the east in the hopes of a brighter tomorrow they could hardly be constant good husbands of their Cambridge patrimony.[35]

Absence on public affairs had not mattered as much in the early sixteenth century when many masters were more *primi inter pares* within their colleges, and had few or no specific responsibilities as heads in the university at large. During the reign of Edward VI a man such as Dr William Mey, president of Queens', had combined a mastership of Requests with the deanship of St Paul's, and in addition was constantly employed on commissions and royal business. Consequently he spent little time at Cambridge.[36] During these years a pattern for absentee masters on official business was established. John Cheke successively combined the provostships of Eton and King's with his tutoring of Prince Edward

---

[32] For the fortunes of Cambridge in parliament see chapter 5.
[33] For a fuller discussion of this aspect of the relationship between the university and the state see chapter 4.
[34] Mullinger 1884, p. 139; *DNB*.
[35] Information on the tenure of chaplaincies by masters has been drawn from a wide range of sources, in addition to the standard biographical dictionaries.
[36] Gray 1926, p. 87; Twigg 1987, pp. 65, 68.

and with other state affairs. Ridley retained the mastership of Pembroke as bishop of Rochester and then of London, while Grindal was for three years master of the same college without ever visiting it. Gardiner, bishop of Winchester, was an absentee master of Trinity Hall.[37] When, in June 1508, Bishop Fisher had resigned the presidency of Queens', alleging inability to reside as his reason, the fellows replied that many other masters did not reside and that they did not expect it of him;[38] no doubt they had in mind that the patronage he could dispense was more than adequate recompense for his absence. James Pilkington had been master of St John's in 1559–61. As bishop of Durham, he wrote to Burghley urging care over the placing of good heads, and proposing the removal of 'the evill'. He claimed that 'some be such thatt I can nott tell whither thei doe lesse harme being absent or present'. Later during the 1560s the incorrigible fellows of St John's were in less doubt. They added the overlong absence of the master to the battery of their complaints against Nicholas Shephard.[39]

This strain of criticism was characteristic of changing conceptions of the role of a master that, starting in mid-century, accelerated rapidly after 1570. It had two main sources. As we have seen, one was rooted in a new conception of the pastoral role of the academic. In its turn this was closely associated with the wider view of the clergy as necessarily resident and preaching pastors of their flocks. In the eyes of contemporaries there was an intimate link between the roles of academic and minister: most academics were clerics; many looked to proceed on to a clerical career; as tutors their functions were closely analogous to those of the caring minister; as scholars and authors they were involved in a combative and proselytising campaign akin to that fought out on the battleground of the parishes by the new militant Protestantism. This newly emergent view of the academic had specific implications for the office of master of a college. For some masters their office was similar to other pastoral charges and required a calling. In 1626, Richard Sibbes had been elected master of St Catharine's. Soon afterwards he was offered the provostship of Trinity College, Dublin, by his friend James Ussher, archbishop of Armagh. Sibbes refused the offer, reporting the 'judgment of my friends

---

[37] Hudson 1980; Collinson 1979, p. 37; Fuller 1665/1840, p. 230. The professional legal involvements in civil law of the members of Trinity Hall necessitated long periods of absence. Henry Harvey (master 1557/8–85) was a master in Chancery and vicar general in the Province of Canterbury. In March 1565 the fellows of Trinity Hall licensed him to be absent at his own discretion, any statutes notwithstanding (Venn, II, p. 7; BL Harl. MS 7029, fo. 225).

[38] Gray 1926, pp. 51, 53; cf. Brooke 1989a, pp. 58, 65 nn. 62–4.

[39] Scott 1907, p. 137; 1909, p. 303.

here is for my stay, considering I am fixed already, and there must be a call for a place'.[40]

But the pastoral role was not the only clerical analogy available. The enlargement of the powers and authority of the masters both within their individual colleges and in the university at large could also be equated with the authority wielded by the episcopacy. It was therefore to be expected that on occasion masters were joined with deans and bishops in puritan attacks on what they conceived to be the biblically unsanctioned hierarchy of the church. This was a view of the master that was readily reinforced on many of the occasions on which they were called upon to exercise their authority. Then, as we have seen, in their roles as master of a college, member of the Consistory, they became the means of enforcing religious conformity in Cambridge.[41] This was the view of a master as the pastor and – as it were – the *episcopus* of his collegiate flock.

The second source of the changing conception of a master derived from their enlarged responsibilities as governors within both the university and their individual colleges. This model drew on the analogy of the public role of the lay magistrate and of the private role of the patriarchal head of a household. Again, it was an analogy reinforced by the practicalities of daily experience. Some of the heads were justices of the peace. On occasion they enforced common or statute laws that had very little direct connection with their academic functions. At the most prosaic level, changes in the statutes and in the social and age composition of colleges combined to encourage the application of the analogy of the domestic household. Much within a college came to depend on the decisions of its paterfamilias.[42] The rights and responsibilities associated with the paternal role were a dominant and, some would argue, an increasingly powerful strain in contemporary thought. The failure to fulfil these responsibilities by a master through his absenting himself in pursuit of his personal advancement was much more than a casual irritant: it was a substantial affront to fundamental values of the period.

There is also the viewpoint of those in the Privy Chamber and the Privy Council in Whitehall. From their perspective, increasingly the universities were testing grounds for able men of business. Having shown their mettle at Cambridge or Oxford, such men could then be promoted to responsibilities outside their confines. At different times both pastoral skills and administrative acumen might serve to recommend a man for

---

[40] Ussher 1847–64, XVI, p. 440. Sibbes could be referring to his lectureship at Gray's Inn, rather than or in addition to his mastership.

[41] Heads were usually, but not invariably, clerics: see above, p. 25.

[42] On the changing statutory responsibilities of masters see p. 78.

promotion. And of course, it was the masters who were best placed to demonstrate these capacities.

The problem was, then, that from the 1570s a series of competing demands came to focus on the masters. First there was the enhanced view of their pastoral responsibilities. Second, there were their enlarged administrative responsibilities. Third, there were the demands placed on them by the exigencies of a state that needed their talents. And while individuals may have benefited from the opportunities that these circumstances created, their conjunction also created a structural conflict within the university. Few masters could satisfy all the demands made on them without alienating either their external patrons or the other members of their college.

Masters faced a dilemma. Increasingly, their colleges came to depend upon their judgement and decision, and much college business could not be conducted without their approval. Absence could easily be interpreted – and sometimes with justice – as absence in pursuit of further personal preferment from those very authorities in church and state for whom the masters seemed the all too ready, pliable and therefore despised instruments for crushing the godly within the groves of academe. Moreover, such absences clashed with a view of the masters' increased responsibilities that was the corollary of their enhanced privileges within the university. Both the pastoral and the gubernatorial models of the master demanded residence and created new expectations of them on the part of religious enthusiasts, and on the part of government. As we will see, those roles and expectations were not always compatible; but they jointly served further to distinguish masters from the mere fellows of colleges.

STIPENDS[43]

On his deathbed, Dr Gostlin, the expiring master of Caius, opined that 'he always held a mastership and governor's place in a College to be a place of honour and credit and not of profit'. This may once have been true, but by the time of Gostlin's demise in 1626 it was no longer necessarily the

---

[43] The archives of most colleges contain substantial sources for examining both their economic fortunes and the fortunes of the regions of the country in which lay the college estates. This is an area in which research on college documents is likely to throw light on an extensive range of other issues of concern to early modern historians. Necessarily, research for this volume has only skimmed the surface of these caches of evidence. Moreover, the purpose has been, as it were, tangential: to use the economic evidence to illuminate the wider theme of this chapter; cf. below, pp. 271 ff. For an exposition of the economic fortunes of Cambridge's sister university see Aylmer 1986.

case. Indeed, Fuller was quite prepared to describe 'The Good Master of a Colledge' as one who 'counts it lawful to enrich himself, but in subordination to the Colledge good'.[44]

At Queens' in the early sixteenth century the habitually absentee masters were paid a stipend of £3-6-8 – only *half* the stipend of a fellow. This appears to have been intended to cover no more than the expenses incurred in occasionally attending at Cambridge on college business. But King's and the new foundation of Trinity College were establishing new standards of munificence in the remuneration of their heads, as in much else. The annual stipend and livery of the provost of King's amounted to £70-10-0, that of the master of Trinity to £104. This compared very well with the remuneration of the heads of other colleges, which ranged between £18-4-0 at St John's to £5 at St Catharine's Hall.[45] As these were set sums fixed by statute, the period of revision of these statutes over the middle decades of the sixteenth century and later provided an opportunity to jack up the master's stipend.[46] In other instances men such as John Jegon rapidly reaped the benefits of the efficient administration he brought with him to Corpus following his election in 1590. Having extricated the college from the debts it had incurred under his predecessors, Norgate and Copcot, by 1600 there was stock in hand, and the grateful fellows acceded to an augmentation of the master's stipend to twice that of a fellow with, in addition, a fee for preaching.[47] Not that all attempts to increase these stipends went through without objection.[48] However, although the proportions varied from college to college, invariably the master now received more than the fellows.[49]

[44] Venn 1897–1901, III, p. 79. In 1640, Samuel Ward claimed that 'My estate hath always been far from any considerable greatness, and the greatest part of it spent maintaining my poor kinred and in buying Books necessary for my profession' (Knappen 1933, p. 135). None the less, Ward was criticised for a pluralism desired to supplement his income. Fuller 1938, I, p. 104.

[45] Gray 1926, p. 51; Peacock 1841, p. 113 n. 1. The master of Trinity was credited with a stipend of £100 in the 'Distribucio' drawn up by Thomas Ansill (Ball 1918, p. 13).

[46] E.g. as at Jesus: £10 in 1557–8 (*VCH Cambs.*, III, p. 423) compared with £6-13-4 some years earlier (Peacock 1841, p. 113).

[47] Lamb 1838, pp. 147–8; and on Jegon's managerial skills see further, below. Similarly, William Fulke took care in managing the finances and property of Pembroke and rewarded himself by increasing the master's stipend from £2 to £7 (Bauckham 1973, p. 105).

[48] In 1582 the master of Gonville and Caius was accused of unstatutably increasing his stipend. The increase was justified, it was claimed, by the additional burdens placed on the master by Dr Caius' revised statutes (BL Harl. MS 7031, fos. 131v, 132); SP 12/127/44, there ascribed to 1578.

[49] Peacock 1841, p. 113 n. 1; *VCH Cambs.*, III, p. 423; NRO, NRS MS 23372, 'The Annall Expenses of the Colledge' (Corpus); Lamb 1838, pp. 147–8; Mullinger 1883, p. 291 (St John's). Later foundations such as Sidney Sussex followed the practice of differentiating between the stipend of the master and those of the fellows, in this instance to the proportions of 2:1 (*Cambridge Documents 1852*, III, pp. 586, 597).

But, ultimately, it was not the relatively trifling increases in fixed stipends that transformed the financial situation of the heads, and to a lesser extent that of those fellows who were on the foundation. Rather, it was the creation of the dividend system, and the varied opportunities for windfall profits that accrued to men in positions of authority such as theirs. As the fellows of University College, Oxford, stated in 1630, the 'sett allowance p.an: is not great . . . but their casuall profits by fines and dividends etc. and specially by paines taken in bearing of Offices, and tuition of scholars' provided their main source of income. By 1649 the master of Corpus was claiming that his fixed stipend represented 13 per cent or less of his regular annual income from the college.[50]

DIVIDENDS AND BENEFICIAL LEASES

The dividend originated as a means of distributing some parts of the surplus income derived from college income, including from rents that accrued over the year after the statutory fixed payments had been made. That the colleges were in the happy position of enjoying these surpluses was partly as a result of the famous 'Corn Act' of 1576, which required that at least one-third of college leasehold rents should be paid in corn or its maximum current market value. Where the rental was expressed in terms of so many quarters of grain – as it almost invariably was – this was of great long-term financial benefit to the colleges as a result of the generally prevailing economic circumstances of the period up to around 1640. These included periodic annual and seasonal high prices, a generally upward drift in the real price of grain, and an overall inflationary situation which created a spiral of burgeoning real incomes for the lucky beneficiaries of profit inflation.[51] Indeed, the benefits of this Act were such that Thomas Baker, the historian of St John's, writing in 1707, remarked that 'it usually made the third part more than the whole', while Thomas Fuller noted that as a result of the Act, 'though their rents stand still, their revenues do increase', and that years of bad harvest (which we now know to have occurred with a fair degree of regularity in a

---

[50] SP 16/281/54; Lamb 1838, p. 179. At an unspecified date it appears that in one year the stipend of the master of Christ's was only half his income from the dividend (CUL, MS Mm. v. 47, fos. 60–1).

[51] 18 Eliz. c. 6. The Act required that monies raised in this way were 'to be expended to the use of the Relief of the Commons and Diett of the said Colledges'; Howard 1935, p. 36; Bowden 1967, pp. 593–695, 814–70; 1985, pp. 1–118. The grain price series for Cambridge are available in typescript in the Beveridge Collection in the manuscript room at the Library of the London School of Economics. But see Bendall in Bendall *et al.* 1999, p. 144, for a college (Emmanuel) which made little use of the Corn Rent Act.

four-year cycle) produced the greatest profit. 'True it is when they have least corn, they have most bread, I mean, best maintenance, the dividends then mounting the highest.' Some no doubt highly speculative contemporary statistics, originally compiled around 1600, suggested that 'in time' the yearly premium of rent corn at Cambridge might increase to between £5,000 and £6,000 per annum *above* 'the auncient revenues'.[52]

In its turn the allocation within each college of dividend as applied to corn rents was regarded as a natural extension of the system whereby the original college revenues had been divided. Again, this redounded to the benefit of the masters of colleges. So, for example, at King's the provost was allotted ten shares for every one granted to a fellow. Similarly, at St John's in 1601, an order was made for distributing the profits made from the bakehouse and the brewhouse. Only those fellows who were at home were to partake of this division, whereas the master was to have a double share whether he was at home or abroad. At the same college, profits were normally shared between fellows and scholars in the ratio of 2:1. However, there were distinctions even amongst the fellows, and by the 1620s the ratio of dividend as between senior and junior fellows was 5:1. At Pembroke, however, it seems that it was not until 1646 that the dividend for the master diverged from that of the fellows.[53]

The Corn Act had applied equally to Oxford and to the colleges of Eton and Winchester as to Cambridge, and as early as 1583 we find the fellows of All Souls taking legal opinion on the disposal of surpluses. They wanted to know whether the income surplus to that required to augment the diet of the college – as originally intended by the statute – could be divided as a monetary payment among the fellows. At this time it is not clear that any such surpluses had arisen. However, by 1587 it was being asserted that the liveries of the college officers of £5 to £5-10-0 had been raised by this means to £13 and 'so the allowance augmented proportionablie to the inferiour sorte'. At Trinity College, Cambridge, during Elizabeth's reign, the surplus revenues or *excresentia* were initially used to finance building operations. However, when these were completed, in the early part of the seventeenth century, the surplus was

---

[52] Mullinger 1883, p. 290; Fuller 1655/1840, p. 274; Willet 1634, p. 1,236; Harrison 1971, pp. 135–55. Contemporary comment on the situation at Cambridge is borne out by the evidence from Oxford (Aylmer 1986, p. 536).

[53] Mullinger 1883, p. 291; Mayor 1865–6, p. 97; Howard 1935, p. 85, see also pp. 38, 137, 143; Pembroke College Treasury B.5, College Orders, 1572–1839, p. 51.

then divided into portions and allotted to members of the foundation. As at other colleges, the number of shares received varied with the collegiate status of the recipient. At St John's the new surpluses were distributed as a weekly money payment known as 'praeter' to the master, fellows and scholars. This practice must have been general by 1610–11 when the vice-chancellor referred to 'the distribution & ordering of such allowances, and ye disposing of all remainders, if any such be' as in the management of the masters and fellows of individual colleges.[54]

Clearly, while all members on the original foundation of a college derived additional income from these surpluses, the system of shares proportioned to the status of one's membership that was extended to this new source of income ensured that the masters were the main beneficiaries of corn rents during a period that was distinguished by what was for the colleges a highly advantageous condition of inflation.[55]

So far the discussion has focussed on the supplementary income derived from the surpluses created by the payment of one-third of rentals in kind. But income from this source was by no means the only way of augmenting fixed stipends, nor, ultimately, the most remunerative. Despite the built-in hedge against inflation provided by the corn rent, by the late sixteenth century the annual rentals charged on the leasehold of college properties was far below an economic or 'rack rent'. The corollary of these low and customarily fixed rents was that the entry fine – the capital sum paid on the making, renewal or assignment in reversion of a lease – was relatively high. It was from these and similar 'casualties' or windfalls that the members of a college derived the greatest addition to their income; as the fellows of

---

[54] 'All Souls v. Lady Jane Stafford 1587' in Fletcher 1885, p. 193. At Trinity in 1609 the Visitor decided that no division of money was to be made: Trinity College Muniments, A: The Masters' Old Conclusion Book, 1607–73, p. 113 (1630), p. 183 (1646); Trinity College Conclusion Book 1646–1811, fo. 6v (The master £200, doctors £60, Bachelors of Divinity £40, MAs £30, BAs £20); Scott 1898, p. 139; Miller 1961, pp. 28–9; Collier 1840, pp. 444–5, and more explicitly in SP 14/61/18. At Pembroke the practice had become a custom by the early seventeenth century, to the extent that money was transferred from one account to another in order to ensure a dividend. In 1615 a loan of £37-5-7 was made from the 'Ladys bag' to the dividend (Pembroke College Treasury, Treasury Accounts, 1530–1641, vol. 1, no foliation, *passim*). As surpluses arose on various accounts, arrangements were made for the proportional allocation of the surpluses, as at Corpus in 1660 (BL Harl. MS 7033, fo. 42v).

[55] Sub-foundations did not normally share in these benefits. This was the case with the Exeter fellows at Clare (BL Harl. MS 7029, fos. 67v, 102v). It should also be noted that the inflation of costs to a college and to its members is very likely to have been below the general level of inflation as calculated by modern historians. This is because the components of expenditure on the part of the colleges and its members were both less flexible (e.g. fees) and more elastic in terms of demand (e.g. building materials) than the 'basket' of basic consumables used to calculate the rate of inflation. For the latter see Brown and Hopkins 1956, pp. 296–314, reprinted in Carus-Wilson 1962, II, pp. 179–96.

All Souls admitted in the 1580s, 'suche beneffitte as commethe to each on[e] for his liverye riseth cheflie by fynes and woodsales'.[56]

The beneficial lease had had its origins in the conjunction of two factors. One was the inherent tendency for all medieval rentals to become fixed. The other was the accelerating inflation of the early sixteenth century. In these conditions the only way of maintaining some semblance of a realistically priced letting was to increase the entry fine relative to the rental.[57] Consequently, as inflation continued on through the sixteenth century an increasing proportion of the total income received from leases was derived from entry fines. Corporate landowners such as the colleges were not alone in employing beneficial leasing; it was also common practice among most of the nobility.[58] However, there were additional reasons for its adoption within the universities, and grounds for believing that its operation was especially pernicious in the academic context.

Initially, the beneficial lease was adopted by the colleges because it was the system that was coming to prevail among the laity from whom they were receiving the majority of their endowments during the sixteenth century.[59] From the viewpoint of the colleges in the last three decades of the sixteenth century and beyond, it had the additional attraction of providing large lump sums when they were needed: during what were years of intense capital investment in building activities.[60] However, the initial incentive to adopt the system of beneficial leasing occurred during

[56] Fletcher 1885, pp. 41, 212; the fullest account of the relation of entry fines and dividends is that for Emmanuel by Sarah Bendall in Bendall *et al.* 1999, pp. 172–5. In 1601 the relationship between fine and rental was explained thus in the case of Cawston manor, Norfolk, and with reference to the situation of the Crown, which did not differ in this respect from that of the colleges. 'All purchases are usually made now a dayes under the Rate 20 years. In purchases from the King that rate is for the most parte doubled, & sometime trebled, & more, according to the proportion of the Leases, both for the number of years in being & for quantity of rents yearly reserved. For the reason is not that men will give the King a better rate then other men, but that the Kinges demaines for the most part have been demised at such an under rate, that a very gainfull improvement may easily be made thereof, to countervaile the seaming high rate of the purchase' (NRO, NRS MS 27218). The author of this description was Roger Rant, an official in the Exchequer (*ibid.*). He lived in the parish of St Botolph, Aldersgate, London, and had been born at North Walsham (Venn, III, p. 421b). The family supplied a number of lawyers and medical men in early seventeenth-century East Anglia. One such was agent for a college (see Lloyd 1931, pp. 88–98). There was not, however, a constant relationship between entry fine and rental from one property to another (see Jones 1938, p. 239; Fletcher 1885, pp. 41, 212). For profits from the sale of college timber at Christ's see Peile 1900, p. 97.

[57] Or to introduce fines where they had not existed before (Jones 1938, p. 236).

[58] Stone 1965, pp. 314, 317. For the situation at Oxford see Aylmer 1986, p. 527.

[59] See Bendall in Bendall *et al.* 1999, pp. 129–56, esp. pp. 129–30.

[60] For some indication of the incidence of building activity see the graph in RCHM, *Cambridge*, I, between pp. lxxxii and lxxxiii. For a sophisticated device desired to allow the alienation of college property for a payment subsequently employed in building activities see Gray 1926, pp. 119–20. For the need for money during building activities at Trinity College, and its relationship to making a lease, see BL Egerton MS 2644, fos. 159, 161, 163.

what were for the universities the depressed and uncertain decades of the
1530s and 1540s when the response to the crisis was to take substantial
fines to meet immediate needs in exchange for the renewal of leases at
the old rents. The personal interests of members of the university must
also have played a part. They had before them the consequences of the
dissolution of religious properties on their former religious. For a time a
similar fate of dissolution was a very real threat to the universities. In this
context the beneficial lease was a means of converting an element of an
insecure capital asset into a certain source of present income.[61]

Unfortunately, the deficiencies of actuarial knowledge at this period
meant that the system of high fines and low rentals rarely produced an
income commensurate with that which would have been received from
an economic or 'rack rent'. The situation was exacerbated by the fact
that, once established, both lessee and lessor had a vested interest in its
continuance. For the lessee, although it might involve considerable effort
and substantial outlays during the two years over which it was customary
to pay the fine, the overall cost of fine-plus-rental was less than a rack
rent. Moreover, the system appealed to the gambling mentality of those
who lived in a world where life was uncertain and the future was insecure.
From the viewpoint of the lessor, Lawrence Stone has shown how difficult
it was for laymen with a life interest in an estate to break with the system.
An increase in future returns for the proprietor or his heirs could be
purchased only at the cost of foregoing immediate returns. This might
be achieved, for example, by allowing existing leases to run their course,
and then renewing at an economic rent. It was even more difficult for
members of a college to break with the system.[62]

As only temporary recipients of the support derived from the college's endowments while they were on the foundation, every member of
the college had every inducement to maximise current rather than future returns. It was this situation that led to sometimes dubious dealings
involving the essentially long-term investments represented by college
woodlands. Neither were there any particularly strong inducements for
the current members of a college to undertake the costs of the survey
that was the necessary preliminary to rack renting in order to increase the
return on capital for future members of the institution. Consequently,
college leases came 'not to imply a rack rent; but such a rent, in some
measure as Colledge-lands use to beare; which may yield some fine at due
times, and may leave to the tenant some competent Livelihood, and may

---

[61] Lamb 1838, p. 59.
[62] Stone 1965, pp. 315–19. Bendall in Bendall *et al.* 1999, pp. 367–71.

probably continue a sure rent to posterity for a perpetuall maintenance of the fellows'. The trouble was that 'a sure rent' did not produce an income sufficient for the needs of 'posterity'. By 1634 the members of University College, Oxford, were complaining that the old long leases made by their predecessors were producing customary rents twenty times smaller than a rack renting would have secured.[63] In the event, some colleges took to rack renting in the eighteenth century, more in the nineteenth.

The system of beneficial leasing was most tenaciously adhered to in the west of England. However, there is evidence to suggest that from the early seventeenth century some lay landlords were successful in introducing rack rents in the southern and eastern parts of the country. With none of the long-term rational inducements for change of these lay landlords, colleges continued to operate the old system. Indeed, an emergent divergence in interests between lay and college landlords may well have increased the demand for leases of college properties, especially where their advantages to the lessee were most evident in comparisons with the rack rents being introduced on some estates in the eastern counties. This suggests that Cambridge, and in particular certain colleges with most of their estates concentrated in this region, was subject to greater pressure than was Oxford, with more of its estates lying in the West Country, where the beneficial lease continued generally to prevail. Certainly, Fuller, whose experience was mainly in the east of England, reported with his usual irony that 'Generally I heare the Muses commended for the best Landladies, and a Colledge-lease is accounted but as the worst kind of freehold.'[64]

To test this supposition, more detailed work would be required than has yet been possible, or would be appropriate in the context of this

---

[63] Fletcher 1885, p. 205; Howard 1935, p. 48; SP 16/281/54; SP 16/28/54. For what follows, see esp. Bendall (as in n. 62).

[64] It is difficult to determine precisely the location of all college estates throughout the period 1560–1750. A notable exception is Emmanuel: see Bendall in Bendall *et al.* 1999, esp. App. 5, pp. 589–649; see also the Caius estate record in Venn 1897–1901, IV. However, early twentieth-century patterns often reflect former distributions. Thus, until the 1920s, a college such as Clare retained the greater part of its property in the eastern counties (Forbes 1928, I, pp. 73, 79). Cf. the map of the location of the estates of St John's in Howard 1935. Cf. the comment of Thomas Fuller 1938, p. 103. There could be considerable sentiment against breaking the continuity of occupation. See, for example, the provisions of 12 Car. II c. 31. This refers to 'John Lord Culpeper the auntient tennant', and to Thomas Clifton's tenure of the parsonage of Kirkham, Lancashire, from Christ Church, Oxford. This 'had long beene in the tenure or occupation' of Clifton 'and his Auncesters by several successive leases', apparently stretching back to before the Dissolution (§§6, 12). John Chicheley's leases from Trinity College and Pembroke Hall were required to be 'restored to his said auntient Possessions'. Sir Francis Barrington was very possessive of property he leased from Trinity College (BL Egerton MS 2644, fo. 157). Cf. Bendall in Bendall *et al.* 1999, pp. 151–3.

present argument. Suffice it to say that there was a continuing demand for the beneficial leases provided by colleges from those would-be lessees who appreciated the lower overall outlay that they required. Moreover, it is worth speculating that the predilection of colleges for the beneficial lease may have favoured particular groups within the countryside and that this preference is likely indirectly to have assisted the processes of economic and social change that have been at the heart of generations of research on the small communities of early modern England.[65] The payment of the relatively large entry fine required a prior accumulation of surplus income and sufficient margin of income over expenditure during the two or so years at the start of the lease when the fine was being paid. Clearly, this arrangement would find most favour with those who already enjoyed relatively high levels of capitalisation and a market orientation. Furthermore, it was these same yeomen and gentry with whom the colleges were most likely to have other connections as sources of students, as alumni and as patrons and benefactors. The development of financial connections between college and countryside based on leases was only one element in a larger and complex nexus of developing relationships.[66]

The beneficial lease had a number of features that laid it open to abuse and university men were not slow to exploit these possibilities. There was always a temptation for a landlord to press for the premature surrender of a lease and the payment of a new entry fine in return for the assurance of the lease to the occupying tenant. This was one means of extracting an immediate lump-sum payment from the system. A variant of this was to sell for present payment the reversion of the tenure after the expiry of the current lease; indeed, these procedures were so openly abused by the colleges and others who 'have from tyme to tyme made Leases for the terme of xxi yeres or three Lyves long before the Expiracion of the former yeres' that a statutory ban was imposed on renewals earlier than three years before the expiry of the existing lease. This put an end to a practice which had, for example, been common at Jesus College up till this time. However, in the 1630s it was still necessary to admonish Gonville and Caius not to make leases *de futuro* of any of their impropriations (that is, tithes from the rectories possessed by the college) for longer than five to ten years, while reversionary leases already made were not to be renewed for more than ten years. As we shall see, it was, perhaps, not surprising that Queen Elizabeth had continued to demand reversionary leases for her servants, while Cecil successfully extracted from King's College a

---

[65] See e.g. Spufford 1970.
[66] Some other aspects of this relationship are discussed in chapter 6.

renewal of the lease of the manor of Ruislip in 1606, eight years before its expiry, even though the college pleaded that they might be permitted the freedom that the Act of Parliament and their local statutes required.[67]

An alternative means of extracting a substantial present payment on entry, to the detriment of subsequent members of the college, was to make 'long and unreasonable Leases'. As the fellows of University College, Oxford, discovered, long leases made by their predecessors not only produced low rentals but also precluded them from benefiting from more frequent entry fines. In 1571 there had been an attempt to abolish this practice by placing a limit of twenty-one years or three lives on these leases from corporations. Unfortunately, the provisions of this Act were complicated by a later amendment which attempted to provide for urban property by permitting leases of up to forty years of houses with less than 10 acres in cities, boroughs, towns corporate, market towns or their suburbs.[68] This opened up a considerable area for abuse, as the definition of a suburb was notoriously inexact. Moreover, coming as it did before major expansion caused metropolitan land prices to soar, this amendment ensured that those who were members of a college when a London lease fell in enjoyed a veritable bonanza – *if* they were allowed to enjoy it, that is. For, as Lawrence Stone has shown, increasingly the nobility were being drawn to London, and were advantageously placed at Court to obtain a favourable lease from a college of a London property. In 1580 the earl of Lincoln was paying £6 a year to King's College as rent for a messuage in the parish of St Andrew's, Baynards Castle (or by the Wardrobe), while in 1590 that bell-wether of aristocratic exploiters, the earl of Essex, was putting pressure on Gonville and Caius College to obtain the lease of a London house for his aunt, Lady Leighton. However, it was the queen who was most favourably placed, and her greatest *coup* came in 1574 when (in a desperate bid to pay off a creditor) she 'persuaded' Magdalene to alienate its Aldgate property perpetually for the derisory yearly rental of £15. Not only did this result in a long-drawn-out series of legal wrangles which the college ultimately lost; it was also contrary to the spirit if not the letter of the statute of 1571 which had attempted to outlaw such depredations.[69]

---

[67] SP 12/260/84, 90; SP 16/315/111; 18 Eliz. c. 11 (1575–6); *VCH Cambs.*, III, p. 423; SP 16/315/111; SP 12/260/84; *HMCS*, XII, p. 21; *HMCS*, X, pp. 449–50, 460; *HMCS*, XVIII, pp. 132–3.

[68] SP 16/281/54. Cf. *HMCS*, III, p. 148, lease for forty years by Magdalene. The Acts are 13 Eliz. c. 10; 14 Eliz. c. 11, §2.

[69] Stone 1965, pp. 385–92; *HMCS*, XIII, p. 178; *HMCS*, VI, p. 73; Hoyle in Cunich *et al.* 1994, pp. 78–83. For other depredations of college property inflicted by Essex see *HMCS*, XIX, p. 391; *HMCS*, III, pp. 147–8; *VCH Cambs.*, III, p. 451.

Finally, the granting of leases for lives provided a further opportunity to realise immediate personal advantage at the expense of future corporate income. Although contemporaries realised that the customarily accepted actuarial basis on which the fines and rentals for leases for lives were calculated was unsound, they were not able, or not willing, to remedy this. The lessee was keen to pay a fine for a form of lease that in practice granted him tenure at an annual rental that would decrease in real terms over its term and that *in toto* underestimated the real exploitable value of the property. On its part the college, or some of its individual members, connived at the practice, for in so doing they were often purchasing 'credit' with a tenant who as a local gentleman impropriator, or as an influential courtier, was a potential source of subsequent personal patronage. At the very least they stood to gain substantially from the annual shareout of the profits from the 'windfall' profits represented by entry fines if those fines occurred during their tenure on the foundation of a college; their successors were left with a modest fixed annual rental for the remainder of the period of the lease. Archbishop Laud rightly saw this as a mortgaging of the future institutional prosperity of corporations and in 1633 persuaded Charles to forbid leases for lives by deans and chapters, and in 1634 these injunctions were extended to include leases by colleges.[70]

Clearly, the system of beneficial leases created temptations which the predominantly transitory members of a college found it difficult to resist, as in an inflationary situation they became ever more dependent on the immediate payment of lump sums as a means of supplementing their fixed stipends. The alternative of reliance on assured rentals spread over a period of years was far less attractive to men who were only temporary beneficiaries of a college's endowments. Moreover, given the large and increasing disproportion in the ratio of entry fine to rental, not even a long-resident master or senior doctor would prefer a regular rental income to the certainty of a juicy windfall profit. Rather, there are some grounds for believing that the system of beneficial leases was particularly advantageous for the masters of colleges, and tended to increase their income far more than that of the fellows.

It was not simply that the shares procedure that already attached to fixed stipends and surplus rentals was extended to the distribution of fines on the passing of leases, with the master always receiving a greater number of dividends than did the fellows. For example, at St John's in 1628–9 the

---

[70] Stone 1965, p. 317; Hill 1956/1971, p. 311; Lamb 1838, p. 173; *VCH Cambs.*, III, p. 424, a resolution in 1634 of Jesus College against granting any more leases for life.

junior fellows received one dividend, the eight senior fellows received one-and-a-half dividends and the master received three dividends from this source.[71] In addition, the irregularity with which entry fines occurred meant that the master was most likely to benefit from them, for in various academic capacities most masters were present in the university for far longer than most of the fellows of colleges. Therefore, they were more likely to encounter entry fines than were the majority of junior fellows who were studying for only three or four years for an MA, and who might miss out on one of these irregular windfalls.[72] Further, as many masters had achieved the office because of their administrative abilities, many had previously served as bursars and therefore had a detailed knowledge of the college properties and their real value; in some colleges it was common for the offices of master and bursar to be combined.[73] Again, a master was in a favourable position for giving the tree a healthy shake whenever he felt the need to increase his income by condoning premature renewals, by encouraging the sale of reversions, or simply by taking a bribe.[74] Finally, he was favourably placed to manipulate the granting of leases by arranging proceedings for those occasions when he knew he could obtain the assent of the majority of the fellows.[75] He might also make leases to members of his own family, or to himself through intermediaries.[76]

In the matter of the personal benefits to be derived from a system of beneficial leases rather than by rack renting, the distinctions between

---

[71] See the preceding discussion of the dividend and Scott 1898, p. 139.

[72] At Corpus this problem was not solved until the mid-eighteenth century. Calculations were then made of the average income from fines over the previous years, and a regular, fixed sum allotted to members for payment from a pooled fund in future years. This remedied many of the inconveniences that had arisen from this variable and irregular source of income (Masters 1831, p. 248).

[73] Bendall in Bendall *et al.* 1999, pp. 93–5, 346–8, 580–1; Fletcher 1885, p. 208. Lancelot Andrewes had been under-treasurer and treasurer at Pembroke (Attwater 1936, pp. 55, 66). In the 1560s, Dr Ithell, master of Jesus, appears to have acted as his own bursar (BL Harl. MS 7033, fo. 71); at King's, in 1569, Roger Goad was accused of acting as his own riding bursar and keeping the college courts (BL Harl. MS 7031, fo. 5v).

[74] An accusation that his enemies did not fail to level at Goad (BL Harl. MS 7031, fo. 5).

[75] The Act, 33 Henry VIII c. 27, had overruled those local statutes of colleges that – somewhat unrealistically – required the unanimous consent of the fellows to the sealing of leases. For this it substituted a simple majority of fellows plus the head. However, it failed to stipulate whether the majority referred to all eligible members, or to those resident at the time of the sealing. For disputes at Corpus over this procedure when extended to other matters of election see Masters 1831, pp. 125–7; *Cambridge Documents 1852*, II, p. 467. The new arrangements of the early seventeenth century required a majority of those present. For complaints in the 1580s over the master's influence on the sealing of leases at St John's see CUL, MS Mm. i, 38, p. 82.

[76] Peile 1900, pp. 115–16. At King's in 1569 the provost, Roger Goad, was said to have grown to great wealth 'by hireing others to purchase councellers Letters for the colledge leases, & by passinge y^m to his owne commoditie in other men's names, some of wch he hath in his owne custodie, & unto his own use' (BL Harl MS 7031, fo. 5v). In the 1620s a similar charge was levelled against Barnaby Gooch, master of Magdalene (HLRO, Main Papers, H.L., 22 March 1623).

master and fellows is not clear-cut – the interests of the more senior and long-serving fellows being more nearly akin to those of the master.[77] Overall, those who were more briefly members of the foundation – junior fellows and scholars – were likely to have achieved a greater aggregate benefit if the regular annual income from rentals had been raised through rack renting. But the matter was as much a question of temperament as of fine financial judgement: there were always those who aspired to a more prolonged membership of the college than actually transpired, while many of the more junior members may have preferred hopes of their tenure coinciding with a windfall bonanza to the dull certainty of a less substantial but assured and regular income.

The chronology of the development of the custom of distributing the income from fines among the members of the foundation is not at all precise. At St John's it was not until the late 1620s that the practice was introduced. Before then it seems to have been expended on various extraordinary costs, such as those incurred on the occasion of royal visits or as gifts in aid to fellows and scholars who were ill.[78] In addition, it was used to help maintain a progression of members through the college by providing lump-sum payments known as *vales* to fellows on their departure. A similar procedure was being employed at King's in the 1590s, where the leases of college rectories were granted to fellows to induce their resignation.[79] Overbury, writing sometime before 1613, described 'A meere fellow of an house' as one who 'prayes as heartily for a sealing, as a *cormorant* doth for a deare yeare: yet commonly he spends that revenue before he receives it'; his '*mockvelvet* or *satinisco*' is not purchased 'without the colleges next leases acquaintance'.[80] On John Jegon's accession to the

---

[77] At King's, Goad was accused of conspiring with the seniors (BL Harl. MS 7031, fo. 7).

[78] The Decree of 27 April 1627 ordered that 'the fine money may be disposed to the best advantage of the whole society' (*Fifth Report from the Select Committee on Education etc.* . . . , Appendix B; Documents, Parliamentary Paper, 1818, IV, pp. 367, 406); Scott 1898, p. 139; Miller 1961, p. 29. See esp. for details on Emmanuel, and other colleges, Bendall in Bendall *et al.* 1999, pp. 172–5.

[79] BL Harl MS 7031, fo. 15. At St John's throughout Elizabeth's reign it was common practice to lease college estates to fellows and ex-fellows (Howard 1935, p. 48). The *vales* could also be used to pay off personal debts to the college (*ibid.*, p. 84; Trinity College Muniments, A: Masters' Old Conclusion Book, 1607–73, p. 113 (1 April 1630), and p. 83, grant to a fellow of the right to receive as his *vale* a payment due to the college from Sir Lionel Tollemache and Mr Cornwallis). Without such assistance a fellow would have found it difficult to contemplate leaving Cambridge. Overbury characterises 'A meere fellow of an house' as one who 'thinkes it a discredit to be out of debt, which he never likely cleares, without resignation money' (Rimboutt 1890, p. 105). Overbury may have been writing from direct observation: he had been a gentleman-commoner at Queen's College, Oxford, in the late 1590s, graduating BA in 1598 (*DNB*). The personal credit that until recently was a characteristic of Oxbridge life at all levels was no doubt in part a residuum from an earlier period when income had been substantial but irregular for both students and fellows.

[80] Rimboutt 1890, p. 105.

mastership of Corpus in 1590 he energetically attempted to rescue the college's finances from the consequences of overenthusiastic expenditure on building. At Jegon's instigation Burghley advised a number of changes in the administration of the college. These included a recommendation that in future the leases were to be let to the best advantage and 'the Fines thereof be whollie received and Used to the Stock of the House', that is, to meet *corporate* expenses. The inference is that they had previously been employed in supplementing the individual incomes of members of the college, a conclusion reinforced by the objections that some fellows made to the change.[81] As early as 1586 a vice-cancellarial visitation of Christ's revealed – in addition to the suspicious circumstance of women bed-makers – that the proceeds from the sale of timber and fines on the passing of leases were being divided between the master and fellows, while a careful study of the leasing procedures at Jesus suggests that the practice of distributing the entry fines may date from the adoption of the beneficial lease in the 1540s.[82] What is certain is that, subject as they were to personal temptation and the pressures exerted by influential laymen, wily masters and fellows continued to contrive ingenious means to circumvent the Elizabethan legislation that had been designed to end the misapplication of college funds.

THE RECIPIENTS OF LEASES

In some degree many of these who were at any one time members of a college stood to benefit financially from high fines and low rentals. But masters and fellows are likely to have differed as to whom the leases should be assigned. For, in addition to the very real financial benefits that they conferred, leases were also units of exchange in client–patron relationships. Indeed, they provided one of the few forms of material recompense with which otherwise completely dependent academics were able to re-pay their patrons. One supplicant to Cecil for the vacant provostship of King's made his dependence explicit. 'For my thankfullnes towards yor Lordship, what is in mee, beeing so meane, & what can I doe to re-quite yor Lordship being so great. Thear is no meanes of gratification or shewing thankfullnes w^{t}hin the power of that place, that shall not wholly bee applied to the desire & commandement of yor Lordship.' Both men knew what was involved in such promises. Cecil had previously bene-fited considerably from obtaining a lease of the manor of Ruislip from

---

[81] Masters, 1831, Appendix N, no. xxxviii, pp. 61–3.   [82] *VCH Cambs.*, III, pp. 423, 433.

the college.[83] The character of this dependence is again evident in an instance concerning Exeter College, Oxford. In March 1592 the fellows were instructed by mandate to choose Thomas Holland as their rector, which they did. In June of 1594 the college was requested to make a lease in reversion to the queen in order that she could assign it to Robert Knollis, a servant at Court and member of an influential courtly family.[84] Clearly, in the circumstances this was not a request that the new rector could easily refuse.

Unfortunately, the differences in past patronage and in hopes of future preferment as between the masters and the majority of fellows found them seeking to satisfy incompatible interests. The majority of the ordinary run of college fellows, with little more than a country living in prospect, would – no doubt – have preferred to gratify the provincial gentry who controlled most of those livings. By way of contrast, masters whose present position and future promotion depended on courtly patronage had every inducement to satisfy the demands from those about the Court.[85]

These demands increased throughout the reign of Elizabeth and during the early years of James' rule. They became incessant from the later 1580s, when Elizabeth began in earnest to use college leases as a device for paying her debts, for recompensing her servants and stuffing the gaping maws of avaricious courtiers. Moreover, the demands made of the colleges were likely to have increased in these years for reasons independent of the increasing impecuniousness of the Crown and the collapse of any real control on private exploitation of the royal prerogative; by 1614 that astute rapporteur of the contemporary scene, Edward Chamberlain, was driven to complain that 'this is no world to thrive in by plaine dealing'.[86] In the case of the universities there were a number of reasons why this was the case.

The property of the church had been increasingly thoroughly expropriated or appropriated. Extension of these activities to the colleges was a temptation that was not long resisted. By contrast with the church, the universities were becoming richer throughout this period as a result of a continuing process of endowment. But they continued to operate a system of beneficial leases that was particularly attractive to the lessee. Further, the humble social backgrounds of the majority of academics, the lack of independent means among the majority of the fellows, and

---

[83] SP 14/53/84; *HMCS*, xii, p. 21; *HMCS*, x, pp. 449–50, 460; *HMCS*, xviii, pp. 132–3.
[84] PRO, S.O. 3/1, March 1592. The nomination arose from a disputed election (*VCH Oxford*, pp. 110b, 114 n. 31).
[85] Morgan 1983, p. 392.   [86] Stone 1965, pp. 488–90; SP 14/78/71.

their desire for ecclesiastical preferment in preference to a continued life in college, made them peculiarly susceptible to external pressures. There was also the fact of the increasing presence of men of future influence resident as students within the colleges. This meant that direct knowledge of the affairs of the universities was more widely disseminated among the elite than ever before. Many of those who had attended university went out into the world with memories of the wealth and sometimes of the quiet local corruptions that attended upon the properties of their Alma Mater. Many again of its alumni in their capacity as provincial gentry or as courtiers were in a position to exploit their knowledge. Many of the clergymen dependent on such men were able to inform them of the rich pickings to be had of their former colleges – witness the accusation in the 1580s that a former member of the college and the then servant to Sir Walter Raleigh had drawn that avaricious courtier's attention to the possibility of depriving All Souls of some of their choicest leases, alluring him 'with intelligence and the savour hereof'.[87] This was not the only occasion on which knowledge of the universities provided the basis for lay exploitation of their wealth.

In another tussle for All Souls' leases a few years later, one of the arguments used against the college was that the warden had previously engineered the lease of the property to his brother; a matter which 'some gentleman that had bin of the house and lived at the Coort' thought fit to report to Sir Francis Walsingham. Sir Henry Wotton used his influence at Court to obtain letters from the queen to New College in order to extract from them a lease of certain of their properties. In a prevaricating response, intended to divert his purpose, the college argued that the lease had already been promised and – somewhat disingenuously one suspects – claimed that otherwise they would have been willing to satisfy Wotton for 'the love we have still borne him (beinge a man brought up amongst us in our college)'.[88] In October 1564 Edward Gascoigne wrote to the Master of Requests, Walter Haddon. Gascoigne reminded Haddon of his familiarity with divers colleges in Cambridge and Oxford, and remarked that 'I could never learn that you obtained a lease for yourself till this day.' Better late than never, suggested Gascoigne, and dangled the prospect of leases of Trinity College rectories, suggesting that any want of money could be supplied. Their past careers had certainly familiarised these two men with the potential for the exploitation of college property. Haddon

---

[87] Fletcher 1885, p. 218. The queen's letters extracted the two leases from the college without the payment of any fine. Raleigh was then reported to have sold them for £1,000 (p. 230).

[88] Fletcher 1885, pp. 161, 183, 204–5, 208–9; *HMCS*, VI, pp. 103, 206; Smith (L.P.) 1907, I, pp. 301–2.

had been successively master of Trinity Hall, and president of Magdalen College, Oxford. Gascoigne had just resigned as master of Jesus College.[89] In 1597 the master and fellows of Trinity College begged Cecil not to demand a lease of one of their rectories for Robert Wright, one of the queen's servants and a former fellow of the college. In this and in other instances the evidence from the universities reinforces in a specific context what we have come to learn of late about the influence wielded by those in service about the person of the monarch.[90]

As the economic and political pressures on the Crown increased during the 1590s, so did the frequency and audacity of the demands directed to soft targets such as the universities. There is both a tone of exasperation and a hint of the fears for what might yet be to come in the expostulation in 1593 of John Cowell at King's: 'her Majesty for divers . . . my lord of Essex for two at the least, Sir Thomas Heneage for one, and more that I now remember not for divers others, have been earnestly requested for a promise beforehand to lease things when they should be leasable'. Two years later the queen was demanding of Queens' College a forty-year lease to her servant, William Jones, of the college's manor of St Nicholas Court, Kent. In addition, the lease was to be renewed immediately, even though there were sixteen years of the old lease to run! The college protested that the suit was against the laws, prejudicial both to them and to their posterity in that house, 'and without example in other Houses of the like done in that order'.[91]

At the same time – in the 1590s – that any former restraint on the part of the Court was being discarded, there are some indications to suggest a decline in the will of the academics to resist the incessant pressures that were now being placed upon them, and a greater willingness to succumb to the temptations of their own immediate advantage. At Christ's the resignation of William Perkins in 1595 may have removed a check on both the theological speculations and the political calculations of his erstwhile colleagues. Certainly, the neurotic Samuel Ward could be found praying that 'ther fallow no ruyne to the colledg, seyng that some fellows

---

[89] *CSPD*, VI, *Addenda 1547–1565*, p. 552; Venn, III, p. 280a; II, p. 199a. In the same year Haddon did indeed receive a grant from the queen, although it was a grant not of college property, but of the site of the abbey of Wymondham, with the manor and lands pertaining to that abbey (*DNB*).

[90] *HMCS*, VII, p. 539. The monarch's personal and household servants are noticeable as obtaining or seeking grants for themselves, or acting as intermediaries on behalf of others, e.g. *CSPD*, IV, p. 300, the queen requiring the grant of a college lease to her tailor, and SP 12/260/84, 90; SP 12/276/2, draft petition regarding a college lease by three servants of the cellar; *HMCS*, IV, p. 613, grant to the son of an officer of the Wardrobe. For a convenient summary and overview of work on the Court and the importance of personal access to the monarch see Starkey 1987.

[91] *HMCS*, IV, p. 611; *HMCS*, V, pp. 448, 480. This implies the existence of an earlier self-denying ordinance in this matter.

begin to use such pollicy without any care of the future good of the colledg'.[92]

James' accession in 1603 immediately added the buccaneering Scots to the indigenous depredators of college possessions.[93] Although there are some crude statistical indications that Court interference with college leases declined somewhat in the second and third decades of the seventeenth century, it was in 1628, after forty years of persistent exploitation, that the university emitted the plaintive cry that 'our goods are but few our household stuffe little, the Circuite of Athens narrow, yet no Riches of Crasus or Midos are sought for after more vehemently by the snares of lewd men, then this unarmed and naked povertie of ours'.[94] Not inappropriately, the cry was directed to one whose exquisite skill as an exploitative courtier meant that he could not fail to be fully appraised of the truth of their complaints: their chancellor, the duke of Buckingham.

PLUNDER AT COURT

The development of Court interference in the allocation of college leases was both encouraged and facilitated by the system that emerged under Elizabeth's rule for the general spoliation of ecclesiastical property. The irony is that in practice the measures intended to curb the misdirection of institutional resources merely had the effect of centralising the process. An additional consequence of this development was that it made it even more important to have good access to influence at Court.

An Act passed at the beginning of the queen's reign had limited leases of episcopal properties to the length of twenty-one years or three lives, *except* when the lease was made to the queen. Effectively this centralised the plunder of the church in the hands of the monarch, with leases to courtiers for periods longer than those permitted by statute initially being made over to the Crown. These limitations on the duration of leases subsequently were extended to other, non-episcopal ecclesiastical property, and to college leases. Although neither of the two relevant Acts explicitly refers to the exception created by the exemption of the Crown from the restrictions imposed by the Act of 1559, the queen proceeded to act as if they permitted her a latitude in dealing with college leases similar to that which she exercised over ecclesiastical properties. Thereafter, even

---

[92] Knappen 1933, p. 109.
[93] Nor did they waste time: see e.g. the letter in favour of Sir James Hey, gentleman of the bedchamber, for a lease from King's College (SP 38/7/28, Feb. 1604).
[94] BL Add. MS 44848, fos. 215–16, copy in BL Sloane MS 1775, fo. 35.

provincial interests seeking the leases of college property on favourable terms, or simply wishing to ensure renewal, were well advised to go through Court intermediaries in pursuit of a royal dispensation or a mandate to the college.[95]

The Corporation of Cambridge did this when a ninety-nine-year lease of Gonville and Caius property came up for renewal in 1604, and so did John Haines, a Devonshire tenant of Corpus Christi College, Oxford. Having been at great expense to defend the title of the college, and to improve the property, he was afraid that at the expiration of the lease it might be granted to someone else. Consequently, he persuaded three servants of the cellar to draft a petition to the queen, requesting that she would write to the college, requiring the grant of the reversion of the lease to her so that subsequently it might be transferred to the sitting tenant. At Cambridge, Roger Kelke, master of Magdalene, was accused of having colluded with the Italian merchant and financier Benedict Spinola. In the lengthy legal proceedings that followed it was alleged that they had agreed that the college should make a lease of London property to the queen, on condition that within three months she should grant the property to Spinola. Subsequent disputes over this particular case made explicit the general problem. It was claimed that the grant to the queen was void, and 'most dishonourable to the said Queene who was onlie used as an instrument to defeat her owne good Lawes'. But in fact the transaction was motivated by the queen's need to pay some of her debts to Spinola.[96] In effect, what happened in these cases was that a courtier inserted himself

---

[95] 1 Eliz. c. 19, §5. For the Acts of 1572 and 1576 see above, pp. 271–3, 278. For letters to deans and chapters requiring the grant of leases to the queen see PRO, S.O. 1/3 *passim*. See also, Hill 1956/1971, pp. 4–15, 30, 311; 13 Eliz. c. 10 and 18 Eliz. c. 11. Assignments of leases to the Crown for this purpose can be found on the Close Rolls. However, the fiction employed means that the ultimate beneficiary is not always specified. Nevertheless, it is sometimes possible to determine this from other sources. For example, in 1583, Sir Walter Raleigh extracted leases from All Souls College. Ostensibly, they were made over to the queen, but in fact they were solicited and ultimately procured by Raleigh (Fletcher 1885, pp. 181–3, 231). When, however, four years later, the queen wrote for the same purpose on behalf of Lady Jane Stafford, she required a direct assignment of the lease to the proposed beneficiary as it was only to be for twenty-one years. But even this procedure was detrimental to the interests of the college, as it was required to be made 'in such manner under the like covenants, rent, and for such fee as hereto fore ye have demised the same at your own choyce' (Fletcher 1885, p. 190). In other words, the assignment was to be made without an appropriate increase in the fine to compensate for inflation and fixed rents. For further assignments of college leases via the queen see SP 12/260/84; SP 12/276/2; *HMCS*, VII, p. 406; X, pp. 449–50; XI, p. 576; XII, pp. 123–4; XIII, p. 171. For permission to lease for a period longer than that permitted by statute, *HMCS*, V, pp. 448, 462, 480; IV, p. 613. For royal letters to King's College, recommending the renewal of leases of college property in Norfolk and Hertfordshire, SP 38/12/20 (June 1622).

[96] *Cambridge Documents 1852*, II, pp. 385–6; *HMCS*, X, p. 80; SP 12/276/2; HLRO, Main Papers (Supplementary), H.C., 8 March 1620/21 (*breviat*). On the Spinola case, see Hoyle in Cunich *et al.* 1994, pp. 77–83, 284.

between the college as lessor, and the ultimate lessee, in order to take a
rake-off of the profits. A lease was made to the courtier, or to the queen if
exemptions from the normal limitations on the duration of college leases
was being sought, or if the college appeared to be unwilling to concede
a grant to the proposed lessee. The lease was then assigned by the queen
to the courtier who – for a price – then made it over to a farmer who
could well be the sitting tenant.

Thus, when James I asked Winchester College for a reversion of the
lease of a parsonage for the benefit of Lord Saye and Sele, the sitting
tenant protested that three times during Elizabeth's reign he had had to
make large payments to buy off the queen's assign for the reversion. In
1599, when the persistent Wotton eventually got his hands on the New
College leases he also obtained permission to sublet.[97]

From the viewpoint of the would-be lessee the snag with this procedure of employing Court intermediaries was that it brought to the
attention of courtiers leases which they might be better able themselves
to exploit by excluding the original supplicant – as we have seen happen in the case of Ruislip manor. From the viewpoint of the long-term
interests of the colleges, the main disadvantage of prospective tenants
having frequent recourse to the Crown was that it habituated courtiers
to meddling in college affairs. The dangers to the college of the attenuated tenancies that resulted from this courtly interference are evident:
no proper control could be exercised over the sub-lessees in order to
maintain the value of agricultural estates, and in the legal intricacies that
ensued upon these leases, property could easily be lost and permanently
alienated.[98] In objections to proposals for an arrangement similar to that
ultimately obtained by Wotton, New College claimed that a proposed
grant contained no mention of the intended assigns and that 'we should
not have known who should be our tenant', as by their statutes they
were required to know. Somewhat belatedly, at Gonville and Caius in
1635, there was an attempt to circumvent this problem by requiring that,

---

[97] *CSPD*, xii, *Addenda*, p. 471; Smith (L.P.) 1907, i, p. 302n.

[98] For example, All Souls had habitually granted a lease of the manor of Whadborough to the priory
of Launde. At the Dissolution this passed with the manor of Halsted into Lord Cromwell's hands.
The college granted a lease of Whadborough to Francis Cave, who assigned it to Gregory, Lord
Cromwell. For three generations the Cromwell family attempted to confuse the two leases, and
at one time to incorporate 700 acres of Whadborough into the manor of Halsted. The college
fought the case through most of the courts in the kingdom, and even when it was eventually given
judgement it could not obtain execution (Fletcher 1885, pp. 196n, 209n, 210n). See also *HMCS*,
xv, p. 103; *HMCS*, xiv, pp. 285, 293; *CSPD*, xii, *Addenda*, p. 471: 'ancient tenants should be
preferred'.

for the future, tenants were to enter a bond to reside on the lands they leased.[99]

Furthermore, the unstatutory privileges obtained by courtiers in seeking leases were at the cost of the colleges' income. As the much molested fellows of All Souls recalled for the benefit of Sir Walter Raleigh's too-short memory, 'our readines as we have often shewed in graunting monie hir Majesties requestes, so especiallie in those 2 our best leases demised to hir Highnes in your Worship's behalf, to our great hinderance in respct of the fines, improvement[,] and the abating of the old rent [all] to your worships more advantage'.[100]

There was also a limit to what the market would bear in the way of inflated prices resulting from courtiers inserting themselves as middlemen. Consequently, even when no special advantages such as those enjoyed by Raleigh had been elicited, the courtiers' profits tended to eat into the income devolving to the college, as the members of New College saw clearly enough. They were not, they wrote, ignorant of 'how much it would endanger the state of our college if our livings should be sold from hand to hand and other reap the profit of that which of right belongeth to us for our poor relief'.[101]

Once solicited, it was up to the Court's main representative in the college, its head, to pleasure his friends and superiors by persuading his fellows to pass the lease. The centralisation in the Court of the patronage involved in the disposal of college leases drew into the process those very courtiers to whom many of the masters were indebted for their present position or future preferment. Consequently, they became peculiarly susceptible to courtly blandishments and bullyings. Moreover, as a result of the blare of publicity that followed the actions of courtiers, and the spawn of rumour that the Court invariably generated, the masters were peculiarly vulnerable to the increasing public and parliamentary criticism of the blatant corruptions in which they participated. In the case of Wotton and New College, the college acknowledged 'The commendations that he brought us from so honourable a personage' as the earl of Essex, while Wotton himself also acknowledged his obligation to Cecil for procuring letters from the queen to the college on his behalf. At King's, a treble

---

[99] *HMCS*, VI, pp. 103–4; SP 16/315/111. Various other means were tried in attempts to overcome this difficulty. When All Souls demised a property to the queen in 1582–3 one of the conditions was that she would not assign it without the consent of the college, and that any assign would be obliged within one year after such an assignment to enter into a bond of £300 to the college to perform the covenants specified in the demise (Fletcher 1885, pp. 233–4). One's impression is that these procedures were never wholly successful.

[100] Fletcher 1885, p. 214. [101] *HMCS*, VI, p. 104.

salt-cellar for the upper table and a silver gilt cup for the provost seem to have smoothed the complications involved in Sir Robert Cecil's acquisition of the college's manor of Ruislip.[102]

It was Humphrey Tredaway, 'one of the auncientest seniors of the college', who – it appears – initially drew Mr Secretary Cecil's attention to the juicy morsel constituted by Ruislip manor. Tredaway acted in gratitude for Cecil's favours bestowed on his brother in Northamptonshire.[103] When, in 1597, Dr Jegon asked Lady Katherine Howard to write on his behalf to Essex and Cecil for the vacant deanery of Canterbury, he also proffered his good offices with one of his fellow masters, Dr Legge of Caius. Jegon offered to help Lady Howard obtain a reversion of the lease of Cambridge mills from Caius College.[104] Four years earlier John Cowell, at that time still only a fellow of King's College, attempted to wriggle out of an invidious situation and in so doing revealed the allegiances of this future master of Trinity Hall. King's had received letters to pass a lease to Mr Fernando (presumably a money-lender). Cowell claimed that a former member of the college, and his former chamberfellow, 'a very dear friend of mine', was currently in possession, and that he 'would give more than a poor man may well spare to be honestly rid of the cause'. However, he also admitted to Henry Brooke, Lord Cobham, that 'Yourself are the man upon whom I profess myself as much to rely as upon any in the world, and therefore I assure you I will not fear to displease him rather than hazard your good favour, if the matter must grow to that point.' Dr Mowtlow, to whom the college had passed a reversionary lease, provided an equally frank display of loyalties when he also wrote to Brooke, protesting that 'If the thing were leasable, though my very near friend and lecture fellow Mr John Smyth should be greatly prejudiced herein, yet would you perceive what a great interest you have in me to command me to anything which by statute or oath I might.'[105]

When an equivalent obsequiousness was not displayed, a variety of pressures were applied to the recalcitrant warden of All Souls to persuade him to succumb to the demands of Lady Jane Stafford for the lease of the College Woods at Edgware. For once a spirited resistance has left us most illuminating evidence of the methods that were employed on these occasions. A bribe of £100 was offered the warden, together with

[102] Smith (L.P.) 1907, I, pp. 301–2; *HMCS*, XVII, pp. 161–2, cf. pp. 123–4.
[103] *HMCS*, VI, p. 565, second son of Robert Tredaway, of Easton-on-the-Hill, Northants. Humphrey was a fellow of King's 1587–1613, and vice-provost (Venn, IV, p. 262b).
[104] *HMCS*, VIII, p. 406. Neither party seems to have been satisfied on this occasion.
[105] *HMCS*, IV, pp. 611, 189, 163.

the promise of future personal patronage, if he would induce the college to grant the lease: 'yf I may anywaie move you and your companie to take better consideration of me I will geve one hundred pounde to you and to thouse which you shall thinke fytte for your goode wills, and frende you in your toulinge to such a thinge as maie be as benefyciall to you as this is to me'. But while Lady Jane claimed that she craved 'Your frendshipe therein and as I can and maie I will acquite it', the stick was far more in evidence than the carrot. Summoned to Court to justify their refusal, the warden and the fellows with him were obliged to leave a catalogue of their names; a procedure that left them not a little ill at ease, 'as we know not . . . to what ende this catalogue may tende'. For his part Lord Hunsdon peremptorily expressed his expectation of compliance. The vice-chamberlain, Sir Thomas Heneage, reminded the college of the queen's pervasive influence over their fortunes, 'and the neede you maie have both in generall and particuler of her continuall gracious favour there is better reason lefte you to satisfy her highness' good pleasure then to dispute against her desire'. He recommended that, 'as it best becometh you and will be best for you, you shall yelde to her Majesties desire herein'. Even Whitgift, their Visitor, felt constrained to warn that 'It will not be well taken' if they failed to satisfy Lady Jane. In two successive private letters to the warden, Sir Thomas Heneage and Sir Walter Raleigh tried to coerce this crucial figure as a means of winning compliance from the college. Heneage wrote:

> I knowe more than ys fytte for me to write how hardly yt wilbe borne, both to the particuler prejudice of yourself, that ys warden, and the generall hynderans to as many as be present felows of your college and shall have hereafter anything to do with her majesty for any of your good and preferment . . . And so hoping and wyshinge you dyd that which may be best for yourselves I commend me hartely unto you.

Commendation indeed! Raleigh was more supple in proffering both personal goads and enticements to the warden, 'for howsoever the company escape[,] the burden of this contempt will light uppon you. And I and other my Lady's friends and Kinsfolkes, that are neare about her majestie, must prosecute yt to the uttermost of oure powers.' But, if the suit was conceded, 'assure yourself that I and other my Lady's friends will bothe excuse you for that ys don and be alwaies willinge to further your preferment in annythinge we may, in such sorte that you shall have cause to thinke this benefyt wel bestowed'. After these forceful efforts one cannot but admire Warden Hovenden's adamant refusal – but then, he was to die still warden, while others, his colleagues, ended their days in episcopal palaces.[106]

The result of the Court's developing interest in college properties was threefold. It deprived the ordinary fellow of any direct utility he may have had in these matters for his potential provincial patron, and further subjected him to the initiative and direction of the master. It reinforced an awareness of the role of the master as the agent of the Court within the college, and on these occasions for business of often dubious propriety. Finally, it engendered resentment amongst those gentry who harboured an almost proprietorial attitude to college properties lying near their own estate and integrated into its economy, who now had to endure the uncertainties and additional expense involved in employing the mediation of their courtier connections. Deprived of the benefits of direct recourse to their friends at the college, such men were the more likely to look critically at the masters of colleges who were the evident agents of the courtly throttlehold on the distribution of leases.[107]

MASTERS, MONEY MANAGEMENT AND OTHER SOURCES OF INCOME

The reputation of the masters of colleges was hardly improved by the other devices they employed to augment their income. There was, perhaps, some justification in William Sancroft the elder's claim that the master's salary at Emmanuel was inadequate. Therefore, he would only accept the job on condition that he was permitted to keep his benefice.[108] But this was a sad falling away from the original standards of grace established by proud Emmanuel, and an unwitting recognition of a changed conception of the style of life appropriately to be maintained by a master. The acquisition of prebendal stalls became an almost necessary adjunct of a mastership. While the accumulation of ecclesiastical preferments in plurality may have been especially obnoxious to the more tender of puritan consciences, the misappropriation of college properties for the personal benefit of the master encountered a broader obloquy. But Warden Hovenden at All Souls, buttressed by three cathedral prebends, was able to resist the demands of despoilers from outside the college.

---

[106] Fletcher 1885, pp. 184, 186, 194, 197–8, 201–2, 203, 218–19, 223; for Robert Hovenden, see *DNB*. Hovenden was an energetic warden on behalf of the college, conserving and improving its properties, and introducing an improved accounting system. He was prebendary of Bath, Canterbury and Lincoln (Horn 1974, p. 21; Horn and Bailey 1979, p. 67; Horn and Smith 1999, p. 54).

[107] Above, pp. 283 ff.

[108] Collinson in Bendall *et al.* 1999, p. 223 and n. 34. Sancroft was uncle to the better-known master, later archbishop of Canterbury.

Sometimes arrangements for the inappropriate exploitation of college property were formalised. At Corpus, Thomas Aldrich was accused of leasing the manor of Wilbraham upon terms very disadvantageous to the college, and of rejecting better offers, in order to assist his cultivation of the local gentry. At Caius in 1605 a lease was made of properties in Cambridge that had only recently been regained from the corporation. The not inconsiderable proceeds were assigned to the master, Dr Legge. At St John's in 1599 the master and seniors agreed that the master should have choice of any lease belonging to the college, thereafter to be permanently annexed to the mastership. Effectively, this was a means of acquiring the lucrative fines on leases, for the accustomed rents, corn rent and other appanages were reserved to the college. Consequently, there was an incentive for masters to maximise income from this source by swopping around the leases that were appended to the mastership whenever a new fine was in prospect. This was not a temptation to be resisted by the masters of St John's: in 1625–6 the governing body agreed that the lease of Clavering should be replaced by that of Ridgwell, which was then available for lease. In 1634 there was a further shift to the lease of Brome Hall. During Beale's mastership (1633–4) the profits of the 'farr walks' by the bowling green were added to those north and south greens which had previously been diverted to the support of the master. As these acquisitions required the agreement of the small body of eight senior fellows who governed the college with the master, it is not perhaps surprising to find them deciding that each in their turn should have the disposing of the seals on the expiration of leases: presumably a mechanism for ensuring an equitable distribution of the *douceurs* bestowed by tenants in expediting renewals.[109]

All these expedients were, in effect, a response by the college to the changing situation that it found itself in: it was an increasingly well-endowed type of institution maintaining customary rentals during a period of rampant inflation; an institution composed of a constantly changing membership whose future careers rendered them markedly susceptible to external influences; an ideologically influential institution – and thus one thought to require a closer supervision by the government of the day, in which the master was the main instrument of that oversight, and consequently an institution in which the concept of the master underwent a magnification that required additional resources to sustain

[109] Lamb 1838, p. 127; *Cambridge Documents 1852*, II, pp. 385–6; *Fifth Report from the Select Committee on Education*, Appendix B: Documents (Parliamentary Paper 1818, IV, 367), pp. 405–7; Scott 1898, pp. 281–5.

it. As one historian of St John's has shrewdly observed: 'In this situation there was resort to expedients which easily became irregularities.'[110]

The fellows of Gonville and Caius were describing a situation the essence of which was often repeated in other colleges in later years when in 1587–8 they complained against their master, Dr Legge, 'that he will chose no stewardes (required by statute) to kepe the College courtes and to give accomptes of perquisites and fines etc. but smothereth up all thinges him selfe, without the knowledg of the fellowes'. On occasion the need to obtain the agreement of the fellows to proposals for the redirection of college funds could be employed as a means of deflecting outside interference – as in 1610 in Cambridge's reply to James' proposal that they should admit Scotsmen. However, in practice the influence of the master was paramount in the management of college finances. The Act 18 Elizabeth c. 6 referred to a *de facto* even if not a *de iure* situation when it implied by its wording that the masters of colleges were the chief movers in the making of college leases. Certainly, Sir Francis Barrington depended upon his cousin, Thomas Nevile, master of Trinity College, for the renewal of his lease of Hatfield Broadoak: 'whose love in this busines I have always found & relyed upon'.[111]

In part this leading role of the master in the financial affairs of a college was a result of the pre-eminent authority that the master had been granted in all spheres of college life by the constitutional changes of the sixteenth century.[112] This position provided him with a considerable leverage that could manifest itself in the *force majeure* against which the fellows of Caius raised their complaints, or in the finesse with which the senior members of St John's were invited to participate in the misappropriation of college income. In part this was the result of the involvement of the colleges in this period in a flurry of fund-raising activities in order to finance an unprecedented spate of building activities.[113] The cultivation of potential patrons, the confidentiality that was often necessary and not least the exceedingly primitive methods of estimating building costs created large funds and uncertain outgoings that were mostly removed from the normal mechanisms of college audit, and wholly in the master's disposing.[114]

[110] Miller 1961, p. 28.

[111] SP 12/152/15; Collier 1840, pp. 445–6; BL Egerton MS 2644, fo. 177 (24 Dec. 1612). For similar intimacies of family and friends with the president of Queens' and again involving the sale and management of college property see Twigg 1987, p. 116.

[112] Above, chapter 3.   [113] Above, pp. 20–1n, 30–1.

[114] Legge was accused of retaining in his own hands money given to purchase lands (CUL, MS Mm. i. 35, pp. 385–6). Even where accounting procedures existed they were not necessarily followed. At Trinity College, from the late 1540s, rentals and other income appear to have been paid to the master who kept the college monies in the treasury in the tower. The bursar in his book

At Corpus, in estimating the price of the new chapel in 1570 the college forgot to allow for what proved to be one of the major items of expenditure – the very substantial cost of transportation.[115] When the building was half-completed the master, Matthew Norgate, contracted that virulent enthusiasm that seems to infect senior academics when building activities are in progress under their auspices.[116] Norgate's insistence at this stage on incorporating a new library in the chapel involved inserting a new floor and raising the roof. Little wonder that it was only two masterships later, under the acute administration of John Jegon, that the college was able to extricate itself from the financial consequences of his predecessor's architectural hubris. But Norgate's mismanagement was less reprehensible than the strong suspicions of peculation that attached to John Hills, the master of St Catharine's. Here, the master had control of the benefactions for building that the college had received during the period 1610–23. The fellows bridled under his mismanagement, and eventually revolted. When the dispute was finally settled in the University Court the master was forced to pay back all the college money in his possession, and to place in the treasury an inventory of all the college property he kept in the master's lodge.[117]

Apart from directly siphoning off college income – an accusation some fellows of Caius did not fail to level against their master Thomas Legge – the enhanced authority of the head within the college made him the obvious target for persuasive presents.[118] John Mill wrote to his father from Corpus Christi College, Oxford, explaining that a chorister's place was about to be bestowed, 'and there are manye labouringe to obtayne it'. His tutor suggested that 'yor Letters to ye Prasident may doe much': the son was more explicit, proposing 'that you wold write unto the President Doctor Cole, to get it for mee, and that yo wold promise him some gift as a reward for his good will, because he will bee the easier moved there unto by promise of reward'. In urgent fear lest his previous letter had

accounted only for such portions of it as were handed to him (Ball 1918, p. 24). At King's the provost received payments and, the fellows complained, 'noe man knowinge what they are' (BL Harl. MS 7031, fo. 5v). At Jesus in the 1620s the fellows complained that the master had not accounted for two years (CUL, MS Mm. i. 38, pp. 53–4).

[115] Sandeen 1959. Sandeen's findings with regard to Sir Nicholas' sponsorship of building at Cambridge are to be found in Sandeen 1962, pp. 23–35.

[116] Similarly, in the 1590s, Thomas Nevile, master of Trinity, indulged his architectural enthusiasms, and created a unified Great Court – although without causing the financial embarrassment to his college that Norgate caused at Corpus. On Nevile's building works, see pp. 20–1n, 24, 38.

[117] *VCH Cambs.*, III, p. 416. At King's the provost was accused of keeping in his own hands fines that should have been paid to the college (BL Harl. MS 7031, fos. 5v, 14v). At Jesus in the 1620s the complaint was that the master, Roger Andrews, kept the rents and dividends in his own hands (CUL, MS Mm. i. 38, pp. 53–4).

[118] SP 12/154/28.

been lost, the younger Mill wrote again urging some promise of reward for his good will.[119] At King's, Goad indignantly rebutted charges of 'Taiking money for my places at Eaton, & being a broker of selling places at Cambr.'[120] But in a sellers' market, from the 1580s, as the pressure for places increased, such unsolicited temptations must have been hard to resist.

In the first decade of the seventeenth century Thomas Nevile, master of Trinity and formerly master of Magdalene, having presided over the building (in part, rebuilding) of Trinity Great Court, loaned his college £3,000 to assist in the building of the new hall. He himself paid for the construction of the second court, which is named after him. Nevile's wealth as a master was exceptional. Bishop Hacket, who had been under him at Trinity, wrote that 'He never had his like for a splendid, courteous and bountiful gentlemen.' Nevile came of a well-to-do armigerous family.[121] But in keeping with the majority of clergy in the late sixteenth and early seventeenth centuries, most masters came from relatively humble social backgrounds, and did not enjoy independent means.[122] Without implying that all practised the corruptions that can be detected amongst some, for the majority of these men it was their masterships that brought them such wealth as they did enjoy. In the eyes of their contemporaries their very evident worldly success contrasted with their humble backgrounds, and with the comparative poverty endured by the majority of fellows. Naturally this engendered a quota of resentment and a portion of suspicion that set them apart from the majority of university men.

The Christmas of 1598 or 1599 saw a performance of the play *The Pilgrimage to Parnassus*, probably at St John's. It and its sequels are suffused with the discontents of disappointed academics and complaints of the poverty that the unlearned invariably assume to be a necessary adjunct of scholarship. One of the characters escaping from academe encounters two of his friends along the way and warns them, 'goe to Parnassus to converse with ragged innocentes? If you be wise, and meane to live, come not there. Parnassus is out of silver pitifullie, pitifullie.'[123] For the majority of

---

[119] SP 46/21/82; SP 46/21/88; SP 46/21/85. Also at Corpus, Oxford, in 1601, Brian Twyne promised to obtain the votes of the fellows of the college for his successor, if the father of the candidate would give him a fee for his service (Twyne 1927, p. 218). As the head of the college had a veto, Twyne would also have had to exercise some persuasion on him.

[120] BL Harl. MS 7031, fo. 7. He was also accused of taking 'privie bribes in letting out leases, where the Colledge received nothinge' (BL Harl. MS 7031, fo. 5v).

[121] Willis and Clark 1886/1988, II, p. 475; *VCH Cambs.*, III, p. 465; Trevelyan 1943/1972, pp. 21, 28–9; above, p. 38.

[122] Stone 1975, pp. 18–23. These remarks on the social background of Cambridge masters are based on a systematic scrutiny of a wide range of biographical sources.

[123] Leishman 1949, pp. 24–6.

academics before the late seventeenth century the rocky slopes of Mount Parnassus did indeed provide only spartan grazing. But not for all. For those masters of colleges who succumbed to internal temptations and acceded to external pressures, the university provided a lushness that was unknown to most of their medieval predecessors and, clearly, was often envied by their less fortunate contemporaries. Until, that is, their evident amenability ensured their elevation to yet richer pastures of ecclesiastical preferment.

MASTERS, FELLOWS AND WOMEN

In the world of early modern Cambridge there was nothing more likely to segregate man from man than womankind. One of the major changes of the Reformation had been the removal of the ban on clerical marriages. Many masters embraced the new possibility with alacrity. At Queens' Dr Heynes (1529–37) was married, and his wife succeeded in retaining her connections with the college after his death by marrying his successor, Dr Mey (1537–53). Sir John Cheke at King's (1548–53) was married, and Matthew Parker married in 1547, while master of Corpus. In the following generation of masters many were married: William Chaderton at Queens' (1568–79), Degory Nicholls at Magdalene (1577–82), Roger Goad at King's (1569–1610), Thomas Preston at Trinity Hall (1585–98), while William Whitaker at St John's (1586–95) was married twice. So too was John Still at St John's (1574–77) and Trinity (1577–93), and married before he became a master. But however it might be for the masters, Elizabeth I's penchant for celibacy prevailed among the fellows: the general decree against marriage in colleges of 1561 was narrowed to fellows in the statutes of 1570.[124] In 1561, Elizabeth complained that she had been informed of late that within individual colleges and cathedral closes 'as well the chief governors as the prebendaries, students and members thereof, being married, do keep particular household with their wives, children and nurses; whereof no small offence groweth to the intent of the founders, and to the quiet and orderly profession of study and learning within the same'. The problem was all the more acute because it occurred at a time when there was an increasing number of students pressing on the limited accommodation, parts of which were being pre-empted by married families. As a result, from henceforth,

---

[124] For this and what follows, Brooke in Bendall *et al.* 1999, p. 420; Strype 1822, I, p. 610; Corrie 1839, p. 12; Cross 1969, pp. 184–5; *HMCS*, xix, p. 357. Unless otherwise stated, biographical information is drawn from *DNB* and Venn; Bendall *et al.* 1999, pp. 30–42, 177–86.

Elizabeth prohibited the maintenance both by the head or by any member of any wife or woman within academic or ecclesiastical precincts under threat of loss of office. Dr Caius' statutes for his refounded college went further and enjoined celibacy upon the master. However, although the revised Elizabethan statutes for the university as a whole required celibacy of the fellows, they may also have given grudging recognition to the different personal circumstances and career patterns of the masters by remaining silent on this point in their case (c. 50, 33). Attitudes were complex. If the head of a college was to be treated on the analogy of the head of a domestic household, should he not also be permitted to marry?

There is some evidence for masters choosing their spouses from university circles. Edmund Barwell at Christ's (1582–1609) married in 1588 Elizabeth Tayler, the widow of a former manciple.[125] Laurence Chaderton married Whitaker's sister-in-law in 1577 while a fellow of Christ's, and as a result he was forced to resign his fellowship. However, he continued to reside in Cambridge and in 1584 was appointed the first master of Emmanuel (1584–1622).[126] A mastership permitted an academic the luxury of married life. As we have seen, Edmund Barwell married after he became a master, as did Clement Corbett at Trinity Hall (1611–26).[127]

The rush into marriage by the masters of Cambridge colleges was probably an unforeseen consequence of the changes in the legislation on clerical marriage. It was widely unpopular. We may even surmise that it was disliked by married masters such as Degory Nicholls who lived to endure the consequences of a combative matrimony. According to the fellows of his college, Magdalene, his wife 'is soe chiding that often she is heard all over the college'. Queen Elizabeth's personal dislike of married clergy is well known, and in this at least the result of the queen's psychological quirks was consonant with the distrust of married academics as expressed in parliament. At Oxford, there were complaints that where the wives and children of married men had been brought into the colleges, their members 'are distracted with the cares of family and posterity, and so neglect learning and government'.[128]

---

[125] Fuller 1655/1840, pp. 286–7; Peile 1910–13, I, p. 83.

[126] Bendall *et al.* 1999, pp. 33–5, 20–1. For married masters of Emmanuel, see *ibid.*, p. 421 n. 23. Henry Smith, master of Magdalene (1626–42), obtained his DD in 1612, and married Sara Byrd at Debden, Suffolk, in December of that year (Venn, IV, p. 99a; CUL, Baumgartner (Patrick) MS 23, fo. 33).

[127] Crawley 1976, p. 84; cf. Heal 1980, pp. 176–8.

[128] Mullinger 1883, p. 330; Heal 1980, pp. 239–47; Strype 1822, I, p. 610.

Marriage did not, however, cease to be a disadvantage in the eyes of the queen when she was considering men for promotion both within the university, and from there into the church. Whitgift had Elizabeth's prejudices in mind in 1602, when he wrote to Cecil asking him to prompt the queen about the filling of vacant bishoprics. In listing three masters of Cambridge colleges as candidates he added that, in addition to all being Cambridge men, only two of them were married – whereas all the candidates from Oxford were married. In the same year, in the disputes that surrounded the election of Thomas Jegon to the mastership of Corpus in 1601, one group of fellows wrote as if his married state *ipso facto* excluded him from the office, and no doubt hoped to engage the queen's sympathy for their candidate as a result. But the prejudice against married masters did not die with the queen. Jegon was again in difficulties over his wife in 1607. Two years later, in the process of settling a dispute surrounding the election of a master of Christ's, James expressed a preference for Valentine Carey from among a shortlist of candidates, 'for that he is a single man without charge of wife or children, a condition which we think prefers him who has it in the choice of a headship of a house before other concurrents, *ceteris paribus*, for it gives him less cause of diverting the revenues of a house to private uses, and has besides less occasion of offence and scandal amongst youth than marriage has'. But it was primarily a suspicion of married masters, and only secondarily a distaste for the diversion of revenues, that aroused parliamentary criticism of the masters of colleges.[129] In these circumstances, the Crown's attempts to enforce a decorous separation of masters from their spouses consumed considerable energies without stifling the essential grounds for suspicion. The fear remained that married men, placed in trust over considerable endowments, and recently granted a considerable accession of power, were more liable to corruption than were single men in a similar position, or at the very least, that married men 'distracted with the cares of family and posterity' were more likely 'to neglect learning and government'.[130]

The queen's periodic curiosity in this matter, and the government's attempts to meet or forestall parliamentary criticism on this sensitive issue ensured that married masters were maintained in a state of nervous apprehension. Following Elizabeth's injunction of 1561 banning women from colleges, married heads were forced to contrive accommodation within

---

[129] *HMCS*, III, pp. 437–8; SP 12/287/21 (February 1603); *HMCS*, xx, pp. 65, 84; *HMCS*, xxi, p. 160, James to the earl of Salisbury, 20 Nov. 1609. For parliamentary criticism of masters see above, pp. 164–72.
[130] Strype 1822, I, p. 610.

the college that segregated their household from that of the fellows and scholars. Alternatively they had to maintain a completely separate establishment outside the college precincts. In reply to criticisms of Thomas Jegon in 1607, the vice-chancellor could for once report the amicable satisfaction of the fellows of Corpus with the domestic arrangements of their master: 'his wife liveth in a very private and convenient lodging on the backside of that College, without any trouble to the Company, burden to the College or offence to any'.[131]

That such exterior habitations did not always provide so happy a solution is evident in the domestic regime that Degory Nicholls and his wife practised in the late 1570s to the affront of the long-suffering fellows of Magdalene. Apart from the reverberations of his wife's chidings, it was complained that 'as for the perfectinge of the scholars it seemeth his least care but rather regardeth the feeding keyne [cattle] which commonlie lie in the Court and often are mylked before the Hall door his wife standing by'. As if this were not enough, 'These keyne bewraye the Hall and Chappel and now and then at mealltymes come and stand in the Hall.'[132] The fellows must indeed have had to wend a wary passage at Magdalene between the master's scolding wife and the cow pats during Nicholl's bucolic but none too peaceful incumbency of the master's lodge.

The master of Christ's appears to have enjoyed the use of a private house, separated from the college. At King's at the turn of the seventeenth century, the provost, Roger Goad, claimed that he had 'a separate lodging after a sort in the town', while his wife and family usually remained in a house he had in the country, about 2 miles distant. But similar arrangements entered into by Jerome Beale, master of Pembroke, following his marriage in the late 1620s, had the opposite effect and aroused the resentment of the fellows at his residing in the town.[133]

In addition to the resentment (or envy?) engendered by the pleasures of the masters in these conjugal establishments, there was always a suspicion that college property was disappearing into the private residence of the master for the use of his family. Witness to this is the claim during the 1630s that the warden's steward at Merton had been terrified of being questioned about the college linen belonging to the lodge, or the need

[131] *HMCS*, xx, p. 84.

[132] *VCH Cambs.*, III, p. 454; Hoyle in Cunich *et al.* 1994, pp. 86–7.

[133] Willis and Clark 1886/1998, III, p. 353 n. 3; *HMCS*, xxi, pp. 191–2. Goad claimed that 'My wyef is not kept within the Quadrant of the Colledge (whereas yet I think she never came twise) but in Lodging being separate apart from the Coll.' (BL Harl. MS 7031, fo. 8); SP 16/160/58.

that emerged at St Catharine's in 1623 to compile an inventory of college property in the master's lodge.[134]

The role of the master as a family man created both irritation and suspicion. In 1582 William Fulke had to apologise to Burghley for his absence from Cambridge, explaining that he had been summoned to his parsonage in Suffolk, 'by occasion that God had taken away one of my children, & my wife opprest with Sorrow & sickness, had the second tyme sent for me'. Once masters were permitted to marry, some celebrated the marital condition with numerous offspring. Roger Goad sired six sons and probably some daughters too. John Duport, master of Jesus, had eight children. His successor, Richard Sterne, had thirteen.[135] With a proliferation of offspring came all the social amenities that a large family might provide. This included the domestic ensemble. In the 1650s the children of Ralph Cudworth, master of Christ's, performed pastoral entertainments in the college. However, not all festivities involving the children of the master were as innocent as this seems to have been. In 1608 an embarrassed tutor had to explain to an irate grandfather that there was no truth in the rumour that his grandson, a student at Jesus, had contracted a marriage with one of the daughters of the master, John Duport: it was merely that the student had drawn the girl in the college lottery for Valentine's the previous February.[136]

But even if the master's wife and children were kept out of the college there were still grounds for suspecting the impartiality of the actions of married masters. In 1609, King James had remarked that there was a danger of married masters 'diverting the revenues of the house to private uses'. The married masters of Christ's certainly seem to have used college leases to provide for their widows. Of course, provision for widows and children was a new problem for the masters of colleges. The legitimate sources of their income terminated on their death, and they must have been sorely tempted while they were alive to use their powers as masters in order to provide for the needs of their families after their own demise. William Whitaker failed to do so, 'for he being wholly given unto his studie' and 'had never leysure, or care, for the providing of more, then was necessarie for verie meane, and scholerlyke dyet and clothing'. As a

---

[134] SP 16/388/75; *VCH Cambs.*, III, p. 416. Queens' College also kept a check on their president (Queens' College Archives, Bk 49, 5 Oct. 1615, 'A note of such stuff as belongeth to the Colledge in oure Masters Lodgeinge').

[135] BL Harl. MS 7031, fo. 132; *DNB*; Jesus College Archives; Venn, I, p. 431a; cf. Laslett and Wall 1972, pp. 154–5.

[136] CUL, MS Mm. i. 47, fo. 105; Halliwell 1845, II, pp. 163–5.

result, Dean Nowell had to write begging letters to Burghley on behalf of Whitaker's widow and children. This was a real problem arising from the changes in the circumstances of the masters, and one that was not resolved by Elizabeth's quirky aversions, James' sanctimonious condemnation or parliamentary attempts to impose a statutory celibacy on the masters of colleges.[137]

We may surmise that the effect of the adverse pressures on married masters was threefold. For the less fortunate, it supplied a recurrent irritant in their already care-worn lives. Second, it is likely to have engendered an enhanced sense of group identity amongst those who – on this issue – were subject to criticism from all sides. This identity may have been assisted through the enforced alliance of the ostracised female partners to these masterly marriages.[138] Third, it served further to cut off the masters from the fellows of their college by forcing them to reside separately within it, or even to split their time between the college and a spouse housed separately in an establishment beyond its precincts.[139]

The adoption of this type of domestic arrangement was but one of a number of developments that increasingly served physically to separate the master from the fellows of his college. The distinctiveness of the emergent lifestyle of the majority of masters was all the greater because it contrasted so markedly with the real circumstances and supposed characteristics of life endured by fellows. The obverse of the feminine presence and the proliferating families enjoyed or endured by many masters was the sexually deprived circumstances and reputed worldly naïveté of other members of the college. If the masters moved in a world accustomed to a feminine presence, most fellows did not. For while the Reformation had removed the ban on the marriage of clergy, the fellows of colleges had been omitted from this liberation. Consequently, they were the butt of much of the humour which previously had attached to the celibate status of the pre-Reformation clergy. Entirely inconsistently but apparently persuasively, this encompassed both their reputed indulgence of the pleasures of the flesh, and their reputed social incompetence with women. The enforced celibacy of the fellows, and the characterisation of them that resulted from this celibacy, served to emphasise the difference between them and the

---

[137] Hatfield MS 128.41; Peile 1900, p. 132; Churton 1809, pp. 430–1. For Whitaker's preoccupation see Fuller 1655/1840, pp. 192–3; HLRO, Parchment Collection, H.L., 6 March 1606.
[138] The evidence for this is scanty, but see the implied familiarity between the wives of two masters (Masters 1831, Appendix, p. 70). For the isolated grandeur of wives of heads of house (and a few married professors) see Brooke 1993, pp. 304–5 and n. 10, citing Shipley 1913, pp. 17–18, 46–51.
[139] See below, pp. 303 ff.

masters.[140] But it was related to another marked difference: the fellows were mostly much younger than the masters – often young men waiting for a benefice and marriage.

THE MASTER'S LODGE

An author nurtured within the brutalist concrete style affected by most of the new universities of the 1960s cannot pretend ignorance of the social influences of architectural artifice.[141] In the early modern period the most evident and daily reminders of the distinction between masters and fellows were the separate lodges that were constructed for the former in most colleges during the latter half of the sixteenth century, and the attendant modifications in their domestic arrangements. Once again, the process of endowment and the frenzy of building activities that characterises this period made possible the separation – in most cases the physical separation – of the master from the fellows of the college. Once again, there was very visible evidence that funds which benefactors had intended for the amelioration of the academic poverty of many might have leaked into the streams that fed the sea of opulence in which were immersed a privileged few. Some change in the domestic arrangements of the master were required by those alterations at the Reformation which enabled masters to marry and therefore to create a domestic establishment separate from that of the college. It is noticeable that it was the first married warden of All Souls, Dr Robert Hovenden, who erected additional accommodation for himself. Similarly, the president's lodgings at Magdalen are attributed to its first married head, Laurence Humphrey.[142]

These new arrangements contrasted with those in the medieval college where the master had eaten with the other members and servants in the college hall. The early sixteenth-century statutes of Christ's required the master and fellows to dine together as a means of encouraging unanimity in the college. As in much else, the ample provision made for the provost of King's in the fifteenth century permitted him to dine apart from the fellows. The changing conception of a master implicit in these arrangements was again expressed in the statutes of Wolsey's foundation at Oxford, Cardinal College, where the dean was expressly

---

[140] The role of women, or the lack of it, in the life of fellows is examined in more detail below, pp. 318–20.

[141] Cf. above, chapter 2. For both similarities to and differences from the lodgings of the heads of colleges at Oxford see Newman 1986, pp. 623–7.

[142] Makower 1895, pp. 222–4; Willis and Clark 1886/1988, III, pp. 345–6.

forbidden to dine with the fellows except on certain specific festivals, on the principle that familiarity breeds contempt. In Cambridge by the early seventeenth century it was customary for the master of St John's to dine separately from the fellows. At Jesus in the 1620s the master, Roger Andrews, was said not to have dined in the college hall for seven years.[143] At Corpus there were complaints that one of the three chambers originally intended for the use of Norwich scholars had been converted by the master to a kitchen for his private use.[144] Roger Goad, provost of King's from 1570 to 1610, claimed that although the statutes provided for his meal on festival days he was not obliged to eat it in hall, and could, if he wished, take it home.[145] By way of contrast, fellows were coerced into dining in hall, as at Jesus in 1632.[146] When they were not dining privately and apart from their fellows, there were occasions when the vice-chancellor, masters of colleges and senior doctors dined together.[147] Changes in the pattern of commensality at Oxford and Cambridge both traced and reinforced the shift in the role of the heads. In turn these changes were both paralleled and made possible by the elaboration of their lodgings.

In the medieval college the master had commonly had a single chamber assigned to him. Over time some provision was made to facilitate his conduct of college business by allocating him an additional chamber for this purpose. At Oxford the separation of masters from fellows is evident at an earlier date than at Cambridge, with nine Oxford colleges incorporating from the beginning a house for the master which either was completely external to the quadrangle or extended beyond it. At Cambridge usually the master's quarters had occupied the first floor adjoining the upper part of the hall, a position roughly equivalent to that of the solar in domestic buildings. At medieval Queens', Cambridge, a modest set of rooms served to accommodate the president. At Gonville Hall three chambers and a private chapel were provided for the master in the 1430s.[148]

---

[143] Willis and Clark 1886/1988, I, pp. 370, 374; III, ch. 4, esp. pp. 331–2; SP 16/249: deposition of Thomas Smith; CUL, MS Mm. i. 38, p. 55. At this point Andrews had been master for nine years.

[144] SP 14/127/41. The truth of the allegation is uncertain. The master denied it, but in no very clear-cut way (Norwich City Muniments, Case 25, shelf d (1361)).

[145] BL Harl. MS 7031, fo. 9. On other occasions, when he had dined in hall, he appears violently to have attacked some of the fellows (fo. 5v).

[146] Jesus College Archives, B.2, Statutes 1 (2), Directions of the Visitor, Dr White.

[147] As at the dinner following the election of the vice-chancellor (CUL, Baumgartner (Patrick) MS 22, fo. 12v).

[148] Willis and Clark 1886/1998, III, ch. 4, esp. p. 336; Ball 1960, p. 138; Watkin *et al.* 1999, pp. 110–13. John Caius approximately trebled the accommodation (*ibid.*, pp. 113–15).

Heads, leases and masters' lodges

The 1506 statutes of Christ's began to break with tradition by assigning to the master a definite location for his lodging in the rooms under those reserved for the use of the foundress. Similar provision was made at St John's (1524) and at Jesus. As in so much else, it was Henry VI's provision for the provost of King's that set new standards for later emulation. Designs for the college included a 'Provostes logging' at the south-west corner of the quadrangle. It was to be staffed by a gentleman-in-waiting and five manservants, supplied with a stable of ten horses; and the provostship itself was further supported by a substantial salary. The sixteenth-century lodges of Trinity, Emmanuel and Sidney Sussex represented a half-way house between the original master's chamber and the fully developed master's house. The latter came to occupy at least half a range in the courtyard form of planning characteristic of the colleges at this time. At Trinity Hall, Henry Harvey (master 1557/8–1585) greatly extended and embellished his lodge. At Gonville and Caius the second founder, John Caius (1559–73), greatly enhanced the master's accommodation. There was creeping expansion at Pembroke, with the addition in the seventeenth century of a wing incorporating a tall bay window.[149] A similar development by incorporation of existing rooms took place at Christ's.[150] At Sidney Sussex, from the outset, special rooms were provided for the master.[151]

The final stage in the separation of the master's lodge from the remainder of the college was marked by the addition of galleries to lodges and the provision of private kitchens and gardens.[152] At this point the

---

[149] Willis and Clark 1886/1988, I, pp. 370, 374, 540–8; II, p. 312; III, p. 331; Clark 1881, pp. 285–312; Ball 1960, pp. 139–41, 147, 305. Bay or oriel windows were also a feature of new building at Oxford in this period (see Newman 1986, pp. 604, 607). 'Lodgings' (the term still current in Oxford) was the term customarily applied to sets of rooms within a larger building. They could, if necessary, function semi-autonomously, separate from the main household establishment. As with the east wing at Blickling Hall in Norfolk, rebuilt in the early seventeenth century, they continued to be incorporated into large buildings, usually as accommodation for guests. For Caius, see n. 148.

[150] CUL, MS Mm. v. 47, fo. 104. This accommodation may not have been occupied personally by the master of Christ's: instead it may have been rented out for his personal profit. Later, during the incumbency of Edward Hawford as master, plots of land were purchased as the site of the master's house (CUL, MS Mm. v. 47, fo. 106v). But the core of the lodge remained, and remains, the chambers originally assigned to the master and the foundress: Brooke, Highfield and Swaan 1988, pp. 147–9 and pls. 100–1.

[151] Willis and Clark 1886/1998, III, p. 332.

[152] Willis and Clark 1886/1998, III, pp. 339–40; NRO, NRS MS 23372 (ground plan of Corpus Christi College, showing the master's lodging and private garden); SP 14/122/128 (complaint that the three chambers allocated to Norwich scholars have been converted to a kitchen for the master's private use). On the development of the long gallery in lay buildings see Coope 1984, pp. 446–55; 1986, pp. 58–72. It is worth noting that urban communities also in some degree emulated the architectural practices of the aristocracy. At Norwich part of the rebuilt Guildhall was used to hang portraits of civic ancestors, as in a long gallery (Morgan 1992, p. 24).

Plate 22 St John's College, the master's long gallery, now the fellows'
combination room, 1599

accommodation for masters could no longer be regarded as a superior
set of chambers, for it had become, in part at least, a functionally distinct
dwelling house. In the provision of a long gallery, as in so much else,
King's led the way. This addition to the provost's lodge was constructed in
1536.[153] The gallery at Queens' was probably built in Elizabeth's reign.[154]
Among other building activities during his rule at Trinity Hall (1557/8–
1585) Henry Harvey oversaw the addition of a modest long gallery to the
master's lodge. At Corpus, in the mid-sixteenth century, Matthew Parker
had built a 70 foot long gallery to the south of the lodge. At Peterhouse
the long gallery was added over the new library of 1590. That at St John's
dates from 1599.[155]

---

[153] Willis and Clark 1886/1988, I, p. 543.
[154] Twigg 1987, pp. 131–2, correcting Willis and Clark 1886/1988, III, p. 340. See Plates 23–4.
[155] *VCH Cambs.*, III, p. 368; Ball 1960, pp. 141–2; Crawley 1976, p. 35 (Trinity Hall); Willis and
Clark 1886/1988, I, pp. 267, 270 (Corpus); II, pp. 248–63 (St John's); Brooke, Highfield and
Swaan 1988, pl. 93 (St John's). The date 1599 is on the gutters of the great long gallery (now
fellows' combination room) at St John's.

Heads, leases and masters' lodges

The separation of the master's lodge from the rest of the college was accompanied by a marked improvement in its internal embellishments. In part this reflected an improvement in the standards of material comfort throughout the college; but in this, as in much else, the provision made for the master outstripped the augmented facilities available to the fellows.[156] Towards the end of the sixteenth century wainscotting became general in the master's lodge.[157] In so far as the gallery was derived from the domestic architecture of gentry housing, it attempted to embody an appropriate degree of ostentation. That erected at Queens' in the late sixteenth century was 80 feet long by 12 feet wide by 9 feet high, and is marked for the beauty of its internal fitments. At Trinity, Nevile's prodigious enthusiasm for building resulted in a remaking of the original lodge of 1554. He doubled its length, adding the present dining room (now much altered) and stately bedrooms. The drawing room was decorated with an embossed ceiling of plasterwork picked out with gold, and provided with a highly ornamented and coloured fireplace displaying the arms of Elizabeth, of the college and of its energetic renovator and master.[158]

In 1610, following the death of Roger Goad, the long-serving provost of King's, the lodge was refurbished for his successor. Items purchased or renovated included 'le great red-leather chaire printed with gould . . . 6 high stooles covered with redd leather and printed with gould . . . a standing . . . bedd, green say curtaines and vallance, a Testar with three Curtan rodds . . . a little back Chaire embrodred . . . a large Arras Coverlett . . . a fether bedd and boulster . . . a quilted woole mattres . . . 12 thrummed quishions [fringed cushions]' and two Arras carpets. By the early seventeenth century the enhancement in the material standards enjoyed by masters was such that they surpassed most other accommodation available locally. One measure of this is the preference for accommodation within the university expressed by the judges of assize. These itinerant

---

[156] See above, pp. 32–7. Emden 1948, pp. 196–8, 'Furniture in the Provost's Lodging'. A systematic study of the probate inventories of Oxford University conveys the impression that the heads of colleges were in the vanguard of improvements in standards of material comfort (Agius 1971, pp. 72–86). Further detailed and systematic work is required on the material culture at Cambridge. Impressionistically one detects a similar improvement. This change in material provision is important not least for its demonstration effect: an awareness of the new patterns of use and consumption practised at the universities was carried back into the countryside by their alumni.

[157] Willis and Clark 1886/1988, III, p. 350. At Trinity Hall, Henry Harvey rounded off work on the new long gallery by the insertion of wood panelling (ibid. I, p. 223; Ball 1960, p. 142).

[158] Twigg 1987, pp. 131–2; Brooke, Highfield and Swaan 1988, pls. 71–2; Willis and Clark 1886/1988, II, pp. 606–9; III, p. 340; Trevelyan 1943/1972, pp. 23, 28.

307

Plate 23 The president's lodge, Queens' College, late sixteenth century, exterior

judges were renowned for seeking – and being offered – the most sump-tuous accommodation available in the places where they stayed. This was some compensation for the rigours and dangers involved in rid-ing circuit. It was also a means of purchasing a kindly disposition to-wards the local community on the part of the judges. So it was that a former alumnus of Trinity, Sir Edward Coke, initiated the practice of

Plate 24 The president's lodge, Queens' College, interior of
the long gallery

partaking of the hospitality of its lodge when he and his fellows rode
circuit.[159]

The cost of achieving these improved standards varied considerably, but
all appeared to be enormous by contrast with the relative frugality endured
by fellows. In 1627, Dr Rowlinson was reported to have expended £400
on building himself a very fair house at Oxford, while in 1638 it was
complained of the warden of Merton College that he had expended
£1,000 of college funds on building and furnishing accommodation for
himself in both Oxford and London.[160]

Once provided with the facilities of a separate lodge and all the com-
forts of a domestic life, the masters of many colleges put them to good use
as a source of profit and a means of generating credit with the influential.

[159] Willis and Clark 1886/1988, III, pp. 352–3. The curtains – almost certainly bed curtains –
the implied elaboration and the quantity of the cushions, and the carpets indicate a very high
level of comfort and therefore of prestige for this period: Queens' College Archives, Bk 49,
5 Oct. 1615, Inventory of furnishings in the master's lodge at Queens'; Trevelyan 1943/1972,
pp. 27–30.
[160] SP 16/87/48; SP 16/387/8. Cf. Martin and Highfield 1997, pp. 201–3.

At Christ's, fellow-commoners and noblemen's sons were accommodated in the rooms allocated to the master. At Trinity in the 1580s, the master, John Still, accommodated the young earl of Essex and other prestigious students in the lodge. Under Goad at King's, the controversial French cleric Peter Baro taught French in the lodge, presumably to the wealthier of Goad's students who could pay for the privilege. At Oxford in 1628, John Prideaux, rector of Exeter College, discoursed to James Ussher upon the dangers inherent in young tutors. He assured Ussher that he intended to tutor a kinsman of Ussher's recently sent to Oxford. 'I have resolved therefore to make your kinsman one of my peculiar, and tutor him whooly myself; which I have ever continued to some especial friends, ever since I have been rector and doctor.' The young student was to be in good company. 'He billets in my lodgings; hath (three) fellow pupils, which are sons to earls.' The especial solicitude and care expected to be shown towards prestigious students made the possession of a wife by a master a positive advantage. The wife of John Wilkinson, principal of Magdalen Hall, Oxford, exercised an evident care over the son of Lady Brilliana Harley. She administered medicine when he was ill, and effectively acted as a surrogate mother. Thus the lodge, and the domestic life that it facilitated, helped to set apart the master and his select group of students. These developments also embodied a changing conception of the role of the master in the life of both college and university, and provided him with a splendour equal to the dignity of the authority with which his office had been newly endowed.[161]

The expansion of the sixteenth-century university through its constituent colleges produced an institution on a scale and with problems for which there were no direct parallels. In particular, they created problems of control. The response to these difficulties was an attempt to assimilate the college to the only model of a permanent residential institution adapted for the control of its members with which the society was widely familiar: the patriarchal household. Within the college the master served as a surrogate 'father', as 'head' of his 'house'.[162] At a subconscious level there appears to have been an emergent perception that equated the domestic establishments of masters with the type of house and of household appropriate for a gentleman. Indeed, this may have been one of the driving forces behind the provision of the greater domestic privacy

[161] Peile 1900, p. 97; CUL, MS Mm. v. 47, fo. 104; BL Harl. MS 7031, fo. 25; Venn, II, p. 38a; BL Harl. MS 7031, fo. 7v; Ussher 1847–64, XV, pp. 419–20; Lewis 1854, pp. 8, 15, 29, 36–8, 66.
[162] Above, pp. 265–6.

afforded masters by the changes in college architecture that occurred especially in the second half of the sixteenth century. This development coincided with the increase in privacy enjoyed by the heads of families in larger domestic households. For although the late sixteenth century is characterised by a greater degree of physical comfort at most social levels, it was only in larger houses that provision was made to ensure greater privacy, and then only for the heads of the household.[163] This distinction in the degree of privacy to be expected at different levels of the domestic hierarchy is epitomised by the squint hole. These enabled the master of the house to survey the activities in hall or chapel from the secrecy of his private domestic apartments – as the Lady Margaret could view both from her lodging at Christ's of 1505–9.[164] In lay society a further stage in the socially segregated and differentiated provision of privacy is associated with the development of the enfilade. This originated in the architecture of Renaissance palaces but was quickly copied by members of the aristocracy. It provided a sequence of rooms with progressively socially differentiated access and increasing privacy for the head of the household and his family.[165] In the universities the emergence of a distinct 'master's lodge' made possible an equivalent development. It is therefore not without significance for our understanding of the contemporary conception of a master that facilities equivalent to those enjoyed by their lay counterparts were provided during the rebuilding activities of the sixteenth and early seventeenth centuries.

Dr Michael Woodward, warden of New College, Oxford, described a visit in 1664 to Dr Gunning, master, of St John's College, Cambridge. He commented on the gallery of the lodgings where a seat was placed for the master, 'if he please, to hear prayers, seeing all the chapel, but the Scholars not seeing him, as in the King's Chapel [i.e., the royal chapel]'.[166] These arrangements dated back to the early sixteenth century at Christ's and St John's and at other colleges too. In addition, at Cambridge (although not at Oxford) the adoption of the gallery as a necessary adjunct of the master's

---

[163] Barley 1961, pp. 60–1,159–60. Privacy and comfort seem usually to develop in tandem, but not necessarily at the same pace. As in France in the late seventeenth century, the presence of women – in this case as the wives of masters – may have contributed to the development of amenities of the master's lodge (cf. Thornton 1981, p. 10). On lack of privacy for fellows and students, see above pp. 32–3.

[164] Willis and Clark 1886/1988, II, pp. 216–17; cf. pp. 193–4 for the date. An excellent domestic example is at Cotehele House, Devon. A number survive in medieval religious houses.

[165] Baillie 1967, pp. 169–99. The practice initiated in palaces filtered down to the so-called 'prodigy' houses of the period: see Summerson 1970, pp. 61–95; Girouard 1980, pp. 81–118; Airs 1982, pp. 40–66.

[166] Willis and Clark 1886/1988, III, p. 335.

lodge was not simply an empty echo of developments in gentry housing. Soon, these galleries resonated with those forms of social intercourse and recreation derived from the lifestyle of the gentry. In doing so they served further to separate a master from the fellows gathered around the hall fire, or in the combination room. Moreover, embodied in the ostentation of the wainscot and strapwork plaster ceilings of the lodge was the equation of the master with the head of a domestic household, imbued with all the authority that such a figure enjoyed at this time.

CONCLUSION

Thus, during the sixteenth century a series of interrelated changes increasingly isolated the master from the fellows of his college. The result was not always happy for the individuals concerned. Amongst the masters of Cambridge colleges in this period there were at least two suicides. The combination of an increased workload with the removal of the master from the supportive fellowship of other members of the college may have played its part. The suicide of Henry Butts, master of Corpus, in 1632 followed three strenuous years as vice-chancellor during a period when the town and university were visited with plague. For his part, in an attempt to stir his melancholy, Barnaby Potter, the puritan master of Queen's, Oxford, took to summoning to his lodgings after supper those scholars of the house who could sing well, sometimes taking a part with them – a poignant attempt to re-evoke the camaraderie of the now forsaken college hall.[167]

One of the original reasons – probably the main reason – for increasing the authority of the masters was to provide a more assured control of university life. In the long term, however, the splendid isolation that had gone along with this accession of power may have made the exercise of that authority more difficult. It was noted that it was only in the exceptional circumstances of trying to drum up support for the election of the duke of Buckingham as chancellor that the master of Trinity College deigned to visit his fellows in their rooms.[168] Certainly, by 1630, Laud was writing to the warden of New College, Oxford, warning him that he lived too solitary a life and that that was not the best position from which to fulfil the responsibilities with which he was charged.[169] Laud was probably right. Within the universities the managerial-coercive had

---

[167] Collinson in Bendall et al. 1999, pp. 213–14; Venn, I, p. 276a; cf. Hair 1970, pp. 36–43; Clarke 1677, p. 394.
[168] BL Sloane MS 1775, fo. 25v.   [169] Lambeth Palace Library MS 943, p. 145.

come to prevail over the fellowship–consensual model. Furthermore, their elevated status laid the masters open to other dangers. First, there was the increasing social gulf that gave an edge to the perennial bickering with the fellows of their colleges. Second, their exposed position made them the natural focus for the criticisms that all the ills of the university engendered during these hectic decades. After all, if they were now the men with ultimate authority in the university, should not its faults be laid at the doors of their splendid new lodgings?

Chapter 9

TUTORS AND STUDENTS

One of the fundamental characteristics of early modern Cambridge was the form of the relationship between tutors and students. Ultimately much of the institutional, political, theological and intellectual life of the university centred in this crucial relationship. It had not always been so and it was not to remain so throughout the whole of the period with which we are concerned. Indeed, one of the main indexes of the changing nature of the university over the course of the seventeenth century is to be traced in the decline in the intimacy and the intensity of the relationship between tutors and students which had characterised the latter part of the sixteenth and the first half of the seventeenth century.[1]

THE ORIGINS OF THE TUTOR–STUDENT RELATIONSHIP

We have already found the government taking an increasingly active interest in the life of the university.[2] This concern with the regulation of the institution extended to reinforcing the authority of the tutor over his students. The tutors had been central to the life of some colleges at least since the fourteenth century. In the later sixteenth century their role was significantly enhanced. The reason for this arose in part from the restricted range of institutional models available to contemporaries. As we have seen, the colleges were equated with great households; the master of the college was equated with the head of the household, the fellows with servants, and the students with children, apprentices or women. It has been argued that throughout society, as part of the central government's desire to maintain order, it reinforced patriarchy.[3] Within the university

---

[1] There was no continuity between the period of intense relationship during the early modern period and the second such period during the late nineteenth century except, that is, in so far as there was some conscious imitation. For the latter period see Rothblatt 1981; Searby 1997, esp. ch. 4; Brooke 1993b, pp. 269–81.

[2] Above, chapters 3–5.   [3] Stone 1977.

the reinforcement of the authority of the tutor also derived in part from this larger inspiration.

The college became the chosen institutional framework for the supervision of students.[4] In its turn this created a need for the college to ensure that students for whom it was responsible met their obligations to the college. Again, the tutor became the regular link between college and student. For example, in 1568 tutors at Trinity Hall were made formally responsible to the college for the payment of their pupils' commons every six weeks.[5] As at Caius, from the 1560s all colleges came to require that one of the fellows should act as surety for each student on his entrance to the college. This was a role which was not necessarily the same as that of a long-term tutor but which seems in most instances to have evolved into this office.

But the emergence of a new type of relationship between tutors and students was not simply a product of administrative convenience imposed from above. Perhaps more importantly it represented changing patterns of teaching. It embodied new aspirations on the part of those who taught.[6] On the part of many it reflected a new model of the purpose of teaching arising from the notion of the university as seminary, an institution charged with the responsibility of producing a preaching clergy and disseminating godliness.[7] The influx of the children of aristocratic families placed new responsibilities on those responsible for their well-being.[8] All these many aspects of change in the university came together to enhance the role of the tutor.

It is artificial to draw too sharp a distinction between students from plebeian and those from aristocratic backgrounds. Indeed, as we will see, the relationship between a tutor and his various students was one of the social mechanisms which drew together the two groups.[9] None the less it is convenient initially to look at the relationship between tutors and students from the viewpoint of these two groups.

---

[4] Above, pp. 32–5. [5] Trinity Hall Archives, Liber Actorum, fo. 47v.

[6] But it was not always apparent to college founders that a change had occurred: Mildmay's statutes for Emmanuel of the 1580s in large measure reproduce Fisher's for Christ's of the 1500s without mention of tutors.

[7] Above, pp. 108–9, and below, chapter 15.

[8] Here as elsewhere 'aristocratic' is used as a convenient and indigenous portmanteau term to encompass all those from gentry no less than those from noble backgrounds. It is preferred to the usage 'patrician' to cover the same groups which has won increasing acceptance in recent years.

[9] In this, my judgement differs from earlier writers on this topic: see Twigg 1987, p. 89 n. 24, and Venn 1913, pp. 191–2.

ARISTOCRATIC REGARD

The preoccupation with the aristocratic element in the universities was evident in a number of ways. In the 1620s it seemed perfectly natural that a tutor at Oxford was able to list the lords then resident in the university. On another occasion the same tutor noted that Mr Goodwin had brought three noblemen's sons to the university.[10] At Cambridge the fame of the mercurial John Preston owed not a little to his ability to attract aristocratic students to his tutelage.[11] When in the mid-sixteenth century the sweating sickness swept through Cambridge it carried off, amongst others, the young Henry Brandon, duke of Suffolk, and his brother Charles. Even some seventy years later the university's historian, Thomas Fuller, was still willing to recall these young boys as 'bulwarks of the land'. At the time of their deaths 'They were much bemoaned of the university', which printed a book of verses on their funerals.[12]

The solicitude on the part of the university and of its individual members for the well-being of the new aristocratic presence was more than matched by the intrusive concern of aristocratic parents. In particular through the careful selection of tutors, those parents sought the assurance of individual supervision of their offspring. To the more discriminating parent, tutorial teaching offered the opportunity of an education tailored to their personal theological and social views – views which they wished to see implanted in their children.[13] For example, the reputation of favouring puritanism which was thought to have damaged John Preston's reputation at Court worked to his advantage as a tutor, for 'Men thought him meet to be trusted with the care of youth; and many had their eyes upon him, for their Sons or Friends.'[14]

The connections outside the university of many of the masters of colleges made them an obvious source of information as to prospective tutors. For example, Sir John Hobart relied upon his friendship with John

---

[10] Boas 1935, pp. 9, 53.

[11] A feature of Preston's near-contemporary biography is the *frisson* of excitement evinced by his repeated hobnobbing with the prestigious and the powerful (Ball in Clarke 1677, p. 481; cf. Collinson in Bendall *et al.* 1999, pp. 214–21).

[12] Fuller 1655/1840, pp. 245, 246; Venn, I, p. 206a.

[13] It has been suggested that parents chose tutors, not colleges (Twigg 1987, p. 91). This could not always be so. Statutory limitations on the one hand and the prospect of eligibility for scholarships on the other both served to constrain choice. Moreover, in some instances, as with St John's and certain schools in the north, and Corpus in its relationship to Norwich, there existed bursaries and tied scholarships. The existence of these mechanisms also served to pre-empt parental choice (see above, p. 190 n. 36; and pp. 189 ff; Morgan 1987, pp. 66–7).

[14] Clarke 1677, p. 82.

Cowell, master of Trinity Hall, for the recommendation of a tutor for his son.[15] In other instances it was natural to invoke the networks of kinship and local connections. When he was contemplating sending his sons up to Cambridge, the Welsh gentleman Sir John Wynn of Gwydir made careful enquiries of one of his kinsmen, William Holland, who was a fellow of St John's. Holland's reply reflected the concerns he expected in his interlocutor. Not unnaturally, he recommended St John's, 'to be *omni exceptione majus*; not inferior to any colledge for the bringinge up of yonge gentlemen'. Holland also realised that Sir John was anxious to obtain the appointment of a suitable tutor, and recommended the means to achieve this end, which depended in part on the mobilisation of their mutual local connections. Finally, Holland again alluded to these connections when he assured his correspondent that 'yf my cosenes come to St John's, they shall want noe Frends in the house'.[16]

The presence in the potentially unhealthy environs of fenny Cambridge of the young men who carried in their person the promise of continuity for their family line was a constant source of anxiety for parents over and above any simple concern about absent offspring. In their turn aristocratic parents expected their anxieties to be translated into a punctilious solicitude for their progeny on the part of their carefully chosen tutor. Thus in the very cold winter of 1607–8 Sir Christopher Heydon wrote to Samuel Ward, tutor to Heydon's ward at Emmanuel. Heydon's wife had heard that Ward and his pupil had travelled at Christmas, and she wanted to know where he had been, 'for except it be to S[ir] John Cottons she doth not lyk he shold be carried any whither'.[17] When, in the autumn of 1608, the term was broken up for fear of infection, John Williams wrote to reassure Sir John Wynn that 'as yeate there is more causeles feare than apparent daunger of infection'. Nevertheless as a precaution he had sent off Sir John's son to live in the country, near to the curate of Williams' living.[18] When illness did strike, the note of anxiety is evident in the tone of a tutor's letter reporting the event, and attempting to exculpate himself from responsibility. In the spring of 1619, one of John Hacket's pupils at Trinity College had been taken ill. Hacket wrote to his pupil's father, Robert Hobart, that 'all the leasure I have from attending my tender patient is to write to you'. In addition to his

[15] Bodl. Tanner MS 283, fo. 188; Tanner MS 285, fos. 28, 60. John Conant, rector of Exeter College, Oxford, was said to have performed a similar role in his college (BL Add. MS 22579, fo. 10).
[16] Yorke 1887, pp. 144–5. Despite these blandishments Sir John appears to have preferred to send his two oldest sons to Lincoln's Inn (*Welsh DNB*, p. 1098). For expressions of similar concerns see John Hammond to Sir Edward Montagu, 6 May 1581 (*HMC* 45: *Buccleuch and Queensberry*, III, p. 22).
[17] Bodl. Tanner MS 75, fo. 247.   [18] Yorke 1887, pp. 145–6.

own 'praiers and carefulness', the tutor had removed his charge from the college to the house of the Cambridge apothecary, Mr Crane: 'I know S^r how little you value charges at the price of his health, and therefore I tooke the most safe course though the most chargable.' Also, by this stage sickness had loosened the errant student's tongue: 'The first occasion of his sickness is now revealed by his own confession. He overcharged his stomach wth a bag pudding eleven daies since and took a surfet. I would to God he had disclos'd that secret sooner. But nothing shall be omitted at this pinch God willing.' Early modern bag puddings were clearly potent concoctions. After the immediate crisis was past the boy was sent off into Norfolk to recuperate, and it was midsummer before he was considered well enough to return to Cambridge.[19]

If the aristocratic student escaped the dangers of Cambridge's unhealthy environment he might yet succumb to the temptations of the flesh that it also provided. Both individual parents and the central government were anxious to avoid the disparagements to the family line and the social hierarchy that might arise from any such indulgences. Again, the first line of defence was a vigilant tutor. From this viewpoint, women at Cambridge were a threat to the social order. They were also, at the most humble social level, a necessary part of the labour force required to serve the domestic needs of the colleges. At St John's, as at many other colleges, they acted as bed-makers.[20] Just what might happen in the intimacies of this activity is at least implied by an order made by Trinity College in 1625. All young women were banished and put out of the college. No woman under the age of fifty or thereabouts, and they also of honest fame, were to come into the college to make beds or to do any other service.[21] The order came none too soon. In the 1590s the young Samuel Ward had been lamenting 'the grievous sinnes' in Trinity College, 'which had a woman which was [carried?] from chamber to chamber on the night tyme'. He confessed to 'My adulterous dream that night'.[22] The drabs of Castle End who once had met the needs of impecunious medieval clerics now had a richer market to ply.[23] Apart from a general desire to reduce 'night gaddinge', the regulations for locking gates and prohibiting the frequenting of town houses were aimed at curbing the opportunities for

---

[19] Bodl. Tanner MS 283, fo. 110; Tanner MS 286, fo. 37. Hacket had become a fellow of Trinity in 1614, and at the time of this letter was aged 26 (Venn, I, p. 278b). For further evidence of parental concern for a son's health at Cambridge see Northamptonshire Record Office, Isham Correspondence, 14: Sir Thomas Isham to his son (9 May 1600).

[20] Marsden 1851, p. 103.

[21] Trinity College Muniments, Masters' Old Conclusion Book, 1607–73, p. 87.

[22] Knappen 1933, p. 111.   [23] Leathes 1897, p. 228 (1534).

nocturnal dalliance in general and on the part of aristocratic students in particular.[24]

Throughout the period there is an evident concern to minimise the likelihood of *mésalliance* among aristocratic students. Especially during the 1620s there were complaints that scholars, gentlemen and others had married wenches from the town.[25] The royal Injunctions of March 1630 urged reform of those circumstances of recent years in which many students were reputed to have made disparaging marriages with women of low birth from Cambridge.[26] The social stigma that thus could be grafted on to the family tree might lead to punitive reprisals on the part of a parent. At Oxford, in 1608, Harvey Bagot reported of his cousin who 'for his good behaviour in mariyinge wth a poore man his daughter . . . hath soffar incurred his fathers displeasure that he will nether alow him any mentainaunce nor suffer him to come in his sight and soe by thease meanes is compelled to forsake the universitie'.[27] At Cambridge in the 1570s a student was sent down who had fallen in love with a young woman from Norfolk 'and would have assured himself unto her without the consent of his friendes'.[28] On another occasion Burghley required to be informed of the relationship between two students at Caius, as he feared it might endanger the inheritance of one who was a charge of the Court of Wards.[29] In 1608 William Boswell, a fellow of Jesus, wrote in haste to the guardian of one of his pupils. Boswell was at pains to deny the rumours that had come to the ears of Sir William Waldegrave that he had permitted his pupil to contract a marriage with one of the daughters of Dr Duport, the master of the college: 'I hope your Worship will not mistrust my watchfull eye over him: at all occasions I will be and am readie to guide him.'[30]

One of the advantages of engaging an astute tutor was indeed that he could often forestall these socially disastrous marriages. The story was told of John Preston's prescience in this respect. Amongst his pupils was a considerable heir, Capel Bedel. This young man's addresses to mistress Jane Newcomb had been encouraged by her father. However, Preston clearly recognised that the safeguarding of Bedel 'was a great trust', and

---

[24] CUA, Lett. 9.B.24.ii.   [25] SP 16/160/58 III (10 Feb. 1630).

[26] CUA, folder in plan press; CUA, Lett. 12.A.29, and the selection of statutes and ordinances relating to the behaviour of students, promulgated by the then vice-chancellor, Henry Butts, in January 1631 (CUA, O.III, CUR 44.1.149a).

[27] Folger Shakespeare Library, MS L.a.50. For an example of the secret marriage of a student at Cambridge, see Searle 1867–71, II, p. 346.

[28] BL Lansdowne MS 33, fo. 105v.   [29] CUA, Lett. 9.C.9.

[30] Venn, I, p. 185a; Halliwell 1845, II, pp. 163–4. The possibility of encounters such as those suggested here was no doubt one of the reasons for the lay dislike of married masters, and for the disapproval of the residence of their families within the college (see above, pp. 297–303).

his 'care was answearable; and because *plus vident oculi* he had his spies', he unearthed the nascent romance. He proceeded to thwart it with all the finesse that he displayed in his manipulation of both university and Court politics. On the pretext of taking his fellow-commoner students to visit Audley End, Preston contrived to stop at Sir Arthur Capel's, where the luckless Capel Bedel was left to cool his ardour in rural solitude.[31]

THE PLEBEIAN PRESENCE

The preceding paragraphs have attempted to convey something of the character of the relationship between aristocratic parents and their children on the one hand and their tutors on the other. It has been possible to do this, because the evident contemporary concern was publicly expressed in administrative documents or in eulogistic print; and also because a quantity of correspondence between tutors and parents has been preserved in the papers of great families. The evidence for those from humbler social backgrounds and of their relationships with their tutors is not so accessible. None the less something can be done. Many of those who came from humble backgrounds ultimately went on to become distinguished clerics whose achievements were recorded in their own autobiographies or in near-contemporary biographies.[32] These sources have their limitations: it is in their nature that they fail to record those who fell by the wayside except as asides about ghastly ends. Moreover, they need to be handled more gingerly than unselfconscious epistolary revelations about bag puddings: as much as the memoirs of modern former cabinet ministers, these biographies were composed with a purpose. Their higher purpose was to provide a series of *exempla* of the godly life. The internal structure of many of the narratives reveals the recurrence of similar motifs. This said, textual analysis reveals much detail that clearly has not been doctored for a purpose. Even the formulaic elements, when recognised as such, can be made to yield insights into university life.[33]

Three features come through very strongly in this biographical literature. One is the importance attached to education by the relatively

---

[31] Clarke 1677, p. 86.

[32] There are parallels to this technique. Margaret Spufford has used the autobiographical writings of authors originating from humble backgrounds in order to analyse the acquisition of literacy: Spufford 1970, 1979.

[33] The main sources used in this section are the compilations by Samuel Clarke. His three volumes are often treated simply as interchangeable editions of the same basic work. They are not. Lives which appear in one volume do not necessarily appear in another. The bibliographical complexities cannot be entered into here but they would repay further study (Clarke 1662, 1677, 1683). Use has also been made of a fairly extensive reading in the biographical fragments contained in the introductory matter to some of the religious literature of the period.

humble and uneducated parents of those lads who ultimately found their way to university. The parents of the young Hugh Clark were 'very carefull of his education, both in Religion and Learning'.[34] Despite the death of his father, Richard Sedgwick's mother, 'being industrious and sparing, out of the little means she had left her, maintained him at Peterhouse'.[35] Education was, of course, a central virtue among the godly because it was seen as a primary means of establishing the new Jerusalem. One would expect this enthusiasm to be evident from the 1570s: by then godliness had become a pervasive presence among sections of English society.[36] However, the reality is not as neat as this. Fragmentary evidence indicates that the enthusiasm for education occurred earlier than did the widespread dissemination of godliness. Moreover, it was not limited to those of a godly disposition. The aim of Arthur Hildersham's papist father was only to send him to a good school frequented by the sons of gentlemen. He was unaware that the school at Saffron Walden was presided over by 'a godly man'.[37] At one stage the young Richard Sedgwick had been adopted as his heir by a childless uncle who put him to school. Despite this, his uncle and his family were 'prophane, hating the power of godlinesse, and wedded to games and sports'.[38]

The widespread enthusiasm for education which was so important in getting poor boys to Cambridge is evident in the extent to which family networks could be invoked for this purpose. The wealthy childless uncle often figures in this scene. As a young boy John Preston was taken up in this way by his maternal uncle, a former mayor of Northampton, 'rich, no children', who sent him to the school there. The uncle was then persuaded to send Preston to a school in Bedfordshire in order to perfect his Greek, from where he was sent up to King's.[39] Sometimes a lad was supported by a patron because the boy displayed exceptional talents which promised to be especially useful to the church in its proselytising mission. John Carter was 'descended of mean parents', but at school in

---

[34] Clarke 1677, p. 27.

[35] Sedgwick's father had been a Norfolk clothier whose financial circumstances had been devastated by a fire (Clarke 1677, p. 157).

[36] There is, of course, a continuing debate about the chronology of the real commitment to reformed practice, and more particularly to the enthusiastic advanced Protestantism encompassed by the notion of godliness. My own conclusions are based on the evidence garnered incidentally in the process of studying its manifestations in and through the university. For the debate see in particular Collinson 1983, 1988; Haigh 1993; Duffy 1992, part II.

[37] Clarke 1677, p. 115.

[38] *Ibid.*, p. 157. He was related to Thomas Sedgwick of Peterhouse and Trinity, Lady Margaret's Professor of Divinity, 1554–6 and Regius Professor in 1557 (*DNB*).

[39] Clarke 1677, p. 75. The Prestons had pretensions to gentility but in the direct line they seem to have fallen into poverty. While Preston was at university his uncle died, leaving his nephew some money (*ibid.*, p. 77).

Canterbury he was perceived to be exceptionally adept at learning and therefore 'likely to be a precious instrument in the Church of Christ'. His parents were unable to sustain him at university but he was supported by a rich man in the town. Over his years at Cambridge, Carter received subventions from his local patron. Neither did this patronage end when he graduated. His first living was acquired for him by his – by then – long-term benefactor.[40]

The career of William Bradshaw illustrates the range of resources that could be called on during the early stages of an academic training. This again demonstrates the influence which was exercised over a range of types of individual by the idea of the virtue of providing education for the able but humble. In this instance the father's desire to 'Train . . . his Son up in Learning' outstripped his financial resources and resort was made first to the wider kin – in this instance a great uncle. Following his death a percipient schoolmaster prevailed upon the parents to maintain William at school. After going up to Emmanuel he was maintained partly by 'some Gentlemen his fellow-pupils under the same Tutor' and partly by subventions from the great puritan patrons Sir Edward and Sir Francis Hastings.[41] After Arthur Hildersham had been disowned by his father and had had to leave Cambridge, he was rescued for scholarship and the godly life by the actions of John Ireton, fellow of Christ's. To Ireton the solution to Arthur's problem was plain: 'thou hast a noble kinsman, whom I will acquaint with thy case: and I doubt not but he will provide for thee'. As Hildersham's noble relative was the godly earl of Huntingdon, Ireton's certainty was well founded.[42] Later in a man's career in the university the opportunity to display his talents might lead to further patronage and financial support. The young John Preston successfully participated in a disputation before James I and his courtiers when they visited Cambridge. Fulke Greville, later Lord Brooke, was so impressed by what he heard that he settled on him a stipend of £50 a year.[43] In the case of John Carter the rewards for ability were on a more humble scale. The lecturer who read the 'themes' composed by freshmen was highly impressed by Carter's effort, declaring it to be the best that he had ever read. In addition he gave him some money for his encouragement. Perhaps of equal importance, he 'always after cast a favourable eye upon him, and sought opportunities to do him good'. Later in his career in the university, Carter's outstanding qualities earned him further patronage from his academic superiors. His

---

[40] *Ibid.*, pp. 132–3. Carter's academic precocity may be evidenced in his age on admission. He would have been 15 when he entered Clare Hall as a sizar and a pupil of its master, Dr Byng, in 1569 (Venn, I, p. 299b). In the college he was noted for the 'ripeness of his years'.
[41] Clarke 1677, p. 25.   [42] *Ibid.*, p. 115.   [43] *Ibid.*, p. 81.

tutor, Thomas Byng, master of Clare, 'out of his singular love to him for his Piety and Learning' gave him the use of a chamber in the master's lodge for over a year.[44]

The second salient feature in the biographical fragments relating to how relatively poor boys got to Cambridge is the crucial role of networks of schoolteachers and university tutors. In many instances these networks appear to have provided the channels through which able boys were forwarded to the universities. As in the case of students from aristocratic backgrounds, but for different reasons, the central role of the tutor is again evident even before the weary aspirant to a scholar's place first glimpsed the chapel turrets of King's as he breasted the top of the Gog Magog hills.

Thirdly, the boundaries between the university and the localities which it served were not as clear-cut as we might tend to assume. Again, tutors often played a key role in maintaining the links which bound them together. Admittedly, in this matter the character of the sources – with their preoccupation with the godly – may bias the interpretation. But even if we restrict our perspective to the practices of the godly we must acknowledge that they constituted a significant element within the university.

The workings both of shared religious commitments and of local connections among tutors and preachers are implicit in the case of Simeon Ash. Ash was admitted as a sizar to Emmanuel in 1613. He later avowed that he 'did more owe himself unto Master Hildersham than to any other man', not least because it was Hildersham who had orchestrated Ash's admission to Cambridge under the tutorship of Thomas Hooker. At the time of Ash's admission Hildersham had for long been first lecturer and then vicar at the centre of radicalism in the east midlands, Ashby-de-la-Zouche. He had left Cambridge in the late 1580s. Hooker was of a later generation; he was born at Markfield, the son of a yeoman of Birstall, Leicestershire, in 1586; he entered the university in 1604. He had attended school at Market Bosworth. Birstall is some 12 miles from Ashby, and both Markfield and Market Bosworth are some 9 miles from it as the crow flies. Certainly, by the time of Ash's admission Hooker was a friend of Hildersham, who may even have performed for Hooker the service which we know he did for Ash. What we have here is a lineage of three generations of religious radicals linking locality and university through the personal associations of tutors and preachers.[45]

---

[44] *Ibid.*, pp. 132–3.

[45] *Ibid.*, p. 123; Venn, I, p. 43b; II, pp. 368b, 403b; *DNB*. The school at Market Bosworth had been endowed by Sir Wolstan Dixie, a benefactor of Emmanuel and friend of its founder (Bendall in Bendall *et al.* 1999, p. 109).

By the 1590s a new factor became significant in both sending and maintaining boys at Cambridge. By then a generation or more of graduates had spread through the English countryside. The importance attached to the pastoral role of these clergy provided a positive incentive to marriage, both to obtain a practical helpmate in the Lord's vineyard and as a means of creating the godly households which did so much by both practice and example to advertise the virtues of the reformed practice. Many of these clergymen sired large numbers of children.[46] Not unnaturally, having benefited so signally from their own education this new generation of the intelligentsia were anxious to ensure a comparable education for their own children. With continuing connections in the university they were well placed to obtain the necessary patronage. Because of the prestige enjoyed by the preaching clergy some were sufficiently well off to be able to pay for the education of their own children. In his day John Carter had required the patronage of a gentleman from his native Canterbury to see him through the university. But in his turn he brought up both his sons as scholars 'and maintained them in the University in good fashion'.[47]

We perhaps need to be cautious about implying the existence of a homogeneous category of those from plebeian backgrounds. Some parents of students from relatively humble backgrounds, such as those of the controversial divine Thomas Cartwright, were nevertheless able to finance the schooling of their son 'till he was fit for the University',[48] and presumably made some contribution between the point when he became a sizar at Clare in the autumn of 1547 and when he migrated to a scholarship at St John's in 1550.

One of the things which enhanced the status of the tutor during the late sixteenth and early seventeenth centuries was the spiritual importance attached to edification. The adept pedagogue was in the front line of the battle on behalf of godliness. A scholar such as Richard Stock of St John's was to become a leading puritan divine. But even while still a student he assisted others in their studies, 'which well also he could do'. This was seen as a presage of his later edificatory skills in the ministry: 'he gave before hand e're he came to it, evident signes of one likely to prove a skilful Master Builder in God's Work, and a winner of many Souls

---

[46] Cf. Hugh Clark, below, n. 88.

[47] Clarke 1677, p. 134. John Carter had entered Clare as a sizar in 1569. His son and namesake entered Corpus as a pensioner in 1596.

[48] Clarke 1677, p. 16; Cartwright later sold parcels of land he had inherited. This included a farmhouse and between 160 and 180 acres of arable land inherited from his father and grandfather (Pearson 1925, pp. 1–2). Thomas' ancestors are described as 'yeomen' in contemporary documents.

unto God'.[49] Similarly, one of the qualities which commended a man such as Paul Baynes to a fellowship and thence to the role of a tutor included 'aptnesse to Teach', which was itself seen as one of the virtues which demonstrated 'fulness of Grace'.[50] The great 'pupil-mongers' such as Preston were held in high esteem. His 'Reputation in the Countrey' increased 'so that now he was acounted the only Tutor'. Such a reputation could be a mixed blessing: Preston certainly 'found himself abridged of his own time'.[51] For each fellow of a college there was an inherent conflict between his role as a tutor and his role as a graduate student – and in the late sixteenth and early seventeenth centuries most fellows were both.

THE INTIMACIES OF LIFE AMONG TUTORS AND STUDENTS

By the late sixteenth century it was a well-established custom in most colleges that most fellows accepted some students and acted as tutors. However, it was not a formal requirement. John Fletcher of Caius, teacher of many mathematicians, is a good example.[52] In addition to the religious imperative to proselytise through the proper education of youth – and for many, the more general, deeply seated desire to instruct in good learning – there were also more mundane inducements. These included the acquisition of the useful connections and the generation of the obligations through the most readily available means: pupils and their parents. Connection and obligation were the essence of early modern patron–client relationships.[53] They were essential to men who for the moment were both fellows and tutors but most of whom had to contemplate a later stage in their lives lived in a wider world. More immediately the private relationship between a tutor and his aristocratic students was also a supplementary source of earnings. While not all tutors were in the position of Preston, who had 'great Incomes from his Pupils', the irregularity and uncertainty of payments from college sources meant that all tutors would have welcomed any additional source of remuneration.[54]

When John Preston first entered King's he was under the tutelage of Matthew Bust. When, some two years later, Bust was made headmaster

---

[49] Clarke 1677, p. 62; *DNB*; Venn, IV, p. 164. For technical reasons Stock twice missed a fellowship. None the less he was held in high regard by the likes of Whitaker, and presumably not least because of his ability as a teacher.
[50] Clarke 1677, p. 22. Baynes was a fellow of Christ's 1600–4 (Venn, I, p. 113b).
[51] Clarke 1677, p. 82.
[52] Venn 1904, pp. 232–3; 1897–1901, I, p. 95. For the earlier history, see above, pp. 25–7, 32–3.
[53] Morgan 1988, pp. 91–116.
[54] Clarke 1677, p. 96. For some of the complexities involved in college finances see pp. 271 ff.

of Eton, Preston was faced with a problem.[55] Because he was not himself from Eton, he was held to be 'uncapable of those preferments in
the Colledge that were of most worth'; and so he migrated to Queens'
where he entered under the tutorship of Oliver Bowles.[56] When in his
turn Bowles was called to the rectory of Sutton in Bedfordshire, Preston
was passed on to yet another Queens' tutor, George Porter.[57] However,
changes such as these, although not unusual for the very reasons exemplified by Preston's case, seem to have been the exception rather than the
rule: most students enjoyed a fairly long-term relationship with a single
tutor. At most, over their undergraduate careers they had a series of two
or three tutors with whom they were usually in close daily contact.

The propinquity of daily domestic living (see pp. 25–7, 33) and the
enthusiasm for shared theological concerns combined to produce intense
personal relationships between some tutors and some students. The conscientious tutor prayed regularly in private with his pupils. This was the
collegiate equivalent of the late sixteenth-century spiritualisation of the
household. Students became their tutors' confidants in their most secret
schemes. In later life grateful pupils frequently recalled the love and care
of their former tutors. When they themselves became fellows, when their
former tutors died they were bequeathed the furniture and belongings
of their deceased tutor's college lodging.[58]

The tutor had three main functions to perform. All required a considerable degree of intimacy between a tutor and his students. First, he was
required to read to his students. Although there is some evidence that
busy tutors deputed at least part of this function to more junior members
of their college it was seen as an important activity and even the busi-
est tutors were obliged to put some effort into this quality-time activity,
especially for their aristocratic pupils.[59] Second, they were responsible
for directing the overall studies of each student. Third, at least in the
case of aristocratic students, the financial obligation of the tutor to the
college as surety for each student seems to have been extended back into
the relationship between tutor, students and parents. Perhaps the largest
single topic in the surviving correspondence is to do with the financial
management of students' affairs. Many of the surviving notebooks of

[55] *Ibid.*, p. 76; probably Matthew Bust, fellow of King's 1596–1612 and headmaster of Eton 1611–30
(Venn, I, p. 271a), although the dates are not entirely congruent.
[56] Clarke 1677, p. 76; Bowles was a fellow of Queens' between 1599 and 1606 (Venn, I, p. 193a).
[57] George Porter, fellow of Queens' 1601–35, later Regius Professor of Civil Law (Venn, III,
p. 382a) – reputed a very learned man and a great philosopher.
[58] Clarke 1677, pp. 92, 108, 113, 115; Hill 1964, pp. 443–81; Collinson 1988, pp. 60–93.
[59] Clarke 1677, p. 82.

fellows and tutors are as concerned with student accounts as they are with matters more strictly academic.[60]

To this we must add two other financial responsibilities with regard to their students which tutors acquired during Elizabeth's reign. The first was a consequence of the influx of aristocratic students. Tutors became responsible to the parents of these students for the management of the expenditure of their offspring. This could mount up, given all the 'extras' of sustenance, clothing and training which these students expected to enjoy. The second arose from a genuine desire on the part of many tutors to sustain and to continue at the university the numerous students from humble backgrounds. This might involve the college politicking necessary to obtain scholarships. It might also involve the invocation of connections outside the university in order to obtain financial support for their most able pupils. In combination all these financial responsibilities of tutors for their students were a considerable burden. They certainly required a detailed familiarity with the doings of individual students and frequent dealings between a tutor and his students on at least a weekly basis. Luckily, not all tutors were like John Dodd, who was said to have been sent into a dangerous fever as a result of being excessively vexed by a dispute with the college bursar over the payment of a considerable sum supposedly owed by one of his pupils.[61]

The best tutors were instrumental in providing a range of learning experiences within their rooms. This was in addition to the teaching which continued to take place outside the college, and the more recently established lectures within some colleges. Sometimes the distinctions between educating pupil-students and the pursuit of a tutor's own intellectual interests must have been blurred. Thus John Preston was joined by distinguished fellow students such as Dodd and Hildersham together with other godly ministers who often came to his chamber. Once he got them to pray with his pupils.[62]

We should not assume that all tutors were averse to the pursuit of the wider range of interests required in the education of an enlarged range of student types. The need to educate a broader spectrum of students permitted tutors to indulge their own interests beyond the bounds of the formal curriculum. Matthew Bust evidently indulged his interest in music with his students at King's.[63] Much of the 'extra-curricula curriculum' which developed in Cambridge during the late sixteenth

---

[60] E.g. D'Ewes, cited Collinson in Bendall *et al.* 1999, pp. 66–7; for the eighteenth century, see Brooke in *ibid.*, pp. 300–2.
[61] Clarke 1677, p. 168.   [62] *Ibid.*, p. 82.   [63] *Ibid.*, p. 76.

century was intended to meet the diverse needs of the university's new aristocratic clientele.[64] It was a curriculum that was either directly provided or indirectly managed by individual tutors. Indeed, the tuition tailored to the individual needs and capacities of aristocratic students and required by their parents could hardly have been provided by any other means. Aristocratic needs played a large part in shaping the tutorial role.

This was not necessarily at variance with the interests or expertise of either the tutors or their more career-orientated pupils. The university was perceived as a religious institution and tutors were expected first and foremost to provide religious instruction to their aristocratic charges. The distinction seems to be that in the case of these students that instruction was often at a more basic level than that required for those intent upon clerical careers. Lady Katherine Paston expected her son to 'ruminat over all thy Psalms and Chapters and textes of scripture', which long since he had learnt by heart and not to forget his *Conduit of Comfort . . .* for they will be to the[e] in time to com, both Comforters and Cownselers . . .'. She also considered that the college provided 'such excelent means' to prepare him to receive his first communion.[65] William Denton expressed to Ralph Verney his hope 'that divinity and especially the pracktique (for knowledge alone doth not save) be ever att both ends of your other studys, for without that there can be noe true content in any study'.[66] When Robert Wilton sent his son Thomas up to Cambridge from Norfolk in April 1621 he confided to his notebook the hope that God would bless him 'with a gr[a]cious progresse in grace and learning in the dewe feare of his heavenly name to my comfort heere & to bothe our endles joyes & comfort everlastingly'.[67] With these ends in view it was only natural that parents should seek to place their sons with 'a very godly and Religious Tutor'.[68] Francis Gardiner wrote to his son's tutor that 'Above all, my desire is, that Sundays, fast days, and the like, may have their particular employment in divine studies, beside his constant reading the scriptures each morning and evening.'[69] William Whiston recalled that in his time as a tutor, in the evenings he sometimes read over to his pupils

---

[64] For a discussion of the aristocratic curriculum, see above, pp. 131–9.

[65] Hughey 1941, pp. 83, 90–1, 102. From Oxford, Anthony Bagot informed his mother that on Saturdays and Sundays he and his companions read parts of Nowell's *Catechisme*, 'wherein I trust we shall so profite as shall be to your desyer and our owne furthereunce' (Folger Shakespeare Library MS L.a.36).

[66] Microfilm of uncatalogued Verney MSS, Claydon House, Bucks., William Denton to Ralph Verney, *c.* 1630.

[67] CUL Buxton MSS, Box 96, Notebook of Robert Wilton, p. 155.

[68] Clarke 1677, p. 115.   [69] Cary 1842, p. 152.

Dr Hammond's *Practical Catechism*.[70] Clearly, for those parents intent upon ensuring that their offspring were provided with a basic induction into the Christian faith the development of the tutorial system at Cambridge furnished them with a very flexible instrument with which to achieve their ends.

Parents, tutors and students all sought, in the main, a balanced diet of divine and secular learning. Lady Katherine Paston expressed to her son the hope that 'that is the plase I trust shall do the[e] good more ways than on[e]', and that her son should come 'from that plase adorned bothe with devine and humayne Learninge', imbued with 'vertuous and Civill behaviour' and 'furnished with grasses as a bee comms laden to her hive'. Her hope that he should 'be furnished with those liberall sciences, which that Nurcery affordethe to the studious and best mindes'[71] would have met with the concurrence of Brian Twyne's father, to whom the son was forced to justify himself: 'I studie not divinity too much. I say unto you father I doe not so . . . I have spent my time in such sort as one of my standinge doth reqyre it, [in] good Liberall artes', although he was brought to admit that 'I have by stelth obtained to some meane knowledge in the Hebrewe toonge.'[72]

THE TUTORIAL GROUP

It is true that a few great pupil-mongers such as Preston specialised in the acquisition of socially prestigious students the majority of whom entered the college as fellow-commoners.[73] However, there were good practical reasons why most tutors would have wished to have at least a few students from humble backgrounds. Most prosaically, such students were able to provide many among the multitude of personal menial services required on a daily basis in a non-technological society. These services ranged from running errands to lighting fires to transcribing notes to mixing the tutor's ink.[74] Moreover, it was not just the tutor who required these services. The more prestigious among his students would not have cared to demean their status by manual labours on their own behalf. The

---

[70] Whiston 1749, p. 10. The biographer of John Conant, rector of Exeter College, Oxford, remarked that 'his first and chief Care was to plant ye fear of God in ye youth there to see that they had well laid ye foundation of sincere Piety & true Religion' (BL Add. MS 22579, fo. 10). While he was a fellow of Queen's, Oxford, Barnaby Potter enjoyed a reputation as 'a very carefull Tutor to many worthy Gentlemans sons, whom he trained up in Learning, but especially in true religion' (Clarke 1677, p. 154).

[71] Hughey 1941, pp. 65, 72, 74, 83.   [72] Twyne 1927, p. 214.   [73] Clarke 1677, p. 86.

[74] An unusual example was that of the Blessed John Fingley, who maintained himself in the Caius of Thomas Legge in the 1570s as the master's butler (Brooke 1988).

inference to be drawn from a few case studies is that some aristocratic students actually patronised at university boys from their home neighbourhood. It is possible to trace some careers in which one student entered a college as a fellow-commoner. On the same date another also entered as a sizar. They both came from the same parish, had the same schoolteacher, and were entered to the same tutor. In one instance the sizar subsequently went on to take a degree and to be presented to a living by his former fellow-student.

The repetition of regulations banning the keeping by students of personal servants in colleges testifies to the felt need for their services. At the same time these regulations stated explicitly that the practice curtailed the opportunities for poor students to work their way through college. The way round this ban was for the aristocratic student to acquire the services of a sizar from among the group of students overseen by his tutor.

There were other pressures on tutors to accept students from humble backgrounds. Analysis of the shared geographical backgrounds or family connections of many students and tutors suggests that what was being articulated by these associations were the mutual obligations of patronage. The favours done by a tutor for a kinsman or neighbour in his home locality helped to maintain the connections which at some future date might be of benefit to the tutor when he was looking to preferment at the end of his fellowship. More immediately, the acquisition by tutors of pupils who were personally obliged to them helped to bolster the position of fellows in the factional rivalries with which some colleges were riven.[75]

There were also non-material inducements for a tutor to acquire pupil-students from humble backgrounds. There must have been an appreciation by academics of bright boys committed to their own intellectual and theological concerns. Here were youths in their own image. Moreover, it was not until the 1620s that fellows from second-generation clerical backgrounds became a strong presence within the university – and even then many or most came from non-clerical families and themselves experienced the translation to a different kind of community. A degree of empathy must have prevailed. Humphrey Tyndall, president of Queens', was said to have 'loved a scholar, and was glad of any opportunity to shew it'.[76]

---

[75] But it is important to remember that not all sizars came from humble homes (Brooke 1985/1996, pp. 117–18; Venn 1913, ch. 9; below, p. 493).

[76] Clarke 1677, p. 78. Arthur Hildersham was launched on his career by his schoolmaster, John Desborough, who 'took great affection to him for his wit and disposition' (Clarke 1677, p. 115). Desborough had himself been a scholar at Trinity in the heady days at Cambridge in the 1560s. He was headmaster at Saffron Walden between 1573 and 1607 (Venn, II, p. 44b).

Finally, there was the force of the religious imperative. Until the reaction which followed the unleashing of the excesses of religious enthusiasm in the mid-seventeenth century, there was a widespread desire to provide a preaching and a proselytising ministry. Although not meritocratic in intent, it was so in effect.[77] Most of the first two or three generations of this new ministry were recruited from relatively humble backgrounds. This imperative created a moral responsibility to educate those who were able and likely to prove lively instruments of further reformation. These were they 'whom God raised up and fitted to send forth into his Harvest, to gather his Corn, then ripe for the Sickle, into his Barn'.[78] This combined with a new enthusiasm for education among the aristocracy which arose from a series of separate motives.[79] It took place at a time when there was not yet that distinct physical separation of social groups which was to emerge in the late seventeenth century and which is reflected in the segregation of social space within large households and in the distancing imposed by the emparkment of the great house.[80] In the early seventeenth century there was simply more propinquity among social groups.

These values and attitudes were realised in the schools from which students came to the university and they were perpetuated in the tutorial groups into which they entered once they arrived. John Ball eked out his meagre income as a cleric by keeping a school within his own household. He took not only the children of 'the poor neighbours, (for he refused none who were willing to learn)' but also 'persons of better quality sent unto him; some whereof were tabled in his own house, and the rest placed in the neighbourhood'.[81] We have already seen that in his days as a student William Bradshaw received financial assistance from 'some Gentlemen his fellow-pupils under the same Tutor'.[82]

The educational responsibilities of tutors extended beyond the confines of Cambridge and did not conclude at term's end. We have already encountered John Preston taking his fellow-commoner students on an ostensibly educational tour of the impressive gallery at Audley End. Apparently trips for art and architectural appreciation were a regular practice on his part.[83] In the long vacation it became customary for fellows to visit their friends and patrons in the country. A variant of this was to take a

---

[77] Thus, although he had 'little acquaintace' there when he was sent up to Jesus as a sizar in 1572, John Dodd's studiousness led to his election first as a scholar and then as a fellow. Venn does not record the scholarship attributed to him by Clarke (Clarke 1677, p. 168; Venn, II, p. 50a; *DNB*, which depends mainly on Clarke).

[78] Clarke 1677, p. 133.   [79] Above, pp. 131–46.   [80] Girouard 1980, pp. 145–9.

[81] Clarke 1677, p. 149.   [82] *Ibid.*, p. 25.   [83] *Ibid.*, p. 86; above, p. 320.

favoured student on a tour of a part of the country with which he was not familiar.[84] Among the not inconsiderable number of the religiously committed, the spiritual oversight provided by tutors within the university was continued at a distance when their charges went forth to proselytise. Simeon Ash had been a pupil of Thomas Hooker at Emmanuel. After graduating he was 'directed and encouraged in his Ministry, by his great Care and Love'.[85]

In the late sixteenth century the Calvinist doctrine of predestination became the accepted doctrine of the English church. For all the disputes over other matters such as church discipline and government, for the greater part of Elizabeth's reign there was a general acceptance of this doctrinal principle. As Whitgift himself acknowledged towards the end of his life, whatever differences he had had with his opponents at Cambridge they had all agreed on this fundamental of doctrine.[86] In the 1580s and especially the 1590s Cambridge University was to have a seminal role in originating the doctrinal debates that in the first four decades of the seventeenth century were to split the church as a whole.[87] But even when this split did come there was always one faction at Cambridge as in the country as a whole – and in both probably the largest faction – which continued to subscribe to a belief in predestination. The particular form of belief in predestination among radical Protestants served to create circumstances in which the years a young man spent at university, and more particularly his relationship with his tutor, took on a crucial importance.

The structure of belief among the godly required that those who were saved received assurance of their salvation by being 'born again in Christ'. This was achieved solely through the assurance of his only saving grace. The acceptance into the 'fellowship of the Saints' required a specific conversion experience. It was often in the hot-house atmosphere of the university that this experience occurred. Among fellow adolescents and under the guidance of their godly tutor, idealistic young men received the psychologically liberating assurance that they were not, after all, destined for eternal damnation. The achievement of an assurance of a state of grace was a source of anxiety not only for the individual but also for those responsible for his education and training. Hugh Clark rejoiced that he 'lived to see to his great comfort, the work of grace wrought in the hearts

---

[84] Clarke 1677, p. 92.
[85] *Ibid.*, p. 123. Hooker was to be silenced by Laud in 1626. He migrated to New England in 1633. He was Dixie Fellow at Emmanuel between 1609 and 1618 (Venn, II, p. 403b). Ashe had been placed with Hooker by Arthur Hildersham (Venn, I, p. 43b).
[86] Trinity College Library, MS O.3.53, fo. 9: Whitgift to Hutton, 7 June 1600.
[87] Below, pp. 441–7; Morgan 1983.

of all his seven children'.[88] The 'conversion experience' was one of 'those memorable passages' in a man's life which usually were recorded in the autobiographical and biographical fragments which often accompanied the post-mortem publication of sermons and other religious works.[89]

In the case of John Preston, his first tutor, Matthew Bust of King's, had introduced him to the study of music, but it was his second tutor, Oliver Bowles of Queens', who weaned him from music and on to a more solid academic diet. Bowles was recalled as a man who combined two characteristics which had close associations at that time: he was both a 'very godly and learned man, and a noted and carefull Tutor'.[90]

AFTER 1640

Not unnaturally, there were considerable fluctuations in the student population of Cambridge between 1640 and 1660 – with an initial sharp decline followed by a marked recovery in the 1650s.[91] But after 1660 the numbers of students at Cambridge steadily declined down to and beyond 1750; and it was indeed not until the mid-nineteenth century that the peak figures of the 1620s were matched and passed. Although a few colleges – most notably St Catharine's[92] – had expanding numbers in the late seventeenth century, most grew smaller. Some of the decline must be due to the growing polarisation between the Church of England and Dissent: Cambridge was for Anglicans alone – or almost alone. Others might come to study; only Anglicans could take their degrees or seek fellowships. But what seems above all to have happened is that the more secular element which had flooded into the university in the sixteenth and early seventeenth centuries gradually withdrew. Where the details can and have been studied, one finds that the solid core of ordinands has survived; the men who went into the law or to managing their estates have gone elsewhere, many of them to the Inns of Court, without the intervening spell at Cambridge so popular in earlier decades. As student numbers fell the proportion of ordinands grew. In Caius – one of the least clerical colleges in the sixteenth century, and one of those where medicine flourished – by the 1780s a community of nearly fifty included only two physicians: the rest were all heading for the clerical profession.

---

[88] Clarke 1677, p. 131.

[89] *Ibid.*, p. 150. This prefatory matter was sometimes, although not always, the source for the truncated biographies brought together by Samuel Clarke during the much changed circumstances of the Restoration in his pious but despondent retrospective on the heroic generations of English Protestantism.

[90] Clarke 1677, p. 76.　　[91] See below, pp. 464–5.　　[92] See above, pp. 33–5.

Within our own period, in the early eighteenth century, Daniel Water-land's *Advice to a Young Student* presupposes that his audience is mainly clerical.[93]

Smaller numbers affected the tutors in a variety of ways. The decline was not accompanied by an equivalent decline in the number of fellows – which tended to be based on statutes and endowments, and to remain stable so long as funds permitted. Thus the need for fellows to be tutors and to teach inevitably declined; and for many fellows between the late seventeenth and the late nineteenth century a fellowship was a prize, carrying a modest stipend and even more modest duties; many came to be non-resident, and the fellowship need only terminate with matrimony or death, whichever came first.[94] Declining numbers meant also a great increase in available space, an end to the days when three or four students shared a room, when the tutor himself lived like an older student, surrounded by his charges. The tutor (and many of his pupils) came to have a room, or suite of rooms, to himself; the society became a little more diffuse, the tutor less intimate with his charges. At the same time, the decline in numbers evidently bred anxiety in the colleges about recruitment, and pupil-mongering (as it was called) – luring pupils to one's tutorial group – was an essential art for the tutor in one of the smaller or less well known colleges. Between 1708 and 1717 Daniel Waterland 'was responsible for the teaching of 64 of the 74 undergraduates admitted'[95] to Magdalene – and doubtless in substantial measure for recruiting them. Whereas the majority of the tutors who lived cheek by jowl with their charges in sixteenth- and early seventeenth-century chambers were young men, teaching in a relatively brief interval between the MA and the country living, it seems likely that an increasing proportion of the tutors in the early eighteenth century were older, more experienced men, dedicated to a life of teaching and celibacy. I say 'seems' because we do not have reliable lists of tutors for most colleges. Though tutors and tutorships were sometimes recognised by college statutes, they were not formal college offices in this period; the tutors were commonly appointed by the master, not by a college meeting; and although they had been central to the life of the colleges for centuries before 1550 and remained so for centuries after 1750, it is not till much later that their appointment is regularly recorded.

---

[93] See below, pp. 526, 529–31; Brooke 1985/1996, pp. 186–7; Waterland 1730 and 1856, IV, pp. 393–415 (written not long after 1705, publ. 1730, 1740); Duffy in Cunich *et al.* 1994, pp. 160–1; Gascoigne 1989, pp. 177–8 – also referring to Johnson 1735, an interesting supplement to Waterland on studies at Magdalene; Searby 1997, p. 152 and nn. 13–14.

[94] On fellows and their duties, see Searby 1997, pp. 94–117.

[95] Duffy in Cunich *et al.* 1994, p. 160.

Thus E.S. Shuckburgh, who knew the Emmanuel records well, was deceived by the lack of evidence he encountered in formal records, and by the wealth of evidence provided by the notebooks of Henry Hubbard, to suppose that Hubbard had been sole tutor. Following a clue given by Dr Sarah Brewer, I was able to reconstruct a complete list of Emmanuel tutors from the 1730s to the 1770s – when they began to be noted (as they were in Caius) in the matriculation registers.[96] It is clear that there were normally two tutors, but that other fellows occasionally acted as tutor – this apart from private tuition provided by men like Richard Hurd (later bishop of Worcester) to the well-to-do. Most of the Emmanuel tutors between 1730 and 1750 were young men waiting for a living – and they departed, some after a few months of tutorship, some after a few years. But Henry Hubbard, appointed in 1736, was to be tutor for thirty years – until 1767. He was a bachelor, and dedicated to the work of the college and the university: he was university registrary for twenty years, and exceedingly active in university business. A contemporary said of him that he would die with a *non-placet* on his lips – a vote against a motion, or grace, in the Senate House; but he was a popular figure and a notable character. His account book shows that he was largely responsible for the financial affairs of the students, probably throughout the college.[97]

Peter Searby has suggested that the decline in the number of tutors in Cambridge in this period was due to the increasing need for specialist teaching in mathematics.[98] Doubtless it was necessary for tutors to be skilled in its intricacies; but as time passed, more and more students came to look for yet more expert and personal guidance from the private coaches who were to dominate the examination scene a century later. There were already private tutors in the eighteenth century, and had been long before, employed by rich and noble families to ensure some measure of good behaviour and study in their sons – and, above all, that they did not make imprudent marriages in Cambridge.[99] But the full development of the private tutor or coach as a regular part of the teaching scene came later. Meanwhile, the tutors were commonly not specialists: they were expected to be able to teach to a reasonable depth in the classics, in philosophy, in mathematics and other sciences and in theology. The examinations were exceedingly specialised; the curriculum was not.[100] Thus while leading wranglers John Oldershaw and Robert Cory were to be successively tutors of Emmanuel at the end of the eighteenth century,

---

[96] Brooke in Bendall *et al.* 1999, pp. 582–3.   [97] Brooke in *ibid.*, pp. 301–2, 582–3.
[98] On the developments leading to the Mathematical Tripos, see Searby 1997, pp. 150–60.
[99] See above, pp. 318–20.   [100] See esp. Wordsworth 1877; Gascoigne 1989.

their colleague William Bennet was a notable classicist whose lecture notes have survived to impress us as they must have impressed his pupils.[101]

The changes in student numbers and teaching needs were clearly an important part of the process which led to a great reduction in the number of tutors, so that by 1721 there may have been only forty-two in the whole university.[102] It is said that in Trinity there were twelve tutors in 1725, while Bentley and his remarkable educational reforms still lived, but eight in 1745 and only two in 1755.[103] Thus the educational work of the colleges fell more and more into the hands of a small group of men, some perhaps as idle as Gibbon believed his tutor to be,[104] but many deeply involved in the welfare and teaching of their pupils.

Three unusual sources may enable us to interview a group of remarkable tutors at work. The celebrated correspondence between Benjamin Whichcote, provost of King's, and his former tutor, now master of Emmanuel, Anthony Tuckney, takes us to the heart of the relationship: it shows that the intimate affection which naturally grew between a tutor and his most brilliant pupil could survive the progressive revelation of deep theological differences. The correspondence of Dr William Bagge, physician and tutor and president of Caius, is of a more humdrum quality; but it reveals a sympathetic and deeply conscientious young tutor holding together a college suffering the agonies of the puritan revolution, preserving a measure of routine and continuity in a rapidly changing world. A generation later, one of the most celebrated Cambridge divines of the first half of the eighteenth century, Daniel Waterland, tutor – later master – of Magdalene, provided a blueprint for a tutor's instructions to his pupils, and their manner of life and their curriculum, which opens a window into the pastoral care and teaching philosophy of one of the most powerful and penetrating minds in the Cambridge of Newton and Bentley.[105]

We shall presently observe the extraordinary variety of religious opinions which grew from the stimulating conversation of the chambers of puritan Emmanuel in the age of puritan revolution.[106] Theologically, the extremes were the hard-line Calvinism of Anthony Tuckney, tutor in the 1630s, master from 1644 to 1653, and the leading Cambridge Platonist Benjamin Whichcote, student in the 1630s, provost of King's in

---

[101] Brooke in Bendall *et al.* 1999, pp. 300–4.   [102] Searby 1997, p. 125.
[103] *Ibid.*, p. 121.   [104] Gibbon 1907, p. 44; also in Murray 1896, p. 67.
[105] What follows is based on Whichcote 1753; cf. Collinson in Bendall *et al.* 1999, pp. 259–62. For Bagge's correspondence see Z.N. Brooke in Brooke 1985/1996, pp. 131–40. For Waterland, see above, n. 93, and below, n. 113.
[106] See pp. 475–82.

the 1640s and 1650s. They were not divided by religious practice – both were equally at home in the puritan simplicity of Emmanuel chapel; nor by doctrines of church and state – for at the Restoration in 1660 both Tuckney (now master of St John's) and Whichcote, provost of King's, were removed from their offices to make way for high churchmen. But Tuckney believed in a strict form of predestination which divided the saved and the damned in divine foreknowledge; Whichcote that God's design was that all might be saved. Tuckney's theology was starkly biblical; Whichcote believed that the light of reason might lighten the darkness of theological speculation. When God created man, he did not create 'a sorry worthless piece for no use', but a creature capable of reasoning, and 'to go against reason is to go against God'.[107] When Whichcote was vice-chancellor in 1651 he made a Commencement address which Tuckney interpreted as a polemic against his own address in 1650; and he wrote to rebuke his old pupil. Whichcote claimed that he was saying nothing new: that he had said it all in exercises in Emmanuel chapel fourteen years before (that is, in 1637 or so). 'You were then but a yonge divine', retorted Tuckney, ' . . . studious and pious and very loving of me . . . but somewhat cloudie in your expressions.'[108] The affection remained, the clouds grew darker, and the differences could no longer be ascribed to youthful enthusiasm. Plato had taken the place of Calvin and the Bible.[109] Tuckney was aware that Whichcote's other tutor, Thomas Hill, now master of Trinity, was on his side, but that Whichcote was supported by a group of his fellow students, 'the Cambridge Platonists'.

William Bagge was one of the ablest of the many physicians who flourished in Caius in the late sixteenth and seventeenth centuries; he became a senior fellow of the college in 1651; he was an MD, and established a flourishing medical practice in the city. In the 1650s he was a tutor, and from 1655 till his early death in 1657 president of Caius – that is to say, the master's deputy. As a physician and a layman, he was not beset by the sectarian demands of the age: he could get on with the work of running the college undistracted by the puritan inquisitors. And he seems to have been on good terms with puritans of various shades of outlook, for he was evidently trusted by the master of Caius, the former army chaplain and enthusiast William Dell.[110] Bagge left his remarkable library – or a

---

[107] Quoted by Collinson in Bendall *et al.* 1999, p. 260.
[108] *Ibid.*, p. 260, quoting Whichcote 1753, pp. 12–13, 28, 36.
[109] *Ibid.*, p. 261; cf. e.g. Whichcote 1753, pp. 38–9, 128–9. On the Cambridge Platonists, see Collinson in Bendall *et al.* 1999, pp. 256–64, and refs. on p. 256 n. 1, esp. to Cragg 1968 and Kroll *et al.* 1992.
[110] On Dell see Brooke 1985/1996, pp. 127–31; Walker 1970.

great part of it – to the college; and from its fly-leaves and pastedowns the assistant librarian of the 1930s, Donald Paige, extracted about seventy letters, clearly from Bagge's files, for most of them are addressed to him, which were studied by the then librarian, Z.N. Brooke, in a paper ultimately published in his son's *History* of Caius.[111] Some of the letters are from grateful parents, some from pupils eager to please him; they all testify to his kindly character and to the responsible manner in which he provided an element of stability and continuity in a time of insecurity and rapid change. The letters from pupils are mostly in rhetorical Latin, to prove that they had learned the lessons of grammar and rhetoric which still formed the basis of the education even of potential medical students. But those who had attained their BAs took the liberty of writing in English. Thus Henry Harcocks BA, in 'a letter which Jane Austen's Mr Collins might have been proud to write':[112]

> Worthy Tutor,
> Rather than show myselfe ungratefull, an illiterate pen (undeckt with flosculent Rhetoricke) have here presumed to commend these impolish'd characters to the candid eye of your acceptance; which though rusticity of style may prompt you to reject with one hand, yett in this am I emboldned, that so ingenuous a nature, so affable a disposition will not be wanting to imbrace with the other

and he goes on to assure his tutor that he will pay his debts when he returns to college – and (in his ingenuous fashion) to petition for a junior fellowship. But though Mr Harcocks failed to win the fellowship he sought, his letter and others less flowery reveal to us as it were in a mirror a genial tutor greatly valued as a good friend and a good tutor by his students and well respected by the parents of his charges.

Daniel Waterland of Magdalene was perhaps the most respected tutor in Cambridge in the early eighteenth century. He was also a man of deep learning, a prolific theologian, strongly orthodox but relatively broad minded. He had no hesitation in recommending the scientific works of Newton and Whiston, little as he cared for their theology. In his warm commendation of the sermons of Archbishop Tillotson, he coolly observed: 'There is one or two points of doctrine, particularly that of hell-torments, justly exceptionable.' Hell-torments apart, there was little or nothing in Tillotson at all unfitting the eyes of a second-year undergraduate.[113]

---

[111] Brooke 1985/1996, pp. 131–40.   [112] *Ibid.*, pp. 136–7.
[113] Waterland 1730, pp. 22–5. For later editions and commentaries see above, n. 93, esp. Duffy in Cunich *et al.* 1994, pp. 160–2, on the *Advice*.

Not long after 1705 Waterland composed for his pupils a small pamphlet full of practical advice. In 1729 it was pirated, and so he felt obliged to print an authorised version, edited to suit a wider audience. 'If a tutor is absent, or busy, or forgetful, or indispos'd, or any other ways hinder'd, the student may go on in his business and his duty, if he will but carefully observe the rules that are here prescrib'd.'[114] He proceeds to lay down rules of conduct and a fairly precise menu of reading for a four-year course to the BA. It is a precious document, for it not only reveals the true nature of the curriculum in early eighteenth-century Cambridge but qualifies two at least of the most widely held views about the Cambridge education of the day – that there was little or no theological education and that serious use of Newton's works was confined to Trinity, Clare and Corpus.[115]

'The generality of students are intended to be clergymen.'[116] He omits law and medicine, because students are few and best dealt with individually by their tutor. His pamphlet is for ordinands. Now, it has often been observed that a high proportion of the students of eighteenth- and early nineteenth-century Cambridge went on to be ordained, and that a curriculum which came to have mathematics as its pinnacle was hardly designed to prepare men for the altar or the pulpit, let alone for their pastoral duties. Ironically, the teaching of pastoral theology had (in principle) been abolished by the Reformation, for it had been a branch of canon law, and the closing of the school of canon law in 1535 had brought to an end its place in the curriculum. In any case, the number of students who went on even to a BD in the seventeenth century was very few; the formal study of theology was for a small minority.[117] But Waterland took it for granted – as did many of his successors down to the mid-nineteenth century – that an arts degree which included a good deal of mathematics and natural sciences was an essential foundation – and beside it, 'Some foundation should be laid in Divinity, within the first four years . . . Because many design for orders, soon after they take a degree; and must therefore be prepar'd in that.'[118] The minimum time allotted comprises every Sunday and holiday, when no work should be done for the arts degree; but those who are to be ordained immediately after the BA will need more time than this. The basic fare in Divinity is the English sermon – 'the easiest, plainest and most entertaining of any books of divinity,'[119]

---

[114] Waterland 1730, p. 2.
[115] See esp. Gascoigne 1989, ch. 6. Gascoigne does also refer to the *Advice* on p. 178; and notes on pp. 143–4 Newton's close friendship with Sir John Ellys, tutor and later master of Caius.
[116] Waterland 1730, p. 7.   [117] Gascoigne 1989, p. 264.
[118] Waterland 1730, p. 12.   [119] *Ibid.*, p. 13.

and one Sunday gives time enough to read and abridge two sermons. It is striking that – although the student is expected to read the Bible morning and night and attend morning and evening prayers in college chapel, Septuagint in hand – no commentaries on Scripture are prescribed; and Pearson on the creeds and Burnet on the Articles are reserved for the later months of the fourth year. There is as much good divinity in good English sermons as anywhere; and they have the special advantage of teaching the student by example the best method of planning a sermon and providing models of 'the English stile and language'.[120] The sermons Waterland commended were from a remarkably wide range of orthodox or moderately orthodox preachers of his own or the immediately preceding generation: the high churchman John Sharp, archbishop of York (1645–1714); Archbishop Tillotson, though Tillotson is usually reckoned a Latitudinarian; Robert South, though South's sermons were 'somewhat too full of wit and satyre'.[121] But they also included the 'very exact and judicious' sermons of Benjamin Hoadly, a theologian of much wider latitude than Tillotson, who had been a tutor at St Catharine's shortly before Waterland wrote – with a moderate Latitudinarian, Edward Stillingfleet, to follow, balanced by the high church Francis Atterbury.[122] His readiness for the student to read Latitudinarians is striking, for he is generally supposed (not without reason) to have been the hammer of the Latitudinarians in Cambridge. In the last edition of the *Advice*, produced at the end of his life in 1740, Waterland added to the already formidable list of sermons, and the additions included Bishop Sherlock, who had been master of St Catharine's early in the century – one of the most notable of eighteenth-century preachers, whose sermons 'represent a plain, intelligible, clear-headed, reasonable, imaginative interpretation of the Christian gospel', with a strong appeal to reason and the moral teaching of the gospel; they justly found a place among Jane Austen's favourite reading.[123]

After three years of sermons came more solid fare in the fourth, including the fundamental classics of Anglican belief: the *Exposition of the Creed* of 1659 by John Pearson, the Cambridge divine who had been bishop of Chester from 1673 to 1686. Waterland also strongly advised further study for ordinands after the BA: they are to 'lay aside all other studies for a few months' to master Hebrew – but Waterland's further list of study, if ordination is not too immediate, largely consists of classical authors and

[120] *Ibid.*
[121] *Ibid.*, p. 22. For these divines, and Hoadly, see *DNB*; for the Latitude men, below, pp. 522–5.
[122] Waterland 1730, p. 22.   [123] Brooke 1999b, p. 130; Waterland 1856, IV, p. 415.

Newton: it is here that the student is set to work on the *Principia* and on Newton's *Algebra*.

Newton was thus the culmination of Waterland's arts course; and we are immediately aware of two of the most striking features of Cambridge at the turn of the seventeenth and eighteenth centuries. Most of the teaching had been concentrated into the hands of a few professional tutors, and this had freed the other fellows of the colleges to be idle or industrious as they wished – and so Newton came to have the freedom he needed for some of the most spectacular intellectual adventures which have occurred within the colleges of Cambridge.[124] As for the tutors, they had taken the syllabus into their own hands. Waterland himself, when pressed late in life by Bishop Gibson to prescribe that ordinands should spend their fourth year in the study of theology, replied that the course of studies for the four years 'is fixed by custom and by the oath they take'.[125] But his own *Advice* shows that custom was not so rigid: it prescribed what the college tutors wished; and although there was a conservative traditional element in it, it was more open to change by personal initiative than at any other time in the history of Cambridge. The four-year course laid down by Waterland comprised what he defined as 'Philosophy' and 'Classics'. He seems to have assumed that the student arrived from his grammar school with a basic knowedge of Latin and Greek grammar: there is no prescription of basic textbooks in these languages as there is with mathematics and other scientific disciplines; their place (strangely enough) is taken by a light course in Terence, followed (as in old-fashioned twentieth-century syllabuses) by Xenophon. The students were then taken through an ample diet of classical authors, concentrating in early days on those best suited to teach the arts of rhetoric. One can discern some relics of the medieval arts course still: its breadth, its emphasis on grammar, rhetoric and logic, with mathematics and astronomy having a crucial role – and with philosophy (in something more like the modern sense) as a higher plane in the arts course. But Aristotle has totally disappeared, and among the sciences Euclid has replaced him – closely followed by other, more recent mathematicians, culminating in Newton. The natural sciences provided the bone structure of 'philosophy' – as the name of the Cambridge Philosophical Society still bears witness – and mathematics is on the way to becoming the centre of the arts course: the Senate House examination slowly evolved in the early eighteenth century, until, from the 1740s, it was primarily mathematical, a prelude

---

[124] See below, pp. 484–7, 494–501.   [125] Quoted in Gascoigne 1989, pp. 263–4.

to the Mathematical Tripos.[126] Meanwhile, the arts course at Magdalene was pretty much what Waterland made it – and this seems to have
had two curious consequences: first, it made possible inspired innovation
by imaginative tutors or educational reformers like Richard Bentley;[127]
but its very informality also made possible the decline of the BA from
a four-year to a three-year, part-time course, as the eighteenth century
went on. It was always the case that for 'reading men' there was plentiful
fare, and ample encouragement from the more enlightened tutors – so
long as the students were not distracted by the numerous rival attractions
preferred by many of the increasing numbers of fellow-commoners and
noblemen.[128]

Thus 'philosophy' involved an ample range of scientific instruction,
from Euclid and Newton's *Trigonometry* in the first year to Newton's
Optics and Gregory's *Astronomy* in the fourth.[129] It also included some
books of philosophy in our sense of the word: almost no classical philosophy – no Aristotle, no Plato – save for Cicero's philosophical works in
the fourth year; and nothing of the most dangerous and influential of the
seventeenth-century moderns, Descartes. But Descartes' disciple John
Locke has a conspicuous place. After an introduction to astronomy, the
second-year student is let loose on Locke's *Essay concerning Human Understanding* (1690). 'Locke's Human Understanding must be read, being a
book so much (and I add so justly) valued, however faulty the author may
have been in other writings.'[130] The 'other writings', one suspects, included his defence of religious toleration, and his defence of reason as the
only safe foundation for religious belief: his belief in the reasonableness of
Christianity was more moderately and (to Waterland and his like) more
acceptably presented in the *Essay*. A visitor from medieval Cambridge
would have been startled to find a stout supporter of orthodox Christianity (without the pope, needless to say) who had abandoned Aristotle
to embrace John Locke.

Thus, in a great variety of ways, Daniel Waterland's *Advice to a young
student with a method of study* . . . is an outstanding monument to the
theory and practice of tutorial instruction in early eighteenth-century
Cambridge.

[126] Searby 1997, pp. 158–9; Gascoigne 1984.
[127] For Bentley, see below, pp. 506–7. But significantly Bentley's reforms were collegiate, though
he hoped to see them influence the university at large – and even so notable a reformer as
William Powell, tutor and master of St John's, was to say in 1774: 'the business of education . . .
is conducted with more success, as it has been conducted for some ages, under the domestic
discipline of each college than it could be under the direction of the Senate' (quoted Searby
1997, p. 164).
[128] Searby 1997, p. 62.   [129] And much else throughout.   [130] Waterland 1730, p. 23.

Chapter 10

THE CAMBRIDGE ELECTORAL
SCENE IN A CULTURE
OF PATRONAGE

We have seen how one set of relationships between state, society and the universities was formulated in the circumstances of the 1520s, 1530s and 1540s.[1] At a less formal level other aspects of those relationships were forged in what were for the universities the increasingly intense circumstances of the reigns of Elizabeth and the first two Stuarts. This becomes evident through an examination of the practices that came to prevail in these years in the management and manipulation of academic elections. It is these which are the focus of the present chapter. Furthermore, in examining the electoral scene in early modern Cambridge we need to understand it within the broader context of the wider political culture of which it was part: here we may be afforded glimpses of the working of elections within the context of a patron–client society. But at the same time a scrutiny of this particular academic arena may well illuminate aspects of that wider political culture. Moreover, it may well be that in looking at elections at Cambridge we will be better able to understand something of the evolution of attitudes to elections over the much longer term.

Today, with us elections have an iconic status. On the one hand there were the images of long and patient queues of first-time voters in the townships of South Africa. Beamed around the world, those images were presented as a hope-filled token of the peaceful alternative to bloody revolution – as indeed they were. On the other hand there is much anguish and soul-searching within the established liberal democracies when, as is currently the case, their complacent (or alienated?) electorates fail to exercise a right hard-purchased by the struggle of their predecessors. Nor is this status of elections as the touchstone of the acceptable all that recent a phenomenon. When, some 200 years ago, a group of provincial English gentlemen established a new state and then set about building a new nation on the eastern fringes of the American continent, they had

---

[1] Above, chapter 1.

343

become so enamoured of enlightenment notions that they settled upon arrangements whereby most public officials were elected, from the dog-catcher even to the head of state. In short, we have come to assume that elections are a marker of modernity. Consequently the implication seems to be that elections were no part of the pre-modern world. This is not true.

At present a debate exists among historians of conventional politics of the Tudor and early Stuart period as to the extent to which parliamentary elections were contested and votes took place.[2] There is an argument that at this level elections were seen as a bad thing and that differences were often underplayed in deference to a notion of consensus. However, the seemingly cataclysmic events of the mid-seventeenth century may have replaced this model of behaviour with one that was more openly 'conflictual'. Certainly, we have understood for over thirty years now that by the late seventeenth and early eighteenth centuries, the political scene is characterised by the 'rage of party' and, consequently, by disputed and highly animated elections.[3] With an electorate that was ever increasing in size there must have been a high level of participation among those who were qualified to vote and, as we now realise, a wider penumbra of awareness of elections, and issues in elections, among even those who were not permitted to vote.[4] Moreover, even though elections at this level were for a national institution – parliament – elections were by their nature local affairs and 'political' issues permeated the provinces. But perhaps an undue amount of attention has been focussed on forms of election which can be made to approximate to those which we know today and which are lineally linked to our own accustomed practices. The pre-modern electoral scene was much wider than this.

Certainly, in large chartered cities such as Norwich the appointment of officials required an unceasing round of elections. Indeed, as is indicated by the evidence from both a city such as Norwich and an institution such as Cambridge University, their constitutions assumed and their practices demonstrated that they were incessantly about the business of elections. Elections were always asimmer and intermittently they boiled over in ways that leave us the evidence for what was going on in the pot. But there was also a world of participation and voting beyond the sphere of those institutions that had formal constitutions. Thus, some historians

---

[2] Hirst 1975; Kishlansky 1986; Underdown 1996.
[3] Harris 1993; Black 1990; see also Hill 1976; Knights 1994. The origins of what was once revisionist and is now the established view lie in Plumb 1967; see also Speck 1970; Holmes 1987. For the new political milieu, see Wilson 1995.
[4] Colley 1982; Rogers 1990, 1994; Wilson 1995.

of early colonial America have argued that the practices of communal organisation found there represent the export of the experience of old England.[5] More recently, English historians have taken up this theme and identified forms of communal participation thriving in the 'small communities' of manor and parish.[6] To these one might add two further loci of participation. First, there is the case of the gentry in the meetings of county quarter sessions. Over the course of the sixteenth century these institutions acquired administrative and political dimensions that were added to their judicial functions. Elections may not have occurred but voting certainly did.[7] What has not yet received adequate attention is the participatory opportunities afforded by the semi-private institutions such as the London livery companies or the craft guilds within other towns and cities.[8] We need to confront the untidy possibility that the hierarchic and in many ways theoretically authoritarian structures of the *ancien régime* – in England at least – also accommodated a remarkable number and frequency of elections.

In examining the entire gamut of elections perhaps we need to distinguish between what might be usefully characterised as 'public' elections and 'private' elections. Today, there may be a more comprehensive right to participate in public elections; but we should note that in the longer term probably there has been a decline in the right to participate in private elections and to determine matters through participation. The realistic and effective exercise of such a right does not accord with the scale, the imperatives and the logic of the institutions of managerial capitalism. Moreover, as the insistent ethos of managerialism becomes ever more dominant in our culture, even those institutions that once carried with them from another age alternative beliefs and practices have succumbed to that ethos.

Of course, we also need to avoid a patronising and unduly critical anachronism. Many of the elections that we are reviewing would not have met the criteria of a modern electoral commission. It is the case that the types of election that we are considering were hedged about by restrictive qualifications and requirements – they were on the cusp between liberties and liberty. Nor were they unfettered in the sense that anyone could stand: often the electorate was presented with a choice between nominees. No doubt this represented a practical embodiment of the balance that was favoured in the political theory of the period

---

[5] Notestein 1954; Demos 1970; Lockridge 1970; Thistlethwaite 1989; Anderson 1991; Thompson 1993; Powell 1963.
[6] Underdown 1995, 1996, pp. 45–67; Braddick 2000; Hindle 2000.   [7] Morgan 1996, 2001.
[8] Thus Norwich, England's largest provincial town: Evans 1979, pp. 26–30; Howard 2000.

between the aristocratic and the popular elements: elements that were seen as components of what was believed to be the healthiest and most stable type of polity – that with a 'mixed' constitution. Furthermore, the monarchical element was also the third essential element in this mix. In turn this may help us to understand why the participation of the monarch as such, and the acceptance of analogues of monarchy – mayors in great cities and masters of houses at Cambridge – were acknowledged part of the electoral scene. In these ways the elections of that period were imbued with the values of their time – just as our elections are permeated by the values of our own age. As such they can provide valuable insights not only into particular events or institutions but also into the wider culture. It is hoped that what follows by way of description of the electoral scene at early modern Cambridge demonstrates this. So, the phenomenon of elections at this time was in some ways a very different beast from the one that we recognise today. None the less, the germ of modern assumption and practice might also be discerned in its progenitor.

Finally, within this larger picture we need to bear in mind what may have been the specific significance of the experience of elections at Cambridge for the increasing numbers who were members of the university from the final quarter of the sixteenth century. A main theme of this volume is the close connection for the greater part of the period that it covers between the university and the wider world of English society. In the context of a consideration of the wider electoral scene we need to contemplate the degree to which the experience of elections at Cambridge seeded the understanding of those who either participated in or observed them at the time. At later stages in their careers these men carried that experience into a wider realm. The different sectors of electoral experience were thus connected. We need to remember this and our debt to the pre-modern world when we elevate elections as a touchstone of modernity.

MASTERS AND ELECTIONS, MANDATES AND THE PREROGATIVE

The nature of the type of constraints, both theoretical and practical, that helped to shape the form of elections in this period in Cambridge is evident if we examine the most prominent category of elections in the university: the election of masters of colleges. In most although not in all colleges the master was supposed to be elected by the fellows, often from among their number. This principle derived from the medieval origins of many of the colleges, and much old college custom adopted by later foundations, in which the master was conceived of as merely a fellow with additional responsibilities.[9] As we have seen, it was a Tudor conception that only came to full fruition under Elizabeth that the obligations of masters were as much to the central government as to the college, as much to the other masters as to the fellows of his own foundation, as much to be distinguished by special rights as by his collegiate responsibilities and as likely to be imposed by his new coercive authority as by the concurrence of the other members of his college.[10] We have also seen that the examples provided by the exceptional circumstances of colleges such as King's, Trinity and Magdalene encouraged the development of those aspects of university life that served to set apart the heads.[11] Again, in the development of attitudes and expectations with regard to the elections of masters, it is possible to detect the influence of a few unusually constituted colleges and of regal rights of nomination elsewhere in the university. These conditions created a habit which was carried over into colleges where there were no such statutory rights.

In the oldest of colleges, Peterhouse, the fellows enjoyed only a restricted freedom of election: they had the right to nominate two candidates to the bishop of Ely, who then chose one as master.[12] At Jesus, a similar procedure was instituted by Bishop West's statutes of 1516–17.[13] It was not only that procedures such as these accustomed the university to the interposition of external authority on the occasion of elections: it also made it easier for the Court to influence elections by concentrating its attentions on one man, the bishop of Ely, rather than dissipating it in attempts to coerce a number of fellows. However, the main attraction of the election procedures at Peterhouse and Jesus from the viewpoint of the Crown was that the right of selection was elevated to the monarch as supreme governor of the church when the bishopric of Ely was vacant. As a wealthy see on a par with Canterbury and Winchester, there were financial inducements to keep it vacant – inducements to which Elizabeth succumbed. As a result, there was no bishop at Ely for nineteen years during Elizabeth's reign, and there was also a briefer vacancy of nearly two years in 1626–8. As a result, the Crown had a direct say in the selection of candidates for the masterships of these two colleges in these years. Indeed, it may well be that control of this additional

---

[9] Thus e.g. at Emmanuel, the master was to be an old member of the college (*VCH Cambs.*, III, p. 474).

[10] Above, chapter 3.   [11] Above, chapters 3, 8.

[12] *VCH Cambs.*, III, p. 338: for the drawbacks of this procedure see the case of 1787 when the bishop chose the wrong man (Winstanley 1935, pp. 284–94).

[13] *VCH Cambs.*, III, p. 422; Gray 1967, p. 95. The bishop's influence also extended to fellowships (Jesus College Archives, Ant. 2, p. 14; cf. Lancelot Andrewes' determination, *ibid.*, Ant. 2. 13.1).

privilege of the bishop of Ely was a further inducement to keep the see vacant.

There was a further group of what might be described as 'proprietorial' colleges. As new institutions the founders, their descendants or the executors of the founders of Emmanuel and Sidney Sussex retained both an informal and a formal authority over their creations during much of the earlier part of this period. This included the right to nominate the masters. At Sidney Sussex this right was exercised three times between 1594 and 1611, when it was finally assigned to the fellows.[14] Dr Caius had been granted a similar privilege with regard to the nomination of his immediate successor following his refoundation of Gonville Hall.[15]

The situation of Magdalene, founded by Thomas, Lord Audley in 1542, was altogether more extreme. Here, there was a strong and continuing connection between the college and the family of the founder – or, more strictly, the inhabitants of the house of Audley End who both acted as Visitor and enjoyed the right of nominating the master.[16] Indirectly this was another means by which the Court was drawn into the college, for during the nonage of Thomas Howard, Lord Audley, in the 1570s, Burghley assumed the right of nomination through his office as Master of the Court of Wards. The outcome of one attempt at nomination also demonstrates the complications that could arise when the Court became involved in affairs at Cambridge. Not least this was because the Court itself was a complex entity housing competing interests. Thus, partly at the request of some of the fellows of the college, Burghley nominated his chaplain, Degory Nicholls.[17] Unbeknown to Burghley, Henry Copinger had obtained letters in his favour from the queen, who claimed that the post was 'in our gyft by our progative by reason of the nonage of Thomas Howard Lord Audley'.[18] The bemused fellows had compared the two conflicting instructions and decided that it was best not to antagonise the queen, and so admitted Copinger. However, Copinger was forced to apologise to Burghley, and soon departed the college, leaving it free for the Lord Treasurer's nominee, who, as we have seen, moved in with his scolding wife and their cows.[19] This proved to be only one of a number of misunderstandings or clashes of interest at Court involving rival nominees to masterships. Also, on the same grounds of the incapacity of the current occupant of Audley End, Elizabeth both

---

[14] *VCH Cambs.*, III, p. 486.   [15] Venn 1897–1901, III, p. 64; Brooke 1985/1996, pp. 62, 77.
[16] *VCH Cambs.*, III, p. 450; Cunich *et al.* 1994, pp. 40–1.   [17] *HMCS*, XII, p. 147.
[18] Hatfield MS 136.10.   [19] *HMCS*, III, pp. 148 ff. See p. 298.

claimed and exercised a right directly to nominate to fellowships at the college.[20]

Apart from the special circumstances of the 'proprietorial' colleges that have just been discussed, there was an overall decline in the powers of the Visitors of the various colleges. This was a corollary of the increase in the authority of the masters, which effectively restricted appeals from the decisions of the master to the Visitors. One consequence was a reduction in the powers exercised by Visitors in college elections. However, the extent of this decline depended on who the Visitor was. For example, Burghley and Whitgift explicitly used their position as Visitors to recommend a new master for St John's.[21] In the case of King's College, Elizabeth, James and Charles all saw fit to exercise a royal proprietorial interest, justified by the claim that it had been founded by their royal predecessors.[22] This was also an argument that could be applied to Trinity College, founded in 1546 by the merger of King's Hall and Michael House,[23] and was applied to St John's.[24] Furthermore, it could be argued that the royal origins of college statutes, under the Great Seal, also created a special relationship, so that, for example, in this capacity, Elizabeth could be claimed as a foundress of Trinity.[25] Of the original foundations that went into the making of Trinity College, King's Hall had always had close connections with the public service, had enjoyed support from the Exchequer and had had its scholars and wardens nominated by the Crown.[26] This tradition was subsumed by the new and larger foundation, and from the beginning the mastership of Trinity was in the gift of the Crown.[27] Along with this went various pieces of ancillary royal patronage, such as presentation to the almshouses associated with the college.[28]

Another creation of the 1540s, the foundation of five Regius Professorships in Divinity, Civil Law, Physic, Hebrew and Greek, provided a further pretext for royal intervention in the running of the university. If Ascham is to be believed, they transformed the depressed circumstances of the time. Two years on he claimed that 'Cambridge is quite another place, so substantially and splendidly has it been endowed by the royal

---

[20] BL Harl. MS 7031, fo. 115; *CSPD 1603–10*, p. 151; S.O. 3/1, 16 July 1587, 16 June 1590 and [22 Jan. 1597].

[21] Cf. CUA, Lett. 10.6.a. The bishop of Ely was Visitor of St John's, Peterhouse and Jesus (cf. Gibbons 1891, pp. 60–6, for eighteenth/nineteenth-century appeals to him in the Ely Archives).

[22] SP 16/427/28.   [23] *VCH Cambs.*, III, pp. 456, 462.   [24] CUA, Lett. 10.6.a.

[25] CUA, Lett. 9.B.3.   [26] *VCH Cambs.*, III, p. 458; Cobban 1969.

[27] *VCH Cambs.*, III, p. 463; see above, p. 8.

[28] E.g. SP 12/262/149.

munificence.'[29] In fact, their foundation can be attributed to Thomas Cromwell, and it was his candidates who were the first appointees.[30]

However, the fiction of their royal origins was available for subsequent manipulation. In 1605 James wrote to the vice-chancellor on behalf of Robert Spalding for the Hebrew lectureship, 'although our meaning be not to prejudice the libertie of the universitie in their election, yet both because our Auncestors are Fownders of the fee belonging to that lecture and the person is otherwise qualified for the place wee will expect that uppon our recommendation you shall preferre him before any other being not of the same meritt as he'.[31]

Elizabeth's ministers had also used the excuse of the royal interest in the Regius chairs as a pretext for intervention. In 1586 Burghley and Whitgift recommended William Whitaker to the mastership of St John's on the grounds that he was as fit for the post as any and as the Queen's Reader in Divinity was the rather to be preferred to any other as a means of assuring his continuance in the university.[32]

Thus the necessary royal involvement in the legal procedures involved in granting corporate existence to all the colleges,[33] together with the Crown's intermittent and piecemeal financial contributions to various parts of the university, provided some justification for the extension of royal oversight.[34] Edward Coke recognised these grounds when he alluded to 'the Colledges and houses of Learning being founded partly by the King's progenitors, and partly by the nobles and other godly and devout men'.[35] And contemporaries would have recognised the Crown's claims when Charles I referred to 'our Colledge of Eton' and to King's as 'our Colledge in our universitie at Cambridge'.[36]

A further reason for royal intervention in university elections occurred because the universities were both equated with promotional procedures in the church, and closely linked with it through personnel. In the church the Crown claimed the right to fill those vacancies created by the

---

[29] Peacock 1841, p. 33; Ascham quoted in Mullinger 1884, p. 52.

[30] Kearney 1970, p. 21; Logan 1977, pp. 271 ff.

[31] CUA, Lett. 11.B.A. Spalding was Regius Professor of Hebrew from 1605 (Venn, IV, p. 162b; Cooper, II, p. 479). It is not known who informed the king on the history of the institution; evidently interested parties had his ear.

[32] CUA, Lett. 10.6.a. Whitaker was Regius Professor of Divinity 1580–95, and master of St John's 1587–95.

[33] See e.g. Brooke 1985/1996, p. 61 and Venn 1904, pp. 43–56, for the charter of King Philip and Queen Mary of 1557 'incorporating' Gonville and Caius College.

[34] E.g. the chairs of Civil Law and Medicine were originally funded from the Court of Augmentations, later from the Exchequer.

[35] CUA, Lett. 11. A.C.36: Edward Coke to the University, 12 March 1604.

[36] The references for these phrases have been mislaid.

elevation of former incumbents to other livings in the royal gift.[37] Thus, in 1585, Elizabeth nominated the new treasurer of St Paul's Cathedral, it being 'in hir majestes disposition' through her promotion of the previous occupant of the office to the bishopric of Hereford.[38] Similarly, Lancelot Andrewes was presented to a prebend in the collegiate church of Southwell (Yorkshire) as a result of the promotion of John Young to the bishopric of Rochester.[39]

By an extension of this royal privilege from the strictly ecclesiastical to the university sphere – a distinction not clearly recognised at the time – the Crown could claim to appoint to masterships or other university offices made vacant by the royal elevation to higher office of former incumbents. As Dr Worthington was to explain it in 1660, 'it is supposed . . . when the King does remove ye present Master to another place, the King doth dispose of yt place, from whence he removed him. So it is in Livings, when the King removes any from thence to be Bps, the King, (not ye respective Patrones) disposes of those places.'[40] Thus, in 1592, John Beaumont was presented by the Crown to the rectory of Hadleigh, Suffolk, which was a peculiar of the archbishopric of Canterbury. This was possible because his predecessor, John Still, had been promoted to the bishopric of Bath and Wells. Still had also been master of Trinity College, and in addition the Crown nominated to that office.[41] Just prior to Elizabeth's death in 1603 a dispute had arisen over the appointment of a master at Corpus.[42] The Crown claimed the privilege of nomination by right of having elevated the previous occupant of the headship to the bishopric of Norwich. An election at the college was said to be void

> for disobedience to the Queen that then was, because the Mastership was resigned by the Bishop of Norwich a little before his consecration to frustrate the Queen's prerogative, who was to appoint a new Master, so soon as the former Master was bishop, as may appear by sundry precedents. The kings of England have authority to stay all elections where express oath, according to the intent of the Founder, doth not require the contrary.[43]

---

[37] 'She giveth all the livings of the persons whom she prefereth, to whose gift or election soever they may appertain' (*HMCS*, VI, p. 207).

[38] S.O. 3/1, Nov. 1585.

[39] S.O. 3/1, April 1589 – although Young had become bishop of Rochester in 1578! There is a marginal note against this entry that the clerk's fee had not been received. For other examples, see S.O. 3/2, Dec. 1603, Nov. 1604, Jan. 1605; S.O. 3/3, Aug. 1606.

[40] BL Harl. MS 7033, fo. 63v. Dr Richard Sterne was nominated bishop of Carlisle, 7 October 1660. However, by 1660 judgement was being given that a mastership was not an ecclesiastical preferment, and therefore fell outside the Crown's gift (*ibid.*, fo. 64).

[41] S.O. 3/2, Feb. 1592; see above, p. 349.   [42] Morgan 1983, pp. 571 ff.

[43] BL Harl. MS 7033, fo. 29.

Here, there is both a recognition of private proprietorial interest but also a demonstration of the prevailing and generally restricted notion of the rights of election.

The general conclusion to be drawn is that the Crown's claim to a proprietorial interest in particular colleges and in the universities as a whole increased during the sixteenth century. At the same time there arose fortuitous opportunities to intervene in the affairs of colleges such as Peterhouse, Jesus and Magdalene. The creation of the Regius chairs habituated both Crown and university to a greater intimacy in each other's affairs. The newly acquired role of the Crown as Supreme Head, and then Supreme Governor, of the church created opportunities to nominate to university places when the previous incumbent was elevated by royal patronage to an ecclesiastical appointment elsewhere. To these constitutional arrangements in the colleges, and accretion of legal rights on the part of the Crown, must be added a variety of other factors that drew the Crown and the universities more closely together over the issue of elections. These are best examined through a general survey of what might be described as the electoral scene at Cambridge in these years. This will be followed by a more detailed analysis of particular elections.

THE ELECTORAL SCENE IN EARLY MODERN CAMBRIDGE

What general circumstances, what immediate influences, activities and attitudes, surrounded elections at Cambridge, and in particular the election of masters? And, in turn, what does this reveal about elections in general in this period? The first thing to note is the frequency with which vacancies had to be filled: the pot was constantly on the boil. There were only twenty-five individual years out of the eighty odd years from 1558 to 1640 in which elections to masterships did not occur. After the revolutionary years 1640–60 there was a downturn in the frequency of elections to masterships. In itself this downturn is an indication of the extent to which the post-Restoration university was becoming uncoupled from the wider world of which once it had been part, constituting, as once it had, a stage in the clerical career pattern. But also, and paradoxically, this calming of the electoral waters in Cambridge coincided with an increase in the storminess of public elections as distinct from the more domestic academic affairs. By the early eighteenth century it is these larger elections that prompted most excitement at Cambridge as the world of party politics came to permeate the university as it did most other parts of

English society. In this as in so many other ways the university had ceased to set the scene.[44]

Elections tended to come in blocks, partly as a result of promotions of masters from one college to another. To this we need to add the effect of the sometimes long-drawn-out disputes that surrounded many elections: they were not necessarily briefly concluded affairs and the heady atmosphere engendered by elections could be sustained over months and sometimes even years.[45] Moreover, because of the various considerations that affected the selection of a master, either by the fellows of a house or by the Crown or Court interests, there was a marked degree of migration from one college to another involved in elections.[46] Consequently, what strictly should have been the business of only the college concerned prompted a more than vicarious curiosity throughout the university and excited the expectations of those presidents, bursars and senior fellows of other colleges who stood in some expectation of promotion. In its turn the possibility of the imminent elevation of one of their senior members excited competition within a college for the vacant senior fellowship that any such promotion would create. Finally, the elections of masters needs to be placed within the context of yet more frequent elections to scholarships and fellowships: the turnover of scholarships, fellowships and masterships, combined with the active creation of new endowments for these purposes in the earlier part of this period, including the creation of two new masterships, made for a constant ferment and agitation at Cambridge in these years that was not to be equalled again until the expansion of the sciences there in the nineteenth century, or, more recently, the competition and career expectations engendered by the creation of the plate-glass universities in the 1960s.

PECUNIARY MOTIVES IN ELECTIONS

Today the assumption seems to be that any financial interest in the conduct or outcome of an election is clear-cut evidence of corruption. In large part this attitude derives from the wider reaction to all that was involved in what became known as the 'Old Corruption' that was swept away by the breathtakingly comprehensive reforms undertaken in the early and mid-nineteenth century.[47] By then, it is true that many practices had achieved a condition of stupendous degeneracy. But in the early

---

[44] See above, nn. 3–4, and below, pp. 533 ff.

[45] For examples, see below, pp. 354, 380 ff. Morgan 1983, App. 9.

[46] See Index under Beale, Holdsworth, Nevile, for examples of masters migrating from college to college.

[47] See e.g. Harling 1996.

modern period many sorts of office-holding were considered to be a negotiable freehold.[48] By extension, the right of election, especially in 'private' elections such as those in the university, was treated as a potentially income-generating asset. In these circumstances we simply cannot impose our own values on behaviour which was coherent and often acceptable within the broader constellation of attitudes of which it formed part. In so far as contemporaries did voice criticisms of conduct in elections these criticisms may themselves be taken as indicative of wider shifts in thinking about property, office, duty and the public sphere.

Pecuniary considerations of more or less justification by the lights of the time were not absent in elevations to masterships, although they were, perhaps, more prevalent in elections to fellowships and scholarships. In 1607, Dr Perse, president and last surviving fellow of the early days of Dr Caius' refoundation, promised that if he was elected master 'he had a full resolution to be answerable to the last founder's gift, and would make assurance to the College of £2000'.[49] There was much to recommend him: 'His ability is three times above the last founder's wealth: a single man, well stricken in years, very wise, honest and learned; and the like opportunity of gratifying the College will not hastily be found in our time.'[50] As it was, the intrigue surrounding this particular election meant that the mastership eluded Perse, although he did prove to be a benefactor to the college, and to the town, on his death in 1615.[51] However, on other occasions there was more likely to have been a loss rather than a potential financial gain to a college as a result of the pursuit of pecuniary advantage in elections.

We have seen the importance of leases in the life at the university.[52] We have also noted the autocratic powers of the master of Magdalene.[53] Therefore, Richard Howland's promotion from Magdalene to St John's in 1577 may not be unrelated to his continued acquiescence in the alienation of college property in London to the Crown. This had been instigated by his predecessor at Magdalene three years earlier. Subsequently there were to be numerous and unsuccessful attempts to regain the lost and increasingly valuable urban property.[54]

Financial considerations can also be detected in elections to fellowships and scholarships. Although not always explicit, resignations in favour

---

[48] Swart 1949; Aylmer 1961, 1973, pp. 91, 134, 293; Hurstfield 1968.

[49] *HMCS*, xix, p. 405: Perse evidently agreed to be a candidate after the failure of Gostlin in a last-ditch attempt to find a candidate within the fellowship (as the college statute prescribed: see below, p. 407n).

[50] *Ibid.*   [51] Brooke 1985/1996, pp. 98–103.   [52] Above, pp. 274–86.   [53] Above, p. 287.

[54] *HMCS*, xii, p. 147; Hoyle in Cunich *et al.* 1994, pp. 77–83 and 284nn.

of a particular successor were likely to involve some form of inducement. Again, what happened along these lines in the university were of
a piece with what happened in the wider world of governmental office-
holding.[55] Thus in an instance at Queens' in 1585 this circumscription
of choice was formalised in an agreement drawn up under the hand
of a public notary: the fellow resigning was to regain his position if his
Court-sponsored successor did not take up the place.[56] Anthony Gawdy's
tutor at Caius, Edmund Michell, was quite explicit with Anthony's uncle,
Framlingham. His pupil had been pre-elected to one of the best scholarships in the college, on Branthwaite's foundation. Michell suggested
that Anthony would benefit both financially and in terms of seniority
if the present occupant was bought out immediately by payment of a
sum commensurate with the profits for that year.[57] These practices were
not peculiar to Cambridge; they are also evident at Oxford. In one of
a number of revealing letters to his father, Bryan Twyne suggested that
he was willing to facilitate the election of a kinsman to the scholar's
place that he was about to resign. Failing a kinsman, Twyne proposed
that his father should tout around for 'any other Gentlemen [*sic*]' who
was willing to give him 'some fee for gettinge ye Fellowes voices for his
sonne', claiming that any such 'would doe very well, and cheape enough
in respect of placinge his sonne elsewhere'.[58] In another Oxford election
there were attempts to buy the votes of the electing fellows, while the
candidate's sister made importunate requests on his behalf to one of the
fellows – what means of persuasion she employed is not recorded.[59] At
Cambridge there are suggestions that by the 1580s such sale and purchase of places was frequent, and that some fellows tried to claim that
the taking of money for resignations was not directly prohibited by the
statutes.[60] Apart from demonstrating the attractiveness of and demand for
academic positions, these arguments were perhaps not quite as specious
as they might at first appear. Their proponents must have had in mind
the extent of very similar practices in the sale of public offices within the
state. If anything, their employment demonstrates the extent to which, in
the eyes of contemporaries, arrangements in the universities were being
approximated to arrangements in the wider world.[61]

However, in so far as such behaviour was considered corrupt even by
the standards of the time, the evidence for it is only adventitious, as in

---

[55] Aylmer 1961; Swart 1949; Hurstfield 1968.   [56] BL Harl. MS 7031, fo. 109.
[57] BL Egerton MS 2715, fo. 234 (17 Oct. 1622).   [58] Twyne 1927, p. 218.
[59] Lambeth Palace Library MS 943, p. 147. For corrupt elections at Oxford, see also Fletcher 1885,
    p. 223.
[60] CUL, MS Mm. i. 38, p. 81.61.   [61] See above, chapters 4–6.

a series of abusive accusations raised by one fellow against another in which one 'spake also as if money had beene given for his fellowshipp, saying he would make it cost him as much as his fellowship did, and with many other words tending to his disgrace'.[62] It may be that what we are hearing here are the beginnings of a half-articulated notion that, in academe at least, considerations of merit should come before advantage and influence. If this is the case, it may be one of the roots of a very different attitude towards elections in general that would take a very long time to prevail. Clearly, the buying and selling of places at elections was disapproved of, but equally clearly it did go on. In fact, Whitgift's general condemnation of the practice suggests that it was endemic: he himself claimed in a letter to Burghley that it 'began to be an ordinary prac- tice for Fellows of Colleges, when they were not disposed to continue, to resign up their fellowships for sums of money', and asked the Lord Treasurer to give straight charge against it.[63] Whitgift's initiative had itself been prompted by a bill with similar aims that had passed both Houses of Parliament some months previously. At the last stage of its legislative progress it had been refused the royal assent as a means of avoiding the disgrace that its passage was thought to call down upon these peculiarly regal institutions.[64] Nevertheless, those who had been thwarted in the parliament of 1576 were pertinacious in their criticisms, and the session of 1588–9 saw the passage of an Act designed to curb these abuses (31 Elizabeth c. vi), and requiring its reading on the occasion of all elec- tions (para. 3) in order to remind fellows of what they were meant not to do. In these comments and in this legislation we are surely seeing the defining of the boundaries through public debate and the redefinition of what was acceptable and what was not. As such this was not only an articulation of the meaning of public good against private rights and op- portunities. It was also through the debates that it engendered in various fora a means by which a pre-modern public sphere was defined and one set of values was transmuted into another.

As the particular instances of bribery that have been cited from throughout this period suggest, legislation did not put an end to cor- rupt practices in elections. However, it may have provided a further in- ducement to exploit patronage connections and resort to the Court in preference to the market uncertainties and now strictly defined illegality of purchase. At the same time, an awareness of the continued indulgence of these comfortable local corruptions provided some pretext for courtly

---

[62] CUL, Baumgartner (Patrick) MS 23, fo. 57v.   [63] Strype 1822, I, pp. 148–50.
[64] Above, p. 159.

intervention while at the same time undermining the moral grounds of those who stood against such interference.

The privileges that the masters came to enjoy in this period, and the enhanced possibilities for cultivating the means to yet further preferment that the office conferred, not unnaturally engendered considerable competition amongst aspirants, inflaming the electoral scene. However, in a peculiar way, the general dislike of the masters seems to have encouraged amongst some of their detractors a belief that they were as well suited as those they criticised to fill these places of power and responsibility. With an intense competition for promotion amongst a locally concentrated group of able men, there were many who would have agreed with the nautical analogy drawn by the earl of Northampton between the university and Jason's ship, 'which in respect of resolution & skill, was sayd to contain as many persons, fit to be Masters, as it held Mariners'.[65]

Overlain on these personal motivations was the jockeying for position amongst the rival religious factions in the university: crypto-Catholic versus puritan in the early decades of Elizabeth's reign, and Arminian versus Calvinist from the 1590s. After the Restoration, Latitudinarianism became the issue.[66] In these circumstances of intensely competitive ideologies the augmented authority of the masters within their colleges, and their pervasive influence in the government of the university as a whole, made victory in the competition for masterships crucial in the propounding and propagating of opposing religious views and, latterly, party-political positions. The Privy Council was drawing on many years' experience of such occasions when in June 1633 it wrote to St John's that, 'Being given to understand of the vacancies of the Mastershipp of your Colledge, and that there is lyke to be some Competition for the place, which (as oftentymes it falls out) may occacon a tumultuous and violent proceeding by the over passionate sideing of parties.'[67] Indeed, in the matter of election to a mastership, the one thing that fellows could not be relied upon to do was 'to demeane [themselves] . . . as temperate and discreete men'.[68]

The detailed evidence suggests that the majority of elections of masters in this period were disputed or contested in some way or other.[69] It was with something of an air of surprise that it was reported in 1626 that the fellows of Caius had been unanimous in electing Thomas Batchcroft as their new master, 'a thing very rare in eleccions'.[70] More frequently, the occurrence of an election to a mastership served only to crystallise existing

---

[65] BL Harl. MS 7031, fo. 203.   [66] Below, pp. 522–6.   [67] PRO, P.C. 2/43, pp. 94 ff.
[68] *Ibid.*   [69] See Morgan 1983, pp. 571–637.   [70] CUL, Baumgartner (Patrick) MS 22, fo. 13.

antipathies. On a previous occasion at Caius, when some interested party had convinced Burghley that an election had not taken place he had complained that, rather than proceeding to an election according to their statutes, the fellows had fallen to 'takinge partes and making Factyons . . . Otherwyse then wyse and Lerned men oughte to doo.'[71] In his time as chancellor, Cecil also had many opportunities to bemoan 'such heat and partiality in the elections of their rulers', and the unfortunate precedent that these disputes provided, for in these elections 'consisteth so much the good estate of the whole body, for commonly the whole House conform themselves *ad exemplum magistri*'.[72] Violence was not unknown on these occasions, as when Thomas Jegon was elected master of Corpus in 1603, for though 'The statute requireth reverence to God conformity to the Senior Fellow at the time of the election, but this election was tumultuous, even with some blows, even in the Chapel.'[73] Nor was this an isolated instance of the violence and physical coercion at the time of elections in early modern Cambridge.

VIOLENCE AND PHYSICAL COERCION

The most likely occasions for wide-scale uproar and disorder arose when the entire university was involved in elections, such as when they exercised their newly gained right to elect MPs. The turmoil created by the clash of interests between the heads and the rest of the university in the parliamentary election in 1614 is reflected in an anonymously compiled report on the incident subscribed by John Duport, the deputy vice-chancellor and master of Jesus.[74] Prior disputes as to the mode of nomination made Duport, the presiding officer, approach the occasion with some trepidation: he exhorted the gathering 'very earnestly that like university men, that is like men of learning wisdom and government, they would peacably and quietly transact all things, that it might not be said of us now as it hath been some-times of late' with 'many earnest exhortations by the Vice Chancellor used for peace and quietness in the transaction'.[75]

The behaviour proscribed by the vice-chancellor gives some indication of the undignified manner in which university elections could be conducted:

---

[71] SP 12/95/10, unsigned draft, 21 Jan. 1574.

[72] *HMCS*, XIX, p. 367, Cecil to James Montague, dean of Salisbury, Dec. 1607.

[73] *HMCS*, XV, p. 350; for details of this election, see Morgan 1983, pp. 605 ff.

[74] For background, see above, chapter 5; cf. Cooper, *Annals*, III, p. 61; Mullinger 1884, p. 463; Rix 1954, pp. 56 ff.

[75] Wright 1868–9, pp. 204–5.

in fine he charged and required them in the name of the Kings majesty and upon virtue of their oath made unto the university 1. that they all should keep the Kings peace unviolably; 2. that every man should keep his seat and standing, and not run on heaps in the Regent house from one seat to another, but patiently abide till they were called up to give their suffrages in writing. 3. that if any of the parties should purpose to come up to move for justice or direction in anything, there should not be above 2 or 3 come together and having preferred their suit discretely and modestly and received answer accordingly, they should then depart back again to their places.[76]

Nevertheless, the returning officer's own inept action in attempting to circumvent the election of Sir Miles Sandys, the popular candidate, precipitated the disturbances the vice-chancellor wished to avoid. Subsequently, he claimed that he dismissed the letters for Sandys 'to the end they might peacably and quietly have dispatched the business, and also because, perceiving the Congregations to begin to be very troublesome, he was afraid it would prove so mutinous and violent in the end that he should not be able to pronounce the election as he would'.[77] While the votes were being checked, 'the Congregation now grew so hot and pressed so hard upon him, that he greatly feared some violence' which 'had surely have come to pass' if he had succeeded in his attempt to stuff the slips containing the votes for Sir Miles Sandys in his pocket.[78] Failing in this, he then stepped into his chair of office to pronounce Sir Miles ineligible. This triggered vehement shouts and cries which became 'yet much more violent by many degrees when he began to say as followeth, which . . . notwithstanding he was continually cried upon and shouted at with the greatest extremity that might be either to hinder him from speaking at all or else to put him out', that Sir Francis Bacon and Dr Barnaby Gooch were elected, then immediately dissolving the Convocation. 'Whereat it is incredible what a noise and shout they made, so as it was sensibly heard a great way off, crying as loud as they could "Let the suffrages be read, Let the suffrages be read", "You do us wrong, You do us wrong", and "a Sandis, a Sandis", etc., the throng being so great that the Vice Chancellor had very much ado with the Bedells before him to get down amongst them.'[79] Such was the school of experience in which prospective preachers and adolescent aristocrats acquired their first close view of the techniques of parliamentary elections.

Violence or the threat of violence was also present on the occasion of other types of election within the university. As might be expected, it

[76] *Ibid.*, p. 205.   [77] *Ibid.*, p. 206.   [78] *Ibid.*, p. 207.   [79] *Ibid.*, p. 208.

359

was most likely to occur in elections to fellowships when, for whatever reason, it was held necessary to expel the existing occupant. In a dispute between the master of Corpus, John Copcot, and one of the fellows, Anthony Hickman, in the late 1580s, the master engineered the election of another fellow to his place '& Mr. Hykman was by extraordinary force, carry'd out of his Chamber, & kept out of the Colledge'.[80] In a not dissimilar incident at King's in 1608, the provost, Roger Goad, had expelled William Lisle for being in contravention of the statutes of the college, and proceeded to the election of Thomas Scamp in his stead. Lisle, who was described as 'a man of a violent and turbulent disposicon', was particularly affronted at Scamp's occupation of his former chamber. Gathering a group of associates about him, he gained access via a study window in an upper gallery and descended upon Scamp, who was asleep in his predecessor's bed.[81]

Violence could also occur in the preliminaries to an election. At Emmanuel in 1618 most of the fellows seem to have determined upon electing Samuel Hildersham to a fellowship.[82] Their intention was in danger of being thwarted by William Ingoldsby,[83] who had obtained a royal mandate requiring his election. Ingoldsby had not yet delivered the mandate, and therefore his opponents contrived means to put him out of circulation until after the crucial day of election. Going to his inn, they pretended to congratulate him on having obtained the royal mandate, and induced him to indulge in some premature celebrations with the intention – it was later claimed – of making him 'drunke with excessive quantie of wyne, and drinke very late in the night . . . intemperately filling him even against his will with most excessive quantities of wyne'. They had arranged for a confederate, one of the university proctors, to break in and arrest them all for causing a disturbance, and lock them in the university prison – the Tollbooth – until the election had been effected. Ingoldsby does not seem to have been sufficiently drunk for their purposes when the proctor broke in, so the latter threw down his staff of office and joined in the carousing, 'purposing with a fresh supplie to drive the said Ingoldsbie unto further distemper', and only subsequently leading them all off to the Tollbooth. Unfortunately for the plotters, their victim seems to have enjoyed a phenomenal resistance to drink, and overheard their mutual self-congratulations while they were all biding their

---

[80] BL Harl. MS 7031, fo. 55; Venn, II, p. 366a. Hickman was restored about a month before his adversary's death in July 1590.

[81] PRO, STAC 8/15/25.

[82] Venn, II, p. 368b. Samuel was the son of the former puritan divine Arthur Hildersham, and religious motives seem to have been behind the dispute (Morgan 1983, p. 482).

[83] Venn, II, p. 448b; Collinson in Bendall *et al.* 1999, pp. 13–17.

time in prison. However, Hildersham was elected and the exploit clearly made a good story: its perpetrators were said to have claimed it 'too bee in themselves most notable and laudable actes of Christian policy and memorable Jestes for their sportes pastime and recreacon to laughe att'. And so no doubt it seemed – until offence was taken at their affront to the royal dignity by attempting to drown the royal mandate, and they were hauled in front of Star Chamber for what others were more inclined to see as their 'wilfull, audacious and contemptuous exploite'.[84]

In the 1590s a more violent and less hilarious scene had accompanied the abortive election of a new master at Catharine Hall. Again, outside interference seems to have exacerbated rather than curbed the violence. The junior fellows had elected Dr Robson of St John's, but they feared that the president of the college – the presiding officer at the election of a master – 'accordinge to his custome forbearinge no practise that may serve his purpose' would lock them out or admit the other and ultimately successful protagonist for the office, Dr Overall. That they had some grounds for their fears is evidenced in the manner in which a senior fellow beat all the scholars out of the college and 'kept the Gates by violence, setting a Man before the Gates with a Sword & Dagger'. In these circumstances the juniors discreetly forbore to seek the admission of their elected candidate until some days later.[85]

All in all, one's impression is that the ivory towers of early modern Cambridge were accustomed to a high incidence of battery in their vicinity, and a fair proportion of this is to be associated with the frequency of all types of elections that took place in the hothouse atmosphere of faction-ridden colleges. Add to this the often make-or-break significance of elections in the careers of many individuals, add the often crucial role of elections in determining the religious complexion of a college or control over its scarce resources and add the frustrations engendered by the supersession of the normal processes of election by the invocation of the *deus ex machina* of courtly interference – and one has a recipe for almost inevitable outbreaks of pent-up violence.

CHARACTERISTICS OF CROWN INTERVENTION IN ELECTIONS

Pre-elections to fellowships and scholarships became increasingly common during the Elizabethan and early Stuart period, as did reversionary

---

[84] *Ibid.*; PRO, STAC 8/28/2, Information.   [85] CUL, MS Mm. i. 38, p. 44.

appointments in the 'civil service'.[86] Essentially, this involved election to the position before it was vacated by the current incumbent. Curiously, however, there is almost no evidence of reversionary interests being granted in masterships.[87] Consequently, the expectation and excitement generated at the time of such an election was all the greater: in the case of the illness of the master of Trinity Hall in 1595, the recommendation for his successor was being penned even before the ailing incumbent had breathed his last.[88] One result of the abruptness of elections was that, despite statutory requirements for their publication in advance, they could be over with before an intending candidate had news of them – as one aspirant found to his cost on the election of a new master at Emmanuel in 1622.[89] On at least one occasion a hastily undertaken election led to subsequent intervention by a competitor who brought down royal letters a week later to override it.[90] If an immediate mandate[91] could not be obtained by a supplicant, if there was disapproval of particular individuals as candidates,[92] or disagreement at Court over the merits of rival candidates, if it was felt necessary to obtain further information about candidates or a disputed election,[93] or in order to permit factional tempers to cool, it was sometimes convenient for the Crown to require the postponement of an election.[94]

The extent of intervention by the Court in academic elections varied, although the impression is that it was increasing throughout Elizabeth's reign. In the 1570s, Burghley thought it necessary only to admonish the fellows of Gonville and Caius to move to an election of their new master,[95] but the outcome of the disputed election at Corpus in 1603 was a report on the circumstances by the archbishop of Canterbury and a recommendation to Cecil as chancellor to move the queen to appoint by her prerogative, or to command by her letters the election of one of the four alternative candidates nominated by Whitgift.[96] Pre-existent factional disputes within a college could themselves induce external intervention on the occasion of the election of a new master in an attempt to impose an authoritative figure able to suppress dissension. After the troubles at St John's in the 1560s and 1570s, John Still and William Whitaker

[86] Aylmer 1961, pp. 104–6; Hurstfield 1968, p. 142.
[87] So also Thomas Baker (on whom see below, pp. 546–7): see his letter to John Anstis, BL Stowe MS 749, fos. 98 ff.
[88] BL Harl. MS 7031, fo. 79.
[89] Shuckburgh 1884, p. 33; cf. Collinson in Bendall *et al.* 1999, pp. 214–15.
[90] CUL, MS Mm. i. 38, p. 45.   [91] See pp. 413 ff.   [92] E.g. SP 12/26/72 (St John's, 1595).
[93] E.g. SP 12/287/181 (Corpus, 1603).   [94] SP 12/287/44 (Corpus, 1602–3).
[95] SP 12/95/10; but see above, p. 358. On factions and clienteles and the distinction between them, see Adams 1991, pp. 265–87; Adams 1995, pp. 20–45.
[96] BL Harl. MS 7033, fo. 29.

were firm-handed masters, although even they did not enjoy undisturbed terms of office. Whitgift at Trinity and John Jegon at Corpus were men of a similar order who met with Court approval during Elizabeth's reign. Although, even here, it was Jegon's financial acumen rather than his ability to control his fellows that is most evident during his period of office. With reference to Trinity Hall in the 1580s, a group of heads recommended Thomas Preston as its new master. Amongst his other virtues, 'we recken it not the least, that he hath always shewed himself voyde of faction: a thyng the reither (in our opinion) to be respected in hym, which shall hereafter be called to goyern theare, for that the Howse at this present (as we hear) is not altogether free from that inconvenience'.[97] For his part, when once installed in office, Preston acknowledged the favour shown in promoting his appointment and expressed his desire to reform those 'owlde & owglie disorders' that had prevailed under his predecessor – although he immediately encountered difficulties with 'the factious crue'.[98] In one instance, that of Roger Andrews at Jesus in the 1630s, the king forced a master to resign as a means of terminating factional disputes.[99] Having gone to this length it was all the more necessary to ensure a suitably qualified successor.

Internal dispute over the election of masters and other college members constituted one of a number of factors resulting in the imposition of royal or courtly authority. As at St John's, it might be that all that was considered necessary – however erroneously as it proved in that case – was a preemptive admonition to virtue: 'Wee have thought good hereby to advise and admonish you so to demeane your selves, in the proceeding to the said Ellecon And that in all other Respects, you so governe your selves, as that on noe parte there may be Cause to trouble his majestie or this Board with any complainte of factions or indirect proceedings concerning the same.'[100] The evidence of the preceding sixty years should have made it clear that such an admonition was unlikely to be effective.

The internal factional disputes that so often led to external interference in the election of masters were, of course, also to be found in disagreements over the election of scholars and fellows. Detailed evidence will be presented later to show the importance of religious differences in fuelling the factional disputes over the elections of masters.[101] The same motives also informed at least some of the contested elections to fellowships. This is evident, for example, in a case that arose at Christ's in the 1580s. In May 1582 the queen had written signet letters on behalf of Thomas Osborne,

---

[97] BL Lansdowne MS 45, fo. 123 (copy in Harl. MS 7031, fo. 79).   [98] *Ibid.*
[99] BL Harl. MS 7033, fo. 64v.   [100] PRO, P.C. 2/43, pp. 94 ff.
[101] Morgan 1983, pp. 571–636; below, chapter 11.

requiring the college to extend by three years the fellowship he already held, even though he had not entered the ministry in due time, as required by the statutes.[102] This was hardly designed to endear him to a college already replete with deserving junior members seeking places, and a college with marked puritan principles that involved a commitment to the creation of a proselytising ministry.[103] The master[104] and fellows therefore took the opportunity of Osborne's breach of a number of the college's statutes to expel him. The resulting dispute tended to resolve itself into an argument over the meaning of the statutes, and who had the right of interpretation.[105] Behind all this was the fact that, against Osborne, the college was maintaining the interests of Hugh Broughton who – contrary to his wishes – had been deprived of the fellowship now so tenaciously occupied by Osborne.[106] Professor Collinson has described Broughton as 'that learned if pugnacious divine'.[107] Learning – or pugnacity – earned Broughton the patronage of leading puritan laymen such as Sir Walter Mildmay and the earl of Huntingdon.[108] At one stage in the dispute there were reports that, in calling a new election for the fellowship, the college intended to 'chose such a one, as hath such friends in ye Court as will maintain [their candidate] . . . in his election when it is done, against whomeso-ever'.[109] It was probably men such as Huntingdon that the puritan element in the college hoped would maintain their interest at Court. As it was, something in the way of a compromise was patched up, with Osborne retaining his fellowship and Broughton being subsidised by the earl of Huntingdon.[110] In all, this dispute had dragged on for nearly five years. It had embroiled leading figures in the university, and beyond them the religious factional interests of Cambridge had called upon leading figures about the Court.

Similar factional conflicts over the election of fellows can be detected at work in the early years of James' reign, at a time when major disputes surrounded the elections of most masters of colleges.[111] Christ's College appeared to have recommended one of their students, John Fish, for a

[102] BL Harl. MS 7031, fo. 39. It was said that Andrew Perne, when vice-chancellor, had thrust him into the college (fo. 35). The consequent dispute started in 1579, and the queen's mandate may have come from Burghley's attempt to settle it (Burghley to Howland, *ibid.*, fo. 39).
[103] Porter 1958/1972, pp. 236–8. William Perkins was a fellow during these years.
[104] Edmund Barwell, who had puritan inclinations and had signed the petition against the statutes in 1572 (Porter 1958/1972, p. 236; above, p. 71). For his dislike of Osborne, see BL Harl. MS 7031, fo. 40.
[105] Peile 1910–13, I, pp. 128 ff.   [106] BL Harl. MS 7031, fo. 35.
[107] Collinson 1967, p. 44. Broughton was said to spend twelve to sixteen hours a day in study and prayer (Porter 1958/1972, p. 219).
[108] Peile 1910–13, I, p. 94; Cross 1966, pp. 261–2.   [109] BL Harl. MS 7031, fo. 40.
[110] BL Harl. MS 7031, fo. 40v; Cross 1966, pp. 261–2.   [111] Morgan 1983, pp. 571–636.

fellowship by mandate.[112] Fish persuaded Viscount Fenton to approach the king on his behalf.[113] Despite the not unexpected willingness of the master and fellows who had recommended Fish to proceed to his election, a further group of fellows procrastinated. This drew down upon the college the demand that it should satisfy the king's request and a threat that not to do so would procure 'stricter Letters'.[114]

But we are not dealing with a situation in which an omniscient Court played with the strings of their wholly dependent puppets at Cambridge. Rather, it could be the case that it was factions in the colleges that drew in the Court by seeking the exercise of royal authority on behalf of their candidate by means of royal letters on his behalf.[115] Such actions did not so much quell as quicken college faction. For their part the patronage brokers at Court – ever in the public gaze – were themselves under pressure to expand their clienteles and to demonstrate the effectiveness of their influence. This combination of needs was near irresistible. The extent to which groups within the colleges had been manipulating the Court was implicitly acknowledged by James right at the end of his reign. The king informed St John's that he understood 'that there is like to be difference amongst yow touching the election of some meete person to a fellowshipp . . . And we have observed that in these choices sometimes affections, grounded upon particular interestes and often moved by lettres, stirre partialities and devisions whereby due respect [is omitted] either to the orders of the house, or care of the advancement of Learning.' Rather, they were now to choose 'the most worthie for learning a[nd] meritt without having respect to persons, Requestes, or private interestes whatsoever'.[116] But by 1623 such admonitions to virtue were rather late and hardly likely to curb practices which arose from the factional divisions that affected most colleges.[117]

Those factional divisions were often based on religious differences within colleges. They could lead to the solicitation and issue of testimonial letters. In turn, these were usually intended to procure the issue of a mandate with the purpose of imposing a candidate upon unwilling

---

[112] SP 14/26/99/1; SP 14/17/43.

[113] Thomas Erskine, Viscount Fenton, was an old Scottish crony of James. They had been educated together, and in 1585 he had been made a gentleman of the bedchamber, and in 1601 a privy councillor in Scotland. At this date he was captain of the Yeomen of the Guard (*DNB*), with convenient access to the king. For a similar Scottish courtier, Lord Bruce of Kinloss, see below, p. 368.

[114] SP 14/26/99. Fish is not recorded as a fellow, but he did take further degrees (Venn, II, p. 141b).

[115] Morgan 1984.

[116] SP 14/140/58 (copy), the king to St John's, 29 March 1623. This was received by the college (Baker and Mayor 1869, I, p. 488, no. 180).

[117] See below, pp. 418–21.

electors. The pursuit of factional ends through resort to the Court inevitably drew courtiers and the Crown into the university. Involvement arising from this cause was in addition to all the other motives that directed the attention of the Court and the prince to the men, the ideas and the endowments represented by the colleges clustered along the Cam.

THE DEVOLUTION OF ELECTIONS

When disputes arose in the course of elections, the resolution of differences and, ultimately, the appointment to office would devolve to a senior official. In disputed elections to fellowships this might be the master, the Visitor, or the vice-chancellor. In the case of disputed elections to masterships, these might ultimately devolve to the chancellor of the university. The increase in the contentiousness surrounding the election of masters thus tended to enhance the influence of the chancellor. As we have seen,[118] from the early sixteenth century the chancellorship was invariably filled by an influential courtier. Consequently, the issues and personalities of university and college politics increasingly found their way to Court in attempts to influence the decisions of chancellors who invariably were also courtiers. Thus, following the dispute that arose in 1607 over the election of a master at Caius, Cecil – acting as chancellor – wrote to the vice-chancellor, naming his nominee, 'the collating of that Mastership resting wholly (by devolution) in me by the statute of that college'.[119] When a similar dispute arose at Christ's College two years later, the nomination again devolved to Cecil as chancellor,[120] while the outcome of the disputed election at Clare in 1601 had again been nomination to the mastership by Cecil.[121] In a dispute arising over the election of a master at Trinity Hall, in 1611–12, two of the fellows appealed to Cecil to nominate a suitably qualified person. They claimed that the power to nominate now rested in Cecil 'by devolution'.[122] This request reveals another facet of these disputes: academic participants were likely positively to encourage the involvement of outsiders if it looked as if this would favour their own interests.

When two aspiring fellows of Jesus College fell into a dispute with their master, John Duport, they appealed to the king to 'direct such course as to your Majesties Royal Wisdom shall seem convenient'. Charles put the issue to arbitration, and warned that if Duport refused to accept

---

[118] Above, p. 93.   [119] *HMCS*, XIX, p. 366. See below, p. 407n.
[120] *HMCS*, XXI, p. 160.   [121] *HMCS*, XI, pp. 114 ff.
[122] Trinity Hall Archives, Misc. Papers, I, no. 11: Thomas Beech to Salisbury, 17 Jan. 1612.

the conclusions of the arbitrators, the matter was to be referred back to him, 'that Wee may according to our Prerogative Royal take such further course as to us shall seem expedient in that behalfe'.[123] These instances should warn us against assuming that all royal intervention in both the universities and elsewhere in this period was simply a gratuitous exercise of power initiated at the centre and at the expense of all those on the periphery of the political arena. Rather, intervention was often sought in pursuit of the interests of contending factions within the university, or elsewhere. Equally, however, to those involved in local disputes, and who were aware of the factional stimulus to such intervention, it could not but appear both arbitrary and unjust. Furthermore, in such circumstances, the royal authority stood in danger of being reviled as evidently no more than the obnoxious instrument of one's opponents: tails have dogs and sometimes they wag them.

ACADEMICS IN PURSUIT OF COURT PATRONAGE

The pressure for places, including that of master of a college, encouraged unsolicited approaches to the Court by academics seeking to assure their appointment through outside influence. This could involve the solicitation of testimonials on the behalf of the candidate from fellow academics who already enjoyed the confidence of the Court: in 1603, Benjamin Carier, an aspirant to the mastership of Corpus, elicited from the heads of houses just such a testimonial directed to 'those who are desirouse to take notice of him in this behalfe'.[124] In one way these testimonials were merely an extension to the masterships of a general practice that was becoming common amongst clerics and academics seeking royal patronage.[125] They were partly the result of the increase in demand for places, and as such an attempt to anticipate the competition. In the university context they appear to be associated with attempts to invoke the royal prerogative in order to overcome constraints imposed on elections by the constitutions of individual colleges. When testimonials are associated with mandates this is clearly evidence for the initiative in these matters originating within the university.

We can trace the process at work in the case of Thomas Some's pursuit of a fellowship at Peterhouse in 1607. On 17 June he obtained a letter addressed to 'anie whomesoever' testifying that he was likely to prove serviceable in church or commonwealth if permitted to continue

---

[123] Jesus College Archives, St. 1.6, fos. 217, 219 (signet letter, Feb. 1637).
[124] SP 12/287/27.   [125] O'Day 1979, p. 89; cf. Knappen 1933, pp. 122 ff.

his studies.[126] Certainly, his credentials appeared to be very respectable: the testimonial was signed by the vice-chancellor, the master of his college, and the dean of Ely. However, even here one may suspect a certain degree of favouritism. The master of his college was his 'cousin' Robert Some.[127] The dean of Ely just happened to be Robert Some's fellow head, Humphrey Tyndall, currently also master of Queens'. Both Tyndall and the elder Some were of the same generation in terms of their university experiences. All three shared common Norfolk origins.[128] Thus equipped, the young Thomas clearly headed for a 'whomesoever' who had some access to the royal source of dispensation, apparently gathering a number of other testimonials on the way.[129] Five days after having obtained his testimonial, he lighted upon Edward Bruce, baron of Kinloss, a long-time servant of James who had come south with the king and had been appointed master of the rolls in 1603.[130] Bruce can then be found writing to Sir Thomas Lake, who as Latin secretary and clerk of the signet had direct access to the king, and was responsible for drafting signet letters[131] – evidently Bruce had already gained a fine sense of the workings of the English Court. He asked Lake to move the king to write letters to Peterhouse on behalf of this poor scholar for his pre-election to a probationary fellowship.[132] Acquiring these letters seems to have taken some time, but Lake evidently obliged and a mandate was drafted. This invoked the royal prerogative to dispense with any statutes, including those limiting fellowships to specific counties, that might have obstructed Thomas Some's election. He duly took his place during 1609.[133]

Similarly, the master and seniors of Trinity College had written a testimonial on behalf of Thomas Smith, which had resulted in an Elizabethan mandate,[134] as did the master and fellows of Christ's on behalf of George Ward.[135] The bishop of Ely (Lancelot Andrewes), Visitor of Peterhouse, recommended Richard Blake for a fellowship at the college. The outcome was a mandate to dispense with the statute of country.[136] St John's

[126] SP 18/27/591.
[127] 'Cousin' in the seventeenth-century sense; the precise relationship is unclear. Though the son of a fisherman, Thomas Some claimed descent from the ancient family of that name (Venn, IV, p. 120a), of which Robert Some was a member.
[128] Venn, IV, pp. 119b, 284a. [129] This can be inferred from SP 14/27/59.
[130] DNB; cf. above, n. 113.
[131] SP 14/27/59. Bruce was master of the rolls and Lake keeper of the records at Whitehall (1595–6: S.O. 3/1, correcting DNB), which may have brought them together.
[132] SP 38/8/18, Dec. 1608. [133] Venn, IV, p. 120a. [134] SP 12/265/84.
[135] SP 14/9A/731 (testimonial), 2 August 1604; SP 14/9A/73 (draft signet letter), 13 Oct. 1604. Ward graduated in Feb. 1604, but the testimonial appears not to have succeeded: there is no record of him as a fellow of Pembroke (Venn, IV, p. 331a).
[136] SP 38/8, 8 Dec. 1618. The docquets sometimes, as here, note by whom a mandate was obtained: these details are not recorded in CSPD.

testified on behalf of Samuel Periam. Armed with this testimonial, Periam petitioned Charles for a mandate to the college for his election.[137] Leonard Mawe, the retiring master of Trinity College, testified to the literary merits of the poet and dramatist Thomas Randolph and successfully requested a mandate to ensure his election to a fellowship.[138]

The recommendations for both Smith and Ward were for fellowships at colleges other than those of which they were currently members, and which had provided the testimonials. Fairly clearly, colleges were anxious to find places for their graduates. Perhaps themselves lacking the resources necessary, they attempted to circumvent the statutory restrictions and the natural reluctance of other colleges to elect non-members. This they did by issuing testimonials intended to elicit mandatory intervention on behalf of their favoured student, but usually in another college. Not unnaturally, this procedure often aroused opposition from the college at the receiving end of these requests. In 1608 Christ's objected to the placing of Gabriel Moore as a fellow by mandate from Trinity College.[139] Gonville and Caius pointed out that their statutes required them to prefer members of their own college.[140] St John's complained of an attempt to place a man from another college in a fellowship. It would, the college claimed, be a 'Great discouragement to our paynefull students, if forreyners and straungers be admytted to their hopes'.[141] Testimonials are likely to indicate an intention to seek external patronage in the pursuit of university places. They often resulted in mandates designed to overcome the reluctance of electors to elect, or to circumvent the statutory inhibitions on the election of unqualified candidates. In pursuit of these particular ends the royal prerogative was being invoked, and increasingly during the reigns of Elizabeth and the first two Stuarts those about the Court were being invited to participate in the affairs of the universities. In this way the exercise of the powers of the Crown were being extended – but not on its own initiative. In these instances the motivation came from provincial academics in pursuit of their own, local, interests. Such patterns of behaviour, here manifested in the context of Cambridge University, are not without interest for our understanding of the wider reaches of politics in early modern England.

Further encouragement to intervention arose from the knowledge of the proprietorial interest claimed by the Crown in colleges such as King's.

---

[137] SP 16/159/17, 171, but without evident effect (Venn, III, p. 346b).
[138] SP 16/148/41. For Randolph, see *DNB* and Randolph 1875. He was elected a fellow in 1629 (Venn, III, p. 420a).
[139] Venn, III, p. 204b; SP 14/28/18 (draft signet letter); S.O. 3/3, 18 June 1608 (docquet of signet letters). The objections failed: Moore got his fellowship.
[140] BL Lansdowne MS 45, fo. 132 (no. 62).   [141] Baker and Mayor 1869, I, p. 477 (1614).

This directed the attention of would-be masters to those Court intermediaries who could exercise influence on their behalf. Following the death
of Dr Goad in 1610, Fogg Newton wrote to Cecil, reporting that he had
been informed that the king was likely to grant the election to the fellows, only requiring that they should choose one of those whom the king
would nominate. Newton assumed that the king would depend on Cecil
and other privy councillors for recommendation of the nominees, and
asked that Cecil might ensure that his name was included.[142] Of course,
the corollary of such supplications as that of Fogg Newton to Cecil was
a commitment to accommodate the courtly patron as occasion and the
newly acquired office might serve – as one supplicant for the provostship
of King's was not unwilling to make clear to Cecil: 'For my thankfullness
towards your Lordshp, what is in mee beeing so meane, & what can I doe
to requite your Lordship beeing so great[.] Thear is no meanes of gratification or shewing thankfullnes within the power of that place, that shall
not wholy bee applied to the desire & comandment of your Lordship.'[143]
Men 'beeing so meane' in degree had little other than that which fell
to them through 'the power of that place' – college property, leases, and
an influential say in the elections to scholarships and fellowships – with
which to satisfy the reciprocal obligations of the patronage relationship
they had invoked as a means of acquiring office. These were elections
conducted within the milieu of a patron–client society.

When, in 1580, the master and fellows of Christ's prevaricated over
letters received from various courtiers on behalf of Robert Hamon for a
fellowship, the matter was referred to the Visitors of the college: the vice-
chancellor, John Hatcher, and two senior doctors. Whereupon, letters
were dispatched to the vice-chancellor by Hamon's patrons, requesting
his admission, and promising that 'we will give you our hearty thanks, &
requite you with any pleasure we may'.[144] Here the flow of obligation was
in the opposite direction to that in the previous instance – and as one of
the last men ever to serve as vice-chancellor who was not already the master of a college, Hatcher no doubt harboured expectations of subsequent
elevation.[145] The pressures to accede to such a request were considerable,
although in this instance Hatcher was never promoted and Hamon did
not become a fellow until 1582.[146] Similarly, in 1622, the provost of King's

---

[142] SP 14/53/83.   [143] SP 14/53/84.
[144] CUL, MS Mm. i. 25, fo. 5. On Hatcher, see Leedham-Green 1986, I, pp. 367–82.
[145] He died in 1587, and was in fact the last but one vice-chancellor not a head of house before the
1990s. In 1586–7 John Capcot was a fellow of Trinity when elected vice-chancellor; master of
Corpus before his term ended (Tanner 1917, p. 24; Winstanley 1935, p. 9).
[146] Venn, II, pp. 329b, 295a.

College, Samuel Collins, was threatened from Court with an unwelcome but not easily declined 'promotion' from the lucrative provostship to the poverty of the see of Bristol.[147] At the time, the friends at Court of Lady Leven were attempting to pressurise Collins into renewing a lease to her, and this unlooked-for patronage was in retribution for 'his so much spoken of slighting and neglect of their letters and personal mediation in her behalf, for renewing the lease she begs of that college'.[148] Collins was forced to ask two of his fellow masters, Valentine Carey and Thomas Bainbridge, to intercede on his behalf with Sir George Goring, who was the courtier supposed to be 'the chiefe in this busines'.[149] An acute contemporary observer assumed that Collins would only avoid 'promotion' by conceding the lease. Some two months later the same observer was reporting that Collins had 'escaped the bishopric':[150] the implication was that Lady Leven had been satisfied. Given the customs of the times other masters were happy explicitly to acknowledge their obligations to those about the Court in the prevailing language of obligation.

The long-serving Elizabethan master of Peterhouse Andrew Perne had well-established connections with Parker, Whitgift and Burghley. It is claimed that through his influence Peterhouse men went on to become masters of colleges.[151] For his part, Perne was willing in both word and action to acknowledge his responsibilities in these mutual relationships with the great and the powerful. When, in 1576, Burghley wrote to Peterhouse on behalf of Ezekiel Hilliard for a fellowship, Perne responded with obliging alacrity, for, 'as I have been always singularlie bound unto your Lord: from tyme to tyme, in any sute that I have had unto your Honor, either for ye universitie or for my selfe: so I take it my bounden dutye in any thinge that maye lye in my small power, to accomplish your Honor's request'. True to his word, Perne ensured that Hilliard was admitted to the fellowship in preference to five other duly qualified competitors for the place.[152]

In its turn the exercise of influence by courtiers on behalf of their academic clients in academic elections reinforced the mutual obligations – and on occasion the competition – in these higher circles. Thus, when

---

[147] 'Dr Searchfield, bishop of Bristol, is lately dead [11 Oct.1622, Horn 1996, p. 10]; but that place is so poor that we have not yet heard of any suitors or pretendants for it' (John Chamberlain to Sir Dudley Carleton, 4 Nov. 1622: Birch 1849, II, p. 348).

[148] Birch 1849, II, p. 349; BL Harl. MS 389, fo. 260.   [149] *Ibid.*   [150] Birch 1849, II, p. 350.

[151] *VCH Cambs.*, III, p. 337; Walker 1930, II, p. 134. For the relations of Perne and Whitgift, see esp. Collinson 1991, pp. 11–12.

[152] BL Harl. MS 7031, fo. 87v, 15 May 1576. Hilliard was formally admitted to a probationary fellowship on 26 May 1576 (for this and his later career, see Walker 1930, II, pp. 1, 15, 26, 28, 70, 85).

Valentine Carey was seeking the mastership of Christ's in 1609, he turned to his old patron, Lord Chancellor Ellesmere. In his turn, Ellesmere wrote to Cecil on behalf of Carey, making it clear that a favour bestowed on the aspiring academic purchased his, Ellesmere's, obligation at Cecil's hands, 'if it may please your Lordship to afford hym your good favor in this his suite, I assure yow, yow shall be[153] it for a verye woorthy man, and I shall be ever most readye with all true thankfullnes to acknowledge it'.[154] And acknowledge it Ellesmere may have been obliged to do, for Carey certainly found his way on to the king's short-list of candidates. Although he did not make it to the provost's lodge at King's he did eventually become master at Christ's.[155] Patronage in academic elections – particularly Court patronage – was not gratuitously exercised, or free of obligations for the Court intermediary, even when he was as eminent a person as the lord chancellor.

Inevitably, there were also occasions on which Court interests clashed in the colleges over the manipulation of elections. In September 1583 the master of Christ's, Edmund Barwell, wrote to Burghley apologising for not having acceded to his letters in favour of Samuel Proctor for a fellowship. Barwell explained that Burghley had been pre-empted by 'our promisses to the Rt. Honourable Walter Mildmay an especiall Benefactor to our House' for another candidate. However, he also saw fit to soften the rebuff by promising to see what he could do for the chancellor's protégé.[156] A few years later, in January 1585, Richard Howland, another of Burghley's clients and his chaplain, was elected to the bishopric of Peterborough.[157] However, he did not resign the mastership of St John's until 25 February 1587,[158] and the delay may be not unrelated to the competition between Burghley and Lord Lumley over the appointment of his successor.

As St John's was his old college, Burghley had a strong personal interest in the foundation – if anything, stronger than that of Mildmay at Christ's. Andrew Perne wrote to him at this time of 'this matter of St Johns, knowing your honourable good affection to benefitt it all kynde of wayes'.[159] However, Lumley was trying to place his chaplain as master in return for bestowing his famous library on the university, and there were fears that either Oxford would get the books or Burghley's interest in his old college would be alienated[160] – 'as for the preferring of his Chapleyn

---

[153] The reading is uncertain.   [154] SP 14/49/100.
[155] On Carey's election, see Morgan 1983, pp. 532 ff.
[156] BL Harl. MS 7031, fo. 40. For a similar clash between the queen and Burghley over the election of a fellow of Queens' in 1585, see BL Lansdowne 45, fo. 115.
[157] Horn 1996, p. 115.   [158] *VCH Cambs.*, III, p. 450a.   [159] BL Lansdowne MS 45, fo. 130.
[160] *Ibid.* Lumley had been a student at Cambridge, but was currently steward at Oxford.

to that place, to loose from the said house such an honourabl'e benefactor and Patrone as your honor is, and may be',[161] wrote Andrew Perne to Burghley, articulating the college's quandary. The outcome of this clash of Court influence was that Burghley and Whitgift jointly nominated William Whitaker to St John's in February 1587,[162] while Oxford got Lumley's books. Acquiring resources for learning was one thing, but the loss of political influence was quite another when two such considerations hung in the balance.

An earlier promotion of Howland from the mastership of Magdalene to that of St John's in 1577 had also occasioned a clash of Court interests at the highest level. The indications are that the parsimoniously minded Burghley was intent upon ringing the maximum patronage advantage from the situation by ensuring that the vacancy created by the promotion of one of his clients was filled by another, ensuring that although the individuals changed, the heads of both the colleges involved remained obliged to him for their preferments. When rumours of Howland's imminent departure for St John's reached Magdalene, the fellows of the latter college wrote to Burghley expressing their desire 'always to fight under the banner of so honourable a patron' as he was, and suggesting that he might care to appoint another of his chaplains, Degory Nicholls,[163] then fellow of Peterhouse, as their master – for the moment they remained blissfully ignorant of the shattered calm that the ultimately successful Nicholls and his newly acquired wife were to call down upon their college.[164] Burghley was not unwilling to accede to these promptings, although there was a delay of almost a month between the receipt of the letter from the fellows and Burghley's sealing of the document appointing Nicholls to the mastership.[165] Matters appeared to be sown up between Burghley and the various authorities at the university, including the vice-chancellor, Dr Roger Goad, who at the end of July had seconded the fellows' recommendation of Nicholls. However, all did not go to plan, and later Goad had to write to Burghley of 'the unlooked for admission' of an unexpected second candidate for office.[166] This was Henry Copinger, on whose behalf the queen had addressed letters to the college at the end of July.[167] Those who acquired these letters on Copinger's behalf appear to have done so without his prior knowledge – or so he claimed in subsequent exculpation to Burghley: 'For He which knoweth all is not ignorant how little I dreamed of any such matter before

[161] *Ibid.*   [162] CUA, Lett. 10.6.a.   [163] *HMCS*, III, p. 147.
[164] Above, p. 300.   [165] *HMCS*, III, pp. 147, 149.
[166] *HMCS*, III, p. 148; *CSPD*, I, p. 552.   [167] *HMCS*, III, p. 149.

it was done, and how mere a stranger I was to the proceeding in it.'[168] In fact, Copinger's Suffolk background, his early university career at St John's in the radical days of the 1560s, and his subsequent presentation to the rectory of Lavenham in his native county strongly suggest that – unknowingly or not on this occasion – he was the protégé of the more puritanically inclined of the Suffolk gentry, who may well have formed an alliance with a courtier of similar disposition, such as Sir Nicholas Bacon or Sir Francis Walsingham.[169] It was this person who must have been responsible for making 'the good report we [i.e., the queen] hear of the learning piety, zeal in religion and other virtues' of Copinger.[170] Confronted with two authoritative instructions to admit different men as master, the fellows were in a quandary. It was a quandary that they resolved by bowing to the highest power and resort to classical justification: they obeyed the queen's command, admitted Copinger, and apologetically explained to Burghley that they had acted 'as piety commands and necessity compels, as saith Ulysses in Homer'.[171] Precisely what happened next is not clear, but Copinger did not long enjoy his victory, for Burghley seems to have prevailed with the queen against his rivals in the matter, and within the year Nicholls had entered on the mastership.[172]

A similar lack of coordination at the highest levels at Court is evidenced in another instance not at Cambridge but in the case of Winchester College – an institution the status and constitution of which was not that different in essentials from the colleges in the universities and which was certainly treated in an equivalent manner by the Court. Rival nominations were made to the wardenship of Winchester. In theory the warden should have been elected by the warden and fellows of New College, Oxford, and have been admitted by their Visitor, the bishop of Winchester. However, in the summer of 1596, the lord treasurer, Buckhurst, wrote purportedly expressing the queen's wish that Winchester should elect Mr John Harmar.[173] The bishop of Winchester replied in some agitation that Henry Cotten had previously obtained letters patent of the queen, who had granted the office by her prerogative. The bishop was anxious not to cross the royal will and ignore a formal instrument of state action in the form of the letters patent: 'If it please Her Majesty to revoke

---

[168] *Ibid.*

[169] On the puritanism of a group of Suffolk gentry round Bury, see Collinson 1967, ch. 5; MacCulloch 1986, pp. 199–207. For the likelihood of local puritan patronage of other Cambridge puritans, the Playferes, see Morgan 1983.

[170] *HMCS*, III, p. 149.   [171] *Ibid.*; see above, p. 348.

[172] See Hoyle in Cunich *et al.* 1994, p. 84.   [173] *HMCS*, VI, pp. 299 ff.

those former letters patent by some sufficient other deed, I shall be very ready to admit any lawfully chosen or named. To undo that done already is not in my power . . . For the matter itself I stand indifferent, any[174] my desire is, before I admit any other warden, I may have my sufficient warrant from Her Highness.'[175]

The quandary that the bishop of Winchester found himself in, in the summer of 1596, and the difficulties experienced by the fellows of Magdalene, confronted with two rival nominees, were the outcome of the structural characteristics of Court patronage during the late sixteenth century. First, there was the opportunity for contesting factions within colleges to solicit the patronage of a variety of courtiers. Second, there was the confusion of roles inherent in the person of individuals such as Cecil or Buckhurst: university chancellor, lord treasurer or secretary of state; patron of particular colleges within the universities; patron of individuals within the universities. Third, there was a further confusion that arose at the highest level, where government officials were also of necessity courtiers and subject to all the pressures of other, non-governmental, courtiers. Finally, there was the highly personalised nature of a system that depended on steps by the monarch in order to initiate official action. This had the effect of concentrating on the Court and those about the monarch the attentions of those seeking the favour of a royal dispensation or grant.[176]

One consequence of the inducements to cultivate Court patronage in the pursuit of university places was that rivalries in academe became entangled in rivalries between clienteles at Court. Indeed, there were occasions on which such Court rivalries were positively exploited and encouraged by academics in pursuit of office. We have already noted the dispute during the 1580s between Thomas Osborne on the one hand and the master and many of the fellows of Christ's on the other.[177] Osborne had obtained letters in his behalf from both Sir Christopher Hatton and Burghley.[178] To counter this influence, Barwell had openly proclaimed to Burghley's agents in the matter that the college intended to elect another in opposition to Osborne, while some of the fellows asserted that they would 'chuse such a one, as hath friends in the Court, as will maintain his election, when it is done, against whomsoever'.[179] All this proved mere bravado, and Osborne retained his place, with due and effusive thanks to Lord Burghley. As Thomas Baker commented dryly later, 'there was

[174] The reading is doubtful.   [175] *HMCS*, VI, p. 300.
[176] For the specific forms of these dispensations and grants, see below, pp. 381–5.
[177] Above, pp. 363–4.   [178] CUL, MS Mm. ii. 25, fos. 5v–6; BL Harl. MS 7031, fo. 39r–v.
[179] BL Harl. MS 7031, fo. 40.

(I doubt) too much of Friendship & affection in the conduct of the whole matter'.[180] No doubt so, but the incident does serve to illuminate the manner in which it was possible for clients to contemplate exploiting their various patrons at Court in order to achieve their particular local ends.

From the viewpoint of the great Court patrons it was necessary to retain, and if possible to enlarge, the number of their dependants at the expense of their rivals. In this context it was politic for would-be suppliants to read carefully the auguries for the relative standing of rival Court clienteles. This is well illustrated by the complicated circumstances that arose following on the death of Thomas Byng, master of Clare Hall, in December 1599.[181] A number of abortive elections and nominations to the mastership took place over the next fifteen months, until William Smith was finally installed, on 24 March 1601. During part of this time the earl of Essex was chancellor of the university, and in normal circumstances it would have been appropriate to request him to intercede with the queen on behalf of the supplicant. But Essex's affairs were in a bad way by this time, he having left his post in Ireland and arrived back in London on 28 September 1599. There he was imprisoned for having treated with Tyrone, and tried before a special court on 5 June 1600, although set at liberty two months later. At the same time, his financial arrangements were collapsing about him, and his creditors were closing in.[182] However, in December 1599 he had given his promise of the mastership of Clare to Dr Branthwaite, although he seems not to have shown any great enthusiasm for imposing his will in the matter.[183] In the meantime, the college had elected one of its own number, William Bois, while the queen's letters had been obtained for another protagonist, Dr Mowtlow.[184] The matter was put out for legal opinion and arbitration, and in the interim various other candidates were promoted by their Court patrons. The heads themselves suggested Richard Neile, Cecil's chaplain,[185] while Sir Horatio Palavicino continued to push the interests of William Bois.[186] Sir Edward Coke and a bevy of noblemen favoured

---

[180] BL Harl. MS 7031, fo. 40. There is circumstantial evidence of the connections which may have lain behind the patronage of Osborne. Sir Christopher Hatton referred to Thomas Osborne as his 'cousin' and they were neighbours in Northamptonshire with houses at Holdenby and Kelmarsh. Other Osbornes were Remembrancers of the Lord Treasurer, Burghley – also an influential figure in Northamptonshire.

[181] On this election see Morgan 1983, p. 596.

[182] *DNB*; James 1986, pp. 416–65. The loss of the farm of the sweet wines spelt his financial ruin (*HMCS*, x, pp. 311 ff).

[183] *HMCS*, xiv, p. 113; x, p. 381.   [184] *HMCS*, xiv, p. 113; xi, pp. 418 ff, 436.

[185] Scott 1909, pp. 19 ff.   [186] *HMCS*, x, p. 38.

Dr Edward Playfere,[187] as did that candidate's former college friend Sir Edward Denny.[188] Playfere seems to have hung about the Court for some weeks before Sir John Stanhope animated his candidature. Andrew Byng was one of the participants in a second but disputed election;[189] but even his godfather, Archbishop Whitgift, to whom he was a chaplain, did not think him suitable for the post.[190] Following a third election Bois withdrew from the fray, and persuaded his patron, Sir Horatio Palavicino, to support Bois' friend, Dr John Overall.[191] This introduced a further complication, for Playfere and Overall were vigorously opposed on theological grounds, and sustained a major encounter at the Commencement in June 1600.[192] During this time, William Smith was also engaged in cultivating his Court connections, although not always with success, partly because of his own social ineptitude, as is evident in his correspondence with Thomas Crompton.[193] Crompton was a functionary of the earl of Essex, who at the time was attempting to maintain the financial and social credit of his beleaguered master.[194] One of the candidates, Playfere, had taken the precaution of obtaining 'express licence' from the earl to sue to other patrons at Court. This was a cautious courtesy on Playfere's part, for as the matter concerned the university this was an area of patronage in which, as its chancellor, Essex had an almost proprietorial interest, even in his current straitened circumstances. Although he claimed that he had sought a like permission, Smith was treated to a 'short and unsweet message' from Crompton.[195] In reply he complained that 'somewhat has been insinuated against me' to the earl 'through sinister suggestion of the adverse competitor'.[196] He went on to justify his proceedings. 'If I have done anything displeasing to his Honour, it must needs arise of one of these three: either that I sued, that I sued to her Majesty, or that I sued by such means', all of which had precedent, he claimed,[197] and 'I could never learn he [Essex] misliked any for using their friends in Court.' And here, of course, was the rub so far as the Essex clientele were concerned, for the queen had referred the settling of the Clare Hall dispute to Cecil and Whitgift, Essex's staunch opponents at Court. Moreover, they also appear to have been involved as alternative patrons in the dispute. Thus, at some time prior to November 1600, Smith had made approaches to Henry, Lord Cobham, Cecil's brother-in-law.[198] Certainly, in the following March Cobham was writing to Cecil to ask if he had yet disposed of

---

[187] *HMCS*, x, pp. 41, 382.   [188] *HMCS*, x, p. 43.   [189] *HMCS*, x, p. 54.
[190] *HMCS*, x, p. 7.   [191] *HMCS*, x, pp. 54, 332–3.
[192] *HMCS*, x, pp. 200–12; see Lake 1982, pp. 235–6, 331.   [193] *HMCS*, x, pp. 311–12, 354.
[194] *Ibid.*   [195] *HMCS*, x, pp. 380–1.   [196] *HMCS*, x, p. 380.   [197] *Ibid.*
[198] This is probably the 'Lord Harry' referred to by Smith at this date (*HMCS*, x, p. 381).

the mastership of Clare, as he wished to reply to Smith's enquiries.[199] But as the earl's fortunes declined, even those within the university, one of his special spheres of influence, saw fit to shift their allegiances in order to achieve their ends, as Smith made abundantly clear. With some justification he claimed with reference to Whitgift and Cecil that they 'could not by me be neglected; being threatened, if I take any other course, to be crossed; if this, I had large promises presently to be despatched'.[200] Thus with both threat and promise Essex's enemies drew his potential clients from him: Smith was admitted master just a month after Essex was led to his execution on Tower Hill. As the convoluted case of the mastership of Clare Hall and the demise of the earl of Essex demonstrates, by 1600 in order to forward their careers aspiring academics required an astute grasp of the niceties of the waxing and waning of influences at Court. Even when they were resident in Cambridge, by the century's turn such men could not afford to take their eyes off Whitehall.

Royal letters mandatory were not the only letters received by the colleges in attempts to determine the outcome of elections. With influential connections, such as we have seen invoked during the election at Clare, some contenders first relied on the direct influence in Cambridge of their courtly patrons. The earl of Shrewsbury had interests in St John's, and his client, David Dolben, depended upon these to effect his entry into a fellowship at that college.[201] Gabriel Harvey successfully induced his family's near-neighbour at Saffron Walden, Sir Thomas Smith, to write on his behalf for a fellowship at Trinity Hall.[202] Smith's long-standing connections both with the college and with the university at large, and his status at Court, certainly recommended him as a patron. Inevitably, however, refusal by a college to accede to these private requests encouraged their influential authors to invoke the mandatory authority of royal letters in support of their clients, and their own dignity which they had engaged on behalf of the client. Thus, in February 1617, the earl of Suffolk recommended his kinsman, Joseph Thurston, for a fellowship at St John's. The master and seniors prevaricated, and attempted to shield themselves from pressure by claiming that the electors would probably not consist of the signatories to the letter in which they attempted to evade Suffolk's request. Thus prevaricated with, Suffolk turned to other means, and by 20 March the earl had obtained a royal mandate for Thurston. This was received on 3 April, and on the 10th the earl's client was pre-elected

---

[199] *HMCS*, XI, pp. 114–15. [200] *HMCS*, X, p. 381. For what follows see SP 12/279/40.
[201] *DNB*; Venn, II, p. 53b; Batho 1971, p. 293; Jamison and Bill 1966, p. 118. Dolben did not get the fellowship, but the college promised to recompense him another way.
[202] Scott 1884, p. 162, for similar private letters, see BL Lansdowne MS 45, fo. 132.

to an Essex fellowship, to which he was fully admitted the following September.[203] Therefore, even when the Crown had no immediate direct interest in the outcome of an election, ultimately the royal authority might be invoked. When academics sought the exercise of influence on their behalf by courtiers there was always the possibility that the courtier would have to use his influence at Court to conclude a matter in which he had engaged his own honour.

The influence of John Preston, the mercurial master of Emmanuel, with the greatest of courtiers, the duke of Buckingham, is well known, and helps to account for his election to the headship of that college.[204] On other occasions courtiers such as the duke of Lennox[205] and Sir George Goring[206] can be detected as key figures in the machinations of those pursuing masterships, or attempting to avoid dismissal from office. During the Elizabethan period, although perhaps to a lesser extent under James and Charles, a wide variety of noblemen and courtiers can be found acting as intermediaries on behalf of those seeking scholarships, fellowships, livings, masterships and leases. These include Sir Christopher Hatton,[207] Sir Walter Mildmay,[208] the earl of Huntingdon,[209] Sir Walter Raleigh,[210] Sir Horatio Palavicino,[211] Sir Julius Caesar,[212] Edward, Lord Bruce of Kinloss,[213] Sir Roger Manners[214] and the earl of Suffolk.[215] At a somewhat less exalted, although no less influential, level about the Court, leverage was exercised and mandates were obtained by the master of the children of the Chapel Royal,[216] with the aim of influencing decisions within the universities. As the personal and factional divisions within the universities increased, so did the importance to academics of access to figures such as these as a means of ensuring a successful realisation of their aspirations.

In pursuit of the Crown's attempt to control the universities and the attempts by courtiers to exploit its resources, the Court was drawn into those institutions. For their part, the pursuit of their personal and factional ends thrust academics into the Court and into the complexities of Court patronage.[217] Consequently, thoughts of the Court – either in fear or in hopeful expectation – were never far away when it came to elections, and especially the election of masters. By 1610 it was natural for both the fellows and the aspirants to the newly vacant provostship at King's

[203] Venn, IV, p. 240a.   [204] Morgan 1983, p. 13; Collinson in Bendall *et al.* 1999, pp. 216–20.
[205] CUA, Lett. 12.A.24 (1635).   [206] BL Harl. MS 389, fo. 260 (1622).
[207] CUL, MS Mm. ii. 25, fos. 5v ff.   [208] BL Harl. MS 7031, fo. 40v.   [209] *Ibid.*
[210] Fletcher and Upton 1885, pp. 181 ff.   [211] *HMCS*, x, p. 38.
[212] S.O. 3/3, 9 Oct. 1607.   [213] *CSPD*, VIII, p. 361.   [214] Morgan 1983, p. 640.
[215] Baker and Mayor 1869.   [216] S.O. 3/3, 25 April 1607.   [217] See above, chapters 1, 4.

to anticipate royal intervention[218] and to expect the directions of their chancellor in the matter: 'Some I suppose of that Societie will attend your Lordship for your direction about their choice.'[219]

Sheer physical stamina was not the least of the requirements for those intending to play for these stakes. Robert Creighton's pursuit of the mastership of Catharine Hall in 1635 had him galloping back and forth to Court,[220] while in the winter of 1584–5, Gabriel Harvey complained that as an aspirant to the mastership of Trinity Hall, 'Truly my Brothers & my self with my Man, have nigh hand killed four good geldings about this cause' in travelling to and from London.[221] In 1614, John Preston ensured the election of John Davenant as master of Queens' through similar efforts. Having 'laid horses and all things ready', Preston rode from Cambridge to London to seek the favour of Viscount Rochester, arriving at Court before the dawn – or the courtier – was up.[222] Even as late as 1660, Dr John Worthington was to assume that he could not obtain the mastership of Jesus College because 'My uncertainty of bodily temper would not permit me take a journey to London' in order to solicit at Court.[223]

THE ELECTION AT CATHARINE HALL, 1635[224]

Some graphic insights into the procedures involved in eliciting the royal favour are contained in the tale of Robert Creighton's attempt upon the headship of Catharine Hall (now St Catharine's College) in 1635. Since 1625, Creighton had been Professor of Greek. Appointed Public Orator in 1627, he acquired a prebend's stall at Lincoln in 1632 and was made treasurer of Wells cathedral (where he was later to be dean and bishop) in 1632, and was subsequently a chaplain to Charles I.[225] He had obtained his fellowship at Trinity College by a royal mandate in 1619.[226] He was already a pluralist and he does not seem to have been an enthusiastic candidate for the Catharine Hall mastership: he subsequently claimed that 'I cared not for it', but that as he intended to resign his place as Professor of Greek 'this might be occasion for me to live still in the Universitie',[227] while 'the faithfulnes of my ten years service might perhaps have prompted me to the hopes of as great a dignitie as the

---

[218] SP 14/53/82, 83.   [219] SP 14/53/84.   [220] Morgan 1984.
[221] BL Harl. MS 7031, fo. 79.   [222] Fuller 1897, p. 56.   [223] BL Harl. MS 7033, fo. 63.
[224] This section is based on Morgan 1984.
[225] *DNB*; Venn, 1, p. 416b; Horn and Smith 1999, p. 46; Horn and Bailey 1979, pp. 2, 6, 15, 80, 110–11.
[226] SP 38/11, 22 Sept. 1619.   [227] CUA, Lett. 12.A.24.

Master-shippe of Catharine Hall, had I beene verie eager on the spurre of ambition'.[228] In fact, the initiative in favour of his election appears to have originated with John Lothian, the senior fellow of Catharine Hall.[229]

It was Lothian who had summoned Creighton to his chamber on a Sunday afternoon in July 1635 to inform him that Richard Sibbes, the incumbent master, had died. Lothian prompted Creighton to try for the office. The deposition of Thomas Buck, the university's senior bedell, who had been present at the afternoon meeting, and had talked with Lothian privately beforehand, suggests that Lothian, while himself not wishing for the office, felt isolated in the college, and wanted support. Lothian told Buck that after the death of Sibbes 'That he was left alone, and had not any one of the fellows to joyn with him', while in their exculpatory depositions the fellows claimed 'That he onely of all the Fellowes had spoken with Mr Crighton [for the mastership] being his Countryman & acquaintance.'[230] Lothian's sense of insecurity may have derived from the means by which he had himself entered the college, as a result of a royal mandate nominating him to a fellowship.[231] Unfortunately, a reading of the statutes of the college, and consultation with Creighton's trusted friend, Thomas Shirley,[232] another fellow of Trinity College, and with Buck, revealed that Creighton was not qualified for election as the statutes required that the master of Catharine Hall should be a bachelor or doctor of divinity, and at this time Creighton was only MA. As Buck subsequently reflected, the means by which Lothian had obtained his own fellowship prompted him to seek the obvious means of overcoming this statutory impediment to his plans: 'and by what I then remembred concerning the manner of Mr Lothians being made fellow of the said hall did conceive that he then intended that Mr Creiton should make suit for no other letteres from his Majestie than those which were to be absolutely Mandatory with a non obstante to their statute and any other thing to the contrary whatsoever'.[233] Creighton claimed that Lothian 'spake to me thus; you see if wee would wee cannot chuse you unles his Majestie dispense with our Statutes; therefore if you will trie your friends at Court to procure his Majesties Letters before the Sun rise on Wednesday morning, I promise you my voice, & best assistance'.[234] Thereupon Creighton 'took horse', galloped off to Court, 'and before the

---

[228] *Ibid.*   [229] Venn, III, p. 106b.   [230] CUA, Lett. 12.A.20–1, 24, 26.
[231] CUA, Lett. 12.A.26.
[232] Venn, IV, p. 67: he entered Trinity in 1611, and was a fellow from 1618.
[233] CUA, Lett. 12.A.26.   [234] CUA, Lett. 12.A.24.

next day at noone I had obtayned his Majesties grant by the intercession of my Gratious Lord and Patrone the Duke of Lennox'.

It was at this stage that difficulties began to occur for, 'finding noe Secretarie of State to attend, I was forced in that straight and narrow compend of time to use mine owne hand in the penning of his Majesties Letters'. Having some compunction about imposing himself upon an unwilling college and being loath to invoke the full force of royal authority, the letters 'I framed whollie dispensatorie, to remove those barres of Statutes', rather than mandatory, obliging the college to elect him. Returning to Cambridge that same night he sent the letters by Shirley to Lothian about 10 p.m. – only to be told by the latter that 'the fellowes had importun'd him and he hadd already passed a Scrutinie, and chosen an other man for the securitie of theire College'. Presumably, Lothian had not been unduly concerned about succumbing to the pressures for an immediate election, as it appears from the reported conversations of the preceding Sunday that he had expected Creighton to obtain letters requiring his election rather than those which simply removed impediments to his candidature.[235] Lothian expressed some regret, 'Wishing the Letters had been Mandatorie, or at least more powerfull, and efficacious', and told Creighton that 'if I brought a mandate what they had done they wuld nullifie if I brought none what they had done should stand for good'.[236] Thus, Lothian had assumed that they had made 'a hypotheticall condicionall election', that could be annulled on the expression of sufficiently strong royal wishes to the contrary. Lothian apparently advised Creighton to take horse once more and 'to returne againe to the Court for letters Mandatory' while he procrastinated over the actual admission of Ralph Brownrigg, the competitor to Creighton for the office and now newly elected.[237]

On being told this, and after all his energetic exertions, Creighton appears to have had enough: 'for my part I was content to sitt downe rather than to entangle mye selfe in a twisted & interfearing busines'.[238] He agreed with Lothian that his expected rival should be admitted and 'that his Majesties lettres should not be mentioned'.[239] He should, perhaps, have been more cautious at the outset of becoming embroiled in Lothian's machinations. For the irony is that this pocket academic Machiavell had at first managed to bungle his own election as a fellow of Catharine Hall for precisely the same reason that had defeated his plans for Creighton! Buck recalled that '(in regard the first letters which it pleased his Majestie to send

---

[235] CUA, Lett. 12.A.26. [236] The last phrase is added to the deposition in Creighton's hand.
[237] CUA, Lett. 12.A.20. [238] CUA, Lett. 12.A.26. [239] CUA, Lett. 12.A.20.

in his [Lothian's] behalf for the said place, were not effectually drawn up) he was enforced to procure his Majesties second letters in a more effectual manner for the obtaining of the said fellowship'.[240] Unfortunately for all the parties involved – Lothian, Creighton and their confidants Shirley and Buck, the fellows of the college and their newly elected master, Ralph Brownrigg – the train of events that Creighton's solicitation of Court favour had set in motion could not so readily be terminated by his opting out at this late stage. The dignity of the Crown had become engaged and what had started as a local academic plot gone awry now called down upon its participants the wrath of the king himself. By royal order Brownrigg was suspended from his newly appointed duties as master, the fellows pleaded their innocence, and the university's chancellor, the earl of Holland, demanded of the heads a full enquiry to determine the truth of the matter, it being alleged that the election was 'not managed with the respect that was due unto his Majesties lettres of dispensation'.[241] For his part Creighton attempted to exculpate himself by asserting that he had called a halt to his efforts on condition: 'alwayes provided they gave his Majestie satisfaction, and my Lord Duke which I thought all parties were bound to doe as well of Loyaltie towards theire Soveraigne as of good manners towards soe great a peere as my Lord Duke'.[242] The ultimate outcome was that the royal sensibilities were mollified and Brownrigg was reinstated in office.

This tale of bungling and irresolution illuminates a number of otherwise obscure aspects of university elections. First, while we know that the election of masters of the larger colleges was a matter for Crown initiative, the situation at Catharine Hall suggests that even under the Spartan discipline and more closely supervised regimen characteristic of the 1630s[243] the prompting for royal interference could still originate from *within* the university. It is only the fortuitous preservation of the records created by the mishandling of the process on this occasion that provides us with this insight: there is nothing about the royal letter itself to suggest that it was prepared in the ad hoc way that in his deposition Creighton reveals was the case.[244] What is ostensibly a royal initiative was in fact instigated from outside the Court, and in effect provided an invitation for Court interference in order to satisfy personal and local ambitions. It is a case of private exploitation of the royal prerogative. It is also a story of a dog and its tail once again. Nor was it an isolated instance of this type of action associated with the university.

---

[240] CUA, Lett. 12.A.26. [241] CUA, Lett. 12.A.19. [242] CUA, Lett. 12.A.24.
[243] Cf. Sharpe 1992. [244] CUA, Lett. 12.A.18.

Sir Edward Coke described how the grant of burgesses to the universities had been obtained. Cecil moved the king for it, who 'graciously graunted and signed it the booke [that is, the grant] being ready drawne and provided'.[245] In 1622 our old acquaintance Robert Creighton had been in competition with Robert Metcalfe for the Professorship of Hebrew. On that occasion Lord Keeper Williams − an old hand at Cambridge politics − had written to his friend Samuel Collins, provost of King's. Williams assured Collins that he would deal with the king if Metcalfe was elected, and if Creighton 'or any other shall procure his Maties letteres'. Equally well versed in Court practices, Williams added that to obtain such letters 'is an easy thing surreptitiously to be effected'.[246] Similarly, in 1631, Thomas Bainbridge, master of Christ's, remarked to Viscount Dorchester that 'if your Honour had procured (as easily I know yow might) that greate hand', then he would be obliged to admit an importunate aspirant to a fellowship.[247] As secretary of state, Dudley Carleton, Viscount Dorchester, was, of course, advantageously placed to obtain the royal signature.

The second main conclusion to be drawn from the story of Robert Creighton's pursuit of the mastership of Catharine Hall reinforces a point that we have already noted in a number of other instances.[248] The role of the Court intermediary, in this case the duke of Lennox, was clearly crucial in obtaining the royal favour.[249] Creighton's activities emphasise once again the importance of such a figure amongst the acquaintance of the aspiring academic.

Thirdly, the Creighton episode illustrates the way in which, once invoked, the dignity of the patron and of the Crown became engaged in the particular and local disputes of their clients and subjects. This was also evident in our earlier examination of the appointment of the master of Magdalene in 1577,[250] and of Clare Hall in 1601.[251]

Finally, the way in which Creighton's suit was treated must raise doubts as to the ethicacy and efficacy of the judgements and procedures involved in dispensing royal favour. Even though Creighton was known at Court, very little judgement or mature deliberation can have been devoted to considering his request. The implication is that in the interstices between other matters the duke of Lennox obtained the royal signature to a form of letters composed by his client on his own behalf. The same conclusion

---

[245] CUA, Lett. II.A.C.3.c; see also Lett. II.A.C.10.a.
[246] Mayor 1865–6, p. 67: but he was not, on this occasion, successful.
[247] SP 16/197/8.   [248] See e.g. p. 379.
[249] For Creighton's connection, see Mayor 1865–6, p. 68n.
[250] Above, pp. 373–4.   [251] Above, pp. 376–8.

applies to the abortive nomination of Henry Copinger to the mastership of Magdalene in 1577. All the relevant considerations had not been
laid before the queen, and she had simply relied on 'the good report'
of Copinger's qualifications with which she had been provided by his
patron-advocates.[252] Further evidence of this lack of due consideration is
that under James there are numerous instances of the king granting the
same thing to different men.[253] Similarly, in a royal mandate for a fellowship at Christ's, in 1631, Charles wrote of being 'given to understand' of
the vacancy of a particular fellowship, and spoke of being 'credibly informed both of the present sufficiency and future' hopes of the candidate
who was seeking his intervention.[254] Given the practices that we have
seen followed on these occasions that credibility must be questioned.

Massive intervention by the Crown in the workings of the university
had had its origins in the unusual circumstances of the 1530s and 1540s.[255]
Subsequent piecemeal intervention was characteristic of a more general
desire minutely to supervise and regulate the workings of the state.[256]
What had had its origins in the assiduous labours of Cromwell in the
1530s was confirmed by the manipulative labours of the Cecils under
Elizabeth and James. The trouble was that this interventionism depended
on a quality of unbiased information to which the Crown rarely had access. At the same time, the increasing propensity for interference created
both the opportunity and the means for all who became involved, to satisfy and to multiply the reciprocal obligations of patronage relationships.
Ultimately, the ostensible purposes of intervention were in danger of being submerged beneath the ever-more-insistent needs of patronage. In
these circumstances – in the hustle and bustle and multiplicity of business
of the early modern Court – the real qualifications of candidates and the
original justification for strategic royal interventions could too easily be
lost to sight in the desire to gratify individual desires. All this is well illustrated by fragments of evidence that can be gathered from Elizabethan
and early Stuart Cambridge. But it is not simply that this aspect of the history of the university in this period illustrates larger forces at work in the
early modern state. It is also the case that the nature of the university itself
was transformed by its ever closer integration within the ambit of that
state. Today the rhetoric of 'targets', 'performance indicators', 'quality

---

[252] *HMCS*, III, p. 148; cf. a similar signet letter for a fellowship for Robert Rayment (SP 12/276/17).
[253] E.g. HLRO, Main Papers (Supplementary), H.L., 26 Feb. 1606, petition of Paul Thompson,
complaining that the king had granted him the advowson of Somersham (Hunts.) in Jan. 1604,
and then, in August, granted it to Cambridge University to augment the stipend of the 'Divinity
Reader' (i.e. the Regius Professor of Divinity). Cf. Morgan 1983, ch. 8.
[254] CUL, MS Mm. ii. 47, fo. 106v.   [255] Above, chapter 1.
[256] Braddick 2000; Morgan 2000.

assurance' and 'research outputs' bandied about within our modern universities represents the intrusion into them of the production orientation of late modern consumer capitalism as internalised by the state itself. So in the early modern period an equivalent process can be detected. A particular type of patron–client relationship had emerged during the course of the sixteenth century. It came to form the ligaments that bound together the formal skeleton of the Tudor state and that articulated the world of curial politics that prevailed in England between roughly 1510 and the 1690s.[257] What we have seen happening within early modern Cambridge is a manifestation of the increasing pervasiveness of that system, roughly from the 1540s onwards. In an especially stark way at Cambridge, and possibly at Oxford too, an existing formal system of selection by election was overlain by the much less formal processes of patronage.

Historians have long understood that it is not possible simply to apply modern moral standards to this system. By drawing a distinction between the manifest and the latent functions of processes such as elections to offices at Cambridge there are those who have argued that the spinning of this multitude of filaments of obligation served to weave substantial parts of the population into the warp and weft of the Tudor state; that this was a means of creating political stability and therefore that it was a 'good thing'.[258] The full ramifications of this line of argument cannot be pursued here. True, the system that evolved was not necessarily and inherently pernicious: under Elizabeth it probably did play an important part in maintaining the hegemony of the state and a much-desired stability. But we have to acknowledge that it was a system that, far more than some others, always carried within it the pathological possibilities of malignant growth. It could be argued that under her successors increasingly this malignant potential was realised. This realisation took a variety of forms. It included the undue dominance over and profligate exploitation of patronage by Buckingham from 1618, 'the conduit through which all largesse doth flow'. This is very evident in his election as chancellor of Cambridge in 1626.[259] It also took the form of the pre-emption of clerical and academic preferment by the Arminian-sacramentalist court-bishops and academics from the mid-1620s. Again, this is evident in the events that make up part of the history of the university at this time.[260] In turn, and cumulatively, this created substantial alienation from rather than concurrence with the status quo. So, even from a purely pragmatic viewpoint, patronage exercised without constraint and predominantly in

---

[257] Morgan 1988.   [258] Cf. MacCaffrey 1961; Hurstfield 1968; Morgan 1988; Patterson 1999.
[259] Morgan 1983, pp. 1–44.   [260] Morgan 1983, and below, chapter 11.

favour of a particular set of interests becomes disfunctional even in terms of its latent purpose of recruiting support for a regime. As the powerful rarely comprehend, the capacity to act, to impose one's will, needs to be tempered by judgement and discrimination as to what the long-term consequences of that action may be. But, then, of course, it is usually only the historian who is privy to knowledge in the long term. We should not expect too much of our fallible predecessors in their uncertain present.

Chapter 11

THE ELECTORAL SCENE AND THE COURT: ROYAL MANDATES 1558–1640

We have seen how, in the three decades from 1520 onwards, the university as an institution, and university men as individuals, became more intimately involved with government and the great affairs of those tumultuous years. A familiarity was established and a series of expectations were laid down. In the last chapter, on the electoral scene, we moved on to consider some aspects of the relationship between the state and the university that came to prevail in the relatively more stable circumstances of what may be broadly described as the 'Jacobethan' period. At first glance the story so far indicates that, for their various purposes, students, fellows and masters were busy importuning potential benefactors and patrons, and both local gentry and well-placed courtiers were frequently intervening in the affairs of the university for their own benefit. Furthermore, for governmental and doctrinal reasons both Crown and archiepiscopacy had come to be intimately involved in its affairs. In these circumstances it might seem that there would be few or none left to oppose intervention and the corruptions thus engendered. Of course this is not so. Those who solicited one type of 'intervention' might oppose other forms of 'meddling'. Beneficiaries on one occasion might be losers on others. One group might consider their intervention as legitimate, that of others as *ultra vires*.

Arising from these circumstances are a series of questions for the historian. Are any patterns discernible, and do they change over time, with changes in the relative advantage of the different groups both within and outside the university? Do the grounds for intervention change in concert with changes in the structure and ethos of the Court or with changes in the respective influence of different religious groupings? What attitudes are manifested towards the different types of involvement, and on what issues is criticism generated? Who are the critics, and where is their criticism articulated?

In seeking the answers to some of these questions three main areas of intervention need to be distinguished: elections to scholarships and fellowships, elections to headships and the allocation of leases.[1] They all have somewhat different characteristics and generate different types and quantities of evidence. This chapter is mainly concerned with intervention in elections, and, more especially, in elections to fellowships and masterships. Here, it is necessary to draw a distinction between the objective incidence of intervention by the Crown on the one hand, and the vociferousness of opposition to that intervention on the other. The two do not necessarily trace the same trajectory and the latter is not a wholly satisfactory index of the former. Nevertheless, a careful reading of the documents can suggest something of the incidence of intervention in circumstances where the unevenness of the sources produces numerical measures of dubious accuracy.[2] Furthermore, it has to be said that an adequate view of Court intervention depends on a more detailed knowledge of the structure and working of the royal Court than we yet possess, despite an outpouring of recent work. Indeed, it may be that an examination of the particular set of relationships between the Court and the university will contribute something to the understanding of the former just as it may help to illuminate facets of the latter.

1558–85

Crown intervention in the affairs of the university in the first three or four years of Elizabeth's reign seems primarily to have been designed to achieve the *expulsion* of those who on religious grounds were likely positively to oppose the new regime and its religious settlement rather than to *intrude* those who might favour it, whoever they might be.[3] This repeats what can be seen happening in the government of the counties through the purging of the commissions of the peace.[4] The 1560s remain a murky period in the history of Cambridge in this as in other respects.[5] It is not until the late 1570s that one begins to hear complaints which suggest that it is in this decade that substantial Court intervention in the election of fellows really began.

---

[1] See above, pp. 282 ff.

[2] For a discussion of some of the technicalities involved in using one of the sources available for measuring rates of intervention, see Morgan 1983, pp. 700–12.

[3] The results of the Commission of 1559 with regard to the tenure of masterships is conveniently summarised in Mullinger 1884, pp. 167–87. See also Swan 1955.

[4] See above, p. 84; Smith 1959b.

[5] But not of the Court: see MacCaffrey 1968, pp. 3–92; Hudson 1980, pp. 9–42. One reason for this murkiness is that many of the older sources for the history of the universities dry up or fossilise during the first half of the sixteenth century, and most of the new sources, both intra-mural and extra-mural, do not commence until the 1570s or 1580s.

The second session (8 February–15 March 1576) of Elizabeth's fourth parliament saw the introduction into the Commons of a bill against the buying and selling of places in the universities and the colleges of Eton and Winchester.[6] Although it passed both Houses it was vetoed by the queen.[7] Whitgift's comments suggest that explicitly the bill was aimed at local corruptions involving the purchase of places in some colleges, but subsequent complaints indicate that, at least by implication, it was also directed at indiscriminate Court intervention.[8] It may have been this parliamentary criticism as much as any positive increase in mandates in the 1570s that, three years later, prompted various heads to write to Burghley complaining of Court intervention.[9] Alternatively, it may just be possible that the criticism in parliament in 1576 of corrupt purchase of places within the universities actually encouraged would-be purchasers to resort to Court in order to obtain the reassurance of an authoritative royal mandate rather than simply spending their money on a 'private' purchase *intra muros*.

Burghley's own position on this issue was equivocal. Certainly, in the mid-1570s, he had had no compunction in making recommendations for fellowships at his old college, St John's, and although the college elected two of his nominees, in its turn it felt able to excuse itself for following conscience and the statutes in declining the other nominations.[10] His attitude is further revealed in his correspondence with the university in the late 1570s. In September 1577 he had written to Corpus on be-half of Remigius Booth for a fellowship. Although the master, Norgate, attempted to accommodate the chancellor's request, he also had other, local, interests to protect, pointing out in reply that in various ways Booth was unqualified, and that the college stood in a bond of £200 to admit none but a Norwich man to the place.[11] On this occasion Norgate was

---

[6] *CJ*, I, p. 110a. The bill received its first reading immediately after the second reading of a bill 'for the maintenance of the Colleges in the universities . . .', first read on 28 Feb. (*CJ*, I, p. 108b). For the subsequent passage through both Houses of the bill against the purchase of places see *CJ*, I, p. 112a, *LJ*, I, pp. 743b, 745a, 746b.

[7] Whitgift assumed that the queen had acted at Burghley's instigation as chancellor of Cambridge, and agreed that it 'was verie graciously done, for it wold have remayned to all posteritie as a perptuall note of ignominie to both the universities'. At the same time Whitgift urged Burghley to write to Cambridge against corrupt dealing (Strype 1822, I, p. 149). For a fuller discussion of parliamentary criticism of practices in the universities see above, chapter 5.

[8] Below, pp. 400–4.

[9] Mandates were formal letters from the Crown under the signet seal. For some discussion of mandates and the related procedures see Morgan 1983, pp. 700–12.

[10] Baker and Mayor 1869, I, p. 395.

[11] SP 12/115/22. The master of Corpus had been born at Aylsham in north Norfolk, and was related to Nicholas Norgate, alderman of Norwich. Nicholas was an associate of Bishop Parkhurst, another Norwich man, and a benefactor of the college (Houlbrooke 1975, p. 118 n. 214). Robert

successful,[12] but a little over a year later the university wrote to both Burghley and the earl of Leicester in terms that made it clear that it was not only private letters that were disturbing the regular course of their elections.[13] These leading courtiers – one on the state, the other on the household side – were asked to diminish the frequency of the queen's mandates for elections to fellowships and scholarships, as a result of which university men were now looking to courtiers as the means of preferment, rather than diligently concentrating on becoming good scholars.[14] Indeed, in the late 1570s, there was what can only be described as a concentrated campaign on the part of the heads in opposition both to private letters and to mandates.

In addition to Norgate's objections in 1577, and the general complaint by the university of March 1579, in 1579 Andrew Perne, master of Peterhouse, had opposed the recommendation by Burghley of Stephen Egerton to a fellowship there,[15] while the formal letter on the same subject from the university[16] had been preceded by a private letter from the then vice-chancellor, Richard Howland, master of St John's, and one of Burghley's clients, reinforced by the verbal report of the university's emissary, John Still, and specific complaints by some of the fellows of Trinity College.[17]

Burghley's answer revealed both the grounds for what many would have accepted as justifiable intervention, and the manner in which those

---

Norgate was also related by marriage to Archbishop Parker, another Norfolk benefactor, Norgate's wife Elizabeth being the daughter of Parker's half-brother, John Baker (*DNB*). It was Parker who is said to have obtained for Norgate his fellowship at Corpus. Later, Norgate was presented to two Crown rectories in Norfolk, Martham and Forncett (Mullinger 1884, p. 288; Venn, III, p. 263a). For locally tied fellowships and scholarships see above, pp. 216 ff.

[12] SP 12/115/33. Booth became a fellow of Gonville and Caius in 1581 (Venn, I, p. 180b).

[13] On 22 March 1579.

[14] CUA, Lett. 2, pp. 460–1. That to Burghley is printed by Strype 1824, II, ii, App., no. xviii, pp. 629–31 and Heywood and Wright 1854, I, pp. 211–13. The original is BL Lansdowne MS 29, fos. 116–17 (no. 50).

[15] Strype 1824, II, p. 198. Egerton was admitted (on this *DNB* is misleading, see Venn, II, p. 91a). Ultimately he entered into a full fellowship on 12 Nov. 1579, having been admitted a probationer fellow on 4 Oct. 1579 (Walker 1930, pp. 56, 38). The evidence of Burghley's recommendation suggests that Walker (p. 56) is not altogether correct in saying that Egerton was 'Fellow in regular course'. As with Stephen Rushbrooke (see below), there are religious implications in Egerton's case. He was later persecuted by Whitgift as a precisian, resulting in his incarceration in the Fleet for three years. (For Egerton's religious proclivities, including his responsibility for the London classis, see Strype 1822, I, p. 537; 1824, II, ii, p. 479; III, i, p. 691; IV, p. 553.) His acquaintance included the religious radicals Barrow, Greenwood and Arthur Hildersham (Walker 1930, p. 7). The careers of Egerton and Rushbrooke at Peterhouse overlapped, and in 1590 we find them cited together as precisians (Strype 1822, II, pp. 6, 13).

[16] CUA, Lett. 2, p. 461.

[17] These other complaints are known through Burghley's reply to them (Cooper, *Annals*, II, pp. 368–9).

grounds had been, and were to continue to be, subverted. As on the occasion of Howland's letters, the lord treasurer rehearsed how he had represented to the queen the complaints of the university. In his transmission of her reply Burghley made it clear that it was their complaint of the frequency and specific form, rather than an objection to the mandate in principle, that he was seconding to the queen, referring to 'the common form of recommendation (a matter not to be misliked except that the same were too frequent)', and, in writings that he had examined, the formula employed by suitors 'conteyned besyde a commendacion of the parties, a maner of a graunt of the roomes being not voyd, and a Commandment to admitte the parties so commended upon their own reports of their habilities'. In other words, peremptory pre-elections were being required by mandates obtained on no firmer ground than the suitors' own request. According to Burghley, the queen's intentions had been perverted, for he 'found her Majestie ernestly offended with such Ministers as had so written her Letters out of all good order, adding that she never ment by her commendations or requests, (howsoever the wordes of her Letters might by abuse be inserted), any violacion of the statuts and orders for elections'.[18] These were aspirations to a level of virtue in the conduct of relationships with Cambridge that the queen and her successors were unable to maintain. Their significance here is that they articulate an ideal from which later practice was to differ so widely.[19] Further, the principal secretaries (as keepers of the signet) were instructed for the future to ensure that nothing should pass 'to the offence of the Statutes of any of your Howses'.[20] The real reason for the subsequent failure to realise this ideal was that the pressures at Court were such that a total embargo was impossible, as Burghley recognised: 'And yet this I cannot but advyse you, that because that it maye be and is not unreasonable that upon some ernest meanes to be made to her Majestie by persons of some valew with her Majestie, she maye at some tymes recommend some persons to be placed in some voyd rooms of the Colledgs.' And who was to judge the validity of these requests? Quite unreasonably, the onus was placed on the impecunious and dependent masters and fellows of colleges who were either to satisfy those thus nominated or to inform the secretaries of state 'of the causes whie the request maye not be fulfilled'.[21] Here was a recipe that would not dissuade importunity at Court but rather encouraged conflict in the colleges and further recourse to those about the queen. It was a recipe the consequences of which we can

---

[18] *Ibid.* p. 369.   [19] See below, pp. 401–4.   [20] Cooper, *Annals*, II, p. 369.   [21] *Ibid.*

see at work in the persistent complaints voiced throughout the 1580s and 1590s.[22]

The statistical evidence indicates that Peterhouse was peculiarly subject to mandates, and Andrew Perne, its master, was one of their most persistent opponents.[23] This was despite his dependence on Burghley. In 1581 he objected to a mandate for Richard Betts on the grounds that as a supernumerary fellow he would further reduce the revenues available to the foundation fellows.[24] Nevertheless, Betts was elected.[25] Less than a year later Perne was again writing of the financial strains imposed by three or four supernumerary fellows, thanking Burghley for excusing the college to the queen for not receiving Stephen Rushbroke as a fellow, and reminding the lord treasurer that at the queen's command, and with his commendation, they had recently accepted three fellows more than they could maintain, 'flatly against diverse Statutes of our House'.[26] The following year, 1583, again saw Perne trying to avert intervention by courtiers on behalf of a would-be fellow. By July of that year he was in receipt of letters: from the queen on behalf of John Munford if a place was void and if not, for the next place vacated; from Burghley, 'at the Speciall suit of my Lord Cobham'; direct from Cobham himself; and from Sir Francis Walsingham. Perne was not prepared to admit Munford even on the recommendation of all these notables, for the college already had its statutory maximum of two fellows from Munford's county of Essex,

---

[22] Strype, who was well acquainted with the sources, noted that 'since that time there were more mandamuses sent down, and dispensations with the statute, than were before' (Strype 1824, II, ii, p. 200). In his remarks on this phenomenon Searle is following Strype (Searle 1867–71, II, pp. 332–3), although in his turn Strype is here paraphrasing a letter from Perne to Burghley (BL Harl. MS 7031, fos. 89–89v). Therefore, the apparent confirmation of these various sources, one by the other, is in fact based on an original contemporary comment that requires independent verification. For some attempt to provide this, see below, pp. 401–4.

[23] All Souls and New College seem to have endured a similar invidious distinction at Oxford. For the religious dimensions of some of these conflicts at Peterhouse, as in the case of Stephen Egerton, see above, n. 15.

[24] SP 12/151/67, 68, 69 (*CSPD 1581–90*, p. 40). Interestingly, the term 'supernumerary' originates in this period and derives from the late Latin, *supernumerarius*, a soldier 'added to a legion after it is complete' (*OED*). In turn this suggests an academic origin for the term such as we find here.

[25] Venn, I, p. 146. The mandate was dated 11 Oct. 1580 (Walker 1930, p. 71). It stated that having been in the university for eight years, Betts had been repeatedly passed over in elections. He was now to be elected despite being doubly disqualified as both an MA and 'Southron' born (Walker 1930, p. 71). Betts was admitted on 9 Sept. 1581 (Walker 1930, p. 85). Perne's letter amongst the State Papers bears out Walker's surmise that Betts was pre-elected. Arthur Purefroy did not resign the fellowship in question in Betts' favour until 1581 (Walker 1930, pp. 279–80). In his turn, Betts' successor in this particular fellowship, Leonard Mawe, was also pre-elected, being admitted fellow on 5 July 1595, whilst Betts did not resign until 6 July 1597 (Walker 1930, pp. 176, 280). This again created a supernumerary fellowship.

[26] *HMCS*, XIII, p. 203, 4; BL Harl. MS 7031, fos. 88v–89, letters of 7 Aug. and 2 July 1582. Rushbrooke took his MA from Peterhouse in 1583, but was never a fellow (Venn, III, p. 499a).

'could have no more thereof', and housed others better qualified than he. Perne would only act when it had 'pleased her Majesty of her prerogative Royall, to dispense with any Statute, custome, or ordinance' of the college that was against the election of Munford. Only then was he prepared to effect Munford's election.[27] In other words, the master of Peterhouse wished to be indemnified against the possible repercussions of a non-statutory election. Recommendations, even recommendations by the queen, did not provide sufficient assurance: what was required was a mandate. Thus objection to intervention from within the university tended to invite more decisive and formal intervention.

Here, then, was a further reason for the encouragement of mandates since, despite her earlier protestations, the queen recommended candidates for places for which they were not statutorily qualified. And, of course, it was for just such places that suitors were most likely to go to Court in order to overcome the restrictions imposed by the 'domestic' statutes of the colleges. Not that Perne appears to have approved of mandates in principle. In the same letter he implored Burghley, on his own behalf, and on behalf of 'the whole university', to request of the queen 'that our free elections be not taken away from us' to the detriment of good learning. He reminded Burghley of his, Burghley's, previous intervention with the queen on their behalf, and of the favourable response in 1579 to a similar request. Yet, said Perne, 'sith that time, there hath been more Mandatums and Dispensations of our Statute[s] . . . then there were before, as your Lordship doth know'.[28] His hopes that Burghley would be able to halt this canker were misplaced. Six months after writing in these terms, Perne was again raising objections to machinations on behalf of Munford. In his earlier letter he had noted that the college could not elect Munford before the fellowship in question was vacated, nor had the queen ever before required this of them.[29] Apparently, Munford had used the mandate as grounds for claiming the income from the fellowship even prior to his election, therefore in effect creating an additional supernumerary fellowship about which Perne had previously complained. Now the college asked Burghley to support in writing an interpretation opposite to that made by Munford.[30] Moreover, they continued to

---

[27] BL Harl. MS 7031, fo. 89. Munford had migrated to Peterhouse from Queens' in 1581, was therefore something of an outsider and, it might be argued, was not technically 'of the house'. He was the fourth son of Thomas Munford of Radwinter, Essex, by his second wife, Alice Trigg, and subsequently became incumbent of that parish (Walker 1930, p. 78). On this occasion Perne seems to have been successful. Munford was not elected to a probationary fellowship until 5 July 1584 (Walker 1930, p. 108) or to a full fellowship until 15 August 1585 (pp. 78, 108).
[28] BL Harl. MS 7031, fo. 89r–v.   [29] *Ibid.*, fo. 89.   [30] *Ibid.*, fos. 89v–90.

oppose the mandate *in toto*, claiming that he was unqualified and 'here we stand at a stay, not knowing how to be resolved', but persuaded – so they claimed – of Burghley's regard for their statutes, requesting 'that we may go forward as erst before with our free elections, according to our Statutes' notwithstanding the former letters.[31] At least technically, this they may have been able to do, for in this case Munford did not get his much-sought fellowship until 15 August 1585,[32] although he may have been pre-elected and maintained himself at his own charges until then.[33] Perne's main concerns were to safeguard the finances of the college; not to discourage other students; to maintain intact at least the word of their statutes; as far as possible to accommodate the supplicant for the fellowship; and finally to ensure that his patron, Burghley, was 'sufficiently pleasured' with the arrangements.

1585–1603

By the mid-1580s it is evident that the Crown was being drawn into the elections of masters no less than of fellows. Following the death of Henry Harvey, the master of Trinity Hall, in February 1585,[34] Burghley and Walsingham wrote on behalf of the queen, inhibiting the fellows from proceeding to an immediate election. A group of fellows replied, urging the two courtiers to ensure that the queen did not 'commende anye to the place of the Master before certayne Enformation howe and in what manner by our Foundation and Statutes, and by vertue of our Corporall Oathes, the said election is to be made, and the Master is to be qualified', for which purpose they forwarded the relevant parts of their statutes.[35] The background to the election is more complicated than might at first appear, but in this context the significant thing is the attempt to deflect the imposition of a prospective royal nominee by merely citing the college statutes: some fellows evidently still assumed they might be respected. In fact, Thomas Preston, the queen's successful candidate, does not seem to have been statutably qualified on his election.[36]

---

[31] *Ibid.*, fo. 89v.   [32] Venn, III, p. 224a.

[33] This is the purport of the conclusion to Perne's letter (BL Harl. MS 7031, fo. 90) and supported by the record of Munford's probationary election on 5 July 1584 (Walker 1930, p. 108).

[34] Crawley 1976, pp. 65–6, 220, gives the date of Harvey's death as 20 Feb., but letters referring to him as 'our late master' are dated 14 and 15 Feb. 1585 (BL Harl. MS 7031, fo. 78v).

[35] BL Harl. MS 7031, fo. 78.

[36] The docquet of the mandate requiring his choice by the fellows as master is dated 7 March 1585 (S.O. 3/1 *sub* date). Preston seems to have been put in by Burghley to sort out the administrative and financial chaos at Trinity Hall (BL Lansdowne MS 45, fo. 123).

Plate 25 Queen Elizabeth, miniature portrait probably by Nicholas Hillyard on her Letters Patent of 11 January 1584, granting licence to Sir Walter Mildmay for the foundation of Emmanuel College

Meanwhile at Queens', the president, Humphrey Tyndall, was trying to extricate himself from a complicated situation in which, at the request of the lord chancellor, Sir Thomas Bromley, he had agreed to a conditional resignation of a fellowship by Bromley's chaplain in favour of Bromley's nominee.[37] The smooth operation of this private corruption had been interrupted by the queen's nomination of yet another candidate! This candidate was still too junior, and Tyndall continued to object to his placement. In trying to bolster his position Tyndall was astute in invoking a major concern on the part of those at Court who oversaw the management of the university. He asked Burghley to support him lest the president's authority was undermined in the college by the faction which had been promoting their youthful candidate through Burghley's mediation.[38]

Tyndall's objections had been to both the specific candidate, and the way in which an election carried against his wishes would undermine his authority. When, some five months later, Perne wrote to Burghley about the election of the new master at St John's, knowingly or not he reinforced Tyndall's argument that external intervention undermined the good order in the university – the good order that Burghley amongst others was insistent that they maintain. 'Your Lordship doth knowe how ernest a suter I have bene for the staying of all such lettres contrarie to the Statutes and godlie Foundacons of the Colledges, the which I knowe will be the greate decay of all good lerning and order in the same universitie, if the elections accordinge to Statutes, both of Masterships, Fellowships, and Schollerships be not observed.'[39] Yet, by the June of 1586, Perne was again writing to Burghley thanking him for reassurances that he would help them to maintain their statutes, but also asking him once more to intercede with the queen in the hope that she would rescind a recent dispensation from the statutes of the college on behalf of two young men

---

[37] The resignation had been done 'by an instrument under the hand of a publique notarie' (BL Harl. MS 7031, fo. 109).

[38] Tyndall's letter to Burghley is dated 9 April 1585 (BL Harl. MS. 7031, fo. 109). The queen's letter for the placement of her nominee, Randolph Davenport, is docqueted as 16 Jan. 1585 (S.O. 3/1 *sub* date). In the interim the college had also received another mandate for the election of Miles Sandys, *non obstante* their statutes (S.O. 3/1 *sub* 24 March 1585). Davenport originally was of Trinity College, but occupied a fellowship at Queens' between 1585 and 1605 (Venn, II, p. 13b). Miles Sandys was the third son of Edwin Sandys, archbishop of York. Originally he had been a member of Peterhouse, and was elected to a fellowship there in 1581. Between 1585 and 1588 he occupied a fellowship at Queens' and – also in 1585 – was made a prebendary at York. In the case of Sandys we may surmise that paternal influence played its part in jobbing him into Queens'. In both cases it is worth noting that mandates were sought in order to effect a migration from another college.

[39] BL Lansdowne MS 45, fo. 125.

who in his judgement deserved not favour but due correction for their misdemeanours.[40] On this occasion what was being sought by means of royal intervention was the retention of fellowships beyond the point when the fellows were required to enter into orders. Perne objected not only because college statutes would be broken but also because such action would deprive Peterhouse of men suitably qualified to maintain the academic exercises required of the college, both internally and, by turns, in the university at large.[41] Evidently Burghley agreed with the master, and acted swiftly on his behalf, for two weeks later Perne was again writing to say that with Burghley's encouragement he had deprived his young adversaries of their fellowships. Once again he took the opportunity to expostulate on the subversive effect of external interference initiated from within the university.[42]

But if Perne had won a battle he had not won the war, although the evidence from the following year does suggest that he had hit upon at least one tactical move that was to be used by many academics with varying success in ensuing years. Perne's objections to the attempts to job John Tenison into a fellowship certainly reveal the wily tenacity of this ageing master. In October 1583 Tenison had obtained a mandate for his election contrary to the statutes.[43] The master's response was to claim that four better-qualified candidates had already been elected to places not yet vacant – this is one of the earliest references to the subsequently frequently played gambit of pre-election. Perne's point was that, however ample the dispensation in the queen's letter, it did not dispense with a prior election. It was a good card to play, and on this occasion Perne played it with some success, but what it illustrates is the process of escalation.[44] Luckily on this

[40] BL Harl. MS 7031, fo. 90r–v. The docquet of the mandate for one of those involved is S.O. 3/1, 7 May 1586. The mandate was for the retention of a fellowship 'contrarie to there statutes' (*ibid.*). If, as seems likely from the ensuing correspondence, this was a joint mandate, this may explain the omission of one of the two names from the summary provided by the docquet book. The characters to whom Tyndall objected were Walter Fare and Nicholas Bownde. Farre had been admitted to a fellowship at Peterhouse on 12 Nov. 1579 on the authority of a mandate. He subsequently served as bursar, 1584–5. His successor in the fellowship was admitted on 9 Aug. 1587 (Walker, 1930, pp. 37, 56). Bownde had been admitted fellow in April 1575 (*DNB* incorrectly says 1570; see Walker 1927, pp. 271, 291; 1930, p. 6 for correction). Part of the argument over Bownde's qualifications for the continued tenure of a fellowship depended on whether he had been ordained priest. The evidence of the Ely Registers is that he was ordained priest on 2 June 1580 (Walker 1927, p. 271). Bownde was again in residence at Peterhouse in Feb. 1595 (Walker 1930, p. 174). It is worth noting the access to Court patronage that was available during the 1570s and 1580s to religious radicals such as Bownde, Egerton and Rushbroke. The last two are discussed above, pp. 391, 393. For Bownde, see Collinson 1967, pp. 186, 372, 377–8, 436, 445–6.

[41] BL Harl. MS 7031, fo. 90   [42] *Ibid.*, fo. 98v.   [43] S.O. 3/1, 10 Oct. 1587.
[44] As a result Tenison did not become a fellow until 1589 (Venn, IV, p. 214a).

occasion a copy of the original signet letter survives, and it is possible to see in what large terms the dispensation had been granted. The letter was 'to will and command you presently upon the sight of these our letters, to chuse and admit him full Fellow of our said Colledge' into a place now void, or the next void 'by any manner of meanes whatsoever. Any Statute, Decree, Act or order to the contrary notwithstanding: for the which we do dispense be these presents, and therefore have no doubt, but that you will accomplish this our pleasure accordingly.'[45] With terms as large as this the mandate was still essentially *negative*, removing limitations on the eligibility of the individual candidate. The danger was that if ruses and excuses, such as that employed by Perne on this occasion, proliferated in response to dispensations, mandates might become *positive*, in that they deprived duly elected scholars, fellows or masters on behalf of royal nominees. The internal dynamic of the situation was one in which the very strenuousness of opposition and objections to mandates was likely to inflate the claims for the discretionary competence of the prerogative.

Furthermore, it is worth noting the broader implications for the state of these processes within the university. At this time, the initiative for invoking the prerogative originated as much in the careerist aspirations of individuals at Cambridge as it did in considerations of policy on the part of those officers of state such as Burghley who were charged with oversight of the university. However, precedents were being set and customs established; attitudes of mind were being created. These could have a far different outcome when a more monolithic regime was established at Court in the 1620s. But for the moment, and in such cases as that under scrutiny, men such as Tenison had access to 'certain worshipfull Friends' who made him an allowance and – we may surmise – had access to the Court or even the queen herself so that she could be 'credibly informed' of Tenison's merits.[46]

On this occasion, as on others, Perne took the opportunity to beg for free elections, albeit his frustration is evident in his words, for although 'upon the sight and knowledge of her Majesties minde [i.e., the mandate]

[45] BL Harl. MS 7031, fo. 91. There is a further copy of the original letter in a letter from Thomas Baker to John Anstis, taken from Burghley's papers, then in the hands of John Strype (BL Stowe MS 749, fo. 108).

[46] BL Harl. MS 7031, fo. 91, Perne to Burghley. The latter phrase is used in the queen's signet letter. It has not been possible to establish who Tenison's friends were. However, John came of the family of Ryhill in Holderness, a family of some standing (Walker 1930, p. 35). It could also be that influence was exercised on his behalf by a parent of any one of a number of students for which there is indirect evidence that he was a tutor (Walker 1930, pp. 35, 138).

we were in all humbleness of duty and reverence willing' to perform her wishes yet he beseeches Burghley:

> to be an honourable meane[s] to her Majesty that whereas at diverse and sundry times heretofore we have performed all due obedience to her Highness in the like Suites, to the manifest violating and infringing of our saidd statutes, we may now at the last be suffered to use the liberty of the same, and namely at this time, when we cannot pleasure the said Tenison, without the manifest prejudice and hurt of so many poore and forward young men.[47]

There is no little irony in the fact that, following Perne's death two years later, Tenison was the first fellow on the foundation bequeathed to the college by its former master.[48]

Precedent, once set, became custom. By 1597, a mandatory letter in favour of Thomas Cordell for a fellowship at Peterhouse was expressing the queen's satisfaction with their past amenability and expectation of their future satisfaction of her wishes, 'because we doe not doubt but do fynde in you a readie disposition to expedite anie thinge that you shall perceave to be gratefull to us'. Therefore, they were not to stand upon their local statutes or other delays 'the which we expect you will not preserve before your duetifull regarde to satisfie us'. Rather, as many as were in the college at the receipt of the letter were to pre-elect Cordell into the next probationary fellowship that became vacant: here was the response to Perne's tactic in the 1580s of pre-emptive elections.[49]

During the vacancy of the see of Ely, Whitgift, as archbishop, acted as Visitor of Peterhouse.[50] In this capacity, on 19 June 1593, when the question of the legality of pre-elections was referred to him, he had given them his approval, provided that the pre-elected fellow had no voice in the affairs of the college until the vacancy of the fellowship to which he had a pre-emptive claim.[51] Subsequently, would-be fellows such as Thomas Cordell, were to seek mandates for pre-election.[52] As a result of Whitgift's judgement of 1593, in the year following, Leonard Mawe was

---

[47] BL Harl. MS 7031, fo. 91v.   [48] Mullinger 1884, p. 291; Walker 1930, p. 143.

[49] SP 12/263/36. The draft of the royal mandate to the college is endorsed 'May 1597' (SP 12/263/37). Cordell was eventually admitted a fellow on 23 June 1598, by authority of a royal mandate dated 11 June 39 Elizabeth, i.e., a month after the draft now in the State Papers (Walker 1930, pp. 158, 192). There is no record of the mandate in the signet office docquet book (S.O. 3/1), which is defective for this date. For Thomas Cordell's influential family associations with the Court see Walker's notes on the family (Walker 1930, pp. 144–5).

[50] See above, p. 97.   [51] Walker 1930, p. 165.

[52] E.g. Robert Rayment in 1600/1 (Walker 1930, p. 177; *HMCS*, x, p. 224); Roger Dereham (mandate of 26 Jan. 1597) in place next after Leonard Mawe, admitted 12 Feb. 1598, took the oath on 22 April 1598, succeeding Ezekiel Hilliard (Walker 1930, pp. 186, 223, 232).

admitted a probationer-fellow on the authority of a royal mandate, with instructions for him to be placed in the next vacant fellowship.[53]

Henceforward, Pelion was upon Ossa. Thus, following on from Cordell's pre-election in 1597, he was admitted on 23 June 1598, and on the same day Robert Kidson was admitted to the next vacant fellowship, while two months later Walter Curll was admitted fellow in the place next vacant following Kidson.[54] In the latter two cases there is no surviving evidence of a mandate, but in the case of Curll there is circumstantial evidence which suggests the influence at Court that is likely to have been exercised on his behalf: the Curlls were dependants of the Cecils. Walter was the younger son of William Curll, auditor of the Court of Wards, itself a Cecilian bailiwick, and Walter had been born near the Cecil country stronghold at Hatfield. Subsequently, there is some evidence that the great family became his patrons.[55]

Peterhouse certainly seems to have been much troubled by royal mandates in these decades. In some degree this must be accounted for by its tightly restrictive statutes of locality,[56] which by the late 1580s had encouraged the procurement of mandates designed not simply to require the choice of specified candidates but which also stipulated that candidates were to be chosen *despite* their statutory ineligibility, with which the royal prerogative dispensed. It was these circumstances, together with the relative wealth and populousness of the college, combined with Perne's genuinely held conviction that intervention undermined the authority of masters, that helped to account for the repeated objections to mandates aimed at Peterhouse. But it was not the only college subject to intervention and from which objections were voiced. Moreover, the phenomenon that we are examining was by no means restricted to Cambridge: in effect, it was a product of the characteristic dependence engendered in the peripheries on the core of the curial state.

Some were more amenable than others. In 1589, the representatives of Magdalen College, Oxford, acknowledged that 'we-take her Majesty's Prerogative to haye authority above all local Statutes, and that Her Majesty may command anything contrary to our Statutes, by virtue of whose commandment divers Fellows of our House at the present hold their places, directly contrary to our Statutes, and obey Her Majesty's

---

[53] Walker 1930, pp. 170–1, mandate of 28 May 1594. On 28 June 1595, having completed his first year of probation, Mawe was sent to Whitgift for confirmation as a foundation fellow. The archbishop declared him admitted into the next fellowship to be vacant.

[54] Walker 1930, pp. 147, 192. Walker says (p. 192) that Curll was pre-elected before 3 Feb. 1597.

[55] Walker 1930, pp. 192–3; *DNB*. Later still, when elevated to the bishopric of Winchester, Curll was to be an active supporter of Laud.

[56] See above, pp. 216 ff.

commandment'.[57] But – even at Oxford – not all colleges were quite as amenable as Magdalen, neither were objections limited to mandates for fellowships. In the 1580s, New College and All Souls seem to have been as frequently subject to intervention as was Peterhouse at Cambridge.[58] At some time during these years Sir Francis Walsingham wrote on behalf of All Souls to the rapacious courtier, Sir Thomas Heneage, Treasurer of the Queen's Chamber, who at that time had further designs upon the property of the college.[59] At the instigation of the fellows, Walsingham pointed out that they 'have often and manie tymes dutifully yealded to the requests of her Majestie's letters not only for placing of Schollers amongst them but also from within theise foure yeares in demising uppon hir letters' two of their best manors to Sir Walter Raleigh without any entry fine paid to the college. Later, Raleigh sold the demise for more than £1,000. But, as the members of All Souls discovered, such amenability served only to whet the appetite of other courtiers, such as Heneage. With rich pickings in prospect for the likes of Raleigh and Heneage the plaintive complaints of the disconsolate fellows to Walsingham proved to be of no avail.[60] Neither did other colleges cease to put up a stream of objections to mandates throughout the 1590s; nor were promises lacking that free elections would be maintained.

A dispute that arose at Christ's in 1590 reveals the resentment engendered by the royal favour obtained and manipulated by some members of the university on their own behalf. Edward Mosley had obtained a mandate for his election to a fellowship. A number of subsequent depositions made it clear that a contemporary fellow of the college, Thomas Murton, took a dim view of such means of election. He was said to have uttered contemptuous words of the queen's mandate, being variously reported to have said that for a place in that house, 'whosoever shuld bring the Queenes Mandate, hee would therefore not chose him', that 'the Mandatum latelie brought to the said Colledge, was a foolish mandat', and that 'whosoever shall but sue for her Majesties letters shall never have my voyce'. Although the master, Cuthbert Bainbridge, denied it, one deponent claimed that the words were spoken in the master's chamber, in his presence and in that of most of the fellows. When charged with these

---

[57] Macray 1894–1915, II, p. 174. The evidence afforded by the signet office docquet books shows a relatively high incidence of intervention at Magdalen.

[58] Miscellaneous evidence suggests that this had begun before the start of the first of the clerk's signet office docquet books in 1584/5, and it is borne out by the entries therein thereafter (S.O. 3/1 *passim*).

[59] See above, p. 291; cf. Penry Williams in McConica 1986, p. 439.

[60] Fletcher and Upton 1885, p. 230.

remarks by his adversary, appearing before the archbishop at Lambeth, Murton hinted that many were of his mind, for he asked Mosley why he did not also charge others 'whoe had sayd that the Queenes letters were foolishe letters'.[61] But it is not only the sense of resentment that comes through in this case. It also illuminates the way in which this resentment at the imposition of candidates who might be considered unworthy could call into disrepute the very means by which such men pursued their ends: the exercise of royal prerogative through letters mandatory.

At Trinity Hall in the mid-1590s the master, Thomas Preston, himself a royal nominee, experienced in his dealings with Clement Corbett the disadvantages of royal intervention.[62] Preston subsequently was to claim that Corbett had been made a scholar of the college 'by mine own mere interest'. However, Corbett's friends had never acknowledged the master's generosity. Consequently, 'I could not thus be plied by their over eager solicitation for further preferment.'[63] Corbett's friends thereupon turned to other means, for in March 1596 they obtained a mandate for his election to the next vacant fellowship.[64] Evidently, Preston prevaricated, writing to Burghley in June claiming, probably with some justification, that the fellows were absent, thus precluding an election, and that within a short space they had already elected three into fellowships on instruction by royal mandate.[65] Ultimately, therefore, the election devolved upon the master. But he did not find this responsibility a comfortable one, 'being mightily perplexed betwixt Her Majesty's gracious pleasure', which had been reiterated in a further letter from Cecil, 'and my duty on the other side towards our Founders statutes. Election is an act religious, heedfully to be undertaken, *medio juramento*.'[66] But prevarication and pleading the college statutes would not satisfy the queen: old age was closing in on Preston, and old ways were fading fast by the mid-1590s.[67] A group of fellows ganged up against their master in Corbett's favour, claiming that

---

[61] CUA, Lett. 10.A.9. This is a letter reporting the depositions in the vice-chancellor's court on 4 April 1590. The 'Acta Curiae' contains a note of these depositions (CUA, V.C. Ct. I. 26, fo. 87v).

[62] See below.

[63] *HMCS*, VI, p. 528 (17 Dec. 1596). Clement was the fourth son of Sir Miles Corbett of Sprowston, near Norwich. He was himself later to become master of Trinity Hall. For a summary of his career see pp. 97, 404, and Levack 1973, pp. 220–1. Levack incorrectly assigns the fellowship to 1592.

[64] S.O. 3/1, fo. 575v (14 March 1597). The mandate seems to have been received sometime in April (*HMCS*, VI, p. 483).

[65] *HMCS*, VI, p. 483.   [66] *HMCS*, VI, p. 483 (Preston to Cecil, 21 Nov. 1596).

[67] *HMCS*, VI, p. 506 (Preston to Cecil, 4 Dec. 1596), and more generally, Stone 1965 pp. 388–9, 488–93; Guy 1995; Morgan *et al.* 2000, pp. xxxix–xl, xiv, xlvii–xlviii.

Preston had placed two as fellows even since receiving the queen's letters for Corbett,[68] while for his part Preston complained of the difficulties of controlling 'some prodigious successors of this nimble age', asserting that Corbett's election was part of a plot hatched in the college 'to yoke the Master's government', which, if it succeeded, would lead to yet further abuses. His earlier favour shown to Corbett had introduced a 'snake into mine own bosom'.[69] Once, again, there is evidence that college faction was intermeshing with Court interests. In this respect, Preston was now ill placed and he seemed to recognise it, for he forlornly expressed the hope that if permitted to supplicate at the queen's knee, he, 'a poor forgotten and shadowed academic might pour out his mournful complaint . . . [and] could make no doubt of finding comfortable relief'.[70] But he seemed to recognise that the old days were passing when now defunct courtiers such as Walsingham and Burghley had at least moderated the demands made on the colleges. Preston's earliest objections had been addressed to Burghley[71] but on 5 July 1596, Burghley's son, Robert Cecil, had been appointed secretary of state,[72] and subsequent correspondence was conducted with him.[73] Even when allowance is made for retrospective idealisation there was some truth in Preston's claim that Burghley had 'always been pleased most tenderly to respect university men in this business [of elections] to solicit seldom, ever to leave us to the freedom of our own consciences, which memorable dealing will justly eternise his Lordship to deserve fame with all posterity'. He expressed the hope that Cecil, representing 'the lively image of your worthy father', would apply a 'like respective favour'.[74] But the old faces and the old ways were fast disappearing: Corbett got his fellowship and went on to become master of his college.[75] Both Preston and Burghley died in 1598.[76] As we have already noted, the structure of the Court and the pressures on it were changing markedly in the 1590s and structural no less than personal factors were in play. But personal factors there were, and the already dubious practices established under Elizabeth were hardly likely to be mitigated by her successor when he came into his own.[77]

Cecil's expressions of respect for college statutes and unfettered elections tended, rather, to be aspirations actually accompanying the nomination of his own candidates. In the case of the election of the master of

---

[68] *HMCS*, VI, p. 487 (certain fellows of Trinity Hall to Cecil, 22 Nov. 1596).

[69] *HMCS*, VI, p. 528.   [70] *HMCS*, VI, p. 528 (Preston to ?, 17 Dec. 1596).

[71] *HMCS*, VI, p. 483 (21 Nov. 1596, alluding to letters of the preceding June).

[72] Fryde *et al.* 1986, p. 117.   [73] *HMCS*, VI, p. 483.

[74] *Ibid.*   [75] Venn, I, p. 396a.   [76] Venn, IV, p. 394a.

[77] The assertion by Corrie that royal intervention *lessened* by the end of Elizabeth's reign is unsubstantiated, and contradicted by the evidence (Corrie 1839, pp. 48–9).

Clare Hall in 1600–1 he expressed his desire 'that in all thinges Elections should be free to their own judgments, and [I] am jealous when I should appoynt, least in my nomination there should be deficiency'.[78] Again, in the election of the master of Gonville and Caius in 1607, Cecil expressed his theoretical position, and then went on to do what in his eyes necessity demanded: 'I should with great contentment have embraced the occasion to give testimony of my great desire that all elections should have free pasage according to the privileges granted to the whole body or to several colleges; and also how indulgent I would have been to the affection of the greater part of such a body in choosing their head' – if they had not descended to factions.[79] Similarly, in a disputed election to a fellowship at Christ's in January 1610 the master referred to Cecil's previously expressed wish 'to have the most worthie firste respected in our Elections according to the statutes of our coll[ege]'.[80]

At least for the moment the aspiration to free election was maintained. But Essex's accession to the chancellorship of the university following the death of Burghley in 1598[81] had ended nearly forty years of Cecilian influence which, even if it had never been exclusive, had always been dominant and moderating in its influence. Even following the election to his father's old office as chancellor of the university, in 1601, Robert Cecil never enjoyed quite the same authority. Indeed, during Essex's brief chancellorship even the Cecil's special domain, St John's, was opened up to Essex's influence.[82]

1603–25

by the early 1600s the practice of intervention had become so habitual, especially in the election of masters, that where before there would have been opposition, now colleges actually began to make prior requests to be permitted the indulgence of the freedom of their elections. When, in 1602, the fellows of Corpus heard that their master had been elevated to the bishopric of Norwich, they wrote to Cecil with their 'humble suit that you would vouchsafe your allowance that we may be permitted, when our Master shall leave, to proceed freely to a new election'. They

---

[78] CUA, Lett. 10.II.8. The letter is dated 25 March 1600, but internal and other evidence proves this to be a misdating for 1601.

[79] *HMCS*, xix, p. 365. For the disputes at Gonville and Caius that precipitated Cecil's intervention, and the recalcitrance of the college in the face of his instructions, see below, pp. 406–7 and n. 89.

[80] Hatfield MS 126.157. For the background to this election see below, pp. 364–5.

[81] Tanner 1917, p. 18.

[82] Baker and Mayor 1869, I, pp. 448, 471 (March 1599; a request for special favour for a fellow of St John's, accompanying Essex into Ireland). For discussion of Essex's role see above, pp. 376–8.

assured Cecil that 'we shall be so careful that we doubt not your Honour will be fully satisfied'.[83] Similarly, following the death of their provost, Roger Goad, in 1610 the fellows of King's wrote to Cecil begging his protection of their society, that their statutes might not be violated, their oaths infringed and their college prejudiced in the ensuing election.[84] But another of Cecil's correspondents, Fogg Newton, had been informed that the election to the provostship was to be granted to the fellows by the king – on the condition that they should elect one of his nominees. Newton assumed that James would depend on Cecil and other privy councillors for the recommendation of nominees, and asked to be included in that number.[85] Evidently Cecil obliged: on 6 May the king did indeed nominate Newton and he was admitted provost nine days later.[86] In the following year a dispute over the election of a proctor at Queens' College led the fellows to request a free election 'earnestly at his Majesty's hands', while Cecil assured them that 'I mean to leave it to a free and fair election.'[87]

No doubt these pleas for free elections were informed by the spectacle of obtrusive royal action against local opposition at Caius in 1607 and at Christ's in 1609,[88] for it should not be thought that the interventions that occurred in the early years of the seventeenth century were all met with the subservience we have seen displayed by the fellows of Corpus in 1602. Indeed, the early 1600s witnessed both new subterfuges and a chorus of opposition in response to an unprecedented level of intervention, which, as one might expect, was ushered in when in 1603 the king came into his own.

In 1607 the fellows of Gonville and Caius took pre-emptive action in order to avoid the imposition of a Crown nominee when their former master, Dr Legge, died. They were said to have acted 'in instanti et primo momento vacationis'. The election 'was called and finished, instantly upon the breath out of the bodye, and some 2 howers before publique notyce therof'.[89] This certainly forestalled the king's letters

[83] *HMCS*, XII, pp. 525–6.   [84] SP 14/53/82 (5 April 1610).

[85] SP 14/53/83. For electoral procedures at King's see above, pp. 369–70.

[86] *VCH Cambs.*, III, p. 408 n. 43.   [87] *HMCS*, XXI, p. 323.   [88] See below.

[89] SP 14/28/39. It was even reported that 'contrary to humanity they elected another before it was absolutely certain he was dead' (*HMCS*, XIX, p. 410). However, it was also said that it was Legge who on his deathbed persuaded the fellows to make a pre-election (*ibid.*). Legge died on the 12th at around 6 o'clock (SP 14/28/39; *HMCS*, XIX, p. 410). The docquet of the signet letter inhibiting an election for sixteen days is dated the 13th, and refers to Legge's death (S.O. 3/3, 13 July 1607). It seems to have arrived at the college the same day (SP 14/28/39). News of the putative election was carried to the Court, and on the 15th further letters were sent, forbidding

inhibiting their election until his further pleasure, which arrived the following day. Thwarted at this stage, two days later further royal letters arrived forbidding the formal admission of the newly elected master. Having gone so far as to elect their preferred candidate, the fellows ignored the royal letters and admitted him. In the altercations and denunciations that followed it was possible to argue that the pre-election was contrary to their statutes and therefore not valid, while in confirming the election 'they have so audaciously carried themselves . . . in contempt of his Majesty's commandment and letters directed to them, that they have incurred the danger of perjury upon the Statutes'.[90] In the end a royal nominee, William Branthwaite, was elected in December 1607.[91] Once again, the dialectic of intervention and opposition had resulted in escalation.

In response to the well-founded fears of prerogative intervention in the election of their master such as they had seen in the elections in other colleges in recent years,[92] the members of Caius, with their strong regional connections,[93] and a continuity derived from thirty-four years

---

election or any other dealing in the matter (SP 14/28/39, but no signet letter is recorded for this date). It seems clear that interested parties had informed the king of the college's reputation for condoning popery (*HMCS*, XIX, pp. 381–3): none of the delaying tactics had any justification in the college statutes, which simply demanded an election within a month – hence the double attempt by Gostlin's supporters to elect him. After the month was over, election devolved on the chancellor (Venn 1897–1901, III, p. 348). On the 26th a further signet letter was dispatched nominating John Richardson as master. (In fact, Richardson was to become master of Peterhouse some two years later, Venn, III, p. 452a.) Whoever drafted the letter clearly envisaged objections as a result of Caius' statutory restrictions on locality – the letter is conditional: for 'if any just occasion of scruple be taken against him by some local statute in regard of his Countrye', then the college was to elect Nicholas Felton, who had been born in Norfolk, and at the time was a fellow of Pembroke (Venn, II, p. 129b). In fact, Felton had to wait another ten years before becoming master of Pembroke, although his friend Lancelot Andrewes tried to get him the job in 1612 (*DNB*). Failing this, the fellows were to suspend the election until they heard further from the king (S.O. 3/3, 26 July 1607). In the event, on 8 August, eight of the twelve fellows met and re-elected their previous choice, Dr Gostlin (*HMCS*, XIX, pp. 211, 409), and when this failed to win approval, Gostlin proposed Perse himself, the senior fellow and president (*HMCS*, XIX, pp. 44, 409). The following months saw a detailed investigation of the dispute (*HMCS*, XIX, pp. 210–11, 309–10, 364–7, 407–11, 466–7; SP 14/28/39). In the end the chancellor, Cecil, appointed William Branthwaite, a securely Protestant fellow of Emmanuel.

90 *HMCS*, XIX, pp. 407–11.

91 Venn, I, p. 207b; *HMCS*, XIX, pp. 364–7. There is no mandate naming Branthwaite recorded in the signet office docquet book for this date. Venn refers to his admission by royal mandate, 9 Dec. 1607 (Venn 1897–1901, I, p. 196). No record of the mandate survives in the college. It seems clear, however, that Branthwaite was admitted master on 14 December, following the devolution of the election to Cecil as chancellor and letters from Cecil in that capacity, nominating Branthwaite (*HMCS*, XIX, pp. 381–3; Venn 1897–1901, III, p. 70).

92 Above, pp. 376–81.

93 Above, pp. 199–201 generally for local connections. Their statutes required preference to be given to a native of the diocese of Norwich (*HMCS*, XIX, p. 407; Venn 1897–1901, III, p. 352). Cf. above, p. 199.

without an election to a mastership, had attempted to forestall any such intervention.[94] But in doing so it was reckoned that they were holding royal wishes in contempt. These provided sufficient grounds for deposing their nominee, but *post hoc* intervention in the election to a headship was a novel and disturbing precedent and it was a precedent that was to be invoked some two years later. At that time Roger Goad and Humphrey Tyndall wrote to Cecil 'Beseeching almighty God in like sort to direct your Lordship in the supply of this governor for Christs Colledge, as not long since for Cayes Colledge.' Moreover, we again see, as in the dispute over the election to a fellowship at Christ's in the 1590s,[95] the way in which the royal prerogative was drawn into contempt by these local disputes, and then its dignity reasserted by an ever more radical re-enforcement of royal authority and right of intervention.

The state of affairs a mere three years after James' accession is evident in the opposition of St John's to the attempts to intrude Ambrose Copinger into their fellowship.[96] Copinger had been a member of Trinity College, but had lost out in the elections to fellowships there, apparently because the king 'by serious letters moved that college lately for some others'. To right this wrong James was then prevailed upon to 'further the preferment of this party rather in some other College than there'. But the 'other college', St John's, complained that within the previous six months the king had sent them 'another more peremptory letter in that kind' to elect the king's nominee, to which they had acceded. They proceeded to send off one of their senior fellows to seek Cecil's intervention, bearing a copy of those of their statutes which disqualified Copinger, claiming that 'without manifest perjury we cannot admit of him'. As in similar cases, so once again, they complained that these heavy-handed interpositions of candidates out of turn discouraged 'young students of good hope brought up in our house'. But it was not just this one case to which they objected. They also asked Cecil 'not only to satisfy his Majesty for the present, but also to stay the like courses hereafter'. These means of advancement both prejudiced learning and discouraged able students who did not have 'friends to procure the like means of their preferment'. As on other occasions, the fellows of St John's harked back to what were now recalled as the balmy days of Burghley's chancellorship and his special relationship with their college, inciting Cecil to follow in his father's

---

[94] Legge had become master in 1573, but even he had not been elected: his predecessor, Dr Caius, had nominated him (above, p. 93).
[95] Above, pp. 402–3. [96] S.O. 3/3, 15 Nov. 1606.

footsteps.[97] In this they may have succeeded, for Copinger did not enter St John's but became a fellow of St Catharine's in 1607.[98] Nor was St John's alone in these difficulties. Christ's evidenced a similar case the following year.

Again James tried to impose as a fellow a member of Trinity College.[99] Again, the members of Christ's enumerated objections very similar to those of St John's and begged to be permitted to make a free election.[100] Again, they recalled the extent of the demands recently made on them: in the previous six months they had already received two other royal letters for the preferment of nominees.[101] Again, they emphasised the inequality of advancement by means of Court influence. Of one nominee, Gabriel Moore, they asserted that he must be rich, and therefore *ipso facto* ineligible, 'because he uses such means of preferment as are chargeable'[102] – in context a clear implication that favour had been purchased at Court, for the college also complained that their own able students would be discouraged 'when they see these preferments, which our honourable foundress provided for the poorest, to be carried away by the rich and such as can make best friends in Court to his Majesty'.[103] Indeed, recent experience had been such that they even professed to fear that '(so great is the number and importunity of such suitors) they may, in time, come to have letters from his Majesty for the most of our places where they be void'.[104] The complaints of Christ's to Cecil seem to have elicited a reassurance from him, and they prepared to make an election according to their statutes. But Cecil was not the only man with

---

[97] *HMCS*, XVII, pp. 353–4. Ambrose Copinger was a member of the Suffolk family of that name. Both his father (Henry) and his uncle (Ambrose) had been fellows of St John's in the 1560s and 1570s. Henry had been briefly master of Magdalene in 1577. Ambrose's brother (William) had also been a fellow of St John's and later was of the Inner Temple. Ambrose succeeded his father as rector of Lavenham (Venn, I, p. 395b; see also for their connections with St John's, Baker and Mayor 1869, I, pp. 173, 384–5, 401, 402). Despite these close family connections with the college, or because of them, a dislike of Ambrose Copinger was manifest. This may have been animated by the unhappy dealings over leases in the previous decades between another of that name (and family?) and the college (Baker and Mayor 1869, I, pp. 403, 454, there described as 'Gent., of Grays Inn').

[98] Venn, I, p. 395b.   [99] S.O. 3/3, [25] April 1607.

[100] For the journeys and expenses involved in opposing the mandates for Gabriel Moore see Peile 1910–13, I, pp. 238–9.

[101] If this was so, they were either not mandates, or if mandates, they are not recorded in the signet office docquet book for the period.

[102] *HMCS*, XIX, p. 405.

[103] *Ibid.* Moore showed a marked aptitude for exploiting the Court. He later became a chaplain to the duke of Buckingham and in 1624 obtained his DD by royal mandate (Venn, III, p. 204b).

[104] *HMCS*, XIX, p. 405.

the king's ear. His letter was followed by a further missive from the king, requiring them to elect Moore.[105] While the fellows of Christ's deliberated on how to square the circle by keeping their statutes and satisfying their monarch, further activity at Court provoked yet another letter from the king which arrived the following day and was of a quite novel type. This authorised the vice-chancellor to make Moore a fellow of the college, in the words of its members, 'after such an extraordinary manner as they have not seen in their times, nor heard of in the days of their predecessors; and after this sort he stands fellow of Christ's College, without election or admission from them'. The general threat posed by this precedent was not lost on them, for they foresaw 'what may ensue by this example, not only to their College, but to others'. They were the more unhappy because of reports that 'some one had incensed the King against them', suggesting that their refusal to elect Moore 'proceeded rather from an obstinate and factious humour than of conscience to observe their Statutes'. As with St John's, but perhaps with greater need, they begged Cecil 'to be a mean to the King for the staying of such proceedings hereafter, and the continuance of free elections, according to their statutes'.[106]

As the college implied, money may have purchased the initial solicitation or royal favour, but as we have seen on the occasion of an earlier election at Christ's in the 1590s,[107] and in the dispute over the election of the master of Caius (which was in fact contemporary with these altercations at Christ's),[108] once the royal dignity was engaged it had to be maintained. A further implication of the bitter remarks by the members of Christ's was that there were those who were willing to stoke the royal indignation at the college's recalcitrance in order to achieve their own immediate ends. The outcome was intervention in a form that created an altogether novel precedent. Again, as with the election of the master of Caius, but with far less justification, opposition had precipitated the forceful and specific assertion of the otherwise vague pretensions to royal rights of intervention in the universities.

At one level, and at a distance in time, these apparently interminable disputes might seem like mildly amusing storms in academic teacups. But when the crockery is examined it can be seen to bear patterns of wider implication. First, at the level of the institution as a whole, it indicates something of the extent, of the changing form, and of the modified expectations inherent at this time in the relationship between the university and the permanent central institution of the early modern state – the

---

[105] SP 14/28/18 (draft signet letters). The docquet is S.O. 3/3, [18] July 1607, cf. *CSPD 1603–10*, p. 364.
[106] *HMCS*, XIX, pp. 212 ff, 405–7.   [107] Above, pp. 402–3.   [108] Above, pp. 406–8.

royal Court. Second, if we take a broader view, what it is possible to read in some detail in the tea leaves at Cambridge has implications for our understanding of both the character and the workings of the early modern state. The primary point that emerges from a perusal of these imbroglios in the university is that a lot of what, superficially, can look like initiatives by the central institutions of the state are in fact manipulations of the centre by interests in the localities in pursuit of their own, local, aims. However, once the power of the state has been invoked, usually in the form of the royal prerogative, the situation could intensify into an assertion of the dignity of that prerogative. Finally, it is evident that the pressure for places at Cambridge, and the pressure on patronage networks at the centre, resulted in an escalation of the terms in which and the means by which the centre intruded in the affairs of the university. All this and more is evident in the election to the mastership of Christ's in 1609.

The engagement of long-established doctrinal factions in the promotion of, and opposition to, the rival candidates in the election to the mastership of Christ's in 1609 was the main cause of the strength of feeling expressed on the occasion of this election.[109] However, this internal dispute was also to become, as contemporaries acknowledged, the cause of a challenge to the exercise of the royal prerogative and the occasion for forcing James to extend its claims.

In writing to Cecil, James asserted that he was 'desirous to preserve the statutes of the house, and the true intentment of the fownders'. It was in pursuit of this intent, and because he could not stomach the election of any of the current members of the college to the mastership, that the king had sought advice on eligible former members of the college.[110] However, both Montagu and Cecil were aware that this constitutional punctiliousness was being challenged by the deviousness of the fellows in their attempt to avoid the imposition of a master they did not want: Montagu reported to the king how Cecil had insistently warned the fellows 'that they should not put a trick uppon the king'.[111] For his part, James clearly was aware of the public affront to his authority threatened by the machinations of the old guard at Christ's. Secretary Lake reported to Cecil that the king thought that the fellows 'abuse him with cavillations, using no manner of sincere dealing'.[112] At the same time James' indignation was stoked by the minority faction of fellows who petitioned 'that his majesty's lettres were not respectively used' by their opponents in the

---

[109] For the doctrinal issues see below, pp. 444–6.
[110] Hatfield MS 128.41   [111] Hatfield MS 128.19.   [112] *HMCS*, XXI, p. 139.

college.[113] James instructed Lake to inform Cecil that, in the deliberate misconstruction put on the royal letters, he 'hath receaved an affront such as he thinketh cannot stand with his honour to suffer',[114] and for his part Lake reported that 'His speeches are earnest wherein he recommends this to your care, in regard his honour is interested in it,' not doubting that Cecil would 'order it well and will have care of his reputation'.[115] The issue had become one of the royal dignity and authority: Cecil was to consult with the archbishop of Canterbury 'what is meet to be don in this matter for the satisfaction of his honour which his majesty takes to be much offended in their contempt'. Nor was the significance of the confrontation limited to the issue of who would be the new master of Christ's: Cecil was to take the more care in the matter 'the rather for that [the King] sayeth he heares from men of good sort that the eyes of the University are cast upon the succese of this busines'.[116] The fellows opposing the king gambled – and as it proved in the outcome, lost – on how far James was willing to stretch the exercise of his prerogative on this issue. The king was not unaware of their ploy: Lake reported that 'they doe but shift as his majesty sayth and put him to the strayning of his prerrogative which is an unpleasing thing in such cases and which he is not willing to use but in case of necesyty'.[117] The Arminian Valentine Carey duly became master.

The significance of the election to the mastership of Christ's in 1609 was that the antagonism of the warring religious factions in the college and their attempts to exploit Court connections ultimately engaged the royal dignity in a confrontation in which the Crown was being forced to extend the exercise of its prerogative powers in order to maintain its own reputation. Competing pressures from the periphery, no less than attempts to impose policies formulated at the centre, could lead to the active exercise and extension of the royal prerogative – a phenomenon which, as we have seen, had already manifested itself on a number of other occasions in the 1590s and early 1600s over elections to a fellowship at Christ's and to the mastership of Caius.[118]

Thus far we have considered the anecdotal evidence for the intervention by the Crown in elections at Jacobethan Cambridge – illuminating and, on occasion, amusing as these anecdotes may be. The detailed comment contained in that evidence is in itself sufficient to suggest that contemporaries perceived a general pattern of escalation in both the rate

---

[113] Hatfield MS 127.173.   [114] *Ibid.*   [115] *HMCS*, xxi, p. 139.
[116] Hatfield MS 127.173.   [117] *Ibid.*   [118] Above, pp. 402–3, 406–8.

and the form of intervention. And, of course, perceptions are part of the reality with which we have to deal. But it would be reassuring if we could ascertain the real as distinct from the perceived level of intervention. Therefore, we need to address the question: what *systematic* evidence is there of the suggested contrast between the pattern of intervention in the latter years of Elizabeth's reign and that which prevailed under her successors? The main *formal* means by which the Crown intervened in the universities was by means of mandates: letters under the signet seal. Considerable time and energy has been expended in attempting to establish a statistical measure of royal intervention in the universities by means of mandates. Some of the originals of these letters, or copies of originals, survive in the archives of the institutions to which they were sent. But, given the random nature of these survivals, and the adventitious evidence for the one-time existence of mandates for which originals no longer survive, any measure based on this type of source is likely to be highly imperfect. The most systematic source of information is the signet office docquet book series. Even these have a number of deficiencies and omissions. Nevertheless, on this documentary basis it is possible to make some very crude statistical comparisons between certain years in the last decade of Elizabeth's reign and the very early years of her successor.[119] It must be emphasised that, given the technical deficiencies of the sources, these are minimum numbers presenting the worst-case scenario for the case here argued.

In the mid-1580s Andrew Perne had written in strenuous opposition to the imposition of fellows on colleges by outside influence.[120] In 1585 there was a minimum of five nominations by royal mandate (Oxford = 1, Cambridge = 4). The following year there were only two, but in 1587 the figure was back at five. Between 1588 and 1590 it hovered around two or three, but from 1591 to 1593 it went up to five or six per year. Even these later Elizabethan years are low when compared with the first Jacobean year for which the docquet book appears to be complete. In 1604 alone there were ten mandates for fellowships at Oxford and seven for fellowships at Cambridge; seventeen in all. The record for the early months of 1605 appears to be defective, with only four mandates

---

[119] The figures that follow are derived from S.O. 3/1–3. These books omit non-mandatory letters, and the statistics also omit mandatory letters relating to scholarships, masterships and leases recorded in the books. These are, however, drawn upon elsewhere for non-statistical purposes. There are grounds for believing that not all mandates have been recorded in the extant docquet books (see discussion in Morgan 1983, pp. 700–12). Therefore, the ensuing figures are very much *minimum* indicators of the real level of intervention.

[120] Above, pp. 393–4.

recorded for the remainder of the year, but in 1606 there were thirteen such mandates (Oxford = 6, Cambridge = 7). In 1607 there are recorded six and eight mandates for Oxford and Cambridge respectively.

In examining this issue we are dealing with circumstances at Court as much as at the university and it would be inappropriate to limit our view to Cambridge alone: in this respect it was caught up in a wider phenomenon. To appreciate what was happening at Cambridge we have to locate the university within the larger landscape. Nor was it simply that the early years of James' reign were characterised by an increase in the total volume of mandates. The free-for-all at the early Jacobean Court created some quite ludicrous confusions that bear ample witness to the fact that no one knew who was granting what to whom.

Take for example the cognate issue of the All Souls leases.[121] In September 1603 the king's letters were sent to the college in favour of Francis Mills, a clerk in the privy seal office, for a lease of certain grounds in Northamptonshire to the value of £20 per annum.[122] The following month the college was instructed to continue as their tenant William Watts, the current lessee, 'notwithstanding any former lettres written in the behalfe of Francis Mylles'.[123] Obviously, counter-action had been taken but the matter was not yet concluded, for in the following February a further signet letter was dispatched to the college promoting the interests in the lease of Francis [?] Miller, notwithstanding the king's former letter in favour of Watts.[124] Similar complications arose over the lease of a property belonging to Winchester College, which in this, as in other respects, was treated very much like the colleges at Oxford and Cambridge: certainly, those with a rapacious eye on their resources made little or no distinction. In July 1606 the king wrote to the warden and fellows recommending the making of a lease to Lord Saye and Sele, 'in regard he is the next heir lineally discended of the founder Colledge'.[125] Again, the would-be beneficiary encountered opposition and by the following September the king was again writing to the warden and fellows, this time to tell them to continue the lease to the current tenant, Richard Venables, despite the earlier letters in favour of Saye and Sele. Nevertheless, they were to 'compensate' his lordship with a lease of similar value.[126]

The situation is no less complicated if we turn from leases to fellowships and scholarships. For example, in January 1604 Magdalen College, Oxford, was instructed to admit Richard Caple, then a demy in that college, as a fellow at the next election.[127] However, two months later

[121] Cf. pp. 290–2.   [122] S.O. 3/2, [17 Sept.] 1603.
[123] S.O. 3/2, 30 Oct. 1603.   [124] S.O. 3/2, 20 Feb. 1604.
[125] S.O. 3/2, July 1606.   [126] S.O. 3/3, [15 Sept.] 1606.   [127] S.O. 3/2, [Jan.] 1603/4.

the president and fellows were told to elect another of their demies, John Warner, to a fellowship about to be resigned by Edward Peacock.[128] The only thing that was clear was that the two letters contradicted each other. This confusion seemed to be resolved the following June when further letters instructed that Caple was to be elected to Peacock's fellowship 'notwithstanding any former L[ett]re written by his Majesty for thellec-con of any other'.[129] But the matter did not rest there, and the workings of college faction may be inferred from the docquet of a letter for the following month which alludes to the testimony of twenty-six of the college in favour of Warner and deprecatory of Caple. We may also infer from this last letter a degree of royal exasperation, for the docquet states that Warner is to be preferred and chosen fellow although 'his majestie remitteth them to a free election to be made according to the statutes of the Colledge'.[130] In this regard Cambridge could display nothing quite so Byzantine as Oxford, but on occasion it did manage to generate a modest complexity.

One way of avoiding confusions such as that at Magdalen was to spec-ify the order in which nominees were to be preferred: but the avoidance of confusion was purchased at the cost of seeing fellowship places pre-empted for months or even years to come. In August 1604 the fellows of Peterhouse were instructed to elect Roger Dereham to a fellowship, but only after William Gibson and Thomas Lowe had been placed.[131] Again, in 1606, the fellows of Trinity College were told to elect George Stanhope, 'gent', currently a student in the college, to a fellowship 'if any such roome be nowe voide or the next that shall be voide – notwithstand-ing any locall statute to the contrary'.[132] When, two weeks later, the king wrote in similar terms for a fellowship for Joshua Bloxton it was neces-sary to provide that Stanhope was given first preference.[133] For those with well-placed connections academic placement became a matter solely of royal favour. In July 1605 the president and fellows of Magdalen College were instructed to accept into their house as a demy one Nathaniel Giles, whose father and namesake was master of the children of the Chapel Royal.[134] Two years later, in April 1607, the college again received a mandate in favour of Giles to be elected to a probationary fellowship. On this occasion it was specifically recorded in the docquet book that the mandate had been granted at the request of his father.[135]

---

[128] S.O. 3/2, 27 March 1604.   [129] S.O. 3/2, [June] 1604, also referred to as 'Pockock'.
[130] S.O. 3/2, 15 July 1604.   [131] S.O. 3/2, [August] 1604.
[132] S.O. 3/3, [15 Sept.] 1606.   [133] S.O. 3/3, [31] Sept. 1606.
[134] S.O. 3/3, 10 July 1605. The letter is dated from Windsor and this may suggest the occasion for access to the royal presence.
[135] S.O. 3/3, [25 April] 1607.

Against all this evidence of intrusion it is clear even from the terse entries of docquets of signet letters that these mandates did not always meet with ready acceptance. For example, in December 1605, the president and fellows of Magdalen College were told to accept John Wilson as a demy.[136] This they appear not to have done, for in May 1607 they were again written to, with a request for Wilson's election 'in regard of his towardlyness in learning and disability of his parentes to beare the charge of his meytennce for whome his Majestie hath heretofore written to the said Colledge'.[137] Similarly, at Cambridge, the master and fellows of Christ's were requested to admit Gabriel Moore to a fellowship.[138] Three months later, there was another letter on behalf of Moore, reiterating the request.[139] He was not finally admitted until 1608.[140]

To the indicative if sometimes enigmatic evidence of opposition to be found amongst the records of the signet office are to be added the evidences of opposition that have been reconstructed from other sources. To these may be further added the explicit and general protest of the Cambridge heads against the mounting volume of indiscriminate intervention in the early years of James' reign, and for which the signet office docquet books have provided us with a statistical – if imperfect and minimum – measure. In July 1607 the vice-chancellor and heads wrote to Cecil in terms that bear out the conclusions derived from our analysis of the docquets for the preceding years.

The heads complained of 'the hindrance of our free elections of Fellowships and Scholarships in our several Colleges by the procurement of his Majesty's letters'. They also noted the increasing number of such letters, 'a thing so frequent as seven or eight Colleges have, specially of late time, this way received trouble and prejudice and so are like still, if remedy be not provided'. This was now become 'so common a grief'.[141] The heads then went on to enumerate the grounds of their objections. Such elections were 'against statutes of foundations, oaths and free choice of the fittest'. They also made it clear that the initiative for the procurement of letters originated in Cambridge: 'such letters procured from home, partly by the boldness of unfit youths moving suit by their parents and partly by the partial affection of their tutors, when they cannot have their pupils preferred as they would, whence also grows faction in houses'. The heads also revealed the means by which letters were procured and the utter failure of the king or his officials to regulate their issue. 'These

---

[136] S.O. 3/3, 15 Dec. 1605.   [137] S.O. 3/3, 18 May 1607.   [138] S.O. 3/3, [25 April] 1607.
[139] S.O. 3/3, [18 July] 1607. For the drafts of signet letters in favour of Moore, and referring to the earlier letters, see SP 14/28/18.
[140] Venn, III, p. 204b.   [141] *HMCS*, XIX, pp. 179–80.

extraordinary ways [are] too ordinarily practiced by mean persons and, it is presumed, for money, and so the poorer sort excluded: several letters sometimes being procured for two scholars for one room at the same time,[142] abusing therein the favour of his Majesty.'

As we have seen, and as the heads remarked, 'some of these letters have been answered but not without trouble and charges to the Colleges'.[143] Moreover, circumvention of the requirements of individual letters was no cure for the general problem, providing 'no stay thereby to importune petitioners'.[144] If the negative evidence of the next four years of the decline in the volume of complaints of intervention is anything to go by, this concerted opposition by the heads seems to have had some effect. This is not to say that mandates ceased, nor that a variety of means were not employed to avoid them. All this is evident in a survey of attitudes and opposition in succeeding decades.

The policy of opposition to external intervention enunciated by the heads in 1607 appears to have been maintained in the following years. Generally, there was a continuing sentiment against the invocation of mandates. In 1612, John Wynn reported to one of his provincial correspondents that the junior proctor at St John's 'was sharpelye rebuked, that he, contrarye to the statute, wolde offer to bringe in one by his Majesty's mandate'.[145] When in January 1609 Robert Some, the ailing master of Peterhouse, seemed near to death, a group of fellows[146] wrote to Dr John Richardson, the Regius Professor of Divinity, that they desired to nominate him as Some's successor, 'and therefore desire you, that you would not be wanting to yourself and us, but use your best meanes to prevent all outward Courses of Mandates from above, that so our election may be free'.[147] In this Richardson seems to have been successful, for he was elected master at the end of January.[148]

It was not only by appeal to potential candidates that colleges attempted to avoid impositions by mandates. Colleges with former members in positions of influence at Court were able to arrange protection against undue interference. This appears to have been what happened on the occasion of the election of a new master at St John's in 1612. By then Richard Neile, bishop of Coventry and Lichfield, had won considerable influence with James,[149] and a few days after the election of Dr Owen

---

[142] A complaint borne out by the evidence to be derived from the signet office docquet books.
[143] As St John's and others had complained: above, pp. 408–9.
[144] *HMCS*, XIX, pp. 179–80.   [145] Mayor 1859, p. 38.
[146] Ironically, they included among their number men such as Leonard Mawe and Roger Dereham: men who owed their own fellowships to mandates.
[147] SP 14/43/9 and copy in BL Harl. MS 7031, fo. 97.
[148] *VCH Cambs.*, III, p. 340a.   [149] Foster 1978.

Gwynn as master, Neile responded to a letter in which he acknowledged the thanks of the new master and the fellows for his part in facilitating the election, alluding to 'that little furtherence which I had opportunity to affoord to the business'. He noted that 'sundry honourable friendes were morre forward and earnest in the particular of your desires then myself was', but he preened himself on the fact that 'for the persuading the King my Master, to abstayne from the interrupting of the due proceedings of the fellowes of Colledges in electing their Masters according to their statutes and foundations, I may be bold to say both the Universities have bene as much beholding to myself as to any man of my ranke, since I had the favoure to speak to his Majestie of things of that kind'.[150] Neile's high-minded remarks should not necessarily be taken at face value: other evidence indicates that the Arminian-inclined Neile actually favoured Valentine Carey against the efforts of another former member of the college, the moderate Calvinist John Williams, who was also beginning to enjoy favour at Court.[151] It was simply that on this occasion a free election appeared to favour the doctrinal principles of those who pursued it. The hypocritical attitude to intervention evident in the election of the master of St John's in 1612 is again evident in an election to a fellowship at that college two years later. In writing for the king on behalf of John Legge for a fellowship, Sir Thomas Lake claimed that this was an exception and that the king did 'not use to meddle with the Elections of houses'.[152] If anyone was likely to know how untrue this was it was a secretary of state. Once again, a disclaimer in principle accompanied intervention in practice.

A comparable attitude was embodied in a signet letter to Corpus following the death of their master in 1618.[153] James wrote that, 'we had resolved not to meddle in the Election of any head of a College, but to leave the fellows to their own freedome in their choice'. However, the king then went on to qualify his abstemiousness: intervention might be

[150] The letter is printed in Scott 1900, p. 274. For a similar appeal to Neile, following the imposition on the college in 1619–20 of the Scotsman, George Seton, see CUL, Mm. i. 38, p. 259. For opposition in general to the imposition of Scotsmen on Cambridge see Morgan 1983, pp. 713–17.

[151] Baker and Mayor 1869, I, pp. 198, 201, and see Williams' letter to Sir John Wynn in which he claims to have been instrumental in excluding Valentine Carey from the mastership (Yorke 1797, p. 153). However, it is also possible that at this time the antagonism between these two former members of St John's was not clear-cut: in 1614, Williams was instituted to a living by Neile (*DNB*).

[152] Baker and Mayor 1869, I, pp. 477–8. The college went into a long-drawn-out avoiding action in response to these letters. Legge had entered the college as a sizar in 1606 and proceeded MA in 1614. He did not obtain the fellowship (Venn, III, p. 71a).

[153] The document used here is Baker's transcription from an earlier copy once in the hands of Mr John Byng (BL Harl. MS 7033, fo. 32v).

necessitated 'by occasion of some distraction among themselves, where our Interposition might settle them in quietness and order'[154] or on those occasions when the king had the privilege and right of nominations.[155] But once again, specific circumstances were now held to justify an exception to these principles. Andrew Byng, fellow of Peterhouse, Regius Professor of Hebrew, a translator of the Bible, and personally known to the king, 'hath moved us to recommend him unto you'. Nevertheless, James was prepared to 'leave you to do what you think fit in your discretions'. The college indulged this discretion with alacrity and the following day elected one of their own number, Samuel Walsall.[156]

Despite these protestations of royal abstention from interference in elections, during this decade there is sufficient evidence to suggest that pre-emptive evasive action was still considered necessary. Thus, on the resignation of John Richardson as master of Peterhouse, in May 1615, one of the fellows was dispatched with a petition to the bishop of Ely for a free election, and with the earl of Worcester apparently acting as their patron at Court.[157] Similarly, in 1617–18 the new master of Peterhouse was in London, trying to circumvent a mandate for one of their students to have a fellowship.[158] The ingenious lengths to which some fellows would go in order to avoid the imposition of a candidate by royal mandate is evident in the tale which emerged from a Star Chamber case that refers to the latter part of 1618.[159] A group of fellows at Emmanuel contrived to intoxicate and imprison William Ingoldsby in order to frustrate the delivery of a mandate he had obtained for his election to a fellowship and in order to elect Samuel Hildersham in his place. It was this contempt for royal letters that led to the appearance in Star Chamber.[160]

The extent to which in the early 1620s mandates were expected on the occasion of elections – despite the expressions of a royal diffidence towards their employment – is reflected in the rather surprised comment of Joseph Mede on the election of a new master at Christ's in May 1622. On the day before the election he reported to his provincial correspondent that 'We heare yet of no mandates no not [even] competitors.'[161] Certainly, towards the end of his reign James seems to have come to the

---

[154] For an example of such a letter over a disputed fellowship election at St John's in 1623, in which the king admonishes the college to elect the most worthy for learning and merit, see Baker and Mayor 1869, I, p. 488, a copy of which is in SP 14/140/58.

[155] For the statutory occasions for royal intervention see above, pp. 349–50.

[156] BL Harl. MS 7033, fo. 32v.

[157] Walker 1930, II, p. 288. For electoral procedure at Peterhouse and how it involved the bishop of Ely see above, pp. 347–8.

[158] Walker 1930, II, p. 298: the student was Oliver Griffin.

[159] PRO, STAC 8/28/2. The story is set out more fully above, pp. 360–1.

[160] See above, p. 361.   [161] BL Harl. MS 389, fo. 196.

realisation that the indiscriminate granting of royal letters for bestowing the favours of the universities was not an unqualified benefit to academe. In March 1623 reports of a potential dispute over the election to a fellowship at St John's elicited from James the not overly astute remark that 'wee having observed that in these choices sometimes affections, grounded upon particular interests and often moved by L[ett]res stirre partialities and devisions'. Therefore they were now to elect according to worth and merit without having respect to persons, 'Requestes, or private interests whatsoever'.[162]

The following year James visited Cambridge, where foreign dignitaries were granted honorary degrees, and – as Chamberlain put it – 'in the crowde some English'.[163] There were consequent remonstrances with the king that led to a restriction on mandatory degrees. The terms in which the king acknowledged the abuses to which the conferral of such degrees was liable could as well be applied to other forms of mandatory intervention. Clearly, the initiative in seeking the grant of this type of degree came from those with a vested interest in their acquisition. As James acknowledged, many of 'our Letters Mandatory' for degrees had been granted 'at the earnest peticons of many our Chaplains and other our loving Subjects'. Without intending to do so, this 'our favour' damaged the university.[164]

However, instead of placing a self-denying ordinance on the royal grant of such letters, the university authorities were required to police their validity. The general signet letter in which these instructions were contained was to provide sufficient authority, 'any commands or authority to be hereafter granted to the contrary notwithstanding'.[165] By 1624 such admonitions to virtue were of little value when addressed from an irresponsible and capricious monarch to dependent and impecunious academics. On the very next day, the master and fellows of St John's penned a circumlocutory letter to the duke of Buckingham in which they acceded to the duke's request that his servant, Robert Mason, a fellow of the college, should be permitted the benefits of his fellowship while absent on royal service.[166] In agreeing to the request they went on to ask that 'the equity and Intention of our statutes; which wee most humbly begg of your Grace (beeing safe in the clearenes and noblenes of you disposition) may (by your pious mediation upon occasion to his Majesty) bee kept inviolable from the partial importunity of those that

---

[162] SP 14/140/58, a copy: the original is in St John's (Baker and Mayor 1869, 1, p. 488).
[163] Chamberlain 1939, II, p. 591, 17 Dec. 1624.
[164] CUA, Folder in plan press: signet letter dated 17 Dec. [1624].
[165] *Ibid.*   [166] CUA, Lett. 11.A (D), part of a letterbook of St John's, fo. 12.

shall attempt it'[167] – hardly the occasion or the man to whom to address such a plea.

1625–40

At the beginning of the new reign Charles was diffident over granting mandates. In May 1625, Secretary Conway wrote to the bishop of Lincoln, John Williams, a former fellow of St John's. The king had been moved by one of his servants to recommend his son, a student at Cambridge, for a fellowship at that college. The servant had told the king that, according to the statutes of the college, he had power to act, 'In which case his Majestie is graciously inclined to write l[ett]res, but desires to be first satisfied in that point.'[168] Williams responded in terms intended to disabuse the king and protect the college, pointing out that 'all the places are appropriated to particular countreyes, as they cannot without Breach of theyr oathes, obeye any direction contrarye to theyr Statutes'. Possibly with the sense of a new broom in the palace, Williams also took the opportunity to expand his remarks into a general objection to intervention in college elections: 'we of the Clergie are all humble suyters upon our knees to his majestye and his great ministres to be as sparinge as maye be, in writinge any letters which may hynder Elections in Colleges whereupon dependes the encouragement of the better schollers, and consequentlye the weale of both the universityes'.[169] In general, and at first, Charles appears to have been far more punctilious than his father in maintaining the letter of statutes of corporations.

In 1633, a dispute arose between Edward Abbot and Robert Creighton over the right to election as a canon residentiary at Wells. Abbot had old letters from James, and Creighton had been recommended by Charles. But the dean and chapter were told to proceed to an election according to their statutes, which 'wee will in noe wise have infringed'. For the future they were 'strictlye [to] observe the order of Succession prescribed in the said statutes'. In the event Creighton was coopted as a residentiary in 1633, Abbot in 1644.[170] Indeed, the late 1620s and early 1630s are characterised by a general 'renovation' of government, and this is evident in relationships with the universities as it is elsewhere. There is a new rigour with regard to the issue of mandates.

---

[167] *Ibid*. There is a discrepancy in dating. Buckingham's letter is dated 12 Dec. 1625; the answer is dated 18 Dec. 1624.
[168] SP 16/2/96.   [169] SP 16/2/96 I.
[170] SP 16/232/72, draft signet letter, 19 Feb. [1633]; Horn and Bailey 1979, p. 110.

It may be that Laud's influence with the king played some part in this.[171] The bishop of London's legalistic punctiliousness is evident in his attempts to place his chaplain as warden at Winchester. In writing to the warden of New College, with which the choice lay, he pointed out the advantages of following his recommendation, but added that if it contravened their statutes 'in any considerable thing, I shall fayrly submit it to your wisdome. For I shall ever consider that God hath disposed of me to the place I beare to keep and preserve the libertyes of Statutes and Elections according to oath, and not to put any stress upon them, but rather to stand as a Barr and a hindrance to my power, when it is attempted by others.'[172] But even Laud did not have everything his own way at Court, and competition could enforce further intervention. A few days later he was writing to say that before he left Windsor he had arranged that no letters should come from the king if his chaplain did not obtain the position, 'Ever resolvinge to keepe me entyre to the deutye of mye place, that Elections might go as Statutes directed, and as merits prevailed.' However, when it became apparent 'that his Majestyes leters were aymed at for another, and in some words that I had noe great cause to like', he then permitted his chaplain to use his friends: 'Yett I ordered it so that the Letters which ar come mighte noe waye trench upon the Libertye of your Election, but keepe neare the precedent which I sawe written for Dr Love.'[173] The disadvantage of such restraint was proven in the outcome: Laud's chaplain failed to become warden of Winchester College.[174] But Laud's was not the only influence at work at this time, and there is some evidence to suggest that in the late 1620s and early 1630s steps were taken to attempt to regulate the signet office, the crucial conduit through which all mandatory exercises of the royal prerogative were required to flow.[175] Again, in order to understand what happened at Cambridge we need to place the university in this larger context.

In 1627 a separate series of docquets of Irish letters was instituted in the signet office together with what aspired to be a stricter secretarial oversight of Irish correspondence.[176] Some four years later, Emmanuel Downing was being told by one of the clerks in the office that a letter he

---

[171] For Laud's attitude, and in particular how this was worked out in his relationship with Oxford, see Sharpe 1989, pp. 123–46.

[172] Lambeth Palace Library, MS 943, p. 141, 10 Sept. 1630.

[173] *Ibid.*, p. 143.   [174] *Ibid.*, p. 145.   [175] See above, pp. 413–16.

[176] PRO, S.O. 1/-. See also Giuseppi 1963, II, p. 259. There the preoccupation is with the role of the signet office as an initiatory stage in the course of the seals leading to grants under the Great Seal. As the preceding discussion amply demonstrates, in this period the office is also important as the direct source for letters missive. A secondary duty of the signet office was to enter all letters under the royal sign manual dispatched from the government to the Lord Lieutenant in Ireland. The change noted here is indicative of a general tightening up in the office.

had delivered to be entered in the book first required the signature of the secretary before it could be sealed, 'for directions are sent into Ireland that such letters shall not take effect unless they be under one of the secretaries hands'.[177] Some attempt appears to have been made to restrict the indiscriminate employment of the royal prerogative by ensuring that letters or grants trenching on major institutions had the prior consent of those responsible for those institutions. This could be done by issuing the clerks of the signet with a caveat against passing certain categories of documents, and by instructing regular recipients, such as heads of colleges, to refer back all such instruments, or to require the fulfilment of certain obligations under the authority granted them by a signet letter of general import.

Evidence of the first procedure is to be found in the objections of the earl of Bridgewater as President of the Council of the Welsh Marches, in July 1632, to a certain grant of lands within his jurisdiction. This had prompted the earl to speak with the king, 'for renewing his warrant to the Signet that nothing concerning the provincial Councils might pass before the President thereof were made acquainted therewith'.[178] Both procedures were applied to matters relating to Cambridge in the late 1620s and early 1630s.

During the king's visit to Cambridge in March 1632 he had issued a signet letter for the granting of sixty mandatory degrees.[179] Some ten days later Charles again wrote to the university, explaining the motives for his actions and rehearsing the objections that had been forwarded to him by their chancellor, the earl of Holland. In most respects these second thoughts recall those of James in 1624.[180] The king had been 'moved by many neare unto us in the behalfe of their chaplains and others to grant our letters Mandatory for their taking such degrees as they severally desired'.[181] However, their chancellor had pointed out 'that the want of performance of such acts and exercises as the statutes of our University do require to be performed by all such as shall there be admitted to any degree may tend much to the prejudice of young students among you'. In future, nominees for mandatory degrees were to put in a surety

---

[177] *HMC* 23: Cooper, *Annals*, I, p. 434.
[178] *Ibid.* Similarly, stops could be placed on specific grants. In 1627, the young duke of Lennox claimed that a 'Caveat was entered in the Signet Office' that on the vacancy of the mastership of Trinity College, his client 'might not be prevented of his Majesties gratious intention by the importunitie of any other suitors' (SP 16/85/50).
[179] CUA, Lett. 12.B.1; Grace Book Z, p. 220. In addition, prior to this date and from 1627, a number of mandates survive for individual degrees, mainly for men in royal service (CUA, Lett. 12.C.11).
[180] Above, p. 420; CUA, Folder in plan press, signet letter dated 17 Dec. [1624].
[181] CUA, Lett. 12.B.2.

that in due time they would perform the exercises necessary for their degrees. As with James some eight years earlier, this general letter was to act as sufficient authority to enforce this requirement, 'any command or authority to be hereafter granted to the contrary notwithstanding'.[182]

The tone of injured innocence in Charles' letter fails to reveal the major row that had precipitated it. According to D'Ewes, who was present at Cambridge during the king's visit, 'the whole body of the University took great offence' at the nominations for doctorates of divinity.[183] Moreover, they accused some of the recipients of bribery, telling the vice-chancellor, Dr Butts, 'in the open Regent's house . . . to his face', that they rejected this begging of degrees,[184] and refused to give their votes for Dr Martin, president of Queens', and the other new doctors, 'yet Doctor Butts carried the business through with much disorder and violence, and pronounced them to have passed, and attained that degree'. D'Ewes attributed Butts' subsequent suicide in part to the opprobrium this affair had called down upon him.[185] Be this as it may, from then on a more rigorous control over the granting of mandate degrees appears to have been enforced.[186]

In the business of tightening up on mandatory degrees the earl of Holland as chancellor was acting as intermediary between the university and the king. There is some evidence to suggest, however, that following his election to office in 1628 in succession to the duke of Buckingham, the earl did play a positive role in attempting to curb Court intervention at Cambridge. This appears to have been in reaction to the excesses perpetrated under his predecessor as chancellor, and provides some indirect evidence by way of contrast with this earlier phase for which regrettably little detailed information survives.[187] In July 1629 Holland wrote to Cambridge that 'It is but lately come to my knowledge, what letters Mandatory have passed his Majesty to your universitye; their number exceedes former Customes.'[188] He claimed that 'All those of myne (not many) had warrant of my hand, as a witnesse how tenderly I preferred them, though by the Kings command.' It was his responsibility, he claimed, to 'see the redresse in others'. The king had granted

---

[182] *Ibid.*   [183] Halliwell 1845, II, p. 68.

[184] 'Istam graduum mendicacionem improbare'.

[185] Halliwell 1845, II, p. 68; on Butts' suicide see Collinson in Bendall *et al.* 1999, p. 214.

[186] For surviving mandates for degrees after this date see CUA, Lett. 12.C.12–15; Subscriptiones I, p. 474 and Grace Book Z, pp. 306, 424. In these letters the requirements of this general letter (CUA, Lett. 12.B.2) normally are reiterated.

[187] For certain aspects of Buckingham's chancellorship see Morgan 1983, pp. 30–6; Maclear 1957–8.

[188] CUA, Lett. 12.D.1; draft in BL Egerton MS 2597, fo. 48. The latter is endorsed 'his Mat[ie]s le[tt]res Mandatory–their abuse'.

him power to oversee 'such as hereafter shall be sent' – this sounds very much like the authority granted the presidents of the provincial councils and in Irish affairs.[189] If letters otherwise came to the heads and they failed to acquaint him with them, 'your owne remissnesse . . . must excuse the neglect of the lybertye you may enioy by your free Elections'.[190] The survival of part of the correspondence with the university of Holland's secretary, William Sanderson, provides some insight into the pressures to which this new regimen was subject over the ensuing months.[191]

In January 1630, Sanderson responded to an enquiry by Dr Butts – then vice-chancellor – as to whether any mandates had been acquired by aspirant fellows for Butts' own college of Corpus. Sanderson assured him that he knew of none, 'And shall bee very unwilling to meete with any Especially to your Howse for you may bee confident, so farr of your Chancelors respect to his Deputy as to allowe his power in his owne College to governe it selfe.' Exceptions to this general restraint would only arise 'where his Majestys especiall command upon especiall occasion alter his Lorships resolution'.[192] That, of course, was a major part of the problem.

The other part was compounded of the pressures to which a chancellor – and courtier – such as Holland was subject and the mercenariness of servants such as his secretary, Sanderson. Thus, in March 1630, Sanderson wrote to Butts in connection with the resignation of a fellowship at Emmanuel. According to Sanderson the fellows were bound not to accept propositions from others or to make prior promises and that therefore a previous letter from Holland had been mistaken, 'that my Lords direction should intimate any application to an Overture of Praescription is certainly misunderstood, themselves being left free to their own Consciences . . . the care of that Colledge to whose statutes his Lordship once took oath makes him tender what to oppose to others Consciences'.[193] Nevertheless, by the same post Sanderson also saw fit to write for a scholarship on behalf of John Harrison of Trinity College. Representations were made on his behalf by his father, 'with the assistance of powerfull mediators for my Lords letters'.[194] Sanderson claimed

[189] For approbatory signatures, above, p. 423 and *HMC* 23: Cowper, *Annals*, I, p. 434.
[190] CUA, Lett. 12.D.1.
[191] CUA, Lett. 12.D.2–19. On Sanderson, Holland and Butts see Collinson in Bendall *et al.* 1999, pp. 212–14.
[192] CUA, Lett. 12.D.2.
[193] CUA, Lett. 12.D.5. Holland had been at Emmanuel in 1603 (Shuckburgh 1904, p. 52; Collinson in Bendall *et al.* 1999, pp. 210–14).
[194] CUA, Lett. 12.D.6.

to have opposed this importunity: 'I persisted against it, because of my promise to take off these troublesome requests and did for the tyme procure deniall.' But 'the good Mans teares for his sonnes preferment' made him relent. He suggested that if, by the 'favour power and meanes' of the vice-chancellor shown to the master and fellows of Trinity 'the young Mans suffitiencye may give waight to the Ballance', it would oblige the supplicants and 'being thus presented by my hand shall also command me'.[195] The old language of patronage and mutual obligation is back. And, of course, the letter does not record at what price this relenting soft-heartedness was purchased of this hard-nosed administrator.

For his part, Holland can be found writing some three months later that 'I have kept my word against Mandates especially for Elections.' Then follows the almost inevitable 'however'. On this occasion the earl was 'persuaded for one Sir Atkinson of Christ's Colledge upon severall testimonies of his sufficiencie, and of his full tyme' to be permitted to proceed MA at the next Commencement, 'I had rather presume of your favours upon my commendacon.'[196] Again, some few months later, Sanderson was writing to Butts on behalf of an old acquaintance, the bearer of the letter, 'Mr. Calvert'. Sanderson admitted that the earlier behaviour of Calvert's son at Caius left much to be desired; nevertheless he recommended him for a fellowship there: 'In good fayth, Charyty to the father makes mee speake for the sonne for your Mediation to the Master and fellowes unlesse in your descretion you find him incapable of this favour which I most humbly recommend.'[197]

The policy of reducing the number of mandates seems only to have increased the number of personal recommendations from those charged with scrutinising the issue of letters missive. At the same time it did not totally stem the flow of formal mandates. In August 1631, Sanderson wrote to Butts of 'a late fellow accepted upon a Mandate which was also without my Lords knowledge. So that you see what troubles these Commands bring upon the Houses and yet yee will not free yourselves.' He also asked Butts to let him know 'who at Court procured the Christs College mandate to you'.[198] Moreover, the policy of cancellarial scrutiny inevitably concentrated power in the hands of his secretary. Sanderson

---

[195] *Ibid.* There were two John Harrisons at the college in these years. The one referred to is almost certainly the Harrison who matriculated as a sizar in 1627 and became a scholar in 1631 (Venn, II, p. 315b).

[196] CUA, Lett. 12.D.7. Undoubtedly a reference to Thomas Atkinson who entered Christ's in 1620. He received his MA in 1627 (Venn, I, p. 54a).

[197] CUA, Lett. 12.D.11. Sanderson's acquaintance was probably Sampson Calvert, citizen of London, whose son Ralph had proceeded MA in 1628. He did not become a fellow (Venn, I, p. 285a).

[198] CUA, Lett. 12.D.17.

more than once asserted his opposition to mandates: 'what refers to mee as an humble Remembrancer I shall discharge the trust as an enemy to them all'.[199] But he was also a member of the second tier of courtiers, as indeed, he was later to describe his role: 'For myself, having lived long in court, and employed (till my grey hairs) more in business than books; far unworthy, I humbly confess, to have any hand to the helm, yet I cabined near the steerage, and so might more readily run the compass of the ship's way.'[200] In the nature of the Court there were those about it such as Sampson Calvert[201] whom Sanderson felt obliged to accommodate, and always there was the temptation of a suitor's bribe – temptation that despite his repeated protestations of antipathy to 'letters' a man like Sanderson found hard to resist.

Writing with the opposition to the mandate degrees in mind in March 1632, D'Ewes gossiped that 'all those doctors had paid Mr Sanderson, the Earl of Holland's secretary, large rate for their doctorships'. The scandal on this occasion was such that Sanderson was said to have been 'about this time turned out of his place' by the earl.[202] The pressure for scholarships, fellowships and degrees was not easily withstood when one of the habitual means to their attainment was through a Court that itself was inherently difficult to regulate. Certainly, from the viewpoint of the recipients of requests, there did not appear to be that parsimony to which Holland may have aspired, and during the 1630s there was continued resentment and opposition to mandates at Cambridge.

In 1633, amongst the accusations levelled at Robert Lane of St John's[203] was that two years earlier (that is, during Sanderson's secretaryship to Holland) he had complained that the chancellor 'is alwaies sending l[ett]res: if the Universitie and Regent House were of my mind wee would chose another Chancellor'.[204] Opposition to mandates also led to anger with the royal authority in which they originated. On another occasion Lane was reported as saying that 'it is the Kings L[ett]res that spoile all elections, if others were of my mind no man should be fellow that brought or procured them'.[205] When asked whether he would fulfil a specific mandate or answer it, 'Dr Lane in very high language said "I care not for them, I will answere them, I will answere them I warrant you"; "then you will answere them" said this deponent, "ye" said Dr Lane

---

[199] *Ibid.*
[200] Sanderson 1656, preface to the 2nd part, refuting Arthur Wilson, quoted in *DNB*, under Sanderson.
[201] CUA, Lett. 12.D.11: above, n. 197.   [202] Halliwell 1845, II, p. 68.
[203] Fellow of the college since 1598, died 11 June 1634 and buried in the college chapel (Venn, III, p. 41b).
[204] SP 16/249, p. 45.   [205] *Ibid.*

"I will answere them".' All this left very little doubt as to his position. Evidently the irascible Lane was in no position fully to refute these words, and in his deposition merely attempted to modify their tenor, claiming that he had not said that the king's letters spoiled elections, 'but he might happily say that if the Kinges L[ett]res were surreptitiously procured and come commonly and ordinarily they might do harme to Elections':[206] the squirming is palpable.

The detailed evidence of attempts to control the procurement of mandates, and of continued opposition within Cambridge to their acquisition by candidates, suggests that even in the late 1620s and in the 1630s the structure of the Court was such that it was still possible for well-connected individuals to acquire them for their personal advancement to scholarships, fellowships and degrees. However, these categories need to be distinguished from mandates for elections to masterships. Because of the powers with which masters had been equipped during the early years of Elizabeth's reign, and because of the contesting religious factions with which the university was riven, by the 1590s at the latest these elections had become matters of considerable political and theological significance for the various interest groups both at Court and in the university. It is these conflicts which inform the elections to masterships in these decades and the specific content of those conflicts is discussed elsewhere.[207] Here, we may conclude this survey of intervention by external interests in Cambridge before 1640 by examining some of the attitudes adopted and means employed to exploit and to oppose external intervention in elections to masterships during the 1620s and 1630s.

Within the first two years of his reign Charles made clear his own interest in the elections of heads of houses when in 1626 he questioned the eligibility of Thomas Batchcroft as the newly elected master of Caius. The king complained to the vice-chancellor and other heads that the choice had been made without due respect to the intentions of the statute 'or care of the honor of our universitie . . . and . . . in the elections of Masters it hath beene the custome to choose some person of note and eminency who by his meritt is either knowne unto our selfe or made knowne unto us by your testimony and recommendacion neither of which in this last hath beene observed'. The king, out of his 'owne Princely affection to the flourishing estate of our universitie, which much depends upon the abilities of governors of particular societies', required an investigation of Batchcroft's qualifications and certification of 'what manifestacion he hath given of his worth by any publick exercise' – the repeated use of the royal

<hr />

[206] *Ibid.*   [207] Below, pp. 444–6.

possessive is to be noted. This ignominious scrutiny of the achievements of one of their number was to be complemented by an investigation by the heads of whether he was 'elected and compleatly qualifyed according unto statute, the libertye whereof shall bee soe farr forth allwayes tender unto us as it crosse not the dignitie of our universitie in general'.[208] Clearly, there was a new, strategic, motivation at work, to which the rights of colleges came a poor second – although, in this case, the root of the objection was that the high church heads reckoned Batchcroft a puritan, even if a moderate one. Moreover the proprietorial air which Charles was to adopt towards the universities throughout his reign is thus evident from its inception. But more contingent circumstances also played a part: the peremptory terms adopted over the election of Batchcroft at Caius in November 1626 were no doubt coloured by events at Corpus in the preceding months. In the event the heads, after some disagreement, confirmed the election of Batchcroft.

A group of fellows at Corpus had complained of the manner of elect-ing John Munday[209] following the death of their former master, Samuel Walsall.[210] Prior to this the duke of Buckingham, as chancellor, asked the king to permit them a free election, 'unto which his Highness most gratiously and willingly condescended'.[211] As a result of the dispute that arose, the matter had been referred to the vice-chancellor and heads so that the college might be provided with 'a discreet, learned and an able Governor'.[212] But in addition to investigating the circumstances of the election they were also to examine 'the sufficiency of the parties elected, and how they and either of them stand affected to the Doc-trine and Discipline of the Church of England, by his Majesty's Laws Ecclesiasticall establisht'. The latter requirement was a clear indication of an increasingly important criterion in university elections. The new king's wider aims in terms of both state and church was to bring with it a more systematic programme of intervention and it was early mani-fest in the universities. This was true even before influential elements of the previous order had been removed. Thus, in sending up a report on the election, the vice-chancellor took the opportunity to enthuse upon Buckingham's generosity: 'for this your high favour expressed out of your free and noble disposicon, by your mediation for the maintaining of the

---

[208] CUL, Baumgartner (Patrick) MS 22, fo. 13 (fo. 8 in Catalogue). On this election see Venn 1897–1901, III, pp. 85–6, quoting a letter of Joseph Mede and the Caius *Annals*.

[209] He had entered Corpus in 1614 as a fellow and became rector of Little Wilbraham in 1626 (Venn, III, p. 227a).

[210] CUL, Baumgartner (Patrick) MS 22, fo. 27.

[211] BL Harl. MS 7033, fo. 32.   [212] *Ibid.*

liberty and freedom of Elections; a favour most gratefull to all our So-
cyeties which they as readily in all duty shall and will be ever bound to
acknowledge as at all times they will earnestly desire to enjoy'.[213] What
was enjoined as a statutory obligation was now being effusively greeted
as a notable favour.[214]

Over many years, piecemeal, faction-driven and often local and personal motivations had induced Cambridge men to seek the exercise of
external influence in pursuit of their aspirations within the university.
The increasing wealth of the colleges, and the increasing familiarity with
that wealth on the part of courtiers and their dependants as a result of
direct experience of the universities; the integration of the university
within a wider world of Court-based patronage – these had all conspired
to create a habit of intervention. But now anarchy was to be replaced by
a purposeful order in pursuit of larger goals.

Opposition on the part of some factions in the university to external
intervention is likely to have been accentuated as increasingly they were
excluded from influence at Court. Thus, in November 1627, and again
in February 1628, the young duke of Lennox wrote to Secretary Conway
in favour of his tutor, Anthony Topham, for the mastership of Trinity
College.[215] The initiative arose from the rumour of the promotion of the
then master, Leonard Mawe.[216] But by this time the exercise of magnatial
patronage on behalf of a personal tutor weighed but lightly in the balance
against the doctrinal considerations which had come to the fore and Mawe
was succeeded by a Laudian fellow-traveller, Samuel Brooke.[217]

The revealing report of the words of Robert Lane that 'the Kings
L[ett]res . . . spoile all elections' to fellowships, which we have earlier

---

[213] CUL, Baumgartner (Patrick) MS 22, fo. 27v.

[214] The outcome was that Henry Butts supplanted the putative master, John Munday, at Corpus.

[215] Topham had been a fellow of Trinity since 1608. Evidence of his favoured standing is to be found
in his DD by royal mandate in 1624 and an accumulating plurality of livings. It was during the
bishopric of John Williams that he became dean of Lincoln in 1629 (Venn, IV, p. 252b; Horn
and Smith 1999, pp. 3, 7). For Lennox's equally unsuccessful mediation on behalf of Robert
Creighton for the mastership of Catharine Hall in 1635 see CUA, Lett. 12.A.20.

[216] SP 16/85/50; SP 16/93/64. If fact, Mawe was nominated as bishop of Bath and Wells on 14 July
1628. His predecessor at Wells, William Laud, had been translated to London on 4 July 1628.
In turn, Laud's predecessor at London, George Montaigne, had been translated to Durham in
February 1628, and it may have been the expectations excited by this general shuffling of the
ecclesiastical hierarchy that led Lennox to put in his plea for Topham (Horn and Bailey 1979,
p. 2; Horn 1969, p. 2 corrected in Fryde *et al.* 1986, p. 242 and Horn, Smith and Mussett,
2003).

[217] For Brooke's doctrinal affiliations with Laud see *DNB* and Trevor-Roper 1962, pp. 112–13.
In fact, Mawe was allowed to retain the mastership for some months in conjunction with his
bishopric (Hembry 1967, pp. 221–2); and the grant of office to Brooke, dated 15 July, was in
the way of being a pre-emptive appointment, only becoming operative when Mawe resigned
(*CSPD 1628–9*, p. 212; *VCH Cambs.*, III, p. 473).

examined, had arisen during an investigation into the circumstances surrounding the election to the mastership of St John's in 1633.[218] Not that Lane's objections to royal letters extended to those which he had obtained of the king for his own election as head of the college following the death of Owen Gwynn and which, in the event, were to result in a protracted dispute and investigation.[219] The problem from Lane's view-point was that the letters that he had obtained in his favour were not mandatory, and this was seized upon by the contrary faction.[220] Again there is evidence that these factions were inspired by conflicting religious beliefs[221] and the issue was further complicated by the absence at this time in Scotland of both the king and the university's chancellor, the earl of Holland. This led to intervention by the Privy Council: an unusual event in university affairs,[222] and one which was clearly based on infor-mation supplied by members of the university intended to subvert the interests of the opposing faction.[223] Indeed, so unusual was intervention from this quarter, that one of Lane's supporters averred that this unwonted threat to their designs on the mastership 'was not matter for the Councell boarde',[224] while for his part Lane refused to open the original council letter of 16 June, returning it to the messenger. This further complicated matters by insulting the council: 'we cannot but marvell thereat, and be verie sensible of soe great an Insolencie and neglect showed to the dig-nitie of this Board', and on the 19th he was summoned to answer for his contumacy.[225]

The most senior fellow willing to support the candidacy of Richard Holdsworth in opposition to Lane was Joseph Thurston. Of Thurston it was reported that on the first reading of the king's letter to the fellows he twice said 'in a rough manner . . . with a loud voice openly, "these letters

---

[218] SP 16/249, p. 45; above, p. 427.

[219] The story of the disputed election at St John's may be reconstructed from the subsequent extensive depositions and subsidiary documents. Tabor, the University Registrary, was to spend 'my whole tyme' from 17 Sept. until 19 Jan. – 18 weeks – 'speeding ingrossing and returning' the commission of inquiry (SP 16/263/63). The college was to object to being charged with the not inconsiderable sum of £89-9-5 for this service (SP 16/263/63). The report of the commission now constitutes a separate volume of 63 pages amongst the State Papers (SP 16/249). For documents generated by the commission of heads appointed by the Crown see CUA, College IV, 1–3 (three packets of documents in a box). For copies of documents and drafts see CUL, Baumgartner (Patrick) MS 22, fos. 17v–22v (from the letterbook of Henry Smith or Smyth, master of Magdalene). Copies of the papers in the University Archives are to be found in Baker MS 27 (now CUL, MS Mm. i. 38, pp. 95–108), and in Baker's note of manuscripts *ex penes* Thomas Dillingham (BL Harl. MS 7029, fo. 256v). See also St John's College Library, MS s.37.

[220] SP 16/249, p. 53.   [221] Below, pp. 444–6.

[222] PRO, P.C. 2/43, pp. 94–5; copy in Henry Smith's near-contemporary collection (CUL, Baumgartner (Patrick) MS 22, fo. 11v).

[223] PRO, P.C. 2/43, p. 94.   [224] PRO, P.C. 2/43, p. 97.   [225] *Ibid.*

are not for Dr Lane" but for the choosing of an able man, and they were left to their liberty'.[226] The role of Holdsworth's proponents in procuring letters from the Privy Council – letters that Lane had refused to open – is implied in Thurston's employment of his 'loud voyce and . . . rude manner' to announce on this occasion 'that there were other letters too to be read'.[227] To the mind of at least one of his antagonists, these 'words . . . the said Mr Thurston used in a menacinge manner'.[228] For his part, as we have heard, Lane had attempted to assure himself of office by obtaining royal letters in his favour. However, as the king was in Scotland at the time, tactically it was necessary to draw out the time for the election as long as possible, while one of Lane's junior supporters, Daniel Ambrose, was dispatched to solicit royal support, as Baker put it, 'upon pretence of giving notice of the master's death, but in reality to procure his majesty's letters'.[229] These royal letters were dated from Berwick on 11 June.[230] Another report had it that Lane 'concealed the masters death one day, caused the bell to be rung all Friday, being the next day [*sic*] and his plott in delaying the eleccion till it hath at length fallen (as he would make it) into the King's hands by lapse'.[231] The dispute dragged on with charges and counter-charges being exchanged until the following February[232] when the king thwarted both protagonists by elevating William Beale from the mastership of Jesus to that of St John's.[233]

The religio-political significance of this dispute would seem to be that, in the unusual circumstances of the king being in Scotland, it was possible for the precisian[234] faction in the college to oppose the recommendatory letters obtained of the king by Lane through appeal to the caretaker Privy Council in London. However, the dispute at St John's also resulted in royal instructions intended to ensure that surreptitious pre-emptive elections

---

[226] SP 16/249, first deposition. But, again, the case was not that of one group being in favour of external intervention and another being against it. Thurston used letters in his own favour to forward his academic career (see Venn, IV, p. 240a; Baker and Mayor 1869, I, pp. 293–479). Rather, attitudes were determined at least in part by which individuals and which interest groups were favoured by intervention on any particular occasion.

[227] An allusion to the Privy Council letters of the 16th, and possibly the 19th, of June (PRO, P.C. 2/43, pp. 94–5, 97), or to letters that were said to have been written by Bishop Williams of Lincoln, and which Lane sent to the king in Scotland (Heywood and Wright 1854, II, pp. 404–5).

[228] SP 16/249, p. 48. On 29 June, Sir John Lambe reported to Laud that Williams was meddling in the matter (*CSPD 1633–4*, pp. 120–1).

[229] Baker and Mayor 1869, I, p. 213.

[230] *Ibid.*, p. 501; St John's College Archives, Register of Letters.

[231] Heywood and Wright 1854, II, pp. 404–5.   [232] Laud 1847–60, VI, I, p. 323; VII, pp. 52, 62.

[233] CUL, Baumgartner (Patrick) MS 22, fo. 16, copy of a signet letter of 14 Feb. [1634], the draft of which is SP 16/260/63. This appointment had obvious implications for the advancement of Arminian interests in the university.

[234] See above. p. 95, n. 125.

were precluded, thereby allowing the government due time to consider suitable candidates. Thus, it appears that the old master, Dr Gwynn, had died sometime before midnight on Wednesday, 5 June, but the 'time of his death was concealed' and it was only the next morning that rumours of his demise began to circulate in the college, 'and then the bell rung out, before which ringing there neither was nor indeed could be any notice taken of his death'. All parties seemed willing to agree that Thursday should be taken as the first day of the notification of the vacancy, but that it was not until Friday that the fellows were summoned together to receive the news, and that notification of the election was fixed to the chapel door.[235]

During the hearing of the ensuing dispute during the last quarter of 1633, and on his return from Scotland, the king dispatched a signet letter intended to regulate further elections to masterships.[236] The letter noted that colleges had statutes 'for the prevention of undue and clandestine eleccons to Masterships and headships of Colledges and Halls'; it rehearsed that on a vacancy the notification of the same and the citation for a new election should be forthwith attached to the chapel door for a period of time specified by the statutes; and it reflected that 'the said Statutes have not of late bene so well observed as they ought to be'. Henceforward, the governors of Cambridge were strictly charged and commanded to ensure that these local statutes were vigorously adhered to. Moreover,[237] no head was to resign his place except in 'a faire and open way before a Publique Notarie' according to the local statutes, and to 'tender the said resignation by himselfe or his Proctor to his next Superior that hath power to admitt the same, and pronounce the place void'. The heads were further charged with overseeing the maintenance of these punctilious standards and instructed to report back on them from time to time to the king.[238] Effectively, what was strictly a matter for individual colleges was now made the joint responsibility of the incumbent masters of all colleges.

---

[235] CUL, Baumgartner (Patrick) MS 22, fo. 12. This report suggests a breach of the strict letter of the college statute II, 'De Electione Magistri', that action should be taken 'tum proximo die' (*Cambridge Documents 1852*, III, p. 249). As Baker remarked, 'Irregular things passed on both sides, the lapse of time, and that the seniors wanted numbers to make an election' (Baker and Mayor 1869, I, p. 214).

[236] Original in CUA, Lett. 12.A.17, copy in SP 16/246/83, both dated 27 Sept. [1633]. Draft by Windebank in SP 16/246/75 endorsed 25 Sept. Subsequent contemporary copy in CUL, Baumgartner (Patrick) MS 22, fo. 30. Printed in Cooper, *Annals*, III, pp. 261–2 from *Statuta Academiae Cantabrigiensis (Statuta 1785)*, p. 290.

[237] Here, I have slightly rearranged the order of the clauses in the original document in order to produce a greater coherence of exposition.

[238] CUA, Lett. 12.A.17.

In itself this reflects the more coherent, policy-driven and programmatic view of the university that had come to prevail at the centre of power.

As with the unsuccessful candidacy of Anthony Topham for the mastership of Trinity in 1627,[239] Lane had also in his time enjoyed noble patronage – in his case from Henry Wriothesley, earl of Southampton, and a Jacobean privy councillor, whose chaplain Lane was.[240] Although the earl's son was briefly at St John's in 1626,[241] despite initially obtaining letters from the king, by 1633 Lane no longer commanded adequate connections at Court.[242] Certainly, he lacked the necessary crucial influence with Laud.[243] The gravamen of the objections to Lane was that he was a dissolute *bon viveur* who failed to attend upon his religious devotions.[244] His opponent, Richard Holdsworth, was, according to Baker, 'suspected as puritanically inclined'.[245] Indeed, in 1637, Holdsworth was to become master of godly Emmanuel,[246] although on that occasion Laud unctuously reported that he had 'done . . . [him] all right to his Majesty'.[247] And he well may have done. In Patrick Collinson's sagacious judgement Holdsworth was an 'extreme moderate': a Calvinist who could stomach Laudian ceremonialism.[248]

The intransigence of the two parties in St John's and the doubts as to the personal qualifications of both candidates ensured that neither *bon viveur* nor scholarly precisian would win.[249] Rather, a Laudian

---

[239] Above, p. 430.

[240] In July 1624, Southampton had written to the college requesting leave of absence for Lane (Baker and Mayor 1869, I, p. 491). This was in preparation for the military expedition to the Low Countries (Chamberlain 1939, II, pp. 562, 567, 575, 590) on which both the earl and his eldest son died in the November of that year (Lee 1972, pp. 317–18). In fulfilment of his intentions, the earl's library was subsequently given to the college (Mayor 1859, p. 60). The origin of Southampton's connection with the college, to which he was admitted in 1585, is to be found in his guardian during his minority, Lord Burghley, who was, of course, a patron of the college.

[241] Mayor 1859, pp. 60–1.

[242] However, it may have been his service as a chaplain in the Low Countries that won him connections at Court. This is suggested by the allusion to him in the royal letter in his favour as one 'who has seen the world abroad in some relation to publique service' (St John's College Archives, Register of Letters, p. 321). Baker comments in passing that, 'notwithstanding some offence then given, [this] gave him an interest and reputation at court, which he unhappily survived' (Baker and Mayor 1869, I, p. 215).

[243] Laud 1847–60, VII, p. 323.

[244] Even allowing for the gross exaggerations of his critics, all the sources pertaining to the election dispute support this conclusion.

[245] Baker and Mayor 1869, I, p. 214.

[246] See below, pp. 478–9.   [247] Laud 1847–60, VI, p. 323.

[248] Collinson in Bendall *et al.* 1999, pp. 224–5, quoted below, p. 479.

[249] See the remarks in the king's signet letter of Feb. 1634 and Laud's terse comment: 'the one be not sober enough for the government, I doubt the other may be found too weak: honest and learned is not enough for government' (Laud 1847–60, VI, p. 323).

Arminian – William Beale – was placed over the college.[250] In its turn, Beale's former mastership at Jesus was filled by Richard Sterne,[251] one of Laud's chaplains and clients, thus increasing the overall influence of that interest amongst the masters.

In many respects the dispute over the election of the master of St John's during the early 1630s marks the culmination of a cumulative process of increasingly intrusive intervention by the Court. In some of its aspects it manifests features characteristic of disputed elections throughout the preceding eighty years. Thus local rivals resorted to support at Court: a resort that ultimately led to the disappointment of both aspirants, the placement of a royal nominee, the escalation of royal claims to supervision, and the enhancement of the responsibility for oversight accorded to the heads of houses. In other aspects, this dispute is indicative of the changes in attitudes and alignments that had occurred by 1630.

The general tenor of the royal handling of the situation articulated in letters from Charles suggests that the Caroline attitude to royal intervention had moved away from the more restrained Elizabethan thinking that we have earlier heard enunciated by Lord Burghley.[252] The articulation of the principles assumed to underlie this change have already been examined.[253] Moreover, the role of religious conviction in shaping factional rivalries at St John's in the 1630s suggests that we need to explore the roots of those rivalries within the university, and the changing balance of power amongst the various religious factions during the preceding decades. To do this we will need to retrace our steps in order to scrutinise the religious dimension to the history of the university in the period between the Elizabethan Settlement and the Long Parliament.[254] Not least, we will need to do this because the university was not only – as has just been indicated – a site of religious conflict: it was also a crucible of religious thinking and devotional experience.

Looking to one partner in the university's relationship with the wider world, the involvement of both lay and clerical courtiers in forwarding the careers of the various aspirants to office whom we have just seen at loggerheads at St John's College in the 1630s reflects our examination of the role of Court intermediaries, and the changes in the balance of influence between the lay and the clerical elements at Court. Looking to another partner, the 'Country', we are reminded of some of the criticisms of corruption and opposition to intervention articulated by the gentry who

---

[250] Baker and Mayor 1869, I, pp. 216–18.   [251] *DNB*.
[252] Above, p. 392.   [253] Above, pp. 392–5.   [254] Below, pp. 441–63.

were sending their sons to the universities, providing the colleges with endowments, and looking to their graduates to provide the preaching ministry that many of them wished to promote. It was in parliament that many of their criticisms were voiced.[255]

Looking forward, we will need to examine the unmitigated disaster that for Cambridge no less than Oxford was the English Revolution. One consequence of it was the myths as to its causes to which it gave rise. Indeed, in the Restoration and beyond, this was to be one of its most long-lasting legacies. The universities did not figure favourably in these myths, and in later chapters we will need to trace the fortunes of Cambridge at a time when it no longer occupied a central place in the public world; when its social forms came to be superseded; its modes of proceeding and latinate culture seemed outmoded; its ways of thinking and its preoccupations appeared to be increasingly peripheral to a newly emergent metropolitan-based and cosmopolitan-orientated culture. But, of course, none of this could have been foreseen as the ultimate consequences of their actions by the selfish careerists, the good college men and the devout believers of every hue as they fought their corners over the burning issues of their moment in pre-Revolution Cambridge. None of us has that degree of prescience.

[255] See above, chapters 4–6.

Chapter 12

LEARNING AND DOCTRINE
1550–1660

A CATENA OF DISCIPLINES

Mordechai Feingold has shown most convincingly that we cannot seek the arts syllabus or the range of disciplines studied in Cambridge in the statutes of 1570; rather they were deliberately drawn up to avoid putting tutors and students in the kinds of straitjackets which afflict their modern successors.[1] In a later chapter we shall pursue that will o' the wisp, the undergraduate syllabus.[2] The conscientious tutor of the early seventeenth century, as summarised by the biographer of Joseph Mede of Christ's (1586–1638), grounded his pupils in 'Humanity, Logick and Philosophy' – that is, in classical literature, philosophy and the natural sciences, led by mathematics and astronomy; or in other words, most of the seven liberal arts of the medieval university. The principal changes which we can discern in the sixteenth and seventeenth centuries were, first, the growing predominance of classical studies in the wake of the Renaissance, and second, the increasing interest in mathematics and astronomy in the seventeenth century, culminating in the intellectual adventures of Isaac Newton. To the natural sciences we shall return; for the classics, it has to be said that Cambridge contributed much to the dissemination of classical studies – Sir John Cheke, Sir Thomas Smith and Roger Ascham were among the pre-eminent teachers of Greek, for example, in mid-sixteenth-century Europe – but little to the original, critical study of Latin and Greek literature and institutions. The changing content of academic study in this region is well illustrated by library catalogues: in the medieval university and college library catalogues and collections which survive, classical texts are relatively ill represented: even allowing that these libraries were primarily for graduate students in the higher faculties, the contrast between their holdings and the inventories of Cambridge dons and the like of the sixteenth and seventeenth centuries edited by Elisabeth

---

[1] Feingold 1984, ch. 1. The statutes are more informative on higher studies.
[2] Below, ch. 15. For what follows see Mede 1677, p. vi.

Leedham-Green is striking: her authors' index contains about 700 items under Cicero, theirs no more than a handful.[3] But Cambridge had to wait for Bentley to make any deep mark on the history of classical scholarship – unless we include Dr Caius' brilliant textual work on the texts of Galen.[4] The classical literature studied came to include the Greek and Roman historians; and under their patronage history entered the undergraduate curriculum. But 'history', though a major subject of academic study throughout our period, had several different faces, each forming quite a separate discipline of its own: as part of classical studies, as part of biblical studies – taking wings in the fanciful studies of biblical chronology of men like Archbishop Ussher and Joseph Mede and reaching their climax, or nadir, in the fantasies of Isaac Newton – and as an exploration of the roots of the English church and English politics. To history in this third, most fruitful sense we shall shortly return: it never formed an integral part of any syllabus, and flourished none the less – perhaps all the more – for that.

The higher studies remained those of the medieval university: medicine, law and theology; but they took on a very different complexion in the wake of the Renaissance and Reformation. For medical studies London and Linacre were at first the chief centre in Britain, though Dr Caius was himself to provide in the 1560s and early 1570s a link between his work in London and in Cambridge. But as time went on, Oxford and Cambridge became increasingly important centres of study and education; and even though Oxford and London carried off Cambridge's most original physiologists, such as William Harvey, a very respectable tradition of medical study persisted through the age of Francis Glisson and the late seventeenth century – worthy of much more attention than we can give it here.[5]

The case of legal studies is a curious one. Notoriously, the study of English law and instruction in it centred in the Inns of Court; the heroic attempt of John Cowell to introduce its study into Cambridge in the opening years of the seventeenth century was stillborn.[6] Cowell was Regius Professor of Civil Law, and civil or Roman law was the only

[3] Of the copies of Cicero's works noted in Clarke and Lovatt 2002, p. 819, only a handful – perhaps not more than half a dozen – can be shown to have been in Cambridge before 1500. This is a surprising figure, since some of Cicero's works were popular in the medieval schools. But it underlines the contrast with the sixteenth- and seventeenth-century evidence indexed in Leedham-Green 1986, II, pp. 209–23.

[4] Brink 1986, p. 13. On Bentley, see below, ch. 14. On Caius, see Nutton 1987.

[5] For Oxford, see R.G. Frank in Tyacke 1997, ch. 8 (and *ibid.*, p. 513 for its flourishing state in Cambridge). For Cambridge, see esp. French 1994, chs. 1–3, 10, and the brief survey in Rook 1971, pp. 49–63; Brooke 1985/1996, pp. 114–15. On Glisson, *ibid.* and refs.

[6] Simon (J.) 1968; Stein 1988, pp. 212–13.

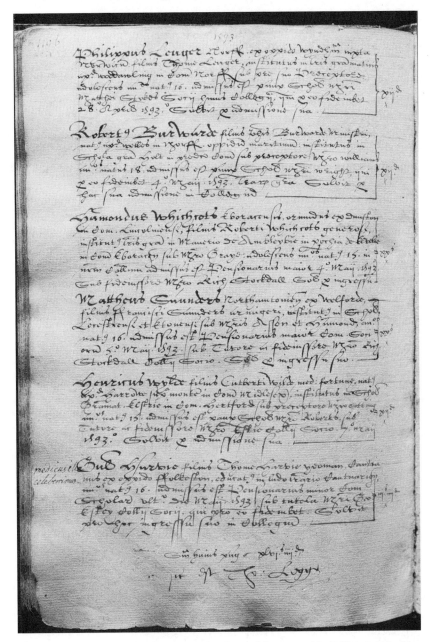

Plate 26 William Harvey's entry at the foot of the page, 'Gul' Harvie', in the Caius Matriculation Register, 1593

subject legally studied in the Cambridge Law Faculty. It was linked to a curious enclave of legal practice in which Roman law prevailed: especially in the Court of Admiralty, which presided over maritime and mercantile cases 'with a foreign element';[7] and this was practised in Doctors' Commons in the city of London, along with canon or ecclesiastical law, and Doctors' Commons was closely linked with Trinity Hall, though neither institution had a monopoly in the other.[8] Not unnaturally, Roman law played a relatively modest part in the academic scene in Cambridge in the late sixteenth and seventeenth centuries: modest, but not insignificant, the more so for its close links with canon law. The Faculty of Canon Law was officially closed in 1535; but Richard Helmholz has convincingly demonstrated that medieval canon law remained the basis of practice in the English ecclesiastical courts for several generations after the Reformation.[9] On how this science was studied and taught he is cautious: 'Some academic study of canon law may well have survived the formal closure of the separate canon law faculties at Oxford and Cambridge.'[10] But the logic of his argument, and the evidence he cites of the mingling of canon and civil law in Cambridge lectures of the seventeenth century, takes us further than this: for although the civilians may have picked up much of their canonical learning on the job in Doctors' Commons, it is hard to believe they were not in a measure prepared for it in Cambridge, and especially in Trinity Hall. Thomas Legge, the genial tutor of Jesus turned master of Caius, bequeathed many law books to the college library; and they include a number of sixteenth-century treatises on canon law. They formed part of the working library of a practically minded practising lawyer, but it is at least possible that he taught canon and civil law to his students.[11] If so, it is perhaps surprising that this was never included among the many charges levelled against him by the discontented fellows of Caius.[12] The finger points inevitably to Trinity Hall as the chief source of learning and teaching in canon law in sixteenth- and seventeenth-century Cambridge.

If the study of canon law is a mystery, there is less that is mysterious about the study of theology, and this must be the central theme of our very selective inspection of learning and doctrinal controversy in Cambridge between 1550 and 1640; though space must be found for the closely

[7] *Ibid.*, p. 210.   [8] See above, p. 50.
[9] Helmholz 1990; cf. below.   [10] Helmholz 1990, p. 153.
[11] On Legge and his books, see Stein 1988, ch. 14, esp. pp. 200–1, 205–8.
[12] Brooke 1985/1996, pp. 89–92; Heywood and Wright 1854, I, pp. 316–26 (from BL Lansdowne MS 33). He was accused of popery, a common charge against canonists, but not specifically of studying and practising Roman canon law.

linked study of medieval history, and for their chief rival, mathematics, to prepare us for the golden age of historical and mathematical studies in the age of Brady and Newton.[13]

THE BIBLE AND THEOLOGY

The pursuit of learning in Cambridge in the generations following the first Reformation had three clear aims: to provide for the education of the young; to create or improve the infrastructure on which Reformation theology was founded; and the pursuit of learning as an end in itself. The first inspired the study of many regions in the very wide traditional syllabus, and especially those to which Renaissance humanism had brought new life. The second and third frequently overlapped and intermingled: a theological animus might inspire a flight of learning, or it might equally be an excuse for it in a man of naturally scholarly inclination. But the Reformation could also inhibit: prelates and politicians kept an anxious eye on the theologians; too eager pursuit of theological speculation could lead to the bonfire or the scaffold, or – much more commonly and less dramatically – close the doors to patronage and promotion.

Central to much of the scholarly endeavour of the age was the study of the Bible. A former generation of scholars, believing implicitly the polemics of the Reformers, firmly believed that the Bible was neglected in the Middle Ages, and brought out into the clear light of day by the Reformers. As so often, polemical writing bore almost no relation to historical fact. It is indeed true that the Reformation coincided with and stimulated study of the Bible; in the translation of the Bible into English the sixteenth and early seventeenth centuries were, very obviously, a golden age. There had been – and remained – considerable anxiety among the hierarchy about the nature and purity of the translations. But in essence the golden age enhanced a notable medieval tradition.[14] Theological study in the late medieval universities always had two main limbs: the study of the Bible and systematic theology based on commentaries on the *Sentences* of the twelfth-century Paris theologian Peter the Lombard. Biblical study was partly geared to understanding what was thought of as the literal, historical sense – which included a good deal more than we would include of prophetic and allegorical interpretation. The English had been pioneers in vernacular translation of the Bible:[15] the Wycliffite Bible was a very popular book in orthodox and heretical circles

---

[13] See below, ch. 14.   [14] For all that follows, see Smalley 1952, 1960.
[15] But not alone: see the surveys in Greenslade 1963–70.

alike, even though officially proscribed. And if we ask where the seedbed of the great translations of the Reformation era lay, one good answer might be: in pre-Reformation Cambridge. The Dominican house (now Emmanuel College) had been for a time the home of Robert Holcot, foremost among the Dominican biblical scholars of the fourteenth century. In the 1520s and 1530s the community of Austin Friars included Brother Miles Coverdale among their number; and William Tyndale himself studied in Cambridge for a while. Both became enthusiastic Protestants and had to pursue their work of translation abroad: it was exile indeed which introduced them to Luther's German Bible, the inspiration for their work; but they had laid essential foundations in England.[16] In the 1520s also, the young Thomas Cranmer was acquiring a deep learning in Bible and liturgy – and the habit of intense and protracted study – which was to enable him as archbishop of Canterbury to compose his liturgies and help draft the homilies to explain and underwrite them.

Biblical scholarship was indeed at the heart of the theological endeavour in Cambridge in the sixteenth and early seventeenth centuries, although it is perhaps ironical that in a primarily Latin culture – in which copies of the Vulgate and other Latin versions of the Bible proliferated in the major libraries of the day – the endeavour revealed itself above all in English translations. None the less, it was so: the Authorised Version is the fruit of a notable scholarly enterprise, and the endeavour was evidently at its most intense in the years from 1604 to 1611, when all the leading theologians of Oxford and Cambridge set to work to prepare the Authorised Version of the Bible. The committees assigned the various books of the Bible met in Westminster, Oxford and Cambridge. The Cambridge teams, who edited the Old Testament from Chronicles to Ecclesiastes and the so-called Apocrypha (that is, the parts of the Old Testament then only known in Greek texts and reckoned second-class citizens in the *Thirty-Nine Articles*),[17] included a notable group of moderate puritans, Chaderton, master of Emmanuel, Branthwaite, fellow of Emmanuel and (from 1607) master of Caius, and Ward, master of Sidney. But the first Westminster team, who created the world with Genesis,

---

[16] For all this, see *ODDC*, s.n. Coverdale, Tyndale and refs.; on Cranmer, see esp. McCulloch 1996. An invaluable study of the English Bible in this period is Hammond 1982. It need hardly be said that the English Reformers continued to have close contacts with their continental allies. In 1549–51, indeed, the Regius Professor of Divinity in Cambridge was the great Strasbourg divine Martin Bucer (see esp. Collinson 1983, ch. 2; Porter 1958/1972, pp. 51–5).

[17] Which is, however, no excuse for the common practice since the nineteenth century of printing the Bible without the Apocrypha, thus depriving readers of Wisdom and Ecclesiasticus, two of the greatest books of the Old Testament. The article is c. 6 (1563): Hardwick 1876, pp. 294–9. The Apocrypha were not listed separately in 1553.

and took the history of Israel past the books of Kings,[18] was led by the deans of Westminster and St Paul's, Lancelot Andrewes, alias master of Pembroke, and John Overall, Regius Professor of Divinity in Cambridge. King James' support for the venture was partly inspired by his dislike of the Geneva Bible, then far and away the most popular version; doubtless its numerous glosses, not always flattering to the cult of monarchy, were his grounds; and the instruction to the editors was to follow the Bishops' Bible and eschew Geneva. In fact the Authorised Version was – and ought to have been – chiefly modelled on Geneva, though with the glosses omitted: only cross-references were allowed or attempted.[19] In addition to the editorial committees there was a revision committee, dominated by the Cambridge scholar Andrew Downes.[20] The consequence of this intensive editorial work over most of the first decade of the seventeenth century was surely crucial to the formation of personal friendships and theological alignments. The cementing of alliances among the moderate puritans in Cambridge is an obvious instance. Equally so is the intimacy of Andrewes and Overall, whose significance will presently appear.

To the Protestant, in the words of the sixth of the *Thirty-Nine Articles*, 'Holy Scripture containeth all things necessary to salvation';[21] to the Catholic, the tradition and the teaching of the church (which had fostered and canonised the canon of Holy Scripture) were of equal importance – though they could never be in conflict with the plain meaning of the Bible.

But there has often been conflict on what the plain meaning of Scripture comprises. Thus St Paul:

> And we know that all things work together for good to them that love God, to them who are called according to his purpose. For whom he did foreknow, he also did predestinate to be conformed to the image of his Son, that he might be the firstborn among many brethren. Moreover whom he did predestinate, them he also called: and whom he called, them he also justified: and whom he justified, them he also glorified

and we are launched into one of the great Pauline rhapsodies, culminating in: 'Neither height nor depth, nor any other creature, shall be able to separate us from the love of God, which is in Christ Jesus our Lord' (Romans 8:28–30, 39).

---

[18] Allen 1970, p. 6, quotes a contemporary list which gives 1 Chronicles both to the first Westminster and the first Cambridge teams.
[19] Hammond 1982, chs. 8–10.   [20] *Ibid.*, pp. 180–92.
[21] *Thirty-Nine Articles*, c. 6, based on the *Forty-Two Articles* of 1553, c. 5 (Hardwick 1876, pp. 294–5).

St Paul had said most emphatically that a man is 'justified' – made just or righteous in God's eyes – by faith, not by the works of the law, by which he meant the Jewish law of the Old Testament.[22] On this foundation, justification by faith and not by works became a pillar of Luther's theology, and of the theology of most of the Reformers; on St James – 'faith, if it hath not works, is dead' (James 2:17) – they trampled mercilessly, while the best of them excelled in all the good works he had commended. For not only St Paul, but St Augustine – supreme among the fathers in the eyes of Protestant and Catholic alike – had been in the business. Augustine had been particularly emphatic that God had predestined some to hell as well as some to heaven – that the number of the elect was limited; and that God's grace alone could justify a man, that he could not earn the entry to heaven by good works. There have always been some – perhaps always many – Christians who protested, silently or noisily, against both doctrines. It is very probable that many would have sympathised with the view of the learned fellow of Christ's Joseph Mede, who, according to his biographer, 'wondered that men would with so great animosity contend about those obscure speculations'.[23] Some may have gone further. If Paul spoke in Romans as if the elect were limited to the faithful, in 1 Corinthians 15:28 he pictured the end as a time when 'all things shall be subdued unto him [the Son] . . . that God may be all in all', which has been interpreted by a distinguished theological tradition coming down from Origen and Gregory of Nyssa to the Cambridge Platonists and beyond to foreshadow the salvation of all and everyone at the latter end – a view partly based on this and other biblical texts, partly on rational moral instincts which rebel against a God less merciful than the best of his creatures.[24] The view that human beings can earn salvation by good works has appealed to the common sense and good feeling of countless Christians, especially to the laity; but professional theologians in every age since the days of St Augustine have shuddered when it is mentioned, for it is the heresy of Pelagius, against which Augustine's choicest thunders were directed. Only God's grace freely given without prejudice, in the view of Augustine's disciples, can determine who is saved. To penetrate the relation of predestination, grace, free will, faith and works is to enter some of the deepest and darkest mysteries of Christian theology; most Christians today would hardly seek precise definitions in this region. But Catholics and Protestants alike were deeply divided among themselves on just these issues, and they inspired

---

[22] Most emphatically, e.g., in Galatians 2:16 and 3:8, 11–12.
[23] Mede 1677, 'Life', p. xviii.   [24] For this tradition, see Ludlow 2000, 2003.

copious polemics in the sixteenth and seventeenth centuries. The official position of the Church of England was firmly set in the Articles of 1553 and 1563, which had the authority of Cranmer and Parker upon them: 'Predestination to life is the everlasting purpose of God' for 'those whom he hath chosen'; and 'As the godly consideration of predestination, and our election in Christ, is full of sweet, pleasant and unspeakable comfort to godly persons', so it is the opposite for 'curious and carnal persons lacking the Spirit of Christ'.[25] This seems, clearly enough, to assume 'double predestination' – that some are predestined for heaven, others for hell, 'before the foundations of the world were laid' (and so before the fall, 'pre-lapsarian' in the curious jargon of the theologians), the doctrine later commonly labelled Calvinist. It is courteously described in Cranmer's best manner, but it seems to an unprejudiced eye little different from the blunt words of the Lambeth Articles of 1595, drafted by William Whitaker, master of St John's, the puritan 'pope' of Cambridge, and approved by Archbishop Whitgift. 'God from eternity has predestined some men to life, and reprobated some to death. The moving or efficient cause of predestination to life is . . . only the will of the good pleasure of God.'[26] In the first instance neither faith nor good works have any say in the matter: that, in all its bleakness, was the official view of the Church of England in the 1590s, when it was first seriously challenged among Anglicans.

The precise nature of God's predestination was the ground of many polemics in the late sixteenth and early seventeenth centuries – and in the twentieth many similar disputes have divided historians trying to discover the reality underlying these polemics. The difference is that in the work of Nicholas Tyacke, Peter Lake, Peter White, Anthony Milton and others a great deal of new learning and insight has been deployed towards the understanding of a very complex interplay of theology and politics ecclesiastical and secular.[27] This makes any extensive study of these polemics redundant in this book – though we have to note the part they played in laying the foundations for the religious divisions of the seventeenth century. The real need in the early twenty-first century is to assimilate the findings of Seán Hughes in his seminal article on the

---

[25] c. 17 both in the *Forty-Two Articles* of 1553 and the *Thirty-Nine* of 1563 (I have modernised the spelling of the English version of 1553): Hardwick 1876, pp. 310–15. Hardwick's book, cited from Procter's edition of 1876, is still fundamental for the history of the Articles. There are minor differences between 1553 and 1563, but not in the words quoted. For the theological setting, see esp. Null 2000.

[26] Hardwick 1876, p. 363, quoted from the translation in Porter 1958/1972, p. 371.

[27] See esp. Tyacke 1987, 2000; Lake 1982, 1988; White 1992; Milton 1995; Como 2000.

English theologies of predestination *c.* 1580–1630.[28] The doctrines of predestination current in the sixteenth century formed a wide spectrum with many subtle variations of colour; and the same – or a very similar spectrum – could be found among both Protestant and Catholic theologians: it has often been observed that there was much in the Lambeth Articles which would have been congenial to St Thomas Aquinas.[29] It is also essential to get behind the labels 'Calvinist' and 'Arminian', which – like later Whig and Tory – started as terms of abuse and were sometimes little more. The real differences which emerge from the 1590s on between theologians who pasted these labels on each other reflect a growing divergence between puritan and high church views of church and sacrament – and between the perception of church and college chapel as the plain house of God, with table and chairs, and God's temple suffused with the beauty of holiness. These very real divergences became entangled with polemic about the justification and election of those predestined to heaven and hell. Hughes has shown how crucial it is to disentangle 'polemic from reality', and has also emphasised the 'enormous diversity of the developing Reformed tradition'.[30] He makes very effective use of the work of John Playfere of Sidney Sussex, who distinguished five types of predestination, according to destiny determined before or after the fall (pre- and post-lapsarian), and various degrees of divine foreknowledge of the responses human beings were to make to the actions of grace upon them.[31] The hardest-line 'Calvinist' position firmly asserted the perseverance of the saints, the assurance of the elect of their own destiny, in 'the "order of salvation" linking regeneration, justification and election in an inseparable and unbreakable "golden chain"'.[32] John Overall's clear rejection of the chain from the 1590s was viewed 'with ever-increasing tolerance by the bulwarks of Jacobean moderate Calvinism'[33] – and so a wedge, or rather a series of wedges, came to insert itself between unyielding believers in the golden chain and those who saw in predestination an element of divine response to the impact of grace on humankind; that is, to those who were ready to allow human merit a place, however modest, in the divine scheme.

Although the polemics on grace and predestination are shot through with biblical texts, the significance of biblical learning is perhaps even more clearly illustrated by the various doctrines of the Eucharist, or the Lord's Supper as the Articles entitle it (no. 28). Every theologian of medieval and early modern times – Catholic and Protestant alike – was

[28] Hughes 1998.   [29] *Ibid.*; and cf. esp. Porter 1958/1972, p. 368.
[30] Hughes 1998, pp. 233–4, 233 n. 18.
[31] *Ibid.*, pp. 233–42.   [32] *Ibid.*, p. 249.   [33] *Ibid.*

bound by the words of Jesus as very amply recorded in 1 Corinthians 11 and the Synoptic Gospels. Here is Paul's version, which is perhaps the earliest: 'And when he had given thanks, he brake it, and said, Take, eat: this is my body, which is broken for you: this do in remembrance of me' – and after supper, he took 'the cup . . . saying, "this cup is the new testament [or covenant] in my blood: this do ye, as oft as ye drink it, in remembrance of me"'.[34] There are minor variations and substantial interpretative additions in the four versions; a somewhat later tradition, incorporated in the Latin mass, added 'mysterium fidei, the mystery of faith'. But St Paul's words contain the essence of the matter. Jesus' words, as recorded, were uncompromising: 'This *is* my body.' But how can bread and wine be body and blood? Catholic interpretations have sought to find some objective change in the elements, and this was described in the decrees of the Third Lateran Council of 1215 and the Council of Trent as the transubstantiation of the elements.[35] But what this means has never been authoritatively defined. The views of medieval theologians varied widely. Thus St Thomas interpreted the change of substance in precise Aristotelean terms – the substance of bread and wine were converted, and only the accidents, the outward semblance of bread and wine remained – or rather, the accidents with something more, since clearly the properties (healthful or otherwise) of bread and wine did not entirely disappear – and this something he called the 'quantity'. But Alexander of Hales and his pupil St Bonaventure – English and Italian professors at Paris and Franciscan friars – rather emphasised the sacramental nature of the experience: and that to receive the sacrament involved not only the acts of eating and drinking but also faith and knowledge, the priest's and the recipient's: it was these that converted the bread and wine into the Body and Blood of Christ and thus united the communicant to the whole body of believers, living and dead. There came to be other interpretations too, though the sacramental theology of St Thomas tended to gain ground in the late Middle Ages, partly because of his prestige, partly because it explained 'transubstantiation' in a manner compatible with fashionable Aristotelean metaphysics. But it was never universally accepted in this period by orthodox Catholics.

Protestant interpretations have varied from objective to subjective change – from Luther's 'consubstantiation' which attempted to solve

---

[34] 1 Corinthians 11:24–5. I give the Authorised Version, which summed up Reformation learning – and there is no ambiguity in the Greek and no substantial differences in the best modern translations.

[35] It is in the form of a participle in 1215: 'transubstantiatis pane in corpus, et vino in sanguinem potestate divina' (Denzinger and Bannwart 1922, p. 190). For all that follows, Macy 1992 is an invaluable guide: popular in form, but based on deep learning and shrewd insight.

Aquinas' problem of 'quantity' by asserting that the substance of bread and wine remained, united to the Body and Blood of Christ, to Zwingli's doctrine, which drove a sharp wedge between the material and the spiritual, and reckoned communion a purely spiritual experience. This, however, was at variance with a powerful tradition going back to the early church – and based ultimately on such passages as St Paul's account of the Resurrection in 1 Corinthians 15 – that too sharp, too absolute a distinction between the material and the spiritual is not acceptable. Whatever the phrase 'the resurrection of the body' in the Apostles' Creed may be taken to mean, it asserts that something more than a disembodied 'soul' survives in heaven; that the personality at least is still there to assume the heavenly body of Paul's exposition. By the same token, John Calvin and other Protestant divines found Zwingli's formula unacceptable, and sought a middle way between transubstantiation or consubstantiation and a purely spiritual sacrament.

These differences of view and interpretation gave plenty of scope for polemic; and the principles on which the arguments were based – especially the attempt to preserve the full meaning of Jesus' words – are a vital element in almost every Christian theological tradition. But neither then nor now are the distinctions entirely plain: a central mystery survives.[36] What was much clearer was the difference in practice; and it is in this region that the real argument – and the most profound differences – must be sought.

The late medieval high mass was a magnificent celebration of the divine presence, with rich vestments, candles and incense – celebrants in chasuble, dalmatic and tunicle, servers in albs, choirmen in surplices, monks in cowls – and so forth. The celebration took place in the sanctuary, separated from the ordinary folk in the nave; or if it were for their behoof, at a nave altar, with much of the solemnity of the high altar about it. High mass and the reserved sacrament were surrounded by screens and hidden in pyxes and tabernacles; they were part of the immensely elaborate devotional apparatus of late medieval England, whose heyday – and its passing – have been so brilliantly evoked in Eamon Duffy's *The Stripping of the Altars*.[37] The laity could and did participate in many elements of such masses; and they could serve or attend the more intimate low masses,

---

[36] 'The Anglican–Roman Catholic International Commission in 1971 reached agreement on Eucharistic doctrine, relegating the term "transubstantiation" to a footnote, in which it is said to affirm the fact of the "mysterious and radical change" rather than to explain how the change took place' (*ODCC*, p. 1,637). This was apparently not the way it was understood by many Protestant polemicists; and they had other grounds for disagreement, especially in doctrines of sacrifice and in eucharistic practice.

[37] Duffy 1992; cf. Brooke 1971.

which either provided individual priests, especially chantry priests, with the occasions for their daily masses which were the centre of their religious obligations, or offered rich families and societies and guilds their own special votive masses. But communion was relatively rare – in some cases confined to special occasions, or even once a year. It was not always nor everywhere so; but broadly speaking the virtue of attending mass lay in being physically present; communion required special preparation, including confession and absolution.

The Reformers read in the New Testament what appeared to them to be descriptions of a common meal utterly different in form and sentiment: a representation or memorial of the Lord's Supper. The Marian exiles in Geneva or Zurich encountered a meeting and an atmosphere which savoured strongly to them of the primitive church: of devout worshippers gathered to a common meal round a table, unencumbered by any of the trappings of the Roman mass. The contrast was complete, and inspiring. This led to a special abhorrence of all vestments which separated the clergy from the community of the faithful gathered under the pulpit and round the Lord's Table – and which carried an inescapable memory of Catholic rituals and vestments. It has sometimes been said that the arguments about the surplice – and the four-square cap and the cope, which Matthew Parker tried to enforce for the Lord's Supper in cathedrals and such places – were superficial expressions of deeper fissures.[38] But in the eyes of the more radical Reformers the surplice was a visible, inescapable symbol of an evil tradition; there was nothing superficial in the reaction to it; and its opponents included not only old Geneva veterans but young men of weight, such as John Whitgift, eventually to become archbishop of Canterbury and to wear the surplice with a good grace.[39]

The Anglican church, in and out of Cambridge, enshrined a variety of different tastes and traditions. In Elizabeth's reign there were many who recalled with nostalgia the splendour of the Catholic mass. The queen herself, though firmly Protestant in doctrine and attitudes, loved ceremonial and the devotional atmosphere of the royal chapels. Her own role in the church, furthermore, presupposed the survival of much of the structure of the medieval church, with the queen performing the

---

[38] Cf. Collinson 1991, pp. 10, 12.

[39] Collinson 1991, p. 12. The Vestiarian controversy had a lighter side. One objector spoke of the 'squealing of chantry choristers, disguised' in 'white surplices . . . imitating the fashion and manner of Antichrist the Pope, that man of sin and child of perdition, with his other rabble of miscreants and shavelings' (Tanner 1930, p. 164 n. 3). A student at King's was accused of not wearing a surplice: but it turned out that he had pawned his surplice to a pastrycook 'for his belly' (Tanner 1930, pp. 165–6 n. 4).

executive and administrative functions of both pope and monarch, while the sacraments were preserved and presided over by bishops, priests and deacons. 'It is evident unto all men diligently readyng the Holy Scripture and auncient authours, that from the Apostles' time there hath bene these orders of ministers in Christ's Church: Bisshoppes, Priestes and Deacons': thus the preface to the rites for ordination in *The Book of Common Prayer*.[40] To most continental Reformers and the more radical British Protestants nothing seemed less evident. But the survival of the episcopate – and of the three higher orders – was essential to the Church of England in all the stages of the Reformation before the 1640s; and this entailed, in the eyes of many leading Anglicans, deep reverence for the traditions of the church. Men of such different religious outlook as Matthew Parker and William Laud were united in regarding themselves as the successors of St Augustine of Canterbury and all his line. This did not necessarily mean that they held the same doctrines of apostolic and episcopal succession: Catholic doctrines of episcopacy seem to have interested the Elizabethan bishops very little.[41] But they believed in tradition, and in the expediency of a monarchical episcopate; and they found a ready ally in the queen, to whom a secure episcopal hierarchy was one of the most essential pillars of what was – to her – a singularly insecure monarchy. James I, who had endured presbyterian church government in Scotland, was for slightly different reasons equally emphatic: to him presbytery and monarchy were notoriously incompatible.[42]

But presbytery – a ministry comprising elders or presbyters each responsible for a single congregation, in some sense or measure democratically chosen and organised – was an alternative to episcopacy in several parts of Europe from Scotland to Switzerland, well known to those Reformers who had been in exile in Mary's reign. Furthermore, it seemed clear to many Protestant scholars that it was the order of the apostolic age. Defenders of episcopacy could say that it was already well established in the course of the second century: it was a venerable institution. But the New Testament portrays a church order much akin to presbytery; and it has something to say of presbyters, only occasionally referring to 'episkopoi', overseers (or 'bishops' in later usage – the word derives from 'episkopoi'), who seem to be originally the equivalent of presbyters.[43]

---

[40] The preface to the Ordinal ('The forme and maner of makynge and consecratyng bysschops, priestes and deacons') in *The Book of Common Prayer* of 1552 – repeated with only spelling differences in 1559 and 1662 – and itself based on the Ordinal of 1549.

[41] As is emphasised in Collinson 1983, ch. 6, esp. pp. 156–8.

[42] His well-known comments – that a Scottish presbytery 'as well agreeth with a monarchy as God and the Devil', and 'no bishop, no king' – are quoted in *ibid.*, p. 155.

[43] See summary accounts in *ODCC*, articles on bishop, presbyter.

These facts are scarcely in dispute; but the interpretation of them as indicators of a divine blessing on a church ruled by presbyters and not by bishops was and is deeply controversial. When Thomas Cartwright, Lady Margaret's Professor of Divinity in Cambridge, gave a course of lectures in Cambridge in 1570, arguing that presbytery was the divinely ordained structure of ministry and church government, the Cambridge establishment was in serious disarray[44] – even the chancellor, Lord Burghley, normally cautious if not sceptical of doctrinal disputes, was deeply stirred: on the initiative of John Whitgift, master of Trinity, Cartwright was removed from his chair and subsequently sent into exile; and the statutes of the university were revised to strengthen the hands of authority. Cambridge, even more than Oxford, was the breeding ground of Elizabeth's bishops; it provided the ideological support the regime so desperately needed. Or so the queen hoped – and so the Cambridge establishment tried to ensure. But Cambridge was the scene of much doctrinal strife in the late sixteenth century; the established episcopal church was under fire from both sides – from the advocates of presbytery and the advocates of Rome.

The threat of a presbytery and the defence of episcopacy raised acutely the problem of their relation to Rome. In 1564 Elizabeth I visited Cambridge, and it was an ideal occasion to clarify the attitude of the Cambridge establishment to the Elizabethan Reformation. Andrew Perne, the conservative master of Peterhouse, won the reputation of being either a fox or a vicar of Bray by surviving the changes of the 1550s and later, and dying master of Peterhouse in 1589.[45] He opened the proceedings in 1564 with an admirable Latin sermon in King's chapel on the text 'Let every soul be subject unto the higher powers' (Romans 13:1), which delighted the queen. But a few days later Perne confronted Matthew Hutton, 'a copper-bottomed Calvinist' in Patrick Collinson's phrase[46] – and a future archbishop of York – on the motion that 'The authority of Scripture is greater than the authority of the Church.' Perne argued that the church was older than the canon of Scripture and had given the canon its authority. His line of argument underlined elements of tradition which (in his view) the Church of England could not do without: so far, he laid before the Elizabethan church and queen an element in Anglican doctrine which was of enormous importance, not only to Catholics undergoing modest reconstruction like Perne, but to Protestants like Matthew Parker who believed in the authority both of Scripture and of the

---

[44] Porter 1958/1972, p. 140; above, chapter 3.
[45] On Perne, see esp. Collinson 1991; see also McKitterick and Leedham-Green in the same volume. For what follows, see Collinson 1991, pp. 7–8.
[46] Collinson 1991, p. 7.

Plate 27 'Andreas Perne': Andrew Perne's note of ownership in Cuthbert Tunstall, *De Arte Supputandi* [On the Art of Reckoning] (1522), Peterhouse, Perne Library

church.[47] But Perne went further, and scandalised his audience by insisting that the Church of Rome – for all its errors – was an essential part of this tradition. Matthew Hutton had inspired this dangerous flight of rhetoric by describing the Church of Rome as 'a shameless whore', 'impudentissima meretrix' – a phrase he was compelled by Perne's arguments to withdraw, or modify. But there is no doubt that – in the context of 1564, and even more after the pope had excommunicated the queen in 1570 – the notion that the Church of Rome was the Babylon of the Apocalypse gained ground. The queen's own position as a legitimate daughter of Henry VIII depended on the rejection of the authority of the papacy; and the Church of England as by then established could have no sound basis if papal authority was in any measure accepted.

Yet how could this be? For no serious student of the history of the medieval church could doubt that St Augustine had derived his authority from Rome; and that Rome's authority had been paramount in the mid and late Middle Ages. That was not the end of the matter: for the English church owed much to other elements in western Christendom apart from Rome; it had retained many independent customs; the English monarchs had asserted considerable authority in it even in the heyday of papal supremacy; papal jurisdiction had been challenged in successive acts of Praemunire and Provisions from the fourteenth century on. And over and above this, tradition could be read in a variety of different ways: a mythical history of the medieval English church could work wonders with the supposed authority of Rome.

Meanwhile, the unity of the Church of England depended on a virulent anti-papalism. 'The Bishop of Rome hath no jurisdiction in this realm of England': Article 37 of the *Thirty-Nine Articles* was agreed by all true Anglicans, and marked the one generally accepted point of Protestant doctrine. But it could be a divisive as well as a unifying principle. Those who believed in tradition were bound, with Perne, to admit some validity in the former actions of the bishop of Rome. To the more radical Protestants, the pope was Antichrist.

Antichrist was a biblical character, noticed as the enemy of Christians in the epistles of St John – and thus often later identified with the beasts of the Apocalypse, also attributed to St John; and there had been much speculation in the late Middle Ages as to the reign of Antichrist and its place in the world's destiny. In the Apocalypse the enemies of the church are especially identified with Babylon, that is, with Rome; and it was natural for Protestants to see this identification as a prophecy of the role

[47] See below, pp. 455–7.

of the papacy in the religious wars of the sixteenth century.[48] But such identifications were difficult for those who believed in tradition to accept; and the right of a national church to have its traditions and its traditional ceremonies and rites was firmly asserted in no. 34 of the *Thirty-Nine Articles*.

TRADITION AND HISTORY

There has been much discussion, and some controversy, about the role and meaning of historical study in the sixteenth and seventeenth centuries.[49] It has been widely held that much of what passed for history really used the past to support some present causes, or to educate the young by moral tales. But in the study of history it is a mistake to separate the search for historical truth and the causes of religion and politics too sharply. On the one hand, a long tradition has inserted in innumerable prefaces to historical works an assertion of the moral value of history; though this was often in part at least an excuse by an author who simply loved to tell historical tales. Furthermore, a deep interest in the past and in the documents and survivals of the past has often gone hand in hand with a serious attempt to relate it to some theological or philosophical or polemical purpose. A medievalist thinks of G.G. Coulton, whose profound love for the documents of medieval history was fuelled and fired by his intense hatred for the beliefs and structures of the medieval Catholic Church – or of Walter Ullmann, equally intense in his passion for medieval scholarship and for those very hierarchical structures Coulton sought to demolish. One cannot deny that bias distorts the vision – but it can easily make it more intense. There have been many historians in whom the love of historical truth has been inspired by argument or controversy. The greatest of all the manuals of scientific history of our period, Dom Jean Mabillon's *De Re Diplomatica* of 1681, was in origin a pamphlet answering the charges of the Jesuit Bollandist Father Papebroch against the honesty of medieval monks.[50] There have been many who loved the past with an equal intensity but studied it with a good deal less of science and fair-mindedness than Mabillon; but it is a false perspective to write them off as pseudo-historians on that account.

[48] On Antichrist, see *ODCC*, p. 76; Reeves 1969/1993. As an example, the young Whitgift, in his doctoral thesis, declared the pope to be Antichrist (Collinson 1991, pp. 11 and 29 n. 56). This was a widespread view in the early seventeenth century, though always controversial even among Protestants.

[49] Admirably summarised by Feingold in Tyacke 1997, pp. 327–40.

[50] On Mabillon see Knowles 1963a, ch. 10; Mabillon 1681.

One such was Matthew Parker. He had been a fellow and master of Corpus in the second quarter of the sixteenth century, and a favourite chaplain of Queen Anne Boleyn; he was one of the saviours of the Cambridge colleges in Henry VIII's last years and prospered as a moderate Protestant reformer under Edward VI. He was eclipsed under Mary and re-emerged in 1559, when Anne Boleyn's daughter Elizabeth was on the throne, as archbishop of Canterbury.[51] He was among the first English Protestants, and his patronage of the *Thirty-Nine Articles* much later in life must indicate that he cast a friendly eye on a good many of the doctrines of John Calvin. But he was also a traditionalist: no one who has contemplated the wonderful collection of manuscripts he left to Corpus could doubt his devotion to English history from the *Anglo-Saxon Chronicle* to Matthew Paris – nor his eye for manuscripts of exceptional beauty. It was Parker furthermore – Parker the eminent Reformer – who preserved the name of his college as Corpus Christi, as did his opposite number in Oxford. The traditional Corpus Christi festival summed up everything the Reformers most distrusted in Catholic religious practice, with adoration of the Reserved Sacrament and magnificent processions accompanying the Reserved Sacrament. And Parker had an alternative ready to hand: it was also known as Benet College, from the church of St Benet or Benedict with which it was closely linked.[52] But to Corpus Christi its founders had dedicated it; and Corpus Christi it remained – and remains.

In Parker's mind the zeal for reform and the love of the past were inextricably mingled. In spite of Elizabeth's role in his promotion, the queen and the archbishop were not good friends: the queen bullied him mercilessly.[53] But Parker was no weakling: remarkably compounded of gentleness and strength, of charm and ruthlessness, of deep learning and credulity, of scholarly conscience and a breathtaking lack of scruple, he gathered a team of helpers and secretaries about him at Lambeth, led by John Joscelyn, formerly fellow of Queens', and employed his leisure time in presiding over a seminar whose aim was to preserve and publish the historical records of early England – to preserve them from destruction, and publish them as evidence above all of the true and natural condition of the English church (as Parker imagined it) before it submitted to the tyranny of the bishop of Rome. It was very doubtful history, but it had some admirable consequences. In 1568 he inspired a Privy Council

---

[51] On Parker, see Strype 1821; Parker 1853; Rupp 1977, ch. 6; on his books see Wright 1951.
[52] The earliest reference to Benet College known to me is of 1515 (Brooke 1993a, p. 10 and n. 14, based on the studies of Catherine Hall).
[53] Cf. Rupp 1977, pp. 79–81. This and the following pages resume some passages in Brooke 1992.

letter which disingenuously observed that the 'Queen's majesty' had 'like care and zeal as diverse of her progenitors have had before times for the conservation of . . . ancient records and monuments' formerly preserved in abbeys; and so the Privy Council announce her pleasure to all and sundry, 'which is, that the most reverend father in God, and our very good lord, the archbishop of Canterbury, should have special care and oversight in these matters aforesaid'.[54] This greatly helped Parker in gathering his rich collections from many sources, including his own cathedral library at Canterbury – thus ensuring their preservation, and greatly enriching the heritage of Corpus. Sir Robert Cotton, in the next generation, showed a zeal very similar to Parker's for collecting manuscripts, especially those related to the medieval English church and the history of parliament; and, also like Parker, he gathered round him a seminar or society of antiquaries – which, had not the king frowned on its undue interest in the liberties of parliament, might have survived to anticipate the foundation of another Society of Antiquaries a century later.[55]

In a curiously confused manner Parker and his colleagues grasped quite firmly the principle that medieval chronicles were the stuff of history: firmly, in that it inspired them to the first systematic attempts to put into print the main chronicles of medieval England; confused, in that they saw no very clear distinction between primary and secondary material, and freely inserted into their editions of one chronicle extracts from another or reflections of their own; and Parker not only scribbled liberally in his manuscripts with the famous red chalk with which all students of medieval English manuscripts are familiar – though it is far from clear how much is due to Parker, how much to his secretaries and his son – but added portions from other sources to complete the story.[56] The edition of Asser's *Life of King Alfred* was printed in a sort of Anglo-Saxon script most lovingly devised by Joscelyn; and it is a work of art. But when one contemplates the interpolations from the annals of St Neot's and Matthew Paris with which it is adorned or disfigured, one can hardly call it a work of scholarship.[57] Yet the idea that history comprises the sources – that the way to grasp the materials for the past is to edit them in a form which enables the student to understand the shape of the history he is studying – has considerable merits, and was taken up by Henry Wharton and others in the heyday of seventeenth-century scholarly endeavour.

[54] Wright 1951, pp. 212–13 (spelling modernised). On Joscelyn, see esp. Graham and Watson 1998.
[55] On Cotton, see Sharpe 1979; Brooke 1985/1996, p. 144 and refs.; Tite 1994, 1996; Wright 1997. For the first Society of Antiquaries, Evans 1956, ch. 1.
[56] Wright 1951, pp. 228–9.   [57] McKisack 1971, pp. 42–3.

Parker's two most significant efforts were his edition (1570) of the major chronicle (*Chronica Maiora*) of Matthew Paris, the thirteenth-century St Albans monk, whose inveterate prejudice against the papal curia did Parker's work for him admirably, and his *De Antiquitate Britannicae Ecclesiae*, on the antiquity of the British church, printed three years before his death, in 1572. His we must call it, and he described in his dedication to William Cecil, Lord Burghley, how he had been 'so spending my wasteful time within mine own walls, till almighty God shall call me out of this tabernacle'; but it was not *his* time only which was spent on it, for most of it seems to have been written by Joscelyn (who later complained that the archbishop had given him too little credit for his works), and some of it by at least one other of the circle.[58] In 1568 Parker's friend John Caius had published his similarly titled *De Antiquitate Cantabrigiensis Academiae*, on the antiquity of the University of Cambridge, attributing it with remarkable effrontery to a citizen of London (where indeed Dr Caius kept his medical practice) – for it is in fact designed to prove that Cambridge is older than Oxford, a project in which he had help and encouragement from the archbishop.[59] Caius' other antiquarian study, his history of the University of Cambridge, has much sound learning in it, as well as occasional flights of fancy. But at its best it can be set beside his work on the text of Galen, which Dr Vivian Nutton has shown to reveal remarkable scholarly acumen.[60] In contrast, the *De Antiquitate* is a miracle of perverted learning, based on a magnificent list of irrelevant authorities. The Carmelite historian of Cambridge of the early fifteenth century, Nicholas Canteloupe or Cantelow, had celebrated (or invented) the noble work of the Spanish prince Cantaber in founding Cambridge in the very remote past – early enough for Paris, Oxford and Cologne to be daughter universities of Cambridge; and this doctrine had been repeated by the best authorities, probably including John Fisher, thus setting in perspective the Oxford claim to have been founded by King Alfred.[61] To this story Caius added a farrago of nonsense. His antiquarian learning, like his medicine, was a curious mixture of sense and nonsense, though his medical practice was based on better authorities than Canteloupe and stood the test – from which his kind of history was marvellously exempt – of experience.

[58] *Ibid.*, pp. 44–8 (spelling modernised).
[59] The edition of 1574 and the *Historia* are reprinted in Caius 1912.   [60] Nutton 1987.
[61] On Canteloupe or Cantelow see Emden 1963, p. 120; Sharpe 1997, p. 385. His *Historiola* is in Hearne 1719, pp. 253–80, which includes the remarkable series of forged papal bulls. For texts of the speech attributed to Fisher, see Underwood 1989, p. 43 n. 22; Lewis 1855, II, pp. 263–72, esp. p. 267.

In the half-century following Parker's death in 1575 Sir Robert Cotton followed Parker's example in preserving manuscripts, and Sir Henry Savile, the notable Oxford savant, edited chronicles, providing tolerable texts of some of the best twelfth-century chronicles – which were later to support Robert Brady's much more scientific historical research in the late seventeenth century[62] – and rescuing the tenth-century chronicle of Æthelweard, which would otherwise have perished in the Cotton fire of 1731.[63]

Meanwhile, in the same circle, a young man not long down from Cambridge called Henry Spelman, of scholarly tastes and of a much more acute and critical mind than Cotton or Savile, was learning the lessons his elders could furnish and pursuing his own path to an understanding of medieval England.[64] Henry Spelman enjoyed the education normal to men of means: he was an undergraduate at Trinity College, Cambridge, and he studied and ate dinners at the Inns of Court. He grew up to be a country gentleman who lived on his ample estates in Norfolk; he was a very conscientious JP, and for a time an MP, and he spent most of his later years in London. As a young man he fell in with the members of the first society of antiquaries, who helped to form his tastes. But his scholarly interests developed on lines of his own, and although he remained in touch with other scholars, especially in Cambridge and London, and was the revered master of many later scholars including his son Sir John Spelman, his virtue as a scholar largely lay in his capacity to follow his own thoughts and interests and enquiries wherever they might lead him. His unhappy experience of lawsuits concerning lands once monastic led him deep into the history of sacrilege: his *History of Sacrilege* combines a very simple traditional interpretation of divine judgement with considerable antiquarian learning.[65] Often his studies led him to good works and the patronage of other good scholars. On a visit to Cambridge he encountered a most remarkable character called Abraham Whelock, university librarian and lecturer in Arabic, and he found that Whelock was just the man to help him in his Anglo-Saxon studies. He employed him first as an amanuensis, then as lecturer in Anglo-Saxon.[66]

---

[62] See below, pp. 488–94.
[63] Brooke, Highfield and Swaan 1988, pp. 176–7 and refs. Of the MS of Æthelweard only fragments remain: Campbell 1962, pp. ix–xii.
[64] On Spelman see *DNB*; Powicke 1930; Cronne 1956; 1961, pp. 43–5; Pocock 1957, ch. 5.
[65] Spelman 1698: the edition of 1846, partly rewritten 'by two priests of the Church of England', is a literary curiosity.
[66] Oates 1986, chs. 7–9.

Abraham Whelock had been a fellow of Clare until he married; he was also vicar of the Holy Sepulchre church and (from 1629) university librarian. He was a notable eccentric, lovable and exasperating, fussy and gentle, 'timorous' as he described himself, yet persistent.[67] The antiquary Thomas Baker wrote of him: 'So vast a knowledge had this thoughtfull soul for words and languages . . . being able to be the interpreter generall not only for the Queen of Sheba to Solomon, or of the Wise Men to Herod, but to Mankind, and to serve as the Universal Character; being by the way . . . the likeliest man to make one.'[68] In 1632 the rich and enlightened City magnate Sir Thomas Adams financed a lectureship in Arabic for Whelock, and in 1638 Sir Henry Spelman made him also lecturer in Anglo-Saxon.

Arabic and Anglo-Saxon seem to us an unlikely combination, though not an impossible one for a gifted linguist. But the combination is extremely significant. In oriental studies Cambridge was trying to catch up with Oxford, where in the 1620s a group of young scholars was fostering the study of Arabic and other oriental languages, and in the 1630s the Laudian Chair of Arabic was established; and where the Bodleian Library could from the same epoch boast the collection of Laud's 600 or so oriental manuscripts.[69] Cambridge could not vie with this, or make a substantial contribution later in the century to the great Polyglot Bible. But it had Abraham Whelock, who – had he lived longer (he died in 1653, just after the scheme for the Polyglot was launched) – would have made a significant contribution to it. By 1653 the general collection of printed books in the University Library had advanced since 1629 from 1,000 to 12,000, and the holdings of Arabic printed text and manuscripts were significant.[70] The inspiration for the study of Arabic was the knowledge that it was a necessary adjunct to the study of Classical Hebrew, and the belief that a knowledge of Arabic – and other oriental languages – was essential to the progress of biblical studies. Other motives could be found: the university, responding to Adams' initiative for creating a permanent chair of Arabic (which came eventually to fruition after the Restoration), emphasised that the study of the language would bring to light 'much knowledge which is as yet lockt up in that learned tongue, but alsoe [prove] to the service [of] the King and State in our commerce . . . and in God's good tyme to the enlarging of Christian Religion to them who now sitt in darknesse'.[71]

---

[67] *Ibid.*, p. 179; cf. *ibid.*, ch. 7 in general. [68] Quoted *ibid.*, p. 175.
[69] Feingold in Tyacke 1997, pp. 477–81. [70] Oates 1986, ch. 9, esp. p. 212.
[71] Quoted in *ibid.*, p. 188.

If Arabic primarily served biblical studies, Anglo-Saxon unlocked some of the doors into the history of the English church in its most crucial phase. Whelock was enlisted to help Spelman carry on, in a more scientific manner, the work of Parker and Joscelyn. Spelman's chief monument in this field was his *Concilia*, the first serious attempt to put together the sources for the legal history of the medieval English church. He published the first volume in 1639, and his notable disciple Sir William Dugdale completed the work in 1664. Dugdale's *Monasticon* and *Baronage* are still of fundamental value to medievalists. Spelman's *Concilia* has earned the compliment of being replaced – by David Wilkins in the eighteenth century and by *Councils and Synods* in the twentieth.[72] Spelman wrote before Mabillon and failed to identify the work of the forgers who had composed some of his texts. He was puzzled by Ingulf's imaginary history of Crowland abbey: he saw that all was not right with it, but he failed to realise it was a spoof, and it led him into some strange errors. His great achievements – partly inspired by his knowledge of continental law books, for he was not an insular scholar – were to perceive that the Norman Conquest had marked a fundamental break in the history of tenure and law; and that parliament was not (as Cotton had supposed) a popular assembly of immemorial origin, but a creation by royal summons of the thirteenth century.[73]

Sir Henry Spelman died in 1641, fortunate to escape the worst of the Civil War. In 1644 Robert Brady entered Caius as sizar; and later in the same year was joined by two of Sir Henry's grandsons, Charles and Roger Spelman. To Roger the Caius library owes its copy of the *Concilia*; and from his friendship with the Spelmans may spring Brady's own historical interests, which certainly owed much to the work of Sir Henry. But Brady belongs to a later chapter.[74]

Ecclesiastical and political history played a very powerful role in the interests of some of the intellectual leaders of Cambridge in the sixteenth and seventeenth centuries. They were of deep interest to some graduates and dons and many alumni; they were not, on the whole, for undergraduates.

But it is not in any one of these single disciplines that the paths were laid which led to Newton and Bentley. By way of epilogue let us contemplate the work of a tutor who was also a polymath.

---

[72] Spelman 1639–64: see esp. Powicke 1930; Wilkins 1737; Powicke and Cheney 1964; Whitelock *et al.* 1981.
[73] See details in Brooke 1992, p. 5.   [74] Below, pp. 487–94.

JOSEPH MEDE[75]

The majority of Cambridge fellows and tutors whose careers can be traced went on in their twenties or thirties to seek the patronage of the great or of the Court if they were ambitious – or a country living, if not. But a few stayed in Cambridge as celibate fellows and life-long tutors. One of the best known and best recorded was Joseph Mede (1586–1638), whose works and 'Life' are a unique revelation of the range of learning possible for an early seventeenth-century scholar – of particular interest for the light they throw on the resources of the college in which Milton was studying in Mede's later years, even though Mede was not Milton's tutor, nor were they of one mind in religion.[76] Mede's most spectacular gift lay in the study of languages, but he was not a narrow specialist: almost every branch of learning was grist to his mill. As a young man he was deeply fascinated by the study of mathematics, and he exchanged notes with other students of mathematics and astronomy throughout his life.[77] A charming story is told of Mede as a student hesitating to buy a book of mathematics for 50 shillings – and eventually succumbing to temptation, encouraged by a chance encounter with his wealthy friend Sir William Boswell.[78] By the same token he had a deep classical learning; but both the classics and mathematics were vital preliminary studies to divinity, on which his main interest was concentrated, and to which they became handmaids. He had learned Hebrew on his own at school,[79] and as a student at Christ's perfected his knowledge of Greek and Latin and read deeply in classical literature. To these languages he added 'Chaldee', that is, Aramaic, which he rightly understood to be the language of the Holy Land in Jesus' lifetime. When he wishes to explain the meaning of the word 'gospel' in the text 'They which preach the gospel should live of the gospel' (1 Corinthians 9:14) he can expound the meaning of 'gospel' as the reward for preaching good tidings in Hebrew, Chaldee, Greek and Latin – all the languages 'that S. Paul was brought up on'.[80] His best-known work was his *Clavis Apocalypsis*, a detailed interpretation of the prophetic meaning of the Book of Revelation, a miracle of misplaced learning and ingenuity in which a deep knowledge of ancient

---

[75] Or Mead: his editors preferred 'Mede', apparently because it was nearer to his own Latin form 'Medus', and we have used this form. What follows is based on the texts and the 'Life' of Mede in the 4th edition published nearly forty years after his death, Mede 1677.

[76] Fletcher 1956–61 made extensive use of Mede's account books as a tutor (preserved in Christ's College Library) in his study of Milton's educational background.

[77] See esp. Feingold 1984, p. 96.   [78] Mede 1677, p. xxxvi.

[79] *Ibid.*, pp. i–ii.   [80] *Ibid.*, p. 79.

and medieval history combines with his love of mathematics to produce some remarkable conclusions.[81] Elsewhere the ten kingdoms of the kings of Revelation 17:12 are interpreted as the Britons, Saxons, Franks, Burgundians, Visigoths, Suevi and Alani, Vandals, Alemanni, Ostrogoths and Greeks (that is, the Byzantine empire), revealing a fairly comprehensive knowledge of late Roman and early medieval political history.[82] But the most dazzling display of learning, much more critically deployed, is to be found in his discussion of the Eucharist. He firmly believed that the Eucharist was a sacrifice, but a commemorative sacrifice only, not a repetition of the sacrifice of the Cross. For this interpretation he finds support in references to the commemorative nature of the liturgy in Clement and a galaxy of Greek liturgies; also in the Roman liturgical tradition in a version of the *Ordo Romanus*, St Ambrose and Ivo of Chartres. For Jewish history he can cite Josephus and he can pursue his argument through the early fathers, Tertullian, Cyprian and – inevitably – Augustine.[83] Another favourite theme was his defence of the word 'altar' for the Holy Table, again marshalling a platoon of fathers, from Tertullian on – to a conclusion, in this case, which must have been anathema to puritan readers; for without overtly defending popish ceremonies he laid some essential foundations for the Laudian devotion to the beauty of holiness in churches and college chapels.[84]

Mede was noted for his moderation; and he liked to be thought independent of parties in religious matters. About four years before his death there were 'great combustions and divisions among the heads of the university in preparation for the Commencement . . . and the more Calvinian part having prevail'd on this occasion . . . I went not . . . this week . . . for fear of being taken to be of a side'.[85] But his denunciation of 'those obscure speculations' and his firm rejection of assurance of faith without works make clear he was not a 'Calvinian'; he left out some vital links in the golden chain; his love of altars attached him to high church practices.[86] Yet he believed that the pope was Antichrist, and even said: if 'the Church of Rome be not an Idolatress or a Spiritual Whore prostituting herself to other Gods, to sticks and stones . . . there never was a Whore in the world'.[87] This is a reminder of how deep anti-papal feeling was, even among men who claimed to be moderate. Some would have thought his claim not to be of a party specious. But he was above all an academic – of firm convictions, yet one who sought to be on good terms with a wide range of colleagues; and his learning was prodigious.

---

[81] *Ibid.*, pp. 419–36. [82] *Ibid.*, pp. 456–63. [83] *Ibid.*, pp. 376–81.
[84] *Ibid.*, pp. 383–90. [85] Mede 1677, 'Life', p. xix.
[86] *Ibid.*, 'Life', p. xviii; *ibid.*, pp. 303–11. [87] *Ibid.*, p. 139.

In his later years Mede was to observe that when he was young he had studied mathematics and natural sciences, 'but ever since neglected them' – a theme repeated by other mathematicians turned theologians in the seventeenth century.[88] Yet he had retained his interest, and continued conscientiously to teach mathematics to his students and put them in touch with up-to-date textbooks.[89] These did not appeal to all his students: in the course of the seventeenth century, mathematics became more technical and its advanced study – even in the Newtonian heyday – was never accessible to all intelligent students. Nor was it clear even to the most original minds of the century where the path of progress lay: William Harvey rejected the astronomy of Copernicus, and Newton's chronology was built on sand.[90] But by the time of Mede's death in 1638 there was in Cambridge a raft of mathematical learning and teaching securely built, on which Isaac Barrow could climb when he entered Trinity in 1646, and Isaac Newton – from the 1660s on – could go 'Voyaging through strange seas of Thought, alone'.[91]

Meanwhile, Cambridge had had to come to terms with the puritan revolution and its aftermath.

---

[88] Feingold 1990, p. 19, quoting Mede 1677, p. 853.
[89] Feingold 1984, pp. 96–8.   [90] *Ibid.*, p. 9; below, pp. 499–500.
[91] On Barrow, see esp. Feingold 1990. The quotation from Wordsworth is from *Prelude* (1850 edn), iii, 63 (see p. 502).

Chapter 13

CAMBRIDGE IN THE AGE OF THE PURITAN REVOLUTION

STUDENT NUMBERS

Two basic facts can be clearly stated at the outset. The second half of the seventeenth century saw a sharp decline in student numbers – in the attraction Cambridge had to offer potential recruits and their parents – at the same time as it saw a marked enhancement of its European fame as a centre of learning. The rhythm in student numbers was similar, though not identical, in Oxford and Cambridge.[1] In Oxford, admissions had risen to a peak by 1600 of over 370 a year, falling slightly in the 1610s, then rising steadily in the 1620s, to 530 a year in the 1630s. The most useful figures for Cambridge give totals for fellows and students, and these rise from 1,783 in 1574 (which may be an underestimate)[2] to 2,911 in 1621, with a slight decline[3] in the 1630s. In both universities there was a sharp decline as the Civil War approached: Cambridge had already fallen to 2,091 in 1641, while Oxford admissions fell to less than half, to 219 a year, in the 1640s. But both had a remarkable recovery in the 1650s and 1660s: Oxford's admissions to 437 a year in the 1650s, 458 in the 1660s; while Cambridge scored totals of 2,848 in 1651 and 2,522 in 1672.

Thereafter decline set in, especially in Cambridge: by the 1690s Oxford admissions were down to 303 a year, while Cambridge – after a steady fall in matriculations – had reached a total of 1,449 in 1727. No serious recovery took place until the early nineteenth century.

The figures suggest that the threat of civil war in 1640, followed by the purges and upheavals of the 1640s, brought chaos to both universities. It is remarkable to observe how thoroughly student recruitment recovered in

---

[1] The figures for Oxford are from Porter in Tyacke 1997, p. 32: he gives both admission and matriculation figures, but as some students never matriculated or did so at some date removed from their admission, the admission figures are more significant, where they can be known. For Cambridge we have the useful lists of college and university totals gathered in Twigg 1990, p. 289. These are very helpful indicators, though some of the sources are probably less reliable than others.
[2] The figures for 1574 may be of students only.
[3] If matriculation figures give a reliable indicator: cf. above, pp. 238–40.

the 1650s, a fact which echoes much evidence that the college authorities tried very seriously to offer a period of stability after the uncertainties of the 1640s. The Restoration saw this trend continue, especially in royalist Oxford; but for little more than a decade. From the 1670s numbers declined in both universities, and by the end of the century they were falling fast. In the 1690s the chambers in Caius Court, Gonville and Caius College – built to house three or four students apiece in the 1560s – were being reordered and wainscotted to house one fellow or student in each.[4]

Doubtless the causes for this decline were complex. As the final outcome was to be that in the eighteenth century the vast majority of students were preparing for clerical careers, it is evident that the lay element which was so prominent in the late sixteenth and early seventeenth centuries among the students had fallen away. But it is not as simple as that: in the late seventeenth century a substantial lay element still played an important role in the student body.[5] In both universities the serious study of theology seems to have become less popular: in Oxford the number of students proceeding to the degree of Bachelor of Divinity had been as high as 217 in the decade 1610–20, and was similar in the 1620s and 1630s; it then fell to ten in the 1640s, rising again to roughly a hundred a decade from 1660 on. The figures for Cambridge for the late seventeenth century were much lower. Yet the fact remains: increasingly the hard core were clergymen to be.

In general terms this decline in numbers must reflect a major shift in fashion. Mordechai Feingold, in his brilliant study of the humanities in seventeenth-century Oxford,[6] has analysed the evidence for this shift. He has unearthed a flow of comment from late seventeenth- and early eighteenth-century writers indicating with more or less vigour a distaste for the pedantry of academic learning – or, alternatively, academic alarm at the flight from learning of the younger generation. Some of these comments are more convincing than others: he cites Anthony Wood and Thomas Hearne, professional grumblers who compared the learning of the past with the philistine ignorance of the present in terms familiar in

---

[4] Brooke 1985/1996, p. 156 and pl. 15; see above, pp. 35–7.
[5] On the destiny of Oxford students, see Porter in Tyacke 1997, pp. 96–101. For a sample of Cambridge students see Brooke 1985/1996, p. 156: the proportion of Caians who became clergymen rose from thirty-six out of 103 admitted between 1680 and 1685 (which may be a considerable underestimate as the destinies of twenty-eight are unknown) to thirty-nine out of forty-five in 1780–5. In a few colleges, notably Trinity and Emmanuel, the fellow-commoners – most of whom were gentlemen of means or entered secular professions – formed a substantial minority throughout the eighteenth century. For Emmanuel, see Brooke in Bendall *et al.* 1999, pp. 307–8, 317–18, 325–6.
[6] Feingold in Tyacke 1997, ch. 5.

every age of recorded history.[7] And the best evidence for a change in fashion remains – not the comments, but the figures of student numbers, so strikingly similar at Oxford and Cambridge. But cumulatively the flow of comment is impressive; and Feingold shows above all how that treacherous former Oxford tutor John Locke undermined his Alma Mater by putting academic attainment very low in his catalogue of educational priorities.[8] Locke doubtless echoed as well as leading fashion; he is certainly a valuable guide to us of some of the reasons why aspiring young students and their parents might turn away from Oxford. It was precisely in the 1690s that Locke levelled his most deadly criticisms of the education offered by the tutors of Oxford and Cambridge.

None the less, there were still plenty of men to whom the pursuit of learning was a worthy ambition; and in the same period that Locke was undermining the assumptions of the constituency from which the students came, men of exceptional scientific ability were providing Cambridge with a European reputation it had never before enjoyed. This has been somewhat obscured from view by the tendency of historians to separate the natural from the humane sciences in their study – following too slavishly the semantic peculiarity of English, which divides the seamless cloak of German *Wissenschaft* and French *science*. It has been observed that Newton and Bentley were friends; but historians of science have not so readily understood that Bentley created a new science in very much the same way as Newton did. It has been pointed out very reasonably that Bentley was building on a notable tradition of European learning: indeed he was. Thus his early friendship with John Mill, the Oxford theologian who was painstakingly accumulating variant readings from manuscripts of the Greek New Testament, played a vital role in preparing the way for his revolutionary studies of the text of the New Testament.[9] They were none the less revolutionary for owing much to the work of Mill; none the less scientific for the range of humane insights on which his creative work was based.

It has also been suggested that the links between Newton and Bentley and Cambridge were not all that close: that Newton's spiritual home was in London, first in the Royal Society, then in the Mint; and that Bentley was a cosmopolitan figure, formed in London and Oxford as much as in Cambridge – and one who would gladly have lived in London if only he had been offered a rich bishopric. The plain fact is that Newton was

---

[7] Cited by Feingold in Tyacke 1997, pp. 240 (Anthony Wood), 261 (Thomas Hearne).
[8] For 'Locke's relegation of learning to the bottom of the gentleman's educational experience', see Feingold in Tyacke 1997, pp. 238–9.
[9] For all this, see below, pp. 503–5.

resident in Cambridge for thirty-five years before he settled in London, and during that time made his most dazzling discoveries and published his *Principia*; and Bentley was master of Trinity – for good or ill – for over forty years, during which time the master's lodge in Trinity formed his principal headquarters. For their role in the history of Cambridge I deploy the evidence more fully in chapter 14; but the paradox that Cambridge declined in popularity just when its wider reputation was rising to a new height needs to be grasped at the outset of this enquiry. But is it so much of a paradox? In the twenty-first century, undergraduate and postgraduate students flock to Cambridge, but they come from quite different constituencies: the postgraduates, in large measure, from the wider world of learning, some from very distant lands, seeking the opportunity to work in celebrated laboratories or faculties under famous masters of their field; something like two-thirds of the undergraduates come from within about 100 miles of Cambridge. There are obvious overlaps between the two constituencies and the kinds of inducement which make Cambridge attractive – there are even postgraduates who seek out Cambridge for its sports – and there are many undergraduates now from the far east and the far west. But the distinction is clear. There is no necessary connection between what makes a university appeal to undergraduates and its international reputation in the natural and humane sciences.

Some historians have sought to relate the rise and fall of the universities' prestige in the eyes of the wider community to the nature of the syllabus and the curriculum to which the students were subjected. The notion has been that the Cambridge syllabus and the Cambridge tutors enforced a medieval scholastic programme based on Aristotle long after the intellectual world had sought new approaches and new divinities. Feingold has shown how little substance there is in this.[10] But it needs to be emphasised that in the senses in which we use the words today – when the minutiae of courses are laid down in ordinances and regulations and what-have-you – there was no syllabus, and the curriculum was what the tutors made it. The statutes of 1570 avoided the fruitless attempts of their medieval predecessors to lay down the courses of study in detail. For undergraduates, they simply prescribed rhetoric to the first year, logic for the second and third – to which philosophy (a word of variable meaning which came to have much of mathematics and natural science in it) should be added in the third.[11] But this perfunctory statement bore little

---

[10] Feingold in Tyacke 1997, chs. 5–6.
[11] Statutes of 1570, c. 6, in *Cambridge Documents 1852*, I, p. 549; cf. Feingold in Tyacke 1997, pp. 213–14. For the medieval statutes see *Cambridge Documents 1852*, I, pp. 360–1; Hackett 1970, pp. 298–9. The syllabus does not figure in the thirteenth-century statutes in Hackett 1970.

relation to the pattern of study, so far as we know it. The evidence of surviving tutors' manuals of the seventeenth and early eighteenth centuries makes it clear that classical learning was the basis of the curriculum as practised by some of the leading tutors; and that they were entirely free – or felt themselves to be so – to modify the pabulum according to their own ideas. Tradition, custom, the very practical needs of university exercises and disputations, acted as a check on their whims and fancies. The tutors could be very conservative. But they could also allow or encourage their charges to read Ramus in the late sixteenth century or Descartes in the mid-seventeenth without doing violence to the prescriptions of the syllabus – for there was none. This helps to explain why some historians have read into these manuals an inveterate conservatism and others have seen them as models for educational advance.

The consequence of these facts is that we know far less than many historians have claimed of what students actually studied. We can cite many instances; we can deduce from Duport's rules for students what happened in Trinity and Magdalene in the mid-seventeenth century, and from Waterland's make a like deduction (of a very different character) for Magdalene in the early eighteenth. We can follow Holdsworth's students from St John's to Emmanuel in the mid-seventeenth century, and find his ideas for the curriculum in a modified form in Joshua Barnes' prescriptions for Emmanuel students in the late seventeenth century.[12] These are fascinating and fundamental documents: but they state the ideals, in each case, of a single tutor in colleges where there were several; and they tell us more of the aspirations of tutors than of the enthusiasms – or the shortcuts – of the young. For these there is some anecdotal evidence; but the area of our ignorance is much greater than has usually been supposed.

1640–60 – BASIC THEMES

The 1640s were a period of catastrophe for both Oxford and Cambridge, though in very different ways. This is well known, but it needs to be repeated, before we can explore the entrancing labyrinth of cross-currents which made the history of Cambridge in these twenty years much more ambivalent and interesting than might have been forecast.[13] The political

---

[12] For Duport see Trevelyan 1943a; cf. Feingold 1990, pp. 13–14. For Holdsworth, see Emmanuel College Library MS 48, printed in Adam 1889–93; cf. Collinson in Bendall *et al.* 1999, pp. 74–5. For Barnes, see Emmanuel College Library MS 179; cf. Collinson in Bendall *et al.* 1999, p. 284; Gascoigne 1989, p. 55. See pp. 511–15.

[13] On all that follows, see Twigg 1990, an admirable and indispensable guide to the history of Cambridge in this period. For case studies, see Collinson in Bendall *et al.* 1999, ch. 8; Brooke 1985/1996, ch. 7. For all that relates to Oxford, Tyacke 1997, esp. chs. 10, 14–15.

upheavals of 1640–1, followed by civil war – by two civil wars – and the execution of the king in 1649 spelt inevitable disruption and economic disaster. The incomes of the colleges fell: their lands were less productive, and rents more difficult to collect; some were cut off from their more distant estates. At the same time their income from students' fees also fell, owing to the many uncertainties and losses in the segments of society which paid the fees.

The universities retained all their importance to the warring factions: they remained the source of educated divines and preachers of the word – vital to the support of every religious complexion in a society in which religion lay near the heart of every turbulence, and loyalty to one side or the other was very much a matter of religious obligation – or, perhaps more commonly, of moral and spiritual perplexity. The leading figures in the universities were inevitably leaders in the religious politics of Westminster and the country at large. But this did not protect the universities from interference: quite the contrary. Cambridge University fell early under the shadow of the MP for the town, Oliver Cromwell, who protected it from its loyal efforts to support the king by sending him money and plate; these were ambushed or forestalled. Then the great local magnate, the earl of Manchester (apparently an abbreviation of Godmanchester, near Huntingdon), was given the task of purging and reforming it. By 1643–4 this seemed an urgent task to the parliamentary leaders in London. They had been saved from military disaster by the support of the Scots, and in return had promised to enforce a presbyterian form of church government in England. It was of the essence to carry the universities with them. So Manchester (in the intervals of campaigning) descended on the University of Cambridge with the Solemn League and Covenant in hand and tried to extract subscriptions to it, purging those who refused to accept the presbyterian mode. The outcome was that many heads and something like half the fellows of the Cambridge colleges lost their offices. This proved to be – for Cambridge – the most violent of the measures taken by the governments of the 1640s and 1650s. When a similar situation arose in 1649–51 in the wake of the execution of Charles I, and the Rump Parliament attempted to win support for the Engagement to recognise the Commonwealth, with no king and no House of Lords, the efforts to enforce it were less instant and less ruthless, and a much smaller number of heads and fellows had to depart – though ironically the victims of the Engagement included Manchester himself in 1651, whose spell as official chancellor, following the execution of the nominal chancellor, the earl of Holland, in 1649, was interrupted in 1651 – only to be resumed in 1660.[14]

Meanwhile at Oxford the early 1640s offered a very different scene: for the city was for a time the headquarters of the royal Court, and remained firmly royalist until the long siege of the mid-1640s ended with its surrender in 1646. After that the university received a new chancellor in the person of Oliver Cromwell himself. The consequence was a more continuous and consistent relationship between Oxford and government, opening with just a single purge, in 1648, of much the same dimensions as Manchester's purge in Cambridge in 1644: many heads, and half the fellows, were removed from office, and strenuous efforts were made to create a new, puritan university. In the 1650s some of the leaders within, as well as the Lord Protector without, were Independents, with radical plans for religious reform; but Cromwell was characteristically inconsistent: at once ruthless and conciliatory – and never commanding the leisure to be an effective controller of a turbulent university.

In recent decades historians have tended to be more interested in the many cross-currents which made this period in the history of the universities so much more complex than the story of the purges might lead us to suspect. Its story has been very lucidly told by John Twigg in *The University of Cambridge and the English Revolution* (1990), and I shall not tell it again, but hope rather, by a series of examples and case studies, to illustrate the fascination of the theme.

It is striking, first of all, that no serious attempt was made at root and branch reform of Oxford and Cambridge, and hardly any to found rival academies.[15] There was plenty of debate in the seventeenth century on the nature and purpose of higher education, and a number of schemes for founding colleges and universities, especially in London. The only practical consequence was the formation of a college in Durham in the late 1650s, a scheme favoured by Cromwell himself as a means of providing godly preachers and pastors for the northern shires. But it was formed too near his own death, and his son and successor, Richard Cromwell, failed to defend it against the vested interests in Oxford and Cambridge. Its failure is symptomatic of the academic policies of the leaders of the English Revolution. They needed (or thought they needed) purges – and they wanted to rebuild what they had in part cast down. But time, energy and resources never quite allowed their enthusiasm to lead to practical consequences. It had taken thirty or forty years for William

[14] Twigg 1990, chs. 5–7, esp. pp. 98, 105, 178 (on the purges), 153, 163, 238, 289 (on Manchester as chancellor).
[15] For what follows, see Twigg 1990, ch. 8, esp. p. 210.

of Wykeham to found New College and Winchester College in the fourteenth century. He was exceptionally long-lived; several foundations of that era foundered or nearly foundered precisely because the men of power, riches and political authority who attempted to found them died too soon.[16] Even Oliver Cromwell only had a brief period of security; and even with him, higher education could rarely be at the top of his agenda. But one has to say that the chief responsibility for the failure of any schemes to broaden or liberalise the universities of seventeenth-century England lies squarely with the vested interests in the ancient universities. When parliament in the early 1640s, and Cromwell in the 1650s, looked for help and advice in bringing reform to the university world, they turned to Oxford and Cambridge to provide it. They had nowhere else to turn. Some of the leaders of the universities were puritans who owed their position to Manchester or Cromwell; many more were not. But with few exceptions, they were loyal to their academic family homes.

It is true, however, that some of the most inspired of the projects for academic reform were the work of a master of Caius, William Dell. He had been a student at Emmanuel, the nursery of college heads of every religious and political complexion; so far, his career conventionally fitted him for headship – but no further. John Wilkins, one of the central figures of the Oxford establishment – though briefly master of Trinity College, Cambridge, in 1659–60 – described Dell as 'an angry fanatick man' who, lacking learning himself, 'would needs persuade others against it'.[17] He had made his name as a fire-eating preacher to the New Model Army, and he made little attempt to come down to earth as a Cambridge head. But he was a man of vision, who inspired Joseph Needham, a twentieth-century master of Caius of similar dreams, to say of him:

> To have said, in the middle of the seventeenth century, that the young men should study geography and mathematics, not philosophy and scholastic theology; to have maintained that they should spend half their time in practical work, in learning an honest trade or profession as well as their book-learning; and finally, to have urged and preached that there should be a university in every great city of the Commonwealth . . . – would make anyone a pioneer covered with glory.[18]

[16] On the lost colleges of medieval Oxford see Highfield 1984, pp. 229–30.
[17] Ward 1654/1970, p. 7, quoted Twigg 1990, p. 230. On Dell, see Walker 1970; Brooke 1985/1996, pp. 127–31; Twigg 1990, pp. 182–5.
[18] Joseph Needham in Walker 1970, pp. v–vi, quoted Brooke 1985/1996, p. 130, q.v. also for what follows. The study of mathematics, however, was not a revolutionary idea in mid-seventeenth-century Cambridge. Twigg 1984 argues that there was none the less a strong conservative element in Dell's writings.

Dell advocated setting up universities or colleges in London, Bristol, Exeter, Norwich and elsewhere; and we may honour him as a minor prophet. But his words failed to impress the academic leaders of his day, and were stillborn. We can indeed understand the anger of the academic establishment, striving to preserve some element of continuity in times of poverty and stress, at what might well seem wild and irresponsible talk – all the worse for sounding so alluring to the ignorant outsider.

THE CROSS-CURRENTS

Let John Wilkins himself stand first among our witnesses of the remarkable cross-currents in the university politics of the 1640s and 1650s. He was a moderate puritan, naturally conservative in matters religious and academic – as these things were understood in the 1640s and 1650s – but an extremely active academic politician who survived the attempts to enforce the Engagement as warden of Wadham from 1648 to 1659, when he was translated to Cambridge. Meanwhile, in 1655 he married Cromwell's sister Robina, widow of his friend Peter French, puritan canon of Christ Church – a strange alliance between the families of the radical chancellor and a leading Oxford conservative. The personal factor frequently cut across all the ideological boundaries.

Next, we may contemplate the one element in Cambridge which was – or could be – exempt from the warring factions: the lay academics. It is a striking fact that through the purges of 1649–51 only two colleges emerged wholly unscathed: one was Cromwell's own Sidney Sussex, a relatively small community under the guidance of the cautious but deeply respected Richard Minshull, master from 1643 to 1688,[19] and Trinity Hall, home of the civil lawyers. A late medieval pope had laid it down that ordained clergy should not study the profane science of Roman or civil law; and it seems that this was the origin of the strange convention in England that civil lawyers must be laymen. But a curious consequence of the Reformation and of Thomas Cromwell's attempts to put down the teaching of canon law in Cambridge was that the study and practice of church law, canon law, fell mainly into the hands of the civil lawyers – and a firm rule came to be established that those who practised in the heartland of civil law, in Doctors' Commons in the City of London, should be laymen. But they were also, many of them, fellows of Trinity Hall; and this was a major cause for the custom that all but one

---

[19] Twigg 1990, pp. 162–3, 239; and on Richard Minshull in Sidney Sussex College, see Goldie 1996, p. 111.

of the fellows of Trinity Hall should be laymen too.[20] As civil lawyers, they had till 1640 largely administered Roman canon law,[21] and for this and other reasons were often suspected of popery; but they were more truly laymen immune (for the most part) to the theological battles of the schools, caring little for the outward forms of religious observance. The surplice, which the clergy either loved or abhorred, was on the whole a matter of indifference to them. They were not a large element in the Cambridge fellowship – but they were a significant one.

Another college in which laymen flourished was Caius, with its strong nucleus of physicians. Here the heady doctrines of the master, William Dell, were balanced by the devoted physician and tutor – and ultimately president (that is, the master's chosen deputy) – William Bagge. His considerable collection of books was left to the college; and by a happy (but strange) inspiration of his executors, some seventy items of his correspondence were inserted as pastedowns in the books, to be discovered in the 1930s.[22] This shows how the college was run in the 1650s. Dell had been slow to make his presence felt, but in 1651–3 he was regularly present at college meetings. Thereafter, he seems to have been a rare visitor, living mainly in his Bedfordshire parsonage, wisely delegating the management of the college to Bagge between 1655 and Bagge's death in the summer of 1657 – a sad event which caused Dell to attend meetings regularly for a while. But all the indications are that Bagge's shrewd, non-sectarian rule in the college helped to see it through the 1650s and avoid the tremors which shook some other colleges in that decade. A college order of 1655 instructed Bagge to continue and perfect the College Annals, which had been inaugurated by Dr Caius and formed one of the monuments to the continuity of college life. In practice, Bagge set his colleague William Adamson to work on a much more significant record: the *Registrum Magnum*, still the most comprehensive guide to the older college records – and indeed, to the not-so-old, for successive bursars' clerks continued to make entries in it till the 1960s. Bagge also held out the hand of friendship to some of the ejected: he consulted the ex-master, Dr Batchcroft, living in exile in Suffolk, and took with him William Moore, ex-fellow and university librarian – and the kindly treatment Moore received from

---

[20] Squibb 1977; Crawley 1976, ch. 4; Brooke 1985/1996, p. 85. A small clerical element was needed in Trinity Hall to maintain the chapel services and spiritual welfare of the students.

[21] Helmholz 1990; see above, p. 440.

[22] See Brooke 1985/1996, pp. 131–40, with supplementary details in Twigg 1990, pp. 184–5. See above, pp. 337–8, where Bagge's correspondence is used to throw light on the relations of tutors and pupils in this period.

his colleagues was duly rewarded in a very notable bequest of medieval manuscripts.[23]

Not all the laity in the colleges worked for peaceful coexistence with the reigning powers, however. It is clear that at least one young medical student of the mid and late 1640s, Robert Brady, was an ardent royalist; and when his brother Edmund was caught and hanged as a royalist 'traitor' in 1650, Robert had to escape from England for a while. Not for long: he resumed his studies in 1652; but he remained an object of suspicion to the higher powers, was refused leave to proceed MD and spent a while in prison. He was then able to pursue his career as a physician, and doubtless benefited from not being a clergyman and not having to declare his religious allegiance. But it is evident that he was an ardent royalist, and his efforts were recognised by Charles II himself. In 1660 William Dell melted away into Bedfordshire, Batchcroft was briefly reinstated as master – and then successfully petitioned the king to insist on Brady's appointment to succeed him. By Christmas Brady was installed as master.[24]

In general the lay masters and fellows of Cambridge formed a peaceful, non-sectarian element in the university. It might well be supposed that the high churchmen[25] – furthest in practice and belief from the leaders of the puritan revolution – would have led the stormiest lives. If we contemplate the successive masters of Peterhouse Matthew Wren and John Cosin, this expectation may seem justified. Wren was bishop of Ely before and after the revolution, and he spent eighteen long winters in the Tower and other prisons. Cosin escaped to Paris and maintained a precarious living as chaplain to the Anglican maids-in-waiting of the Catholic Queen Henrietta Maria – precarious, since the pious queen did not see why she should pay a salary to a man engaged in fierce anti-Catholic propaganda. But Cosin, though impoverished and living on charity, was allowed to remain in Paris until the Restoration – when he found himself suddenly enriched as bishop of Durham. So rich did he become, indeed, by grinding the faces of rich and poor alike in his diocese that he was able to give Peterhouse and Caius (his first college) ample endowments, to fill the castle and the cathedral at Durham with

---

[23] Brooke 1985/1996, p. 135.

[24] *Ibid.*, p. 145 and references. On Brady, see below, pp. 487–94.

[25] The phrase 'high churchman' came into fashion at the end of the seventeenth century, and immediately ambiguities arose in its use – whether it was a term of abuse, or related to religious observance and the beauty of holiness, or to the authority of bishops and priests, or to the relation of church and monarchy, or to some theological positions: see *OED*, and esp. Walsh *et al.* 1993, pp. 34–5. But it remains preferable, in my view, especially for the period before 1660, to the more fashionable words Laudian and Arminian, which are even more deceptive. See below, p. 477.

beautiful Gothic woodwork of the 1660s and 1670s, and to die a wealthy man.[26]

When Cosin went to Durham, he gathered to him, among others, two Emmanuel men – distinguished products of the college formerly supposed a puritan stronghold. John Sudbury, dean of Durham, 1661/2–1684, was evidently close to Cosin; but William Sancroft the younger, Cosin's chaplain, prebendary of Durham (1662–1674) and rector of Houghton-le-Spring, was closer still – and Sancroft was destined to go on to the deaneries of York and London and the archbishopric of Canterbury.[27] The most notable architectural monuments of the high churchmen of seventeenth-century Cambridge are the chapels of Peterhouse, Pembroke and Emmanuel. Peterhouse chapel was begun by Matthew Wren in the 1630s and finished by Cosin in the 1660s. Pembroke and Emmanuel were both designed by Matthew Wren's nephew, Christopher Wren, in the 1660s: Pembroke was the final monument to Matthew Wren, and Emmanuel chapel was built on the initiative of William Sancroft.[28]

What had happened in Emmanuel in the 1630s and 1640s to pave the way for what Collinson calls its transmogrification?[29] In the case of John Sudbury, we can give no sort of answer. Sancroft is much better documented – and for that reason the most puzzling of all. We can say at once that Emmanuel in the 1630s and 1640s was exceptionally large and intellectually alive, and when we come to contemplate the Cambridge Platonists we are forced to see that in the chambers of Emmanuel in the mid-seventeenth century a great diversity of ideas and ideals was initiated and discussed. William Sancroft the younger was nephew and protégé of his namesake, a conventional Emmanuel puritan who had been master of the college from 1628 to 1637,[30] and had been brought up to be a member of the Emmanuel establishment. How there came to be a high church element in the Emmanuel fellowship is one of the deepest mysteries in the history of that society. Collinson conjectures that the tutor of Sancroft the younger, Ezekiel Wright, to whom he was evidently devoted, had high church tendencies.[31] What is abundantly clear is that Emmanuel came in the 1630s and 1640s to contain every shade of theological opinion in the Protestant fold of the day, from high church to puritan to what we would

[26] On Cosin, see Brooke 1985/1996, pp. 110–14.

[27] Collinson in Bendall *et al.* 1999, p. 269. On Sancroft, Collinson, in *ibid.*, pp. 247–56, 265–75; Horn *et al.* 2003.

[28] See above, pp. 44–7.

[29] Collinson in Bendall *et al.* 1999, ch. 9: 'Restoration and transmogrification'.

[30] Collinson, in *ibid.*, pp. 221–4.   [31] Collinson, in *ibid.*, pp. 252–3.

call broad church. The labels are anachronistic and perhaps inappropriate; but at least they convey the great range – and the curious way in which the fellows and scholars of Emmanuel lapped over the boundary lines historians like to set.

William Sancroft the younger is one of the best-documented characters of the seventeenth century; and partly for that reason the workings of his mind are often very difficult to follow. But his cast of mind and manner of life have in recent years been much illuminated by Patrick Collinson;[32] although he is hard put to it to explain how such a blatant royalist and high churchman survived in his fellowship at Emmanuel so long. 'Sancroft's correspondence leaves us in no doubt about the fierceness of his church-and-king royalism as revolutionary politics led to Civil War. He avoided subscription to the Covenant, which he called "the thing out of the North"; "to comply would be to throw a foule aspersion upon the whole Church of God in England since the Reformation".' When Holdsworth was removed from the mastership in 1644 for a royalism no less blatant – though no doubt more conspicuous, since Holdsworth was a very senior figure in the Cambridge establishment, and Sancroft a novice – Sancroft observed: '"I had not thought they would have beheaded whole colleges at a blow; nay, whole universities and whole churches too". "They" were worse than the Emperor Caligula, who had lopped off the head of Jupiter in the Capitol, replacing it with his own.' And 'they' were soon to be identified with Oliver Cromwell, of whose abhorrence Sancroft made no secret among his friends. He could take a pleasant vacation at Fressingfield in Suffolk, his family home; but when he returned to Cambridge, he found Anthony Tuckney installed both as master of Emmanuel and as vice-chancellor, to his horror. Tuckney was a hard-line puritan and a good servant of the government: he only left Emmanuel in 1653 to become master of St John's; and his successor, William Dillingham, was a conservative puritan who struggled to govern a divided college. Meanwhile, amazingly, Sancroft was left in his fellowship till 1651. Collinson cites evidence which suggests that he was protected by Ralph Brownrigg, former master of St Catharine's and bishop of Exeter. Brownrigg was indeed a deeply respected puritan; but his acceptance of a bishopric from the king in 1642 had made him an object of suspicion; and in 1645 he was ejected from the mastership of St Catharine's.[33] How he came still to exercise influence in 1650 is a mystery – and it is equally mysterious that Sancroft should have been

<hr>

[32] Collinson, in *ibid*, esp. p. 247–56, 265–76: what follows is especially based on *ibid.*, pp. 252–6.
[33] Twigg 1990, pp. 56–7.

sheltered so long. It seems likely that the authorities in Emmanuel turned a blind eye to the shocking opinions of one whom they had nurtured; and outside Emmanuel he was still relatively obscure. In December 1650 he wrote to Brownrigg: 'When the cedars fall and when Lebanon shudders, who can be sensible that a poor shrub suffers?' – or even exists?[34] In any case, the desultory expulsions of 1649–51 seem to have depended on pressure from insurgent students who wished to enjoy their fellowships. Early in 1651, it seems, Sancroft preached a sermon comparing the republican regime to the tyrannies of Diocletian and Caligula. In April 1651 came a'humble petition' from Thomas Brainford issuing in a formal notice that Sancroft must immediately subscribe to the Engagement or lose his fellowship.[35] From 1651 he was an exile in Fressingfield, alternately keeping silence and issuing violent attacks on the regime: his 'mordant best seller, *Modern Policies*' contains passages which 'leave us in no doubt that Oliver Cromwell was his target'.[36] From 1658 to 1660 Sancroft enjoyed a foreign tour, with long periods in Utrecht and visits to Switzerland and Italy. In 1660 news reached him – in Rome – of the Restoration of Charles II; and by 1662 Sancroft was master of Emmanuel.

Studies of Cambridge theologians of the seventeenth century have tended to polarise them into Calvinists and Arminians, Laudians and puritans. But some of the most eminent Cambridge men fell into neither category, and it is striking that two of these were students and fellows of St John's in the early years of the century – and both are largely remembered today for their libraries. John Williams was a fellow from 1603, but rapidly achieved patronage at Court, becoming a notable pluralist and a leading adviser to the duke of Buckingham: he rose to be Lord Keeper of the Great Seal to James I and bishop of Lincoln. To political historians he is seen above all as William Laud's principal rival and enemy on the bench of bishops, and he suffered in consequence imprisonment in the Tower, 1637–40. When the clouds encompassed Laud, Williams was rewarded with the archbishopric of York in 1641 – ironically, for episcopacy was in the shadows during the rest of his life. But his last years, 1645–50, were spent alternately in efforts to make peace and in retirement. It is striking that he was not a Calvinist or a puritan: he held the middle ground, despised perhaps both by puritans and Laudians as a worldly, easy-going prelate; but he was not, in the long run, a time-server. He seriously attempted to make the middle way a viable meeting point between the fell opposed points of mighty opposites. In the 1620s he gave St John's

---

[34] Quoted by Collinson in Bendall *et al.* 1999, p. 254.
[35] Collinson, in *ibid.*, p. 255.   [36] Collinson, in *ibid.*, pp. 225–6 (also for what follows).

its magnificent library, evidently designed to be a monument to himself as well as a major contribution to learning and scholarship within the college. But Williams was not himself a great book collector; others had to fill its echoing spaces – indeed, it was partly inspired by the rapid growth of the collection in the previous generation.[37]

Richard Holdsworth was one of the notable characters of Cambridge of the era: he was archdeacon of Huntingdon in the diocese of Lincoln, John Williams' see, from 1634; he was offered the bishopric of Bristol in 1641; he was dean of Worcester from 1646; but his life was spent between London, where he was rector of St Peter le Poer and a noted preacher, and Cambridge. He was a fellow and tutor of St John's and from 1637 master of Emmanuel, and in the early 1640s vice-chancellor: it was the singular misfortune of this admirable and attractive man that he was an ardent royalist in the days of the Long Parliament. He spent his last years, from 1643 on, in prison in London, separated from his friends and colleagues in Cambridge, and from his books. For Holdsworth had the largest private library of the age: the largest personal collection recorded in Cambridge before the eighteenth century. Andrew Perne had died in 1589 master of Peterhouse and owner of over 3,000 books, a formidable collection of extraordinary range.[38] The bequest of William Branthwaite, founder fellow of Emmanuel and master of Caius from 1607 to 1619, to the Caius library, is a noble collection of over 1,000 books; William Sancroft was to leave over 5,000 to Emmanuel. But Holdsworth amassed slightly more than 10,000.[39] Two generations later John Moore, bishop of Ely, a fanatical book-collector, put together a collection which was bought by George I and presented to Cambridge and so became the Royal Library in the Cambridge University Library after his death; and this was estimated at over 30,000 books, including manuscripts.[40] Moore had enjoyed long years of book-collecting and the income first of an arch-pluralist and then of the wealthy see of Ely; but it still puts all earlier collections – and the infinitely more modest libraries of the colleges and the university before his day – into perspective.

None the less, Holdsworth's collection was an amazing achievement, especially as he was only a very modest pluralist and his chief benefice – his archdeaconry – came relatively late. It is very wide ranging, including for example 316 medical books (comprising medicine, botany and cookery) – though they wear a slightly old-fashioned look as William Harvey is not among the authors.[41] Similarly the philosophical texts (714 of them)

---

[37] On the library of St John's, see above, pp. 52–3.   [38] McKitterick 1991, esp. pp. 35–69.
[39] Oates 1986, pp. 327–8.   [40] McKitterick 1986, chs. 3–5, esp. p. 152; see above, p. 58.
[41] Oates 1986, p. 329; for Holdsworth's library, see *ibid.*, ch. 13 *passim.*

contained a very impressive array of late medieval and early modern commentaries on Aristotle, while mathematics claimed only 62 titles. Literary
and grammatical texts abound – mostly Greek and Latin classics, but also
including Chaucer, Spenser, Sidney and several copies of More's *Utopia*.
Not surprisingly, the theological books provide far the largest sector, and
it is characteristic of this kind of collection that – though Holdsworth
was a fervent Protestant – Catholic theological works far outnumbered
Protestant. In his case this may partly reflect the special tastes of an antiquarian bibliophile: the collection included 186 manuscripts and over
200 incunabula. It is the collection of a man who loved books and who
wanted a representative library covering all a scholar's proper interests;
it is a tutor's library calculated to inspire naturally gifted students with
the love of learning. Although it contained 972 'Libri controversiarum',
it was the library of a peace-loving theologian. Patrick Collinson, while
observing that Holdsworth was 'probably the best master Emmanuel ever
had', characterises him as an anti-Arminian moderate, 'a central churchman, an establishment Calvinist, even an extreme moderate. Such men
were to suffer most in the upheavals to come' in the 1640s.[42]

Collinson goes on to say: 'Holdsworth was a man who aroused real
devotion' and quotes the encomia of two very different pupils: of the
old-fashioned Calvinist Symonds d'Ewes, who noted in his diary after a
sermon by Holdsworth in d'Ewes' Suffolk parish, that he 'began to love
him even better than ever'; and Sancroft, his disciple in Emmanuel who
was to end as a leading high churchman: 'Your counsell was both card and
compasse . . . your favor the gale that fill'd my sails.'[43] Holdsworth was
warm-hearted, enthusiastic, occasionally hot-tempered (if we may believe
Fuller) – but quick to recover; a man who immersed himself and his pupils
in books, a much-admired exponent of a fairly traditional course of study.
Of his 'Directions for Students' Collinson says, less kindly, that he was
'an academic Polonius'; and the 'Directions', like the library, reflect the
rhetorical bias in the literary studies he prescribed in great detail – as well
as a very ample dose of Aristotle.[44] The men who sought the middle
way may have had ill treatment at the time; but their heritage survives:
John Williams' library building is one of the glories of Cambridge and
Holdsworth's library (which he really meant to go to Emmanuel) was the
core of the University Library before the advent of John Moore's.

The leading puritans of Cambridge were mostly of a presbyterian persuasion, at home with the Solemn League and Covenant, less so with the

---

[42] Collinson in Bendall *et al.* 1999, pp. 224–5.   [43] Collinson, in *ibid.*, p. 226.
[44] Fuller 1662, p. 305; and on Holdsworth's 'Directions for Students', see below, p. 515; Collinson
in Bendall *et al.* 1999, p. 74.

Engagement. Among the most eminent and admirable were the 'three old Calvinist warhorses' Anthony Tuckney, Thomas Hill and John Arrowsmith.[45] Tuckney and Hill were the characteristic sons of traditional, Calvinist Emmanuel: they were deeply convinced Calvinists, puritans in religious practice, ready supporters of the presbyterian modes of the Solemn League and Covenant; Arrowsmith was their natural ally, a product of that wing of the St John's fellowship more deeply Calvinist than Holdsworth. And they were rewarded: Tuckney with the mastership of Emmanuel (1644–53) and St John's (1653–61); Hill with the mastership of Trinity (1645–53); Arrowsmith with the mastership of both St John's and Trinity (1644–53, 1653–9). By these means the parliamentary and puritan establishment, and the government of the 1640s and 1650s, sought to manage the three most populous colleges of the day.[46] But they were far from being stooges of the government: they were Cambridge men through and through. They were all equally convinced that the vocation of Cambridge was to produce puritan preachers, and all found pulpits outside Cambridge and enjoyed links with a wider network of puritan preachers.[47] All three engaged in political activity in the early 1640s and were members of the Westminster Assembly, engaged in reforming the church and (in the process) the universities, and Tuckney was one of its most prominent members.[48] So much involved was he in Westminster that he was in effect an absentee master for his first three years as master of Emmanuel, only becoming an effective presence in Cambridge itself when he was vice-chancellor in 1647–8: but the weight of his hand was felt before that.[49] Yet Tuckney had been a very effective and pastoral tutor: the extraordinary correspondence between him and his former pupil Benjamin Whichcote – when Whichcote was provost of King's and was propounding the doctrines of the Cambridge Platonists – reveals a human relationship which could overcome sharp differences of ideology.[50] By the same token, both Arrowsmith and Hill encountered opposition and division in their colleges, but John Twigg has shown that the troubles in St John's under Arrowsmith were exaggerated, and those under Hill at Trinity much exaggerated: that Hill, for all his stern convictions, was a fairly tolerant master who – after a difficult start – restored order and a measure of good fellowship to the college.[51] Doubtless as convinced opponents of traditional episcopacy and Anglican modes of

---

[45] Collinson, in *ibid.*, p. 261.   [46] See table in Twigg 1990, p. 289.
[47] *DNB.*   [48] Twigg 1990, pp. 111–15.
[49] Cf. Collinson in Bendall *et al.* 1999, pp. 244–5.   [50] See above, pp. 336–7.
[51] On Arrowsmith at St John's, see Twigg 1990, pp. 123–7; on Hill at Trinity, *ibid.*, pp. 127–8.

worship, they were revolutionaries; but they were also highly responsible Cambridge men who hoped to see order and peace restored in the new Jerusalem.

In this they were to be disappointed: after 1660 came the counter-revolution, as repressive in its way as the regimes it replaced. Hill and Arrowsmith had the good fortune to live out their lives in their respective lodges, and die before the Restoration. Tuckney was deposed from St John's in 1661 after a petition from twenty-four fellows had claimed that when the Book of Common Prayer was reintroduced in the chapel of St John's the master absented himself. In 1665 he was arrested for preaching of a nonconformist character; he died in 1670, after nine years in the wilderness.[52]

But neither the high church of Sancroft nor the middle track of Holdsworth nor the puritan mode of Tuckney, Hill and Arrowsmith prepared the way for the new model of the Cambridge Platonists. All the protagonists of the older modes believed in predestination, though there was a large variety of subtle differences in their definition of it – as there had been in the Catholic Church before the Reformation. To put it crudely, they all believed that hell was populous, but they differed considerably on the size of its population. The Cambridge Platonists doubted if it was inhabited at all.

It is a commonplace to say that the Cambridge Platonists, by their own submission, were not a party or a club, but a group of individual academics, most of them sprung from Emmanuel, some from Christ's, with many ideas in common. It is also held that some of the ideas they propounded in both theology and the natural sciences led down cul-de-sacs and were not in the end fruitful. It may well be so. But they opened many windows into fresh and exciting ideas; and as to predestination, they indicated or hinted that God had intended to save us all – a view which many have found in some passages in St Paul – and that heaven might not be confined to a small body of elect. Above all, they stood for reason and rational enquiry: no new idea – so had the medieval school-men whose books lined the shelves of college and university library, and of those of the reformed divines, Perne, Branthwaite and Holdsworth. But they subjected received theological opinion to rational enquiry with a fresh vigour often at variance with orthodox Calvinism. They were puritan in religious sentiment; the chapel of Emmanuel – as it was under Tuckney – answered to their ideas of religious devotion. They were

[52] Twigg 1990, p. 251; *DNB*.

great preachers in the tradition of Emmanuel. They opened windows into a world of ideas which must belong to a later chapter;[53] we can only make a brief acquaintance with them here. But this chapter would be woefully incomplete without them. For out of the Emmanuel of the elder Sancroft, Holdsworth and Tuckney, emerged Benjamin Whichcote and Ralph Cudworth – and Whichcote had Tuckney and Hill for his tutors, nor did they reject or repudiate his friendship, though Tuckney was mightily surprised by his views.[54] Nor were they obscure or fugitive heretics. Whichcote was provost of King's till the Restoration restored his predecessor, and Cudworth was master of Clare and Christ's: he died master in 1688, shortly after the death of the third and perhaps the most remarkable of all the Platonists, Henry More, fellow of Christ's throughout his middle and later life. If we contemplate Sancroft, Tuckney, Whichcote and More, we must conclude that Emmanuel and Christ's – and in a measure Cambridge as a whole – was fertile in a wider variety of outlook and imagination in the age of the puritan revolution than seems quite to fit the title of this chapter.

Oliver Cromwell died in 1658; his son Richard abdicated in 1659. On 29 May 1660 Charles II resumed the throne he had held (in royalist theory) since 1649. Cambridge briefly endured another purge; but for all the triumphalist and persecuting ambitions of many leading Anglicans of the Restoration era, Cambridge was not to suffer a like persecution again.

---

[53] See below, pp. 522 ff; and see Collinson in Bendall *et al.* 1999, pp. 256–64 and refs. on p. 256 n. 1.
[54] See above, pp. 336–7.

Chapter 14

CAMBRIDGE AND THE
SCIENTIFIC REVOLUTION

BRADY, NEWTON AND BENTLEY

The scientific revolution is out of fashion. John Gascoigne called his fundamental study of curriculum and science, religion and politics *Cambridge in the Age of the Enlightenment*; but this chapter is not about curricula, nor mainly about the broader trends in education and intellectual life. The word revolution suggests rapid and violent change, and that cannot be in question in intellectual movements, whatever the fellows of Trinity may have felt when Dr Bentley was let loose among them. Nor do I question recent arguments that crucial changes in the study of mathematics and the natural sciences came more gradually than was once supposed. But the natural sciences are not the only sciences, and were assuredly not the only ones affected by the winds that blew in the seventeenth and early eighteenth centuries. If Newton and the new physics formed the most dramatic and widely known of these, a change equally fundamental can be discerned in some of the humanities, especially in the study and editing of Greek and Latin texts and in scientific research in medieval history. It would be universally accepted that the academic career of Richard Bentley was a major turning point in the criticism of classical texts; it can equally be seen as a fundamental staging post in the study of the New Testament, and it is ironical that Bentley won the Regius Professorship of Divinity by chicanery, yet contributed as much as most of his line to theological research. Bentley's work was of prime importance on a European plane; Robert Brady's was perhaps more parochial. He was the most acute and brilliant of a group of scholars who laid the foundations of medieval English history; he put Domesday Book and the public records on the map as sources for intelligible and scientific history. We cannot claim for him the European role of Bentley, though there are indications that he was aware of the work of continental scholars. The key study of the Maurist Father Jean Mabillon, *De Re Diplomatica* (1681), which set in motion the two sciences of palaeography and diplomatic (the technical study of charters and other documents) is in the Caius College library, in which Brady worked: tantalisingly, we cannot be sure that he read it. But it was certainly studied by other British scholars of the age, and it would be very strange if he had not.[1]

The question is: what had all this to do with Cambridge? Was it more than chance that Newton was resident there and Brady and Bentley masters of colleges? In the case of Newton, some of the answer is immediately plain. The steward's accounts in the Trinity archives establish that as a fellow he was continuously resident in Trinity for twenty-eight years from 1668 to 1696 – which included the most creative years of his life – and it seems that he rarely left Cambridge during the thirty-five years from 1661 to 1696 for more than a few days, or at most a very few weeks, save in the plague years 1665–7 and for his brief duties as an MP in 1689–90.[2] These are the most significant purely biographical facts about him.

Although Brady and Bentley had both been students at Cambridge – at Caius and St John's – it became their home in middle life: Brady, at 33, was made master of Caius in 1660, and it remained his headquarters till his death in 1700. But the redit books of Caius show him often absent; and we know that he had many calls on his time – a Norfolk estate, an appointment as royal physician, and above all as keeper of public records, until the Revolution of 1688 ended his favour at Court and excluded him from the records. Cambridge undoubtedly provided intellectual stimulus and a firm academic base; his materials as a historian lay mainly in the archives and libraries of London. Bentley was 38 when he returned to Cambridge as master of Trinity, and from then on, for forty-two years, Trinity was his base. His earlier career had been partly spent in Oxford, partly in London, where he was a very active royal librarian for a time. He never forgot Cambridge, and was much involved in the revival of

---

[1] On Brady, see Brooke 1985/1996, ch. 8; Hallam 1986, pp. 124–7; Pocock 1950–2, 1957, pp. 195–228; Douglas 1951, ch. 6. A characteristic example of the attempt to diminish the originality of the scholars of the late seventeenth century is A. Grafton's study in Feingold 1990, pp. 291–2, who regards Brink 1986 as 'a learned and critical version of the traditional view', which he wishes to refute. But he seems to me not to have grasped the true nature of Bentley's achievement, and he ignores the work of Brady and Mabillon and the scientific historians of the period. I admit that the phrase 'the scientific revolution' is open to objection; but so also is any attempt to minimise the difference between the three who are the theme of this chapter and their predecessors of earlier generations.

[2] The precise weeks of Newton's residence each year were noted in Edleston 1850, p. lxxxii, though without specific indication that they derive from the steward's accounts on which they must be based; he also gave in meticulous detail (which only requires correction in very minor details) the evidence of the exiit and redit book, 1662–96, and of the buttery books, 1686–1702, which largely confirm the details (*ibid.*, pp. lxxxv–xc); his table is copied in Gjertsen 1986, pp. 585–6. I am very grateful to Jonathan Smith for his help with these sources in the Trinity College Archives. Westfall 1980 is an admirable biography marred by a strong prejudice against Newton's Cambridge.

Plate 28 Isaac Newton's garden, Trinity College, with his rooms behind, from
David Loggan, *Cantabrigia Illustrata, c.* 1690

the Cambridge University Press as a great house for printing scholarly
books even before his return.[3] In Trinity and Cambridge, he had a few
disciples and friends, in theology and the natural sciences as well as the
classics; and he had many enemies. With Brady one is involved in a more
difficult, and with Bentley in a more subtle enquiry to determine the
role of Cambridge in their scholarly work. But it is immediately evident
that to all three, Cambridge was in some measure and for some reasons
a congenial base for major adventures of the mind.

The reputation of Cambridge in this period has been fluctuating. To
some, it has seemed axiomatic that the era of Newton and Bentley must –
in some senses at least – be a golden age in Cambridge history. To J.A.
Westfall, who was to publish the standard modern life of Newton in 1980,
'the catastrophic decline of the university after the Restoration left it an
intellectual wasteland'.[4] John Gascoigne, in *Cambridge in the Age of the
Enlightenment*, steered a middle course. Far from being a wasteland, it was
a centre of great intellectual activity; Newton's was far from being a lone

[3] McKitterick 1998, ch. 3, esp. pp. 46–67 – and cf. *ibid.*, Index, s.v. Bentley.
[4] Westfall 1975, p. 194, cited Gascoigne 1989, p. 6; Collinson in Bendall *et al.* 1999, p. 283.

voice. The latest fashions in mathematics and philosophy were slowly overtaking the old scholastic syllabuses, and preparing the way for the triumph of Newtonian science and the formation of the Mathematical Tripos in the eighteenth and nineteenth centuries. But Gascoigne indicated very clearly that the beneficiaries of this lively intellectual world were relatively few; above all, that it was perhaps only in Trinity, Caius, Clare and Corpus that we can discern the more advanced intellectual tendencies, and educational methods, of the Enlightenment.[5] Dr Bentley would have agreed, up to a point. He devoted his early years as master of Trinity to extensive, and often uncomfortable, educational reforms; and he always had a group of admirers about him. But they were a small group: he left no one in any doubt that most of the fellows even of Trinity were inferior scholars beneath his contempt. It is indeed a fundamental problem in writing the history of scholarship that in any age journeymen outnumber profound and original scholars; and in the early modern period a scholar of genius, like Bentley, may hardly seem to belong to his own age. None the less, it is sufficiently clear that Cambridge was a congenial home to Brady the historian and physician, to Newton the mathematician and physicist, and to Bentley the classical and New Testament scholar – a place where they had just sufficient intellectual companionship and stimulus to foster their extraordinarily wide and deep scholarly interests. Brady was happy to stay there so long as he could commute to London and the royal Court; Newton tied himself to Cambridge while his original inspiration lasted, and until a practical, administrative post in the Royal Mint made London seem suddenly very attractive; and Bentley stayed in Trinity waiting for the rich bishopric which never came.[6]

The width of their interests is as astonishing as the depth – though they would have made no impact if the depth and penetration of their minds had been in any sense impaired by the range of their interests. It is undoubtedly true that Brady might have made a more original contribution to medicine if he had not been so fertile a historian; that when Newton tried to advance the scientific study of chronology he wrote nonsense; and that Bentley floundered when he turned his knowledge of Greek and Latin poetry to the hopeless task of improving the text of *Paradise Lost*. In one of his most cynical passages, A.E. Housman observed that 'though Bentley's faculty for discovering truth has no equal in the history of learning, his wish to discover it was not so strong'. Not only did he treat 'the MSS much as if they were fellows of Trinity . . . His buoyant

---

[5] Gascoigne 1989.
[6] Bentley refused the bishopric of Bristol in 1724 – it was not sufficiently well endowed (Monk 1830, p. 499).

mind, elated by the exercise of its powers, too often forgot the nature of its business, and turned from work to play; and many a time when he feigned and half fancied that he was correcting the scribe, he knew in his heart (and of his *Paradise Lost* they tell us he confessed it) that he was revising the author.'[7] This is neither quite right nor quite fair. He saw some real problems in the text of Milton; but his treatment of them involved absurd errors of judgement; it is unlikely that he really admitted as much. Bentley was exuberant and arrogant; he was also naturally litigious, and played with his adversaries with great panache, whether they were broken metres or vulgar errors in editions of classical authors, or inferior scholars maintaining the authenticity of spurious texts, or the fellows of Trinity striving to make headway against him in the lawcourts. Not for nothing did the House of Lords vote to meet on a Saturday (an unheard of event, I believe) to enjoy a day's entertainment from the affairs of Trinity.[8] Thus Bentley illustrates the strength and weakness of Cambridge, and his adventures reduced the academic process in Cambridge and Trinity to farce. Small wonder that when George II witnessed fifty-eight candidates being presented by Bentley for the doctorate of Divinity – not fifty-eight budding theologians, but fifty-eight would-be Whig voters in the senate – he went off to his German principality to help found the University of Göttingen.[9] Yet there are many indications in the scholarly works of Bentley of the historical period he lived in and the intellectual culture he adorned. So it was with Brady and, most obviously, with Newton.

ROBERT BRADY

Robert Brady entered Caius in 1644, as a tutorial pupil of Thomas Batchcroft, the master, with whom he seems to have remained on friendly terms, though his studies turned soon to medicine and his sympathies to the exiled king. In 1660, at the Restoration of Charles II, Batchcroft was restored to the mastership he had lost for being, though a puritan, not puritan enough. He had reached the respectable age of 88, and came in only as a caretaker; and he and King Charles arranged that Brady was rapidly appointed to succeed him, in reward for services to the royal cause we cannot now identify. Brady rose to be Regius Professor of Physic in 1671, and royal physician in the 1680s. He attended Charles II in his last illnesses, and James II after Charles' death. He attended James (with

---

[7] Housman 1903/1937, p. xviii (on Housman, see Brooke 1993b, pp. 211–16); for comment on Bentley's Milton, see Brink 1986, pp. 80–3.

[8] Monk 1830, p. 596, cited Brooke 1985/1996, p. 163 n. 15.

[9] Brooke, Highfield and Swaan 1988, p. 246, citing Monk 1830, pp. 542–3.

some discomfort, he later declared) when he visited Oxford in an attempt to reform it in a papist direction; and he was present at the birth of the Old Pretender. He was a notable physician, and made some original contributions to the science of medicine, though not on the same scale as his predecessor in the chair, his fellow-Caian Francis Glisson.[10] He is better known as the author of lively political pamphlets of a royalist tendency. The Whig historians of the seventeenth century had defended the proposition that all authority derived from parliament and so from the people; and that parliament was as old as the hills, or at any rate older than the Norman Conquest.[11] Brady was able to show that parliament was an invention of the thirteenth century; that it owed its existence to royal summonses; that even the treasured liberties of Magna Carta were in form grants from King John and his successors.

He derived this knowledge from three sources. First of all, he was a disciple of one of the most notable scholars of an earlier generation, Sir Henry Spelman, whose glossary of medieval terms and studies on knight service showed the way to the use and understanding of the great medieval archive preserved (at that time) mainly in the Tower of London. Spelman died in 1641, and Brady cannot have known him personally. But two of his grandsons were contemporaries of Brady's in Caius as students, and it may be that the young medical student learned something of the achievements of the great antiquary from his family.[12] He also owed much to William Prynne, the learned and eccentric archivist – both from his published work, especially his book on parliamentary writs, which appeared in 1662, and from his pioneer work in rescuing and arranging the medieval records in the Tower. It was an ironical debt, since in politics and religion they were poles apart – Prynne a fiery puritan, Brady a lively and dedicated royalist.

The third and most crucial source of Brady's historical learning was the public records themselves, which he came to study personally and through a research assistant over long periods in the 1670s and 1680s. After his death the seat in the Tally Court at the Exchequer of Receipt on which he worked was remembered by his younger colleagues.[13] There presumably he studied Domesday Book, for he was the first modern scholar seriously to appreciate its riches. There he studied the rolls and petitions which unfolded to him the history of parliament and of royal government. If his most spectacular achievement was to prove beyond cavil (working on

---

[10] Gascoigne 1989, pp. 60–1. For all these details, and full refs., see Brooke 1985/1996, pp. 143–50.
[11] For this and what follows, see Pocock 1950–2; Brooke 1985/1996, pp. 143–5.
[12] See Brooke 1985/1996, pp. 141–2; for Spelman, see esp. Spelman 1662, 1664, 1687.
[13] Brooke 1985/1996, p. 144 and n. 4; Hallam 1986, pp. 124–7.

Spelman's foundations) that parliament was a new invention of the thirteenth century, equally lasting was his careful, scholarly elucidation of the precise details of English political history in the thirteenth and fourteenth centuries.[14] He had the good fortune to be keeper of the best-preserved royal archive in Europe: only the records of the Crown of Aragon at Barcelona are of comparable richness and systematic preservation; and he saw the possibility this opened up for scientific historical research. The details he patiently teased out of the records provided a wealth of information which was to be quarried by innumerable historians for over two hundred years: only in the twentieth century did the publication of the Public Record Office *Calendars* give scholars ready access to information closer to the source than Brady's *Complete History* and its *Continuation*.

It seems so obvious to medievalists today that one culls the details of political and constitutional history from the rolls and files of the PRO that the scale and depth of Brady's achievement is easily underestimated. It is true that he was greatly helped by the achievements of his predecessors and younger contemporaries in publishing the major chronicles of medieval England. A hundred years earlier, Matthew Parker had attempted to tell the story of the medieval English church by editing (and sometimes fudging) its sources. To Parker goes the credit of the first printing of *Asser's Life of King Alfred*, and the discredit of interpolating material from other sources, of his own or of his aides' fancies, into it.[15] Some of Parker's successors were greatly superior to him in accuracy and scholarly integrity; and the collections edited by (or under the name of) Sir Henry Savile (1596) and Sir Roger Twysden (1652) – and the editions by William Wats of Matthew Paris (1640) – meant that many of the fundamental narrative sources of the twelfth and thirteenth centuries were available to Brady in tolerable editions. One of the most notable events of Brady's own time was the edition of lives and annals of English bishops and bishoprics in Henry Wharton's *Anglia Sacra* (1691). Wharton had been a student at Caius, and it is highly probable that he had begun his studies in the Caius library (to which he presented a copy of the book); it is likely too that he owed something to Brady's advice and encouragement – though curiously, there is no record of contact between them, and no acknowledgement to Brady in the preface. Wharton was not so precise and meticulous as Brady: he worked at breath-taking speed

---

[14] Brady 1685, 1700. The first has a preamble down to 1200; but the most valuable part is the period from *c.* 1200 covered by the public records.

[15] McKisack 1971, ch. 2, esp. pp. 42–3; Stephenson 1904/1959, pp. xiv–xxi. For the background to Brady, see esp. Douglas 1951, chs. 1–6.

and had published numerous books and pamphlets as well as *Anglia Sacra* before his early death at the age of 30.[16]

The editing of texts had indeed greatly advanced in the seventeenth century. In particular, the great collections of Roger Dodsworth and Sir William Dugdale had issued in the *Monasticon Anglicanum* (1655–73). They reflect a circle of scholars who understood the need for accurate texts and knew where to find medieval charters. Beyond that, they had little critical sense: a contemporary observed that it was unfortunate that Dugdale printed spurious and genuine charters together without comment.[17] The Copernican revolution in the critical study of medieval documents came with Mabillon's *De Re Diplomatica* (1681). The impulse which led to it was not so much the urge to expose the forged as to defend the genuine. Dom Jean Mabillon was the most notable of the group of Benedictine scholars who worked and flourished in the Congrégation de Saint-Maur from the mid-seventeenth century until the French Revolution.[18] They studied the historical records of their own order and a wide circle of patristic and medieval texts. Their chief rivals in the critical study of medieval texts were the Jesuit Bollandists, founded in the early seventeenth century to study the lives of the saints, and still in the twenty-first century (after a pause in the late eighteenth and early nineteenth centuries, when their Order was suppressed) at work upon them. Needless to say, the Bollandists had to wade knee-deep in spurious legends and doubtful miracles, and they were very much aware of it; the problem of distinguishing genuine tradition from pious and not-so-pious legend sharpened their critical faculties. The most notable scholar among the early Bollandists, Father Daniel Papebroch, produced a stately preface, or Prolegomena, to a volume of the *Acta Sanctorum* in 1675 in which he claimed that many or most early charters were forgereies, especially those from the abbey of Saint-Denis – then a member of the Maurist Congregation. This greatly disturbed the normally mild Dom Mabillon, and he set to work to devise a scientific set of criteria by which to distinguish genuine from false. From his studies sprang the *De Re Diplomatica* (1681), a massive folio pamphlet, in which two sciences were born – and Papebroch was flattened: in a light-hearted aside, Mabillon proposed brave punishments for those who accuse documents falsely.[19] Mabillon studied both the history of handwriting, providing the first scientific

---

[16] On Wharton, see Brooke 1985/1996, pp. 147–50; *ibid.*, p. 150 for Collier (cf. below, p. 493).
[17] Sir Roger Twysden, quoted in Douglas 1951, p. 36.
[18] On the Maurists, see Knowles 1963b, ch. 2; on Mabillon, Knowles 1963a, ch. 10; on the Bollandists (below), Knowles 1963b, ch. 1.
[19] Mabillon 1681, p. 242 no. viii.

treatise on medieval palaeography, and the forms and formulae of medieval documents, from which sprang the science of diplomatic. Its influence in England is not easy to gauge, for British scholars were shy of admitting to the study of Roman Catholic scholarly literature, especially in the age of the Popish Plot and of James II. But its presence in the Caius library is suggestive, and there is no doubt of its influence on the next generation of scholars, especially those trained in Oxford. Among the most distinguished of these was Humphrey Wanley, Harley's librarian and the most notable palaeographer of his day, whose ambition was to produce a 'De Re Diplomatica Angliae' whose title leaves no doubt of its inspiration.[20] This was also the era of Thomas Madox, in whom the tradition of Brady and Mabillon met: for his two most notable works were a history of the Exchequer, in which he showed a profound understanding (like Brady) of the public records, and his *Formulare Anglicanum* (1702), which is a systematic analysis of medieval documents – of which he printed specimens from the public records – the essential foundation of English diplomatic.

There were two marked symptoms of the scientific approach to the study of historical records in this period: an attempt to apply rational, scientific principles of analysis to them, and a determination to get the precise historical facts correct. The first shows British historians at work in a larger world, with its centre in France and the Low Countries, but with its disciples spread widely about Europe. Of the second, the successive editions of Francis Godwin's *De Praesulibus Angliae Commentarius* – a catalogue of English bishops designed to establish the apostolic succession in the Church of England – are an early example. Godwin himself was an Elizabethan divine who earned a bishopric by the first edition of 1601, and revised the book in 1615–16. It was prefaced with a history of episcopacy which is not a serious contribution to scholarship; but the lists reflected decent, laborious antiquarian research of its day. In 1743 William Richardson, master of Emmanuel College, Cambridge – who had originally settled in Cambridge to work on the book – published a revised edition. Richardson was not an original scholar of the calibre of Brady, and he owed much to some recent predecessors, notably Henry Wharton and John Le Neve, author of the *Fasti* of all cathedral clergy (1716).[21] He allowed too much of Godwin to stay in print. But he

---

[20] On British scholarship in this period, see Douglas 1951; Brooke 1985/1996, ch. 8; Fox 1956. On Wanley (below), see the bibliographical note in Gneuss 2001, p. 145 n. 1; Douglas 1951, ch. 5 is a helpful introduction.

[21] Le Neve's *Fasti* has been twice revised, most recently under the auspices of the Institute of Historical Research in London, by Joyce Horn, Diana Greenway and others. On Godwin and Richardson, see Brooke in Bendall *et al.* 1999, pp. 296–7 and n.

corrected him with great care and learning, so that the edition of 1743 remained for over a hundred years the source of precise information on episcopal chronology that Brady's books were for royal. Even when, in 1858, the young William Stubbs – later to be one of the creative figures in the Oxford history school – published his *Registrum Sacrum Anglicanum*, while revising with care the chronology of episcopal succession, Stubbs was often content to repeat Richardson's date for a bishop's death, which has commonly not been replaced in books of reference until the advent of the new Le Neve in recent times.

Rational argument and precision were at the heart of all the scientific advances of the seventeenth and eighteenth centuries. It was not all advance: the great age of historical scholarship of Brady and his immediate successors was followed by an age mainly of journeymen – and though Edward Gibbon in the 1770s and beyond might add much to historical literature, he added little to its scientific methods. Furthermore, there was plenty of room for incompetent and backward-looking scholars, as the list of those who fell before Richard Bentley's lance bears witness. Still, the modern scholar who takes the trouble to open the folios of this era is immediately aware of kinship: reason and precision govern these works as never before. Of the British scholars in this field, Robert Brady was one of the ablest, most brilliant, most precise.

If we ask, at the end of this survey, how many of his achievements Robert Brady owed to Cambridge – and how much he gave to Cambridge – there are no easy answers. His early medical training and his wide learning doubtless owed much to his early years in Caius and Cambridge; and he encountered notable Caius physicians – Francis Glisson, his predecessor in the Regius Chair, and Sir Charles Scarburgh, his colleague as a royal physician – in his medical career.[22] There were distinguished medievalists in Cambridge over the years when Brady was student and master: such were Abraham Whelock, who died in 1653, who had combined a precocious knowledge of oriental languages, especially Arabic and Persian, with pioneer work in Anglo-Saxon studies.[23] To a later generation belonged the scholar who first provided the learned world with a first-rate edition of Bede's *Ecclesiastical History*, John Smith – who, though a canon of Durham, was a frequent visitor in London and Cambridge, and the first serious student of the Moore Bede, one of two surviving copies written very shortly after the author's death in his own monastery at Monkwearmouth, then in the bishop of Ely's collection, soon to be one of the treasures of the Cambridge University

---

[22] Cf. Brooke 1985/1996, pp. 114–15, 126.   [23] *DNB*; Oates 1986, chs. 7–9.

Library.[24] But there is no evidence of direct contact between Brady and these scholars: his inspiration came rather from the Spelman family in Norfolk and the public records in London.

Even more tantalising is the difficulty of establishing his relation to the Cambridge historians and antiquaries of the next generation. We have spoken of Henry Wharton.[25] Some influence he must have felt from the master, but he never spoke of it in his writings. Similarly Jeremy Collier, a student in Caius from 1666 to 1676, and later a leading non-juror, wrote an *Ecclesiastical History*, a complement to Brady's political history of medieval England, and in its own way very influential in establishing current views of the Middle Ages in eighteenth-century England. But he again makes no mention of Brady, though his political as well as his historical interests strongly suggest some influence from the master. Brady was close to James II, but drew back at the Revolution of 1688–9, and was instrumental in saving his college and his colleagues from becoming non-jurors. Wharton was close to Archbishop Sancroft, most eminent of non-jurors, but stepped back from the brink just in time to make the oaths to the new regime and lose the confidence of Sancroft. Collier went steadily forward, ministering to a non-juring congregation in London, rising in 1713 to the non-juring episcopate. It is tantalising that we know so little of the links between these three notable scholars, united by their allegiance to Caius in the late seventeenth century.

Brady was born about 1627; Newton in 1642; Bentley in 1662. They came to Cambridge aged about 16, 18 and 14 respectively: Bentley's youth (by no means exceptional in that century) and Newton's age reflect a difference between a very positive and a reluctant family background. All alike came from moderately well-to-do homes and entered their colleges as sizars – an interesting commentary on the old-fashioned doctrine that sizars were socially deprived members of society – and rose to be scholars. Newton became a fellow of Trinity; Brady and Bentley were prevented by politics or college statutes from becoming fellows – Brady was a royalist in the age of puritan revolution, Bentley, one of the Yorkshiremen whose number in St John's was limited by statute – but they rose to be masters of Caius and of Trinity by royal mandate and royal appointment. There were many parallels in the careers of the three, and Bentley and Newton were friends. But it is hard to imagine three more different characters; and their personal qualities were vital to their achievements.

Of the three, Brady is the least well documented: we can discern a lively, brilliant, subtle, attractive personality, not above a slight devious

---

[24] See above, p. 58. On Smith, see Colgrave and Mynors 1969, p. lxxii.   [25] See above, pp. 489–90.

twist here and there when the politics of the 1690s demanded it. But we cannot meet him face to face as we can Newton and Bentley, two of the best documented among the giants of scholarship and science.

ISAAC NEWTON

Nature and Nature's laws lay hid in night:
God said, 'Let Newton be', and all was light.

It did not last: the Devil howling 'Ho!
Let Einstein be!' restored the status quo.

A mere historian, struggling amid the fearsome Latin of Newton's *Principia*, could be forgiven for suspecting that he would find himself more at home in *The Meaning of Relativity*: that he might even be tempted to reverse the roles of Pope's epitaph on Newton and J.C. Squire's addendum to it, and assign darkness to Newton and to Einstein, light. A brief acquaintance with Newton's work on alchemy and ancient chronology might lead him to approve J.M. Keynes' whimsical proposal: Newton 'was not the first of the age of reason. He was the last of the magicians, the last of the Babylonians and Sumerians.'[26] A magician he undoubtedly was. It cannot be reasonably questioned that Newton added a dimension to human understanding of the universe, and of the capacity of mind and mathematics to penetrate its mysteries. By brilliant intuition, by combining deep theoretical speculation with constant ingenious experiments, he added greatly to scientific knowledge and to the prestige of science. Furthermore, he was no narrow specialist. It was indeed partly the width of his interests which enabled him to see so deeply into many scientific problems old and new – to link the apple tree in his mother's garden (if such there was) with the movements of the stars and the planets; to include in the second edition of the *Principia* a Scholium explaining the relation of his scientific theories to the nature of God.

But he was not a rationalist, and in a great part of his work the age of reason, as ordinarily understood, is scarcely apparent. Reason as we naturally understand the term suffered a severe reverse in the seventeenth century. It has had no more fervent disciples in the history of thought than Aristotle and St Thomas Aquinas, both of whom attempted systematically to apply rational thinking and argument to every part of the cosmos and of human experience. But St Thomas was removed from the curriculum at the Reformation – though not from the libraries even of

[26] Quoted in Mandelbrote 2001, p. 141.

the most Protestant of learned divines – and Aristotle was dethroned by Descartes and other moderns in the mid and late seventeenth century.[27] In the early 1660s, Newton was still set to learn physics and metaphysics from the pages of Aristotle and his interpreters.[28] But he was soon to learn that Aristotle's views on the natural world and on physics were outmoded, and Aristotle played little part in his later thinking, deeply as he studied some ancient authors. He helped to accelerate a process which reached its peak in the early eighteenth century, when the *Advice to a Young Student* of Daniel Waterland, tutor and later master of Magdalene, a leading Whig but also the most distinguished defender of orthodox Anglican doctrine in the Cambridge of Newton's later years, wholly excluded Aristotle from his syllabus. In his place came Descartes and other moderns – and, for the fourth-year student, Newton's *Principia*.[29] Waterland had no use at all for Newton's theology, but revered him as a 'natural philosopher' – as we should say, as a mathematician, physicist and astronomer: he acknowledged the difficulty of understanding Newton, which was proverbial, but reckoned that no serious student should complete his course without some acquaintance with 'The Mathematical Foundations of Natural Philosophy', *Philosophiae Naturalis Principia Mathematica*. There were other tutors who thought differently, no doubt; and the independence of the colleges gave wide opportunity for differences of academic doctrine and practice. But Newton won early recognition in Cambridge in the 1660s and international recognition in the 1680s as one of the thinkers of genius of his age. Under Newton's guidance what might have been the age of reason, became the age (in Cambridge) of mathematics.

Newton was the son of a prosperous country squire in Lincolnshire, who however died before his son was born; the young Newton was brought up by his widowed mother, who hoped he would become a gentleman farmer like his father. Newton was not in the habit of throwing away his papers or his notebooks; and the result is that, like Archbishop Sancroft, he is documented almost to excess.[30] But that has not prevented the growth of legend; indeed, he evidently enjoyed fostering it himself. Three examples must suffice. He spent very little of his adult life with his mother at Woolsthorpe, save in the plague years 1666–7, when he had

---

[27] See below, pp. 513–15.   [28] Mandelbrote 2001, p. 15.   [29] See above, pp. 341–2.
[30] Mandelbrote 2001 catalogues an exhibition which gave an admirable idea of the range of the Archive, now scattered about the world, but much of it in Cambridge. A great part of it is garnered in Newton 1959–77, 1967–81 and 1978. Westfall 1980 is the standard biography (see n. 2 above). Gjertsen 1986 is a mine of useful information on a wide variety of Newtonian themes, the most accessible guide to scholarship on Newton; and I have given as many references to it as possible in consequence.

ample opportunity to meditate in her orchard. The descendants of the apple tree in his mother's garden at Woolsthorpe have been successfully grown elsewhere; and there is abundant evidence that he himself in later years told the tale that he first conceived the doctrine of gravitation from observing an apple fall from it 'perpendicularly to the ground'.[31] But it is reasonably certain that an early attempt to relate such a theory to the moon's orbit foundered because he lacked the essential information on the best current estimates when he was at Woolsthorpe.[32] He apparently did not return to the theme until the late 1670s.

The most distinguished mathematician and theologian among the fellows of Trinity in Newton's early years was Isaac Barrow, who rose to be master in 1673 – not long before his early death in his late forties in 1677, but long enough for him to launch the scheme for the new Trinity library. Naturally many legends arose about Newton's relations with Barrow, the most improbable of which are the story that Barrow examined him in Euclid in 1664 and found him wanting – and that in 1669 Barrow was so impressed by Newton's mathematical skills that he instantly resigned the Lucasian Chair so that Newton could succeed him in it.[33] It is characteristic of Newton legends that the former seems to go back to Newton himself, and the latter was undoubtedly derived from the Abbé Conti, an ambiguous source, since he was one of those friends of Newton who eventually fell out with him. In 1664, the date of the first story, it is in fact highly probable that Newton had made his acquaintance with Descartes' version of Euclid and learned to prefer his use of algebra to the purer geometry of Barrow's own edition. It is equally probable that he met Descartes' work first in Barrow's library, to which he evidently had ready access in the years which followed – until the days in 1677 when he arranged its disposal after the master's death.[34] That Barrow found Newton's precocious interest in Descartes matter for comment is not at all improbable; more certainly, Barrow observed with admiration the rapid progress of his very remarkable protégé soon turned colleague. 'It remains true . . . and without too much exaggeration', wrote Derek Gjertsen, 'that in a remarkably short period the twenty-four-year old student [we are in 1666–7] created modern mathematics, mechanics and optics.'[35] It is also true that there is not much direct evidence of contact

---

[31] Gjertsen 1986, pp. 29–31, conveniently summarises the evidence.   [32] *Ibid.*, p. 238.

[33] The evidence for the origins of these is laid out in *ibid.*, pp. 54–5.

[34] On Barrow's library see Feingold 1990, ch. 7, and on Newton's use of it, esp. pp. 336–8. The edition of 1659–61 of Descartes' *Geometria* is no. 317 in Barrow's library catalogue (*ibid.*, p. 349); Barrow's edition of Euclid (1656 edn) is no. 367 (p. 351).

[35] Gjertsen 1986, p. 24.

between Barrow and Newton: here the archives fail us, because they lived in the same college and had little occasion to put their discussions on paper. The fragments of positive evidence – and the overwhelming quantity of circumstantal evidence – leave no doubt that Barrow was Newton's patron, who helped him to his Trinity fellowship, to the Lucasian Chair (1669) and the dispensation of 1675 which enabled him to hold both without being ordained.[36] It is true that Newton rapidly surpassed the master; but that is not uncommon. One is reminded of the relationship between the pure mathematician G.H. Hardy and the self-taught Indian Ramanujan, whom he transported from Madras to Trinity in 1913–14, and who had of his own native genius mathematical insights beyond Hardy's own experience.[37] What is abundantly clear is that Isaac Barrow was a generous-minded man who saw the promise of the young Isaac Newton and fostered it. What is reasonably certain is that the immediate ground for Barrow's resignation from the Lucasian Chair of Mathematics in 1669 was his own wish to serve God, and his perception that 'he could not make a bible out of Euclid';[38] and that he helped Newton to the chair he had vacated. It may well be indeed that contemplation of the difference between his own talents and Newton's had helped to encourage him to hand on the Lucasian baton to Newton. Nor was the combination of mathematics and theology, so characteristic of Barrow, lost on Newton. Indeed, in some respects Newton even surpassed the master in theological studies, for Barrow's inventory reveals fourteen Bibles, while Newton had thirty.[39] But there was this difference: as in so many fields of enquiry, Newton pursued his own studies of the Bible, and came to his own eccentric conclusions. From it (in large measure) stemmed his strange chronological theories, in which good astronomy and bad history were to mingle in unequal proportions; and from it too came his conviction that the doctrine of the Trinity had no secure foundation in Scripture. In this he showed his independent critical faculty, and it led him to serious doubts as to whether he could seek ordination – essential if he was to preserve his fellowship and his chair. Barrow must have had some sympathy for his doubts, or at least a strong determination to keep Newton in Cambridge; and the outcome was a royal dispensation in 1675 from the statutes of the university and college.[40]

---

[36] On Barrow's influence on, and services to, Newton, see summaries in Gjertsen 1986, pp. 54–5; Feingold 1990, pp. 111–12, 148, 151, 336–8.
[37] Brooke 1993b, pp. 483–4 and refs.   [38] Quoted from *DNB* by Gjertsen 1986, p. 54.
[39] Feingold 1990, p. 344; Gjertsen 1986, pp. 69–70.
[40] Mandelbrote 2001, pp. 22–3 (with facsimile of the original letters patent of 27 April 1675 in the Cambridge University Archives).

The third legend is that Newton's creative work was all done when he was young: that his later years were entirely given over to administering the Mint and rehashing his early discoveries. There is no doubt that his most original work was done in Cambridge and in Trinity between the mid-1660s and the mid-1690s; and that he left Cambridge in large measure because a more active professional life of a different kind at the hub of the universe beckoned him to London. But in fact he never ceased work on one or other of his scientific projects; and new editions of the *Principia* appeared in 1713 and 1726 – largely the work of disciples and friends, but all containing something of Newton in them; new editions of *Opticks* with new propositions from his fertile mind continued to appear down to 1717;[41] and of his work on ancient chronology and biblical prophecy there was no end.

No one, least of all a historian who has no expertise in physics or astronomy, can summarise Newton's achievement, for it spread into almost every region of academic activity in his day, spreading light and darkness as it went. Among the earliest and most crucial of his studies was precisely the study of light. By brilliantly ingenious experiments with a variety of prisms and a minimum of other equipment, he greatly advanced knowledge of how light actually operates – of the spectrum, of the formation of white light, of the light shed from sun and stars. By even more brilliant mathematics he was able to interpret and systematise his discoveries. This first brought him fame and opposition: he wished his work to be known, and forged links with the Royal Society from the early 1670s on with this in view. But he found argument very trying, and in this and other fields he became a fierce and relentless controversialist. Meanwhile, Newton had affirmed, and reaffirmed, his conclusion that light was not carried on waves but formed of tiny particles. In this Newton was wrong, as was perceived by the best continental scientists of his day. But in England his doctrine held sway until the age of Thomas Young at the turn of the eighteenth and nineteenth centuries, who firmly established the wave theory – whether or not he conceived it by contemplation of ripples set up by swans swimming on the pond in the Fellows' Garden at Emmanuel, which play the role in the legendary history of Thomas Young of the apple tree in Newton's.[42]

But Newton will always be associated above all with the doctrine that gravity is a force universal to the sun and its planets, including the earth. Gravity in various forms had been studied long before; but it had been assumed, or argued, that it was a local phenomenon – at most, that every

---

[41] Gjertsen 1986, pp. 420–1, 475–7.   [42] See Bendall *et al.* 1999, p. 319.

planet had its own gravity. Descartes believed gravity to be the work of a small vortex between the moon and the earth, rotating with it. A similar view was held by Leibniz. Nearer to Newton was the theory of Robert Hooke, who sought in 1670 a universal explanation of gravity. Meanwhile, Newton himself was beginning to provide the links in a chain of reasoning and evidence which produced the mature doctrine of universal gravitation – as a mutual force in sun and earth and planets – by 1685. What Newton could not offer – to the contempt of Leibniz – were the causes of gravity: 'I frame no hypotheses', he grandly concluded, in a famous, and disingenuous, phrase. Newton has been vindicated in his belief in gravitation, though it has become wound up in a much more complex web of physics. But in his refusal to frame hypotheses, he was covering his tracks: his *Opticks* are full of them.[43]

If his advances in optics were the fruit of intensive experiment and deep mathematics, his understanding of gravity owed much to a wider spectrum of disciplines, including astronomy – and the search, which marks the greatest scholars and scientists, for simplicity at the heart of very complex data. In his studies of ancient chronology he widened the spectrum still further, to take in surviving sources for ancient history and Greek science, and ancient mythology: his book *The Chronology of Ancient Kingdoms Amended*, on which he was working from about 1680 till the very end of his life is a miracle of scholarship combined with perverse ingenuity. When he began, current chronological learning had placed the siege of Troy earlier than the founding of the Temple of Solomon. This was contrary to a firm assumption of Newton's, that Jewish civilisation was older than Greek. After much effort he was able to put the siege of Troy in its place by mobilising the following principles.

1. One can never rely on oral evidence: there is no history of Greece before 'Cadmus brought letters into Greece'; biblical history, written down from the time of Moses (as he believed), had a unique continuity.

2. That the king-lists which provided the basic data for the antiquity of the siege were misleading: they provided only three reigns to a century, when his own historical researches showed that on average five reigns fit a century. The siege of Troy came forward in a satisfactory degree.

3. That chronology could be determined by astronomical data; and here (naturally enough) Newton was a pioneer in a technique of dating which has seen notable advances in recent times. But he tried to carry historical sources giving information about eclipses, and, even more significantly, about the precession of the equinoxes, into a time when no such sources

---

[43] There is a useful summary on gravity in Gjertsen 1986, pp. 236–41.

could possibly exist. His 'reasoning was impeccable; his data unfortunately were highly questionable'.[44] The use of astronomy was highly rational; it was Newton's knowledge of ancient history which was at fault; and that was even more evident in his final, and most crucial principle.

4. That the heroes of epics and myths were real people. The constellations are not named after the heroes of the Trojan wars, but from Perseus and Andromeda and other characters related to the age of the Argonauts; thus ingeniously he dated them all within a short period of twenty or twenty-five years when the heroes of Greek myth were recently dead.

By manipulating these curious principles Newton was able to date Solomon's Temple to 1015 BC and the launching of the Argo to 937 BC. The whole work is a masterpiece of misplaced ingenuity; and it is strange to reflect that in Bentley, already master of Trinity before Newton completed his massive book, Newton had a friend who could in an instant have put his finger on the fallacies on which it was based. Thus it is notorious that – heroic as were the dimensions of Newton's interests, vital as was the width of his vision to his most original insights – his understanding of historical documents and of the Bible was very limited indeed. He was more of a specialist than he cared to believe.

These details – lightly as they scratch the surface of the immense landscape of Newton's achievement – are essential for us to have any grasp of the significance of his legacy. This was not all positive; nor was his reputation, great as was his fame in his own day. Newton was admired and worshipped and hated – the last two in about equal proportions – in his lifetime. The most famous of his controversies were those with Leibniz, which ranged from the question who first invented the calculus in mathematics to Newton's views on natural theology. International endeavours to make peace between them had showed little signs of success when the argument was stilled by the death of Leibniz in 1716. To this dispute the temperaments of the two parties contributed in fairly equal measures. In two of his other controversies, Newton was unlucky in his opponents: Robert Hooke was eccentric and provocative by nature, and the preposterous Astronomer Royal, John Flamsteed, as he grew older, developed something like a mania for scoring off Newton. At one point he told the Princess of Wales, the future Queen Caroline – who knew Newton and Leibniz personally and greatly admired both of them – that Newton was 'a great rascal', and that he had stolen two of Flamsteed's stars. The princess very reasonably greeted this 'with a fit of giggles'.[45]

---

[44] *Ibid.*, p. 114; cf. *ibid.*, pp. 112–15, 564–7.
[45] *Ibid.*, p. 97. For a summary of his disagreements with Hooke and Leibniz, see *ibid.*, pp. 257–61, 300–7.

Newton's disciples included theologians like Samuel Clarke, polymaths after his own mould like William Whiston, and men of culture and learning like the notable antiquary William Stukeley, one of the founders of the Society of Antiquaries, and Martin Folkes, the only man to have been president both of the Royal Society and of the Antiquaries. This brief list already indicates the wide range of early eighteenth-century learned and cultured society: his influence and his genius were acknowledged by men of every discipline and of none. The *Principia* was admired and the *Opticks* read throughout the learned world – though perhaps among the greatest scientists and mathematicians of the age the roles were reversed, for they undoubtedly studied the *Principia* closely and accepted the *Opticks* with reserve. His work enormously enhanced the prestige of mathematics and the natural sciences in Cambridge, and made Cambridge (for a time) the centre of the scientific world. What this meant in terms of syllabuses we have investigated elsewhere.[46] It undoubtedly enhanced the tendency in Cambridge to set these disciplines upon a pedestal, though Newton cannot be blamed for the cult of examinations which led in the mid-eighteenth century to the Senate House Examination and later to the Mathematical Tripos, absorbing a wholly disproportionate share in the time and energy and ambition of able students until the late nineteenth century.

But our final, and most significant question is: how much did Newton owe to Cambridge? The answer must be that Cambridge in the mid and late seventeenth century provided an ideal setting for an independent-minded student of brilliance and initiative, who none the less needed the resources of international science to help him on his way. To reduce the answer to its simplest terms, it offered Descartes and much else in the way of ancient and very modern mathematics; Newton found in Barrow a patron sufficiently learned and exceptionally sympathetic – a notable academic who lives in the monuments erected by two of his friends, the Wren Library and the works of Isaac Newton; and it gave him freedom to work and to think. The third was perhaps the greatest asset of all: freedom from the examinations which hampered later students, and from the trammels of modern syllabuses. Trinity was a society offering plentiful scope and variety of learning: but the syllabus, though a very elaborate affair and rich in variety, was flexible, and could readily be adapted to the needs and interests of a scholar of original mind. The age of Newton was a golden age in Cambridge for two reasons: because it was the era of Newton, and because he and many others had freedom to explore,

---

[46] See below, pp. 516–22; for what follows, see Searby 1997, pp. 158–63, 176–86.

as Wordsworth said of him: 'Voyaging through strange seas of Thought, alone'.[47]

I am aware of the limited truth in such statements: from the early 1670s he was corresponding with the Royal Society; in later years he presided over the Royal Society. His work came to depend on contacts in a far wider world than that of Cambridge. But so it must be in an academic society: Cambridge has only been a major intellectual centre when the world has come to visit it – and when its leading scholars have had contacts far and wide.

I am also aware of the paradox involved in such a claim. Newton's biographer, we recall, thought Cambridge was an intellectual wasteland.[48] But we have also investigated some of the reasons why he was mistaken; and in any case it is impossible so to regard the academic society which fostered first Brady, then Newton, and finally Bentley.

RICHARD BENTLEY

Richard Bentley was at St John's from 1676 to 1680, and then, after an interlude as a schoolmaster, became private tutor to one of the sons of Edward Stillingfleet, formerly fellow of St John's, from 1678 dean of St Paul's. We know little of his early education save that his mother taught him Latin and he went on via a village school and Wakefield Grammar School to Cambridge at a very early age. It is clear that at St John's he laid vital foundations in Latin and Greek and also in his wider interests, for he knew enough of theology and cosmology to give brilliant Boyle Lectures on natural religion in the 1690s, and enough mathematics and astronomy to read Newton's *Principia* seriously in 1691 and to edit the second edition of it in the 1710s.[49] But it was in the classics, and especially in Greek literature very widely interpreted, that he penetrated most deeply from an early age – compassing its first beginnings, its classical heyday, and much later Greek, from the Bible to a Byzantine chronicle of the eighth or ninth century. He also had some knowledge of Hebrew and Syriac, for the study of the Bible was always a central interest with him. Charles Brink credits him with being 'a devout Anglican'.[50] He was certainly an Anglican; he was archdeacon of Ely for over forty years (1701–42). But he was scarcely venerable, and the readiness with which he

---

[47] *Prelude* (1850 edn), iii, 63, quoted in Brooke, Highfield and Swaan 1988, p. 259.
[48] See above, p. 485.   [49] On Bentley and Newton, see Gjertsen 1986, pp. 60–1.
[50] Among the best modern guides to Bentley as a scholar is Brink 1986, chs. 2–4, with references to other literature. The classic biography, still unsurpassed, is Monk 1830; the most justly famous commentary is in Housman 1903/1937.

abandoned attendance at college chapel when the vice-chancellor's court deprived him of his degrees in 1718 does not suggest deep attachment, at least to the outer forms of religious observance.[51] Yet his interest in the New Testament especially, and in some of the fathers, and in late Greek literature as well as early, was a persistent theme, opening his eyes to many unusual sources of knowledge.

He owed something to personal influences. Clearly Stillingfleet himself was a highly cultivated and learned man, whose tendency to toleration in matters of religion influenced Bentley — even if it did not teach him tolerance towards the fools and knaves with which he believed the world, and especially Trinity College, to be mainly peopled. His tutorial charge went to Oxford, and his tutor with him: there Bentley met, among others, John Mill, principal of St Edmund Hall, who was amassing materials for the first serious attempt at an edition of the Greek New Testament by recording the readings of all available manuscripts.[52] But Stillingfleet's most notable service to Bentley — and scholarship — was the opportunity he was able to give him for extensive reading in exceptionally well-furnished libraries: in Stillingfleet's own and the Bodleian. From 1694 Bentley was Keeper of the King's Libraries, especially of the Royal Library in St James's Palace. In these places he read voraciously; and he remembered what he read, in spite of a specious claim that his memory was not of the best: almost every line in his scholarly writings proves the opposite.

John Mill was also engaged in a collaborative edition of the eighth- or ninth-century Byzantine chronicler Malelas, whose work would by now have been justly forgotten but for a promise Bentley made to Mill (during his sojourn in Oxford) to allow him to print some glosses on the chronicle. Bentley soon found that the text of Malelas was prodigiously dull; but Mill was relentless, and the fruit of Bentley's promise, quaintly called the *Epistola ad Millium*, is a fascinating medley of disjointed notes, revealing a whole spectrum of remarkable techniques for finding gold in a vein of lead. Newton aspired to be an alchemist; Bentley, in this sense, unquestionably was. Here he first revealed his very shrewd and sure feeling for history. Brady had developed his in the relative security of the public records. Bentley showed historical understanding while traversing farragos of myth and invention and (in the Phalaris affair) mere fraud. Brady's best work began in the eleventh century AD; Bentley could venture into the second millennium BC. The most notable novelty of his *Epistola* lay in his grasp of the history of sentiment. The editors of Malelas

---

[51] Monk 1830, pp. 494–6, 555–6 and 556 n.   [52] Mill 1707. On Mill and Bentley, see Fox 1954.

had been excited by its account of a lost play by Sophocles, ostensibly of the fifth century BC, which Bentley was able to show had been influenced by Christian writers. He was also able to throw new light on Euripides, by a dazzling display of learning on Greek verse metres and ancient botany.[53]

Bentley was exceptionally gifted, with an intuition to separate true from false, ancient from not quite so ancient. But this he could only acquire by deep and accurate learning. For choice he studied ancient authors where he could acquire a precise knowledge of the techniques they themselves had used. His devotion to Manilius – as that of Housman two hundred years after him – owed much to the fact that a deep knowledge of the intricacies of metre and an even deeper knowledge of ancient astronomy were essential foundations for a secure judgement on his text. Thus he acquired exceptional scholarly tools and a shrewd and sure judgement. But there were other elements in his make-up: like Newton, he was aware of his own talents; he loved to play with a text as on a musical instrument; his self-confidence was abounding, and his mind excessively ingenious. This came out most forcibly in his love of another great discipline, the law.

Meanwhile the *Epistola ad Millium* had been followed by his Boyle Lectures, *The Confutation of Atheism* in 1692 and by the *Dissertation upon the Epistles of Phalaris* in 1697. Like Malelas, Phalaris would long since have been forgotten had not Bentley aimed his lance at him. Phalaris was a tyrant of Agrigentum in the sixth century BC and was supposed the author of a collection of letters, in fact a much later forgery. Yet many believed in their authenticity, and a fine new edition appeared in 1695. Bentley's *Dissertation* attacked them on many grounds. There were anachronisms – several cities referred to were not founded till long after the days of Phalaris; Syracuse was credited with a coinage from a later age. He detected a hidden quotation from Euripides, ostensibly deployed well over a century before Euripides wrote the words. Equally remarkable is the display of philological learning: Bentley could show that the language was post-classical Attic, not pre-classical Sicilian. Most remarkable of all, perhaps, was his perception that the use of fundamental concepts, 'philosopher', 'tragedy' and others, revealed a much later cultural milieu.[54] Here is an intriguing contrast. Both Bentley and Newton were deeply learned in ancient, classical and biblical literature;

---

[53] Bentley 1691, summarised in Brink 1986, pp. 41–9, esp. pp. 45–6.
[54] Bentley 1697/1699 (2nd edn); Brink 1986, pp. 49–60.

and they were friends. But whereas Bentley's understanding of ancient history, literature and mythology has been triumphantly vindicated, and his judgement shown to be fundamentally sound – in spite of his wayward intellectual adventures – Newton's historical speculations have gone away on the wind, along with his studies of alchemy. On the other hand, Bentley only edited – could not conceivably have written – the *Principia*.

Bentley's historical sense remained important for his later work – important for his editions of Horace and Manilius, fundamental for his New Testament studies. The quality of sixteenth-century editions of the Greek New Testament lay in the beauty of their print, not in the value of their texts. The textual study of the New Testament started afresh in the seventeenth century, when the need for the study and comparison of the numerous surviving manuscripts came to be fully appreciated, and the presence in Cambridge (since the 1550s) of the Codex Bezae of *c.* 400 AD, in which Greek and Latin texts of the Gospels and Acts are set opposite one another, and in London (since the 1620s) of the Codex Alexandrinus, gave English scholars a special incentive for the work. John Mill laid the essential foundations by collecting material. Around these materials Bentley's fertile genius played, and he established one of the fundamental principles of New Testament criticism: the significance of agreement between the earliest known Greek and Latin witnesses to the text. In particular, he observed Greek texts which were quoted by Origen in the early third century in a form identical to those in the Latin Vulgate of the late fourth century; and reckoned by such means to establish the text of the New Testament as it had been at the time of the Council of Nicaea in 325 AD. Since the earliest codices are of the fourth century, that remained the most realistic ambition of textual critics until the discovery of numerous earlier papyrus fragments in the nineteenth and twentieth centuries. Bentley did much original work and inspired it in others; but the most he ever put into print was a *Proposal* or prospectus for a new edition of the Greek New Testament, issued in 1720, with two specimen pages. 'A New Testament text edited by Bentley', Stephen Neill coolly observed, 'would almost certainly have been brilliant, illuminating, and perverse. Yet, in the two specimen pages which he did produce, in spite of the limited materials at his disposal he set forth a text which is almost as correct as anything in the most modern editions.'[55]

---

[55] Neill and Wright 1988, p. 70. For an appreciation of Bentley's biblical scholarship by an eminent classical scholar, see Kenney 1974, pp. 100–1, 115.

In 1700 Bentley was translated to Cambridge by royal letters patent appointing him master of Trinity. For the next forty years he was to enchant a minority and infuriate the majority of the fellows of Trinity. He was diverted from the pursuit of pure scholarship by his ambitious – and in some ways inspired – plans to make Trinity a centre of educational reform and by the almost ceaseless litigation against his colleagues in the college and the university inspired by his tactless, arrogant, arbitrary and tyrannical conduct. In his litigation he was nearly always successful. This is perhaps a comment on the state of the law, which made possible the kind of piracy Bentley enjoyed performing in the courts; nor can the House of Lords be acquitted of giving Bentley and his adventures plenty of rope.[56] But that is not the whole truth. In his long-running dispute with Thomas Gooch, who as Tory vice-chancellor had deprived the Whig Bentley of his degrees for contumacy, the Court of King's Bench, in an epoch-making decision, determined that the manner of his condemnation in the vice-chancellor's court had been contrary to natural justice.[57]

In after days the masters of Caius used to show a hole in the panelling in their master's lodge which was alleged to have been made by a bullet fired by a supporter of Bentley. But the dispute had

> a happier epilogue. Both men were fond of children: Bentley made his son a member of the college at ten, a fellow at fifteen; Gooch was more modest, only admitting his sons at sixteen, and only making one of them a fellow, when he was twenty. Bentley's grandson recalls how 'Once, and only once, I recollect [my grandfather] giving me a gentle rebuke for making a most outrageous noise in the room over his library and disturbing him in his studies; I had no apprehension of anger from him, and confidently answered that I could not help it, as I had been at battledore and shuttlecock with Master Gooch, the bishop of Ely's son.'[58] 'And I have been at this sport with his father', he replied; 'but thine has been the more amusing game; so there's no harm done'.[59]

The fellows of Trinity indeed, when Bentley was nearing the end of his life, also felt that they could play a more peaceful game with the master, and offered a truce. But the old man could not dispense with strife, and shortly died.

---

[56] Monk 1830, p. 596; Brooke 1985/1996, p. 163.
[57] Monk 1830, pp. 494–6, 556n.; cf. Brooke 1985/1996, p. 166.
[58] Gooch was successively bishop of Bristol, Norwich and Ely – while remaining master of Caius (Brooke 1985/1996, pp. 163–70).
[59] Brooke 1985/1996, pp. 166–7, quoting Monk 1830, p. 650.

To come near to any assessment of Bentley's role in the history of the University of Cambridge, one has finally to grapple with three themes: his educational reforms in the college; the libraries which were the source of his learning and the means of preserving it and passing it to posterity; and the legacy of his inspired gifts as a textual critic.

Bentley lacked nothing in self-confidence. In his first two years as master, he took his turn as vice-chancellor, assumed office as archdeacon of Ely, and married Joanna Bernard – the start of a happy home life in the master's lodge in marked contrast to the strife of hall and combination room. He also embarked, without delay, on reforms intended to raise the standard of election to scholarships and fellowships.[60] Newton had recently left Cambridge for the Mint; and though still a fellow of Trinity, he was by now a rare visitor in Cambridge. But his legacy was the most obviously creative element in the academic life of Cambridge, and Bentley was determined to garner it for Trinity first and foremost. He planned to found a 'School of Natural Philosophy' to be a centre of scientific learning and to foster Newtonian science.[61] As a practical measure he established an observatory over the Great Gate of Trinity for Roger Cotes, a young protégé whom he had helped to establish as Plumian Professor of Astronomy, and William Whiston, Newton's closest disciple and successor as Lucasian Professor.[62] After Cotes' early death, he was succeeded by Robert Smith, one of Bentley's most faithful disciples and ultimately his successor as master. In similar fashion, Bentley provided the distinguished Italian chemist Giovanni Francesco Vigani with a laboratory in Trinity. Nor were his adventures confined to the natural sciences. A leading German orientalist, H. Sike, was encouraged to seek the Regius Chair of Hebrew and made a fellow of the college.[63] At a time when study and syllabuses were very much at the mercy of college initiatives, Bentley's programme was of great importance in making Cambridge a centre of academic distinction. What he gave with one hand, however, he took away with the other: he made Trinity a battleground and encouraged the mediocre majority among the fellows to pursue their own way regardless of him. But the legacy survived: Trinity retained much of its pre-eminence.

It is sufficiently evident, from all that has gone before, that Bentley's learning depended on access to a number of first-rate libraries. In early days he had enjoyed the run of Stillingfleet's and lorded it in the Royal Library in St James's Palace – in all the king's libraries indeed. When

---

[60] For this and what follows, see Brink 1986, pp. 30–3 and refs. on p. 202, esp. to Monk 1830.
[61] Brink 1986, p. 31; Monk 1830, p. 203.
[62] Brink 1986, p. 31; Monk 1830, pp. 229–30.   [63] Brink 1986, p. 32.

he returned to Cambridge, he could enjoy the magnificent new library which was Isaac Barrow's supreme legacy to the college, designed by his friend Christopher Wren. Doubtless one of the attractions of the master's lodge was the more ample space for his own books which it could offer, though one has to admit that both the charges levied against him by the fellowship for extravagance and chicanery, and his own defence, lay more emphasis on space and grandeur and wainscotting, to make the regal palace of the master of Trinity fit to receive its princely guests.[64] He must at least have had space for the Codex Bezae, which he had on loan for over five years from the University Library, and for the many books he borrowed from the library of his friend John Moore, the bishop of Ely – which was to become Cambridge's Royal Library, the richest treasure of the Cambridge University Library, after Moore's death.[65] Moore's main residence was at Ely House in London, the seat of his 'London library' – a phrase presumably implying he also kept books in his palace at Ely.[66] It is hardly surprising that there were plans afoot as soon as Moore died to attract the library to Cambridge – and rival plans to join his library to Harley's. But there is no evidence as to Bentley's involvement in these schemes; indeed there is no evidence at all as to what lay behind the offer Lord Townshend (a good King's man) was able to make on behalf of George I of the Royal Library to Cambridge in 1715.[67] Once the library was in Cambridge, Bentley was a leading member of the various syndicates which struggled to find it space – at first with little success; but gradually, as new rooms were fitted out and the Senate House built so that the Regent House and other parts of the Old Schools could provide shelter for the masses of books, the Royal Library was made accessible, a process only completed in the 1730s, with an epilogue in the 1750s when the east wing of the Old Schools was finally rebuilt.[68] No modern librarian would dream of allowing the Codex Bezae to pass into a private library for one day, let alone five years; but it is ironical to recall that during the five years in which it lay in the master's lodge at Trinity – during which Richard Bentley could contemplate Greek and Latin texts in apposition – it may well be that the science of New Testament textual criticism was born.

---

[64] Willis and Clark 1886/1988, II, pp. 614–16. On the Wren Library see esp. McKitterick 1995.

[65] Jayne Ringrose in Fox 1998, ch. 6; McKitterick 1986, pp. 71–3 (Bentley and Moore), 173 (Codex Bezae), and chs. 3–5 on the Royal Library. On the Codex Bezae see David Parker in Fox 1998, ch. 2.

[66] See McKitterick 1986, p. 151, for evidence that the books were at Ely House; *ibid.*, pp. 47–8 for a visit of Francis Burman with Bentley to Moore's 'London library'.

[67] *Ibid.*, pp. 147–50.   [68] *Ibid.*, pp. 153–66.

Bentley's love of fine books as a vehicle of scholarship had been illustrated even before his return to Cambridge in his plans to revive the Cambridge University Press.[69] His inspiration, persistence and rapacity ensured the successful production of many beautifully printed books, and the avarice and rapacity of which the Trinity fellows so often complained ensured a modest but adequate financial success. Yet it was ungrateful and disingenuous in Newton – or perhaps merely whimsical – to say, when asked why he had allowed Bentley to handle the second edition of the *Principia*: 'Why, he was covetous, and I let him do it to get money.'[70]

Bentley's fame in later centuries, however, rests firmly on his work as a textual critic. In two respects one may reckon his legacy had harmful consequences. His mode of textual criticism depends on a combination of learning and imagination and sheer intellectual brilliance rarely found among mortals; and in lesser hands it has often turned gold back into lead. His bold statement that better, and more secure, results come from conjecture than from manuscripts[71] encouraged ingenious minds to ignore the need to study manuscript texts – which was far from Bentley's own practice. Good textual criticism remains a fairly esoteric mystery. But Bentley is hardly to be blamed if his work has often fallen into the hands of journeymen; and it has not always been so. Jeremiah Markland among his younger contemporaries showed something of the flair one would expect from a disciple of Bentley; and in much more recent times he has found worthy successors in A.E. Housman and D.R. Shackleton Bailey and others.[72] But there has also been a backlash. Bentley's arrogance led some scholars to attack his findings and his manner of work, just as Housman was later to be accused (not altogether unjustly) of frightening would-be classicists away into safer fields of enterpise. An early example of Bentley's negative influence was Richard Dawes of Emmanuel, whose fine critical faculty was perverted by an urgent desire to score off Bentley after his death.[73] Nor did Bentley's influence inspire English scholars to the kind of systematic study of grammar and metre which seems now clearly to be the next step from Bentley's inspired pioneering advances. That was to be undertaken by German scholars in the nineteenth century. Yet his books remained to inspire scholars of later generations. It is not chance that Manilius – who has few readers outside

---

[69] See above, n. 3.   [70] Gjertsen 1986, p. 61.

[71] Brink 1986, p. 66, from Bentley 1711, Praefatio ad Lectorem.

[72] Brink 1986, pp. 84–9 (Monkland), and ch. 9 (Housman). For Shackleton Bailey see Bailey 1956 and 1960, the latter leading to his great edition of Cicero's *Letters ad Atticum* (1965–70).

[73] Brink 1986, pp. 89–92.

a small circle of experts – inspired both the most remarkable work of Bentley's later years and the book on which Housman's fame as a textual critic[74] is securely based: the manuscripts are bad, and the critic needs, above all, knowledge of Greek astronomy and Latin metre and critical flair. Furthermore, Bentley made England and Cambridge names to be reckoned with in international classical scholarship – and the Cambridge of Newton and Bentley was never again to stand so high in the academic spectrum of the learned world until Ernest Rutherford returned there in 1919.

[74] And as a writer of vitriolic English prose: Housman 1903/1937; cf. Brooke 1993b, pp. 211–16.

Chapter 15

THE SYLLABUS, RELIGION AND POLITICS 1660–1750

THE SYLLABUS

The Cambridge arts syllabus in the mid and late seventeenth century has often been abused as medieval, conservative, tied to the apron strings of Aristotle. A kindlier breeze, inspired by Mordechai Feingold, John Gascoigne and others, has found parts at least of the university more receptive – one might say, much more receptive – of new ideas and new philosophies than some had supposed. If the Cambridge into which the young Isaac Newton came in the early 1660s had been quite so hidebound as the 'intellectual wasteland' of his modern biographer's fancy he would hardly have stayed a year in Trinity, let alone thirty-five.[1] Between the Restoration and the mid-eighteenth century there scarcely was such a thing as an undergraduate syllabus, in the senses in which we use the term. The statutes of 1570 say: 'the first year will teach rhetoric, the second and third dialectic; the fourth adds philosophy', and prescribes lectures and disputations. That is all.[2] The statutes have a little more to say about the activities of BAs and MAs, and rather less about the five-year courses for bachelors of theology, law and medicine; less still for the doctorates: 'After such a mighty labour and such dangers and examinings [the statute on doctors of theology concedes] we would not impose more labour on the doctors than they of their own free will wish to undertake – save that once in the year of receiving the degree they propound a question in the public schools whose ambiguities and difficulties – while they make clear both sides of the issue – they will define and determine', under penalty of 40 shillings to be paid to the university.

The vagueness of the statutes allowed considerable freedom of movement and choice, kept in check by the force of tradition, the framework of university lectures and the need to prepare for the compulsory

---

[1] Westfall 1975, p. 194; cf. Gascoigne 1989, p. 6.
[2] *Cambridge Documents 1852*, I, p. 459 no. 3. For what follows see *ibid.*, I, pp. 460–2, cc. 10–18, esp. c. 11 on theology. For the informal syllabus for 'aristocratic' students, see above, pp. 131–46.

disputations. The force of tradition ensured a very wide-ranging group of studies. This was undoubtedly medieval in concept; and that ensured that the students were prevented from narrow specialisation and taught above all to think and argue – taught the nature and uses of reason. I emphasise this because a hoary tradition associates medieval scholasticism with superstition and unreason; and historians of science still tend to associate it with a blind acceptance of the teaching of Aristotle. But there are two sides to Aristotle: the Aristotle of the logical treatises and Aristotelean natural science. The first is a profoundly rational system, and whatever one may think of its logical and philosophical validity, had ensured a deep faith in the possibilities of human reason. So much was this so that, notoriously, Aristotle is as important as the Bible in understanding late medieval treatises on systematic theology. None the less, we would readily agree that the dosage of Aristotle in a statute of the late fourteenth century was excessive.[3] It provided for something of the Philosopher for every year of the four-year arts course, and a particularly heavy dose in the second and third. Another statute of much the same period added two short contemporary textbooks on logic. It is clear that in this period Aristotelean logic was the heart of the system. But it was part of a much wider frame which helped to ensure that the Cambridge undergraduate was offered a wide spectrum of disciplines from the thirteenth to the eighteenth century – though what most of them made of the offering we cannot tell.

The arts course in medieval universities traditionally comprised the *trivium* of grammar, rhetoric and logic followed by the *quadrivium* of the 'mathematical arts' of arithmetic, music, geometry and astronomy.[4] The latter played a relatively minor part in the Cambridge syllabus of the late middle ages – but they were there; they were recognised as part of the arts degree; they were capable of development if fashion changed. Meanwhile it seems to have been assumed that the undergraduate had acquired in his grammar school the basic knowledge of Latin and how to speak it; rhetoric was relatively underdeveloped territory compared with logic – the emphasis was on the nature of argument rather than on its formal presentation in elegant Latin. The new learning of the Renaissance changed this – changed, not the framework, which remained intact, but the balance of its content. In 1488 three salaried lectureships were established, in 'the books of *humanitas*', logic and 'philosophy', that is in the subjects of the *trivium*.[5] The holder of the first came to be known

---

[3] Hackett 1970, pp. 397–9; Leader 1988, p. 93.
[4] Leader 1988, ch. 5, esp. p. 139 for 'artes mathematicales'.   [5] *Ibid.* p. 118 and n. 39.

as the 'Terence' lecturer, for the Latin comic playwright was to remain for several centuries the favourite entry into ways of talking idiomatic classical Latin. In the course of the sixteenth and seventeenth centuries rhetoric tended to take the place of logic as the principal theme of the *trivium*, the core of undergraduate studies; Cicero and Quintilian found a substantial place in libraries and lectures. And the arts course provided an umbrella for the study of Greek. Few men played a more crucial part in the development of humanist studies – and the preservation of collegiate Cambridge – than John Cheke of St John's and his pupil Roger Ascham, tutor respectively to Edward VI and Elizabeth I, and among the earliest Regius Professors of Greek. In a moment of high enthusiasm in 1542, Ascham described how 'Aristotle and Plato . . . are now heard by the boys in the original. Herodotus, Thucydides, Xenophon are read more than Cicero and Terence.'[6] Possibly so; but Cicero and Terence and Latin rhetoric remained at the heart of the syllabus.

None the less, as we have seen, none of these characters plays any role in the statutes of 1570, in contrast to their medieval predecessors. In part this is of the nature of university and college statutes: they rarely tell one either what actually happened or even what was meant to happen. In this case the statute-makers hoped to create a set of statutes which would last: as we saw at length in chapter 3, they attempted to enhance the authority of a small oligarchy of heads, and diminish the opportunities for mischief of the democracy of the young, of the regent and non-regent masters. Nothing in the regulations of a university is more likely to require amendment than a statute or ordinance prescribing the set books in a syllabus. So they were omitted in 1570, and the relevant statutes lasted, unamended, until the 1850s.

The sixteenth century saw several reformations, in literary studies, in philosophy, in science as well as in religion. In recent commentaries much has been made of Ramus and the Ramists, who attempted to un- seat Aristotle and provide shorter cuts to the logic required in theological dispute than had Aristotle, the Greek agnostic. But we do well to listen to Feingold on Ramus. 'The sweeping reform promised by Petrus Ramus [in the third quarter of the sixteenth century] – which was enthusias- tically embraced by many Protestants following Ramus's martyrdom at the St Bartholomew Day Massacre [in 1572] – was little more than a reckless iconoclastic critique of Aristotle and an irresponsible attempt to reorder the disciplines.'[7] Ramus had none the less had many followers in

---

[6] *Ibid.*, p. 342 and refs.; above, pp. 6–7.
[7] Feingold 1990, p. 13. For what follows, see Collinson in Bendall *et al.*1999, p. 76 and n. 30.

Cambridge, and the vice-chancellor's court, attempting to quell a riot at the turn of the century, had been forced to declare: 'Albeyt wee of the universitye for Philosophye matters have preferred Aristotle, yet Ramus is not to be abused with reprochefull words.'

Feingold was commenting on a critical reference to Ramus in the 'Rules' composed by the celebrated Cambridge tutor James Duport in the mid-seventeenth century – which has been taken as an example of Duport's supposedly obscurantist refusal to accept modern philosophy and mathematics in preference to Aristotle.[8] But Feingold shows that Duport's concern was to preserve the central place of liberal studies in a broad sense of the term. He was quite aware that Aristotle's scientific authority had been seriously challenged, but that in logic Aristotle – studied in Greek – was still a vital authority.[9]

A part of the evidence for Duport's view of Aristotle comes from his manual for the use of his students, one of a series of such manuals from the seventeenth and early eighteenth centuries which are perhaps the best evidence we have of the nature of student studies in this period.[10] Doubtless what a tutor imagined his students might study and what they actually accomplished were not the same; and the manuals were aimed 'mainly to instruct the student in matters of religion, morals and academic conduct . . . not to stipulate rigidly which philosophical systems to follow or authorities to obey': thus Feingold on Duport.[11] Duport offered his students his own philosophy of education and his own tastes: mathematics and science he left to other tutors. He was allowed to combine the roles of college tutor and Regius Professor of Greek, until ejected from the chair in 1654 as a palpable royalist, but he remained a leading tutor until his promotion to be master of Magdalene in 1668. In religion he was remarkably moderate, an Anglican who commended to his pupils not only Bible reading (preferably in Hebrew and Greek) but the works of puritan divines balanced by the poetry of the high church ex-fellow of Trinity, George Herbert.[12] His own interests lay primarily in language and literature, and rhetoric and poetry meant more to him than logic – great as was his respect for Aristotelean logic. 'Duport made use of the Trinity College fountain as a metaphor for his lifelong devotion to the classics, particularly his passion for Greek poetry. Although he extolled the pure fountain of Aristotle, in the depth of which "truth" shines, his real subject was not Aristotelean philosophy, but rhetoric and poetry,

---

[8] For what follows, see Feingold 1990, pp. 10–15. [9] *Ibid.*, p. 13.
[10] For Waterland's *Advice*, see above, pp. 338–42. [11] Feingold 1990, p. 13.
[12] Duffy in Cunich *et al.* 1994, p. 148.

Cicero and Livy, and the greatness of the Athenian and Roman heritage.'[13] He is still remembered as an enthusiastic commentator on Homer.[14] Duport was not an obscure figure on the periphery of the Cambridge scene, but a leading Trinity tutor for over twenty years whose students numbered 180 or so.[15] His 'Rules' show clearly that in his eyes the *trivium* was still supreme, that literature and rhetoric – and poetry – were the basis of his theory and practice of education. Yet his most famous pupil was Isaac Barrow, who was to be the first Lucasian Professor of Mathematics and the patron of Isaac Newton. Duport's influence remained a vital part of Barrow's very broad academic interests; but at the same time Duport had not prevented Barrow studying mathematics and reading Descartes, under advice from other tutors.

A little earlier, perhaps in the 1630s, Richard Holdsworth had composed his 'Directions' for his students in St John's – and carried the 'Directions' with him when he became master of Emmanuel in 1637. They were still being copied there in the early eighteenth century.[16] At first sight there is much in common with Duport's scheme. Both are concerned for the good life – Holdsworth is full of advice against wasting time in the evening and not getting up early in the morning. He shows the same concern to teach rhetoric, instructing his students to advance by way of 'a plain, easy and familiar' style through something 'more raised and polished' to adorning their university acts with 'quaint and handsome expressions'.[17] He tried to ensure that 'poetry, classical oratory and history' shall be studied every afternoon. But the morning is devoted to logic and philosophy, which included an element of the quadrivial sciences; and although Holdsworth's library reveals that he himself had little interest in mathematics, he had an immense collection of late medieval and early modern commentaries on Aristotle and a respectable sprinkling of recent science.[18] Aristotle seems to have lost little of his authority in Holdsworth's scheme. We can indeed see the decline and fall of Aristotle in the 'Directions' of Holdsworth of the 1630s, the 'Rules' of Duport of the mid-seventeenth century and the 'Advice' of Waterland of the early eighteenth century. In Holdsworth Aristotle still dominates the morning study; the main qualification to his dominion is that rhetoric and literature fill the afternoons and were clearly of great importance to Holdsworth. This is even more the case with Duport, who seems almost aware of fighting a rearguard action to preserve some at least of Aristotle. In Waterland's 'Advice' he is nowhere to be found.[19]

[13] Feingold 1990, p. 12.   [14] *Ibid.*, p. 147; Monk 1826.   [15] Feingold 1990, pp. 10–11.
[16] Collinson in Bendall *et al.* 1999, p. 75.   [17] *Ibid.*, p. 74.   [18] Oates 1986, pp. 328–9.
[19] For Waterland, see above, pp. 334, 338–42.

If mathematics were of little interest to Holdsworth, that was not the universal view of Cambridge tutors and students of his time. John Aubrey tells the story of Thomas Batchcroft, the moderate puritan master of Caius, visiting his students' chambers and finding the young Charles Scarburgh reading a commentary on Euclid by the eminent German Jesuit mathematician Christopher Clavius (1537–1612) – best known today as the author of the Gregorian calendar – 'Clavius upon Euclid'. 'The old Dr. had found in the title ". . . e Societate Jesu", and was much scandalised at it. Said he, "By all means leave off this author, and read Protestant mathematical books."'[20] We may doubt if the young Scarburgh was inclined by Clavius to the Roman faith; but it is curious to recall that in 1688 Sir Charles Scarburgh and Robert Brady (Batchcroft's successor as master of Caius) were to meet, as royal physicians, at the queen's bedside for the birth of the Old Pretender.

Stories such as this – of the young Scarburgh deep in Clavius in the 1630s – illustrate a major theme in mid-seventeenth-century Cambridge. Cambridge benefactors had been relatively slow to pursue the example of Sir Henry Savile at Oxford, who founded chairs of geometry and astronomy early in the century. But the researches of Feingold have unearthed a series of lecturers and a group of libraries which clearly indicate a strong interest in mathematics particularly, and help to explain the background of the most notable Cambridge mathematician of the generation before the rise of Newton, Isaac Barrow.[21] Especially significant (it seems) were the lectures of one of the Cambridge Platonists, John Smith of Queens', from 1648 on, which are probably the first indication of the serious study of Descartes' *Geometry* in Cambridge.[22] We have no means of knowing how widespread interest in Descartes and other apostles of the new mathematics was among the tutors and students of mid-seventeenth-century Cambridge; but we know they had access to the literature of the subject, and its spirit was sufficiently abroad to alarm some conservative scholars. Needless to say, Descartes came among them in two guises: as a philosopher whom some supposed to be spreading ideas conducive to atheism; and as a mathematician who had attempted to rewrite Euclid. As a student in the late 1640s and early 1650s Barrow himself could find both within and without Trinity, his own college, opportunities for advanced study of mathematics. These he himself was greatly to enhance when he became first Lucasian Professor of Mathematics in 1663. Euclid was only

[20] Aubrey 1898, I, pp. 94–5; quoted Brooke 1985/1996, p. 126 (also for what follows).
[21] Feingold 1984, esp. pp. 52, 156–7; 1990, esp. pp. 18–20.
[22] *Ibid.*, pp. 19–20; for Smith's library, see Saveson 1958.

a part of Barrow's mathematics; but it was a significant part. When he died in 1677 his library contained his own Euclid of 1656 and Clavius' of 1612; it also contained six volumes of Descartes, including the crucial edition of 1659–61 of his *Geometria*, which pointed the path away from Euclid which Newton and others were to tread, and may have passed into Newton's own hands.[23] Barrow's library also included his own study of optics and a number of other scientific works as well as a broad range of classical, biblical, patristic and other theological works. It is evident that it was freely available to his pupils and disciples and friends, especially in Trinity; and its catalogue is the best evidence of the congenial environment Barrow provided for Newton: even if Barrow was not Newton's tutor, his library was.[24] And symbolic of Barrow's interests and influence is the great monument he planned, but did not live to see completed: the Wren Library at Trinity.[25]

Thus Cambridge was open in the mid and late seventeenth century to the scientific and especially the mathematical winds which blew from many parts of western Europe. Their actual effect we must not exaggerate. 'There was . . . less interest in Cambridge in the new science than at Oxford', wrote John Gascoigne of the Restoration period. 'Thus an attempt to found an equivalent to the Oxford Philosophical Society at Cambridge in 1685 foundered (as Newton reported) because of "the want of persons willing to try experiments". Hans' analysis of the careers of 680 scientists from 1660 to 1785 shows that Oxford consistently produced more scientists than Cambridge until the 1690s. As Frank points out, on the basis of Hans' figures, in the cohort educated at Oxford in the period 1660–88 there were four times as many future scientists as at Cambridge, while in the first three decades of the eighteenth century, by contrast, there were twice as many future scientists at Cambridge as at Oxford. Cambridge's rather tepid interest in the experimental sciences is reflected in the university's tenuous involvement with the Royal Society. Of the 443 members elected between 1660 and 1688 only seventy-six (16%) were Cambridge graduates, and of these thirty-two (42%) were physicians, most of whom had left Cambridge after graduation. In the same period a mere twenty fellows of the Royal Society held fellowships at Cambridge and, apart from the work of Newton and – to compare great things with small – that of Newton's young friends Edward Paget and Francis Aston (both fellows of Trinity) who were active in the institutional

---

[23] Feingold 1990, p. 349 (items 317, in 2 vols., and 318–21); cf. p. 351. For what follows, see *ibid.*, pp. 333–72.
[24] Cf. above, pp. 496–7.   [25] See above, p. 54.

life of the Society, Cambridge contributed little to the Society in this period.'[26]

None the less, after 1690, and still more in the first half of the eighteenth century, 'nature and nature's laws' became of prime importance to the leading academics, and above all to the tutors, of Cambridge. The old disputations and other acts and exercises survived until 1839; but long before that they had been overtaken by an examination – first oral, then partly written, and finally (from the mid-eighteenth century) the fully fledged Senate House Examination which was to grow into the Mathematical Tripos. For already, as the early eighteenth century advanced, the content of the exam was becoming increasingly mathematical. The tutors remained (so far as we can tell) as much wedded to the classical foundations of their pupils' education as ever; but they came increasingly to look beyond the foundation, for the more promising of them, to a higher flight in maths. In the end there was a curious reversal of fortune. In earlier days classics had come first; mathematics, the quadrivial disciplines, followed. But when at last, in 1824, the Classical Tripos found a place beside the Mathematical, for a time it could only be attempted by those who had already taken the Maths Tripos.[27] The old disputations had continued to the end of our period and beyond to ensure that ambitious candidates were still able to hold forth in presentable, and preferably eloquent, Latin – even though from about 1750 the Examination came to be conducted in English.

The history of the Examination is both fascinating and obscure. It grew out of tests which down to about 1700 were less important than the acts and disputations: it helped to sort the sheep from the goats, but the 'Order of Seniority', *Ordo Senioritatis*, which had set all the candidates for the BA into a kind of order since the late fifteenth century, presumably reflected the examiners' reactions to their performance in the disputations. I say presumably, for very little is known about how the Order was arrived at, and it is likely that the examiners, and even more the proctors, had some influence in enhancing the position of their own tutorial pupils. However that may be, it seems certain that the gradual remodelling of the whole exam system, so that by 1750 the Examination was of first consequence, the disputations increasingly formal, was not the product of formal decisions by university bodies. Rather the examiners themselves, step by step, modified the exam and the method of recording it. In 1747–8 the

---

[26] Gascoigne 1989, p. 58, citing Newton 1959–77, II, p. 415; Hans 1951, pp. 32–3; Frank 1973, p. 240; Hunter 1982 cf. Hunter 1981.

[27] On all this and what follows, see Searby 1997, pp. 147–86 and refs., esp. to Gascoigne 1984.

results were printed for the first time – and so 1748 has become the tra-
ditonal date assigned for the foundation of the Maths Tripos. From 1753
'the merit or honours group [were divided] into three classes instead of
two – the wranglers, and the senior and junior optimes'.[28] In the historical process which led to the modern tyranny of exams and syllabuses
these were momentous events. Since many of the examiners were also
college tutors, we may probably see here a spontaneous development by
agreement – not necessarily or in any likelihood among all – but among
a powerful group of college tutors. Ironically, they had found a way to
surrender that freedom of choice and movement which was so conspicuous a feature of the tutorial initiative as represented in the programmes
of study of Holdsworth, Duport and Waterland. If one had to attempt an
answer to the question of when the medieval liberal arts, the *trivium* and
the *quadrivium*, ceased to rule in the Cambridge Arts School, the answer
seems to be, about 1750. That they lasted so long is a measure not of the
blind conservatism of the Cambridge tutors, but of the enlightenment of
their medieval predecessors.

No one doubts that this development reflects in large measure the
growing prestige in Cambridge of Newtonian mathematics and Newtonian science in general. But it seems that we can go further, and deduce
from the nature of the change – which was not in any visible way dictated
by government or heads or by votes of the regents – that the study of the
new mathematics had taken hold in many or most of the colleges by the
time the process was complete.

John Gascoigne has investigated in meticulous detail such positive evidence as can be found for the reception of Newton in the colleges.
Naturally, the first and principal centre of Newton's fame in Cambridge
was in his own college, Trinity. Although Newton himself seems to have
had relatively few pupils, and left Cambridge in the late 1690s, the influence of his work there was greatly enhanced by the arrival of Richard
Bentley as master in 1700. Bentley was not only a friend and admirer
of Newton; he had already, before his return to Cambridge, been very
active in propagating some of the doctrines of the *Principia* in his Boyle
lectures on natural religion in the early 1690s. Although Bentley's own
expertise lay primarily in the classics and theology – especially in the critical and historical study of classical authors and of the New Testament –
he was very much concerned to preserve and enhance the reputation of
Trinity as a centre of Newtonian science. He provided William Whiston
of Clare, Newton's closest disciple, with rooms in Trinity to conduct

[28] Searby 1997, pp. 158–9.

his scientific work and the first-known college laboratory for the Italian Professor of Chemistry G.F. Vigani. He rode roughshod over the plans of the Astronomer Royal, John Flamsteed, for the disposal of the endowment of Thomas Plume, setting up Plume's observatory in the college and seeing to the appointment of his brilliant protégé Roger Cotes as first Plumian Professor. Together Bentley and Cotes set to work to prepare the second edition of Newton's *Principia*, Cotes providing the scientific expertise, Bentley the driving force; and Newton himself took the credit.[29] Yet 'Cotes's preface to the second edition of the *Principia* was one of the most influential documents in popularising Newton's work both in England and on the Continent.'[30] Nor was he the only distinguished disciple of Newton in Trinity: among others Robert Smith, a cousin and close friend of Cotes, was to succeed him as Plumian Professor and to succeed Bentley as master of Trinity, where he reigned till 1768.

When Gascoigne turns to look for signs of Newtonian influence in other colleges, he finds it first in Caius. In 1694 Samuel Clarke, later to be celebrated as a disciple of Newton, a notable heretic and a popular London preacher, based an undergraduate exercise in the schools on a proposition in Newton's *Principia*. Gascoigne points out that Clarke's tutor, John Ellys, was a close friend of Newton. Ellys was a layman, a medical fellow of Caius, whose whole life was dedicated to the college, as tutor and master; his career ended in extreme old age in sad conflicts with the fellows which won him the title 'the devil of Caius'. But in his earlier career he had been a conscientious and much-respected tutor and one of the closest colleagues of the master, Robert Brady, physician and medieval historian. As such, we may probably assume that in politics Ellys was a Tory; as a layman he was not involved in religious controversies, and there is no reason to suppose that he was interested in Newton's or Clarke's Arianism. All that is certain is that he was a proponent of the new scientific methods: he set Clarke to translating Rohault's *Physica*, a textbook of Cartesian natural philosophy, and introduced Clarke – and doubtless others – to the works of Newton.[31]

The most devoted of all Newton's disciples was William Whiston, who was later to promulgate Newton's theology as well as his physics; and by

---

[29] Gascoigne 1989, pp. 149–51. Gascoigne seems to suggest that Newton prevented Bentley himself from being editor of the second edition. But it seems doubtful if Bentley had ever intended to be more than entrepreneur (cf. Mandelbrote 2001, p. 124) – and in the event he amended Newton's Latin here and there. Newton's own preface makes no mention of Cotes.

[30] Gascoigne 1989, p. 151.

[31] *Ibid.*, pp. 142–3; Brooke 1985/1996, pp. 154, 159–60; Venn 1897–1901, III, pp. 110–14. Ellys was also vice-chancellor in 1704–5, and was knighted by Queen Anne during a royal visit to Cambridge.

his own account he was first inspired to study the *Principia* by reading a paper by the Edinburgh professor David Gregory, who in 1691 became Savilian Professor in Oxford, carrying Newton's fame with him at a time when the prophet had relatively little honour in his own land. Whiston read Gregory's paper in or soon after 1691, when Whiston was a fellow of Clare; and only in 1694 did he come to know Newton personally, though they lived within 200 yards of one another.[32] Whiston and other fellows of Clare thus came to teach Newton's works in Clare, though with Bentley's help Whiston also taught in Trinity.[33]

The celebrated physician and antiquary William Stukeley provides in his diary of his Corpus career (1704–8) remarkable evidence of the spread of Newtonian influences in Corpus, especially by Cotes' friend Robert Danny, who taught him 'arithmetic, algebra, geometry, philosophy, astronomy, trigonometry' with the help of many advanced scientific textbooks and 'all Newtons and Boyles works'. Stukeley's tutor, Thomas Fawcett, taught him the humanities, including theology, but encouraged the young man's scientific interests and provided a room for his experiments.[34]

Some of the most impressive evidence of Newtonian influence from the opening decades of the eighteenth century comes from Magdalene, especially (as we have seen) in the *Advice* of Daniel Waterland, a leading orthodox theologian and a very active tutor, later master of Magdalene.[35] Waterland's book was written for his own pupils about 1706 and printed in editions of 1730 and 1740. Undergraduates are offered Newton in the guise of textbooks by Gregory, Whiston and Clarke, and in their fourth year, the *Principia* itself. From the 1730s Gascoigne adduces two other student guides to natural philosophy from Magdalene: Thomas Johnson, who showed students how to use Newton in disputations, and John Rowning, who produced a popular *Compendious System of Natural Philosophy* in 1735.[36]

The other colleges whose tutors are known to have lectured on Newton or published introductions to Newtonian physics were St John's and Emmanuel. In St John's two of the leading tutors of the mid-century, William Powell, later master and a noted educational reformer – whose ideas of reform, however, did not include any diminution of the independent role of college tutors in determining the syllabuses of their students – and Thomas Rutherforth both published systematic expositions for serious students in the late 1740s. In Emmanuel, Gervase Holmes is known

---

[32] Gascoigne 1989, pp. 144–5.   [33] *Ibid.*, pp. 151–3.   [34] *Ibid.*, pp. 159–60.
[35] See above, pp. 338–42.   [36] Gascoigne 1989, p. 178.

to have given lectures on similar themes, and the best-known Emmanuel tutor of the mid-eighteenth century, Henry Hubbard, gave 'lectures on Newtonian optics, mechanics and astronomy'.[37] Hubbard was the leading mathematician in Emmanuel, holding the 'Algebra Lectureship' for over twenty years; but he was also a leading Tory in one of the most persistently Tory colleges of the century, a powerful defender of the Anglican establishment and a popular, sociable man and university registrary.[38] Gascoigne shows an interesting web of links between the early proponents of Newtonian physics and cosmogony, the Latitudinarian divines and the early Whigs. He admits that there are exceptions to this pattern; and we do well to recall that Tory Caius came very early in our list of colleges (even though partly as the first home of Samuel Clarke, later an energetic Whig), and we can observe that when Henry Hubbard is lecturing on Newton in Emmanuel, Newton has become established in the heart of the Tory world. By such means we can glimpse the extraordinary revolution in tutorial teaching in Cambridge which lay behind the apotheosis of the Mathematical Tripos in the generations which followed 1750. Gascoigne cites evidence to show that some in Cambridge in the 1690s reckoned Newton hopelessly obscure – and much of the *Principia*, especially in its original Latin dress, is notoriously difficult. There were also voices raised – especially but not exclusively among the non-jurors and high churchmen – who found Newton's cosmology seriously objectionable: a threat to revealed religion; but many more, including such staunchly orthodox theologians as Daniel Waterland, did not. Newton and mathematics did not conquer the academic world of Cambridge without a fight; but by 1750 their triumph was all but complete.

RELIGION

Our understanding of the religious and political landscape of Cambridge and England between 1660 and 1750 is beset, or rather bedevilled, by a cluster of party labels of doubtful and ambiguous meaning: puritan, Calvinist and Arminian had survived from the previous generations; to these came to be added 'Latitude men' or 'Latitudinarians' or Platonists and high and low churchmen – and a variety of ancient heresies whose names were revived, chiefly Arians and Socinians; in politics, Whig and Tory. And in a world in which religion and politics were so closely intertwined – when the battle to define and control the established church

---

[37] *Ibid.* On Powell, see Searby 1997, pp. 140–1, 145, 164. On Hubbard (also for what follows), see Brooke in Bendall *et al.* 1999, pp. 301–2, 582–3.
[38] See also above, p. 335.

lay near the heart of the political scene – religious and political labels met and mingled and became embrangled, as they have been in the writings of modern historians. For the most part, they originated as terms of abuse, and their meaning often lies hidden in the smoke of seventeenth-century polemic – which we, not trained in the arts of classical polemical rhetoric as were seventeenth-century Cambridge academics, tend to take too much at face value.

Of all these labels perhaps 'Latitude men' was the most ambiguous. It started its career in Cambridge (so far as we know) in the reaction of puritan and high church rigorists to the Cambridge Platonists. 'They push hard at the Latitude men as they call them', wrote the Cambridge Platonist Henry More to his friend Lady Conway in 1663; 'some in their pulpitts call them sons of Belial, others make the Devill a latitudinarian'.[39] Possibly so; but More was not so isolated as he wished Lady Conway to believe. He stayed securely in his fellowship in Christ's till his death, having refused two bishoprics.

After the Revolution of 1688–9 'Latitude' was given a new meaning. In the bitter polemics of the non-jurors against Anglicans who had (as they thought) sold the pass by taking the oaths to William and Mary, it was one of the favourite titles of abuse applied to the leaders of the church who had taken over from Sancroft and the other bishops who refused the oaths – and especially to Archbishops Tillotson and Tenison. Even the saintly Thomas Ken, the very symbol of the high church spirituality in the Restoration period, described Richard Kidder, who had replaced Ken as bishop of Bath and Wells, and his accomplices, the bishops who had accepted the sees of non-jurors, as 'Latitudinarian traitours, who would betray the baptismal faith'.[40] After the second crisis for the non-jurors with the accession of the Hanoverian George I in 1714, 'Latitude' became a yet broader term; and it almost lost all meaning when it was applied to Benjamin Hoadly (1676–1761), who argued that the church was a human institution which should be wholly subjected to royal authority and taught a eucharistic doctrine which evacuated the sacrament of most of its mystical meaning. The former gave rise to the celebrated Bangorian controversy – when Hoadly was bishop of Bangor – in which his chief opponent was the Cambridge theologian, master of St Catharine's, Thomas

---

[39] Nicolson 1930, p. 243, cited Gascoigne in Feingold 1990, pp. 276, 289 n. 170; cf. Nicolson 1929–30. On More, see *DNB* and below, n. 44. I make minimal use of the phrase 'low church' which in this period, when it came into use, was usually the equivalent of Latitudinarian – in marked contrast to its use in the twentieth century. Cf. esp. Goldie 1993, p. 144 and n. 4.

[40] Quoted Gascoigne 1989, p. 78. On Hoadly (see below), see *DNB*; on Sherlock (below), see Carpenter 1936; for penetrating studies of the Anglican church in this period, see Taylor 1995a, 1995b, 1998, 1999.

Sherlock; the second called out an answer from Daniel Waterland, master of Magdalene. Both were orthodox theologians very much open to reason and rational discussion in theology; to both, Hoadly seemed to have sailed beyond the confines of latitude. Ironically, Sherlock's career was in some respects a mirror image of Hoadly's. Hoadly's career also began in St Catharine's, of which he was a fellow; later he had passed through the bishoprics of Bangor, Hereford and Salisbury on his way to Winchester (1734–61). Sherlock followed him through Bangor and Salisbury to London (1748–61) – and the offer, which he refused, of two primacies.

'Reason' is perhaps the most ambiguous word of all; but it was the key to the thought of the Platonists, the first Latitude men. Christianity was a reasonable faith. Thus Benjamin Whichcote: 'If there were no other argument in the world to prove there is a God, a man is an argument sufficient to himself. For thus a man feels that he is; and he doth prove that by his acting: I act, therefore I am; I do, therefore I have being; and if I am, either I made myself, or was made by another. But it was not I, but God who made me.'[41] We may hear an echo of Descartes – 'cogito, ergo sum: I think, therefore I am' – and behind him a tradition going back to Augustine and Anselm. Contemporary Calvinists were inclined to say that Whichcote was immersed in 'Plato and his schollers above all' rather than the Bible, preaching 'a kind of moral Divinitie . . . nay a Platonique faith'.[42] Curiously, the same charge was made by experimental scientists, that Platonism 'or other high and aery speculations of Divinity or Philosophy' kept them from down-to-earth scientific enquiry.[43] This charge might be made of the most intellectually inquisitive of them, Henry More, fellow of Christ's from 1639 to 1687, whose academic range included theology, philosophy, mathematics, a variety of sciences sufficient to make him an ornament of the Royal Society, alchemy, chronology and ghosts. The list has brought on him the patronising contempt of some historians of science.[44] Yet some parts of the list are strikingly reminiscent of Newton. There is little precise evidence for any direct influence of More on Newton, but it is highly likely and generally accepted – and seven of More's books were on Isaac Barrow's shelves, and at least two of these may well have passed into Newton's library after Barrow's death.[45]

These details illustrate how widely it was possible for the original ideas of Henry More to spread among intellectuals in Cambridge (and

---

[41] Quoted Collinson in Bendall *et al.* 1999, p. 260.
[42] Anthony Tuckney, quoted in *ibid.*, p. 261. [43] Thomas Smith, quoted in *ibid.*, p. 260.
[44] This is even true of the essentially sympathetic study, Hall 1990.
[45] Feingold 1990, pp. 358 (nos. 657–63) and 371 (nos. 31–2); Gjertsen 1986, pp. 369–70.

elsewhere), whether his disciples or not. More was at work in Christ's from 1639 to 1687, and published many books. Whichcote may have addressed an even larger audience; for he was above all a preacher. He became a fellow of Emmanuel as early as 1633, and from 1644 to 1660 was provost of King's. From 1636 he was lecturer, that is a regular preacher, in Holy Trinity church in Cambridge, and as provost and vice-chancellor often entered the university pulpit in Great St Mary's. He ceased to be provost at the Restoration and most of the rest of his long life (he died in 1683) was spent in London, latterly as vicar of St Lawrence Jewry, a key City church in process of rebuilding by Wren – so that Whichcote had the neighbouring Guildhall as his preaching house, where he commanded a large popular following. 'Whichcote in his London pulpit was a godfather to the Church of Archbishops Tillotson and Tenison', the Latitudinarian primates of the Revolution of 1688 and its aftermath.[46]

Emmanuel, the puritan college, was ironically the chief breeding ground of the Platonists, and this helps us to answer the question of whether they really formed a group or not. The label was applied by their enemies, and it has been fashionable recently to deny that they had much common ground or worked closely together. Neither doubt seems justified. The other three leading Platonists, Ralph Cudworth, Nathaniel Culverwell and John Smith, were all products of Emmanuel in the 1630s. Culverwell and Smith both died in their early thirties, and their works were published after their deaths. In them '"the candle of the Lord" burned, and shone, more brilliantly and fiercely than in any other Cambridge Platonist works, for both were brilliant stylists', says Collinson of them. 'Both exalted the role, and power, of reason, and both grappled with the problem of reconciling reason with revelation.' Thus Culverwell: 'To blaspheme reason is to reproach heaven itself and to dishonour the God of Reason, to question the beauty of the image.'[47] The Dominican divines who lay buried in the precinct of what had now been for two generations Emmanuel College would have been proud of them. The fourth of the leading Emmanuel Platonists, Ralph Cudworth, has not had such a good press in recent years.[48] But he was a Renaissance scholar of immense if eccentric learning, and an acute philosopher who was one of the first and fiercest critics of Hobbes, and he could see flaws in the fashionable Descartes. Like Whichcote, he was not an obscure figure: he was fellow and tutor in Emmanuel, master both of Clare (1645–54) and

---

[46] Collinson in Bendall *et al.* 1999, p. 262. On Whichcote see also *DNB*, and above, pp. 336–7.
[47] Collinson in Bendall *et al.* 1999, pp. 263–4.
[48] Cf. Passmore 1951, p. 17 and Levine 1992 with the just comments of Collinson in Bendall *et al.* 1999, pp. 262–3; and see *ibid.* for what follows.

Christ's (1654–88), and one of the few survivors of the Restoration among the Cambridge heads. At Christ's he was colleague and patron of Henry More. The links among the leading Platonists were strong. They were all personalities of markedly individual character; but they were united in a love of learning and teaching or preaching, in devotion to Cambridge, and in independence of some of the central features of the dominant Calvinism of the Cambridge of the 1640s and 1650s. This did not preclude them from close friendship with Calvinist tutors and colleagues – the case of Whichcote and Tuckney is the best-documented example of this; and it seems clear that in religious sentiment and preferred forms of worship they were contented children of puritan Emmanuel.[49] Perhaps too much has been made of the battles over predestination which raged in the schools and pulpits and printing presses of Cambridge in the late sixteenth and seventeenth centuries; and not only then, for the Dominicans had disputed the matter in the precincts of Emmanuel long before. But it can hardly be questioned that the dominant views, whether hard-line Calvinist, moderate Calvinist or Arminian, severely restricted the population of heaven and provided hell with ample recruits. The Cambridge Platonists denied the whole structure of Calvinist predestinarian doctrine and even questioned whether hell was populated at all. In the *Advice* to students of the orthodox Daniel Waterland there is a striking commendation of the sermons of the Latitudinarian Archbishop Tillotson, who had been a fellow of Clare when Cudworth was master in the early 1650s; but he warns: 'There is one or two points of doctrine, particularly that of Hell-torments, justly exceptionable.'[50]

Ten masters were ejected in 1660; by 1662 three more had gone by death or dismissal. Only three remained: the popular, gentle divine John Lightfoot at St Catharine's, the most notable Hebrew scholar of his age, who inaugurated the renaissance of his college still visible in its buildings, and died master in 1675;[51] Ralph Cudworth of Christ's who survived, not without challenge, to die as master in 1688; and Richard Minshull of Sidney, the one genuine Calvinist survivor in the most lastingly puritan college.[52] He and his colleagues were assuredly not the only Calvinists in Cambridge after 1660; but the winds of change had blown most of them away. The Toleration Act of 1689, though very limited in its scope, giving very little ground for dissenters in great areas of the land, including the universities, was a public recognition that the Church of England no

---

[49] See above, pp. 336–7. [50] Waterland 1730, p. 24. [51] See above, pp. 33–5.
[52] Goldie 1996, p. 111; cf. Twigg 1990, p. 239 for the changes of 1660.

longer had – or could seriously hope to recover – a monopoly of religious allegiances in the country.[53] From then on, the heirs of the puritan tradition most obviously flourished in the dissenting churches. None the less, though it is very difficult to penetrate the religious sentiment of most fellows of Cambridge colleges, we need not doubt that variety and diversity remained, and that many of the attitudes of the mid-seventeenth-century puritans survived here and there as they did in the country – to prepare the way for the evangelical movements of the eighteenth century.

Meanwhile, the dominant exterior influences on the churchmanship of Cambridge between 1660 and 1689 were high church. Once again there were many Cambridge men on the bench of bishops: those most intimate with Cambridge and its colleges were William Sancroft at Lambeth (1678–90) and the bishops of Ely, of whom Matthew Wren (1638–67) and Peter Gunning (1675–84) laid the deepest mark on Cambridge. The supreme devotion of Wren's life was to Pembroke, the home of his student days and fellowship. There he left a minor monument in a very remarkable collection of antiquarian notes, chiefly on the alumni of Pembroke – and a major monument in its chapel. As master of Peterhouse in the 1620s and 1630s he built the college chapel, later embellished by his like-minded successor, John Cosin. Wren was one of the bishops closest to William Laud: devout, determined and intolerant; and he paid the penalty by many years' imprisonment in the Tower of London. When the Restoration came he was well over 70, but still extremely active; as was John Cosin at Durham, a very vigorous bishop in his mid-sixties, still in close touch with Cambridge, gathering like-minded men about him, including William Sancroft himself.[54] The Anglican church of the Restoration was partly ruled by old men in a hurry, who wished to see a regime not much different from Laud's reintroduced. Some of them, including Sancroft, may possibly have learned a measure of tolerance as they grew older; not so Wren or Cosin or Gunning. To them the church of the Restoration was not only the Church Militant (that is, doing its service) on earth, but (in their dreams) the Church Triumphant. They rejoiced greatly in the revival of the rich liturgies of their early days, in the ceremonial, the candles, the altars and altar rails – in the beauty of holiness, which carried with it its own genuine spirituality, of which Gunning himself was a notable exponent, though its greatest champion, Jeremy Taylor of Caius and All Souls, had long since departed

---

[53] See esp. Goldie 1991.

[54] See above, pp. 474–8. Sancroft was a prebendary at Durham from 1662 to 1674 (Horn *et al.* 2003). For the bishops' dates, Horn 1992, p. 8.

for a bishop's throne in Ireland. But if we had to find a definition of high church principles in this age, which fairly allowed for the immense diversity of opinion and practice which had grown up in the course of the century, we should seek it rather in politics. It found its apotheosis, as well as its nemesis, in the trial of the seven bishops in 1688. In 1660, monarchy and bishops were both restored; and the bishops rejoiced to be the loyal servants of the king – so long as the king was equally loyal to the church and to the status of the church which the bishops enshrined. Charles II's conversion to Catholicism posed an exceedingly awkward problem, softened by his determination to keep it secret. James II's open Catholicism was infinitely more difficult: the high church bishops saw him as the true king, but were torn apart by his determined trampling on some of their most treasured principles. High churchmen and Latitudinarians were equally determined to defend England from the Roman Catholics: however little they might condone the appalling libels of Titus Oates, their own strong, often bitter, opposition to the Roman Catholic faith and to the pope helped to create an atmosphere congenial to the horrors of the Popish Plot. And when James II declared toleration for Catholics as well as dissenters, they felt bound to refuse to promulgate his decree. But most of the same bishops were faced in the course of 1688–9 with the spectacle of an anointed king, a king by divine right, driven out of the country; and this too they could not accept. Two of the central pillars of the high churchmen of the age were thus affronted: most of the seven bishops refused the oaths to William and Mary and had to relinquish their sees.

Peter Gunning was fortunate to die before this supreme test: his successor Francis Turner was to be deprived as a non-juror early in 1690.[55] Gunning had been one of the most courageous and outspoken of royalists in the 1640s and 1650s, first in Cambridge, then in Oxford – finally, at the centre of a group who maintained an Anglican form of worship at Exeter House in the Strand in London. In 1660–1 he had his reward: mastership of two colleges and two professorships in turn. From the master's lodge in St John's and as Regius Professor of Divinity he kept as tight a grip as he could on the faith and morals of the university. From 1670 he was bishop of Chichester, then, from 1675 to his death in 1684, bishop of Ely; and from Ely he kept almost as close an eye on Cambridge as John Fell, bishop of Oxford – also dean of Christ Church – did on Oxford from his deanery till his death in 1686.[56] Fell left his mark on Christ Church

---

[55] *DNB*; for their dates, Horn 1992, p. 8 (Ely); Horn 1971, p. 3 (Chichester).
[56] On Fell, see R.A. Beddard in Tyacke 1997, chs. 17 and 18, esp. pp. 807, 824–5, 829, 870–6.

by calling in Christopher Wren to design Great Tom over the entry to Tom Quad. Less dramatically, Peter Gunning left his mark on St John's by presiding over the plans for the completion of the Third Court, for which (it seems) he also consulted Wren, and which was being built as he departed for Chichester in 1670.[57]

After 1689, with the virtual destruction of the high church element in the hierarchy, especially under the regimes of Tillotson and Tenison, Latitudinarian winds blew from Lambeth and there was a notable alliance between the earl of Nottingham, the central figure in episcopal appointments in William III's early years – though himself personally a convinced high churchman – and Cambridge Latitudinarians. But Nottingham's closest friend in the episcopate, John Sharp, archbishop of York (1691–1714), was a more orthodox, right-wing figure, and grew away from Tenison in his later years, becoming the leader of the orthodox Tory bishops. The pattern of relationships was infinitely complex.[58] In Ely, by the same token, the non-juring bishop was replaced by Simon Patrick. But soon the whole issue of the relations of Cambridge and the Court and the episcopate had become entangled with the issues of Whig and Tory, and can be more clearly understood in that context below.

Meanwhile, Cambridge had become a seminary – at least in the sense that the large majority of undergraduates were destined for a clerical career. 'The generality of students are intended to be clergymen', said Daniel Waterland, 'and, as such must take the Arts in their way.' And he proceeded to outline an immensely broad structure of learning, which must precede any specifically theological study.[59] Waterland himself saw that there was a problem: ordinands needed an opportunity to study the Bible and theology. But to us it is extremely puzzling that so few of them went on even to a BD (bachelor of divinity, that is, theology) degree, let alone a DD. While 11,000 BAs were awarded between 1660 and 1727, only 438 received BDs.[60] One might imagine that the religious strife of the mid-seventeenth century had bred suspicion of too much theological speculation in the young – and anyone who had contemplated the Emmanuel of 1630–60 might well deduce that a flourishing theological education was the seedbed of diversity, division and perhaps heresy. Very likely this has something to do with the decline of specifically theological education in the eighteenth century. But this does not explain the marked difference between Cambridge and Oxford in the production of BDs: at

---

[57] Willis and Clark 1886/1988, II, pp. 271–4. As the foundation stone was laid in 1669, we may presume that Gunning had taken the lead in planning the building.

[58] Gascoigne 1989, pp. 74–9. On Sharp see esp. *ibid.*, p. 76 and Hart 1949.

[59] Waterland 1730, p. 7.   [60] Gascoigne 1989, p. 264.

Oxford in the same period about 650 BDs were granted, and the number (after a brief decline in the 1710s and 1720s) remained fairly steady for the rest of the eighteenth century at approximately one BD for fourteen or fifteen BAs.[61] But we have little idea of the standards imposed or the course of study which lay behind these figures; and the whole issue of how, and how much, candidates for orders received theological training in this period is extremely obscure. As for pastoral theology, it had been in the medieval syllabus a part of canon law, whose study was forbidden by the injunctions of 1535; to what extent it crept back in practical advice from tutors is altogether unknown. Waterland himself saw the problem: he insisted on some measure of theological instruction for those going on immediately to ordination, though it had to be fitted into gaps in the normal academic programme – into Sundays and holidays; and for most it was at once practical and elementary. 'I advise by all means to begin with English Sermons', from which so much good divinity, and, more important still, models for future preaching, might be found. After these sermons, 'a general view of the several controversies . . . and some knowledge of Church History', from very basic textbooks; and then 'if you have time, Pearson on the Creed, Burnet on the Articles' – works which one might have supposed were in the hands of every Anglican clergyman of the age.[62] Waterland was a Whig, and 'cannot sensibly be described as a high churchman';[63] but he well illustrates the weakness of every attempt to divide the clergy of Cambridge and England into theological and political camps. He was a pillar of orthodoxy, and, as such, the natural ally of Edmund Gibson, bishop of London from 1723 to 1748 and for many years Walpole's chief adviser on the appointment of bishops and ecclesiastical affairs in general, yet as orthodox as Waterland and much concerned to avoid spreading any infection of the Arian views of Samuel Clarke and William Whiston (not to mention Isaac Newton) and other heresies rampant or threatening at the time. To this end he proposed to Waterland that the university might consider making it a rule that fourth-year studies for ordinands should comprise theology. Naturally, there was some appeal to Waterland in the proposal: but 'There seems to be no way of changing the course of their studies for the first four years. It is fixed by custom and the oath they take' – whatever that might mean.[64] Waterland was being somewhat disingenuous; yet his words are extremely revealing. His *Advice* is the best evidence we have of the freedom of powerful tutors to arrange the syllabus to suit their personal views and

[61] This is based on table 3 in Stone 1975, p. 94.
[62] Waterland 1730, pp. 12–17; see above, pp. 338 ff.
[63] Duffy in Cunich *et al.* 1994, p. 162.   [64] Quoted Gascoigne 1989, pp. 263–4.

tastes – and so to let in Locke in spite of his doubtful views on some matters, to propagate Tillotson in spite of his weakness on hell-fire, and spend much time in the earlier years preparing his students for the supreme encounter with Newton's *Principia* in the end. And yet there is an equally powerful inspiration which is deeply conservative: granted the tutors' freedom to innovate, they were also agents of a centuries-long tradition. It might be better for the ordinands to go forth with some knowledge of theology – better still to be BDs or (like Waterland himself) DDs – but that was secondary; first and foremost they must have a broad education in the liberal arts. The *trivium* and the *quadrivium* – 'the mathematical arts'[65] – which had founded the university in the thirteenth century were still alive and well.

Thus the university can only be called a seminary in respect of the future careers of its alumni: however important a liberal arts degree might seem – may have been – to the future welfare of the Anglican clergy, it often gave them no specific training for their task. In two respects, however, it may well be that Cambridge and the parochial ministry were drawing closer together in this period. More and more of the rectors and vicars of the seventeenth and eighteenth centuries had university degrees. This was the end of a long process, and its details are still imperfectly known; there was still a large underclass of curates, some of whom presumably did not have degrees. None the less, the parish priest in many parts of the country represented an element of Oxford or Cambridge in the countryside or the town. To find their way to suitable livings they had to contend with all the complexities of patronage, which in a large majority of cases meant a lay patron – a squire, a magnate or the Crown. But there were also college livings, available to the privileged few, that is, in the main to the fellows. They had come increasingly to seem to young fellows tied to celibacy the most significant part of a college's endowment, the path by which marriage and a wider career might be open to them. In some colleges this was reflected in attempts to increase the number of college livings. Too little research has been done to propound any general statements; and, as so often, what we know emphasises differences between colleges more than their common interests.[66] Thus Emmanuel, which had been relatively well endowed in its early years – with thirteen livings by 1625 – had to be content with two additions in the late seventeenth

---

[65] See above, p. 512.

[66] What follows is chiefly based on material collected for the histories of Emmanuel and Caius. For Emmanuel, on some details see Bendall *et al.* 1999, Index, s.v. Emmanuel, livings; for the nineteenth-century purchase, *ibid.*, livings, Dixie fund. For Caius, esp. Brooke 1985/1996, pp. 160–1.

century, provided by William Sancroft and his successor as master, John
Breton. No further increases came until the nineteenth century, when
competition had become especially severe among the fellows, and they
managed to arrange for the purchase of some nine more out of college
endowments. Meanwhile in Caius, between 1660 and 1736 the number
of advowsons had been more than doubled. Gonville Hall had enjoyed
six before 1500, to which Caius added one, and one more came in 1632.
The Restoration period saw two additions, the 1690s one more, bringing the total to eleven; then, between 1700 and 1736, ten more were
added. These were partly the result of purchase by the college, mainly
gifts from benefactors, including a lay master, Robert Brady, and a lay
president, John Gostlin, conscientiously helping to speed their colleagues
on their way – though not, it should be said, until the benefactors were
dead.[67] Although the lay element in the Caius fellowship never wholly
disappeared – and was strongly represented in the eighteenth century by
Sir James Burrough, architect and antiquary, tutor and master – it was
on the way to becoming for a time a conventional clerical college, with
as high a proportion as any of clergy to be, presided over, from 1737
to 1754, as we shall see, by a master who was also a bishop. Not so
Trinity Hall, which had emerged from the Middle Ages relatively well
provided for a small college, with eight livings. But as it became in the
sixteenth century a predominantly lay society, its advowsons seemed of
little value to the fellowship, and most of them were sold or otherwise
disposed of in the sixteenth century or later.[68] It is frustrating not to
be able to pursue this theme through all the colleges; but we need not
doubt that in most or all the others would-be benefactors were liable to
encounter a strong plea that the college's first need was to enhance its
advowsons. This remained a constant theme in fellows' minds until the
late nineteenth century, when the departure of the celibacy rules and the
secularisation of the university began the process by which the advowsons
have become a curious survival from a lost world. But in the eighteenth
century, and the early nineteenth, they were at the heart of many men's
ambitions. Thus when, in 1798, Samuel Blackall, fellow of Emmanuel,
was tempted to matrimony by a visit to Jane Austen and her family in
Hampshire, he already had his eye on the living of North Cadbury in
Somerset. But he had to wait till 1812–13: then at last the college was able
to present him to it, and he then sought another young woman to be his
wife.[69]

---

[67] Brooke 1985/1996, pp. 160–1; Venn 1897–1901, III, pp. 280–1, 311–22.
[68] Crawley 1976, p. 15 and n. 1.   [69] Brooke in Bendall *et al.* 1999, pp. 315–16.

The syllabus, religion and politics 1660–1750

TORIES, WHIGS AND THOMAS GOOCH

Nowhere is the confusion of labels more baffling than among the politicians. The division between Tory and Whig was, notoriously, the product of late Stuart politics, when the Court could no longer present a single face to the country – as it had done, or attempted or pretended to do, in spite of many factions and other differences, in Tudor and early Stuart days. The labels began, as always in that era, as terms of abuse, and the early history of the parties is much obscured by the difficulty of determining in what measure labels were simply attached by enemies or by-standers, in what measure by the party men themselves. Ambiguity, furthermore, was of their essence from the start. In the Exclusion Crisis of 1679, the Tory defence of divine right emphasised the legal claims of James II to succeed. But when the Revolution of 1688–9 followed James II's exceedingly unpopular adventures, the Tories were divided, and those prepared to accept William and Mary (or Mary and William) played a major role in James' departure. To put the matter very crudely, William and Mary were commonly more at home with the Whigs, Anne with the Tories – but both groups or factions or parties played an active part in the complex interweaving of British politics between 1689 and 1714.

The universities meanwhile were no longer under the constant scrutiny of Court and parliament described by Victor Morgan in the earlier chapters of this book. But that is not to say that they had won any real independence of government and secular politics. In the Restoration period an immense number of appointments to masterships, fellowships and degrees were made by royal mandate; and royal mandates came for a time to play something of the role that papal provisions had played in the late Middle Ages: a rerouting of normal methods of appointment and patronage to suit those energetic or ambitious or (in some cases) unscrupulous enough to seek the fountainhead of all patronage. In the early 1660s mandates had especially been used to put right (as it was then understood) the wrongdoing of the previous twenty years, and some notably good appointments were made or ratified, as well as some less easily justified. But if Charles II and his ministers used the system with a characteristic mixture of kindness, incaution and absent-mindedness, under James II the mandates became major instruments of policy; and his attempts to infiltrate Roman Catholics into key positions in Oxford and Cambridge discredited the whole system. The tactics of the Restoration era were not tried again.[70] But that did not mean an end to state

---

[70] Twigg 1990, pp. 266–74 (Charles II), 277–85 (James II).

interference; far from it. It could very crudely be said that the universities were caught between the Scylla of Tory Jacobitism, or, in the longer run, of Tory insistence on the crucial role of the church in government, and the Charybdis of Whig corruption. From the former, Cambridge tended to suffer less than Oxford, although in 1689 there were actually relatively few in Oxford who refused the oaths – only twenty-five or so. The efforts of James II to subvert university and college statutes had been frustrated, and Cambridge, on the whole, welcomed the king's deposition. Naturally, there were many tender consciences, and in St John's – so recently ruled over by Peter Gunning – between twenty-five and thirty fellows refused the oath to William and Mary; but the total of non-jurors for the whole of Cambridge was little more than forty.[71] The master of Caius, Robert Brady, a noted Tory who had accompanied James II as a royal physician in his Oxford visitation, suffered a good deal from James' fall: he was ousted from his place as keeper of public records and cut off from the major sources for his historical research. But he was able to steer the college through the shoals. It remained predominantly Tory indeed throughout the eighteenth century, and two of the students of Brady's mastership, Jeremy Collier and Richard Welton, were to become non-juring bishops; but only one or two fellows refused the oaths. In what was probably a disingenuous statement in 1691, Robert Brady affirmed that all but two had sworn, and one of the two was out of his wits, and the other out of Cambridge.[72] The second was Bartholomew Wortley, a very long-serving fellow under Brady's regime; and it seems most probable that he refused the oaths and certain (if so) that the master succeeded in shielding him. For in 1705 the college presented him to the living of Bratton Fleming in Devon, where he ended his days, retaining into his mid-nineties, as well he might, 'a strong attachment to the place of his education', in the stately words of the college Commemoration of Benefactors. He left the whole of his substantial fortune to Caius, partly to found two new fellowships, one for a man always to bear the name Wortley (but not Wortley Montague or Montague Wortley), the other for a man from Bratton Fleming or its immediate neighbourhood. The college established the fellowships and enjoyed his money, but ignored the stipulations. We have reached the year 1749.[73] Meanwhile, in 1714, there was much less agonised heart-searching than in 1689, though it was to be many years before the new regime could be wholly secure of the

---

[71] Twigg 1990, p. 286 and n. 78: the evictions from St John's have been variously estimated at twenty-six and twenty-eight. On Oxford non-jurors, see Gascoigne 1989, p. 73. For the wider political scene, see reference above, p. 528 n. 56 and Marshall 1999.
[72] On Caius non-jurors, see Brooke 1985/1996, pp. 150–2.   [73] Ibid.

support of the universities – especially of Oxford. Only ten fellows lost their fellowships for refusal of the oath to the Hanoverian succession, and some of these were very gently treated: Thomas Baker, the celebrated antiquary and long-serving fellow of St John's, was ever after 'ejected fellow – *socius ejectus*', but he lived on till his death in 1740 in his college rooms.[74]

The career of Thomas Gooch (1675–1754) spanned almost the whole space between the Revolution of 1688–9 and the mid-eighteenth century; and among the Tories and Whigs of this, our final phase, he is one of the best recorded. He came to Caius in 1691 as a pupil of John Ellys and was almost an exact contemporary of Samuel Clarke. But whereas Clarke was led by Ellys into the orbit of Newton, and became one of his most fervent disciples and (in the long run) a heretic and a Whig, Gooch remained in early life staunchly Tory. He was a fellow of Caius from 1698, and held a series of college offices, culminating as bursar, a post he relinquished in 1710. Meanwhile he was proceeding through the theological degrees, culminating in DD in 1711.[75] Although he had been at some point domestic chaplain to Henry Compton, bishop of London, it was evidently from his successor, the Tory diplomat John Robinson (1713/14–1723), that Gooch won his first taste of ecclesiastical plurality. In 1714, at midsummer, Gooch resigned his fellowship in order to marry Mary Sherlock, daughter of the dean of St Paul's and sister of Gooch's lifelong friend Thomas Sherlock, master of St Catharine's from 1714 to 1719. In July Gooch was made archdeacon of Essex and in the same year rector of St Clement Eastcheap and St Martin Orgar in the City of London, a joint living which seems to have given him a home in London, since his first wife was buried in the parish in August 1720.[76] Meanwhile, in 1716, he was elected master of Caius, and he remained master through all the vicissitudes of his ecclesiastical career till his death in 1754. From 1717–20 he was also vice-chancellor. In 1715 Sherlock had become dean of Chichester and in 1719, doubtless through Sherlock's influence, Gooch became a residentiary canon there; from 1730 he was also a prebendary of Canterbury. In 1737, he was consecrated bishop of Bristol, accepting translation to Norwich in 1738 and to Ely in 1748.

[74] Twigg 1990, p. 286 and n. 79; *DNB*.
[75] On Gooch, see Venn 1897–1901, III, pp. 115–24; Brooke 1985/1996, pp. 163–70; and esp. for what follows Brooke, Horn and Ramsay 1988. For Gooch as archdeacon of Essex, *ibid.*, pp. 550–4 and Horn 1969, p. 9.
[76] Brooke, Horn and Ramsay 1988, p. 550 and n. 21. For all details relating to Chichester and Canterbury which follow, see *ibid.*, pp. 550–5. For the union of the two parishes see Newcourt 1708–10, I, p. 417.

His long career illustrates many of the themes of this book. In his early years as vice-chancellor he was one of the leading Tories of Cambridge, deeply involved in Cambridge politics and, in particular, in conflict with the great Whig master of Trinity, Richard Bentley. He was also a pluralist; and surviving records, to a quite unusual extent, enable us to trace the extent of a pluralist master's residence in his various homes. A happy providence, in the shape of Bishop Bateman (1355), had dictated that the master, fellows and scholars of Caius were fined 12 pence a week for absence from the college at any time of year,[77] and this was one of the early statutes which was effectively enforced down to about 1800 – all the more readily, one may suppose, because the sum was never raised, and by Gooch's day was a relatively minor matter. But the Exiit Books were thus financial records, and so carefully kept – and in Caius and other colleges are a mine of information on residence, with many secrets still to reveal.[78] The chapter records are not so precise or complete, but while I tracked Gooch in the Exiit Book, Joyce Horn was able to monitor his residences in Chichester and Nigel Ramsay in Canterbury; and a relatively full picture of an eighteenth-century pluralist and his residences emerged. We learned nothing of his visits to his London parish, which he held till 1732, after 1720. We learned a little from London diocesan records of his occasional visitations as archdeacon of Essex, which occupied a few days or a few weeks in several years between 1720 and 1736. At Chichester the cathedral statutes laid down that he was due to reside for three months in the year; and in his early days as a canon he evidently performed his residence. Indeed, he was very much at home at Chichester, in spite of the death of his first wife, the dean's sister, in 1720. He consoled himself by marrying a daughter of Sir John Miller of West Lavant, near Chichester; and after Sherlock had departed for his first bishopric, Bangor, in 1727, Gooch became a dominant figure in the chapter.

Meanwhile, Gooch had been from 1717 to 1720 a very active Tory vice-chancellor in Cambridge. The office at this time normally rotated annually and went to one of the junior heads. But political feeling in the university ran so high in the late 1710s that Gooch was nominated by the Tory heads three times. In the first election he defeated his rival, the Whig master of Corpus, Dr Bradford, by ninety-five votes to fifty-one. Gooch followed up his success by proceeding against Dr Bradford: the vice-chancellor was Visitor of Corpus, and Bradford had had his son elected a fellow, a precedent which was to be followed by both Gooch and

---

[77] Bateman's statute of 1355 is in Venn 1897–1901, III, p. 350.

[78] It is the equivalent of the redit book in Trinity which helps to record Newton's long residence there.

Bentley. Bradford, however, had more influence at Court: he received a royal Order in Council inhibiting Gooch from interfering in Corpus – and was promoted bishop of Carlisle.[79]

But Gooch's main endeavour was against the master of Trinity. 'The first Whig, according to Dr Johnson, was the devil: the first Whig in Cambridge – in stature though not in time – was Dr Bentley.'[80] He was the real enemy of the Cambridge Tories, and the ground for Gooch's re-election as vice-chancellor. A trivial dispute was brought to the vice-chancellor's court by Conyers Middleton, a distinguished Latitudinarian, later to be head of the University Library. He was one of the fellows of Trinity most active in resistance to Bentley, and used the vice-chancellor's court as a means of attacking the master. Bentley was summoned time and again before the court and paid no attention – save only to visit the Caius lodge to assure Gooch that 'he would not be judged by him and his friends over a bottle'.[81] Gooch consulted the other heads and in the end pronounced sentence on Bentley: he was to be deprived of all his degrees. The sentence was in due course confirmed by the Senate. But if Gooch had won the first battles, Bentley characteristically won the war. A good while later the Court of King's Bench – in a celebrated application of the principles of natural justice – decreed the judgement of the vice-chancellor's court null and void, because Bentley had not stated his case before it.

The years passed, and Gooch enjoyed his residences at Chichester, and sometimes visited his archdeaconry. But he was an ambitious career ecclesiastic, looking for a bishopric, and by 1727 or so he had despaired of finding the path to a mitre. It was probably in that year that he confessed to Dixie Windsor, Tory MP for the university and an old friend, that he was in process of conversion. Windsor complained that the university was deserting its Tory allegiance: if the Whigs sent a broomstick as candidate, they would vote for it – 'and so must I too', Gooch is reported to have replied.[82] Ironically, it was in the same year that his brother-in-law and mentor, Thomas Sherlock, began his progress along the episcopal bench, which was to lead him eventually to London, and the offer (not accepted) of a primacy – and to becoming the duke of Newcastle's chief ecclesiastical adviser – all achieved without surrendering his allegiance to the Tory interest. Gooch reaped his reward for becoming a Whig much more slowly. In 1730 he was collated to a prebend in Canterbury

79 Brooke 1985/1996, p. 165.   80 *Ibid.*, p. 163.
81 *Ibid.*, p. 165, citing Monk 1830, p. 373: *ibid.*, pp. 372–83, gives the classic account of this saga. For what follows see esp. *ibid.*, pp. 494–6.
82 Brooke 1985/1996, p. 167 and n. 33.

cathedral. This meant in principle that he would be absent from Cambridge for six months of the year: three months at Chichester, three at Canterbury. He offered the senior fellows of Caius to resign as master; but the offer was not accepted – a refusal they were later to regret. For Gooch became ever more openly Whig, and a client of Newcastle; and increasingly, an absentee master. His first long absence from the master's lodge came between April 1732 and May 1733, when visitations in Essex were followed by residence in Canterbury and Chichester – and then by a repetition of his ecclesiastical round. Thereafter his clerical routine became more erratic; but he evidently tried to keep some measure of balance between his three homes until 1737 took him to Lambeth to be consecrated bishop, and 1738 took him to London to perform the political duties of a bishop. He surrendered his archdeaconry in 1737, and his two canonries on his translation to Norwich in October 1738.

Meanwhile, Gooch had become a satellite of the duke of Newcastle. In 1735 he had added to his prebend at Chichester the wardenship of St Mary's Hospital, doubtless a sinecure; and in October he wrote to the duke protesting his loyalty to him. In January 1736, a client of Newcastle in the Chichester chapter assured the duke that he could depend on Gooch so long as Gooch could hope for a bishopric.[83] In 1737 the duke sought election as High Steward of the University of Cambridge, and on 12 June 1737 Gooch was consecrated bishop of Bristol.

It was extremely unusual at this date for the head of a college to retain his headship on consecration as a bishop. There were venerable precedents: Laurence Booth, bishop of Durham (1457–76) and archbishop of York (1476–80), had been master of Pembroke throughout his episcopal career: he was one of a succession of episcopal masters of Pembroke. More briefly, St John Fisher had been president of Queens' while bishop of Rochester.[84] What was special about Gooch's case was that his ambition was to become bishop of Ely, and Newcastle was the supreme maker of bishops. But the route to Newcastle's patronage lay above all in Cambridge. From 1737, as High Steward, Newcastle was able to begin that process of manipulation among the masters and fellows of Cambridge which was to be his hobby – even after his fall from office in Westminster – till his death in 1768. In this process, the key events came in 1737–8, when he was elected High Steward and Gooch became in quick succession bishop of Bristol and then of Norwich, and in 1748, when Newcastle was elected chancellor and Gooch was translated to Ely. In the

---

[83] Brooke, Horn and Ramsay 1988, p. 549 and n. 16.
[84] See Brooke 1989a, pp. 50–1, 58.

meantime the notable Caius antiquary Francis Blomefield had dedicated the first volume of his *History of Norfolk* to the bishop, with a prayer 'that it would please God long to preserve him amongst us'. 'I am apt to think', commented the sharp-tongued high Tory William Cole, 'that the bishop did not heartily say Amen to this, as he had an eye to a future translation to Ely.'[85] In 1747–8 Newcastle anxiously watched the old chancellor die, and prepared his campaign with the aid, among others, of 'our old friend' Dr Gooch. In 1748 Newcastle was elected chancellor – and Gooch was translated.[86] To fulfil his role and his ambitions, Gooch needed to remain master of Caius.

There was a price to pay. In his last years, relations between master and fellows in Caius seriously deteriorated. So far as we can discern the motives at work, both sides seem to have proceeded with malice; and Gooch, busily occupied in Ely House in the Strand and the House of Lords, proceeded also by neglect and inadvertence.[87] The senior fellows who, in 1730, were content to have him absent half the year, found the Whig bishop intolerable, and found that when his attention was securely fixed in Cambridge, it was in the interests of promoting the great Whig manipulator to the highest office in the university. The Tory fellows (and most of them were Tory) doubtless reckoned, as we must, that Newcastle's patronage had corrupted the master. It is an extreme case of a theme often repeated in these pages, of the ambitious pluralist master seeking higher office. Although interference in the university's affairs was a much rarer event than before 1700, the Court and the government were always present realities in Cambridge. In the years following the Hanoverian succession and the rebellion of 1715, Archbishop Wake and the earl of Macclesfield planned a revival of the 'visitation general' of the universities to ensure their loyalty.[88] But the plan failed, and lords spiritual and temporal alike increasingly relied on personal influence and intrigue. Newcastle was the supreme example of the patronage broker – 'even fathers-in-God sometimes forget their maker', he is alleged to have complained after his fall from power in Westminster.[89] But he was not the last. The Tories, triumphant in Cambridge in the late 1710s, had gradually lost way. The Whigs conquered Cambridge under Newcastle's flag, while the Tories retained a minority in most colleges and a majority in very few. But later in the century, when the younger Pitt was both

---

[85] Quoted in Brooke 1985/1996, pp. 167–8.
[86] *Ibid.*, p. 168 and n. 37. For Bristol, Norwich and Ely, Horn 1992, pp. 9, 40; 1996, p. 13.
[87] Details in Venn 1897–1901, III, pp. 119–21. For what follows, see Searby 1997, pp. 391–4, and Winstanley 1922, pp. 37–54.
[88] Gascoigne 1989, p. 92.   [89] Quoted in *ibid.*, pp. 110–11.

member for the university and prime minister, there was a marked Tory
revival – and Pitt became a very popular figure, especially on his visits to
Cambridge.[90] The labels Whig and Tory were, indeed, of very variable
meaning, and in high politics almost of no meaning in the 1750s. Those
who would seek a definition even in the 1720s and 1730s must reckon
with the Tory Thomas Sherlock progressing through the mainly Whig
hierarchy. But in Cambridge the labels always had a very real (if often an
obscure) significance.

Thomas Gooch was one of those men whose personality is clearly
reflected in his career. Two sources enable us to come a little closer to
him. A modest dossier of family papers has survived: it was not available
to me when I was writing on Gooch in *A History of Gonville and Caius
College*, but by the generosity of Sir Timothy Gooch it is now in the College Archives. Much of the correspondence concerns Gooch's younger
brother William, who was lieutenant-governor of Virginia and was made
a baronet. On his brother's death without heirs Thomas Gooch inherited the baronetcy. There is also a sheaf of letters from Thomas Sherlock,
confirming the impression of him as a warm-hearted, kindly man, close
to the Gooches: they include a leg-pull in which he tells his brother-in-
law what a poor thing a baronetcy is – less than nobility; fitting doctrine
perhaps for two lords spiritual. But the letters tell us little of college or
university.[91] The other sources are the notebooks of William Cole, a
hostile witness, for he could hardly be expected to forgive Gooch for his
conversion to Whigcraft. But he appreciated Gooch's social gifts.

> As I have hinted that he was a man of as great art, craft, design, and
> cunning, as any in the age he lived in, so I must also bear my testimony
> that he was as much of a gentleman in his outward appearance, carriage,
> and behaviour as ever it was my good fortune to converse with. He was
> a man also of the most agreeable, lively, and pleasant conversation, full of
> merry tales and lively conceits, yet one who well knew the respect that
> was due to his character . . . always free and easy of access to all those who
> had any sort of pretension to it.[92]

We have made the acquaintance of Waterland and Sherlock, two of the
most admirable heads of house Cambridge has known. Waterland has spoken to us chiefly through his *Advice*, exceptionally revealing evidence of
the Cambridge syllabus – or lack of it – in the hands of a conscientious and
imaginative tutor of the early eighteenth century. It would be good – had

[90] Searby 1997, pp. 412–14.
[91] Gonville and Caius College Archives, File of Gooch Correspondence, not paginated.
[92] Quoted Brooke 1985/1996, p. 164; Venn, 1897–1901, III, pp. 118–19.

we the time – like Jane Austen, to relish Sherlock's sermons. 'I am very fond of Sherlock's Sermons, prefer them to almost any', said that shrewd observer of the eighteenth-century pulpit. I am not as deeply read in sermons as she was; but they are strikingly attractive: 'a plain, intelligible, clear-headed, reasonable, imaginative interpretation of the Christian gospel', with a strong appeal to reason and the moral teaching of the church; yet firmly orthodox.[93] Beside Waterland and Sherlock, there were less admirable men in the lodges of Cambridge, among whom we should place Sir Thomas Gooch. He started his career as a good college man; he strove to be an effective Tory leader in Cambridge; he wanted to stand comparison with his brother-in-law as a conscientious career ecclesiastic. But he was subject to the frustrations and temptations of his position and of his aims; he stayed in the master's lodge too long. And so we can see in his career, as in a mirror, a whole spectrum of aspects of university life in his time. Gooch reminds us that interference from afar was by no means stilled in the eighteenth century; and that it had many forms and twists. In 1733 the House of Lords devoted a whole Saturday to an extended debate upon the affairs of Trinity College.[94] Gooch was not yet a lord spiritual; but some of his former colleagues may well have been there. In any case we have come full cycle: the high court of parliament and the University of Cambridge were not strangers to one another.

---

[93] First quotation, Jane Austen, letter of 28 Sept. 1814, in Le Faye 1995, p. 278, quoted in Brooke 1999b, p. 130; second quotation, Brooke *ibid*. It is suggested there that 'Sherlock' might conceivably refer to William, Thomas' father: this is just possible, but most unlikely. It is noteworthy that a new edition of a collection of Thomas' sermons was published in 1812.

[94] Monk 1830, p. 596.

Chapter 16

EPILOGUE

In recent chapters we have explored the variety and ambivalence of university life between 1660 and 1750: in the lofty achievements of Brady, Newton and Bentley; in the humdrum of study and syllabus; in shifting patterns of religious allegiance; in the corrupt politics of Newcastle and Gooch. As final expressions of this ambivalence, I have chosen three moments in the history of the university, in 1684, in 1716 and in 1724, to illustrate the variety of experience and interest which this book has attempted to portray.

1684

In 1684 the sculptor Joseph Catterns completed the monument in Christ's College chapel to a remarkable friendship between two devout Christ's men, which is also recorded in two portraits now in the Fitzwilliam Museum.[1] Sir John Finch (1626–82) was the younger brother of Heneage Finch, Lord Nottingham, whose son Daniel was to play a dominant role in the ecclesiastical politics of the 1690s.[2] John Finch went to Christ's as a pensioner in 1645, where he met Thomas Baines (1622–80), and formed a friendship of such intimacy that they were rarely apart in later life – and were reunited in Christ's chapel after their deaths. In the 1650s they were in Italy, studying medicine in Padua: Finch for a time was the English consul in Padua and held a chair in the University of Pisa. After the Restoration they returned to England, and stayed there long enough to become Honorary Fellows of the Royal College of Physicians and Fellows of the Royal Society. In 1665 Finch resumed his diplomatic career and became minister to the grand duke of Tuscany; and it was during his

[1] For the tomb, see Pevsner 1970, p. 52 and plate 46. For the portraits, see Plates 29 and 30.
[2] See above, p. 529.

Plate 29 Carlo Dolci, portrait of Sir John Finch, Fitzwilliam Museum, Cambridge

residence in Florence that he and Baines had their portraits painted by Carlo Dolci. In 1672 they moved to Constantinople, where Finch was ambassador, and where Baines was to die in 1680. Two years later Finch returned to England, but himself died soon after, having ensured that he and Baines would be remembered as substantial benefactors to their

Plate 30 Carlo Dolci, portrait of Sir Thomas Baines, Fitzwilliam Museum,
Cambridge

college – and be buried in its chapel side by side. The tomb is a dramatic
and moving reminder of the magic spell a Cambridge college can cast
over some of its alumni – though perhaps only over a few in any age; and
of the friendships which are its most lasting legacy.[3]

---

[3] This paragraph is based on the entries in *DNB*, corrected by Venn, I, p. 114; II, p. 138.

Epilogue

1716

In 1716 a young fellow of Emmanuel, William Law – a worthy disciple of Archbishop Sancroft, a high churchman and a Tory – refused to take the oaths to the Hanoverian dynasty which were imposed in the wake of the rebellion of 1715, and resigned his fellowship. The rest of his life was spent away from Cambridge, first as Edward Gibbon's private tutor, then in retirement, with two devoted women companions, who formed what was almost a religious community, devoted to prayer, study and charitable good works. The three comprised strongly marked personalities, all eccentric in their ways, but also genuinely devout; and Law's own writings included very notable polemics against the Latitudinarians, especially against Bishop Hoadly, and his celebrated classics of the spiritual life, *A Practical Treatise on Christian Perfection* (1726) and *A Serious Call to a Devout and Holy Life* (1729).[4] The eighteenth-century church is celebrated for its rationalism, its worldliness and its complacency – not without cause. But it was infinitely various; and these eloquent treatises, which deeply influenced men as diverse as John and Charles Wesley and Samuel Johnson, are a constant reminder of an age of ardent spiritual endeavour. The Emmanuel which bred the young William Law is to us a silent society: of the life of the college which had been richly documented in the mid-seventeenth century we know very little in his time. But it is abundantly clear that William Law had learned some substantial part of the Christian message of his maturer years during the decade, from 1705 to 1716, spent in Cambridge: in his lively style of portraying the devout life to the prosperous, middle-class Englishmen from whom he sprang, we can see in a mirror the ideals and aspirations set before him in early eighteenth-century Emmanuel.

1724

In 1724 King George I, at the behest of Bishop Edmund Gibson of London, established the Regius Professorship of Modern History. It is a striking fact that this event occurred at a time when the study of history flourished exceedingly in Cambridge, but that the attempt to foster a formal role for history among undergraduates was stillborn.

We left the study of the history of Cambridge a while ago in the hands of charlatans, Parker and Caius. It was a natural consequence of

---

[4] On Law, see esp. Rupp 1986, ch. 15, and Collinson in Bendall *et al.* 1999, pp. 285–92, with bibliography on p. 285 n. 1.

the more scientific study of history of the age of Robert Brady that the records of Cambridge itself should benefit, and Brady's own notebooks in the Caius library indicate that he made some shrewd investigations of the history of his own college.[5] From 1679 to 1740 another antiquary of great distinction was resident in St John's, compiling an immense collection of transcripts of historical records, whose centre lay in his projects for histories of St John's and of the University of Cambridge. He published neither in his lifetime, but in the nineteenth century his college history was edited by another learned eccentric, J.E.B. Mayor, and his material for a university history formed the core of Cooper's *Annals*.[6]

Under the inspiration of Peter Gunning in the 1660s, St John's had become the leading high church college in Cambridge; it was a nursery of devout high churchmen, and no less than three of the seven bishops who resisted James II's attempts at religious toleration were Johnians. Nemesis came with the Revolution of 1688–9, when many of the fellows proved unwilling to swear the oaths of allegiance to William and Mary. In 1693 the master, Humphrey Gower, was ordered 'to eject twenty of the fellows who had refused the oath'. The master himself had taken the oath, and, like Brady in Caius, was determined to protect his colleagues. So he did nothing, and was haled into court. Gower argued that a fellowship was a freehold, 'and Magna Carta and many other statutes forbade a man to be put out of his freehold save by due process of law'.[7] The argument suggests that he had antiquarian advisers among his non-juring colleagues, as well as a doughty ally in the obscurity of the common law, for the case failed owing to a technical flaw and the fellows remained in possession of their freeholds until 1717, when a more stringent demand for an oath to the Hanoverian succession led to the resignation of the surviving non-jurors. Among these was Thomas Baker. A non-juror in 1689 and in 1717, Baker was at last compelled to resign his fellowship and ever after 'inscribed his books *socius ejectus*; but', as Edward Miller observes in his history of St John's, 'his severance from the college was far from complete. He continued to reside in third court until the afternoon in 1740 when he was found lying in his rooms, his tobacco pipe broken by his side.'[8]

Among Baker's heroes was John Cosin, bishop of Durham, an elder statesman in the formative years of Peter Gunning. Baker possessed

---

[5] Gonville and Caius College MSS 709/695 (and 617/549 and 617*) contain his version of the Caius Annals. There are also short pieces in MSS 602/278, fo. 37; 607/279, fos. 1 ff. MSS 580/685, 581–4/329–32 are transcripts for his historical works: see above, pp. 488–9. What follows on Thomas Baker resumes Brooke 1992, pp. 8–9. The chief source for his life is Masters 1784.

[6] Baker and Mayor 1869; Cooper, *Annals*.   [7] Miller 1961, pp. 44–5.   [8] *Ibid.*, p. 45.

a portrait of Cosin as bishop which he left to a young Tory of like antiquarian interests, James Burrough of Caius, and it now hangs in the Caius hall.[9] We may well suppose that Cosin and Gunning were the gods of Baker's early life who inspired him to his lifelong devotion to church and king. Late in life, after his dedication to the non-juring cause had deprived him of his one benefice, the rectory of Long Newton, as well as his fellowship, he had ample leisure for his antiquarian research in the collections in Cambridge and London, which have made his transcripts, now divided between the Harleian collection in the British Library and the Cambridge University Library, a goldmine for students of medieval and early modern religious and academic history. His career is remarkably parallel to that of Thomas Hearne, the Oxford non-juror, save that Hearne succeeded in publishing numerous volumes of texts and studies in his own lifetime. Baker had also in common with Hearne a natural gift for accuracy – an impressive innate tendency to get his texts right.

It is remarkable that neither the church history of Parker, nor the parliamentary history beloved of Cotton, impinged on students' syllabuses, so far as surviving tutorial manuals reveal them. This is all the more noteworthy, since history was a vital part of the humanist arts course of the period; but this was history as transmitted by texts which also taught Greek and Latin grammar and style and rhetoric – and ethics and political theory.[10] It has sometimes been suggested that English political history was too dangerous for young men to be exposed to it: Charles I found it necessary to separate Sir Robert Cotton from his library in Cotton's last years.[11] Study of early church history too could be used to justify a presbyterian form of church government – or stir polemic between puritans and high churchmen. But this line of objection would not have applied to church history as practised by Matthew Parker. At least, the Anglican establishment could – and many of them did – take comfort from current interpretations of the history of episcopacy; and Francis Godwin's treatise on episcopal succession, as well as providing a largely mythical account of the origins of episcopacy and a somewhat more reliable catalogue of English bishops, won him a bishopric from Queen Elizabeth.[12] But these matters did not, as far as our evidence goes, impinge on undergraduate courses. History won high prestige, but it was the history of Greece and Rome. Cotton might arrange his medieval and early modern texts in book cases surmounted by statues of the Roman emperors – so that they are still labelled MS Cotton Augustus, Tiberius, Claudius

---

[9] Masters 1784, p. 135; cf. Venn 1897–1901, III, p. 293.
[10] Feingold in Tyacke 1997, pp. 327–57, esp. pp. 340–2.
[11] Brooke 1992, p. 4.   [12] On Godwin, see *DNB* and above, pp. 491–2.

and so forth – but no such harmony in historical studies attracted the Cambridge tutors. Richard Holdsworth's *Directions* of the second quarter of the seventeenth century introduced the first-year student at once to a survey of Greek and Roman history; and he passed late in his second year through Florus, Sallust and Quintus Curtius to Livy and Suetonius in his fourth year. For the advanced student, he reserved Plutarch, Xenophon, Herodotus, Thucydides and Tacitus.[13] It is abundantly clear that history is conceived as a branch of the classics; that the authors are chosen to mark stages in the development of the students' linguistic skills. Only the advanced student has material offered him which would stimulate serious reflection on political theory and ethics.

The pabulum offered by Daniel Waterland two generations later was similar, but not identical. In the first year, Xenophon marked (then, as in mid-twentieth-century syllabuses) first steps in Greek; the *Cyropaedeia* also introduced some Greek ideas on the formation of a ruler. In the second year, after an ample course in rhetoric, the student was to read Caesar and Sallust. The third year was fallow, unless Homer be accounted a historian; but the fourth year brought forward Thucydides and Livy, the heart and core of classical history, as well as other works on the history of Greek thought.[14] There is copious evidence to confirm the impression from these manuals that Greek and Roman history comprised a major academic subject in seventeenth- and early eighteenth-century Oxford and Cambridge;[15] and that other kinds of history depended on the personal inclinations of students and their tutors. Much might depend on the availability of books and libraries: the young Henry Wharton in the 1680s and the young Francis Blomefield in the 1720s evidently found materials in the Caius library which started them on their major works.[16] The extreme flexibility of the syllabus meant that young men who had congenial and sympathetic tutors might follow their interests to considerable depth. Blomefield enjoyed the patronage and encouragement of his tutor James Burrough, himself a notable antiquary as well as an even more notable amateur architect. But where such support was lacking, access to books and academic support were likely also to be lacking.[17]

Edmund Gibson, bishop of London from 1723 to 1748, was a conscientious man who combined deep learning – he was known as 'Dr Codex' on account of his learned codification of English canon

---

[13] Feingold in Tyacke 1997, p. 341. On Holdsworth, see above, p. 515.
[14] Waterland 1730, pp. 18–28. The list of historians was extended in the later editions to include Clarendon, Burnet and Paul's *History of the Council of Trent*. Waterland 1856, pp. 412, 414.
[15] Feingold in Tyacke 1997, p. 341.   [16] Brooke 1985/1996, pp. 147–50, 177.
[17] On the tutors and the syllabus, see above, pp. 333–42, 511–22.

law – and considerable political influence. Though an Oxford man, he took an equal interest in the improvement (as he hoped to see it) of the syllabuses of both universities. He encouraged the study of theology for ordinands in Cambridge;[18] and he planned courses in modern history and modern languages in both Oxford and Cambridge to provide relevant instruction for young men engaged in diplomatic service or tutoring the sons of the gentry and aristocracy.[19] In 1724, at Gibson's behest, George I established regius professorships in both universities for the study of modern history and – through the medium of assistants – of modern languages. So far as Cambridge was concerned, the scheme was stillborn. The tutors paid no attention; the first professor gave only one lecture; some modest language teaching was provided; and the Whig ministry had a moderately valuable sinecure added to its patronage. Modern history was simply not on the tutors' lists of eligible subjects; and when a conscientious professor eventually emerged in the person of John Symonds – he succeeded the poet Thomas Gray in 1771 – 'he had to agree with the heads of houses that not more than twenty-six might attend' lectures on so frivolous or possibly (for Symonds was a radical Whig) so dangerous a theme.[20] With hindsight we may think that Bishop Gibson and King George had the final say; but they had to wait a very long time before college tutors conceded that modern history was a serious branch of historical study.

This forward glance puts in perspective the very powerful role of ecclesiastical and political history in the interests of some of the intellectual leaders of Cambridge in the sixteenth and seventeenth centuries. They were of deep interest to some graduates and dons and many alumni; they were not, on the whole, for undergraduates. Once again we glimpse the ambivalence of the Cambridge scene in the eighteenth century: a remarkable mingling of opportunities overlooked and opportunities grasped.

---

[18] See above, p. 341. On Gibson, see esp. Taylor 1995a.
[19] For what follows, see Searby 1997, pp. 233 ff.   [20] *Ibid.*, p. 235.

BIBLIOGRAPHICAL REFERENCES

Adam, J., 1889–93, 'Dr Richard Holdsworth's "Directions for students in the Universitie"', *Emmanuel College Magazine*, 1, 2 (1889), 51–8; 4, 1 (1892), 1–10; 4, 2 (1893), 89–100

Adams, S.L., 1991, 'Factions and favourites at the Elizabethan court', in *The Court at the Beginning of the Modern Age, c. 1450–1650*, ed. R.G. Asch and A.M. Birke, Oxford, 1991, pp. 265–87

  1995, 'The patronage of the crown in Elizabethan politics: the 1590s in perspective', in Guy 1995, pp. 20–45

Agius, P., 1971, 'Late sixteenth and seventeenth century furniture in Oxford', *Furniture History*, 7 (1971), 72–86

Airs, M., 1982, *The Buildings of Britain, Tudor and Jacobean: A Guide and Gazetteer*, London, 1982

Allen, W., 1970, *Translating for King James*, Nashville, 1970

Anderson, C.A., and Schnaper, M., 1952, *School and Society in England: Social Backgrounds of Oxford and Cambridge Students*, Washington, DC, 1952

Anderson, V., 1991, *New England's Generation: The Great Migration and the Formation of Society and Culture in the Seventeenth Century*, Cambridge, 1991

Atherton, I., and Morgan, V., 1996, 'Norwich Cathedral 1630–1730', in *Norwich Cathedral: Church, City and Diocese, 1096–1996*, ed. I. Atherton, E. Fernie, C. Harper-Bill and A. Hassell Smith, London, 1996, pp. 540–75

Attwater, A., 1936, *Pembroke College Cambridge: A Short History*, Cambridge, 1936

Aubrey, J., 1898, *Brief Lives*, ed. A. Clark, 2 vols., Oxford, 1898

Auerbach, E., 1954, *Tudor Artists*, London, 1954

Aylmer, G.E., 1958, 'Charles I's Commission on Fees, 1627–40', *Bulletin of the Institute of Historical Research*, 31 (1958), 58–67

  1961, *The King's Servants: The Civil Service of Charles I, 1625–1642*, London, 1961

  1973, *The State's Servants: The Civil Service of the English Republic 1649–1660*, London, 1973

  1986, 'The economics and finances of the colleges and university *c.* 1530–1640', in McConica 1986, pp. 521–58

Bailey, D.R. Shackleton, 1956, *Propertiana*, Cambridge, 1956

Bibliographical references

1960, *Towards a Text of Cicero, Ad Atticum*, Cambridge, 1960

ed., 1965–70, *Cicero's Letters to Atticus*, 2 vols., Cambridge, 1965–70

Baillie, H.M., 1967, 'Etiquette and planning of the state apartments in Baroque palaces', *Archaeologia*, 101 (1967), 169–99

Baker, T., ed. J.E.B. Mayor, 1869, *History of St John's College*, 2 vols., Cambridge, 1869

Baldwin, T.W., 1944, *William Shakespeare's Small Latine and Lesse Greeke*, 2 vols., Urbana, 1944

Ball, M.A.V., 1960, 'University and collegiate planning in the later sixteenth and seventeenth centuries', University of London, Courtauld Institute, MA thesis, 1960

Ball, W.W. Rouse, 1918, *Cambridge Papers*, London, 1918

Barley, M.W., 1961, *The English Farmhouse and Cottage*, London, 1961

Barnes, T.G., 1961, *Somerset 1625–1640: A Country's Government during the 'Personal Rule'*, London, 1961

Barton, T.E., ed., 1964, *The Registrum Vagum of Anthony Harison*, NRS, 33, 1964

Batho, G.R., ed., 1971, *A Calendar of the Shrewsbury and Talbot Papers in Lambeth Palace Library and the College of Arms, II, Talbot Papers in the College of Arms*, London, 1971

Bauckham, R., 1973, 'The career and thought of Dr William Fulke (1537–1589)', University of Cambridge, PhD thesis, 1973

1975, 'Marian exiles and Cambridge puritanism: James Pilkington's "Halfe a Score"', *Journal of Ecclesiastical History*, 26 (1975), 137–48

Beales, D.E.D., and Nisbet, H.B., eds., 1996, *Sidney Sussex College Cambridge: Historical Essays in Commemoration of the Quatercentenary*, Woodbridge, 1996

Beier, A.L., 1985, *Masterless Men: The Vagrancy Problem in England 1560–1640*, London, 1985

Bendall, S., Brooke, C.N.L., and Collinson, P., 1999, *A History of Emmanuel College, Cambridge*, Woodbridge, 1999

Bentley, R., 1691, *Epistola ad Cl. V. Joannem Millium* [Appendix to J. Mill's edn of Malelas], Oxford, 1691

1697/1699, *A Dissertation upon the Epistles of Phalaris* (in W. Wotton, *Reflections upon Ancient and Modern Learning*, 2nd edn, London, 1697); 2nd edn (as a separate book), London, 1699

1711, *Horatius Flaccus*, Cambridge, 1711

Bindoff, S.T., 1961, 'The making of the Statute of Artificers', in Bindoff *et al.* 1961, pp. 59–94

Bindoff, S.T., Hurstfield, J., and Williams, C.H., eds., 1961, *Elizabethan Government and Society: Essays Presented to Sir John Neale*, London, 1961

Birch, T., 1849, *The Court and Times of James the First*, ed. R.F. Williams, 2 vols., London, 1849

Black, C.J., 1966, 'The administration and parliamentary representation of Nottinghamshire and Derbyshire, 1529–1558', University of London, PhD thesis, 1966

Bibliographical references

Black, J., 1990, *Robert Walpole and the Nature of Politics in Early Eighteenth-Century Britain*, Basingstoke, 1990

Blackstone, W., 1829, *Commentaries on the Laws of England*, ed. T. Lee, 4 vols., London, 1829

Blomefield, F., Parkin, C. *et al.*, 1739–75/1805–10, *An Essay towards a Topographical History of the County of Norfolk*, 5 vols., Fersfield etc., 1739–75, cited from the edn, 11 vols., of London, 1805–10

Bloxam, J.R., ed., 1853–5, *A Register of the Presidents, Fellows, Demies . . . of Saint Mary Magdalen College in the University of Oxford*, 2 vols., Oxford, 1853–5

Boas, F.S., ed., 1935, *The Diary of Thomas Crosfield*, London, 1935

Bond, D.F., ed., 1965, *The Spectator*, 5 vols., Oxford, 1965

Bond, M.F., ed., 1962, *The Manuscripts of the House of Lords*, n.s., IX, *Addenda 1514–1714*, London, 1962

Bossy, J., 1975, *The English Catholic Community 1570–1850*, London, 1975

Bourne, J.M., 1986, *Patronage and Society in Nineteenth-Century England*, London, 1986

Bowden, P., 1967–85, 'Agricultural prices, farm profits, and rents', in *The Agrarian History of England and Wales*, IV–V, ed. J. Thirsk, Cambridge, 1967–85, IV, pp. 593–695, 814–70; V, pp. 1–118

Bowers, F., 1941–2, 'Thomas Randolph's salting', *Modern Philology*, 39 (1941–2), 275–80

Braddick, M.J., 2000, *State Formation in Early Modern England, c. 1550–1700*, Cambridge, 2000

Bradshaw, B., and Duffy, E., eds., 1989, *Humanism, Reform and the Reformation: The Career of Bishop John Fisher*, Cambridge, 1989

Brady, R., 1685, *A Complete History of England . . . from Julius Caesar unto the End of the Reign of King Henry III . . .* , London, 1685

  1700, *A Continuation of the Complete History of England: containing the Lives and Reigns of Edward I, II, III and Richard the Second*, London, 1700

Branford, C., 1988, 'Carriers and carrying in early modern Norfolk', University of East Anglia, MA thesis, 1988

Brentnall, D.J., 1980, 'Regional influences in the House of Commons 1604–10', University of East Anglia, MPhil thesis, 1980

Bridenbaugh, C., 1968, *Vexed and Troubled Englishmen 1590–1642*, Oxford, 1968

Bright, G., ed., 1684, *The Works of the Reverend and Learned John Lightfoot, D.D.*, 2 vols., London, 1684

Brink, C.O., 1986, *English Classical Scholarship: Historical Reflections on Bentley, Porson and Housman*, Cambridge, 1986

Brook, V.J.K., 1962, *A Life of Archbishop Parker*, Oxford, 1962

Brooke, C.N.L., 1957, 'The earliest times to 1485', in *A History of St Paul's Cathedral*, ed. W.R. Matthews and W.M. Atkins, London, 1957, pp. 1–99, 361–5

1971, 'Religious sentiment and church design in the later Middle Ages', in Brooke, *Medieval Church and Society* (London, 1971), ch. 8

1985/1996, *A History of Gonville and Caius College*, Woodbridge, 1985, corr. repr. 1996

1985a, 'The churches of medieval Cambridge', in *History, Society and the Churches: Essays in Honour of Owen Chadwick*, ed. D. Beales and G. Best, Cambridge, 1985, pp. 49–76

1987, 'Allocating rooms in the sixteenth century', *The Caian*, 1987, pp. 56–67

1988, 'Blessed John Fingley', *The Caian*, 1988, pp. 110–14

1989a, 'The University Chancellor', in Bradshaw and Duffy 1989, pp. 47–66, and 'Chancellors of the University of Cambridge, *c.* 1415–1535', pp. 233–4

1989b, 'Oxford and Cambridge: the medieval universities', *The Cambridge Review*, 110 (1989), 162–5

1989c, *The Medieval Idea of Marriage*, Oxford, 1989

1992, 'Cambridge and the antiquaries, 1500–1840', *Proceedings of the Cambridge Antiquarian Society*, 79 (1992 for 1990), 1–14

1993a, 'The dedications of Cambridge colleges and their chapels', in Zutshi 1993, pp. 7–20

1993b, *A History of the University of Cambridge*, IV, *1870–1990*, Cambridge, 1993

1998, 'The University Library and its buildings', in Fox 1998, ch. 15

1999a, 'Urban church and university church: Great St Mary's from its origin to 1523', in *Great St Mary's: Cambridge's University Church*, ed. J. Binns and P. Meadows, Cambridge, 1999, pp. 7–24

1999b, *Jane Austen: Illusion and Reality*, Cambridge, 1999

1999c, *Churches and Churchmen in Medieval Europe*, London, 1999

Brooke, C.N.L., Highfield, J.R.L., and Swaan, W., 1988, *Oxford and Cambridge*, Cambridge, 1988

Brooke, C.N.L., Horn, J.M., and Ramsay, N.L., 1988, 'A canon's residence in the eighteenth century: the case of Thomas Gooch', *JEH*, 39 (1988), 545–56

Brooke, C., and Ortenberg, V., 1988, 'The birth of Queen Margaret of Anjou', *Historical Research*, 61 (1988), 357–8

Brown, E.H. Phelps, and Hopkins, S.V., 1956, 'Seven centuries of the prices of consumables, compared with builders' wage-rates', *Economica*, n.s., 23 (1956), 296–314, repr. in *Essays in Economic History*, II, ed. E.M. Carus-Wilson, London, 1962, pp. 179–96

Bujak, E., 1992, 'The Herald's Visitation, 1530–1686: an inquiry into the growth and decline of a system of armorial regulation in England', University of East Anglia, MA thesis, 1992

Burnet, G., 1865, *The History of the Reformation of the Church of England*, ed. N. Pocock, 7 vols., Oxford, 1865

Burton, R., 1621/1932, *The Anatomy of Melancholy*, Oxford, 1621; Everyman edn, London, 1932

Bibliographical references

Bussby, F., 1953, 'An ecclesiasticall seminarie and college general of learning and religion, planted and established at Ripon', *Journal of Ecclesiastical History*, 4 (1953), 154–61

Caius, J., 1912, *The Works of John Caius, M.D.*, ed. E.S. Roberts, Cambridge, 1912

Cambridge Documents 1852: Documents Relating to the University and Colleges of Cambridge . . . published by direction of the [University] Commissioners, 3 vols., London, 1852

Cameron, E., 1991, *The European Reformation*, Oxford, 1991

Campbell, A., ed., 1962, *Chronicon Æthelweardi: The Chronicle of Æthelweard*, Nelson's Medieval Texts, 1962

Campbell, L., 1985, 'The women of Stiffkey', University of East Anglia, MA thesis, 1985

Carpenter, E., 1936, *Thomas Sherlock, 1678–1761*, London, 1936

Carus-Wilson, E.M., ed., 1962, *Essays in Economic History*, II, London, 1962

Cary, H., 1842, *Memorial of the Great Civil War in England from 1646 to 1652*, 2 vols., London, 1842

Catto, J., ed., 1984, *The History of the University of Oxford*, I, *The Early Oxford Schools*, Oxford, 1984

Chamberlain 1861: *Letters written to John Chamberlain during the Reign of Queen Elizabeth*, ed. S. Williams, Camden Society, o.s. 79, 1861

Chamberlain, J., 1939, *The Letters of John Chamberlain*, ed. N.E. McClure, 2 vols., Philadelphia, 1939

Charles, A.M., ed., 1971, *The Williams Manuscript of George Herbert's Poems: A Facsimile Reproduction*, Durham, NC, 1971

Charlton, K., 1965, *Education in Renaissance England*, London, 1965

Chartres, J.A., 1977, *Internal Trade in England 1500–1700*, London, 1977

Christie, W.D., 1871, *A Life of Anthony Ashley Cooper, First Earl of Shaftesbury*, 2 vols., London, 1871

Churton, R., 1809, *The Life of Alexander Nowell, Dean of St Paul's*, Oxford, 1809

CJ: House of Commons Journals

Clark, J.W., 1881, 'On the old Provost's Lodge of King's College', *Proceedings of the Cambridge Antiquarian Society*, 4 (1881), 285–312
　　ed., 1892, *Letters Patent of Elizabeth and James the First*, Cambridge, 1892
　　1904, *Endowments of the University of Cambridge*, Cambridge, 1904
　　1906, *The Riot at the Great Gate of Trinity College, February 1610–11*, Cambridge, 1906

Clark, P., ed., 2000, *The Cambridge Urban History of Britain*, II, *1540–1840*, Cambridge, 2000

Clark, P., and Slack, P., eds., 1972, *Crisis and Order in English Towns 1500–1700: Essays in Urban History*, London, 1972
　　1976, *English Towns in Transition 1500–1700*, Oxford, 1976

Clark, P., Smith, A.G.R., and Tyacke, N., 1979, *The English Commonwealth: Essays in Politics and Society Presented to Joel Hurstfield*, Leicester, 1979

Bibliographical references

Clarke, P.D., and Lovatt, R., eds., 2002, *Corpus of British Medieval Library Catalogues*, 10, *The University and College Libraries of Cambridge*, London, 2002

Clarke, S., 1662, *A Collection of the Lives of Ten Eminent Divines*, London, 1662

    1677 (1651), *A General Martyrologie, containing a Collection of all the greatest Persecutions which have befallen the Church of Christ . . . whereunto is added the Lives of Thirty Two English Divines*, 3rd edn, London, 1677, also referred to in the edn of 1651

    1683, *The Lives of Sundry Eminent Persons in this Later Age . . .* , London, 1683

Cliffe, J.T., 1960, 'The Yorkshire gentry on the eve of the Civil War', University of London, PhD thesis, 1960

    1969, *The Yorkshire Gentry from the Reformation to the Civil War*, London, 1969

Cobban, A., 1969, *The King's Hall within the University of Cambridge in the Later Middle Ages*, Cambridge, 1969

Coby, D.J., 1992, 'St Andrew's Norwich (1550–1730): parochial prestige in an urban context', University of East Anglia, MA thesis, 1992

Cole, J., 1969–70, 'A note on Hugo Glynn and the statute banning Welshmen from Gonville and Caius College', *National Library of Wales Journal*, 16 (1969–70), 185–91

Colgrave, B., and Mynors, R.A.B., ed. and trans., 1969, *Bede's Ecclesiastical History of the English People*, Oxford Medieval Texts, Oxford, 1969

Colley, L., 1982, *In Defiance of Oligarchy: The Tory Party 1714–1760*, Cambridge, 1982

Collier, J.P., ed., 1840, *The Egerton Papers*, Camden Society, o.s. [12], 1840

Collinson, P., ed., 1960, *Letters of Thomas Wood, Puritan, 1566–1577*, Bulletin of the Institute of Historical Research, Special Supplement, 5, London, 1960, repr. in Collinson 1983, pp. 45–107

    1961, 'John Field and Elizabethan Puritanism', in *Elizabethan Government and Society . . .* , ed. S.T. Bindoff *et al.*, London, 1961, pp. 127–62, repr. in Collinson 1983, pp. 335–70

    1964, 'The "nott conformyte" of the young John Whitgift', *Journal of Ecclesiastical History*, 15 (1964), 192–200, repr. in Collinson 1983, pp. 325–33

    1967, *The Elizabethan Puritan Movement*, London, 1967

    1979, *Archbishop Grindal 1519–1583: The Struggle for a Reformed Church*, London, 1979

    1983, *Godly People: Essays on English Protestantism and Puritanism*, London, 1983

    1988, *The Birthpangs of Protestant England: Religion and Cultural Change in the Sixteenth and Seventeenth Centuries*, Basingstoke, 1988

    1991, 'Andrew Perne and his times', in McKitterick 1991, pp. 1–34

Colvin, H.M., 1988, *The Canterbury Quadrangle, St John's College, Oxford*, Oxford, 1988

Commons Debates 1621: see Notestein, Relph and Simpson 1935

Como, D., 2000, 'Puritans, predestination and the construction of orthodoxy in early seventeenth-century England', in Lake and Questier 2000, pp. 64–87

Bibliographical references

Coope, R., 1984, 'The gallery in England: names and meanings', *Architectural History*, 27 (1984), 446–55

1986, 'The long gallery', *Architectural History*, 29 (1986), 58–72

Cooper, Cooper, *Annals*: C.H. Cooper, *Annals of Cambridge*, 5 vols. (v, ed. J.W. Cooper), Cambridge, 1842–1908

Cooper, J.P., 1967, 'The social distribution of land and men in England, 1436–1700', *Economic History Review*, 2nd series, 20 (1967), 419–40

Corfield, P., 1972, 'A provincial capital in the late seventeenth century: the case of Norwich', in Clark and Slack 1972, pp. 263–310

1976, 'The social and economic history of Norwich, 1650–1850: a study in urban growth', University of London, PhD thesis, 1976

Corrie, G.E., 1839, *Brief Historical Notices of the Interference of the Crown with the Affairs of the English Universities*, Cambridge, 1839

Cosin 1869–72: *The Correspondence of John Cosin, D.D., Lord Bishop of Durham*, [ed. G. Ornsby], 2 vols., Surtees Society, 1869–72

CPR Eliz.: *Calendar of the Patent Rolls preserved in the Public Record Office, Elizabeth*, 1–, London, 1939–

Cragg, G.R., 1968, *The Cambridge Platonists*, New York, 1968

Crawley, C., 1976, *Trinity Hall: The History of a Cambridge College, 1350–1975*, Cambridge, 1976

Creighton, C., 1965, *A History of Epidemics in Britain*, 2nd edn, 2 vols., London, 1965

Cressy, D., 1970, 'The social composition of Caius College, Cambridge, 1580–1640', *Past and Present*, 47 (1970), 113–15

1972, 'Education and literacy in London and East Anglia, 1580–1700', University of Cambridge, PhD thesis, 1972

1980, *Literacy and the Social Order: Reading and Writing in Tudor and Stuart England*, Cambridge, 1980

Crofts, J.E., 1967, *Packhorse, Wagon and Post*, London, 1967

Cronne, H.A., 1956, 'The study and use of charters by English scholars in the seventeenth century: Sir Henry Spelman and Sir William Dugdale', in Fox 1956, pp. 73–91

1961, 'Charter scholarship in England', *University of Birmingham Historical Journal*, 8 (1961), 26–61

Cross, C., 1966, *The Puritan Earl: The Life of Henry Hastings Third Earl of Huntingdon, 1536–1595*, London, 1966

1969, *The Royal Supremacy in the Elizabethan Church*, London, 1969

1976, *Church and People 1450–1650: The Triumph of the Laity in the English Church*, London, 1976

1977, 'From the Reformation to the Restoration', in *A History of York Minster*, ed. G.E. Aylmer and R. Cant (Oxford, 1977), ch. 5

CSPD: *Calendar of State Papers, Domestic Series* [1st series, 1547–1625], 12 vols., Public Record Office, London, 1856–72

Bibliographical references

Cunich, P., Hoyle, D., Duffy, E., and Hyam, R., 1994, *A History of Magdalene College, Cambridge, 1428–1988*, Cambridge, 1994

Curle, J.S., 1999, *A Dictionary of Architecture*, Oxford, 1999

Curthoys, M.C., and Howarth, J., 'Origins and destinations: the social mobility of Oxford men and women', in *The History of the University of Oxford*, VII, ed. M.G. Brock and M.C. Curthoys, Oxford, 2000, pp. 571–95

Curtis, M.H., 1959, *Oxford and Cambridge in Transition, 1558–1642*, Oxford, 1959
1967, 'The alienated intellectuals of early Stuart England', repr. in *Crisis in Europe 1560–1660*, ed. T.H. Aston, Garden City, NY, 1967, pp. 309–31

Cust, R., 1992, 'Parliamentary elections in the 1620s: the case of Great Yarmouth', *Parliamentary History*, 11 (1992), 179–91

Cust, R., and Hughes, A., eds., 1989, *Conflict in Early Stuart England: Studies in Religion and Politics 1603–1642*, Harlow, 1989

Dashwood, G.H., Bulwer, W.E.G.L., *et al.*, eds., 1878–95, *The Visitation of Norfolk in the year 1563, taken by William Harvey . . .* , 2 vols., Norfolk and Norwich Archaeological Society, Norwich, 1878–95

Davenport, A., ed., 1949, *The Collected Poems of Joseph Hall, Bishop of Exeter and Norwich*, Liverpool, 1949

Davis, N.Z., 1975, 'The Reason of Misrule', in Davis, *Society and Culture in Early Modern France*, London, 1975, pp. 97–123

d'Avray, D.L., 2001, *Medieval Marriage Sermons*, Oxford, 2001

Dawson, J.E.A., 1984, 'The foundation of Christ Church, Oxford, and Trinity College, Cambridge, in 1546', *Bulletin of the Institute of Historical Research*, 57 (1984), 208–15

Dean, D.M., 1990, 'Parliament and locality', in Dean and Jones 1990, pp. 139–62
1996, *Law-Making and Society in Late Elizabethan England: The Parliament of England, 1584–1601*, Cambridge, 1996

Dean, D.M., and Jones, N.L., eds., 1990, *The Parliaments of Elizabethan England*, Oxford, 1990
1998, *Parliament and Locality, 1660–1939*, Edinburgh, 1998

Demos, J., 1970, *A Little Commonwealth: Family Life in Plymouth Colony*, New York, 1970

Denzinger, H., and Bannwart, C., eds., 1922, *Enchiridion Symbolorum definitionum et declarationum de rebus fidei et morum*, 14th–15th edn, ed. J.B. Umberg, Freiburg im Bresgau, 1922

Dewar, M., 1964, *Sir Thomas Smith: A Tudor Intellectual in Office*, London, 1964

D'Ewes 1682: *The Journals of all the Parliaments during the Reign of Queen Elizabeth*, London, 1682
1942: *The Journal of Sir Simonds D'Ewes from the first Recess of the Long Parliament to the Withdrawal of King Charles from London*, ed. W.H. Coates, Yale Historical Publications, Manuscripts and Edited Texts, 18, New Haven, 1942

Bibliographical references

Dickens, A.G., 1952, 'Aspects of intellectual transition among the English parish clergy of the Reformation period: a regional example', *Archiv für Reformationsgeschichte*, 43 (1952), 51–70

   1963, 'The writers of Tudor Yorkshire', *Transactions of the Royal Historical Society*, 5th series, 13 (1963), 49–76

DNB: *Dictionary of National Biography*

Douglas, D.C., 1951, *English Scholars 1660–1730*, 2nd edn, London, 1951

Dowling, M., 1986, *Humanism in the Age of Henry VIII*, London, 1986

Dowsing 2001: *The Journal of William Dowsing*, ed. T. Cooper, London and Woodbridge, 2001

Duffy, E., 1992, *The Stripping of the Altars*, New Haven, 1992

Dyer, G., 1824, *The Privileges of the University of Cambridge, together with Additional Observations on its History, Antiquities, Literature and Biography*, 2 vols., London, 1824

Earle, J., 1629, *Micro-Cosmographie*, London, 1629 (facsimile edn of Autograph Manuscript, Leeds, 1966)

Edleston, J., 1850, *Correspondence of Sir Isaac Newton and Professor Cotes*, London, 1850

Edwards, G.M., 1899, *Sidney Sussex College*, Cambridge, 1899

EHR: *English Historical Review*

Eland, G., 1935, 'The annual progress of New College by Michael Woodward, Warden 1659–1675', *Records of Buckinghamshire*, 13 (1935), 77–137

Eliot 1832: *De Iure Maiestatis and the Letter Book of Sir John Eliot*, 2 vols., London, 1832

Elton, G.R., 1953, *The Tudor Revolution in Government*, Cambridge, 1953

   1965, *The Tudor Constitution: Documents and Commentary*, Cambridge, 1965

   1972a, *Policy and Police: The Enforcement of the Reformation in the Age of Thomas Cromwell*, Cambridge, 1972

   1972b, 'The rule of law in the sixteenth century', in *Tudor Men and Institutions*, ed. A.J. Slavin, Baton Rouge, 1972, pp. 265–94

   1973, *Reform and Renewal: Thomas Cromwell and the Common Weal*, Cambridge, 1973

   1974–83, *Studies in Tudor and Stuart Politics and Government*, 3 vols., Cambridge, 1974–83

   1979a, 'Reform and the "Commonwealth-Men" of Edward VI's reign', in Clark, Smith and Tyacke 1979, pp. 23–38

   1979b, 'Parliament in the sixteenth century: functions and fortunes', *Historical Journal*, 22 (1979), 255–78

   1986, *The Parliament of England 1559–1581*, Cambridge, 1986

   1988, 'Tudor Government', *Historical Journal*, 31 (1988), 425–34

Emden, A.B., 1948, *Oriel Papers*, Oxford, 1948

   1963, *A Biographical Register of the University of Cambridge to 1500*, Cambridge, 1963

1964, 'Northerners and southerners in the organisation of the university to 1509', in *Oxford Studies Presented to Daniel Callus*, Oxford Historical Society, new series, 16, Oxford, 1964, pp. 1–30

Eulenburg, F., 1904, *Die Frequenz der deutschen Universitäten*, Leipzig, 1904

Evans, J., 1956, *A History of the Society of Antiquaries*, London, 1956

Evans, J.T., 1979, *Seventeenth Century Norwich: Politics, Religion and Government 1620–1690*, Oxford, 1979

Everitt, A., 1957, 'Kent and its gentry, 1640–1660: a political study', University of London, PhD thesis, 1957

    1966, *The Community of Kent and the Great Rebellion 1640–1660*, Leicester, 1966

    1967, 'The marketing of agricultural produce', in *The Agrarian History of England and Wales*, IV, *1500–1640*, ed. J. Thirsk, Cambridge, 1967, pp. 467–90

    1969a, *The Local Community and the Great Rebellion*, Historical Association, London, 1969

    1969b, *Change in the Provinces: The Seventeenth Century*, University of Leicester, Dept of English Local History Occasional Papers, 2nd series, 1, 1969

Feingold, M., 1984, *The Mathematician's Apprenticeship*, Cambridge, 1984

    ed., 1990, *Before Newton: The Life and Times of Isaac Barrow*, Cambridge, 1990

Ferguson, A.B., 1965, *The Articulate Citizen and the English Renaissance*, Durham, NC, 1965

Fifth Report from the Select Committee on Education, Parliamentary Paper 1818, IV

Finch, J., 1989, '"And God created all men equal". Status differentiation, expression and legitimation in funeral monuments, 1350–1850', University of East Anglia, MA thesis, 1989

Fincham, K., 1990, *Prelate as Pastor: The Episcopate of James I*, Oxford, 1990

Firth, C.H., ed., 1886, *The Life of William Cavendish, Duke of Newcastle, to which is added the true Relation of my Birth, Breeding and Life, by Margaret, Duchess of Newcastle*, London, 1886

Fletcher, C.R.L., and Upton, C.A., eds., 1885, 'All Souls College *versus* Lady Jane Stafford, 1587', in *Collectanea*, I, Oxford Record Society, Oxford, 1885, pp. 179–247

Fletcher, H.F., 1956–61, *The Intellectual Development of John Milton*, 2 vols., Urbana, 1956–61

Fletcher, J., 1983, 'Destruction, repair, and renewal: an Oxford college chapel during the Reformation', *Oxoniensia*, 48 (1983), 119–30

Flower, R., 1935, 'Laurence Nowell and the discovery of England in Tudor times', *Proceedings of the British Academy*, 21 (1935), 47–73

Forbes, M.D., 1928, *Clare College, 1326–1926*, 2 vols., Cambridge, 1928

Foster, A.W., 1978, 'A biography of Archbishop Richard Neile (1562–1640)', University of Oxford, DPhil thesis, 1978

    2000, 'Archbishop Richard Neile revisited', in Lake and Questier 2000, pp. 159–78

Foster, J., 1891–2, *Alumni Oxonienses*, 4 vols., Oxford, 1891–2

Bibliographical references

Foster, R., ed., 1966, *Proceedings in Parliament 1610*, Yale Historical Publications, Manuscripts and Edited Texts, New Haven, 1966

Fox, A., 1954, *John Mill and Richard Bentley: A Study of the Textual Criticism of the New Testament, 1675–1729*, Oxford, 1954

Fox, A., and Guy, J., 1986, *Reassessing the Henrician Age: Humanism, Politics and Reform 1500–1550*, Oxford, 1986

Fox, L., ed., 1956, *English Historical Scholarship in the Sixteenth and Seventeenth Centuries*, London, 1956

Fox, P., ed., 1998, *Cambridge University Library: The Great Collections*, Cambridge, 1998

Frank, R.G., 1973, 'Science, medicine and the universities of early modern England: background and sources', *History of Science*, 11 (1973), 194–216, 239–69

French, R., 1994, *William Harvey's Natural Philosophy*, Cambridge, 1994

Friedman, T., 1984, *James Gibbs*, New Haven, 1984

Fryde, E.B., Greenway, D.E., Porter, S., and Roy, I., eds., 1986, *Handbook of British Chronology*, 3rd edn, Royal Historical Society Guides and Handbooks, 1986

Fuller, M., 1897, *The Life, Letters and Writings of John Davenant, D.D., 1572–1641, Lord Bishop of Salisbury*, London, 1897

Fuller, T., 1655/1840, *The History of the University of Cambridge since the Conquest*, [London], 1655, cited from edn of 1840

  1662/1840, *The History of the Worthies of England*, London, 1662, cited also from edn of London, 1840

  1938, *The Holy State and the Profane State*, ed. M.G. Walton, 2 vols., New York, 1938

Gammon, S.R., 1973, *Statesman and Schemer: William First Lord Paget, Tudor Minister*, Newton Abbot, 1973

Garrard, B., 1986, 'Inns and innkeepeers in late sixteenth- and early seventeenth-century Norwich', University of East Anglia, MA thesis, 1986

Gascoigne, J., 1984, 'Mathematics and meritocracy: the emergence of the Cambridge Mathematical Tripos', *Social Studies of Science*, 14 (1984), 547–84

  1989, *Cambridge in the Age of the Enlightenment*, Cambridge, 1989

Gaskell, P., and Robson, R., 1971, *The Library of Trinity College, Cambridge: A Short History*, Cambridge, 1971

Gibbon, E., 1907, *Autobiography*, edn of London, 1907; see also Murray

Gibbons, A., ed., 1891, *Ely Episcopal Records: A Calendar and Concise View of the Episcopal Records Preserved in the Muniment Room of the Palace at Ely*, Lincoln, 1891

Girouard, M., 1980, *Life in the English Country House: A Social and Architectural History*, New Haven, 1978, cited from edn of Harmondsworth, 1980

Giuseppe, M.S., 1963, *Guide to the Contents of the Public Record Office*, revised edn, 2 vols., London, 1963

Gjertsen, D., 1986, *The Newton Handbook*, London, 1986

Glanville, J., 1768, *Laws Concerning the Election of MPs*, London, 1768

Gleason, J.H., 1969, *The Justices of the Peace in England, 1558 to 1640*, Oxford, 1969

Gneuss, H., 2001, 'Humfrey Wanley borrows books in Cambridge', *Transactions of the Cambridge Bibliographical Society*, 12, 2 (2001), 145–60

Godwin, F., 1601, *A Catalogue of the Bishops of England*, London, 1601 (2nd edn, 1615)

1616, 1743, *De praesulibus Angliae commentarius*, 2 parts, London, 1616; ed. W. Richardson, London, 1743

Goldie, M., 1991, 'The theory of religious intolerance in Restoration England', in *From Persecution to Toleration*, ed. O. Grell, J. Israel and N. Tyacke, Oxford, 1991, pp. 331–68

1993, 'John Locke, Jonas Proast and religious toleration 1688–1692', in Walsh, Haydon and Taylor 1993, pp. 143–71

1996, 'Joshua Basset, popery and revolution', in Beales and Nisbet 1996, pp. 111–30

Goose, N., 1980, 'Household size and structure in early-Stuart Cambridge', *Social History*, 5 (1980), 347–85

Graham, T., and Watson, A.G., eds., 1998, *The Recovery of the Past in Early Elizabethan England*, Cambridge Bibliographical Society Monograph 13, Cambridge, 1998

Graves, M.A.R., 1985, *The Tudor Parliament: Crown, Lords and Commons, 1485–1603*, Harlow, 1985

Graves, M.A.R., and Silcock, R.H., 1984, *Revolution, Reaction and the Triumph of Conservatism: English History 1558–1700*, Auckland, 1984

Gray, J., 1967, 'Thomas Alcock, master of Jesus College, Cambridge, in 1516', *Proceedings of the Cambridge Antiquarian Society*, 60 (1967), 91–5

Gray, J.H., 1926, *The Queens' College of St Margaret and St Bernard in the University of Cambridge*, Cambridge, 1926

Greenslade, S.L., Lampe, G.W.H., Ackroyd, P.R., and Evans, C.F., eds., 1963–70, *The Cambridge History of the Bible*, 3 vols., Cambridge, 1963–70

Greven, P.J., 1970, *Four Generations: Population, Land and Family in Colonial Andover, Massachusetts*, Ithaca, 1970

Griffiths, E., and Smith, A. Hassell, 1987, *'Buxom to the Mayor': A History of the Norwich Freemen and the Town Close Estate*, Norwich, 1987

Guy, J., ed., 1995, *The Reign of Elizabeth I: Court and Culture in the Last Decade*, Cambridge, 1995

ed., 1997, *The Tudor Monarchy*, London, 1997

Hackett, M.B., 1970, *The Original Statutes of Cambridge University: The Text and Its History*, Cambridge, 1970

Haigh, C., 1993, *The English Reformation: Religion, Politics and Society under the Tudors*, Oxford, 1993

Hair, P.E.H., 1970, 'A note on the incidence of Tudor suicide', *Local Population Studies*, 5 (1970), 36–43

Hall, A.R., 1990, *Henry More: Magic, Religion and Experiment*, Oxford, 1990

Bibliographical references

Hall, C.P., and Ravensdale, J.R., 1976, *The West Fields of Cambridge*, Cambridge Antiquarian Records Society, 3, 1976

Hallam, E., 1986, *Domesday Book through Nine Centuries*, London, 1986

Halliwell, J.O., ed., 1845, *The Autobiography and Correspondence of Sir Simonds D'Ewes Bart. during the Reigns of James I and Charles I*, 2 vols., London, 1845

Hammond, G., 1982, *The Making of the English Bible*, Manchester, 1982, repr. 1988

Hans, N.A., 1951, *New Trends in Education in the Eighteenth Century*, London, 1951

Harbage, A., 1952, *Shakespeare and the Rival Traditions*, New York, 1952

Hardwick, C., 1876, *A History of the Articles of Religion*, 3rd edn, ed. F. Procter, London, 1876

Hargreaves-Mawdsley, W.N., 1963, *A History of Academical Dress in Europe until the End of the Eighteenth Century*, Oxford, 1963

Harling, P., 1996, *The Waning of 'Old Corruption': The Politics of Economical Reform in Britain, 1779–1846*, Oxford, 1996

Harris, T., 1993, *Politics under the Later Stuarts: Party Conflict in a Divided Society 1660–1715*, Harlow, 1993

Harrison, C.J., 1971, 'Grain price analysis and harvest qualities, 1465–1634', *Agricultural History Review*, 19 (1971), 135–55

Harrison, W., 1968, *The Description of England*, ed. G. Edelen, Ithaca, 1968

Harrison, W.J., 1953, *Notes on the Masters, Fellows, Scholars and Exhibitioners of Clare College*, Cambridge, 1953

Hart, A. Tindal, 1949, *The Life and Times of John Sharp*, London, 1949

Harte, N.B., 1976, 'State control of dress and social change in pre-industrial England', in *Trade, Government and Economy in Pre-Industrial England: Essays Presented to F.J. Fisher*, ed. D.C. Coleman and A.H. John, London, 1976, pp. 132–65

Hasler, P.W., ed., 1981, *The History of Parliament: The House of Commons 1558–1603*, 3 vols., London, 1981

Heal, F., 1975–6, 'The parish clergy and the Reformation in the diocese of Ely', *Proceedings of the Cambridge Antiquarian Society*, 66 (1975–6), 146–63

   1980, *Of Prelates and Princes: A Study of the Economic and Social Position of the Tudor Episcopate*, Cambridge, 1980

Heal, F., and Holmes, C., 1994, *The Gentry in England and Wales, 1500–1700*, Basingstoke, 1994

Hearne, T., ed., 1719, *Thomas Sprott, Chronica*, Oxford, 1719

Helmholz, R.H., 1990, *Roman Canon Law in Reformation England*, Cambridge, 1990

Hembry, P., 1967, *The Bishops of Bath and Wells, 1540–1640: Social and Economic Problems*, London, 1967

Hexter, J.H., 1950/1961, 'The education of the aristocracy in the Renaissance', *Journal of Modern History*, 22 (1950), 1–20, repr. in Hexter, *Reappraisals in History*, London, 1961, pp. 45–70

1968, 'The English aristocracy, its crises, and the English Revolution, 1558–1660', *Journal of British Studies*, 8, 1 (1968), 22–78

Heywood, J., ed., 1838, *The Statutes of Queen Elizabeth for the University of Cambridge*, London, 1838

1840, *Collection of Statutes for the University and Colleges of Cambridge*, London, 1840

1855, *Early Cambridge University and College Statutes in the English Language*, 2 vols., London, 1855

Heywood, J., and Wright, T., eds., 1854, *Cambridge University Transactions during the Puritan Controversies of the Sixteenth and Seventeenth Centuries*, 2 vols., London, 1854

Highfield, J.R.L., 1984, 'The early colleges', in Catto 1984, pp. 225–63

Hill, B.W., 1976, *The Growth of Parliamentary Parties 1689–1742*, London, 1976

Hill, (J.E.)C., 1956/1971, *Economic Problems of the Church from Archbishop Whitgift to the Long Parliament*, Oxford, 1956, 2nd edn, London, 1971 (pagination unaltered)

1958/1962, *Puritanism and Revolution*, London, 1958, cited from the edn of 1962

1963a, *The Century of Revolution 1603–1714*, Nelson's History of England, Edinburgh, 1963

1963b, 'Puritans and "The dark corners of the land"', *Transactions of the Royal Historical Society*, 5th series, 13 (1963), 77–102

1964/1966, *Society and Puritanism in Pre-Revolutionary England*, London, 1964, 2nd edn, 1966

Hindle, S., 2000, *The State and Social Change in Early Modern England, 1550–1640*, Basingstoke, 2000

Hirst, D., 1975, *The Representative of the People? Voters and Voting in England under the Stuarts*, Cambridge, 1975

HMC 23 Cowper: Historical Manuscripts Commission [23], *The Manuscripts of the Earl Cowper, K.G., Preserved at Melbourne Hall, Derbyshire*, 3 vols., London, 1888–9

HMC 24: The Manuscripts of His Grace the Duke of Rutland, G.C.B., preserved at Belvoir Castle, 4 vols., London, 1888–1905

HMC 45: Historical Manuscripts Commission [45], *Report on the Manuscripts of His Grace the Duke of Buccleuch and Queensberry, K.G., K.T. . . .* , 3 vols. in 4, London, 1899–1926

HMC 47: Historical Manuscripts Commission [47], *The Manuscripts of Shrewsbury and Coventry Corporations . . .* , London, 1899

HMC [70] *Pepys: Report on the Pepys Manuscripts Preserved at Magdalene College, Cambridge*, London, 1911

HMCS: Historical Manuscripts Commission 9, Calendar of the Manuscripts of the Most Hon. the Marquis [al.Marquess] of Salisbury, K.G., preserved at Hatfield House, Hertfordshire, London, 1883–

Holmes, C., 1980, 'The county community in Stuart historiography', *Journal of British Studies*, 19 (1980), 54–73

Holmes, G., 1987, *British Politics in the Age of Anne*, 2nd edn, London, 1987

Horn, J.M., 1969, 1971, 1974, 1986, 1992, 1996, 2003, John le Neve, compiled by Joyce M. Horn, *Fasti Ecclesiae Anglicanae 1541–1857*, I, *St Paul's London*, II, *Chichester Diocese*, III, *Canterbury, Rochester and Winchester Dioceses*, VI, *Salisbury Diocese*, VII, *Ely, Norwich, Westminster and Worcester Dioceses*, VIII, *Bristol, Gloucester, Oxford and Peterborough Dioceses*, X, *Coventry and Lichfield Diocese*, London, 1969–2003

Horn, J.M., and Bailey, D.S., 1979, John Le Neve, compiled by J.M. Horn and D.S. Bailey, *Fasti Ecclesiae Anglicanae 1541–1857*, V, *Bath and Wells Diocese*, London, 1979

Horn, J.M., and Smith, D.M., 1975, 1999, John le Neve, compiled by J.M. Horn and D.M. Smith, *Fasti Ecclesiae Anglicanae 1541–1857*, IV, *York Diocese*, IX, *Lincoln Diocese*, London, 1975, 1999

Horn, J.M., Smith, D.M., and Mussett, P., 2003, John Le Neve, compiled by J.M. Horn, D.M. Smith and P. Mussett, *Fasti Ecclesiae Anglicanae 1541–1857*, XI, *Carlisle, Chester, Durham, Manchester, Ripon, Sodor and Man Dioceses*, London, 2003

Houlbrooke, R.A., ed., 1975, *The Letter Book of John Parkhurst, Bishop of Norwich, Compiled during the Years 1571–5*, NRS, 43, 1975

Housden, J.A.J., 1903, 'Early posts in England', *EHR*, 18 (1903), 713–18

Housman, A.E., ed., 1903/1937, *M. Manilii Astronomicon Liber Primus*, London, 1903, cited from 2nd edn, Cambridge, 1937

Howard, H.F., 1935, *An Account of the Finances of the College of St John the Evangelist in the University of Cambridge, 1511–1926*, Cambridge, 1935

Howard, P., 2000, 'Norwich craftsmen in wood 1550–1750: a study of communities', University of East Anglia, MPhil thesis, 2000

Hoyle, D., 1986, 'A Commons investigation of Arminianism and popery in Cambridge on the eve of the Civil War', *Historical Journal*, 29 (1986), 419–25

Hudson, W.S., 1980, *The Cambridge Connection and the Elizabethan Settlement of 1559*, Durham, NC, 1980

Hughes, S.F., 1998, '"The problem of 'Calvinism'": English theologies of predestination *c.* 1580–1630', in Wabuda and Litzenberger 1998, pp. 229–49

Hughey, R., ed., 1941, *The Correspondence of Lady Katherine Paston, 1603–1627*, NRS, 14, 1941

Humberstone, T.L., 1951, *University Representation*, London, 1951

Hunter, M., 1981, *Science and Society in Restoration England*, Cambridge, 1981
1982, *The Royal Society and Its Fellows 1660–1700*, British Society for the History of Science Monographs, 4, Chalfont St Giles, 1982

Hurstfield, J., 1958, *The Queen's Wards: Wardship and Marriage under Elizabeth I*, London, 1958

Bibliographical references

1967, 'Was there a Tudor despotism after all?', *Transactions of the Royal Historical Society*, 5th series, 17 (1967), 83–108

1968, 'Social structure, office-holding and politics, chiefly in western Europe', in *The New Cambridge Modern History*, III, *The Counter-Reformation and the Price Revolution, 1559–1610*, ed. R.B. Wernham, Cambridge, 1968, pp. 126–49

Ives, E.W., 1986, *Anne Boleyn*, Oxford, 1986

Jackman, W.T., 1962, *The Development of Transportation in Modern England*, London, 1962

Jackson-Stops, G., 1979, 'The building of the medieval college', in *New College, Oxford, 1379–1979*, ed. J. Buxton and P. Williams, Oxford, 1979, pp. 147–92

James, M.E., 1967, 'The fourth duke of Norfolk and the North', *Northern History*, 3 (1967), 150–2

1986, *Society, Politics and Culture: Studies in Early Modern England*, Cambridge, 1986

Jamison, C., and Bill, E.G.W., eds., 1966, *A Calendar of the Shrewsbury and Talbot Papers in Lambeth Palace Library and the College of Arms*, I, *The Shrewsbury Papers in Lambeth Palace Library (MSS 694–710)*, London, 1966

JEH: Journal of Ecclesiastical History

Johnson, T., 1735, *Quaestiones philosophicae*, Cambridge, 1735

Jones, G., 1969, *A History of the Law of Charity 1532–1827*, Cambridge, 1969

Jones, M.K., and Underwood, M.G., 1992, *The King's Mother: Lady Margaret Beaufort, Countess of Richmond and Derby*, Cambridge, 1992

Jones, T.I. Jeffreys, 1938, 'A study of rents and fines in South Wales in the sixteenth and early seventeenth centuries', in *Harlech Studies: Essays Presented to Dr Thomas Jones, C.H.*, ed. B.B. Thomas, Cardiff, 1938, pp. 215–44

Jones, W.R.D., 1970, *The Tudor Commonwealth, 1529–1559*, London, 1970

Jordan, W.K., 1959, *Philanthropy in England 1480–1660: A Study of the Changing Pattern of English Social Aspirations*, London, 1959

1960, *The Charities of London 1480–1660: The Aspirations and Achievements of the Urban Society*, London, 1960

1961, *The Charities of Rural England*, London, 1961

ed., 1966, *The Chronicle and Political Papers of King Edward VI*, London, 1966

Kearney, H., 1970, *Scholars and Gentlemen: Universities and Society in Pre-industrial Britain*, London, 1970

Keene, D., 1982, 'Town into gown: the site of the College and other College lands in Winchester before the Reformation', in *Winchester College: Sixth-Centenary Essays*, ed. R. Custance, Oxford, 1982, pp. 37–75

Kenney, E.J., 1974, *The Classical Texts*, Cambridge, 1974

Key, J., 1993, 'The letters and will of Lady Dororthy Bacon, 1597–1629', in *A Miscellany*, NRS 56, 1993, pp. 77–112

Kibre, P., 1947, *The Nations in the Mediaeval Universities*, Medieval Academy of America Publications, 49, Cambridge, Mass., 1947

Bibliographical references

Kinge, J., 1597, *Lectures upon Jonas, delivered at York in the Year of Our Lord 1594*, Oxford, 1597

Kishlansky, M.A., 1986, *Parliamentary Selection: Social and Political Choice in Early Modern England*, Cambridge, 1986

Knappen, M.M., 1933, *Two Elizabethan Puritan Diaries*, Chicago, 1933

Knights, M., 1994, *Politics and Opinion in Crisis, 1678–1681*, Cambridge, 1994

Knowles, D., 1955, 1959, *The Religious Orders in England*, II, *The End of the Middle Ages*, III, *The Tudor Age*, Cambridge, 1955, 1959

    1963a, *The Historian and Character and Other Essays*, Cambridge, 1963

    1963b, *Great Historical Enterprises: Essays in Monastic History*, London, 1963

Kroll, R., Ashcraft, R., and Zagorin, P., eds., 1992, *Philosophy, Science and Religion in England 1640–1700*, Cambridge, 1992

Kussmaul, A., 1981, *Servants in Husbandry in Early Modern England*, Cambridge, 1981

Lake, P., 1978, 'Laurence Chaderton and the Cambridge moderate Puritan tradition', University of Cambridge, PhD thesis, 1978

    1982, *Moderate Puritans and the Elizabethan Church*, Cambridge, 1982

    1988, *Anglicans and Puritans? Presbyterianism and English Conformist Thought from Whitgift to Hooker*, London, 1988

    1995, 'Presbyterian propositions', *Journal of Ecclesiastical History*, 46 (1995), 110–23

Lake, P., and Questier, M., eds., 2000, *Conformity and Orthodoxy in the English Church, c. 1560–1660*, Woodbridge, 2000

Lamb, J., ed., 1838, *A Collection of Letters, Statutes and Other Documents from the MS Library of Corpus Christi College, Illustrative of the History of the University of Cambridge during the Period of the Reformation, from AD MD to AD MDLXXII*, London, 1838

Laslett, P., 1948, 'The gentry of Kent in 1640', *Cambridge Historical Journal*, 9 (1948), 148–64

Laslett, P., and Wall, R., 1972, *Household and Family in Past Time*, Cambridge, 1972

Laud, W., 1847–60, *Works*, ed. W. Scott and J. Bliss, Library of Anglo-Catholic Theology, 7 vols., London, 1847–60

Lawson, J., 1963, *A Town Grammar School through Six Centuries: A History of Hull Grammar School against Its Local Background*, Oxford, 1963

Leader, D.R., 1988, *A History of the University of Cambridge*, I, *The University to 1546*, Cambridge, 1988

Leathes, S.M., ed., 1897, *Grace Book A*, Cambridge, 1897

Lee, M., ed., 1972, *Dudley Carleton to John Chamberlain, 1603–1624: Jacobean Letters*, New Brunswick, 1972

Leedham-Green, E., 1981, 'A catalogue of Caius College library, 1569', *Transactions of the Cambridge Bibliographical Society*, 8, 1 (1981), 29–41

    ed., 1986, *Books in Cambridge Inventories*, 2 vols., Cambridge, 1986

    1991, 'Perne's wills', in McKitterick 1991, pp. 79–119

Bibliographical references

1996, *A Concise History of the University of Cambridge*, Cambridge, 1996

Le Faye, D., ed., 1995, *Jane Austen's Letters*, Oxford, 1995

Legge, T., 1992, *The Complete Plays*, ed. D.F. Sutton, New York, 1992

Leishman, J.B., ed., 1949, *The Three Parnassus Plays (1598–1601)*, London, 1949

Leonard, H., 1970, 'Knights and knighthood in Tudor England', University of London, PhD thesis, 1970

Levack, B.P., 1973, *The Civil Lawyers in England, 1603–1641*, Oxford, 1973

Levine, J.M., 1992, 'Latitudinarians, neoplatonists and the ancient wisdom', in Kroll *et al.* 1992, pp. 85–108

Lewis, I., ed., 1977, *Symbols and Sentiments: Cross-cultural Studies in Symbolism*, London, 1977

Lewis, J., 1855, *The Life of Dr John Fisher*, 2 vols., London, 1855

Lewis, T.T., ed., 1854, *Letters of the Lady Brilliana Harley*, Camden Society, 58, London, 1854

Linnell, C.L.S., 1955, in *Gresham's School History and Register*, ed. A. B. Douglas, Holt, 1955, pp. 11–30

Lipincott, H.P., ed., 1974, *'Merry Passages and Jeasts': A Manuscript Jestbook of Sir Nicholas Le Strange (1603–1655)*, Salzburg, 1974

LJ: House of Lords Journals

Lloyd, A.H., 1931, 'John Rant, a college lawyer of the seventeenth century', *Proceedings of the Cambridge Antiquarian Society*, 31 (1931), 88–98

Lloyd, H.A., 1968, *The Gentry of South-West Wales, 1540–1640*, Cardiff, 1968

Loach, J., 1991, *Parliament under the Tudors*, Oxford, 1991

Loades, D., 1992, *The Tudor Court*, 2nd edn, London, 1992

Lobel, M.D., and Johns, A.H., 1975, *Atlas of Historic Towns*, II, *Cambridge* fascicule, 1975

Lockridge, K.A., 1970, *A New England Town, the First Hundred Years: Dedham, Massachusetts, 1636–1736*, New York, 1970

Logan, F.D., 1977, 'The origins of the so-called Regius Professorships: an aspect of the Renaissance in Oxford and Cambridge', *Studies in Church History*, 14 (1977), 271–8

Lovatt, R., 1981, 'John Blacman: biographer of Henry VI', in *The Writing of History in the Middle Ages: Essays Presented to Richard William Southern*, Oxford, 1981, pp. 415–44

LP: Letters and Papers, Foreign and Domestic, of the Reign of Henry VIII, ed. J.S. Brewer, J. Gairdner and R.H. Brodie, 36 vols., London, 1862–1932

Luckett, R., 1973, 'Church and college 1660–1745', in Rich 1973, pp. 110–37

Ludlow, M., 2000, *Universal Salvation: Eschatology in the Thought of Gregory of Nyssa and Karl Rahner*, Oxford, 2000

2003, 'Universalism in the history of Christian theology', in *Universal Salvation: The Contemporary Debate*, ed. R. Parry and C. Partridge, Carlisle, 2003, forthcoming

Lyons, C., 1910, 'The old plate of the Cambridge colleges', *Burlington Magazine*, 17 (1910), 214–20

Bibliographical references

Mabillon, J., 1681, *De Re Diplomatica*, Paris, 1681

MacCaffrey, W.T., 1961, 'Place and patronage in Elizabethan politics', in Bindoff *et al.* 1961, pp. 95–126

1965, 'England: the crown and the new aristocracy, 1540–1600', *Past and Present*, 30 (1965), 52–64

1968, *The Shaping of the Elizabethan Regime*, Princeton, 1968

McConica, J., 1965, *English Humanists and Reformation Politics under Henry VIII and Edward VI*, Oxford, 1965

1973, 'The prosopography of the Tudor university', *Journal of Interdisciplinary History*, 3 (1973), 543–54

1975, 'Scholars and commoners in Renaissance Oxford', in Stone 1975, pp. 151–82

1977, 'The social relations of Tudor Oxford', *Transactions of the Royal Historical Society*, 5th series, 27 (1977), 115–34

ed., 1986, *The History of the University of Oxford*, III, *The Collegiate University*, Oxford, 1986

MacCulloch, D., 1986, *Suffolk and the Tudors: Politics and Religion in an English County, 1500–1600*, Oxford, 1986

1996, *Thomas Cranmer: A Life*, New Haven and London, 1996

McDowall, R.W., 1950, 'Buckingham College', *Proceedings of the Cambridge Antiquarian Society*, 44 (1950), 1–12

McKisack, M., 1971, *Medieval History in the Tudor Age*, Oxford, 1971

McKitterick, D., 1984, *Four Hundred Years of University Printing and Publishing in Cambridge, 1584–1984*, Cambridge, 1984

1986, *Cambridge University Library: A History. The Eighteenth and Nineteenth Centuries*, Cambridge, 1986

1991, *Andrew Perne: Quatercentenary Studies*, Cambridge, 1991, including D. McKitterick, 'Andrew Perne and his books', pp. 35–69

ed., 1995, *The Making of the Wren Library, Trinity College, Cambridge*, Cambridge, 1995

1998, *A History of the Cambridge University Press*, II, *Scholarship and Commerce, 1698–1872*, Cambridge, 1998

Maclear, J.F., 1957–8, 'Puritan relations with Buckingham', *Huntington Library Quarterly*, 21 (1957–8), 111–32

McMahon, C.P., 1947, *Education in Fifteenth-Century England*, Baltimore, 1947 (repr. New York, 1968)

Macray, W.D., ed., 1894–1915, *A Register of the Members of St Mary Magdalen College, Oxford, from the Foundation of the College*, new series, 8 vols., 1894–1915

Macy, G., 1992, *The Banquet's Wisdom*, New York, 1992

Maitland, S.R., 1847–8, 'Archbishop Whitgift's college pupils I–VI', *British Magazine and Monthly Register of Religious and Ecclesiastical Information*, 32 (1847), 361–79, 508–28, 650–6; 33 (1848), 17–31, 185–97, 444–63

Bibliographical references

Makower, F., 1895, *The Constitutional History and the Constitution of the Church of England*, London, 1895

Mallet, C.E., 1924–7, *A History of the University of Oxford*, 3 vols., Oxford, 1924–7

Mandelbrote, S., 2001, *Footprints of the Lion: Isaac Newton at Work. Exhibition at Cambridge University Library 9 October 2001–23 March 2002*, Cambridge, 2001

Marsden, J.H., 1851, *College Life in the Time of James the First as Illustrated by an Unpublished Diary of Sir Symonds D'Ewes*, London, 1851

Marshall, A., 1999, *The Age of Faction: Court Politics 1660–1702*, Manchester, 1999

Martin, G.H., 1976, 'Road travel in the Middles Ages: some journeys by the warden and fellows of Merton College, Oxford, 1315–1470', *Journal of Transport History*, 3 (1976), 159–78

Martin, G.H., and Highfield, J.R.L., 1997, *A History of Merton College, Oxford*, Oxford, 1997

Mason, R.H., 1884, *The History of Norfolk*, London, 1884

Masson, D., 1859, *The Life of John Milton, Narrated in Connexion with the Political, Ecclesiastical and Literary History of His Time*, London, 1859

Masters, R., 1753, 1831, *The History of the College of Corpus Christi and the B. Virgin Mary (commonly called Bene't) in the University of Cambridge*, Cambridge, 1753; also cited in edn of J. Lamb, 1831

   1784, *Memoirs of the Life and Writings of the late Rev. Thomas Baker . . . from the Papers of Dr Zachary Gray*, Cambridge, 1784

Mayor, J.E.B., 1859, 1865–6, 'Letters of Archbishop Williams, with material for his life', *Cambridge Antiquarian Communications*, 2 (1864 for 1859), 25–66; 3 (1879 for 1865–6), 61–106

   ed., 1893, *Admissions to the College of St John the Evangelist in the University of Cambridge . . . , January 1629–30 July 1915*, Cambridge, 1893

Mede [Mead], J., 1648–50, 1677, *Works*, London, 1648–50, cited from 4th edn, 1677

Mill, J., ed., 1707, *Novum Testamentum*, Oxford, 1707

Miller, E., 1961, *Portrait of a College: A History of the College of St John the Evangelist, Cambridge*, Cambridge, 1961

Miller, E.H., 1959, *The Professional Writer in Elizabethan England*, Cambridge, Mass., 1959

Mills, G., 1990, 'School and university: an examination of the pupils/students who attended the King Edward VI Free Grammar School, Bury St Edmund's, and Cambridge University, 1550–1750', University of East Anglia, MA thesis, 1990

Milton, A., 1995, *Catholic and Reformed: The Roman and Protestant Churches in English Protestant Thought, 1600–1640*, Cambridge, 1995

Moir, T.L., 1958, *The Addled Parliament of 1614*, Oxford, 1958

Monk, J.H., 1826, *Memoir of Dr James Duport*, 1826

   1830, *The Life of Richard Bentley, D.D.*, London and Cambridge, 1830 (cited from one-vol. edn)

Bibliographical references

Moorman, J.R.H., 1952, *The Grey Friars in Cambridge, 1225–1538*, Cambridge, 1952

More, J., 1594, *Three godly and fruitful Sermons*, 1594

Morgan, V., 1968, 'The community of the county 1540–1640', University of East Anglia, BA thesis, 1968

    1975, 'Cambridge University and "the Country", 1560–1640', in Stone 1975, I, pp. 183–245

    1978, 'Approaches to the history of the English universities in the sixteenth and seventeenth centuries', in *Bildung, Politik und Gesellschaft*, ed. G. Klingenstein, H. Lutz and G. Stourzh, Vienna, 1978, pp. 138–64

    1979, 'The cartographic image of "The Country" in early modern England', *Transactions of the Royal Historical Society*, 5th series, 29 (1979), 129–54

    1980, 'L'università di Cambridge e il suo retroterra sociale 1560–1640', in *L'Università nella società*, ed. L. Stone (Bologna, 1980), pp. 203–80

    1983, 'County, Court and Cambridge University, 1558–1640: a study in the evolution of a political culture', University of East Anglia, PhD thesis, 1983

    1984, 'Whose prerogative in late-sixteenth and early-seventeenth century England?', *Journal of Legal History*, 5 (1984), 39–64

    1986, 'Su alcune forme di padrinaggio nell'Inghilterra dei secoi XVI e XVII', *Cheiron*, 5 (1986), 23–45

    1987, 'Cambridge University, religion and the regions, 1560–1640', in *Regional Studies in the History of Religion in Britain since the Later Middle Ages*, ed. E. Royle, Humberside [1987], pp. 57–79

    1988, 'Some types of patronage, mainly in sixteenth- and seventeenth-century England', in *Klientelsysteme im Europa der frühen Neuzeit*, ed. A. Mączak (Munich, 1988), pp. 91–116

    1992, 'The Norwich Guildhall portraits: images in context', in *Family and Friends: A Regional Survey of British Portraiture*, ed. A. Moore and C. Crawley, London, 1992, pp. 21–9

    1996, 'The Elizabethan shirehouse at Norwich', in *Counties and Communities: Essays on East Anglian History Presented to Hassell Smith*, ed. C. Rawcliffe, R. Virgoe and R. Wilson, Norwich, 1996, pp. 149–60

    1999a, 'Perambulating and consumable emblems: the Norwich evidence', in *Deviceful Settings: The English Renaissance Emblem and Its Contexts: Selected Papers from the Third International Emblem Conference*, ed. M. Bath and D. Russell, New York, 1999, pp. 167–206

    1999b, 'The construction of civic memory in early modern Norwich', in *Material Memories*, ed. M. Kwint, C. Breward and J. Aynsley, Oxford and New York, 1999, pp. 183–97

    2001, 'Government, Local', 'Justice of the Peace' and 'Sheriff', in *Tudor England: An Encyclopaedia*, ed. A.F. Kinney, D.W. Swain, E.D. Hill and W.B. Long, New York, 2001, pp. 298–300, 403–4, 643–4

    forthcoming, 'The election of the duke of Buckingham as chancellor of Cambridge University: an episode in national politics', forthcoming

Bibliographical references

Morgan, V., Key, J., and Taylor, B., eds., 2000, *The Papers of Nathaniel Bacon of Stiffkey*, IV, *1596–1602*, NRS, 64, 2000
Morison, S.E., 1935, *The Founding of Harvard College*, Cambridge, Mass., 1935
Morris, B., and Withington, E., eds., 1967, *The Poems of John Cleveland*, Oxford, 1967
Mousley, J.E., 1956, 'Sussex country gentry in the reign of Elizabeth', University of London, PhD thesis, 1956
Mullinger, J.B., 1867, *Cambridge Characteristics in the Seventeenth Century*, London, 1867
    1873, *The University of Cambridge from the Earliest Times to the Royal Injunctions of 1535*, Cambridge, 1873
    1883, 'Cambridge life in the latter part of the sixteenth century', *The Eagle* 12 (1883), 285–93, 321–30
    1884, *The University of Cambridge from the Royal Injunctions of 1535 to the Accession of Charles the First*, Cambridge, 1884
    1911, *The University of Cambridge, Volume III, from the Election of Buckingham to the Chancellorship in 1626 to the Decline of the Platonist Movement*, Cambridge, 1911
Murray, J., ed., 1896, *The Autobiography of Edward Gibbon*, London, 1896
Neale, G.W., 1909, *The Early Honours Lists (1498–9 to 1746–7) of the University of Cambridge*, Bury St Edmunds, 1909
Neale, J.E., 1953, *Elizabeth and Her Parliaments, 1559–81*, London, 1953
    1957, *Elizabeth and Her Parliaments, 1584–1601*, London, 1957
Neill, S., and Wright, T., 1988, *The Interpretation of the New Testament, 1861–1986*, Oxford, 1988
Nelson, A.H., ed., 1989, *Records of Early English Drama: Cambridge*, 2 vols., Toronto, 1989
    1994, *Early Cambridge Theatres: College, University, and Town Stages, 1464–1720*, Cambridge, 1994
Newcourt, R., 1708–10, *Repertorium ecclesiasticum parochiale Londinense*, 2 vols., London, 1708–10
Newman, J., 1986, 'The physical setting: new building and adaptation', in McConica 1986, pp. 597–641
Newton, I., 1959–77, *The Correspondence of Isaac Newton*, ed. H.W. Turnbull, J.F. Scott and A.R. Hall, 7 vols., Cambridge, 1959–77
    1967–81, *The Mathematical Papers of Isaac Newton*, ed. D.T. Whiteside, 8 vols., Cambridge, 1967–81
    1978, *Isaac Newton's Papers and Letters on Natural Philosophy*, ed. I.B. Cohen, Cambridge, Mass., 1978
Nicholls, J., 1812–16, *Literary Anecdotes of the Eighteenth Century*, 9 vols., London, 1812–16
Nicolson, M.H., 1929–30, 'Christ's College and the Latitude-men', *Modern Philology*, 27 (1929–30), 35–53

Bibliographical references

ed., 1930, *Conway Letters: The Correspondence of Anne, Viscountess Conway, Henry More and their Friends, 1642–1684*, New Haven, 1930

Notestein, W., ed., 1923, *The Journal of Sir Simonds D'Ewes from the Beginning of the Long Parliament to the Opening of the Trial of the Earl of Strafford*, Yale Historical Publications, Manuscripts and Edited Texts, 7, New Haven, 1923

1954, *The English People on the Eve of Colonisation: 1603–1630*, New York, 1954

1971, *The House of Commons 1604–1610*, New Haven, 1971

Notestein, W., Relf, F.H., and Simpson, H., eds., 1935, *Commons Debates 1621*, Yale Historical Publications, Manuscripts and Edited Texts, 14, 7 vols., New Haven, 1935

Null, A., 2000, *Thomas Cranmer's Doctrine of Repentance*, Oxford, 2000

Nutton, V., 1987, *John Caius and the Manuscripts of Galen*, Cambridge Philological Society, Supplementary Volume 13, Cambridge, 1987

Oates, J.C.T., 1986, *Cambridge University Library: A History from the Beginnings to the Copyright Act of Queen Anne*, Cambridge, 1986

O'Day, R., 1979, *The English Clergy: The Emergence and the Consolidation of a Profession 1558–1642*, Leicester, 1979

1982, *Education and Society 1500–1800: The Social Foundations of Education in Early Modern Britain*, Harlow, 1982

ODCC: *The Oxford Dictionary of the Christian Church*, 3rd edn, ed. F.L. Cross and E.A. Livingstone, Oxford, 1997

O'Donohoe, J.A., 1965, 'The seminary legislation of the Council of Trent', in *Il Concilio di Trento e la Riforma Tridentina*, Rome, 1965, I, pp. 157–72

OED: *The Oxford English Dictionary*

Ong, W.J., 1959, 'Latin language study as a Renaissance puberty rite', *Studies in Philology*, 56, 2 (1959), 103–24

Osborne, H., n.d., *Earle: Microcosmography*, London, n.d.

Owens, G.L., 1970, 'Norfolk 1620–1641: local government and central authority in an East Anglian county', University of Wisconsin, PhD thesis, 1970

Oxford DNB: *The Oxford Dictionary of National Biography*, Oxford, forthcoming, 2004

Parker, M., 1572, *De Antiquitate Britannicae Ecclesiae*, London, 1572

1853, *The Correspondence of Matthew Parker*, ed. J. Bruce and T.T. Perowne, Parker Society, 1853

Parker, R., 1721, *The History and Antiquities of the University of Cambridge*, Cambridge, 1721

Parker, R., 1983, *Town and Gown: The 700 Years' War in Cambridge*, Cambridge, 1983

Parsons, D., ed., 1876, *The Diary of Henry Slingsby*, London, 1876

Partridge, A.C., 1969, *Tudor to Augustan English: A Study in Syntax and Style from Caxton to Johnson*, London, 1969

Passmore, J.A., 1951, *Ralph Cudworth, an Appreciation*, Cambridge, 1951

Patten, J., 1978, *English Towns 1500–1700*, Folkestone, 1978

Bibliographical references

Patterson, C.F., 1999, *Urban Patronage in Early Modern England: Corporate Boroughs, the Landed Elite, and the Crown, 1580–1640*, Stanford, 1999

Peacock, G., 1841, *Observations on the Statutes of the University of Cambridge*, London, 1841

Pearson, A.F. Scott, 1925, *Thomas Cartwright and Elizabethan Puritanism 1535–1603*, London, 1925

Peel, A., ed., 1915, *The Seconde Parte of a Register*, 2 vols., Cambridge, 1915

Peile, J., 1900, *Christ's College*, London, 1900

    1910–13, *Biographical Register of Christ's College, 1505–1905*, 2 vols., Cambridge, 1910–13

Penry, J., 1960, *Three Treatises concerning Wales*, ed. D. Williams, Cardiff, 1960

Pevsner, N., 1970, *The Buildings of England: Cambridgeshire*, 2nd edn, Harmondsworth, 1970

Plumb, J.H., 1967, *The Growth of Political Stability in England 1675–1725*, London, 1967

Pocock, J.G.A., 1950–2, 'Robert Brady, 1627–1700. A Cambridge historian of the Restoration', *Cambridge Historical Journal*, 10 (1950–2), 186–204

    1957, *The Ancient Constitution and the Feudal Law*, Cambridge, 1957

    1975, *The Machiavellian Moment: Florentine Political Thought and the Atlantic Republican Tradition*, Princeton, 1975

Porter, H.C., 1958/1972, *Reformation and Reaction in Tudor Cambridge*, Cambridge, 1958; corr. repr., Hamden, Conn., 1972

Pound, J.F., 1962, 'An Elizabethan census of the poor', *Birmingham University Historical Journal*, 8 (1962), 135–61

    1971, *The Norwich Census of the Poor 1570*, NRS, 40, 1971

    1988, *Tudor and Stuart Norwich*, Chichester, 1988

Powell, S.C., 1963, *Puritan Village: The Formation of a New England Town*, Middletown, Conn., 1963

Powicke, F. M., 1930, 'Sir Henry Spelman and the "Concilia"', *Proceedings of the British Academy*, 16 (1930), 3–37

Powicke, F.M., and Cheney, C.R., eds., 1964, *Councils and Synods with Other Documents relating to the English Church*, II, *A.D. 1205–1313*, 2 parts, Oxford, 1964

Prest, W.R., 1965, 'Some aspects of the Inns of Court, 1630–39', Oxford, DPhil thesis, 1965

    1972, *The Inns of Court under Elizabeth I and the Early Stuarts, 1590–1640*, London, 1972

Prestwich, M., ed., 1985, *International Calvinism*, Oxford, 1985

Purnell, E.K., 1904, *Magdalene College*, London, 1904

Quintrell, B.W., 1965, 'The government of the County of Essex, 1603–1642', University of London, PhD thesis, 1965

Rabb, T.K., 1967, *Enterprise and Empire: Merchant and Gentry Investment in the Expansion of England 1575–1630*, Cambridge, Mass., 1967

Bibliographical references

Rackham, O., 1987–8, 'The making of the Old Court', *Letter of the Corpus Association*, 66 (1987), 33–48; 67 (1988), 45–55

Raleigh, W., 1829, *Works*, Oxford, 1829

Randolph, T., 1875, *Poetical and Dramatic Works*, ed. W.C. Hazlitt, 2 vols., London, 1875

Rashdall, H., 1936, *The Universities of Europe in the Middle Ages*, ed. F.M. Powicke and A.B. Emden, 3 vols., Oxford, 1936

RCHM, *Cambridge*: Royal Commission on Historical Monuments for England, *City of Cambridge*, 2 parts, London, 1959

Rees, J., 1971, *Fulke Greville, Lord Brooke, 1554–1628: A Critical Biography*, London, 1971

Reeves, M.E., 1969/1993, *The Influence of Prophecy in the Later Middle Ages: A Study in Joachism*, Oxford, 1969, 2nd edn, 1993

   1969a, 'The European university from medieval times with special reference to Oxford and Cambridge', in *Higher Education: Demand and Response*, ed. W.R. Niblett, London, 1969, pp. 61–84

Report of the Commissioners appointed to Inquire into the . . . University and Colleges of Cambridge [Graham Commission Report and Evidence], Parliamentary Papers 1852–3, HC xliv [1559], 1852–3

Rex, M.B., 1954, *University Representation in England 1604–1690*, Etudes présentées à la Commission internationale pour l'histoire des assemblées d'états, 15, London, 1954

Rex, R., and Armstrong, C.D.C., 2002, 'Henry VIII's ecclesiastical and collegiate foundations', *Historical Research*, 75 (2002), 390–407

Rich, E.E., ed., 1973, *St Catharine's College, Cambridge, 1473–1973*, London, 1973

Rimboutt, E.F., ed., 1890, *The Miscellaneous Works in Prose and Verse of Sir Thomas Overbury, Kt.*, London, 1890

Ringrose, J., 1993, 'The medieval statutes of Pembroke college', in Zutshi 1993, pp. 93–127

   1997, 'The foundress and her college', in *Pembroke College Cambridge: A Celebration*, ed. A.V. Grimstone, Cambridge, 1997, pp. 1–12

   1998, 'The Royal Library: John Moore and his books', in Fox 1998, ch. 6.

Roach, J., 1962, 'The Victoria County History of Cambridge', *Proceedings of the Cambridge Antiquarian Society*, 54 (1962 for 1960), 112–26

Rogers, N., 1990, *Whigs and Cities: Popular Politics in the Age of Walpole and Pitt*, Oxford, 1990

   1994, 'The middling sort in eighteenth-century politics', in *The Middling Sort of People: Culture, Society and Politics in England, 1550–1800*, ed. J. Barry and C. Brooks, Basingstoke, 1994, pp. 159–80

Rook, A., ed., 1971, *Cambridge and Its Contribution to Medicine*, London, 1971

Roots, I., 1968, 'The central government and the local community', in *The English Revolution, 1600–60*, ed. E.W. Ives, London, 1968, pp. 34–47

Rosenberg, E., 1955, *Leicester, Patron of Letters*, New York, 1955

Bibliographical references

Rothblatt, S., 1981, *The Revolution of the Dons: Cambridge and Society in Victorian England*, 2nd edn, Cambridge, 1981

Rubin, M., 1987, *Charity and Community in Medieval Cambridge*, Cambridge, 1987

Rubinstein, W.D., 1983, 'The end of "Old Corruption" in Britain, 1780–1860', *Past and Present*, 101 (1983), 55–86

Rupp, G., 1977, *Just Men*, London, 1977

Russell, C., 1976, 'Parliamentary history in perspective, 1604–1629', *History*, 61 (1976), 1–27

   1979, *Parliaments and English Politics 1621–1629*, Oxford, 1979

   1983, 'The nature of a parliament in early Stuart England', in *Before the Civil War: Essays on Early Stuart Politics and Government*, ed. H. Tomlinson, London, 1983, pp. 123–50

Russell, E., 1977, 'The influx of commoners into the University of Oxford before 1581: an optical illusion?', *English Historical Review*, 92 (1977), 721–45

Ryan, L.V., 1963, *Roger Ascham*, Stanford, 1963

Salway, P., 1996, 'Sidney before the college', in Beales and Nisbet 1996, pp. 3–34

Sandeen, E.R., 1959, 'The building activities of Sir Nicholas Bacon', University of Chicago, PhD thesis, 1959

   1962, 'The building of the sixteenth-century Corpus Christi College chapel', *Proceedings of the Cambridge Antiquarian Society*, 55 (1962), 23–35

Sanderson, W., 1656, *A Compleat History of the Lives and Reigns of Mary Queen of Scotland and her Son . . . James*, 2 parts, London, 1656

Saunders, H.W., 1932, *A History of the Norwich Grammar School*, Norwich, 1932

Saunders, J.W., 1964, *The Profession of English Letters*, London, 1964

Saveson, J.E., 1958, 'The Library of John Smith, the Cambridge Platonist', *Notes and Queries*, 203 (1958), 215–16

Savile, H., ed., 1596, *Rerum Anglicarum Scriptores post Bedam*, London, 1596

Scarisbrick, J., 1968, *Henry VIII*, London, 1968

SCH: Studies in Church History

Schochet, G.J., 1975, *Patriarchalism in Political Thought: The Authoritarian Family and Political Speculation and Attitudes, especially in Seventeenth-Century England*, Oxford, 1975

Scot, T., 1623, *The Highwaies of God and the King*, London, 1623

Scott, E.J.L., ed., 1884, *Letter-book of Gabriel Harvey, A.D. 1573–1580*, Camden Society, new series, 33, 1884

Scott, R.F., 1897, 'Notes from the College Records', *The Eagle*, 19 (1897), 137–45

   1898, 'Notes from the College Records', *The Eagle*, 20 (1898), 281–300

   1900, 'Notes from the College Records', *The Eagle*, 21 (1900), 269–89

   1907, 'Notes from the College Records', *The Eagle*, 28 (1907), 135–63

   1908, 'Notes from the College Records', *The Eagle*, 29 (1908), 130–61

   1909, 'Notes from the College Records', *The Eagle*, 31 (1909), 4–37, 281–316

Scott-Giles, C.W., 1975, *Sidney Sussex College: A Short History*, Cambridge, 1975

Searby, P., 1997, *A History of the University of Cambridge*, III, *1750–1870*, Cambridge, 1997

Searle, W.G., 1867–71, *The History of Queens' College of St Margaret and St Bernard in the University of Cambridge, 1446–1662*, 2 vols., Cambridge Antiquarian Society, 1867–71

Seaver, P.S., 1970, *The Puritan Lectureships: The Politics of Religious Dissent, 1560–1662*, Stanford, 1970

Shadwell, L.L., ed., 1912, *Enactments in Parliament Specially Concerning the Universities of Oxford and Cambridge, the Colleges and Halls Therein, and the Colleges of Winchester, Eton, and Westminster*, 4 vols., Oxford Historical Society, 58–61, Oxford, 1912

Sharpe, K., 1979, *Sir Robert Cotton*, Oxford, 1979

1981, 'Archbishop Laud and the University of Oxford', in *History and Imagination: Essays in Honour of H.R. Trevor-Roper*, ed. H. Lloyd-Jones, V. Pearl and B. Worden, Oxford, 1981, pp. 146–64

1989, *Politics and Ideas in Early Stuart England*, London, 1989

1992, *The Personal Rule of Charles I*, New Haven, 1992

Sharpe, R., 1997, *A Handlist of the Latin Writers of Great Britain and Ireland before 1540*, Brepols, 1997

Sheavyn, P., 1967, *The Literary Profession in the Elizabethan Age*, 2nd edn by J.W. Saunders, Manchester, 1967

Shipley, A.E., 1913, *'J.': A Memoir of John Willis Clark*, London, 1913

Shrewsbury, J.F.D., 1970, *A History of Bubonic Plague in the British Isles*, Cambridge, 1970

Shuckburgh, E.S., 1884, *Laurence Chaderton, D.D. . . . Richard Farmer, D.D. . . . : An Essay*, Cambridge, 1884

1904, *Emmanuel College*, London, 1904

Siebert, F.S., 1965, *Freedom of the Press in England*, Urbana, 1965

Simon, B., 1954–5, 'Leicestershire schools, 1625–40', *British Journal of Educational Studies*, 3 (1954–5), 42–58

ed., 1968, *Education in Leicestershire: A Regional Study*, Leicester, 1968

Simon, J., 1968, 'Dr John Cowell', *Cambridge Law Journal*, 26, 2 (1968), 260–72

Siraut, M.C., 1978, 'Some aspects of the economic and social history of Cambridge under Elizabeth I', University of Cambridge, MLitt thesis, 1978

Skinner, Q., 1978, *The Foundations of Modern Political Thought*, I, *The Renaissance*, Cambridge, 1978

Slack, P., 2000, 'Great and good towns, 1540–1700', in Clark 2000, pp. 347–76

Smalley, B., 1952, *The Study of the Bible in the Middle Ages*, 2nd edn, Oxford, 1952

1960, *English Friars and Antiquity in the Early Fourteenth Century*, Oxford, 1960

Smith, A.G.R., 1967, *The Government of Elizabethan England*, London, 1967

1968, 'The secretariats of the Cecils *circa* 1580–1612', *English Historical Review*, 83 (1968), 481–504

Smith, A. Hassell, 1959a, 'The Elizabethan gentry of Norfolk: office holding and faction', University of London, PhD thesis, 1959

  1959b, 'The personnel of the commissions of the peace, 1554–64: a reconsideration', *Huntington Library Quarterly*, 22 (1959), 301–12

  1967, 'Justices at work in Elizabethan Norfolk', *Norfolk Archaeology*, 34 (1967), 93–110

  1974, *County and Court: Government and Politics in Norfolk, 1558–1603*, Oxford, 1974

  1979, 'Militia rates and militia statutes 1558–1663', in *The English Commonwealth, 1547–1640: Essays in Politics and Society Presented to Joel Hurstfield*, ed. P. Clark, A.G.R. Smith and N. Tyacke, Leicester, 1979, pp. 93–110

  1989, 'Labourers in late sixteenth-century England: a case study from north Norfolk', *Continuity and Change* 4, i (1989), 11–52

Smith, D.L., 1999, *The Stuart Parliaments, 1603–1689*, London, 1999

Smith, J., 1673, *Select Discourses of John Smith*, Cambridge, 1673

Smith, L.B., 1953, *Tudor Prelates and Politicians, 1536–1558*, Princeton, 1953

Smith, Logan Pearsall, ed., 1907, *The Life and Letters of Sir Henry Wotton*, 2 vols., Oxford, 1907

Speck, W.A., 1970, *Tory and Whig: The Struggle in the Constituencies, 1701–1715*, London, 1970

Spelman, H., 1626, 1664, 1687, *Glossarium Archaiologicum*, edns of London, 1626, 1664, 1687

  ed. [with W. Dugdale in vol. II], 1639–64, *Concilia, Decreta, Leges, Constitutiones in re ecclesiarum orbis Britannici*, 2 vols., London, 1639–64

  1698, *A History of Sacrilege*, London, 1698; also edns of 1846 and [ed. C.F.S. Warren] 1895

Spufford, M., 1970, 'The schooling of the peasantry in Cambridgeshire, 1575–1700', in *Land, Church and People: Essays Presented to H.P.R. Finberg*, ed. J. Thirsk, Suppl. to *Agricultural History Review*, 18 (Reading, 1970), pp. 112–47

  1979, 'First steps in literacy: the reading and writing experiences of the humblest seventeenth-century spiritual autobiographers', *Social History*, 4 (1979), 407–35

Squibb, G.D., 1977, *Doctors' Commons: A History of the College of Advocates and Doctors of Law*, Oxford, 1977

Starkey, D., 1977, 'Representation through intimacy: a study of the symbolism of monarchy and court office in early modern England', in Lewis 1977, pp. 187–224

  ed., 1987, *The English Court from the Wars of the Roses to the Civil War*, Harlow, 1987

  1989, 'A reply: Tudor government: the facts?', *Historical Journal*, 31 (1989), 921–31

Statuta antiqua in *Cambridge Documents 1852*, I, 308–453

Bibliographical references

Statuta 1785: *Statuta Academiae Cantabrigiensis*, Cambridge, 1785

Statutes 1570 in *Cambridge Documents 1852*, I, 454–95; translated in Heywood 1838

Statutes of the Realm, The, 11 vols. in 12, Record Commission, London, 1810–28

STC: A Short-Title Catalogue of Books Printed 1475–1640, ed. W.A. Pollard and G.R. Redgrave *et al.*, 2nd edn, 3 vols., London, 1976–91

Stein, P., 1985/1988, 'Thomas Legge, a sixteenth-century English civilian and his books', in *Satura Roberto Feenstra*, ed. J.A. Ankum *et al.*, Fribourg, 1985, pp. 545–56, repr. in Stein 1988, ch. 14

    1988, *The Character and Influence of the Roman Civil Law*, London, 1988

Stephenson, W.H., ed., 1904/1959, *Asser's Life of King Alfred*, Oxford, 1904, 2nd edn by D. Whitelock, Oxford, 1959

Stone, L., 1964, 'The educational revolution in England, 1560–1640', *Past and Present*, 28 (1964), 41–80

    1965, *The Crisis of the Aristocracy, 1558–1641*, Oxford, 1965

    ed., 1975, *The University in Society*, 2 vols., Princeton and London, 1975

    1977, *The Family, Sex and Marriage in England, 1500–1800*, London, 1977

Stow, J., 1908, *A Survey of London*, ed. C.L. Kingsford, 2 vols., Oxford, 1908

Strong, R., 1969, *The English Icon: Elizabethan and Jacobean Portraiture*, London, 1969

Strype, J., 1812, *Memorials of Thomas Cranmer*, edn of Oxford, 1812, with additions by Henry Ellis

    1821, *The Life and Acts of Matthew Parker*, London, 1711, cited from edn of London, 1821

    1822, *The Life and Acts of John Whitgift*, London, 1718, cited from edn of London 1822

    1824, *Annals of the Reformation and Establishment of Religion . . . during Queen Elizabeth's Happy Reign*, 4 vols., London, 1709–31, cited from edn of London, 1824

Stubbings, F.H., ed., 1983, *The Statutes of Sir Walter Mildmay Kt . . . authorised by him for the Government of Emmanuel College Founded by Him*, Cambridge, 1983

Summerson, J., 1953/1970, *Architecture in Britain 1530–1830*, Harmondsworth, 1953, 5th edn, 1970

Surtz, E., and Murphy, V., eds., 1988, *The Divorce Tracts of Henry VIII*, Angers, 1988

Sutton, D., ed., 1992, *The Complete Plays: Thomas Legge*, New York, 1992

Swan, C.M.J.F., 1955, 'The introduction of the Elizabethan Settlement into the Universities of Oxford and Cambridge, with particular reference to Roman Catholics', University of Cambridge, PhD thesis, 1955

Swart, K.W., 1949, *Sale of Offices in the Seventeenth Century*, The Hague, 1949

Talbott, J.E., 1971, 'The history of education', *Daedalus*, 100 (1971), 133–50

Tanner, J.R., 1917, ed., *The Historical Register of the University of Cambridge*, Cambridge, 1917 ed., 1930, *Tudor Constitutional Documents A.D. 1485–1603*, 2nd edn, Cambridge, 1930

Taylor, J., 1637, *The Carriers Cosmographie*, London, 1637

Taylor, S., 1995a, '"Dr Codex" and the Whig pope: Edmund Gibson, bishop of Lincoln and London, 1716–48', in *Lords of Parliament: Studies 1714 – 1914*, ed. R.W. Davis, Stanford, 1995, pp. 9–28, 183–91

1995b, 'The government and the episcopate in mid-eighteenth-century England: the uses of patronage', in *Patronage et clientélisme 1550–1750 (France, Angleterre, Espagne, Italie)*, ed. C. Giry-Deloison and R. Mettam, Villeneuve d'Ascq, 1995, pp. 191–205

1998, 'Queen Caroline and the Church of England', in *Hanoverian Britain and Empire: Essays in Memory of Philip Lawson*, ed. S. Taylor, R. Connors and C. Jones (Woodbridge, 1998), pp. 82–101

1999, 'Bishop Edmund Gibson's proposals for church reform', in *From Cranmer to Davidson: A Church of England Miscellany*, ed. S. Taylor, Church of England Record Society, 7, Woodbridge, 1999, pp. 169–202

Thirsk, J., ed., 1967–85, *The Agrarian History of England and Wales*, IV, V, Cambridge, 1967–85

Thistlethwaite, F., 1989, *Dorset Pilgrims: The Story of West Country Pilgrims Who Went to New England in the Seventeenth Century*, London, 1989

Thomas, K., 1976a, 'Age and authority in early modern England', *Proceedings of the British Academy*, 62 (1976), 205–48

1976b, *Rule and Misrule in the Schools of Early Modern England*, Stenton Lecture 9, Reading, 1976

Thompson, E.P., 1972, 'Rough music: le charivari anglais', *Annales*, 27 (1972), 285–312

Thompson, G.S., 1918, 'Roads in England and Wales in 1603', *EHR* 38 (1918), 234–43

Thompson, Roger, 1993, '*The uprooted* or "worlds in motion": East Anglian founders of New England, 1629–1640', *Parergon*, 11, 2 (1993), 1–15

Thornton, P., 1981, *Seventeenth-Century Interior Decoration in England, France and Holland*, New Haven, 1981

Tite, C.G.C., 1994, *The Manuscript Library of Sir Robert Cotton*, London, 1994

1996, 'Sir Robert Cotton, Sir Thomas Tempest and an Anglo-Saxon gospel book: a Cottonian paper in the Harleian Library', in *Books and Collectors, 1200–1700: Essays Presented to Andrew Watson*, London, 1996, pp. 429–40

Tittler, R., 1991, *Architecture and Power: The Town Hall and the English Urban Community, c. 1500–1640*, Oxford, 1991

Townshend, T., 1680, *Historical Collections: An Exact Account of the Last Four Parliaments of Elizabeth*, London, 1680

Trevelyan, G.M., 1943/1972, *Trinity College*, Cambridge, 1943, also cited from edn of 1972

1943a, 'Undergraduate life under the Protectorate', *Cambridge Review*, 64 (1943), 328–30

Bibliographical references

Trevor-Roper, H.R., 1953, *The Gentry 1540–1640, Economic History Review Supplement*, I, 1953

   1957, *Historical Essays*, London, 1957

   1962, *Archbishop Laud, 1573–1645*, 2nd edn, London, 1962

Twigg, J., 1984, 'The limits of "Reform": some aspects of the debate on university education during the English Revolution', *History of Universities*, 4 (1984), 99–114

   1987, *A History of Queens' College, Cambridge*, Woodbridge, 1987

   1990, *The University of Cambridge and the English Revolution, 1625–1688*, Woodbridge, 1990

Twyne 1927: 'Some correspondence of Brian Twyne, Part I', *Bodleian Quarterly Record*, 5, 4 (1927), 213–18

Tyacke, N., 1987, *Anti-Calvinists: The Rise of English Arminianism, c. 1590–1640*, Oxford, 1987 (2nd edn, 1990)

   1997, ed., *The History of the University of Oxford*, IV, *Seventeenth-Century Oxford*, Oxford, 1997

   2000, 'Lancelot Andrewes and the myth of Anglicanism', in Lake and Questier 2000, pp. 5–33

Tyler, P., 1967, 'The status of the Elizabethan parochial clergy', *SCH* 4 (1967), 76–97

Ullmann, W., 1961, *Principles of Government and Politics in the Middle Ages*, London, 1961

   1979, *Law and Politics in the Middle Ages*, London, 1979

Underdown, D., 1995, 'Regional cultures? Local variations in popular culture during the early modern period', in *Popular Cultures in England c. 1500–1850*, ed. T. Harris, Basingstoke, 1995, pp. 28–47, 222–7

   1996, *A Freeborn People: Politics and the Nation in Seventeenth-Century England*, Oxford, 1996

Underwood, M., 1989, 'John Fisher and the promotion of learning', in Bradshaw and Duffy 1989, pp. 25–46; see also Jones and Underwood

Ussher, J., 1847–64, *Works*, ed. C.R. Elrington and J.H. Todd, 17 vols., Dublin and London, 1847–64

VCH: Victoria History of the Counties of England, esp. *Cambs.* III, ed. J.P.C. Roach, Oxford, 1959

Venn: Venn, J. and J.A., eds., *Alumni Cantabrigienses*, Part I, *To 1751*, 4 vols., Cambridge, 1922–7

Venn, J., ed., 1897–1901, *Biographical History of Gonville and Caius College*, I–III, Cambridge, 1897–1901 (followed by vols. IV–VIII)

   ed., 1904, *The Annals of Gonville and Caius College by John Caius*, Cambridge Antiquarian Society, 1904

   ed., 1910, *Grace Book* Δ . . . *1542–89*, Cambridge, 1910

   1913, *Early Collegiate Life*, Cambridge, 1913

Venn, J. and S.C., 1887, *Admissions to Gonville and Caius College . . . March 1558/9 to June 1678–9*, London and Cambridge, 1887

Bibliographical references

Wabuda, S., and Litzenberger, C., eds., 1998, *Belief and Practice in Reformation England: A Tribute to Patrick Collinson from His Students*, Aldershot, 1998

Walker, E.C., 1970, *William Dell: Master Puritan*, Cambridge, 1970

Walker, T.A., 1912, *Admissions to Peterhouse or St Peter's College* [1615–1911], Cambridge, 1912

    1927, *A Biographical Register of Peterhouse Men*, I, *1284–1574*, Cambridge, 1927

    1930, *A Biographical Register of Peterhouse Men*, II, *1574–1616*, Cambridge, 1930

    1935, *Peterhouse*, 2nd edn, Cambridge, 1935

Wall, A.D., 1966, 'The Wiltshire Commission of the Peace 1590–1620: a study of its social structure', University of Melbourne, MA thesis, 1966

Walsh, J., Haydon, C., and Taylor, S., eds., 1993, *The Church of England c. 1689–c. 1833: From Toleration to Tractarianism*, Cambridge, 1993

Ward, S., 1654/1970, *Vindiciae Academiarum*, Oxford, 1654, facs. edn in *Science and Education in the Seventeenth Century: The Webster-Ward Debate*, ed. A.G. Debus, London, 1970

Wardale, J.R., ed., 1903, *Clare College Letters and Documents*, Cambridge, 1903

Waterland, D., 1730, 1856, *Advice to a Young Student with a Method of Study for the First Four years*, London, 1730, also cited from Waterland, *Works*, ed. W. Van Mildert, 3rd edn, Oxford, 1856, IV, pp. 393–415

Waters, J.J., 1968, 'Hingham, Massachusetts, 1631–1661: an East Anglian oligarchy in the New World', *Journal of Social History*, I (1968), 351–70

Watkin, D., Brooke, C., and Richmond, H., 1999, 'The Master's Lodge', *The Caian*, 1999, pp. 110–25

Watson, F., 1916, *The Old Grammar Schools*, Cambridge, 1916

Watson, J.B., 1959, 'The Lancashire gentry, 1529 to 1558', University of London, MA thesis, 1959

Wayment, H., 1972, *The Windows of King's College Chapel, Cambridge, Corpus Vitrearum Medii Aevi*, Great Britain, Supplementary Volume I, London, 1972

Webster, T., 1997, *Godly Clergy in Early Stuart England*, Cambridge, 1997

Welsby, P.A., 1958, *Lancelot Andrewes, 1555–1626*, London, 1958

Welsh DNB: The Dictionary of Welsh Biography down to 1940, Honourable Society of Cymmrodorion, London, 1959

Westfall, R.S., 1975, 'The role of alchemy in Newton's career', in *Reason, Experiment and Mysticism in the Scientific Revolution*, ed. M.L. Righini Bonelli and W.R. Shea, London, 1975, pp. 189–232

    1980, *Never at Rest: A Biography of Isaac Newton*, Cambridge, 1980

Wharton, H., ed., 1691, *Anglia Sacra*, 2 vols., London, 1691

Whichcote, B., 1753, *Moral and Religious Aphorisms Collected from the Manuscript Papers of the Reverent and Learned Doctor Whichcote* (ed. Samuel Salter) . . . *To which are added Eight Letters which Passed between Dr Whichcote, Provost of King's College, and Dr Tuckney, Master of Emmanuel College in Cambridge*, London, 1753

Bibliographical references

Whiston 1749: *Memoirs of the Life and Writings of Mr William Whiston*, London, 1749

White, P., 1992, *Predestination, Policy and Polemic: Conflict and Consensus in the English Church from the Reformation to the Civil War*, Cambridge, 1992

Whitelock, D., Brett, M., and Brooke, C.N.L., eds., 1981, *Councils and Synods with Other Documents Relating to the English Church*, I, *A.D. 871–1204*, 2 parts, Oxford, 1981

Wilbraham, R., 1821, 'An attempt at a glossary of some words used in Cheshire', *Archaeologia*, 19 (1821), 13–42

Wilkins, D., ed., 1737, *Concilia Magnae Brittaniae et Hiberniae, A.D. 446–1717*, 4 vols., London, 1737

Willet, A., 1601/1634, *Synopsis Papismi*, 2 edns, London, 1601/1634

Williams, P., 1986, 'Elizabethan Oxford: state, church and university', in McConica 1986, pp. 397–440

Williams, R., 1965, *The Long Revolution*, London, 1965

Willis, R., and Clark, J.W., 1886/1988, *The Architectural History of the University of Cambridge and of the Colleges of Cambridge and Eton*, 4 vols., Cambridge, 1886; repr. ed. D.J. Watkin, 3 vols., Cambridge, 1988

Willson, D.H., ed., 1931, *The Parliamentary Diary of Robert Bowyer 1606–1607*, Minneapolis, 1931

  1940, *The Privy Councillors in the House of Commons 1604–1629*, Minneapolis, 1940

Wilson, K., 1995, *The Sense of the People: Politics, Culture and Imperialism in England, 1715–1785*, Cambridge, 1995

Winstanley, D.A., 1922, *The University of Cambridge in the Eighteenth Century*, Cambridge, 1922

  1935, *Unreformed Cambridge: A Study of Certain Aspects of the University in the Eighteenth Century*, Cambridge, 1935

Winthrop Papers: *The Winthrop Papers*, ed. G.W. Robinson *et al.*, 6 vols., Boston, Mass., 1929–47

Woodman, F., 1986, *The Architectural History of King's College Chapel*, London, 1986

Wordsworth, C., 1877, *Scholae Academicae*, Cambridge, 1877

Wren, C. and S., 1750, *Parentalia or Memoirs of the Family of the Wrens*, London, 1750

Wright, C.E., 1951, 'The dispersal of the monastic libraries and the beginnings of Anglo-Saxon studies: Matthew Parker and his circle: a preliminary study', *Transactions of the Cambridge Bibliographical Society*, 3 (1951), 208–37

  1958, 'The Elizabethan Society of Antiquaries and the formation of the Cottonian Library', in *The English Library before 1700*, ed. F. Wormald and C.E. Wright, London, 1958, pp. 176–212

Wright, C.J., ed., 1997, *Sir Robert Cotton as Collector*, London, 1997

Wright, W.A., 1868–9, 'An account of the election of Sir Francis Bacon and Dr Barnaby Goche as burgesses in parliament in 1614, written by Dr Duport,

Bibliographical references

Deputy Vice-Chancellor', *Cambridge Antiquarian Communications*, 3 (1868–9), 203–10

ed., 1904, *The Schoolmaster: English Works of Roger Ascham*, Cambridge, 1904

Wyatt, A., 1989, 'Localism, patronage and the university', University of East Anglia, MA thesis, 1989

Wyatt, T.S., 1996, 'The building and endowment of the college', in Beales and Nisbet 1996, pp. 43–53

Yorke, P., 1799/1887, *The Royal Tribes of Wales . . . to which is added an Account of the Fifteen Tribes of North Wales*, Wrexham, 1799, and ed. R. Williams, Liverpool, 1887

Zutshi, P., ed., 1993, *Medieval Cambridge: Essays on the Pre-Reformation University*, The History of the University of Cambridge: Texts and Studies, 2, Woodbridge, 1993

INDEX

Note: page references in *italics* denote illustrations.

Index

Berkley family, 192
Betts, Richard, fellow of Peterhouse, 393
Bible, 441–54; authority, 443, 451–3; Polyglot, 459; textual study, 466, 483, 502, 503, 505, 508; translations, 441–3; *and see* chronology
Blackall, Samuel, fellow of Emmanuel, 532
Blake, Richard, fellow of Peterhouse, 368
Blickling Hall, Norfolk, 305n149
Blomefield, Francis, 538–9, 548
Blomfield, Sir Arthur, 47
Bloxton, Joshua, 415
Blundell, Peter, and Sidney Sussex, 208, 214, 244
Blythe, Dr, of Clare, 216
Bodleian Library, Oxford, 49, 52, 372–3, 459, 503
Bois, John, MP, 166
Bois, William, fellow of Clare, 376–7
Bollandists, 490
Bonaventure, St, 447
Booth, Laurence, master of Pembroke, archbishop of York, 538
Booth, Remigius, 390–1
Borage, John, of North Barsham, 193
Boswell, Sir William, tutor of Jesus, 301, 319, 461
Botesdale, Suffolk, 191
Bowles, Oliver, tutor of Queens', 326, 333
Bownde, Nicholas, fellow of Peterhouse, 237, 398n40
Bowyer, Robert, 171
Boys, Edward, fellow of Corpus Christi, 125
Brackley, manor of, 224
Bradford, Samuel, master of Corpus Christi, bishop of Carlisle, 536–7
Bradford Grammar School, 190
Bradshaw, William, 137n179, 322, 331
Brady, Edmund, 474
Brady, Robert, master of Gonville and Caius, Regius Professor of Physic, 474, 487–94; Cambridge connection, 484, 486, 492–3; and Gonville and Caius, (undergraduate), 484, 487, (master), 474, 484, 487, 532, 534, (work on records), 545–6; historical work, 440–1, 458, 483–4, 486, 488–92, 503, 545–6, (and Public Records), 483, 484, 488–9, 493, 534; London and Court connections, 484, 486, 487–8, 493, 516, 534; medicine, 484, 486, 487–8, 492, (James II's physician), 484, 487–8, 493, 516, 534; personality, 493–4; politics, 474, 493, 520, 534; and Spelman family, 460, 488, 493
Brainford, Thomas, 477

Brandon, Henry and Charles, dukes of Suffolk, 316
Branthwaite, William, fellow of Emmanuel, master of Gonville and Caius, 376, 442, 481; benefactions, 355, 478; election, 407, 407n89, 407n91
Brasenose College, Oxford, 189–90, 191, 216, 244
Bratton Fleming, Devon, 534
Breton, John, master of Emmanuel, 46
brewers, Cambridge, 253
Bridges, John, 113n72, 130n156
Bridgewater, earl of (John Egerton), 423
Bristol, 207; bishopric, 370–1, 486n6; *and see* Felton; Gooch, Sir Thomas
Brome Hall, 293
Bromley, Sir Thomas, Lord Chancellor, 397
Brooke, Baron (Fulke Greville), 104, 261, 322
Brooke, Henry (Baron Cobham), 290, 377–8, 393
Brooke, Samuel, master of Trinity, 91n104, 430
Broughton, Hugh, fellow of Christ's, 364
Browning, John, fellow of Trinity, 131
Brownrigg, Ralph, master of St Catharine's, bishop of Exeter, 105n25, 382, 383, 476–7; religious views, 112, 476–7, (public recantation), 95n123, 130
Bruce, Edward (Baron Bruce of Kinloss), 368, 379
Bucer, Martin, Regius Professor of Divinity, 442n16
Buck, Thomas, senior bedell, 381, 382–3
Buckeridge, John, bishop of Rochester and Ely, 97n133
Buckhurst, Baron (Thomas Sackville), chancellor of Oxford University, 166, 217, 374–5
Buckingham, duke of (George Villiers), chancellor, 157, 477; and college elections, 227, 420–1, 429–30; election as chancellor, 83, 86n85, 156, 172, 227, 257, 312, 386; patronage, 286, 379, 386
Buckingham College, 5, 17; *and see* Magdalene College
buildings, 13–62, *14*; academic quarter, 13, 15, 17, 21–5, 242–3; dissolution and, 17–21; funding, 193, 243, 246, 261, 272–3, 274, 294–5; housing for poor, 243; impact on town, 242–3, 244–6, 253; lay element and, 25–31; in local towns, by gentry, 246; pensionaries, 120; of university, *see under* Cambridge University; *and see* attics; chambers; chapels; friaries; galleries, long; gates; Gothic style; halls; halls, college; libraries; lodges, masters'; *and individual buildings, and under individual colleges*

Index

Index

commissions: for dissolution of monasteries, 2–3; of 1540s, on universities, 3, 5–9, 18–19; of 1559, 389n3; of 1620s, on fees, 162

commonplaces, college, 126

Commonwealth, concept of, 108, 109

Commonwealth period, *see* puritan revolution

communications, 225–9

Communion, *see* Eucharist

community of the country, 183n6, 237–8

Compton, Henry, bishop of London, 535

Conant, John, rector of Exeter College, Oxford, 136, 317n15, 329n70

Congregation, 69–70

Consistory, 74, 77–8, 95–6, 149

constitution of university, 63–98, 102; change in origin of authority, 76, 82, 88, 96–8, 143; *and see individual elements and jurisdiction; statutes*

Conti, Abbé, 496

Conway, secretary of signet office, 421

Cooke, Thomas, fellow of Gonville and Caius, 218–19

Cooper, Anthony Ashley (earl of Shaftesbury), 130, 145–6, 249–51

Cooper, Charles Henry: *Annals of Cambridge*, 546

Cooper, Thomas, fellow of Magdalen College, Oxford, vice-chancellor of Oxford University, 75

Copcot, John, master of Corpus Christi, vice-chancellor, 90n100, 91, 270, 360

Copernicus, Nicolas, 463

Copinger, Ambrose, fellow of St Catharine's, 408–9, 409n97

Copinger, Henry, master of Magdalene, 348, 373–4, 384–5, 409n97

Corbett, Clement, master of Trinity Hall, 97, 106, 298, 403–4

Cordell, Thomas, fellow of Peterhouse, 400, 401

corn rents, 271–3

Cornwallis, Mr (creditor of Trinity), 281n79

Cornwallis, Sir William, 181

Cornwallis, William, undergraduate at Trinity, 141, 142

corporations, civic, 193, 205; *and see under* Norwich

Corpus Christi College: as Benet College, 455; building, 26, 43, 295, 304, 306, (chambers), 214, 304, (chapel), 42, 43, 295; elections, (fellows), 217, 390–1, 425, (masters), 91, 299, 351–2, 358, 362, 367, 405–6, 418–19, 429–30; estate management, 188; finances, 219–20, 270,

273n54, 280n72, 295; foundation, 43, 242; Hickman expelled, 360; leases, 280n72, 280n75, 281–2, 293; library, 214–15, 455, 456; masters, 260, 304, (income), 270, 270n49, 271, 293, (*and see* Aldrich; Bradford, Samuel; Butts, Henry; Copcot; Jegon, John; Jegon, Thomas; Munday; Norgate; Parker; Walsall); name, 43, 455; Newtonian science, 339, 486, 521; Norfolk connections, 199–201, 202, 203, 206, 214–15, 217, 219–20, 390, (Norwich), 97–8, 106, 194, 199–201, 214–15, 217, 219–20, 304, 390; Parker and, 7–8, 43, 306, 390–1n111, (benefactions), 186–7, 193, 199–201, 214–15, 455, 456; statutes, 190–1n37, 199–201; town interest in, 43, 242; Visitors, 96n130

Corpus Christi College, Oxford, 43, 155n30, 217, 287, 295–6, 455

correspondence, 181, 225–8, 338; tutors', 320, 336, 337–8; *and see* Whichcote (and Tuckney)

Cory, John, tutor of Emmanuel, 335

Cosin, Edmund, master of St Catharine's, vice-chancellor, 90n100

Cosin, John, master of Peterhouse, vice-chancellor, bishop of Durham, 90n100, 105n25, 474–5, 527, 546–7; and Peterhouse chapel, 43–4, 475, 527

Cotes, Roger, Plumian Professor of Astronomy, 507, 520

Cotten, Henry, and Winchester College, 374–5

Cotton, Sir Robert, 456, 547; library, 457–8, 547–8

Coulton, G.G., 454

country, 181; alumni in, 205–6, 222, 229–38, 531, (*and see* clergy (graduates)); calendar, 222–5, 262; and college life, 183–6, 204, 206–21; communications, 225–9; community of, 183n6, 237–8; endowments, 186–210, 212, 215; gentry's involvement with colleges, 188–9, 201–4, 222, 316n13; local groupings in colleges, 214–15, 317; mind and character by locality, 213–14; regional speech, 212–13; sermons by university men, 171–2, 179, 228–9, 479, 480; tutors' links with, 202–4, 317, 323; and university as a whole, 221–9; visits to, 222–5, 262, 331; *and see* statutory limitations

Court, 99, 100–1, 533–5, 539; academics invoke influence, 9, 99, 102, 104–5, 251, 366–80, 537; alumni at, 103, 104–5, 106–7, 417–18, 421; and Chantries Act,

Index

Index

Mey, John, master of St Catharine's, vice-chancellor, bishop of Carlisle, 66, 70, 105n25

Mey, William, president of Queens'; annexes Carmelite friary, 5, 18; on Commission of 1540s, 7, 8, 19; influence at Court, 103, 266; marriage, 297; prebends, 7, 266

Michaelhouse, 8, 13, 19, 24, 42–3

Michaelmastide, 223, 224

Michell, Edmund, tutor of Gonville and Caius, 355

Middle Ages: religious ceremonial, 448–9; syllabus, 437, 441–2, 494–5, 512, (influence), 341, 467, 511, 519

Middle Temple, 38, 166, 170

Middleton, Conyers, fellow of Trinity, university librarian, 537

Middleton, Lancs., 189–90, 191

Midsummer fair, 96

Mildmay, Sir Walter, chancellor of the exchequer, 25, 364, 372, 379; founds Emmanuel, 21, 40, 46, 171, 396

Mill, John, principal of St Edmund Hall, Oxford, 466, 503–4, 505

Mill, John, of Corpus Christi, Oxford, 295–6

Miller, Sir John, of West Lavant, 536

Mills, Francis, of privy seal office, 414

Milton, John, 461, 486–7

Milton Abbas church, 3

Minshull, Laurence, 141

Minshull, Richard, master of Sidney Sussex, 472, 526

Mint, Newton at, 466, 498, 507

misrule ceremonies, 143, 145, 146, 251

monarch: access to, 106–7; appointments in gift of, 349, 350–2, 493, 505–6; control over universities, 107, 163; divine right theory, 180; on influence of university, 108–9; intervention initiated within university, 366–7, 383–4, 392–3, 411, 416, 430; and leases, 286–7, 354, 414; and parliament, 148–9, 163, 389–90; proprietorial attitude to universities, 115, 148–9, 163, 349, 350, 369–70, 428–9; and Regius Professorships, 349–50, 352; *and see individual monarchs*; charters, royal; elections (Crown intervention); injunctions; mandates; prerogative, royal; visitors to Cambridge (royal); *and under* King's College; Trinity College

monastic establishments: sponsorship of colleges, 121–2, 184; *and see* Augustinian canons; Carmelite friary; dissolution; Dominican friary; Franciscan friary; St Radegund's nunnery

Monasticon Anglicanum, 490

Montagu, Sir Edward, 138n185

Montagu, James, master of Sidney Sussex, bishop of Winchester, 91n104, 105n25, 106, 263

Moore, Sir Francis, 166

Moore, Gabriel, fellow of Christ's, 369, 409–10, 416

Moore, John, bishop of Ely: library, 58–9, 478, 492–3, 508

Moore, William, fellow of Gonville and Caius, university librarian, 473–4

More, Henry, fellow of Christ's, 482, 523, 524, 525, 526

More, John, minister of St Andrew's, Norwich, 237

Morrell, Robert, college tutor, 138

Mosley, Edward, fellow of Christ's, 402

Mowtlow, Dr, fellow of King's, 290, 376–7

Munday, John, master of Corpus Christi, 429–30

Munford, John, fellow of Peterhouse, 393–5

Murton, Thomas, fellow of Christ's, 402–3

music: in curriculum, 137, 512; music-making, 223, 301, 312, 327, 333

nationes, continental, 195

Naylor, Oliver, fellow of Gonville and Caius, 226–7

Neile, Richard, fellow of St John's, bishop of Coventry and Lichfield, 106–7, 376–7, 417–18

Nevile, Thomas, master of Trinity, vice-chancellor, dean of Canterbury, 105, 144, 262–3, 294, 296; building at Trinity, 19–20, 24, 38, 296, 307

Neville, Francis, of Trinity, 143

New College, Oxford, 289, 312, 402, 470–1; buildings, 26, 35, 38; leases, 284, 288, 289; and Winchester College, 374, 421–2

'new learning', 4, 102–3

Newcastle, duke of (Thomas Pelham-Holles), chancellor and high steward, 61–2, 537, 538, 539; election, 538, 539; and Gooch, 538–9

Newcastle, duke of (William Cavendish), 138–9

Newcomb, Jane, 319–20

Newmarket, 89–90

newsletters, 225, 228

Newton, Fogg, provost of King's, vice-chancellor, 90n100, 369–70, 406

Newton, Isaac, fellow of Trinity, Lucasian Professor of Mathematics, 437, 440–1, 494–502; alchemy, 494, 505; astronomy, 494, 495–6, 498–500; and Barrow, 496–7, 501, 524; and Bentley, 466, 493, 500, 502, 504–5, 509, 519, 520; Cambridge

601

Index

Pearson, John: *Exposition of the Creed*, 340, 530

Peasants' Revolt (1381), 43

Pelagius, heresy of, 444

Pembroke College (previously Pembroke Hall): chapel, 42, 45, 44–7, 475, 527; finances, 120, 261, 270n47, 272, 273n54, 280n73; local endowments and limitations, 190, 197, 202, 203; lord of misrule, 142–3; master's lodge, 305; masters, 270n47, 538, (*and see* Andrewes; Beale, Jerome; Booth, Laurence; Felton; Fulke; Grindal, Edmund; Harsnett; Hutton; Lany; Ridley; Young, John); property, 120, 191, 215, 276n64; size, 120, 120n107; statutes, 197, 211; Matthew Wren and, 44, 475, 527

pensionaries, 120

pensioners, 201–3, 204

Periam, Samuel, of St John's, 368–9

Perkins, William, fellow of Christ's, 285–6

Perne, Andrew, master of Peterhouse, vice-chancellor, 85, 94–5n120, 246, 451, 481; and Burghley, 108, 371, 391, 393, 397–400; and Court intervention, 371, 372–3, 391, 393–5, 397–400, 413; disputation with Hutton, 451–3; library, 452, 478; religious views, 18, 108, 451; and statutes, 70, 76

Perse, Stephen, fellow of Gonville and Caius, 18, 32, 354, 407n89

Perse Grammar School, Cambridge, 5, 18

Peterhouse: chapel, 40, 42, 43–4, 45–6, 475, 527; Cosin's endowments, 474; elections, 347, 348, 352, 367–8, 391, 393–5, 397–402, 417, 419; founding, 42; hostel, 246; local preferences and limitations, 196, 202, 203, 368, 393–4, 401; long gallery, 306; master's ambling nag, 10, 259; masters, *see* Cosin, John; Mawe; Perne; Richardson, John; Seaman; Some, Robert; Wren, Matthew; size, 120n107; statutes, 196, 368, 393–4, 401; Visitors, 97, 196, 368, 400–1

Petre, Sir William, 8

philosophy, 341, 342, 513, 521; in curriculum, 335, 341, 437, 467, 511, 515

Physic, Regius Professorship of, 349, 487; *and see* Brady, Robert; Glisson

Physicians, Royal College of, 542

Physwick Hostel, 8, 19, 24

pigs, Hammond's, 254–5

Pilgrimage to Parnassus, The (drama), 296–7

Pilkington, James, master of St John's, bishop of Durham, 105n25, 267

Pisa, University of, 542

Pitt, William the younger, 539–40

plague, 222, 224, 247–8, 312

plasterwork, 307, 312

plate, 214

Platonists, Cambridge, 481–2, 522, 524–6; and predestination, 336–7, 444, 481, 526; and puritans, 336–7, 480, 523, 526; *and see* Cudworth; Culverwell; More, Henry; Smith, John; Whichcote

Playfere, Edward, 376–7

Playfere, John, fellow of Sidney Sussex, 446

plebeian students, 132, 320–5; and aristocratic students, 141–2, 315, 322, 327, 329–30, 331; financial support, 320–3, 324, 327, 329–30; and tutors, 320–5, 327, 329–31

Plume, Thomas, and Plumian Professorship, 520; *and see* Cotes; Smith, Robert

pluralities, academic and ecclesiastical, 90, 262–6, 292, 477, 478; parliamentary attacks on, 165–6, 171–2, 177–8; *and see under* Gooch, Sir Thomas; Jegon, John; Preston, John; Ward, Samuel

Pocklington School, 190, 191

poetry, 181, 231, 514–15

Pole, Cardinal Reginald, chancellor, archbishop of Canterbury: Ordinances, 63, 84, 85, 128, 132; and seminaries, 114

poor: relief, 247, 254; townspeople, 243, 245, 247, 248, 252–3; *and see* plebeian students

Pope, Alexander: epitaph on Newton, 494

Popham, Sir John, chief justice, 121

popish plot, 528

population, 247, 248–9

Porie, Dr, 85

Porter, George, tutor of Queens', 326

Potter, Barnaby, president of Queens', 312, 329n70

Powell, William, master of St John's, 342n127, 521

praeter (weekly allowance at St John's), 273

praevaricator, 223

preachers and preaching: academics in country, 171–2, 179, 228–9, 479, 480; at assizes and quarter sessions, 237, 238; commemoration of benefactors, 211; education of preaching ministry, 229–30, 233–7, 243, 267, 315, 330–1; at Great St Mary's, 79, 126, 525; heads of houses, 79, 171–2, 179, 270; itinerant, 206; state control, 124–7, 130–1, 481; Whichcote's, 337, 525; *and see* lectureships; sermons

precisians, *see* puritans

predestination, 332–3, 336–7, 443–6, 481, 526

pre-election, 355, 361–2, 378–9, 392, 398, 400–1, 407

Index

Wren, Matthew, master of Peterhouse, vice-chancellor, bishop of Ely, 86n85, 111n59, 474, 527; bishoprics, 97n133, 105n25; and Pembroke, 44, 475, 527; and Peterhouse chapel, 43, 475, 527
Wren family chronicle, *Parentalia*, 44
Wright, Ezekiel, tutor of Emmanuel, 475
Wright, Robert, fellow of Trinity, 285
Wright, Stephen, architect, 61–2
Wriothesley, Henry, *see under* Southampton
Wriothesley, Sir Thomas, lord chancellor, 10

Wycliffe, John, 441–2
Wymondham, Abbey of, 285n89
Wynn, Sir John, of Gwydir, 317
Wynn, John, on royal mandate, 417

year, rhythm of, 222–5, 262
Young, John, master of Pembroke, bishop of Rochester, 90n100, 105n25, 351
Young, Thomas, and wave theory of light, 498

Zwingli, Huldreich, 448